PROGRAMMING IN **BASIC**

BASIC A COMPLETE COURSE

MARGARET McRITCHIE

HOLT, RINEHART AND WINSTON OF CANADA, LIMITED   TORONTO

Published simultaneously in the United States of America by Holt,
Rinehart and Winston, Publishers, New York, N.Y.

Canadian Cataloguing in Publication Data

McRitchie, Margaret
Programming in BASIC
Includes index.
ISBN 0-03-920148-1
1. Basic (Computer program language). I. Title.
QA76.73.B3M37   001.64′24   C82-094168-9

Editor: F.L. Barrett
Production Editor: Jocelyn Van Huyse
Cover and Interior Design: Maher & Murtagh Inc.
Typesetting, Assembly and Technical Art: Trigraph Inc.

Printed in the United States of America
5   032   86 85 84

Contents

Preface

The prime purpose of this book is to teach the computer language BASIC in the context of personal and practical real-life situations. Although a few mathematical problems are presented, the reader need not have a mastery of mathematics in order to progress through the book. The approach is simple and well suited to those who have had no experience with computers. The book is written for time-sharing, batch, and microcomputer systems and may be used as a self-teaching text or as a text in a formal instructional environment. This makes the book suitable to a wide audience of readers, from students in schools, colleges, and universities to the non-professional computer user who has a computer at home or in the office.

The chapters are organized in the following manner:

1. A list of objectives at the beginning of each chapter gives the concepts that will be introduced.
2. The chapters are divided into sections. The majority of sections consist of four parts:

(a) A new concept is explained. This is accomplished by the use of a short program in which the concept is incorporated.
(b) A sample program is listed with statements fully explained. In many sections, several programs are given. A RUN is shown for every sample program.
(c) A "Your Turn" unit gives the reader the opportunity to experiment with the skill just learned by solving exercises and writing programs.
(d) Solutions are provided for the "Your Turn" exercises and programming problems.
Another section is started and the process is repeated.

3. A summary at the end of each chapter reviews the most difficult concepts.
4. Questions, exercises, and programming problems complete a chapter, depending on its content. The majority of chapters include the three types.

Sample programs, "Your Turn" problems, and assignment problems are deliberately simple and are designed to help readers concentrate on learning BASIC programming rather than on deciphering a problem. Explicit instructions prevent a reader from using a preferred method to perform a routine with the possibility of forgetting other options. Calculations to be performed in a program are clearly defined. With few exceptions, every program — whether it be a sample program, a "Your Turn" problem, or an assignment problem — has its RUN shown. Beginning programmers feel more confident and gain better programming skills when goals (the results) are clearly and concisely laid out for them. A simple flowchart using the basic symbols is introduced at the beginning of the book and is methodically developed as other symbols become necessary. Flowcharts are given for some of the "Your Turn" problems and for the more difficult assignment problems at the end of a chapter.

I wish to express my thanks to Bob Kennedy and John Spisich of Computerland™ of Winnipeg and to the staff at Radio Shack® Computer Centre, Winnipeg, for their willing help and advice and for providing the latest hardware and software products. Gratitude is also extended to the University of Manitoba and to the Superintendent's office of the River East School Division No. 9 for the loan of their hardware and software, and to the students who tested portions of the manuscript. Finally, I wish to express my thanks to Mr. Anrep-Matthiesen for his thorough review of the manuscript and for his many helpful suggestions.

Margaret McRitchie

ONE COMPUTERS AND COMPUTER LANGUAGES

Through the study of this chapter, you will become familiar with:
1. The functions of the analog computer and the digital computer.
2. The MARK I, ENIAC, and BINAC computers.
3. The stored-program principle.
4. The advantages of transistors over vacuum tubes.
5. Large Scale Integration (LSI).
6. The generations of computers.
7. The history of the microcomputer.
8. Software.
9. The fundamental units of a computer system.
10. Peripherals.
11. External media for mass storage of information.
12. The two main components of a microprocessor.
13. Registers in a microprocessor.
14. RAM, ROM, byte.
15. Serial and parallel interfacing.
16. Data bus, address bus, and control bus.
17. The term microcomputer-on-a-chip.
18. The terms machine language, symbolic language, high-level language.
19. Interpreters and compilers.
20. The reasons for the development of ALGOL, FORTRAN, PL/I, COBOL, BASIC.
21. The history of the BASIC language.

1.1 THE ELECTRONIC COMPUTER

The impact of the electronic computer cannot be minimized. It has affected almost every one of us in one way or another. From the vital function of data processing in business and government to the modern technologies of medicine, space travel, and national defense, computers have extended man's capabilities and knowledge. They are now found quietly at work in such diverse places as banks, department stores, hospitals, oil refineries, airports, pulp and paper mills, schools, and newspaper offices.

What is a computer and why has its impact been so great? The computer is an electronic device that uses stored data and instructions to generate information. Its dramatic effect on most of us is due to its untiring performance and fantastic speed. When properly programmed, a computer is able to outperform thousands of office clerks in speed and accuracy and is even capable of making logical decisions.

Although the digital computer will mainly be discussed, you should be aware that there are two kinds of electronic computers — the analog computer and the digital computer. The digital computer is a machine that counts data in discontinuous form, while the analog computer is a machine that measures values continuously. By using gauges and meters, physical conditions, such as pressure, voltage, temperature, and velocity, can be measured by analog computers. Digital computers operate on numbers, letters of the alphabet, and other symbols which are transformed into discrete binary (base two) electronic signals. They solve problems by following instructions which have been submitted in the form of a program.

The development of the electronic digital computer will quickly be reviewed. The first machine designed with features that are found in today's computers was conceived by Charles Babbage, a professor at Trinity College in Cambridge, England. A mathematical genius, he developed a computing machine in 1822 that was capable of calculating logarithmic tables automatically. He called it the **Difference Engine**. Realizing that computing machines should be able to solve any numerical problem, he became interested in designing a general purpose machine. This change in plans resulted in the withdrawal of the financial aid he was receiving from the English government, and his work on the Difference Engine was abandoned. For the remainder of his life, Babbage concentrated his efforts on a machine that he called the **Analytical Engine**. Embodying many of the principles used in modern computers, it included an arithmetic unit, a storage unit, and a control unit. Instructions were submitted on punched cards, and results were printed by an output unit. Unfortunately, Babbage worked on ideas that surpassed the technology of metallurgy, and his Analytical Engine, begun in 1830, was never completed. It was not until the twentieth century that his original ideas were incorporated in the first operable computer.

In 1939, Professor Howard Aiken developed an electromechanical machine known as the **HARVARD MARK I**. Successfully completed in 1944, it is considered the world's first workable machine capable of solving a series of mathematical and logical problems. However, it was not fully electronic, since it used mechanical devices to perform these calculations. The MARK I was huge. It had a mass of five tonnes and consisted of over seventy devices connected by hundreds of kilometres of wiring. A set of sequential instructions punched into paper tape automatically controlled its operations. Punched cards supplied the data, and output was either punched into new cards or typed. Although the MARK I could provide results faster than any machine of its time, it is considered slow by today's standards because of its electromechanical design.

In 1946, J. Presper Eckert and John Mauchly built the first all-electronic computer called the **ENIAC** (**E**lectronic **N**umerical **I**ntegrator **A**nd **C**omputer). The electromechanical devices used by the MARK I were replaced by a large number of vacuum tubes. Electronic pulses flipped these vacuum tubes on and off much like turning an electrical switch on and off. The computer received its instructions by means of plug boards (control boards) which had to be hand-wired by highly skilled technicians. Its size was enormous. With over 18 000 vacuum tubes, it covered more than 135 m² (the floor space of an average-sized house) and generated so much heat that it had to be cooled by extensive air-conditioning systems. Before each program could be **RUN**, 6 000 switches had to be set and its 18 000 tubes had to be in functioning order. Still, the ENIAC was a remarkable machine. With no moving parts other than its input and output units, calculations could be performed one thousand times faster than by the MARK I, since electric currents move more quickly than electromechanical devices. A union had taken place between electronics and computers, one that has flourished right up to the present.

It soon became apparent that the formidable, time-consuming task of wiring in a program was unnecessary. If instructions and data could be stored in the memory of the computer, new programs could be written without making changes in hardware. The concept of the **stored program** was the contribution of John von Neumann, a mathematician, who helped design the **EDVAC** (**E**lectronic **D**iscrete **V**ariable **A**utomatic **C**omputer), the first digital computer that used the principle of a stored program. The notion of internal programming proved to be a breakthrough in computer design, and even with today's advanced technology, it remains a feature of modern computers.

The year 1949 heralded a new dimension in computer design. A much superior machine called the **BINAC** introduced magnetic tape for mass storage of information, and its crystal diodes replaced the many vacuum tubes as switches. It used binary (base two) arithmetic by transmitting electronic pulses through tubes that were filled with liquid mercury. The presence of an electronic pulse represented one binary digit. Its improvements reduced the size of computers from a machine occupying 135 m^2 of floor space to one occupying the space of two over-sized filing cabinets. After BINAC, improvements in electronic computers progressed with amazing speed. In 1951, the **UNIVAC I** (**Univ**ersal **A**utomatic **C**omputer) carried out statistical analysis and processed business data, rather than scientific and engineering information. It marked the beginning of automatic data processing.

By 1959, computers no longer depended on vacuum tubes for any of their operations. Transistors replaced these tubes and computers were now referred to as **solid state** computers. The machines required very little power, generated minimal amounts of heat, and were much more compact and reliable. Computing power increased and new types of input/output equipment were introduced.

The year 1965 saw a revolution in the computer industry with the development of the **integrated circuit** (**IC**). Transistorized circuits were mounted on a silicon chip by photoelectrically etching the design on the chip. At first only a few transistors were etched on a chip the size of a quarter. Since then, densities have increased rapidly. Today, the technique is so refined that transistorized circuits can be laid down on a chip about the size of the period at the end of this sentence. A **L**arge **S**cale **I**ntegrated (**LSI**) circuit, more complicated than the ENIAC which had a mass of 30 t, can now be placed on your fingertip!

Traditionally, computers have been categorized into **generations**, with each generation introducing a drastic change.

(a) The first generation used vacuum tubes (1946).
(b) The second generation used transistors (1959).
(c) The third generation used integrated circuits (1965).

Since the appearance of the integrated circuit, component densities have increased to such an extent that many people believe computers are now in the fourth generation (LSI) or even in the fifth generation (**VLSI** — **V**ery **L**arge **S**cale **I**ntegration).

1.2 THE MICROCOMPUTER

The history of the microcomputer is understandably brief, since its introduction to the general public has just recently taken place. Commercial Large Scale Integration (LSI) first appeared in 1971, developed by companies that were new in the computer business and that found a potential market for their product in the form of desk and pocket calculators. The first general purpose microprocessor (an LSI component that holds most of the functions of a conventional computer) was developed in 1971 and was expanded upon the following year. Placed on the market to promote memory chips, its sales took everyone by surprise. The dynamic market for the microprocessor sent the original manufacturer and his competitors scurrying to redesign the faulty processor.

Microcomputers were first sold in 1975 as computer kits directed mainly at the electronic hobbyist and engineer. The first completely assembled microcomputer designed for non-technical personnel was introduced to the general public in 1977. From the humble beginnings of an LSI chip, a new industry emerged, brought about by the declining cost of the assembled product and by its dramatically reduced size. Today, many individuals and small business firms can afford computing power with the result that several related industries and support services have come into being. These include computer consultants, who provide software (programs), publishing companies that issue computer magazines and books, computer stores that provide both sales and service, and computer clubs, shows, and conferences. Of these developments, the provision of software has become the most crucial. Before a computer can function, it must be told what to do. Detailed instructions written for the computer are called programs (software), and unless one can write one's own, they must be purchased. (They are stored on either cassette tapes or on magnetic disks.) Today, software is being developed at an alarming rate, ranging from accounting systems to word processing, from scientific applications to computer games. Most of these are mass-produced and sold in cassette form. Should an individual wish to have a tailor-made program, it must be written by either the individual or by a professional programmer. It is interesting to note that in recent years, software is becoming more expensive than some of the hardware. This phenomenon has come about because of the reduced cost of electronic components and the increased cost of programming.

The structure of a microcomputer system is basically similar to that of a conventional computer system, since it comprises the same five fundamental units. These include the **Control Unit** (**CU**) and the **Arithmetic-Logical Unit** (**ALU**), which together form the **Central Processing Unit** (**CPU**), memory, an input module, and an output module.

First, the internal structure of a microcomputer (the CPU or microprocessor unit, the main memory, and the interface circuitry)

I. History of the Microcomputer

II. Architecture of the Microcomputer System

will be examined. This will be followed by a brief discussion of external devices usually referred to as **peripherals**.

1. The Microprocessor Unit (MPU)

The heart of a microcomputer is the tiny silicon chip called the microprocessor chip. In spite of its minuscule size, this LSI component incorporates all the functions of a traditional CPU. The features that make microcomputers so different from other computer systems are their reduced cost and size brought about by the microprocessor. The cost of a processor is presently one of the least expensive components in a microcomputer, while its compactness has reduced the size of a microcomputer system to such an extent that a computer can now be placed on the top of a desk. But what is truly remarkable about the microprocessor chip is its programmability, a feature that makes it so versatile that it is now considered a peripheral to other equipment, such as pocket calculators, digital watches, microwave ovens, and video games. The microprocessor in a computer system includes the following units:

(a) The Arithmetic and Logical Unit (ALU), which contains the circuitry that performs arithmetic operations, such as addition, subtraction, multiplication, and division, and makes logical decisions, such as determining the relationship between two values;

(b) The Control Unit, which supervises the functions of the computer by generating and regulating all control signals so that the system's operations and the flow of data are synchronized. Its main function is to retrieve, interpret, and execute instructions that are stored in the computer's main memory.

Microprocessors are equipped with several **registers** that act as small memories to store information temporarily. Examples of such registers are the instruction register that holds the current instruction, the address register (or registers) that stores the address of the data item or instruction, and a program counter that holds the address of the next instruction.

2. The main memory

The main **memory** of a microcomputer system comes in the form of specialized memory chips mounted on printed circuit boards. There are two types of memory: one type is called **R**andom **A**ccess **M**emory (**RAM**), to which information can be written and from which information can be read; the other is called **R**ead **O**nly **M**emory (**ROM**), from which information can only be read. Microprocessor programs and frequently used instructions are written permanently into ROM, making this type of memory unavailable to the user. Information in RAM is lost when the computer is turned off, while the information in ROM is permanent and is always available.

Memory consists of thousands of storage locations called **bytes**. Each byte is capable of storing one character, which usually consists of eight **b**inary dig**its** generally referred to as **bits**. Since the bits are operated on as a unit, a byte is the smallest accessible part of memory. The memory section of a microcomputer contains one or more printed circuit boards with a storage capacity that usually ranges from 4**K** to 64**K** bytes (**K** represents one thousand). Not all of this is users' programmable memory. Some of it is taken up as ROMs and some of it is used as a work space, particularly for the **D**isk **O**perating

A. The Internal Structure of a Microcomputer

System (**DOS**), when a disk drive is used to store and retrieve information. On the whole, most of the computer's memory is users' K (RAMS).

3. Input/Output interface chips

The rates of data transmission for input/ouput devices such as keyboards, printers, and readers are much slower than the transmission rate of a microprocessor. A special printed circuit board called an **interface** must be installed to enable an external device to communicate with the MPU. There are two types of interfaces, **serial** and **parallel**. Serial interfacing transmits bits in a series, one bit following the other at an exact rate. Parallel interfacing sends bits simultaneously. If eight bits are transmitted, then eight wires are needed to transfer the bits side by side. Teletypes, cathode ray tubes, and other communication terminals require serial interfacing; printers, keyboards, paper tape readers, and card readers need parallel interfacing.

Communication lines, grouped by function, connect all internal components of a microcomputer. Each group is called a **bus**. There are generally three types of buses to provide this communication: the **data bus**, which transmits data; the **address bus**, which selects the location (origin or destination) of the data to be transferred; and the **control bus**, which transmits control signals. A cabinet, referred to as the **mainframe**, houses the microprocessor, memory, interfaces, and bus lines. Today, the technology of LSI circuits has advanced to such an extent that all the functions of a simple computer (microprocessor, memory, and peripheral circuitry) can be incorporated on a single chip, the microcomputer-on-a-chip. However, most microprocessors require non-resident memories (the main memory) and external input/output circuitry (interface chips).

B. External Devices (Peripherals)

1. Mass storage

Since memory boards have a limited capacity, mass quantities of information must be transferred to external storage media, such as magnetic tapes and disks. This is accomplished by means of external devices (cassette tape recorders and disk drives). The external device (peripheral) must be interfaced with the computer and is driven by instructions issued from the computer. These instructions are translated by a device controller that often resides on the same printed circuit board as the interface.

2. Input/Output terminals

Input/output devices provide the means by which man can communicate with the computer. These peripherals must also be interfaced with the computer. The usual input device is a keyboard, while typical output devices are video monitors and printers.

1.3 COMPUTER LANGUAGES

A computer is unable to function automatically unless it receives explicit instructions. This series of instructions is called a **program** and the procedure for developing the series is called **programming**. The first programs, written in the early 1950s, were in machine language — a numeric language expressed as a combination of ones and zeros. Based on the binary numbering system, machine language lends itself perfectly to the two possible conditions of a circuit which can be turned either on or off. Since the controlling circuitry of the central processing unit understands these conditions, no translation of the language is necessary. However, this causes the language to be machine-dependent, making it necessary for the programmer to fully understand the internal structure of the computer being used. Programming, therefore, becomes cumbersome, onerous, and subject to many errors. This is especially true when instructions and data must be referenced by their storage locations.

To ease the programmer's task, symbolic (assembly) languages were developed. These employ symbols (alphabetic characters referred to as mnemonic codes) to denote the machine language instructions. Since operation codes, such as **ADD**, **SUBT**, and **DIV**, more closely resemble the English language, programmers find symbolic languages simpler to learn and easier to use, especially after they become familiar with the required op-codes (symbols). An assembly language cannot be used directly by a computer. It must first be translated or assembled into machine language instructions. The computer performs this translation by using a special program called an **assembler** supplied by the manufacturer. The assembly language usually has a one-to-one correspondence with the machine language and is therefore assembled on this basis. This results in a program that has the same instructions as the original program but in machine-language form. Because of this close relationship with machine language, an assembly language continues to be dependent on the model of computer in use. Although not as complex to write, programming in an assembly language remains a detailed and time-consuming task.

The need for a problem-oriented language, and one that more closely resembles the human language, soon led to the development of several **high-level** languages such as **FORTRAN**, **COBOL**, **ALGOL**, **PL/I** and **BASIC**. Working in this type of language, a programmer need not be involved with the details of computer operation and is able to shift his concentration to the development of a program. The languages are easier to learn and, because of their machine-independent feature, can be used on a variety of computers with only minor modifications. However, these problem-oriented languages must be translated into machine language by a manufacturer-supplied program. This is either a compiler or an interpreter, depending on the language being translated. An interpreter executes (processes) each statement immediately after it is translated, while a compiler translates a whole program and executes it at a later time. Each language has its own compiler or interpreter. For example, each of the languages FORTRAN and COBOL requires its own compiler, while interpretive BASIC, the version adopted by most microcomputers, is translated by an interpreter. Programs written in high-level languages are called **source** programs; their translated versions are referred to as **object** programs. Here is a brief summary of some of the high-level languages currently in use.

ALGOL is an algorithmic language especially oriented toward algebraic and logical processes. It is not meant to handle large amounts of data (although large amounts can be processed), and little attention is given to the type of data involved. ALGOL concerns itself mainly with the presentation of concise and well-defined procedures to solve arithmetic and logical problems. It was developed by international computer experts to standardize an algorithmic language.

ALGOL (Algorithmic Oriented Language)[1]

FORTRAN is a mathematical and scientific language designed to solve algebraic equations. First developed by International Business Machines (IBM), it is now extensively used by other manufacturers. Many versions of FORTRAN exist, however with minor changes, it can be adapted easily to different computers.

FORTRAN (Formula Translation)

PL/I is a general-purpose language well suited to both commercial and scientific applications. It combines the mathematical notations of FORTRAN with the desirable parts of ALGOL and the data processing features of COBOL. It is characterized as being less English than COBOL, simpler than FORTRAN, and incorporates fewer rules and restrictions than either language.

PL/I (Programming Language/I)

A widespread, business-oriented language, COBOL was designed to process large quantities of data in a repetitive routine. Its near-English form provides a means of communicating its problem-solving process with non-programmers. Its English-like notation also makes for ease in training, promotes accuracy in programming, and reduces programming time. With minimum modification, a program written in COBOL can be used on a wide variety of makes and models of computers. It is presently one of the leading commercial programming languages.

COBOL (Common Business Oriented Language)

BASIC is a FORTRAN-like language designed primarily for interactive and time-sharing environments.[2] Most microcomputers use some version of BASIC. It is considerably easier to learn than FORTRAN, yet with its extensions, it is capable of solving scientific, mathematical, and engineering problems. It can be used in a great variety of commercial applications, such as accounting, inventory control, and word processing. BASIC can also be employed in such diverse areas as medicine; economics; the administration of student records in schools, colleges, and universities; and in the maintenance of personal records in the home. Because of the simplicity of the language, coupled with the declining cost of computers, an increasing number of educational institutions are becoming interested in BASIC as a means of teaching programming. In addition, its interactive feature makes it especially useful for individualized instruction.

BASIC (Beginner's All-Purpose Symbolic Instruction Code)

1. An algorithmic language is a procedure-oriented language which solves a problem by setting up a series of well-defined steps (procedures). A detailed set of instructions to solve a specific problem is called an **algorithm**.

2. Interactive programming allows an individual to work interactively with the computer, as if in a two-way conversation. The user gives information to the computer and receives information from it while the program is being processed. In a time-sharing system, several remote terminals have simultaneous access to a centrally located computer. Telephone lines connect the terminals to the computer.

1.4 BASIC

The introduction of time-sharing in the late 1950s soon revealed that the programming languages in use at the time were too difficult for this type of system. The language used in a time-sharing environment should be simple to write to enable a user sitting at a remote terminal to correct a programming error easily. To rectify the situation, in the mid-1960s, John Kemeny and Thomas Kurtz of Dartmouth College developed a simpler version of FORTRAN which they called BASIC. Since its introduction, many computer manufacturers have incorporated this language into their machines.

At first the BASIC language was quite limited, consisting of approximately 20 words. The inadequacy caused manufacturers to expand their compilers, thereby extending BASIC's vocabulary. BASIC that has been extended is referred to as **Extended BASIC** or **Level II**, as opposed to **Level I**. Unfortunately, the manufacturers did not consult one another when writing their extensions, so that now there are many "dialects" of BASIC. The net result is that there is no standard version of the language, thus making it necessary to modify a program before it is executed on a different make of computer.

A SHORT SUMMARY

The history of the electronic computer is divided into several generations. Each generation introduced a drastic change that resulted in greater speed, greater reliability, lower costs, and a reduction in size. The first generation of computers used vacuum tubes (1946), the second generation used transistors (1959), and the third generation used integrated circuits (1965). Many people believe that computers are now in the fourth generation (LSI—Large Scale Integration) or even in the fifth generation (VLSI—Very Large Scale Integration).

Microcomputers were first sold, in 1975, as computer kits. In 1977, the first completely assembled microcomputer was introduced to the general public. This opened up such new businesses as computer shops that sell hardware and consulting services that provide software. The internal structure of a microcomputer is basically the same as that of a conventional computer, namely, the Control Unit and the Arithmetic-Logical Unit (each is part of the Central Processing Unit), memory, and input/output facilities. The outstanding feature of the microprocessor is its programmability. Because of its versatility and its reduced size and cost, a microprocessor can be considered a peripheral to other electronic equipment. Today, technology has advanced to such an extent that all of the functions of a simple computer can be mounted on a single chip—the microcomputer-on-a-chip.

In the early 1950s, computer programs were written in machine language and later in symbolic language. Most programmers now write their programs in one of several high-level languages designed to ease the programmer's task by being less machine-dependent and by more closely resembling the human language. Symbolic and high-level languages cannot be used directly by the computer and must be translated first into machine language instructions. BASIC, one of the many problem-oriented languages in use today, was designed primarily for interactive situations and is currently the language adopted by most microcomputers.

QUESTIONS FOR REVIEW

1. State the function of
   (a) The analog computer.
   (b) The digital computer.
2. (a) What two computing machines did Charles Babbage design?
   (b) What was the reason for the development of each machine?
   (c) State some of the principles embodied in his second machine that are included in today's computers. Why was it not possible to completely build a modern machine during his time?
3. (a) Who designed the MARK I?
   (b) When was it successfully completed?
4. (a) Who developed the ENIAC?
   (b) Give a brief description of this computer.
5. What was the main difference between the MARK I and the ENIAC?
6. What important contribution did John von Neumann make in the design of a computer?
7. What three features did the BINAC introduce?
8. State four improvements that solid state computers had over computers that used vacuum tubes.
9. (a) What do the letters LSI mean?
   (b) Briefly describe how an LSI circuit is made.
   (c) How has the density of its circuitry changed?
10. Computers have been categorized into generations. Characterize each generation, giving its introductory year.
11. Briefly summarize the history of the microcomputer.
12. (a) What is meant by software?
    (b) In what two ways can software be purchased?
    (c) What is the recent trend with respect to software and hardware?
13. What five fundamental units do all computer systems possess?
14. (a) What is meant by a peripheral?
    (b) Give three examples.
15. (a) Name the two main components of a microprocessor and state the functions of each.
    (b) Why are microprocessors equipped with several registers?
16. (a) Give the definition and purpose of
       (i) RAM,
       (ii) ROM.
    (b) What is a byte?
17. (a) What is the purpose of an interface chip?
    (b) What is the difference between serial interfacing and parallel interfacing?

18. State the purpose of each of the following.
    (a) Data bus
    (b) Address bus
    (c) Control bus
19. What is meant by a microcomputer-on-a-chip?
20. Give two examples of external media used for mass storage of information.
21. (a) State two features that differentiate machine language from symbolic languages.
    (b) What feature makes them similar?
22. Other than being easier to learn, what advantage do high-level languages have over machine and symbolic languages?
23. What is the difference between an interpreter and a compiler?
24. State the main purpose for the development of each of the following high-level languages.
    (a) ALGOL
    (b) FORTRAN
    (c) PL/I
    (d) COBOL
    (e) BASIC
25. At first BASIC was limited to approximately 20 words. How has this been rectified and what is the resultant problem?

TWO INTRODUCING BASIC

A. Through the study of this chapter, you will become familiar with:
   1. The structure of a BASIC program.
   2. The rules that must be observed when writing a BASIC program.
   3. REMARK statements.
   4. Executable and non-executable statements.
   5. Flowcharting symbols.
   6. Integers and floating-point numbers.
   7. The BASIC symbols for arithmetic operations.
   8. The hierarchy of operations including parentheses.

B. You should be able to:
   1. Operate the system commands on an interactive system.
      (a) Clear the computer's memory.
      (b) Transmit a typed statement or command to the computer's memory.
      (c) Display a program.
      (d) Clear the screen.
      (e) Terminate a program.
   2. Make corrections in a BASIC program using an interactive system.
   3. Delete and insert lines in a BASIC program using an interactive system.
   4. Draw flowcharts for simple BASIC programs.
   5. Evaluate BASIC expressions.
   6. Produce the output of programs.
   7. Convert arithmetic problems into BASIC expressions and vice versa.
   8. Convert numbers from arithmetic notation to scientific notation and vice versa.
   9. Write BASIC programs using PRINT statements that
      (a) Leave blank lines.
      (b) Evaluate expressions.
      (c) Print messages (strings).
      (d) Use commas to separate items.
      (e) Use semicolons to separate items.
      (f) Print strings and numeric values on one line.
      (g) Use a comma or a semicolon at the end of the first of two PRINT statements to output two items on one line.
      (h) Counteract the comma or semicolon placed at the end of a PRINT statement.

2.1 SYSTEM COMMANDS[1]

To communicate with a computer, it is necessary to be familiar with the system's commands. Only those most commonly used will be

---

1. These commands are for use in an interactive or time-sharing environment. If you are not using this type of system (teletype, cathode ray tube, or microcomputer), you may ignore this section.

discussed, since there are many commands. After they have been explained, you will be given a number of short programs to key into the computer so that you can determine which commands are required by your computer system. Consult your reference manual for the required variation if you find that those given cannot be used. The notations in this section represent two different ways of entering the commands. A box around a command (representing a key) means that only the key must be depressed, for example, the RETURN key. If a command is not in a box, it must be typed out in full. For example, **NEW** must have three letters typed: an **N**, an **E**, and a **W**. Commands will be introduced in almost the same order as they are used.

1. Cursor

Although this is not a command, you should know the meaning of the word, since a cursor is used in an interactive computer system. A cursor is a light (often blinking) that appears on your screen in the form of a square, an arrow, an underscore, or some other character. It indicates the position of the next entry. Every time an entry is made, the cursor advances one position to the right. On some computers, special keys allow you to move the cursor up and down, as well as backwards and forwards.

2. Clearing the computer's memory

It is important that you erase any ''old'' program that is stored in the computer's memory before typing in a new program. On most computer systems, this command does not clear the screen. **Type** one of the commands shown below, then press RETURN or ENTER or CR.
NEW or **SCR** or **CLEAR** or **START** or **SCRATCH** or **N.** or **NE** or **DELETE** or **DELETE ALL**
On some systems, the command sets numeric variables currently in memory to zero and string variables to the **null** string. A string, which is a series of characters, is explained in Section 2.4 and variables are explained in Chapter Three. Turning the machine off also erases programs from memory, but this method is not recommended.

3. The RETURN or ENTER or CR key

One of the above keys must always be pressed after each statement or command is **typed**. The appropriate key transmits the typed statement or command to the computer's memory. Similar to the carriage return on a typewriter, it allows you to type the next entry at the beginning of a new line. Throughout this book, RETURN will be used for this particular command. However, many computer systems do not require a RETURN signal if another command key, such as STOP, has been depressed.

4. Displaying a program on the screen

To display a program currently stored in memory, type **LIST** (or **LIS** or **LI** or **L**), then press the RETURN key. Most versions of BASIC automatically list the line numbers in ascending order, regardless of the sequence of their entry into the computer. There are several LIST commands.

(a) LIST without a line number displays your whole program.
(b) LIST 100 displays only line 100.

(c) LIST 40,100 displays lines 40 and 100.
(d) LIST 40 – 100 displays lines 40 to 100 inclusive.
(e) LIST – 40 displays all lines up to and including line 40.
(f) LIST 40 – displays all lines from 40 to the end of your program (including line 40).

It is quite possible that not all of these commands can be used on your computer. If not, you will need to refer to your manual for the required variations.

5. Executing (processing) instructions

The **RUN** or **RU** command instructs the computer to execute your program, starting with the lowest line number and terminating when either an **END** statement, a **STOP** statement, or the highest line number is reached. Type RUN or RU, then press the RETURN key. If there are errors in your program, the computer will show you which lines are incorrect and will print diagnostic messages to tell you what is wrong. It is a good idea to LIST your program before RUNning it, just to make sure that your instructions are correctly stored in memory.

6. Clearing the screen

To clear the entire screen without erasing your program from memory, depress the **CLR** key, or type **CLS** or **HOME**, then press RETURN. On some computer systems, the CLR command not only clears your screen, it also deletes the line you are currently typing. All the lines previously typed remain in memory.

7. Making corrections

(a) To correct a character in a line before the RETURN key is pressed, press the left arrow key ← or the BACKSPACE key or the DEL key or the RUBOUT key. Each time the key is pressed, a character is deleted from memory. After all the incorrect characters have been erased, type the correct ones.
(b) To correct a character in a line after the RETURN key has been pressed, type the original line number, key in the correct statement, then press RETURN. On some systems the character cannot be corrected as in Part (a) since the statement has already been transmitted to the computer's memory. Some computers have built-in **EDIT** programs that allow you to change lines after they have been submitted to memory.
(c) To delete an entire line type the number of the line, then press RETURN. On some computer systems, you can delete one or more lines by typing the command **DELETE** or **DEL**, the line number (or numbers) to be deleted, then pressing RETURN.

DELETE 50 erases line 50.
DELETE 50,51 erases lines 50 and 51.
DELETE 45 – 50 erases lines 45 to 50 inclusive.
DELETE – 50 erases all lines up to and including line 50.
DELETE 50 – erases all lines from 50 to the end of your program (including line 50).

To erase all the lines at once, use one of the commands listed on page 13 under ''Clearing the Computer's Memory.''

(d) To insert a line, type the line with its appropriate line number under your original program and the computer will insert the statement in proper sequence.

8. Terminating a program

Sometimes a programmer may wish to terminate the execution of a program before it has been completely processed. There are many different commands for this function. Try the following, but remember, you may have to press RETURN after the command key has been depressed, depending on your computer system.

(a) Press the STOP key.
(b) Hold the CTRL key down, depress the C key.
(c) Press the BREAK key.
(d) Press the ESC key.
(e) Press the ALT MODE key.
(f) Press the S key.
(g) Press the PAUSE key.

On many systems, execution may be resumed from the point where it was stopped by typing **CONT** or **CONTINUE**.

9. READY or OK or DONE

These are not commands. One of them, or something similar, is displayed on the screen to inform you that the computer is ready to receive further instructions or commands.

2.1 SYSTEM COMMANDS—Your Turn

Even though you may not understand what you are typing, it doesn't matter. The main concern of this section is to give you an opportunity to use the different system commands. You will be asked to key in several programs, each one stressing a different set of commands. Try all those given for a particular operation, and if none of them work, consult your manual or ask someone who knows. The page number where the command was introduced is typed after each exercise.

1. Clear the computer's memory of all old instructions. (Page 13)
2. Enter the following program into the computer. Remember to press RETURN after each statement has been typed. (Page 13)

I. Commands Required to Enter a BASIC Program into the Computer and to Execute the Program

```
10 PRINT
20 LET A=1
30 PRINT A
40 LET A=A+1
50 IF A>5 THEN 99
60 GO TO 30
99 END
```

3. Display the program on your screen. (Page 13)
4. Execute the program. (Page 14)
   Your RUN should produce the following results.

```
RUN

1
2
3
4
5
```

5. Clear the screen. (Page 14)
   Your screen should now be blank. LIST the program again. If everything went right, the program should reappear on your screen.

II. Making Corrections

1. To correct a character in a line before the [RETURN] key is depressed:
   (a) Erase the old program from memory.
   (b) Key in the statement.

   20 PRIMT A   Do not [RETURN]

   (c) Change PRIMT to PRINT. (Page 14)
2. To correct a character in a line after the [RETURN] key has been depressed:
   (a) Erase the above statement from memory.
   (b) Key in the following program.

```
10 LET A=1
20 LET B=2
30 PRIMT A
40 PRINT B
99 END
```

   (c) After you have typed the five statements, change PRIMT in line 30 to PRINT. (Page 14)
3. To delete a line:
   (a) Delete lines 20 and 40 from the above program. (Page 14)
   (b) LIST your program. Lines 20 and 40 should no longer be included in your program.
4. To insert a line:
   (a) In the same program, insert the line **15 PRINT A+2**. (Page 15)

(b) LIST your program. Notice how the inserted line has been placed in proper sequence.

```
10 LET A=1
15 PRINT A+2
30 PRINT A
99 END
```

1. Erase the old program from memory.
2. Key in the following program.

```
10 LET A=1
20 PRINT A
30 LET A=A+1
40 GO TO 20
99 END
```

3. LIST and RUN the program. Your RUN should produce the following.

```
RUN
 1
 2
 3
 4
 5
 6
 7
 .
 .
```

Notice that the computer continues to process the instructions.

4. Terminate the program. (Page 15)

III. Terminating Execution of a Program

2.2 A BASIC PROGRAM

A number of rules must be observed when you write a BASIC program. Refer to the sample program on page 18 as the rules are being presented. Do not enter the program into your computer; it is here merely as an aid to help you understand the rules.

```
01 REM THIS PROGRAM FINDS THE AVERAGE
02 REM OF 4 NUMBERS
03 REM K--COUNTER
04 REM S--SUM
05 REM N1--"NUMBER" OF NUMBERS
06 REM N--NUMBERS TO BE AVERAGED
07 REM A--AVERAGE

100 REM INITIALIZE THE VARIABLES
110 PRINT
120 LET K=1
130 LET S=0

200 REM READ THE DATA
210 READ N1
220 READ N
230 DATA 4,67,85,79,93

300 REM ADD, PRINT THE NUMBERS
301 REM AND THE ACCUMULATED SUM
310 LET S=S+N
320 PRINT N,S

400 REM INCREMENT THE COUNTER
410 LET K=K+1
420 IF K>N1 THEN 500
430 GO TO 220

500 REM FIND THE AVERAGE
510 LET A=S/N1

600 REM PRINT THE AVERAGE
610 PRINT
620 PRINT "THE AVERAGE IS:";A

999 END

RUN

    67          67
    85          152
    79          231
    93          324

THE AVERAGE IS: 81
```

1. All BASIC programs consist of statements.   Rules
2. Each statement may not exceed a certain number of characters.
   Some versions of BASIC allow seventy-two characters, some
   allow seventy-nine characters, and others allow even more. If the
   allowed maximum is exceeded, either the excess characters are
   ignored or the entire statement is ignored. An error message

may or may not be given. Check your computer manual for the maximum number of characters allowed on your system.

3. Each statement must begin with a line number that is unique. (No other statement may have the same line number.) These numbers must be positive integers[2] and may range from 1 to 99999 inclusive, depending on the computer system being used. Again, check your manual.

4. Unless there is a branch, statements are always executed according to line number (from lowest to highest). On many computer systems, statements are processed in this manner regardless of the sequence of their entry; on other systems, they must be entered in the same order as their lines are numbered.

5. It is customary to number statements in multiples of a specific number (say, 10) so that additional statements may be inserted at a later time.

6. On many computer systems, programs must terminate with an END statement. If the END statement is required, most of these systems insist that it be the highest-numbered statement in the program. If the END statement is not required, execution terminates with the highest numbered statement.

7. **REM (REMARK)** statements may be inserted anywhere in the program. They are used to identify the program, to identify the variables, and to describe a routine. REM statements are not executable instructions but are merely comment statements that document[3] a program.

8. To distinguish between the number $\emptyset$ and the letter O, most programmers place a slash through one of them. For example:

Number 0 . . . . . .$\emptyset$,   Letter O . . . . . .O.

Turn to the sample program on page 18. It has been numbered and documented in an extreme fashion, but this is the way it is often done when programs are very long.

1. REM (REMARK) statements are placed at the beginning of the program (numbered from 01 to 07) to identify the program and the variables used.

2. Line numbers are segregated into groups of hundreds. Each multiple of 100 is a routine different from the others and each is headed by a REM statement. For example:
    (a) The READ routine has statements numbered in the 200 range.
    (b) The summation routine has statements numbered in the 300 range.
    (c) The PRINT routine has statements numbered in the 600 range.

3. For ease in reading, a blank line is inserted between each routine and before the word RUN.

4. Throughout the book, a slash is drawn through the number zero to distinguish it from the letter O.

```
130 LET S=0
```

2. An integer is a number that has no decimal point.
3. Programs are documented by inserting explanations throughout the programs to make them easier to understand.

5. The programs in this book include END statements. The END statement will be the highest-numbered statement in a program. In the sample program, the END statement is numbered 999.

```
999 END
```

6. Programs are made up of executable statements and non-executable statements. An executable statement is an instruction, one to which the computer can respond by following a direction. A non-executable statement is not an instruction, therefore, the computer does not execute (process) this type of statement. Examples taken from the sample program are

Executable statements:

```
220 READ N
410 LET K=K+1
620 PRINT "THE AVERAGE IS:";A
```

Non-executable statements: The REM statements

There are a few terms you should know before going on to some simple BASIC programs. They are data, coding, and debugging. Information entered into the computer to be processed is called data. In the sample program, the data items are: 4,67,85,79,93. The process of writing BASIC statements is referred to as coding, while that of identifying and correcting errors is called debugging.

2.3 FLOWCHARTING

When a program is long and complicated, a chart of its steps is often drawn before the program is written in order to give a pictorial representation of the procedure it follows. This representation is called a flowchart. Its purpose is to clearly define an overall plan so that a programmer can more readily visualize the logical flow of the program. Standard symbols of various shapes and sizes are used to denote the different operations. These symbols are connected by lines and arrows to show the direction of the flow.

An oval represents a terminal point, either the beginning or the ending of a program.

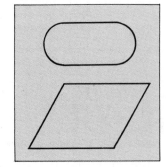

A parallelogram indicates an input or an output operation.

A rectangle denotes a processing operation.

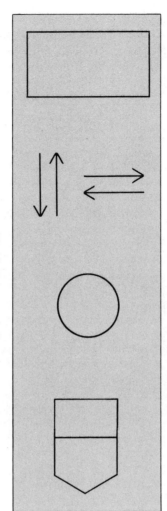

Lines of flow connect two symbols. Arrowheads show the direction of programming logic.

Circles, called connectors, are used instead of lines and arrows to connect symbols when processing lines are long and complex. With an appropriate letter or number inside, one connector denotes an exit from one part of the flowchart, while a second connector indicates the entry to another part of the flowchart, thus maintaining a continuous flow of logic.

An off-page connector indicates that the flowchart is continued on another page.

As concepts are developed throughout the book, other symbols will be introduced and flowcharts will be drawn to help you understand more easily a program's logic.

Although flowcharts vary in detail, a few basic rules are usually observed.

1. Construct the flowchart so that the direction of programming logic flows from top to bottom and from left to right.
2. Connect all symbols with lines and arrows, or connectors.
3. When there are several entries to one symbol, point the lines to the main line entering the symbol.

Permitted   Not permitted

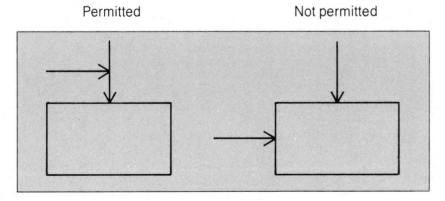

4. Place a description of the operation inside each symbol.
5. Use a **template** to draw a flowchart. A template is a piece of plastic usually 10 cm long and 25 cm wide in which the symbols have been cut.

2.3 FLOWCHARTING — Sample Program

Shown below is a flowchart for a program that adds two numbers, then prints their sum. Do not be too concerned if you don't understand how the computer processes some of the statements. This will be covered in another chapter. At the moment, all that is required is to learn to flowchart a simple BASIC program.

The program

```
01 REM N1--FIRST NUMBER
02 REM N2--SECOND NUMBER
03 REM S--SUM

10 READ N1,N2
20 DATA 7,5
30 LET S=N1+N2
40 PRINT S
99 END
```

The flowchart

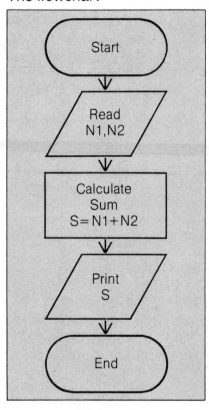

```
10 READ N1,N2
20 DATA 7,5



30 LET S=N1+N2



40 PRINT S



99 END
```

2.3 FLOWCHARTING—Your Turn

Draw a flowchart for the following program. This program subtracts
one number from another, then prints the difference. Opposite each
symbol, write the appropriate statement(s).

```
01  REM N1--FIRST NUMBER
02  REM N2--SECOND NUMBER
03  REM D--DIFFERENCE

10  READ N1,N2
20  DATA 12,5
30  LET D=N1-N2
40  PRINT D
99  END
```

2.3 FLOWCHARTING—Solution for "Your Turn"

N1 — FIRST NUMBER
N2 — SECOND NUMBER
D — DIFFERENCE

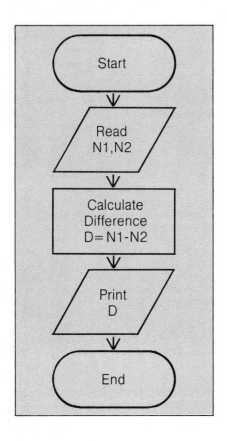

```
10  READ N1,N2
20  DATA 12,5



30  LET D=N1-N2



40  PRINT D



99  END
```

2.4 THE PRINT STATEMENT

The PRINT statement gets information out of the computer so that you are able to see it. This information is either displayed on a screen or typed on paper and is in the form of numbers and messages. Some PRINT statements also leave blank lines wherever you wish to have them in your output. Here are two simple programs using PRINT statements that leave blank lines.

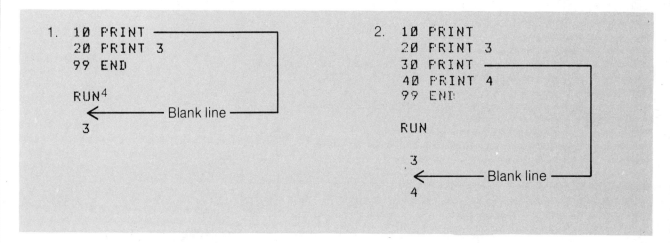

In Program 1, the statement **10 PRINT** leaves a blank line just *before* the output. In Program 2, the statement **30 PRINT** leaves a blank line *between* the two values in the output. Most programs in this book leave a blank line right after the word **RUN** (in other words, before the output). To achieve this and to be consistent, the PRINT statement is placed just before the one that prints the results.

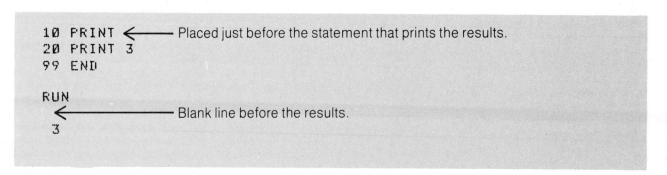

Some computer systems allow you to type a question mark instead of the word PRINT. For ease of reading, it is better to use the word.

Printing messages

Besides printing numbers and blank lines, a PRINT statement can also print messages which are referred to as **strings**. A message must follow the word **PRINT** and must be enclosed in either double or single quotation marks, depending on the computer system used. The message may contain letters of the alphabet, digits, special

4. If you are not using an interactive system, ignore the word RUN shown before each output.

characters, and spaces, but not the quote that delimits the string. The computer prints exactly what has been placed within the quotation marks.

```
10 PRINT
20 PRINT "HI"
99 END

RUN

HI
```

Notice that no quotation marks are printed in the output. Messages are often used as headings or to identify results. For example, **THE AVERAGE IS: 81**.

A program that prints both a string and the result of a calculation is shown below.

```
10 PRINT
20 PRINT "6+7"
30 PRINT 6+7
99 END

RUN

6+7
13
```

Statement 20 causes the computer to print **6+7** while statement 30 tells the computer to evaluate 6+7 then print the answer. You have probably noticed by now that every time the computer encounters a PRINT statement, output is printed on a new line. In the above program there are three PRINT statements; in the RUN there are three lines of output — a blank line, **6+7**, and **13**.

2.4 THE PRINT STATEMENT — Your Turn

If you are using a microcomputer, remember to clear any old instructions from the computer's memory before keying in a new program. (It is assumed that you will remember this from now on.) Page numbers are given for programs similar to the ones you are to write, so that you can refer to these pages if you need any help.

1. Write a program that prints your name on one line, **12+5** on the next line, and the answer to **12+5** on the last line. Leave one blank line after the word **RUN**. (Page 25)

```
   RUN

   JOHN SMITH
   12+5
    17
```

2. Rewrite the above program so that a blank line is left after your name, as well as before it. (Page 24)

```
   RUN

   JOHN SMITH

   12+5
    17
```

2.4 THE PRINT STATEMENT—Programs for "Your Turn"

```
1.  10 PRINT                    2.  10 PRINT
    20 PRINT "JOHN SMITH"           20 PRINT "JOHN SMITH"
    30 PRINT "12+5"                 30 PRINT
    40 PRINT 12+5                   40 PRINT "12+5"
    99 END                         50 PRINT 12+5
                                    99 END
```

2.5 THE PRINT STATEMENT WITH COMMAS OR SEMICOLONS

Until now, only one value or message per line has been printed, using a separate PRINT statement for each line of output. It is possible to print several items on one line with just one PRINT statement. The items are printed across the line with a specific number of spaces between each item. The values listed in the PRINT statement must be separated by either commas or semicolons. On most computer systems, a comma tells the computer to print the items spread widely across the page or screen, while the semicolon causes the items to be printed closer together. However, there are exceptions. A few computers do not recognize the comma in a PRINT statement, but treat it as a semicolon instead. Thus, the output is always closely spaced.

I. Commas in the PRINT Statement[5]

Commas in a PRINT statement usually divide an output line into zones of fixed and equal width. The number of zones and the width of each zone are dependent on the computer system. Most computers have either four or five zones with 10, 15, or 16 characters to each zone. Only one item is printed in a zone.

It was mentioned earlier in the chapter that pressing the RETURN key transmits a statement to the memory of the computer. Suppose the last character of a statement is in the last print position of a line and that the cursor has automatically dropped down to the beginning of the next line. To transmit the statement to memory, you must still press the RETURN key, even though the cursor is positioned on a new line. It was also mentioned that the number of characters to a statement varies among computers. To be consistent, all programs in this book are written for a computer that allows 79 characters to a statement but permits only 40 characters to a display line. This means that a statement can use 40 print positions in the first line and 39 in the second. In the first nine chapters, statements are brief so that they fit a 40-character line. Statements in the other chapters are longer. It should also be mentioned that, wherever possible, output is given to help you understand a new concept in a sample program and to indicate the results you should obtain for a "Your Turn" problem or a programming problem. The output that is given is from a computer that has four zones to an output line with ten characters to a zone.

Now, try some sample programs. A comma between two items in a PRINT statement causes the second item to be printed on the same line but in the next available zone. If there are more items than zones, the computer prints the remaining items on successive lines, using all the zones in one line before going on to the next line.

```
10 PRINT
20 PRINT 1,22,333,4444,55555,666666
99 END

RUN

1          22          333         4444
55555      666666
```

Zones of fixed widths

Notice that the zone widths are all the same. Spacing between items, then, depends on the number of characters in each zone. Also, on most systems the first position in a zone is reserved for the sign. If the number is positive, the position is left blank; if the number is negative,

5. If your computer does not recognize a comma but treats it as a semicolon, your output will always be closely spaced. The computer used for programs in this book distinguishes a comma from a semicolon.

it is filled in with a minus sign. The following is an example of a RUN with positive and negative numbers.

```
10 PRINT
20 PRINT 1,22,333,4444
30 PRINT -1,-22,-333,-4444
99 END

RUN

   1          22         333        4444
  -1         -22        -333       -4444
```

Strings usually start in the first position of each zone.

```
10 PRINT
20 PRINT "HI,","HOW","ARE","YOU?"
99 END

RUN

HI,         HOW        ARE        YOU?
```

First position of each zone

It is common practice to use one PRINT statement to print a combination of strings and numbers. Here is an example.

```
                        Space
10 PRINT
20 PRINT "2+3 =",2+3
30 PRINT "2-6 =",2-6
99 END

RUN
        Space
2+3 =          5
2-6 =         -4
```

Notice the space before the equals sign in line 20 and in line 30. Since this space is part of the string, it is included in the output.

II. Semicolons in the PRINT Statement

Depending on your computer system, semicolons in a PRINT list cause the computer to leave one, two, or possibly three spaces between printed items. The number of zones in one line depends on the number of characters in a printed item and on the maximum number of characters allowed in each zone (16 is the usual maximum number allowed, which includes the spaces, if any, before and after a number). Thus, while a comma causes zones of fixed width, the semicolon sets up zones of varying widths. Usually, the first position in each zone is reserved for the sign. A space is left if the number is positive; a minus sign is inserted if the number is negative.[6]

```
10 PRINT
20 PRINT 1;22;333;4444;55555
30 PRINT -1;-22;-333;-4444;-55555
99 END

RUN

 1  22  333  4444   55555
-1 -22 -333 -4444  -55555
```

Zones of varying widths

Do not be too concerned if your output turns out differently. Some computer systems leave one space before and one space after the number in each zone, regardless of whether the number is signed or unsigned. As a result, numbers no longer line up. Compare the output below with the one just shown.

```
RUN

 1   22   333   4444    55555
-1   -22   -333   -4444    -55555
```

One space before and one space after each number

Other computers leave one space before and no space after each signed or unsigned number. The output looks like this.

```
RUN

 1 22 333 4444 55555
-1 -22 -333 -4444 -55555
```

One space before each number

6. In this book, regardless of the type of punctuation used in a PRINT statement, a space is left before a positive number and a space is left after any number, whether it is positive or negative. If the number is negative, the space before the number is filled in with a minus sign.

For computers that leave no space between numbers in the output, it is necessary to insert a space. Examine the following program.

```
10 PRINT
20 PRINT 1;" ";22;" ";333;" ";4444;" ";5
5555
99 END
```

To obtain a space between two output numbers, one space, enclosed in quotation marks, is placed between two numbers in the PRINT statement. Notice, also, that the PRINT statement exceeds 40 characters and is continued on the next line, starting in the first position of the line.

Semicolons separating strings in a PRINT statement cause messages (strings) to be printed with no space between them. This is because each string starts in the first position of a zone.

```
10 PRINT
20 PRINT "HI,";"HOW";"ARE";"YOU?"
99 END

RUN

HI,HOWAREYOU?
└──┴──┴──┴──┘
```
First position of each zone

To print a more legible line, each string that is followed by another string should have a trailing space coded within its quotation marks.

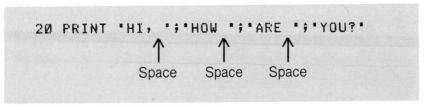

Another solution is to code a leading space in each string that is preceded by another string.

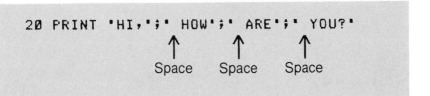

A RUN of a program using either one of the above statements now produces the following.

```
RUN

HI, HOW ARE YOU?
```

Here is a program that combines a string with a number in the PRINT statement. The program on page 28 used a comma to separate the items; this one uses a semicolon.

```
10 PRINT
20 PRINT "NUMBER:";4
99 END

RUN

NUMBER: 4
```

Notice that the output has one space before the number 4. If the number had been negative, the computer would either insert a minus sign in this space or (as mentioned on page 29) leave a space before the signed number.

Depending upon the computer being used, the output may be as follows.

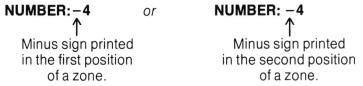

NUMBER:−4   *or*   **NUMBER: −4**

Minus sign printed   Minus sign printed
in the first position   in the second position
of a zone.   of a zone.

A comma or a semicolon at the end of a PRINT list causes the items of the next PRINT statement to be printed on the same line as those of the former PRINT statement.

III. Comma or Semicolon at the End of a PRINT Statement

1. Using a Comma   2. Using a Semicolon

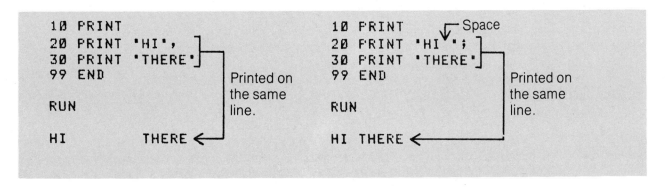

```
10 PRINT                        10 PRINT          Space
20 PRINT "HI",                  20 PRINT "HI";
30 PRINT "THERE"                30 PRINT "THERE"
99 END              Printed on  99 END              Printed on
                    the same                        the same
RUN                 line.       RUN                 line.

HI        THERE                 HI THERE
```

Notice the space in the string **"HI "** in Program 2. This space is needed, otherwise your output will be **HITHERE**. The PRINT statements in Program 1 will run the words together if you are using a computer that treats a comma as a semicolon. To get a space between the two words, line 20 in Program 1 should be changed to **20 PRINT "HI ",**.

If your computer leaves a space before a number, no trailing space needs to be coded in the string that precedes the number.

```
10 PRINT
20 PRINT "NUMBER";
30 PRINT 4              ↑
99 END              No space

RUN

NUMBER 4
       ↑
    Space
```

There is a technique to counteract the comma or semicolon that appears at the end of a PRINT list. Have a **PRINT** (the one that prints a blank line) as the next PRINT statement. This causes the output of a subsequent **PRINT** to be placed on a new line. It's the same as not having a comma or a semicolon after **"HI"** in the above programs.

1. Using a Comma   ### 2. Using a Semicolon

```
10 PRINT                               10 PRINT
20 PRINT "HI",   Counteracts           20 PRINT "HI";   Counteracts the
30 PRINT ←——→ the comma                30 PRINT ←——→ semicolon
40 PRINT "THERE"                       40 PRINT "THERE"
99 END                                 99 END

RUN                                    RUN

HI                                     HI
THERE                                  THERE
```

Note that no space is inserted in the string **"HI"** in Program 2 since the next word (**THERE**) is printed on a new line.

2.5 THE PRINT STATEMENT WITH COMMAS OR SEMICOLONS—Your Turn

You will now have the opportunity to try the various PRINT statements on your own. There are many sample programs in the previous unit;

refer to them if you need help. The page numbers are given for easy reference.

For each of the following problems, leave one blank line after the word **RUN**. (It is assumed that your computer differentiates between a comma and a semicolon.)

1. Write a BASIC program that prints the numbers 1,2,3,4 on one line, then −1,−2,−3,−4 on the next line. The items in both lines of output are to be widely spaced. (Page 28)
2. Rewrite the above program so that the items in both lines are closely spaced. (Page 29)
3. Write one BASIC program that prints **COMMAS OR SEM-ICOLONS** in the three ways listed below. Each PRINT statement must have three strings. (Pages 28 and 30)
   (a) Widely spaced across the line
   (b) With no spaces between the words
   (c) With one space between each word
4. Write one BASIC program that calculates 6+3 and 6−9 and prints the results as follows. (Pages 28 and 31)
   (a) The string **6+3 =** followed by the answer. Output is widely spaced.
   (b) The string **6−9 =** followed by the answer. Output is widely spaced.
   (c) The string **6+3 =** followed by the answer. Output is closely spaced.
   (d) The string **6−9 =** followed by the answer. Output is closely spaced.
5. Write a BASIC program that uses two PRINT statements (in addition to the one that leaves a blank line) to print the words **YOUR TURN** widely spaced on one line. (Page 31)
6. Rewrite the above program so that your output is closely spaced. Use the same number of PRINT statements as in Problem 5. Leave one space between the words. (Page 31)
7. Modify the following program so that your output is printed on two lines. Do not change lines 20 and 30 in any way. (Page 32)

```
10 PRINT
20 PRINT "LAST",
30 PRINT "QUESTION"
99 END
```

Your RUN should be as follows.

```
RUN

LAST
QUESTION
```

2.5 PRINT STATEMENT WITH COMMAS OR SEMICOLONS—Programs for "Your Turn"

```
1.  10 PRINT
    20 PRINT 1,2,3,4
    30 PRINT -1,-2,-3,-4
    99 END

2.  10 PRINT
    20 PRINT 1;2;3;4
    30 PRINT -1;-2;-3;-4
    99 END

3.  10 PRINT
    20 PRINT "COMMAS","OR","SEMICOLONS"
    30 PRINT "COMMAS";"OR";"SEMICOLONS"
    40 PRINT "COMMAS ";"OR ";"SEMICOLONS"
                    or
    40 PRINT "COMMAS";" OR";" SEMICOLONS"
    99 END

4.  10 PRINT
    20 PRINT "6+3 =",6+3
    30 PRINT "6-9 =",6-9
    40 PRINT "6+3 =";6+3
    50 PRINT "6-9 =";6-9
    99 END

5.  10 PRINT
    20 PRINT "YOUR",
    30 PRINT "TURN"
    99 END

6.  10 PRINT              or   10 PRINT
    20 PRINT "YOUR ";          20 PRINT "YOUR";
    30 PRINT "TURN"            30 PRINT " TURN"
    99 END                     99 END

7.  10 PRINT
    20 PRINT "LAST",
    25 PRINT
    30 PRINT "QUESTION"
    99 END
```

2.6 INTEGERS, FLOATING-POINT NUMBERS, HIERARCHY OF OPERATIONS

There are two terms you should be familiar with before you start working with BASIC expressions.[7] One is the term **integer** and the other is the term **floating-point**. Both refer to numbers. An integer is a number that has no decimal point; a floating-point number is one that has a decimal point. Floating-point means that the decimal point "floats" or moves within the number depending on the value you want. For example, the number 257 may be changed to 25.7 or 2.57 or .257 or .0257, etc., by moving the position of the decimal point. In BASIC, numbers (whether integer or floating-point) are operated on by arithmetic operators. These operators must be in a form that is understood by the computer. You have already had examples of addition and subtraction in the previous sections. Here is a complete list.

Operation	Symbol in BASIC
Addition	+
Subtraction	−
Multiplication	*
Division	/
Exponentiation[8]	↑ or ** or ∧
(The act of raising a number to a power — for example, $4^2 = 4 \times 4 = 16$.)	

When two or more operators appear in one statement, confusion may arise as to which one is processed first. This is solved by a set of rules known as the **hierarchy of operations**. The order of execution is as follows.

1. **Exponentiation**
2. **Multiplication and division** — Multiplication and division have equal priority, therefore these operations are performed in the order they appear in a statement. (The computer always processes a statement in a left-to-right direction.)
3. **Addition and subtraction** — As in multiplication and division, addition and subtraction have equal priority, which means that these operations are also processed in a left-to-right order.

When a statement contains parentheses, the operations within the parentheses are executed first, starting with the innermost pair of parentheses, then moving outwards to the second innermost pair, then to the third innermost pair, etc. If there are two sets of parentheses, one following the other, the computer clears the first set of parentheses before clearing the second. In the expression

$$(2+3)/(7-2)$$

7. When arithmetic operators connect numbers or variables or a combination of one or more numbers with one or more variables, a BASIC expression is formed.
8. Throughout this book the symbol ↑ will be used to represent exponentiation.

the computer performs the addition in the first set of parentheses, then the subtraction in the second set of parentheses, and finally the division. Parentheses can alter the normal order of execution. For example:

$$2+(3*4) = 14 \quad but \quad (2+3)*4 = 20$$

On some computer systems, two arithmetic operators may not be written consecutively. The expression **3*−4** is invalid, while **3*(−4)** is valid. More than one expression can be coded in a PRINT statement.

```
10 PRINT
20 PRINT 0+1,0+1+2,0+1+2+3,0+1+2+3+4
99 END

RUN


 1              3              6              10
```

2.6 INTEGERS, FLOATING-POINT NUMBERS, HIERARCHY OF OPERATIONS – Sample Problems

1. The following BASIC expressions will be evaluated twice; first by hand and then by the computer. Go over each step so that you understand how the computer follows the rules of hierarchy. Note that just one arithmetic operation is performed at a time.

(a) 5*3−4/2+1
    15−4/2+1
    15−2+1
    13+1
    14

(b) 6+3↑2/(5−2)−4
    6+3↑2/3−4
    6+9/3−4
    6+3−4
    9−4
    5

(c) 7*2−(4↑2−8)/(3+1)
    7*2−(16−8)/(3+1)
    7*2−8/(3+1)
    7*2−8/4
    14−8/4
    14−2
    12

(d) 8−(2*(3+4)−6)+1
    8−(2*7−6)+1
    8−(14−6)+1
    8−8+1
    0+1
    1

(e) $15-(2\uparrow3-2*(3*(7-5)-5))$

$15-(2\uparrow3-2*(3*2-5))$

$15-(2\uparrow3-2*(6-5))$

$15-(2\uparrow3-2*1)$

$15-(8-2*1)$

$15-(8-2)$

$15-6$

9

(f) $(4\uparrow2+5)/(2\uparrow3-5)+7$

$(16+5)/(2\uparrow3-5)+7$

$21/(2\uparrow3-5)+7$

$21/(8-5)+7$

$21/3+7$

$7+7$

14

2. Now, key in and RUN the programs shown below. Do you get the same answers on the computer as you did when the calculations were done by hand?

(a) ```
10 PRINT
20 PRINT 5*3-4/2+1
99 END

RUN

 14
```

(d)  ```
10 PRINT
20 PRINT 8-(2*(3+4)-6)+1
99 END

RUN

 1
```

(b) ```
10 PRINT
20 PRINT 6+3↑2/(5-2)-4
99 END

RUN

 5
```

(e)  ```
10 PRINT
20 PRINT 15-(2↑3-2*(3*(7-5)-5))
99 END

RUN

 9
```

(c) ```
10 PRINT
20 PRINT 7*2-(4↑2-8)/(3+1)
99 END

RUN

 12
```

(f)  ```
10 PRINT
20 PRINT (4↑2+5)/(2↑3-5)+7
99 END

RUN

 14
```

2.6 INTEGERS, FLOATING-POINT NUMBERS, HIERARCHY OF OPERATIONS – Your Turn

1. Evaluate the following BASIC expressions. Do one calculation at a time.

   (a) $4\uparrow2 - 9/3 + 1$
   (b) $2*5\uparrow2/(10-8)+3$
   (c) $6*3 - (8/2\uparrow2)/(6-4)$
   (d) $16-(2*(9/3+1)-4)+2$
   (e) $7-(2*(3*(8/4-1)+2)-6)+5$
   (f) $9-(9/3+1)/(7*2-12)+3$

2. Write six BASIC programs to evaluate the above expressions. RUN the programs on your computer and compare the answers with the ones you arrived at when the calculations were done by hand. The answers for each expression should be the same.

2.6 INTEGERS, FLOATING-POINT NUMBERS, HIERARCHY OF OPERATIONS – Solutions for "Your Turn"

1. (a) $4\uparrow2 - 9/3 + 1$
       $16 - 9/3 + 1$
       $16 - 3 + 1$
       $13 + 1$
       14

   (b) $2*5\uparrow2/(10-8)+3$
       $2*5\uparrow2/2+3$
       $2*25/2+3$
       $50/2+3$
       $25+3$
       28

   (c) $6*3 - (8/2\uparrow2)/(6-4)$
       $6*3 - (8/4)/(6-4)$
       $6*3 - 2/(6-4)$
       $6*3 - 2/2$
       $18 - 2/2$
       $18 - 1$
       17

   (d) $16 - (2*(9/3+1) - 4) + 2$
       $16 - (2*(3+1) - 4) + 2$
       $16 - (2*4 - 4) + 2$
       $16 - (8 - 4) + 2$
       $16 - 4 + 2$
       $12 + 2$
       14

(e) $7-(2*(3*(8/4-1)+2)-6)+5$

$7-(2*(3*(2-1)+2)-6)+5$

$7-(2*(3*1+2)-6)+5$

$7-(2*(3+2)-6)+5$

$7-(2*5-6)+5$

$7-(10-6)+5$

$7-4+5$

$3+5$

8

(f) $9-(9/3+1)/(7*2-12)+3$

$9-(3+1)/(7*2-12)+3$

$9-4/(7*2-12)+3$

$9-4/(14-12)+3$

$9-4/2+3$

$9-2+3$

$7+3$

10

---

2. (a)
```
10 PRINT
20 PRINT 4T2-9/3+1
99 END

RUN

 14
```

(b)
```
10 PRINT
20 PRINT 2*5T2/(10-8)+3
99 END

RUN

 28
```

(c)
```
10 PRINT
20 PRINT 6*3-(8/2T2)/(6-4)
99 END

RUN

 17
```

(d)
```
10 PRINT
20 PRINT 16-(2*(9/3+1)-4)+2
99 END

RUN

 14
```

(e)
```
10 PRINT
20 PRINT 7-(2*(3*(8/4-1)+2)-6)+5
99 END

RUN

 8
```

(f)
```
10 PRINT
20 PRINT 9-(9/3+1)/(7*2-12)+3
99 END

RUN

 10
```

2.7 CONVERTING FROM ARITHMETIC INTO BASIC AND VICE VERSA

When writing BASIC programs, it is often necessary to convert arithmetic problems into BASIC expressions. You should also be able to do the reverse.

1. Here are some arithmetic problems that have been changed to BASIC expressions.

Arithmetic	BASIC	
(a) $2+3(6-4)$	$2+3*(6-4)$	— Don't forget the asterisk!
(b) $2+\dfrac{3}{4+5}-7$	$2+3/(4+5)-7$	— Note the parentheses.
(c) $\dfrac{2+3}{4+5}-7$	$(2+3)/(4+5)-7$	— Notice two sets of parentheses.
(d) $6+\dfrac{(5-2)^2}{3+4}$	$6+(5-2)\uparrow2/(3+4)$	— Be careful what you square — just $5-2$.
(e) $\dfrac{(7-3)^3+8^2-4}{5+2}$	$((7-3)\uparrow3+8\uparrow2-4)/(5+2)$	— This is a tough one. Notice that all of the numerator must have parentheses around it, which results in two left parentheses in front of $7-3$.

2. These convert BASIC expressions into arithmetic problems.

BASIC	Arithmetic	
(a) $3+5\uparrow2-4/6+7$	$3+5^2-\dfrac{4}{6}+7$	— Note 4 divided by 6.
(b) $3+5\uparrow2-4/(6+7)$	$3+5^2-\dfrac{4}{6+7}$	— This time 4 is divided by $6+7$.
(c) $(3+5\uparrow2-4)/(6+7)$	$\dfrac{3+5^2-4}{6+7}$	— Notice the numerator now — it consists of several numbers and operators.
(d) $8-(4+2)\uparrow3+5/(9-2)$	$8-(4+2)^3+\dfrac{5}{9-2}$	— Watch the parentheses.
(e) $(4\uparrow3+(8-3)\uparrow2)/(6-2)-7$	$\dfrac{4^3+(8-3)^2}{6-2}-7$	— Another tough one. The numerator has parentheses within it. Also, the denominator does not include the number 7.

2.7 CONVERTING FROM ARITHMETIC INTO BASIC AND VICE VERSA—Your Turn

1. Convert the following arithmetic problems into BASIC expressions.

   (a) $\dfrac{6}{2} + 4(9-3)$

   (b) $\dfrac{6}{4-2} + \dfrac{4^2-8}{3}$

   (c) $\dfrac{6+2}{4-2} + \dfrac{8-(5+4)}{7}$

   (d) $\dfrac{3^2+6}{9-5} + \dfrac{10-4}{3}$

   (e) $\dfrac{(3+2)^2 - 4^3}{5-3} + 6$

   (f) $\dfrac{3^2 - 4(12-(7+3)+9)}{7-1} + 5^2$

2. Convert the following BASIC expressions into arithmetic problems.

   (a) 2↑3/4− 10/5
   (b) (6− 2)↑3+ 8/4+ (5+ 7)/2
   (c) (5+ 4)↑3+ 8/(4+ 3)− (6− 4)/2
   (d) (7+ (3+ 6)↑2)/(4+ 3)− 9/(7− 4)
   (e) ((6− 2)↑3+ 8)/(4+ 3)+ (8− 2)/(5+ 1)
   (f) (2*(3+ (7− 5)↑2− 9))/(4+ 5)− 7

2.7 CONVERTING FROM ARITHMETIC INTO BASIC AND VICE VERSA—Solutions for "Your Turn"

1. Arithmetic into BASIC

   (a) 6/2 + 4*(9 − 3)
   (b) 6/(4 − 2) + (4↑2 − 8)/3
   (c) (6 + 2)/(4 − 2) + (8 − (5 + 4))/7
   (d) (3↑2 + 6)/(9 − 5) + (10 − 4)/3
   (e) ((3 + 2)↑2 − 4↑3)/(5 − 3) + 6
   (f) (3↑2 − 4*(12 − (7 + 3) + 9))/(7 − 1) + 5↑2

2. BASIC into Arithmetic

   (a) $\dfrac{2^3}{4} - \dfrac{10}{5}$

   (b) $(6-2)^3 + \dfrac{8}{4} + \dfrac{5+7}{2}$

(c) $(5+4)^3 + \dfrac{8}{4+3} - \dfrac{6-4}{2}$

(d) $\dfrac{7+(3+6)^2}{4+3} - \dfrac{9}{7-4}$

(e) $\dfrac{(6-2)^3 + 8}{4+3} + \dfrac{8-2}{5+1}$

(f) $\dfrac{2(3+(7-5)^2 - 9)}{4+5} - 7$

2.8 PRINTING NUMBERS

Many computer systems print whole numbers without decimal points even when the numbers are entered as decimal fractions with zeros. Thus, 132 is printed 132 when entered as 132.00. A number that includes a decimal point has all the leading and trailing zeros dropped. For example, 01.20 appears as 1.2, with the leading zero and the trailing zero left off. Remember, not all computer systems print numbers as described above. See what your computer prints by RUNning the following program.

```
10 PRINT
20 PRINT 132.00,01.20
99 END
```

What does your output look like?

Any number that contains more digits than the computer allows (usually 6 to 15) is converted to **scientific notation**, sometimes known as **E format** or **E specification**.

Mantissa	Exponent
8.12345678	E +09

In the above example:

1. The letter E separates the mantissa from the exponent.
2. The exponent indicates the power of 10 to which the number is to be raised. In this case, the decimal point is moved nine places to the right, which results in the number 8,123,456,780. If the exponent had been negative, the decimal point would be moved 9 places to the left. The resultant number would now be .00000000812345678.
3. There is one digit to the left of the decimal point.

4. There are several digits to the right of the decimal point, with the last permissible digit usually rounded off. Suppose a computer prints eight digits to the right of the decimal point, then

1 123 456 789	becomes	1.12345679E+09,
.001987654326	becomes	1.98765433E−03.

On some computer systems, all trailing zeros to the right of the decimal point are dropped when the number is expressed in scientific notation.

1 234 500 000	becomes	1.2345E+09
12 000 000 000	becomes	1.2E+10

A number of computer systems print a sign before the exponent (**E+09** or **E−09**); others omit the sign when the power is positive (**E09**). Also, some computers print a two-digit power (**E+09**); others print just one digit when the exponent is less than ten (**E+9**).

How does your computer print a number in E format? RUN the following program.

```
10 PRINT
20 PRINT 1234567866666666666
30 PRINT .00001234567866666666666
40 PRINT 123000000000000000000
99 END
```

What does your output look like? Check the following:
1. How many digits are there to the right of the decimal point?
2. Is the last digit rounded off?
3. Are trailing zeros to the right of the decimal point dropped?
4. Does the exponent have a sign when it is positive?
5. How many digits are printed to express an exponent that is less than 10?

2.8 PRINTING NUMBERS—Sample Problems

Suppose that your computer expresses a number in scientific notation as follows:
— Allows eight digits to the right of the decimal point.
— Rounds off the last permissible digit.
— Prints a two-digit, signed exponent.
— Drops all trailing zeros.
1. The problems shown below convert numbers from arithmetic notation to scientific notation (E format).

  (a) 7 123 456 885.

The decimal point is moved from the last position in the number to the position immediately after the 7, a total of 9 moves.

7.123456885   Scientific notation: 7.12345689E+09

9 moves   Last permissible digit is rounded

The exponent must be +09 to indicate that the decimal is to be moved 9 places to the right in order to convert the number back to arithmetic notation.

---

7 123 456 890.

9 moves

Notice that accuracy is lost; the result is 7 123 456 890 instead of 7 123 456 885.

(b) 14 000 000 000 000.

The decimal point is moved from the last position in the number to the position immediately after the 1, a total of 13 moves.

1.4000000000000   Scientific notation: 1.4E+13

13 moves

The exponent must be +13 to indicate that the decimal is to be moved 13 places to the right in order to convert the number back to arithmetic notation.

---

14 000 000 000 000.

13 moves

(c) .009876543218

The decimal point is moved from the first position in the number to the position immediately after the 9, a total of 3 moves.

009.876543218   Scientific notation: 9.87654322E−03

3 moves   Last permissible digit is rounded

The exponent must be −03 to indicate that the decimal is to be moved 3 places to the left in order to convert the number back to arithmetic notation.

.00987654322

3 moves

Once more, accuracy is lost. The result is .00987654322 instead of .009876543218

(d) .00000000081234

The decimal point is moved from the first position in the number to the position immediately after the 8, a total of 10 moves.

0000000008.1234   Scientific notation: $8.1234E-10$

10 moves

The exponent must be −10 to indicate that the decimal is to be moved 10 places to the left in order to convert the number back to arithmetic notation.

.00000000081234

10 moves

2. These problems convert numbers from scientific notation to arithmetic notation.

Scientific Notation	Arithmetic Notation
(a) $1.23456789E+10$	12 345 678 900

Two zeros must be added to 1.23456789 before moving the decimal 10 places to the right.

(b) $5.8E+14$ 580 000 000 000 000

Thirteen zeros must be added to 5.8 before moving the decimal 14 places to the right.

(c) $1.23456789E-04$ .000123456789

Three zeros must be placed in front of 1.23456789 before moving the decimal 4 places to the left.

(d) $7.65E-07$ .000000765

Six zeros must be placed in front of 7.65 before moving the decimal 7 places to the left.

2.8 PRINTING NUMBERS—Your Turn

1. Convert the following numbers from arithmetic notation to scientific notation. In which questions is accuracy lost?

   (a) 3 987 654 328
   (b) 123 987 654 321
   (c) 12 300 000 000 000
   (d) 12 000 000 000 000 000
   (e) .000002345678987
   (f) .0000000123

2. Convert the following numbers from scientific notation to arithmetic notation.

   (a) 4.1234567E+10
   (b) 3.12345E+12
   (c) 7.5E+13
   (d) 2.45678E−02
   (e) 9.123E−06

2.8 PRINTING NUMBERS—Solutions for "Your Turn"

1. Arithmetic notation to scientific notation

   (a) 3.98765433E+09 Accuracy is lost. Arithmetic notation is 3 987 654 330 instead of 3 987 654 328.
   (b) 1.23987654E+11 Accuracy is lost. Arithmetic notation is 123 987 654 000 instead of 123 987 654 321.
   (c) 1.23E+13
   (d) 1.2E+16
   (e) 2.34567899E−06 Accuracy is lost. Arithmetic notation is .00000234567899 instead of .000002345678987.
   (f) 1.23E−08

2. Scientific notation to arithmetic notation

   (a) 41 234 567 000
   (b) 3 123 450 000 000
   (c) 75 000 000 000 000
   (d) .0245678
   (e) .000009123

A Short Summary

A number of system commands were introduced in this chapter. These are required in order to operate a computer system and execute a program. Many of these are machine dependent, so it may be necessary for you to refer to your computer manual for the required variations. Flowcharting and a few flowchart symbols were also introduced. As concepts are developed in this book, techniques and other symbols used in flowcharting will be explained. Several rules must be observed in the writing of BASIC programs. They will become more familiar to you as you write your own programs in successive chapters.

The computer evaluates a BASIC expression in a specific order known as the hierarchy of operations. The order of execution is as follows.

1. Exponentiation
2. Multiplication and division, whichever appears first
3. Addition and subtraction, whichever appears first

When a statement contains parentheses, the operations within the parentheses are executed first.

Quite often the writing of BASIC programs involves the conversion of arithmetic problems into BASIC expressions. For example, $\frac{(4+5)^2}{6}+7$ in arithmetic becomes $(4+5)\uparrow2/6+7$ in BASIC. You should also be able to do the reverse. Numbers that contain more digits than the computer allows are converted to scientific notation. Results vary depending on the computer being used.

Information is displayed or printed by means of a number of PRINT statements.

1. A PRINT statement with no list leaves a blank line.
2. A PRINT statement with commas prints items widely spaced across a line.
3. A PRINT statement with semicolons prints items closely spaced on a line.
4. A PRINT statement with messages (strings) must have the strings enclosed in quotation marks.

Questions and Exercises[9]

1. State the system commands required by your computer to:
   (a) Clear the computer's memory.
   (b) Transmit a typed statement or command to the computer's memory.
   (c) Display a program on the screen.
   (d) Execute a program.
   (e) Clear the screen.
   (f) Terminate a program.
2. On your computer system, what operations are required to:
   (a) Correct a character in a line before the RETURN key is pressed?
   (b) Correct a character in a line after the RETURN key is pressed?
   (c) Delete a line?
   (d) Insert a line?

9. If you are not using an interactive system, you may ignore Problems 1 and 2.

3. (a) A BASIC program consists of a number of _____.
   (b) What maximum number of characters does your computer allow in one statement?
   (c) In what order are BASIC statements executed? Give one exception.
   (d) State three reasons why REMARK statements are used.
4. What is the difference between an executable statement and a non-executable statement? Give an example of each.
5. Draw a flowchart for the following program. The program multiplies one number by another, then prints the product. Notice the extra PRINT statement that leaves a blank line. Opposite each symbol, write the appropriate statement(s).

```
01 REM N1--FIRST NUMBER
02 REM N2--SECOND NUMBER
03 REM P--PRODUCT

10 READ N1,N2
20 DATA 3,9
30 LET P=N1*N2
40 PRINT
50 PRINT P
99 END
```

6. What is the difference between an integer and a floating-point number?
7. List the five arithmetic operations used in BASIC and give their BASIC symbols.
8. List the hierarchy of operations, including parentheses within parentheses. Should two operators of equal priority appear in one statement, explain the order of execution.
9. Evaluate the following BASIC expressions. Do one calculation at a time.

   (a) $3+16/2\uparrow3+6/3$
   (b) $8-12/4*(2\uparrow2+1)/5$
   (c) $(3\uparrow2+5)/(2\uparrow3-1)+6$
   (d) $3+4/2+(8-(4+2))\uparrow2$
   (e) $6+4*3*(9/(6-3)-2)-7$
   (f) $30-(2*(8/4+3*(7-5)+5))$

10. Show the RUNS for the following programs.

```
(a) 10 PRINT
    20 PRINT "I";" SPEAK";" BASIC"
    30 PRINT "I ";"SPEAK ";"BASIC"
    40 PRINT "I";"SPEAK";"BASIC"
    50 PRINT "I","SPEAK","BASIC"
    99 END
```

```
(b) 10  PRINT
    20  PRINT "8+4  =",8+4
    30  PRINT "8-12 =",8-12
    40  PRINT "8+4  =";8+4
    50  PRINT "8-12 =";8-12
    99  END
```

```
(c) 10  PRINT
    20  PRINT 10,200,3000,40000
    30  PRINT -10,-200,-3000,-40000
    40  PRINT 10;200;3000;40000
    50  PRINT -10;-200;-3000;-40000
    99  END
```

```
(d) 10  PRINT
    20  PRINT "MY",
    30  PRINT "PROGRAM"
    99  END
```

```
(e) 10  PRINT
    20  PRINT "MY";
    30  PRINT "PROGRAM"
    99  END
```

```
(f) 10  PRINT
    20  PRINT "MY ";
    30  PRINT "PROGRAM"
    99  END
```

```
(g) 10  PRINT
    20  PRINT "MY";
    30  PRINT
    40  PRINT "PROGRAM"
    99  END
```

11. Convert the following arithmetic problems into BASIC expressions.

(a) $\dfrac{8}{2} - 3(6+4)$

(b) $\dfrac{9}{4-2} + \dfrac{3+4}{5+2}$

(c) $\dfrac{3^2}{6+3} + \dfrac{(8-3)^2}{4}$

(d) $8^3 - (3(2+5)^2 - 4)$

(e) $\dfrac{4+6-3(5-2)^2}{7} + \dfrac{6}{5+1}$

(f) $\dfrac{8-(3(6-2)+4)}{9-2}$

12. Convert the following BASIC expressions into arithmetic problems.

(a) 3+2/(8−6)+(5−2)/7
(b) (3+1)↑2−(4+1)/(6−2)
(c) ((5−1)↑3+9)/(7+6)
(d) 2*(3+(5−1)↑2)−4/(7−3)
(e) (6+4)↑3/(4−(3*(7+2)−9))
(f) (7−(5*(3↑2−2)+8))/(4+5)

13. Convert the following numbers from arithmetic notation to scientific notation. In which questions is accuracy lost?

(a) 1 234 567 869
(b) 12 345 678 900
(c) 15 000 000 000 000 000
(d) 9 876 543 211 000
(e) .0001234567847
(f) .0000002345

14. Convert the following numbers from scientific notation to arithmetic notation.

(a) 6.123456E+10
(b) 3.12345678E+13
(c) 6.1E+15
(d) 5.4321E−05
(e) 5.4E−08

Programming Problems

Write BASIC programs to evaluate the following arithmetic problems.

1. $\dfrac{4^2 - 2}{3+4}$

RUN

2

2. $\dfrac{8}{2} + \dfrac{9-(6-3)}{9-6}$

RUN

6

3. $25 - (3+2)^2 + \dfrac{4^2}{8-6}$

   RUN

   8

4. $4(2(6-2)-3)+5$

   RUN

   25

5. $5(12-(3(9-7)^2-6)+4)$

   RUN

   50

6. $\dfrac{20}{3+2} + 4(6-3)^2$

   RUN

   40

For the following problems, it is assumed that your computer differentiates between a comma and a semicolon. In each output, leave one blank line after the word **RUN**.

7. Write a BASIC program that prints **HOW ARE YOU DOING?** spread widely across the page or screen.

8. Rewrite the above program so that your RUN produces **HOWAREYOUDOING?** Use four strings in your PRINT statement.

9. Write the program once more to make your output more legible by leaving a space between each word. Use two different PRINT statements to obtain two identical lines of output.

10. Write one BASIC program that prints the numbers 1,22,333,4444 widely spaced on the first line of output, then closely spaced on the next line. Do the same for the negative numbers $-1, -22, -333, -4444$ on the following two lines of output.

11. Write a BASIC program that evaluates $6+3$. Use two PRINT statements to produce two lines of output, each one starting with the string **6+3 =**, followed by the answer. The first line should have the string and the answer widely spaced apart, while the second line should print them closer together.

12. Write a BASIC program to evaluate $6-12$. As in Problem 11, use two PRINT statements — one to print a string and the answer widely spaced apart, and the other to print them closer together. Change the string to **THE ANSWER IS:**.

13. Write two BASIC programs to evaluate $13-6$. Each program must use two PRINT statements (in addition to the one that leaves a blank line) to print the string **13−6 =** and the answer on *one* line. One program prints the output widely spaced; the other prints the output closely spaced.

14. Modify the program on page 52 so that your output is printed on two lines. Do not change lines 20 and 30 in any way.

```
10 PRINT
20 PRINT "LAST",
30 PRINT "PROGRAM"
99 END
```

Your RUN should be as follows.

```
RUN

LAST
PROGRAM
```

THREE ENTERING DATA INTO THE COMPUTER

A. After completing this chapter, you should be able to write BASIC programs and complete skeletal BASIC programs that

1. Enter data into the computer using LET statements.
2. Enter data into the computer using INPUT statements.
3. Enter data into the computer using READ/DATA statements.
4. Retain values of variables for use in subsequent statements.
5. Transfer (copy) values from specific storage locations and place them into other storage locations.
6. Use prompts to identify values entered into the computer by means of INPUT statements.
7. Use one or several READ statements in conjunction with one or several DATA statements.
8. Reassign values in DATA statements by means of RESTORE statements.

B. In addition, you should be able to

1. Define a variable and give examples.
2. Display and label a LET statement.
3. Explain how a LET statement is executed.
4. Explain how a statement such as **A=A+1** is entirely logical in BASIC.
5. Define initialization.
6. Summarize the response made to an INPUT statement.
7. State the purpose of
   (a) the READ statement.
   (b) the DATA statement.
8. Correct invalid program segments that use
   (a) LET statements.
   (b) INPUT statements.
   (c) READ/DATA statements.
   (d) RESTORE statements.
9. Explain how a RESTORE statement is executed.
10. Produce the RUNS of programs.

3.1 VARIABLES

A variable is a symbol that is used in programming to represent a number or a string. It refers to that place in the computer's memory where the number or string is stored. In other words, a variable can be thought of as an address that designates a location in storage. This location contains a value which may vary as the program is being executed. In this chapter, you will be working with numeric variables. String variables are explained later on in the book.

A numeric variable may consist of one or several characters, depending on the computer system; however, the first character must always be alphabetic. The remaining characters may be letters or digits. The following rules may have to be observed, depending upon the version of BASIC being used.

(a) Only two letters may be allowed in a numeric variable; the rest would be ignored. This means that variables **AA**, **AAB**, and **AACD** are all the same, since the **B** of **AAB** and the **CD** of **AACD** are dropped.

(b) It may be necessary for the second character of the variable to be a digit. Thus, **A1** would be valid while **AA** would not be valid.

After you have learned about the LET statement in the next section, try the different symbols for variables and see which ones work on your computer system. Here are some examples of numeric variables. **A** is used as the first character; however, any letter of the alphabet may be used.

A
A1
AB   (The second character may be invalid,
          since it is not a digit.)
ABC   (The third character may be ignored
          by the computer, leaving this variable
          the same as the previous one.)

3.2 THE LET STATEMENT

The LET statement is one of three methods by which data may be entered into the computer. The general form is as follows.

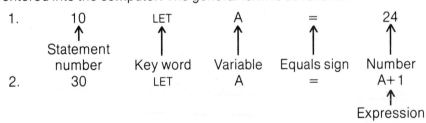

	10	LET	A	=	24
1.	↑	↑	↑	↑	↑
	Statement				
	number	Key word	Variable	Equals sign	Number
2.	30	LET	A	=	A+1
					↑
					Expression

The LET statement is composed of a statement number, the word **LET**, a variable, and an equals sign followed by a number or another variable, expression. In example one, the number 24 to the right of the equals sign is **assigned** to the variable **A** on the left. This means that 24 is stored in address **A**. Notice that the item on the left-hand side of the equals sign must be a simple numeric variable, not an expression. The assignment **A=A+1** in example two is particularly worthy of comment. It seems to resemble an algebraic equation, yet mathematically it doesn't make sense. However, in BASIC it is entirely logical. The equals sign does not denote the usual algebraic operation but rather **assigns** the result of **A+1** to the variable on the left-hand side of the equals sign. (The computer adds one to the value of **A** then assigns this new value back to **A**.) The former value stored in address **A** is lost.

There is one more term you should know. When a variable is assigned a value for the first time (before it is used in an expression), it is said that the variable has been **initialized**. Although variables can be initialized by the other statements covered in this chapter, the LET statement is most often used to perform this function. Here are two examples.

```
10 LET A=1    — Initializes A to 1.
20 LET S=0    — Initializes S to 0.
```

These two statements should be executed only once. The intention is to initialize the variables prior to using them in an expression. If a variable is not initialized, the following may occur:

1. The computer may give an error message.
2. The computer may give the non-initialized variable a value of zero.
3. The value of the non-initialized variable may continue to be the value that was assigned to it in a previous program if the program is not cleared from memory.

Variables may be initialized in any order. If there are two variables to initialize, say **A** to 1 and **S** to 0, **A** may be initialized first and then **S**, or vice versa.

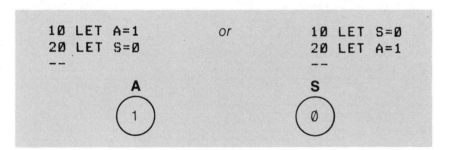

It doesn't matter how these values are stored in the computer's memory, just as long as they are stored in their *respective* addresses.

It was mentioned that the LET statement in the second example (**30 LET A=A+1**) destroys the original contents of **A**. This is not always desirable, since you may want to retain the original data item. To do this, you can assign the value of the term **A+1** to a different variable, say **B**, then ask the computer to print the values of both **A** and **B**.

```
10 LET A=24      — Initializes A to 24.
20 LET B=A+1     — Increments (increases) the value of A by 1, then assigns the new
                   value to B.
30 PRINT         — Leaves a blank line after the word RUN.
40 PRINT A,B     — Prints the values of A and B.
99 END           — Terminates program execution.

RUN

  24            25
```

Notice that the values of **A** and **B** are printed, not the letters **A** and **B**. Also note that the variable **A** is assigned a value of 24 in line 10 prior to its use in the expression in line 20. Remember, a variable must be assigned a value before it is placed in a statement on the right-hand side of the equals sign.

Data can also be transferred (**copied**) from one storage location to another without altering the contents of the first location.

```
10 LET A=4          — Initializes A to 4.
20 PRINT            — Leaves a blank line after the word RUN.
30 PRINT "A =";A    — Prints the variable and its value.
40 LET B=A          — Copies the value that is stored in A and places it in B.
50 PRINT "B =";B    — Prints the variable and its value.
99 END              — Terminates program execution.

RUN

A = 4
B = 4
```

The number 4 is now stored in address **A** and in address **B**. Also, lines 30 and 50 each prints a variable as well as its value. The statement **30 PRINT "A =";A** asks the computer to print two separate parts:

(a) `"A ="` — The computer prints   A = (Remember **strings** in Chapter Two?)

(b) `;A`   — The computer prints   4   (The current value of **A**.)

— The semicolon stops automatic line spacing so that the 4 is printed on the same line as the **A =**.

The final result is

     A = 4

Suppose you want to print the values of **A** and **B** along with their respective variables on one line. Your PRINT statement should look like one of the following:

(a) `50 PRINT "A =";A,"B =";B` — The comma causes the item **B = 4** to be printed in the next available **fixed** zone.

        A = 4   B = 4

(b) `50 PRINT "A =";A;"B =";B` — The semicolon leaves one, two, or possibly three spaces after the item **A = 4**.

        A = 4 B = 4

Instead of assigning the result of an expression to a variable, and then printing the value of the variable, an expression may be placed directly in a PRINT statement. The following programs each produce the same result.

(a) Expression Assigned to a Variable

(b) Expression Placed in a PRINT Statement

```
10 LET A=2                10 LET A=2
20 LET B=A+2              20 PRINT
30 PRINT                  30 PRINT "B =";A+2
40 PRINT "B =";B         99 END
99 END
                          RUN
RUN
                          B = 4
B = 4
```

In some versions of BASIC, you may use one LET statement to assign the same value to several variables. For example

```
10 LET A=B=C=D=1
```

assigns 1 to each of the variables **A,B,C**, and **D**. This is known as a multiple-assignment statement. It should also be mentioned that the key word **LET** may be omitted on many computer systems. That is, **10 LET A=1** gives the same result as **10 A=1**. Throughout this book, the word **LET** is retained.

Just one or two hints before you go through a sample program. It's a good idea to assign as many data items as possible to variables before any calculations are made. In this way, all data is stored and ready for use. The second hint is this: Try to use variables that represent the types of data assigned to them. For example, the variable **D** could mean deposit while the variable **W** would stand for withdrawal.

3.2 THE LET STATEMENT—Sample Programs

1. This program prints the whole numbers 1,2,3 using only one variable.

```
10 LET A=1    —Initializes A to 1.
20 PRINT      —Leaves a blank line after the word RUN.
30 PRINT A    —Prints the current value of A (1) before making any changes to
                its value.
```

```
40 LET A=A+1        — Increments the value of A by 1.
50 PRINT A          — Prints the current value of A (2) before making any changes to
                      its value.
60 LET A=A+1        — Increments the value of A by 1.
70 PRINT A          — Prints the current value of A (3).
99 END              — Terminates program execution.

RUN

1
2
3
```

First   A = 1   A

                                (1)

Then   A = A + 1   A
               = 1 + 1
               = 2   (2)

Finally   A = A + 1   A
               = 2 + 1
               = 3   (3)

Notice that the address **A** contains only one number at a time. The previous number in **A** is replaced by the latest one stored. This is important to know, because if you wish to have the old value printed, you must do this *before* making any changes to the value of the variable.

2. The previous program can be written more efficiently by using more than one variable. In this way, you don't have to worry about losing values before they are printed.

```
10 LET A=1          — Initializes A to 1.
20 LET B=A+1        — Increments the value of A by 1, then stores the result in B.
30 LET C=A+2        — Increments the value of A by 2, then stores the result in C.
40 PRINT            — Leaves a blank line after the word RUN.
50 PRINT A          — Prints the current value of A.
60 PRINT B          — Prints the current value of B.
70 PRINT C          — Prints the current value of C.
99 END              — Terminates program execution.
```

```
RUN

1
2
3
```

First   A = 1   A
                                     (1)

Then   B = A + 1   B
               = 1 + 1
               = 2   (2)

Finally   C = A + 2   C
               = 1 + 2
               = 3   (3)

In this program, no value is destroyed since each value is assigned to a *different* variable (1 is assigned to **A**; 2 is assigned to **B**; and 3 is assigned to **C**). The contents of variables **A,B**, and **C** may be printed any time after each variable has been assigned a value.

3.2 THE LET STATEMENT—Your Turn

1. Identify the errors, if any, in the LET statements shown below.

```
(a) 10 LET A=1 AND 2     (d) 10 LET A=A+2
(b) 10 LET A-9=B         (e) 10 LET 5=A
(c) 10 LET A=16          (f) 10 LET 1A=1
```

2. If the values of **A, B**, and **C** are initially 1, 2, and 3 respectively for *each* of the following program segments, what will be their values after execution of each program segment? In which program segments do the values of **A** and **B** interchange? The first one has been done for you.

```
(a) 40 LET C=A           40 LET C=A
    50 LET A=B               C = 1
    60 LET B=C           50 LET A=B
                             A = 2
                         60 LET B=C
                             B = 1
```

The values of **A** and **B** are interchanged in this program segment, since **A** is now equal to 2 and **B** is now equal to 1.

```
(b) 40 LET A=C        (d) 40 LET A=B
    50 LET B=A            50 LET C=A
    60 LET C=B            60 LET B=C

(c) 40 LET C=B
    50 LET B=A
    60 LET A=C
```

3. What is the output of each of the following programs?

```
(a) 10 LET A=3        (c) 10 LET A=6
    20 LET A=AT2          20 LET B=A
    30 PRINT             30 LET C=B+2
    40 PRINT A           40 LET A=C
    99 END               50 PRINT
                         60 PRINT A,C
                         99 END

(b) 10 LET A=3        (d) 10 LET A=2
    20 PRINT             20 LET B=AT2
    30 PRINT A           30 LET A=B+2
    40 LET A=AT2         40 LET B=AT2
    50 PRINT A           50 PRINT
    99 END               60 PRINT A,B
                         99 END
```

4. In each of the following programs, what initial value should **A** have in order to produce the RUN shown?

```
(a) 10 LET A= _____   (b) 10 LET A= _____
    20 LET B=A             20 LET B=A+2
    30 PRINT              30 PRINT
    40 PRINT "B =";B      40 PRINT "B =";B
    99 END                99 END

    RUN                   RUN

    B = 12                B = 6
```

```
(c) 10 LET A= _____   (d) 10 LET A= _____
    20 LET B=A*2            20 LET B=A-4
    30 LET C=B             30 LET C=B+2
    40 PRINT               40 PRINT
    50 PRINT "C =";C       50 PRINT "C =";C
    99 END                 99 END

    RUN                    RUN

    C = 9                  C = 10
```

5. Write a program that prints the numbers 2, 4, 6, 8. Use only one variable.

```
RUN

 2
 4
 6
 8
```

6. Rewrite the above program so that you incorporate the following changes.

   (a) Use one variable, say **A**, to store the initial value, then use other variables to store the remaining values.
   (b) Instead of incrementing **A** each time, increment the variable that has just been assigned the latest number.
   (c) Have the computer print the numbers horizontally instead of vertically.

```
RUN

 2       4       6       8
```

7. Suppose you had $400 in your bank account. What amount would you have if you deposited $600 at the beginning of this month? How much would you have left in your account if you withdrew $250 one week later?

   (a) Use LET statements to enter the data.
   (b) Current Balance = 400.
   (c) Don't forget to print the Current Balance before making any changes to its value.

(d) Current Balance = Current Balance + Deposit
(e) Again, have the computer print the Current Balance before changing its value.
(f) Current Balance = Current Balance − Withdrawal
(g) A flowchart is drawn to help you follow the flow of logic. Notice that when several consecutive statements perform the same type of operation, all descriptive material is placed in one symbol with the items listed on separate lines.

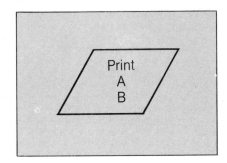

If several items are coded in one statement, they will be listed on one line within the symbol.

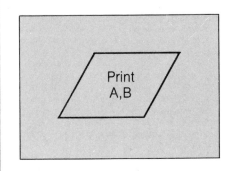

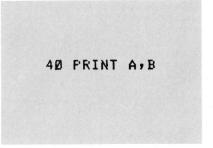

Also note that REM statements and messages in PRINT statements are not displayed in a flowchart.

```
RUN

CURRENT BALANCE: 400
DEPOSIT: 600
CURRENT BALANCE: 1000
WITHDRAWAL: 250
CURRENT BALANCE: 750
```

Problem 7

C — CURRENT
    BALANCE
D — DEPOSIT
W — WITHDRAWAL

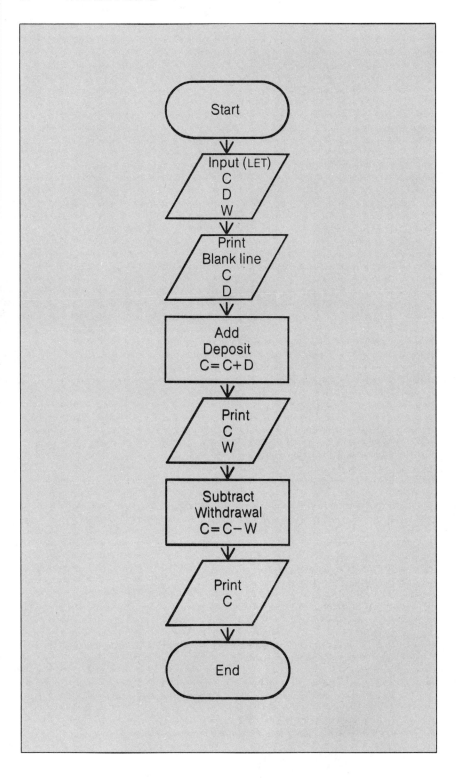

3.2 THE LET STATEMENT—Solutions for "Your Turn"

1. (a) Only one value may be assigned to **A**.

```
10 LET A=1
20 LET B=2
```

(b) The item on the left-hand side of the equals sign must be a numeric variable, not an expression.

```
10 LET B=A-9
```

(c) Nothing is wrong.
(d) Nothing is wrong.
(e) The item on the left-hand side of the equals sign must be a numeric variable, not a number.

```
10 LET A=5
```

(f) The first character of the numeric variable **1A** must be alphabetic.

```
10 LET A1=1
```

2.

```
(b) 40 LET A=C          (d) 40 LET A=B
          A = 3                   A = 2
    50 LET B=A              50 LET C=A
          B = 3                   C = 2
    60 LET C=B              60 LET B=C
          C = 3                   B = 2

(c) 40 LET C=B
          C = 2
    50 LET B=A
          B = 1
    60 LET A=C
          A = 2
```

The values of **A** and **B** are interchanged in program segment (c).

3.

(a) RUN	(c) RUN
9	8 8
(b) RUN	(d) RUN
3 9	6 36

4.

(a) `10 LET A=12`	(c) `10 LET A=3`
(b) `10 LET A=4`	(d) `10 LET A=12`

5.

```
10 LET A=2
20 PRINT
30 PRINT A
40 LET A=A+2
50 PRINT A
60 LET A=A+2
70 PRINT A
80 LET A=A+2
90 PRINT A
99 END
```

6.

```
10 LET A=2
20 LET B=A+2
30 LET C=B+2
40 LET D=C+2
50 PRINT
60 PRINT A,B,C,D
99 END
```

7.

```
01 REM C--CURRENT BALANCE
02 REM D--DEPOSIT
03 REM W--WITHDRAWAL

10 LET C=400
20 LET D=600
30 LET W=250
40 PRINT
50 PRINT "CURRENT BALANCE:";C
60 PRINT "DEPOSIT:";D
70 LET C=C+D
80 PRINT "CURRENT BALANCE:";C
90 PRINT "WITHDRAWAL:";W
100 LET C=C-W
110 PRINT "CURRENT BALANCE:";C
999 END
```

3.3 THE INPUT STATEMENT[1]

The **INPUT** statement is another way by which data may be entered into a computer. Consider the following program using the LET statement.

```
10 LET A=2
20 PRINT
30 PRINT A
99 END

RUN

   2
```

In this program you entered and then printed just one value. Suppose you want to input and print three values, the numbers 2, 31, and 49. If you do not add any statements to the above program, you would have to RUN the program three times and modify the LET statement after each RUN. For the first RUN, line 10 would be **10 LET A=2**; for the next RUN, line 10 would be changed to **10 LET A=31**; and for the last RUN, line 10 would be changed to **10 LET A=49**. Now, what if there were more than three values to be

1. This method of entering data is used in an interactive or in a time-sharing environment. If you are not using this type of system (teletype, cathode ray tube, or microcomputer), you may wish to ignore this section.

assigned to **A**? Surely there must be some other method by which data can be entered into the computer without having to modify the LET statement after each RUN. There is! You can reduce the amount of work by the use of an INPUT statement. Here is an example.

```
10 PRINT
20 INPUT A
30 PRINT A
99 END

RUN

?
```

When the computer encounters the INPUT statement during execution of the program, it displays a question mark and then waits for the programmer to enter a value. The user types the number 2 immediately after the question mark, then presses the RETURN key.

```
RUN

? 2   —The user types the number 2 then presses RETURN.
```

The value 2 is stored in address **A** and displayed on the screen.

```
RUN

? 2
 2
```

To change the contents of **A** from 2 to 31, the user RUNs the program a second time. Again the computer displays a question mark and waits for a data item to be keyed in. The user types the number 31 after the question mark and presses the RETURN key. The result is shown below.

```
RUN

? 31
 31
```

The above process is repeated for the number 49.

Take another look at the program.

```
10 PRINT    —Placed before the INPUT statement.
20 INPUT A
30 PRINT A
99 END

RUN
    ←——————— Blank line
? 2
  2
```

Notice that a PRINT statement is placed before the INPUT statement. This leaves a blank line after the word **RUN**, that is, before the display of the keyed-in value. In the other two methods of entering data, a PRINT statement is placed (in most programs) just before the PRINT that prints the results. For example, when the LET statement is used to enter data, the PRINT statement is placed as follows.

```
10 LET A=2
20 PRINT    —Placed just before the PRINT that prints the results.
30 PRINT A
99 END

RUN
    ←——————— Blank line
  2
```

The previous program used the INPUT statement to enter just one value into the computer for each RUN. There may be a time when you may want to enter several data items but RUN the program only once. The program shown below INPUTs two numbers (12 and 4), then subtracts one number from the other. There are two ways (using the INPUT statement) by which these two numbers may be entered into the computer.

1. The first method uses two INPUT statements.

```
10 PRINT              —Leaves a blank line after the word RUN.
20 INPUT A            —Requests data, user enters the value for A.
30 INPUT B            —Requests data, user enters the value for B.
40 LET C=A-B          —Subtracts the value of B from the value of A
                       and stores the result in C.
50 PRINT "A =";A,"B =";B,"C =";C  —Prints the values of A, B, and C.
99 END                —Terminates program execution.
```

```
RUN

? 12                                    —Enter 12, then press RETURN.
? 4                                     —Enter 4, then press RETURN.
A = 12     B = 4      C = 8
```

Lines 20 and 30 allow the user to assign two values — one to each of the INPUT variables **A** and **B**. However, the two question marks in the RUN are not too informative since they do not tell you what type of a response to make. To identify the values to be entered, you should add two more statements to the above program so that the computer will prompt you as to what it wants when it displays a question mark.

```
10 PRINT                                —Leaves a blank line after the word RUN.
20 PRINT 'VALUE FOR A';                 —Identifies the value to enter (a prompt).
30 INPUT A                              —Requests data, user enters the value for A.
40 PRINT 'VALUE FOR B';                 —Identifies the value to enter (a prompt).
50 INPUT B                              —Requests data, user enters the value for B.
60 LET C=A-B                            —Subtracts the value of B from the value of A
                                          and stores the result in C.
70 PRINT 'A =';A,'B =';B,'C =';C        —Prints the values of A, B, and C.
99 END                                  —Terminates program execution.

RUN

VALUE FOR A? 12                         —Enter 12, then press RETURN.
VALUE FOR B? 4                          —Enter 4, then press RETURN.
A = 12     B = 4      C = 8
```

Now when you RUN the program, the computer prints two messages (**VALUE FOR A?** and **VALUE FOR B?**), which tell you what two data values should be entered. Notice the semicolon at the end of line 20 and another at the end of line 40. The semicolon stops automatic line spacing with the result that the question mark and the keyed-in item are displayed on the same line as the prompt. The INPUT statement makes the computer wait for the data to be entered. After the data is keyed in and the RETURN key is pressed, program execution resumes.

On some computer systems, the prompt is part of the INPUT statement. The two statements

```
20 PRINT 'VALUE FOR A';
30 INPUT A
```

are replaced by the one statement

```
20 INPUT "VALUE FOR A";A
```

2. The second method by which two values may be entered uses just one INPUT statement.

```
10 PRINT              — Leaves a blank line after the word RUN.
20 INPUT A,B          — Requests data, user enters the values for A and B.
30 LET C=A-B          — Subtracts the value of B from the value of A and
                        stores the result in C.
40 PRINT "A =";A,"B =";B,"C =";C   — Prints the values of A, B, and C.
99 END                — Terminates program execution.

RUN

? 12,4                — Enter 12 and 4 then press RETURN.[2]
A = 12     B = 4      C = 8
```

As in part 1, the question mark in the RUN tells you very little. This program, too, should print an identifying message (a **prompt**) to indicate to you what the computer expects. Here is the program again, but with a prompt added.

```
10 PRINT                        — Leaves a blank line after the word RUN.
20 PRINT "VALUES FOR A,B";      — Identifies the values to enter (a prompt).
30 INPUT A,B                    — Requests data, user enters the values for A
                                  and B.
40 LET C=A-B                    — Subtracts the value of B from the value of A
                                  and stores the result in C.
50 PRINT "A =";A,"B =";B,"C =";C  — Prints the values of A, B, and C.
99 END                          — Terminates program execution.

RUN

VALUES FOR A,B? 12,4            — Enter 12 and 4, then press RETURN.
A = 12     B = 4      C = 8
```

Take another look at that last RUN. Notice that the values of **A** and **B** are displayed twice—once after the prompt and again in the line

2. On some systems, each value is keyed in on a separate line. The computer displays a question mark on a new line after each value is entered (except after the last value).

below the prompt. Since a data item is always displayed when it is typed in response to an INPUT statement, there is no need to have a special PRINT statement to print the data item again. From now on, most of the programs using the INPUT statement will have their data displayed only once, and this will be directly after the question mark. Eliminating this duplication, the program and its RUN now look like this:

```
10 PRINT                      — Leaves a blank line after the word RUN.
20 PRINT "VALUES FOR A,B";    — Identifies the values to enter (a prompt).
30 INPUT A,B                  — Requests data, user enters the values for A and B.
40 LET C=A-B                  — Subtracts the value of B from the value of A and
                                stores the result in C.
50 PRINT "C =";C              — Prints only the value of C, since the values of A and
                                B are already displayed.
99 END                        — Terminates program execution.

RUN

VALUES FOR A,B? 12,4          — Data displayed only once.
C = 8
```

When assigning values to multiple variables in one INPUT statement, several rules must be observed.

1. The variables listed in the INPUT statement must be separated by commas, with no comma before the list and no comma at the end of the list.

2. The values keyed in must be separated by commas with no comma before the list and no comma at the end of the list.

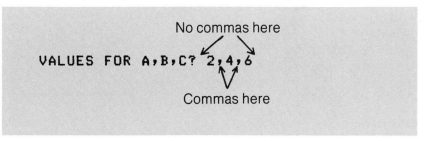

3. There must be a one-to-one correspondence between the values keyed in and the variables listed in the INPUT statement.

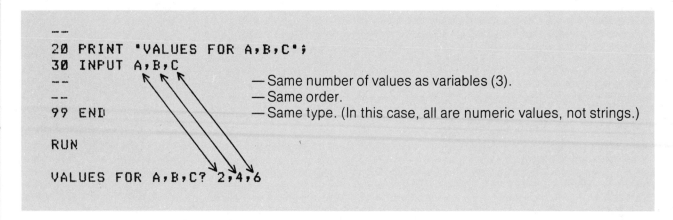

```
--
20 PRINT "VALUES FOR A,B,C";
30 INPUT A,B,C                    — Same number of values as variables (3).
--                                — Same order.
--                                — Same type. (In this case, all are numeric values, not strings.)
99 END

RUN

VALUES FOR A,B,C? 2,4,6
```

4. When insufficient data is supplied, your computer may perform one of the following:

   (a) It may print a message asking for more data (often in the form of one or two question marks on the next line);
   (b) It may simply wait for more data;
   (c) It may terminate execution.

   Suppose you inadvertently forget to enter the value for **C** when you RUN the following program. It is assumed that when insufficient data is entered, your computer types two question marks on the line immediately below the one where the values for **A** and **B** are keyed in.

```
10 PRINT
20 PRINT "VALUES FOR A,B,C";
30 INPUT A,B,C
40 PRINT A,B,C
99 END

RUN

VALUES FOR A,B,C? 2,4      — Forgot to key in the value for C.
??                        — Computer displays two question marks on the next line.
```

The value for **C** should now be typed right after the last question mark.

```
RUN

VALUES FOR A,B,C? 2,4
?? 6   — Value for C entered.
```

After you press the RETURN key, program execution resumes.

5. When too much data is supplied, the computer either ignores the extra data or terminates execution. Here is a RUN that one computer system produces when a user supplies too much data in response to an INPUT statement.

```
10 PRINT
20 PRINT "VALUES FOR A,B,C";
30 INPUT A,B,C
40 PRINT A,B,C
99 END

RUN

VALUES FOR A,B,C? 1,2,3,4   —User enters too
?EXTRA IGNORED                  much data.
  1           2           3
```

3.3 THE INPUT STATEMENT—Sample Programs

1. Suppose you purchased the following items.

Quantity	Item	Unit Price
2	Coat	$132
3	Jacket	58

This program finds the cost of the two coats, the cost of the three jackets, and the total cost of all the items.

(a) Use two INPUT statements to enter the quantity and the unit price of each item.
(b) Cost of Coats = Quantity × Unit Price
(c) Cost of Jackets = Quantity × Unit Price
(d) Total Cost = Cost of Coats + Cost of Jackets

```
01 REM Q1--QUANTITY (COATS)
02 REM U1--UNIT PRICE OF COATS
03 REM Q2--QUANTITY (JACKETS)
04 REM U2--UNIT PRICE OF JACKETS
05 REM C--COST OF COATS
06 REM J--COST OF JACKETS
07 REM T--TOTAL COST

10 PRINT                              —Leaves a blank line after the word RUN.
20 PRINT "COATS--QTY,UNIT PRICE";     —Identifies the quantity and the unit price
                                       of the coats (Q1 and U1)—a prompt.
```

```
30 INPUT Q1,U1                              — Requests data, user enters the values
                                              for Q1 and U1.
40 PRINT "JACKETS--QTY,UNIT PRICE";         — Identifies the quantity and the unit price
                                              of the jackets (Q2 and U2) — a prompt.
50 INPUT Q2,U2                              — Requests data, user enters the values
                                              for Q2 and U2.
60 LET C=Q1*U1                              — Finds the cost of the coats and stores
                                              the result in C.
70 LET J=Q2*U2                             — Finds the cost of the jackets and stores
                                              the result in J.
80 LET T=C+J                               — Finds the total cost of all the items
                                              and stores the result in T.
90 PRINT "COATS:";C                        — Prints the cost of the coats.
100 PRINT "JACKETS:";J                     — Prints the cost of the jackets.
110 PRINT "TOTAL COST:";T                  — Prints the total cost of all the items.
999 END                                    — Terminates program execution.

RUN

COATS--QTY,UNIT PRICE? 2,132
JACKETS--QTY,UNIT PRICE? 3,58
COATS: 264
JACKETS: 174
TOTAL COST: 438
```

2. The program shown in Part 1 is now rewritten, this time using only one INPUT statement to enter the values.

```
01 REM Q1--QUANTITY (COATS)
02 REM U1--UNIT PRICE OF COATS
03 REM Q2--QUANTITY (JACKETS)
04 REM U2--UNIT PRICE OF JACKETS
05 REM C---COST OF COATS
06 REM J---COST OF JACKETS
07 REM T--TOTAL COST

10 PRINT                                    — Leaves a blank line after the word
                                              RUN.
20 PRINT "QTY,UNIT PRICE--COAT,JACKET";     — Identifies the quantities and unit
                                              prices of the coats and jackets
                                              (Q1,U1,Q2,U2) — a prompt.
30 INPUT Q1,U1,Q2,U2                        — Requests data, user enters the
                                              values for Q1,U1,Q2,U2.
40 LET C=Q1*U1                              — Finds the cost of the coats and
                                              stores the result in C.
50 LET J=Q2*U2                             — Finds the cost of the jackets and
                                              stores the result in J.
```

```
60 LET T=C+J                    —Finds the total cost of all the items
                                  and stores the result in T.
70 PRINT "COATS:";C             —Prints the cost of the coats.
80 PRINT "JACKETS:";J           —Prints the cost of the jackets.
90 PRINT "TOTAL COST:";T        —Prints the total cost of all the items.
99 END                          —Terminates program execution.

RUN

QTY,UNIT PRICE--COAT,JACKET? 2,132,3,58
COATS: 264
JACKETS: 174
TOTAL COST: 438
```

3.3 THE INPUT STATEMENT—Your Turn

I. Suppose that you have set aside $12.50 for lunches for the next
five days. Find the average amount you can spend each day.

(a) Use one INPUT statement to enter the total amount you have
set aside and the number of days that you will be buying
lunch.

(b) Average Amount Each Day = $\dfrac{\text{Total Amount}}{\text{Number of Days}}$

(c) Fill in the missing lines.

```
01 REM T--TOTAL AMOUNT
02 REM D--DAYS
03 REM A--AVERAGE AMOUNT EACH DAY

10 PRINT
20 PRINT "TOTAL AMOUNT,DAYS";
30
40
50
99 END

RUN

TOTAL AMOUNT,DAYS? 12.50,5
AVERAGE AMOUNT EACH DAY: 2.5
```

1. Which statement should be coded in line 30?

```
(a) LET T=12.5
(b) LET T=12.5,5
```

```
(c) INPUT T
(d) INPUT D,T
(e) INPUT T,D
```

2. Which statement should be coded in line 40?

```
(a) LET T=D/A
(b) LET T=A/D
(c) LET A=D/T
(d) LET A=T/D
(e) LET D=T/A
```

3. Complete line 50 with a PRINT statement.

II. An employee in a furniture factory is paid according to the number of pieces produced. Write a program that finds the total number of pieces produced in 8 hours if the output was 6 pieces per hour.

(a) Use two INPUT statements to enter the number of hours and the number of pieces per hour.

(b) Total Pieces = Number of Hours × Number of Pieces per Hour

```
RUN

HOURS? 8
PIECES PER HOUR? 6
TOTAL PIECES: 48
```

III. Modify the flowchart for Problem II and rewrite the program so that you use one INPUT statement instead of two to enter your data.

```
RUN

HOURS,PIECES PER HOUR? 8,6
TOTAL PIECES: 48
```

Problem II

H — HOURS
P — PIECES PER
          HOUR
T — TOTAL PIECES

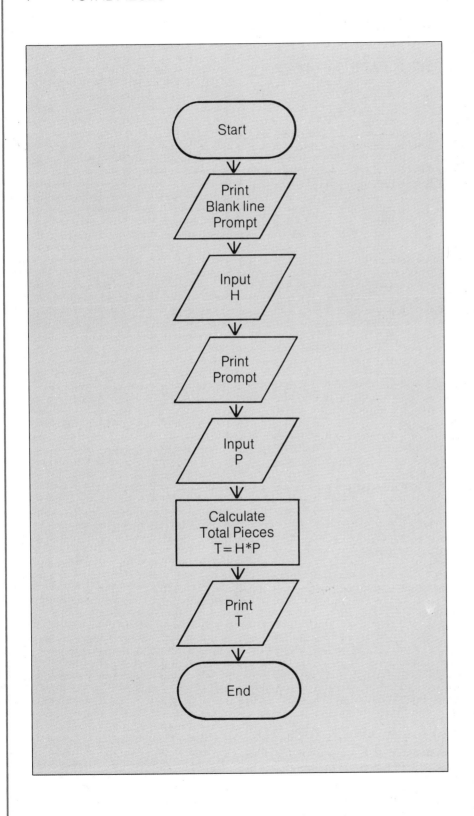

3.3 THE INPUT STATEMENT—Solutions for "Your Turn"

I.

```
1. (e) 30 INPUT T,D
2. (d) 40 LET A=T/D
3. 50 PRINT "AVERAGE AMOUNT EACH DAY:";A
```

II.

```
01 REM H--HOURS
02 REM P--PIECES PER HOUR
03 REM T--TOTAL PIECES

10 PRINT
20 PRINT "HOURS";
30 INPUT H
40 PRINT "PIECES PER HOUR";
50 INPUT P
60 LET T=H*P
70 PRINT "TOTAL PIECES:";T
99 END
```

III.

```
01 REM H--HOURS
02 REM P--PIECES PER HOUR
03 REM T--TOTAL PIECES

10 PRINT
20 PRINT "HOURS,PIECES PER HOUR";
30 INPUT H,P
40 LET T=H*P
50 PRINT "TOTAL PIECES:";T
99 END
```

PROBLEM III

H — HOURS   T — TOTAL PIECES
P — PIECES PER
     HOUR

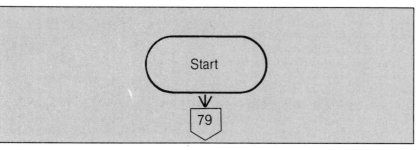

Start

79

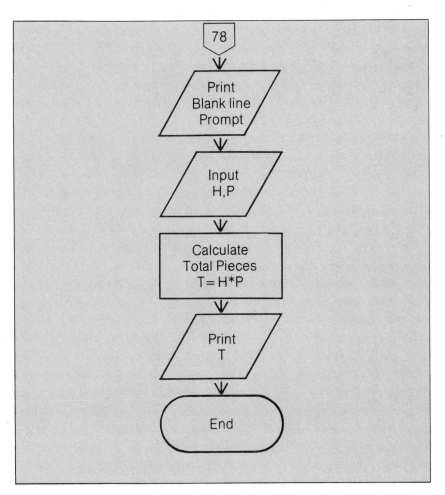

The off-page connector is used in the flowchart of this program. The symbol on the previous page indicates that the flowchart is continued on page 79. The symbol on this page indicates that the flowchart is continued from page 78.

3.4 THE READ/DATA STATEMENTS

The **READ** statement combined with the **DATA** statement is the third method by which data may be entered into the computer.

```
10 READ A,B,C
20 DATA 24,25,26
```

A READ statement is always associated with a DATA statement. The READ statement directs the computer to locate the DATA statement and to assign (in sequential order) the values listed in the DATA statement to the variables that are coded in the READ statement. Perhaps the best approach in explaining this method of entering data into the computer is to list a few rules. As each rule is mentioned, it will be accompanied by a program or a program segment to try and make it as easy as possible for you to understand what the rule is all about.

1. A READ statement must have at least one accompanying DATA statement.

```
10 READ A,B,C
20 DATA 24,25,26
30 PRINT
40 PRINT A,B,C
99 END
```

The DATA statement supplies the READ statement with values. The first number in the DATA statement (24) is assigned to the first variable in the READ statement (**A**). The second number in the DATA statement (25) is assigned to the second variable in the READ statement (**B**). Finally, the third number (26) is assigned to the third variable (**C**). Should there be more numbers and more variables, the computer assigns values until it runs out of numbers and variables.

2. The variables listed in the READ statement must be separated by commas with no comma before the list and no comma after the list.

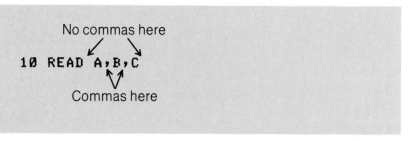

3. The values listed in the DATA statement must be separated by commas with no comma before the list and no comma after the list.

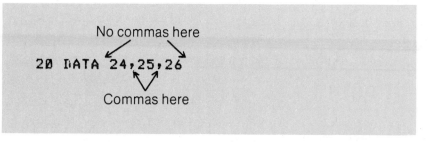

Suppose your computer allows two lines per statement and that a program requires three lines of data. Two DATA statements are used in the following program segment.

```
20 DATA 85,13,24,96,...............,64,123    —Number completed in the next line.
45,67,149,2,37,...................,352         —No comma after the last item when
                                                the line is followed by a statement.

30 DATA 425,14,98,510
```

Notice that the number 12345.67, which is incomplete in the first line of the first DATA statement, is completed in the second line starting in the first position of the line. The second line must not end with a comma, since this line is followed by a statement (in this case, by another DATA statement).

4. Some computer systems are not particular about where the DATA statement is placed; others insist that its line number be less than that of the END statement. Try the following program to find out what your computer does when the DATA statement is placed after the END statement.

```
10 READ A,B,C
20 PRINT
30 PRINT A,B,C
40 END
50 DATA 24,25,26
```

Here are two more examples.

```
(a) 10 DATA 24,25,26        (b) 10 READ A,B,C
    20 READ A,B,C               20 PRINT
    30 PRINT                    30 PRINT A,B,C
    40 PRINT A,B,C              40 DATA 24,25,26
    99 END                      99 END
```

In example (a), the computer ignores the DATA statement in line 10 until it finds the READ statement in line 20. It then assigns values from the "skipped" DATA statement and resumes execution, starting at line 30. In example (b), the computer ignores the two PRINT statements in its search for a DATA statement, assigns values, and then returns to line 20. As shown in the above programs, the READ statement may have a line number that is either higher or lower than that of the DATA statement.

5. The DATA statement must have at least the same number of values as the READ statement has variables, and there must be a one-to-one correspondence between the values and the variables. Excess data is ignored, while insufficient data causes an error message.

```
10 READ A,B,C        —Same number of values as variables (3).
                     —Same order.
30 DATA 24,25,26     —Same type. (In this case, all are numeric values, not strings.)
```

(a) Excess Data

```
10 READ A,B,C
20 DATA 24,25,26,27  — Extra value.
30 PRINT
40 PRINT A,B,C
99 END

RUN

  24          25          26    — Number 27
                                  is not printed.
```

(b) Insufficient Data

```
10 READ A,B,C
20 DATA 24,25   — Insufficient data.
30 PRINT
40 PRINT A,B,C
99 END

RUN

?OUT OF DATA ERROR IN  10 — Error message,
                            or something similar.
```

6. A program may have several DATA statements for one READ statement.

```
10 READ A,B,C
20 DATA 24,25
30 DATA 26
40 PRINT
50 PRINT A,B,C
99 END
```

The computer reads items starting at the lowest-numbered DATA statement and continues reading from sequentially higher-numbered DATA statements until the READ statement is satisfied.

7. A program may have several READ statements accompanied by only one DATA statement.

```
10 READ A,B
20 READ C
```

```
30 DATA 24,25,26
40 PRINT
50 PRINT A,B,C
99 END
```

In this program, the READ statement in line 10 assigns 24 to **A** and 25 to **B**. When the computer encounters line 20, it remembers that 24 and 25 have already been assigned, so it continues to the third value and assigns 26 to **C**.

8. Variables, expressions, and numbers with commas (for example, the number 1,000) are invalid data items.

```
20 DATA X,D/2,1,000
```
Invalid

3.4 THE READ/DATA STATEMENTS—Sample Program

The sample program in Section 3.3 is rewritten and shown below using the READ/DATA statements to enter the data instead of the INPUT statement. Here is the problem once more.

Suppose you purchased the following items.

Quantity	Item	Unit Price
2	Coat	$132
3	Jacket	58

This program finds the cost of the two coats, the cost of the three jackets, and the total cost of all the items.

(a) Use the READ/DATA statements to enter the quantity and the unit price of each item.
(b) Cost of Coats = Quantity × Unit Price
(c) Cost of Jackets = Quantity × Unit Price
(d) Total Cost = Cost of Coats + Cost of Jackets

```
01 REM Q1--QUANTITY (COATS)
02 REM U1--UNIT PRICE OF COATS
03 REM Q2--QUANTITY (JACKETS)
04 REM U2--UNIT PRICE OF JACKETS
05 REM C--COST OF COATS
06 REM J--COST OF JACKETS
07 REM T--TOTAL COST
```

```
10 READ Q1,U1,Q2,U2          — Reads the quantities and unit prices of the coats and
                               jackets from the DATA statement.
20 DATA 2,132,3,58           — Supplies the READ statement with data.
30 LET C=Q1*U1               — Finds the cost of the coats and stores the result in C.
40 LET J=Q2*U2               — Finds the cost of the jackets and stores the result in J.
50 LET T=C+J                 — Finds the total cost of all the items and stores the
                               result in T.
60 PRINT                     — Leaves a blank line after the word RUN.
70 PRINT "COATS",Q1,U1       — Prints the quantity and unit price of the coats.
80 PRINT "COST PRICE:";C     — Prints the cost price of the coats.
90 PRINT                     — Leaves a blank line.
100 PRINT "JACKETS",Q2,U2    — Prints the quantity and unit price of the jackets.
110 PRINT "COST PRICE:";J    — Prints the cost price of the jackets.
120 PRINT                    — Leaves a blank line.
130 PRINT "TOTAL COST:";T    — Prints the total cost of all the items.
999 END                      — Terminates program execution.

RUN

COATS        2           132
COST PRICE: 264

JACKETS      3           58
COST PRICE: 174

TOTAL COST: 438
```

3.4 THE READ/DATA STATEMENTS—Your Turn

I. To have enough cash on hand to make change, a grocer starts the day with $80.

 1. How much cash does the grocer have at the end of the day if $431 was received?

 2. How much cash does the grocer have if $431 was received *and* $16.50 was paid out?

   (a) Use the READ/DATA statements to enter the amount of change, the amount of cash received, and the amount of cash paid out.
   (b) Current Balance = Change
   (c) Current Balance = Current Balance + Receipts
   (d) Current Balance = Current Balance − Payments
   (e) Fill in the missing lines.

```
01 REM C--CHANGE
02 REM R--RECEIPTS
03 REM P--PAYMENTS
04 REM B--CURRENT BALANCE

10 READ C,R,P
20
30 PRINT
40
50
60
70 LET B=C
80
90 PRINT
100
110
120 PRINT "CHANGE,RECEIPTS,PAYMENTS:";B
999 END

RUN

CHANGE: 80
RECEIPTS: 431
PAYMENTS: 16.5

CHANGE,RECEIPTS: 511
CHANGE,RECEIPTS,PAYMENTS: 494.5
```

1. Complete line 20 with a DATA statement.

2. Complete lines 40, 50, and 60 with PRINT statements.

3. Which statement should be coded in line 80?

```
(a) LET B=B+R
(b) LET B=B-R
(c) LET B=R-B
(d) LET R=R-B
(e) LET R=R+B
```

4. Complete line 100 with a PRINT statement.

5. Which statement should be coded in line 110?

```
(a) LET P=B-P
(b) LET P=B+P
```

```
(c) LET B=P-B
(d) LET B=P+B
(e) LET B=B-P
```

Here are two problems from the "Your Turn" unit of Section 3.3. Write programs using the READ/DATA statements rather than the INPUT statement to enter the data.

II. Suppose that you have set aside $12.50 for lunches for the next five days. Find the average amount you can spend each day.
   (a) Use the READ/DATA statements to enter the total amount you have set aside and the number of days that you will be buying lunch.
   (b) Average Amount Each Day $= \dfrac{\text{Total Amount}}{\text{Number of Days}}$
   (c) Notice that the DATA statement is not included in the flowchart.

```
RUN

TOTAL AMOUNT: 12.5
NUMBER OF DAYS: 5
AVERAGE AMOUNT EACH DAY: 2.5
```

III. An employee in a furniture factory is paid according to the number of pieces produced. Find the total number of pieces produced in 8 hours if the output was 6 pieces per hour.
   (a) Use the READ/DATA statements to enter the number of hours and the number of pieces per hour.
   (b) Total Pieces = Number of Hours × Number of Pieces per Hour.
   (c) Draw a flowchart before you write the program.

```
RUN

HOURS: 8
PIECES PER HOUR: 6
TOTAL PIECES: 48
```

Problem II

T — TOTAL AMOUNT
D — DAYS
A — AVERAGE
      AMOUNT

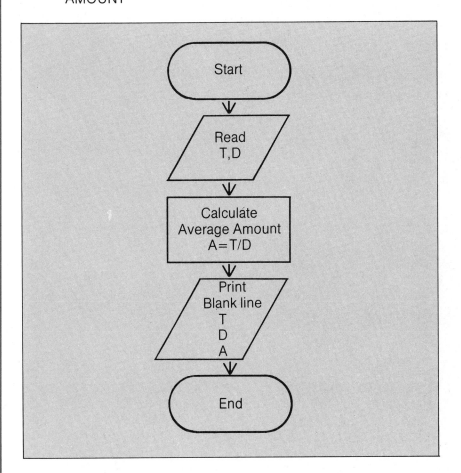

3.4 THE READ/DATA
STATEMENTS—Solutions for "Your Turn"

I.

```
1. 20 DATA 80,431,16.50
2. 40 PRINT "CHANGE:";C
   50 PRINT "RECEIPTS:";R
   60 PRINT "PAYMENTS:";P
3. (a) 80 LET B=B+R
4. 100 PRINT "CHANGE,RECEIPTS:";B
5. (e) 110 LET B=B-P
```

II.

```
01 REM T--TOTAL AMOUNT
02 REM D--DAYS
03 REM A--AVERAGE AMOUNT EACH DAY

10 READ T,D
20 DATA 12.50,5
30 LET A=T/D
40 PRINT
50 PRINT "TOTAL AMOUNT:";T
60 PRINT "NUMBER OF DAYS:";D
70 PRINT "AVERAGE AMOUNT EACH DAY:";A
99 END
```

III.

```
01 REM H--HOURS
02 REM P--PIECES PER HOUR
03 REM T--TOTAL PIECES

10 READ H,P
20 DATA 8,6
30 LET T=H*P
40 PRINT
50 PRINT "HOURS:";H
60 PRINT "PIECES PER HOUR:";P
70 PRINT "TOTAL PIECES:";T
99 END
```

Problem III
H — HOURS
P — PIECES PER
      HOUR
T — TOTAL PIECES

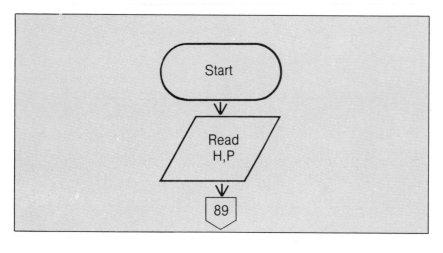

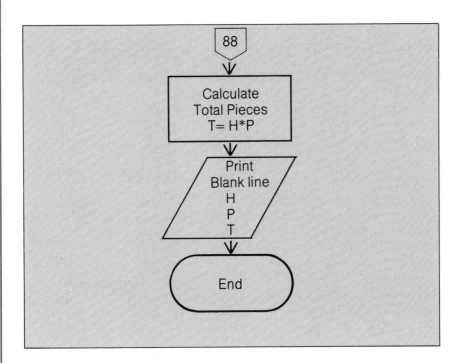

3.5 THE RESTORE STATEMENT

Sometimes you may want to read the data items from one DATA statement several times during execution of a program. This can be accomplished by the use of a **RESTORE** statement. When the computer encounters a RESTORE, it goes back to the first item in the DATA statement that has the lowest line number. These data items are reassigned when the computer executes the next READ statement. Here is an example.

```
10  READ A,B
20  DATA 1,2
30    --
40    --
50  RESTORE
60  READ L,M
70    --
99  END
```

The first READ statement assigns 1 to **A** and 2 to **B**. The RESTORE statement makes all the items in the DATA statement available for reassignment. This means that when the computer encounters the READ statement in line 60, numbers 1 and 2 are reassigned, but this time to **L** and **M**.

The program on page 90 prints the values of all the variables to help you trace through the logic of the RESTORE statement.

```
10 READ A,B
20 DATA 1,2,3,4,5
30 PRINT
40 PRINT "A =";A,"B =";B
50 RESTORE
60 READ L,M,N
70 PRINT "L =";L,"M =";M,"N =";N
99 END
```

The first READ statement assigns 1 to **A** and 2 to **B**. The numbers 3, 4, and 5 are ignored. The RESTORE statement causes the computer to go back to the beginning of the DATA statement with the result that when the computer encounters the READ statement in line 60, 1 and 2 are reassigned, but this time to **L** and **M**, while 3 is assigned to **N**. The numbers 4 and 5 are ignored. A RUN produces the following.

```
RUN

A = 1      B = 2
L = 1      M = 2      N = 3
```

Without the RESTORE statement, the computer does not go back to the beginning of the DATA statement after assigning 1 to **A** and 2 to **B**. Instead, the remaining values 3, 4, and 5 are assigned to **L, M,** and **N** respectively. A RUN now produces the following.

```
RUN

A = 1      B = 2
L = 3      M = 4      N = 5
```

3.5 THE RESTORE STATEMENT — Sample Program

This sample program changes original data (10, 20, 30) first by adding 10 to each value and then by subtracting 10 from each value.
(a) Use the READ/DATA statements to assign the original values to **A, B, C**.
(b) Change the values of **A, B, C** by adding 10 to each.
(c) Use a RESTORE statement and another READ statement to reassign the numbers in the DATA statement to variables **X, Y, Z**.
(d) Change the values of **X, Y, Z** by subtracting 10 from each. Note: The original values of **A, B, C** and **X, Y, Z** must be printed before they are changed.

```
10 READ A,B,C                          — Reads the values of A, B, C from the DATA
                                         statement.
20 DATA 10,20,30                       — Supplies the READ statement with data.
30 PRINT                               — Leaves a blank line after the word RUN.
40 PRINT "A =";A,"B =";B,"C =";C       — Prints the original values of A, B, C.
50 LET A=A+10                          — Adds 10 to the value of A and stores the
                                         result back into A.
60 LET B=B+10                          — Adds 10 to the value of B and stores the
                                         result back into B.
70 LET C=C+10                          — Adds 10 to the value of C and stores
                                         the result back into C.
80 PRINT "A =";A,"B =";B,"C =";C       — Prints the new values of A, B, C.
90 RESTORE                             — Causes the computer to go back to the
                                         first item in the DATA statement that has the
                                         lowest line number.
100 READ X,Y,Z                         — Reassigns the values in the DATA
                                         statement to variables X, Y, Z.
110 PRINT                              — Leaves a blank line.
120 PRINT "X =";X,"Y =";Y,"Z =";Z      — Prints the original values of X, Y, Z.
130 LET X=X-10                         — Subtracts 10 from the value of X and
                                         stores the result back into X.
140 LET Y=Y-10                         — Subtracts 10 from the value of Y and
                                         stores the result back into Y.
150 LET Z=Z-10                         — Subtracts 10 from the value of Z and
                                         stores the result back into Z.
160 PRINT "X =";X,"Y =";Y,"Z =";Z      — Prints the new values of X, Y, Z.
999 END                                — Terminates program execution.

RUN

A = 10     B = 20     C = 30
A = 20     B = 30     C = 40

X = 10     Y = 20     Z = 30
X = 0      Y = 10     Z = 20
```

3.5 THE RESTORE STATEMENT — Your Turn

1. Identify the errors, if any, in the program segments shown below.
   Make the necessary corrections. Note: Part (a) has two errors.

```
(a) 10 READ A,B,C        (b) 10 READ A,B,C
    20 DATA 1,2,3            20 DATA 2,4,6
    --                       --
    60 RESTORE D,E,F         60 RESTORE
    --                       70 READ D,E
    99 END                   --
                             99 END
```

```
(c) 10 READ A,B,C        (d) 10 READ A,B,C
    --                       20 DATA 4,8,12
    40 RESTORE               --
    50 READ D,E,F            60 RESTORE 4,8,12
    60 DATA 2,3,4            70 READ D,E,F
    --                       --
    99 END                   99 END
```

2. What is the output of each of the following programs?

```
(a) 10 READ A,B,C
    20 DATA 3,6,9
    30 PRINT
    40 PRINT "A =";A,"B =";B,"C =";C
    50 RESTORE
    60 READ P,Q,R
    70 PRINT "P =";P,"Q =";Q,"R =";R
    99 END

(b) 10 READ A,B,C
    20 DATA 3,6,9,12,15
    30 PRINT
    40 PRINT "A =";A,"B =";B,"C =";C
    50 READ P,Q
    60 PRINT "P =";P,"Q =";Q
    99 END

(c) 10 READ A,B
    20 DATA 5,10,15,20
    30 PRINT
    40 PRINT "A =";A,"B =";B
    50 RESTORE
    60 READ P,Q,R
    70 PRINT "P =";P,"Q =";Q,"R =";R
    80 READ A
    90 PRINT "A =";A
    99 END
```

3. A customer is shopping for two items, a chair and a table lamp. These items are originally marked at $80 and $60 respectively at two different stores. The first store is offering a discount of $10 on each item, while the second store is offering a discount of $20 on each item. Write a program that finds the reduced price of each item in each store.

   (a) Use the READ/DATA statements to assign the original prices to variables **C1** (chair in first store) and **L1** (lamp in first store).

   (b) Change the values of **C1** and **L1** by subtracting $10 from each (discount offered by first store).

   (c) Use a RESTORE statement and another READ statement to reassign the original prices to variables **C2** (chair in second store) and **L2** (lamp in second store).

(d) Change the values of **C2** and **L2** by subtracting $20 from each (discount offered by second store).

(e) Remember to print the original values of **C1, L1** and **C2, L2** before the values are changed.

(f) A new symbol is introduced in the flowchart. A six-sided figure, called the preparation symbol, indicates that the computer is getting prepared for a routine. Preparations vary. The computer may initialize a variable, set up a FOR/NEXT loop (explained in Chapter Six) or, as in this flowchart, RESTORE data that has already been read.

```
RUN

FIRST STORE
CHAIR: 80          LAMP: 60
REDUCED: 70        REDUCED: 50

SECOND STORE
CHAIR: 80          LAMP: 60
REDUCED: 60        REDUCED: 40
```

Problem 3

C1 — CHAIR IN FIRST STORE   C2 — CHAIR IN SECOND STORE
L1 — LAMP IN FIRST STORE   L2 — LAMP IN SECOND STORE

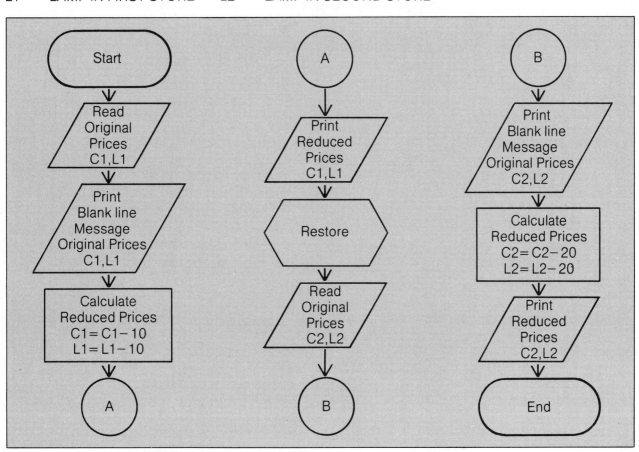

3.5 THE RESTORE STATEMENT—Solutions for "Your Turn"

1. (a) The key word RESTORE should not be followed by a list of variables. The RESTORE statement should be followed by a READ statement.

```
10 READ A,B,C
20 DATA 1,2,3
----
60 RESTORE
70 READ D,E,F
----
99 END
```

(b) Nothing is wrong.
(c) Nothing is wrong.
(d) The key word RESTORE should not be followed by a list of numbers.

```
10 READ A,B,C
20 DATA 4,8,12
----
60 RESTORE
70 READ D,E,F
----
99 END
```

2.

```
(a) RUN                                    (c) RUN

    A = 3      B = 6      C = 9               A = 5      B = 10
    P = 3      Q = 6      R = 9               P = 5      Q = 10      R = 15
(b) RUN                                       A = 20

    A = 3      B = 6      C = 9
    P = 12     Q = 15
```

3.

```
01 REM C1--CHAIR IN FIRST STORE
02 REM L1--LAMP IN FIRST STORE
03 REM C2--CHAIR IN SECOND STORE
04 REM L2--LAMP IN SECOND STORE
```

```
10 READ C1,L1
20 DATA 80,60
30 PRINT
40 PRINT "FIRST STORE"
50 PRINT "CHAIR:";C1,"LAMP:";L1
60 LET C1=C1-10
70 LET L1=L1-10
80 PRINT "REDUCED:";C1,"REDUCED:";L1
90 RESTORE
100 READ C2,L2
110 PRINT
120 PRINT "SECOND STORE"
130 PRINT "CHAIR:";C2,"LAMP:";L2
140 LET C2=C2-20
150 LET L2=L2-20
160 PRINT "REDUCED:";C2,"REDUCED:";L2
999 END
```

3.6 A WAGE PROGRAM

Here is a sample program that will be rewritten in subsequent chapters but with additions and modifications so that it reflects newly learned concepts. The program determines the wages of an employee who works a certain number of hours at a specific rate per hour. Deductions are made for income tax, union dues, and a registered pension plan. Here is the data needed for this program.

Hours Worked	Rate	Income Tax Ded.	Union Dues	Pension Ded.
37	$11.54	$75	$2	$2.50

(a) Use the READ/DATA statements to enter the number of hours worked, the rate per hour, and the deductions.
(b) Remarks are placed in strategic spots to help you understand the program.
(c) Blank lines have been inserted only for clarity.
(d) Calculations:
Gross Pay = Hours × Rate
Total Deductions = Income Tax Deduction + Union Dues + Pension Deduction
Net Pay = Gross Pay − Total Deductions

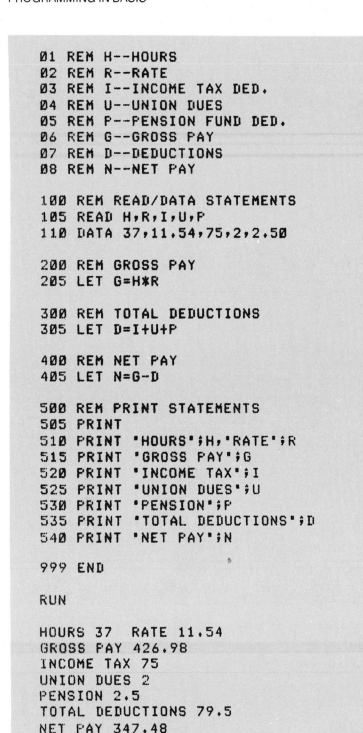

```
01 REM H--HOURS
02 REM R--RATE
03 REM I--INCOME TAX DED.
04 REM U--UNION DUES
05 REM P--PENSION FUND DED.
06 REM G--GROSS PAY
07 REM D--DEDUCTIONS
08 REM N--NET PAY

100 REM READ/DATA STATEMENTS
105 READ H,R,I,U,P
110 DATA 37,11.54,75,2,2.50

200 REM GROSS PAY
205 LET G=H*R

300 REM TOTAL DEDUCTIONS
305 LET D=I+U+P

400 REM NET PAY
405 LET N=G-D

500 REM PRINT STATEMENTS
505 PRINT
510 PRINT "HOURS";H,"RATE";R
515 PRINT "GROSS PAY";G
520 PRINT "INCOME TAX";I
525 PRINT "UNION DUES";U
530 PRINT "PENSION";P
535 PRINT "TOTAL DEDUCTIONS";D
540 PRINT "NET PAY";N

999 END

RUN

HOURS 37  RATE 11.54
GROSS PAY 426.98
INCOME TAX 75
UNION DUES 2
PENSION 2.5
TOTAL DEDUCTIONS 79.5
NET PAY 347.48
```

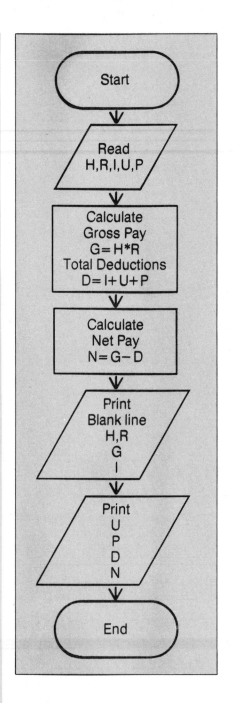

1. Which two statements enter data into the computer?

```
*********************************
105 READ H,R,I,U,P
110 DATA 37,11.54,75,2,2.50
```

2. Which statement calculates the gross pay?

```
******************************
205 LET G=H*R
```

3. Which statement calculates the total deductions?

```
******************************
305 LET D=I+U+P
```

4. Which statement calculates the net pay?

```
******************************
405 LET N=G-D
```

5. Which statement prints the gross pay?

```
******************************
515 PRINT "GROSS PAY";G
```

6. Which statement prints the net pay?

```
******************************
540 PRINT "NET PAY";N
```

A SHORT SUMMARY

There are three ways by which data may be entered into a computer. In a LET statement, the value on the right-hand side of the equals sign is assigned to the variable on the left-hand side of the equals sign. The LET statement may also be used to assign the result of an expression to a variable. The INPUT statement allows data to be keyed into the computer during execution of a program. When the READ/DATA statements are used, the values listed in the DATA statement are assigned, in sequential order, to the variables listed in the READ statement.

Each of the following programs prints the numbers 1, 2, 3 on one line and the squares of these numbers (1, 4, 9) on the next line. Pay close attention to the RUNs. Notice that the programs using the LET statement and the READ/DATA statements produce the same RUN. The program that uses the INPUT statement produces a RUN that is different, since data is displayed immediately after a prompt. There is no need to have this data printed again.

1. Using the LET statement

```
10 LET A=1
20 LET B=2
30 LET C=3
40 PRINT
50 PRINT A;B;C
60 PRINT AT2;BT2;CT2
99 END

RUN

   1   2   3
   1   4   9
```

2. Using the INPUT statement

```
10 PRINT
20 PRINT "VALUES FOR A,B,C";
30 INPUT A,B,C
40 PRINT AT2;BT2;CT2
99 END

RUN

VALUES FOR A,B,C? 1,2,3
   1   4   9
```

3. Using the READ/DATA statements

```
10 READ A,B,C
20 DATA 1,2,3
30 PRINT
40 PRINT A;B;C
50 PRINT AT2;BT2;CT2
99 END

RUN
```

```
1   2   3
1   4   9
```

Items listed in a DATA statement may be reread by means of a RESTORE statement and its accompanying READ statement. The program shown below assigns 1, 2, and 3 to variables **A, B**, and **C**, then reassigns these values to variables **L, M**, and **N**.

```
10  READ A,B,C
20  DATA 1,2,3
30  PRINT
40  PRINT "A =";A,"B =";B,"C =";C
50  RESTORE
60  READ L,M,N
70  PRINT "L =";L,"M =";M,"N =";N
99  END

RUN

A = 1       B = 2       C = 3
L = 1       M = 2       N = 3
```

The preparation symbol, a six-sided figure, was introduced in this chapter. It indicates that the computer is getting prepared for a routine. New techniques in flowcharting were also explained. These included the placement of consecutive and similar operations in one symbol and the omission of irrelevant material.

Questions and Exercises[3]

1. Give the definition of a variable.
2. What must be the first character of a numeric variable?
3. Display and label a LET statement. Explain how a LET statement is executed.
4. The assignment **A=A+1** seems to resemble an algebraic equation, yet mathematically it makes no sense. Explain how such a statement is entirely logical in BASIC.
5. Explain the term **initialization of a variable**. Give an example. Is there any particular order in which two variables should be initialized?
6. A programmer wishes to have the value of **A** printed each time a number is assigned to the variable. What is wrong with the following program? Make the necessary corrections.

3. Questions and exercises that involve the INPUT statement may be omitted if you are not using an interactive system. This applies to the remaining questions and exercises in this book.

```
10 LET A=1
20 LET A=A+1
30 LET A=A+1
40 PRINT
50 PRINT 'A ='iA
99 END
```

The programmer would like to have the following RUN.

```
RUN

A = 1
A = 2
A = 3
```

7. Write a short program that copies a value stored in location **A** and places it in location **B**. Use a LET statement to enter your data into the computer. Print the values of both **A** and **B** and show the RUN of your program.

8. What is wrong with the following program? Make the necessary correction.

```
10 LET A=1
20 LET C=A+B
30 PRINT
40 PRINT 'C ='iC
99 END

RUN

C = 10
```

9. If the values of **A, B**, and **C** are initially 1, 2, and 3 respectively for *each* of the following program segments, what will be their values after execution of each program segment? In which program segments do the values of **A** and **B** interchange?

```
(a) 40 LET C=A          (c) 40 LET A=B
    50 LET A=B              50 LET B=C
    60 LET B=C              60 LET C=A

(b) 40 LET B=C          (d) 40 LET C=B
    50 LET A=B              50 LET B=A
    60 LET C=B              60 LET A=C
```

10. (a) What happens when the computer encounters an INPUT statement?
    (b) How does the programmer respond?
11. Write two programs, each of which INPUTs two values and PRINTs two values. In one program use two INPUT statements to enter the data; in the second program use only one INPUT statement. Show the RUN for each program.
12. Using prompts, modify the following program so that the values of **A** and **B** can be identified. Show the RUN for the modified version of the program.

```
10 PRINT
20 INPUT A
30 INPUT B
40 PRINT "A+B =";A+B
99 END

RUN

? 2
? 4
A+B = 6
```

13. Indicate the errors, if any, in the program segments and screen messages shown below. Make the necessary corrections.

(a) 10 LET B-4=A
    --
    99 END

Let A=B-4
or B=A+4

(b) 10 LET S1=10
    --
    99 END

(c) 10 LET 1S=10
    --
    99 END

Let S1=10

(d) 10 LET A=10 AND 12
    --
    99 END

A=10
B=12

(e) 20 INPUT,X,Y,Z
    --
    99 END

input X,Y,Z
or
input W,X,Y,Z

(f) 20 PRINT "VALUES FOR X,Y,Z";
    30 INPUT X,Y,Z
    --
    99 END

    RUN

    VALUES FOR X,Y,Z? 2,4

need one more number too

(g) 20 INPUT I,J,K
    --
    99 END

    RUN

    ? 2,3,4

10 PRINT "ENTER 3 numbers"

```
(h)  20 PRINT "VALUES FOR A,B,C";
     30 INPUT A,B,C
     --
     99 END

     RUN

     VALUES FOR A,B,C? A,B,C
```

14. What is the purpose of each of the following statements?
    (a) The READ statement
    (b) The DATA statement
15. Write a program segment in which three READ statements are satisfied by one DATA statement.
16. Write a program segment in which one READ statement is satisfied by three DATA statements.
17. Identify the errors, if any, in the program segments shown below. Make the necessary corrections.

```
(a)  20 READ A,B,C           (f)  20 READ A,B,C
     --                           30 DATA 1,1+1,3
     99 END

(b)  20 READ A,B,C           (g)  20 READ,A,B,C
     --                           30 DATA 48,49,50
     60 DATA 2,3

(c)  20 DATA 16,17,18        (h)  20 READ A,B,C
     --                           --
     60 READ A,B,C                60 END
                                  99 DATA 98,99,100

(d)  20 READ A,B,C           (i)  10 READ A,B,C
     30 DATA,10,11,12             20 DATA 10,20,30
                                  --
                                  60 RESTORE I,J,K
                                  --
                                  99 END
                             (Note: There are two errors.)

(e)  20 READ 1,2,3           (j)  10 READ A,B,C,D
     30 DATA A,B,C                20 DATA 2,4,6,8
                                  --
                                  60 RESTORE
                                  70 READ I
                                  --
                                  99 END
```

18. Using a sample program, explain how a RESTORE statement is executed.
19. Show the RUNS for the following programs.

```
(a) 10 LET B=4
    20 PRINT
    30 PRINT B
    40 LET B=B+6
    50 PRINT B
    99 END
```

blank line
↑4
↑10

```
(b) 10 LET C=2
    20 LET D=C+1
    30 LET C=CT2
    40 LET D=C+1
    50 PRINT
    60 PRINT C,D
    99 END
```

2+1 3   C+1 5
c=4   4.5

blank line show a wide spacing
C 5
4

```
(c) 10 LET I=8
    20 LET J=I
    30 LET K=J-5
    40 LET I=K
    50 PRINT
    60 PRINT I,K
    99 END
```

blank line wide spacing
3   C   3

8.5 3
3 3

```
(d) 10 READ A,B
    20 DATA 1,2,3,4,5
    30 PRINT
    40 PRINT "A =";A,"B =";B
    50 RESTORE
    60 READ I,J,K
    70 PRINT "I =";I,"J =";J,"K =";K
    99 END
```

Blank line
A = 1   B = 2   K = 3
↑5   ↑5   ↑5
I = 1   J = 2
↑5   ↑5

```
(e) 10 READ A,B
    20 DATA 1,2,3,4,5
    30 PRINT
    40 PRINT "A =";A,"B =";B
    50 READ I,J,K
    60 PRINT "I =";I,"J =";J,"K =";K
    99 END
```

Blank line
A = 1   B = 2   K = 5
↑5   ↑5   ↑5
I = 3   J = 4
↑3   ↑5

20. Write three program segments, each of which assigns the four values 1, 2, 3, and 4 to four variables. In each program segment, use one of the three methods introduced in this chapter to enter data into the computer.

10 Read A, B, C, D
20 PRINT "A = "; A,

Programming Problems[4]

For each of the following problems, write three separate programs, each one entering data in a different way. One program uses the LET statement, the second program uses the INPUT statement, and the third program uses the READ/DATA statements. Remember, the RUNS for programs that use LET statements are the same as the RUNS for programs that use READ/DATA statements.

1. Suppose you own 5 bonds, each having a par value of $1000. If the interest rate is 12%, what will be your annual interest income?
   (a) Interest Income = Number of Bonds × Par Value × Rate of Interest (.12)

4. Throughout the book, flowcharts are drawn for the more difficult problems. To understand the flow of logic, you should draw flowcharts for the remaining problems in the book. Always draw the flowchart before you write the program. Programs that use the INPUT statement to enter data may be omitted in this chapter if you are not using an interactive system.

Using the LET Statement and the READ/DATA Statements

```
RUN

NO. OF BONDS: 5
PAR VALUE: 1000
RATE OF INTEREST: .12
INTEREST INCOME: 600
```

Using the INPUT Statement

```
RUN

NO.,PAR VALUE,RATE? 5,1000,.12
INTEREST INCOME: 600
```

2. If you were working in the furniture department of a store and received a basic salary of $100 a week and a commission of 10% based on sales, and if you sold $2200 worth of furniture last week, how much commission would you receive? What would your income be for the week?
   (a) Use S for Salary.
   (b) Use A for Amount of Sales.
   (c) Commission = Amount of Sales × Rate of Commission (.10)
   (d) Income = Salary + Commission

Using the LET Statement and the READ/DATA Statements

```
RUN

SALARY: 100          RATE: .1
AMOUNT OF SALES: 2200
COMMISSION: 220
INCOME: 320
```

Using the INPUT Statement

```
RUN

SALARY,RATE? 100,.10
AMOUNT OF SALES? 2200
COMMISSION: 220
INCOME: 320
```

Problem 2

S — SALARY   A — AMOUNT OF SALES   I — INCOME
R — RATE   C — COMMISSION

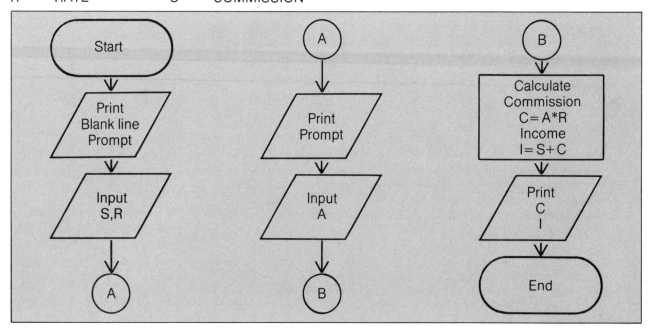

3. A retailer purchases 50 pairs of shoes at a total cost of $2000 and sells them for $3100. Operating expenses amount to $500. Write a program that finds the profit before expenses are paid (gross profit) and the profit after expenses are paid (net profit).
   (a) Gross Profit = Sales − Cost
   (b) Net Profit = Gross Profit − Expenses

Problem 3
S — SALES
C — COST
E — EXPENSES
G — GROSS PROFIT
N — NET PROFIT

Using the LET Statement and the READ/DATA Statements

```
RUN

SALES,COST,EXPENSES:  3100   2000   500
GROSS PROFIT: 1100
NET PROFIT: 600
```

Using the INPUT Statement

```
RUN

SALES,COST,EXPENSES?  3100,2000,500
GROSS PROFIT: 1100
NET PROFIT: 600
```

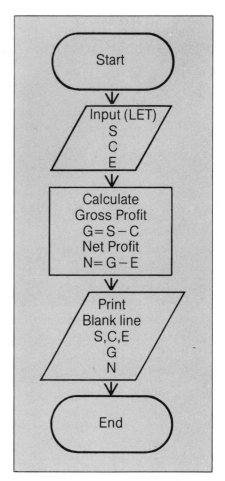

4. Suppose you received $550 as your salary on May 1. If you made payments amounting to $350 to cover rent, food, clothes, and miscellaneous items, what amount did you save? What amount is saved if you received another $550 on May 15 but spent only $125? Initially you had no savings.
   (a) Amount Saved = 0
   (b) Amount Saved = Amount Saved + Salary − Payments
   (c) In the flowchart, notice the preparation symbol that initializes A to zero.

Using the LET Statement and the READ/DATA Statements

Using the INPUT Statement

```
RUN

SALARY: 550
PAYMENTS: 350
AMOUNT SAVED: 200


SALARY: 550
PAYMENTS: 125
AMOUNT SAVED: 625
```

```
RUN

SALARY? 550
PAYMENTS? 350
AMOUNT SAVED: 200


SALARY: 550
PAYMENTS? 125
AMOUNT SAVED: 625
```

Problem 4

A — AMOUNT SAVED   P1 — FIRST PAYMENTS
S — SALARY   P2 — SECOND PAYMENTS

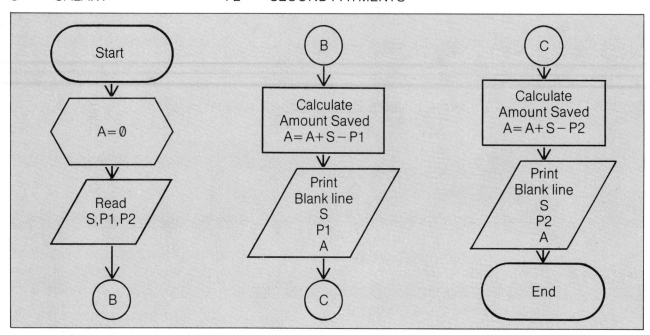

5. Convert 77°F to degrees Celsius. The conversion formula is as follows.

$$C = \frac{5}{9}(F - 32)$$

Using the LET Statement and the READ/DATA Statements

Using the INPUT Statement

```
RUN

FAHRENHEIT: 77
CELSIUS: 25
```

```
RUN

FAHRENHEIT? 77
CELSIUS: 25
```

6. Use the READ/DATA statements to assign 2000, 5000, and 8000 to three variables. Print these values. Using the RESTORE statement, copy the contents of these three storage locations by storing the values in three different locations in the computer. Print the contents of these last three locations.

```
RUN

A = 2000   B = 5000   C = 8000
X = 2000   Y = 5000   Z = 8000
```

FOUR BRANCHING AND LOOPING I

A. After completing this chapter, you should be able to write BASIC programs and complete skeletal BASIC programs that use:
  1. GO TO statements.
  2. IF/THEN statements.
  3. ON...GO TO statements.
  4. Counters (positive and negative).
B. In addition, you should be able to:
  1. Differentiate between conditional and unconditional branches.
  2. Define
     (a) A branch.
     (b) A loop.
  3. Summarize what happens when the index of an ON...GO TO statement is a number that contains a decimal fraction.
  4. List the six BASIC relational operators and their meanings.
  5. Terminate loops by means of
     (a) IF/THEN statements that test the data.
     (b) IF/THEN statements that test counters.
     (c) ON...GO TO statements.
  6. State the number of alternative transfers allowed in
     (a) GO TO statements.
     (b) IF/THEN statements.
     (c) ON...GO TO statements.
  7. State the differences in execution between
     (a) GO TO statements.
     (b) IF/THEN statements.
     (c) ON...GO TO statements.
  8. Find and correct errors in invalid
     (a) GO TO statements.
     (b) IF/THEN statements.
     (c) ON...GO TO statements.
  9. Find errors in programs.
  10. Produce the output of programs.
  11. (a) State the restrictions that limit the index of an ON...GO TO statement.
      (b) Explain how a computer may respond to an ON...GO TO statement whose index is out of the range.
  12. Summarize the purpose of each of the three statements required to set up a counter that controls a loop.

4.1 THE GO TO STATEMENT

Until now, statements have been executed sequentially, from lowest line number to highest. Sometimes, you may want to change the order of execution. One statement that alters the normal sequence is the **GO TO** statement. (Some computer systems require **GOTO**.) Here is how it works.

```
→ 10    --
  20    --
  30    --
  40 GO TO 10
   --
   ...
  99 END
```

Line 10 is executed, then line 20 and then line 30. On reaching line 40, control is transferred back to line 10. Lines 10, 20, and 30 are executed a second time. Again, line 40 causes the computer to transfer back to line 10. Lines 10, 20, and 30 are executed for the third time. Line 40 causes control to transfer to line 10. Notice that control keeps going back to line 10, and that the execution of lines 10, 20, and 30 never stops. The program is in a **loop** and the GO TO statement is referred to as an **unconditional branch**, since there is no alternative except to GO TO line 10. In other words, the GO TO statement offers no conditions under which the computer may choose another path.

A GO TO statement may also transfer control to a higher-numbered statement, ignoring all the intervening statements in the process. This transfer is called a **branch**. Here is an example.

```
10    --
20 GO TO 50
30    --
40    --
50    -- ←
```

When the computer reaches line 20, control is transferred to line 50, where execution resumes. Lines 30 and 40 are skipped.

In the first example, the GO TO transfers control to a lower-numbered statement. In example two, control is transferred to a higher-numbered statement. It should be noted that a GO TO statement must not reference itself, since this results in a continuous loop.

4.1 THE GO TO STATEMENT—Sample Programs[1]

The GO TO statement will now be used in a program that prints the whole numbers 1, 2, and 3. Three variations of this program are given,

---

1. If you are not using an interactive system, omit programs that use the INPUT statement to enter data.

each of which enters data into the computer in a different way. The first one uses the LET statement, the second one uses the INPUT statement, and the third one uses the READ/DATA statements. Trace through the logic of each program, then key it in and RUN the program. Compare the three RUNS.

1. Using the LET statement

```
   10 LET A=1          — Initializes A to 1.
   20 PRINT            — Leaves a blank line.
   30 PRINT 'A =';A    — Prints the current value of A.
   40 LET A=A+1        — Increments A by 1.
   50 GO TO 20         — Transfers control back to line 20. Execution resumes sequentially
                          until line 50.
   99 END              — Not executed, but may have to be included.

   RUN

   A = 1

   A = 2

   A = 3

   ---
```

The program is in a continuous loop. How do you abort (stop) the program? It depends on your computer system. A number of commands to terminate a program were given in Chapter Two on page 15. The list is shown again below. Remember, you may have to press RETURN after the command key is pressed. If you are not using an interactive system, turn off the machine and consult your manual.

(a) Press the STOP key.
(b) Hold the CTRL key down; press the **C** key.
(c) Press the BREAK key.
(d) Press the ESC key.
(e) Press the ALT MODE key.
(f) Press the **S** key.
(g) Turn off the machine.
(h) Consult your manual.

2. Using the INPUT statement

```
   10 PRINT               — Leaves a blank line.
   20 PRINT 'VALUE FOR A';— Identifies the value to be entered.
   30 INPUT A             — Requests data, user enters the current value for A.
   40 PRINT 'A =';A       — Prints the value of A.
   50 GO TO 10            — Transfers control to line 10. Execution resumes
                            sequentially until line 50.
   99 END                 — Not executed, but may have to be included.
```

```
RUN

VALUE FOR A? 1
A = 1

VALUE FOR A? 2
A = 2

VALUE FOR A? 3
A = 3

VALUE FOR A?
```

The computer keeps asking for more data! How do you abort this program? See Program 1 where you were in a continuous loop.

3. Using the READ/DATA statements

```
→10 READ A              —Reads the values of A one at a time from the DATA statement.
 20 DATA 1,2,3          —Supplies the READ statement with data.
 30 PRINT               —Leaves a blank line.
 40 PRINT "A =";A       —Prints the current value of A.
 50 GO TO 10            —Transfers control to line 10. Execution resumes sequentially until
                          line 50.
 99 END                 —Not executed, but may have to be included.

RUN

A = 1

A = 2

A = 3

?OUT OF DATA ERROR IN  10
```

After **A** is assigned a value of 3, the computer attempts to read another value. Since all the items in the DATA statement are already assigned, the computer prints a message something like the one above, then stops.

4.1 THE GO TO STATEMENT—Your Turn

Write three programs for each of the following two problems. Each program is to use one of the three methods by which data can be entered into the computer. RUN your programs to see what your computer system prints when a program is in a continuous loop (using the LET statement), when the computer requests more data (using the INPUT statement), and when the computer informs you that it is out of data and stops (using the READ/DATA statements). The RUNS are shown below.

1. Print the whole numbers 2, 4, 6.

The LET Statement	The INPUT Statement	The READ/DATA Statements
A = 2	VALUE FOR A? 2 A = 2	A = 2
A = 4	VALUE FOR A? 4 A = 4	A = 4
A = 6	VALUE FOR A? 6 A = 6	A = 6
--	VALUE FOR A?	?OUT OF DATA ERROR IN 10
----		

2. A customer buys 3 watches, one priced at $40, a second one priced at $50, and the third one priced at $60. If a sales tax of 5% is added to the retail price, what is the total cost of each watch?

(a) Sales Tax = Retail Price × .05
(b) Total Cost = Retail Price + Sales Tax
(c) In the flowchart, notice that a GO TO statement is represented by a line and two arrows. These are drawn from the PRINT symbol (from the symbol that includes the statement just before the GO TO) to the READ symbol. The flowchart is drawn for the program that uses the READ/DATA statements.

The LET Statement	The INPUT Statement	The READ/DATA Statements
RETAIL PRICE: 40 SALES TAX: 2 TOTAL COST: 42	RETAIL PRICE? 40 SALES TAX: 2 TOTAL COST: 42	RETAIL PRICE: 40 SALES TAX: 2 TOTAL COST: 42
RETAIL PRICE: 50 SALES TAX: 2.5 TOTAL COST: 52.5	RETAIL PRICE? 50 SALES TAX: 2.5 TOTAL COST: 52.5	RETAIL PRICE: 50 SALES TAX: 2.5 TOTAL COST: 52.5
RETAIL PRICE: 60 SALES TAX: 3 TOTAL COST: 63	RETAIL PRICE? 60 SALES TAX: 3 TOTAL COST: 63	RETAIL PRICE: 60 SALES TAX: 3 TOTAL COST: 63
-- --	RETAIL PRICE?	?OUT OF DATA ERROR IN 10

Problem 2

R — RETAIL PRICE
T — TAX
C — COST

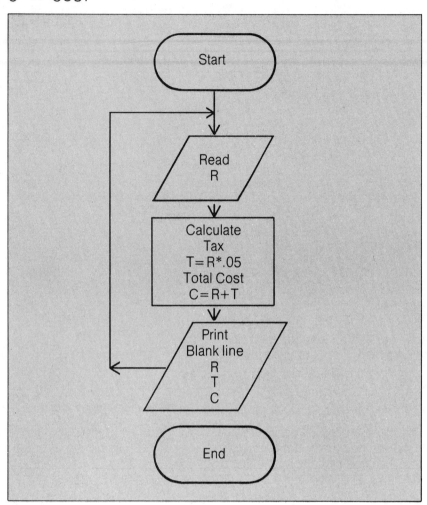

4.1 GO TO STATEMENT—Programs for "Your Turn"

1.

Using the LET Statement	Using the INPUT Statement

```
10 LET A=2
20 PRINT
30 PRINT "A =";A
40 LET A=A+2
50 GO TO 20
99 END
```

```
10 PRINT
20 PRINT "VALUE FOR A";
30 INPUT A
40 PRINT "A =";A
50 GO TO 10
99 END
```

Using the READ/DATA Statements

```
10 READ A
20 DATA 2,4,6
30 PRINT
40 PRINT "A =";A
50 GO TO 10
99 END
```

2.

Using the LET Statement

```
01 REM R--RETAIL PRICE
02 REM T--TAX
03 REM C--COST

10 LET R=40
20 LET T=R*.05
30 LET C=R+T
40 PRINT
50 PRINT "RETAIL PRICE:";R
60 PRINT "SALES TAX:";T
70 PRINT "TOTAL COST:";C
80 LET R=R+10
90 GO TO 20
99 END
```

Using the INPUT Statement

```
01 REM R--RETAIL PRICE
02 REM T--TAX
03 REM C--COST

10 PRINT
20 PRINT "RETAIL PRICE";
30 INPUT R
40 LET T=R*.05
50 LET C=R+T
60 PRINT "SALES TAX:";T
70 PRINT "TOTAL COST:";C
80 GO TO 10
99 END
```

Using the READ/DATA Statements

```
01 REM R--RETAIL PRICE
02 REM T--TAX
03 REM C--COST

10 READ R
20 DATA 40,50,60
30 LET T=R*.05
40 LET C=R+T
50 PRINT
60 PRINT "RETAIL PRICE:";R
70 PRINT "SALES TAX:";T
80 PRINT "TOTAL COST:";C
90 GO TO 10
99 END
```

4.2 THE IF/THEN STATEMENT

The programs in Section 4.1 should be modified. They were either in a continuous loop (using the LET statement), requested more data (using the INPUT statement), or gave an error message (using the READ/DATA statements). They should be changed so that the computer can get out of the loop in order to execute the rest of the program.

```
 ┌→10    --
 │  20    --
 │  30    --
 └─ 40 GO TO 10
    --
    99 END
```

In this example, the END statement is never executed. To abort the first two programs, you had to type in a system command. Although you didn't have to abort the program using the READ/DATA statements (because it gave an error message instead), it, too, never reached the END statement. There must be some other method by which looping can be stopped so that termination of a program is automatic and not user dependent. In other words, the END statement is executed. One of the solutions is the IF/THEN statement, an important decision-making statement. Here is an example.

```
    20 --
    30 IF A=6 THEN 99 ┐
    --                │
    60 GO TO 20       │
    --                │
    99 END ←──────────┘
```

In statement 30, the key word IF is followed by a relationship (in this case, between **A** and 6); the key word THEN is followed by a statement number which specifies the statement to which control must be transferred when the relationship is true. In the example above, if **A** is equal to 6, the computer branches to line 99. The program is now out of the loop; in fact, it has reached the END statement. If **A** is not equal to 6, the computer goes on to the next line and execution resumes sequentially until line 60.

Some computer systems accept the words GO TO instead of the word THEN. Others accept THEN GO TO, while still others allow an executable statement such as PRINT, END, or an assignment statement after the word THEN. Here are some examples of the different ways the statement may be written.

```
40 IF A=26 THEN 120
50 IF B=10 GO TO 100          or    50 IF B=10 GOTO 100
60 IF C=49 THEN GO TO 999     or    60 IF C=49 THEN GOTO 999
70 IF D=58 THEN PRINT C
80 IF E=14 THEN D=DT2
90 IF F=67 THEN END
```

Take another look at the IF part. The relationships in the examples so far have been between a variable and a number. This does not always have to be the case. The relationships may also be between:

(a) A variable and another variable.

20 IF A = C THEN 40

(b) A variable and an expression.

20 IF A = B*C THEN 40

(c) Two expressions.

20 IF A/2 = B*C THEN 40

Here is a simple table showing the BASIC relational operators and their meanings.

RELATIONAL OPERATOR	MEANING
=	is equal to
>	is greater than
>=	is greater than or equal to
<	is less than
<=	is less than or equal to
<>	is not equal to

4.2 THE IF/THEN STATEMENT—Sample Programs

The three sample programs in Section 4.1 will now be modified so that the computer can pass out of the loops. Each program prints the whole numbers 1, 2, 3, but enters data into the computer in a different way. This time the IF/THEN statement will be used to automatically stop program execution by transferring control out of the loop to the END statement. Trace through the logic of the following programs. Key in and RUN the first program in each of parts 1, 2, and 3 (not the program segment).

1. Using the LET statement

```
10 LET A=1              — Initializes A to 1.
20 IF A>3 THEN 99       — Tests the current value of A.
```
    (i) If **A** is greater than 3, control is transferred to the END statement where the program terminates.

    (ii) If **A** is not greater than 3 (less than 3 or equal to 3), the computer proceeds to the next statement. Execution resumes sequentially until line 60.

```
30 PRINT                — Leaves a blank line.
40 PRINT "A ="; A       — Prints the current value of A.
50 LET A=A+1            — Increments A by 1.
60 GO TO 20             — Transfers control back to line 20.
99 END                 — Terminates program execution.

RUN

A = 1

A = 2

A = 3
```

There is usually more than one way to write a program. Here is another method by which the relationship between **A** and 3 can be tested.

```
10 LET A=1              — Initializes A to 1.
20 IF A<=3 THEN 40      — Tests the current value of A.
```
    (i) If **A** is less than 3 or **A** is equal to 3, control is transferred to line 40, where execution resumes sequentially until line 70.

    (ii) If **A** is greater than 3, the computer proceeds to the next statement.

```
30 GO TO 99             — Transfers control to the END statement, where the program terminates.
40   --  ⎫             — Executable statements.
50   --  ⎭
60 LET A=A+1            — Increments A by 1.
70 GO TO 20             — Transfers control back to line 20.
99 END                 — Terminates program execution.
```

2. Using the INPUT statement

```
10 PRINT                    — Leaves a blank line.
20 PRINT 'VALUE FOR A';     — Identifies the value to be entered.
30 INPUT A                  — Requests data, user enters the value for A.
40 IF A>3 THEN 99           — Tests the current value of A.
                               (i) If A is greater than 3, control is transferred to the
                                   END statement.
                               (ii) If A is not greater than 3 (less than 3 or equal to 3),
                                    the computer proceeds to the next statement.
                                    Execution resumes sequentially until line 60.
50 PRINT 'A =';A            — Prints the current value of A.
60 GO TO 10                 — Transfers control back to line 10.
99 END                      — Terminates program execution.

RUN

VALUE FOR A? 1
A = 1

VALUE FOR A? 2
A = 2

VALUE FOR A? 3
A = 3

VALUE FOR A? 4
```

Notice the number 4 that was entered as the last value for **A**. This
entry may be any number greater than 3 in order to stop the program.
An alternative method of testing **A** would be as follows.

```
10    --
20    --
30 INPUT A                  — Requests data, user enters the value for A.
40 IF A<=3 THEN 60          — Tests the current value of A.
                               (i) If A is less than 3 or A is equal to 3, control is transferred to line
                                   60, where execution resumes sequentially until line 70.
                               (ii) If A is greater than 3, the computer proceeds to the next
                                    statement.
50 GO TO 99                 — Transfers control to the END statement.
60    --                    — Executable statement.
70 GO TO 10                 — Transfers control back to line 10.
99 END                      — Terminates program execution.
```

3. Using the READ/DATA statements

```
10 READ A          —Reads the values of A one at a time from the DATA statement.
20 DATA 1,2,3,3.5  —Supplies the READ statement with data.
30 IF A>3 THEN 99  —Tests the current value of A.
                      (i) If A is greater than 3, control is transferred to the END statement.
                      (ii) If A is not greater than 3 (less than 3 or equal to 3), the
                           computer proceeds to the next statement. Execution resumes
                           sequentially until line 60.
40 PRINT           —Leaves a blank line.
50 PRINT 'A =';A   —Prints the current value of A.
60 GO TO 10        —Transfers control back to line 10.
99 END             —Terminates program execution.

RUN

A = 1

A = 2

A = 3
```

In the above program an extra value is listed in the DATA statement,
the number 3.5. As in the program that uses the INPUT statement, this
value may be any number greater than 3 in order to stop execution.
An alternative version of the above program would be as follows.

```
10 READ A          —Reads the values of A one at a time from the DATA statement.
20 DATA 1,2,3,4    —Supplies the READ statement with data.
30 IF A<=3 THEN 50 —Tests the current value of A.
                      (i) If A is less than 3 or A is equal to 3, control is transferred to line
                          50, where execution resumes sequentially until line 70.
                      (ii) If A is greater than 3, the computer proceeds to the next
                           statement.
40 GO TO 99        —Transfers control to the END statement.
50   --  ⎤
60   --  ⎦        —Executable statements.
70 GO TO 10        —Transfers control back to line 10.
99 END             —Terminates program execution.
```

4. The branch out of the loop does not necessarily have to be to the
   END statement. Control may be transferred to another statement
   outside the loop.

```
10 READ A
20 DATA 1,2,3,3.5
```

```
30 IF A>3 THEN 100 ─┐
--                  │
90 GO TO 10         │
100    --    ◄──────┘
--
999 END
```

Statement number 100 could be the start of a new routine, such as a routine that reads in another set of numbers and finds the largest number in the set. The program terminates when the END statement is reached.

5. In the sample programs and program segments just shown, the test on **A** is performed before its value is printed. You may want to perform the test after the value is printed. Here is an example. Notice that the relationship is between **A** and 2 in order to produce the same RUN as those produced in Programs 1 and 3 on pages 116 and 118.

```
10 LET A=1          — Initializes A to 1.
20 PRINT            — Leaves a blank line.
30 PRINT "A =";A    — Prints the current value of A.
40 IF A>2 THEN 99   — Tests the current value of A.
```
     (i) If **A** is greater than 2, control is transferred to the END statement.
     (ii) If **A** is not greater than 2 (less than 2 or equal to 2), the computer proceeds to the next statement. Execution resumes sequentially until line 60.
```
50 LET A=A+1        — Increments A by 1.
60 GO TO 20         — Transfers control back to line 20.
99 END              — Terminates program execution.

RUN

A = 1

A = 2

A = 3
```

4.2 THE IF/THEN STATEMENT — Your Turn

In Section 4.1, you were asked to write three programs for each of the two problems presented. The programs for each problem were to use the three methods by which data can be entered into the computer. Rewrite these programs. This time use IF/THEN statements to transfer control out of the loops. Here are the two problems again.

1. Print the whole numbers 2, 4, 6. Your programs should produce the following RUNs.

Using the LET Statement and the READ/DATA Statements

Using the INPUT Statement

```
RUN

A = 2

A = 4

A = 6
```

Handwritten:
```
10 Let A=2
20 If A > 6 THEN 70
30 PRINT
40 PRINT "A = "; A
50 Let A = A+2
60 GOTO 20
70 End
```

```
RUN

VALUE FOR A?
A = 2

VALUE FOR A? 4
A = 4

VALUE FOR A? 6
A = 6

VALUE FOR A? 8
```

Handwritten:
```
10 PRINT "Value for A";
20 PRINT A
30 If A > 6 THEN
40 PRINT
```

2. A customer buys three watches — one priced at $40, a second one priced at $50, and a third one priced at $60. If a sales tax of 5% is added to the retail price, what is the tax and what is the total cost of each watch?

   (a) Sales Tax = Retail Price $\times$ .05

   (b) Total Cost = Retail Price + Sales Tax

   (c) The decision symbol, a diamond-shaped figure, is introduced in the flowchart. It indicates that the computer is about to make a decision. The four points of the symbol represent incoming and outgoing flows of logic. The top point is usually reserved for an incoming path of logic, while the other three are used to show the various outgoing paths of logic. A symbol with two outgoing branches usually has the word **YES** and the word **NO** marked on the exit paths to show the respective result of an IF/THEN test. A decision symbol with multiple branches will be shown in the next section. The flowchart is drawn for the program that uses the INPUT statement.

   (d) Your programs should produce the following RUNs.

Handwritten:
```
10 Let A = 40
20 If A > 60 THEN 110
30 Let S = A×0.5
40 Let T = A+S
50 PRINT "&
60 PRINT "Retail Price"; A
70 " "Sales Tax"; S
80 " "TOTAL COST"; T
90 Let A = A+10
100 GOTO 20
110 End
```

Using the LET Statement and the READ/DATA Statements

Using the INPUT Statement

```
RUN

RETAIL PRICE: 40
SALES TAX: 2
TOTAL COST: 42

RETAIL PRICE: 50
SALES TAX: 2.5
TOTAL COST: 52.5
```

```
RUN

RETAIL PRICE? 40
SALES TAX: 2
TOTAL COST: 42

RETAIL PRICE? 50
SALES TAX: 2.5
TOTAL COST: 52.5
```

```
RETAIL PRICE: 60          RETAIL PRICE? 60
SALES TAX: 3              SALES TAX: 3
TOTAL COST: 63           TOTAL COST: 63

                          RETAIL PRICE? 70
```

Problem 2

R — RETAIL PRICE
T — TAX
C — TOTAL COST

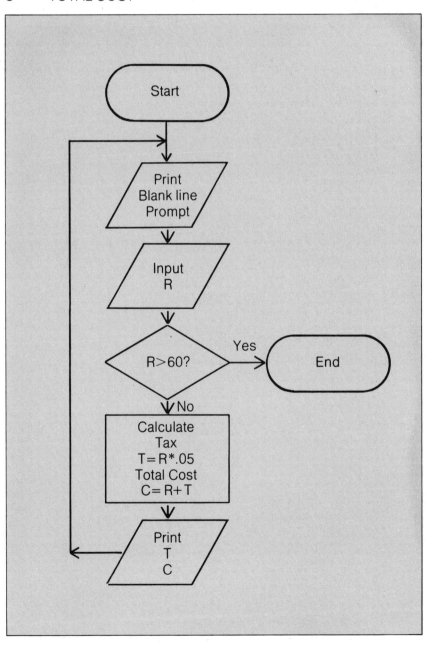

4.2 THE IF/THEN STATEMENT—Programs for "Your Turn"

1. Using the LET Statement

```
10 LET A=2
20 IF A>6 THEN 99
30 PRINT
40 PRINT "A =";A
50 LET A=A+2
60 GO TO 20
99 END
```

Using the READ/DATA Statements

```
10 READ A
20 DATA 2,4,6,8
30 IF A>6 THEN 99
40 PRINT
50 PRINT "A =";A
60 GO TO 10
99 END
```

Using the INPUT Statement

```
10 PRINT
20 PRINT "VALUE FOR A";
30 INPUT A
40 IF A>6 THEN 99
50 PRINT "A =";A
60 GO TO 10
99 END
```

2. Using the LET Statement

```
01 REM R--RETAIL PRICE
02 REM T--TAX
03 REM C--TOTAL COST

10 LET R=40
20 IF R>60 THEN 999
30 LET T=R*.05
40 LET C=R+T
50 PRINT
60 PRINT "RETAIL PRICE:";R
70 PRINT "SALES TAX:";T
80 PRINT "TOTAL COST:";C
90 LET R=R+10
100 GO TO 20
999 END
```

Using the READ/DATA Statements

```
01 REM R--RETAIL PRICE
02 REM T--TAX
03 REM C--TOTAL COST

10 READ R
20 DATA 40,50,60,70
30 IF R>60 THEN 999
40 LET T=R*.05
50 LET C=R+T
60 PRINT
70 PRINT "RETAIL PRICE:";R
80 PRINT "SALES TAX:";T
90 PRINT "TOTAL COST:";C
100 GO TO 10
999 END
```

Using the INPUT Statement

```
01 REM R--RETAIL PRICE
02 REM T--TAX
03 REM C--TOTAL COST

10 PRINT
20 PRINT "RETAIL PRICE";
30 INPUT R
40 IF R>60 THEN 99
50 LET T=R*.05
60 LET C=R+T
70 PRINT "SALES TAX:";T
80 PRINT "TOTAL COST:";C
90 GO TO 10
99 END
```

4.3 THE ON...GO TO STATEMENT

The last two sections discussed the GO TO and the IF/THEN statements. The GO TO statement is referred to as an **unconditional** transfer, since there is no choice but to GO TO a specific statement. The IF/THEN statement is referred to as a **conditional** transfer. This is because the computer branches to another statement only when a certain condition is met. The IF/THEN statement offers a two-way choice. Conditions can be either true or false. If the condition is true, the computer branches to the statement specified; if the condition is false, there is no transfer and the computer proceeds to the next line.

Here is another conditional control statement. This one offers a multiple-way choice for control to be transferred. It is called the **ON...GO TO** statement (some computer systems require **ON... GOTO**), and it allows the computer to branch to one of several statements, depending on the current value of a certain variable or expression. This variable or expression is called the **index** of the ON...GO TO. Here are two examples, one using a variable as the index and the other using an expression as the index.

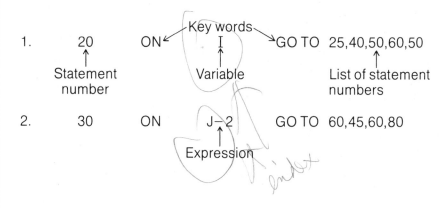

If the numeric value of the index is either 1 or 2 or 3, etc., control is transferred to either the first or second or third, etc., statement number in the list. In the example **20 ON I GO TO 25,40,50,60,50,**[2] if **I** = 1, control is transferred to statement 25, the *first* number in the list. If **I** = 2, control is transferred to statement 40, the *second* number in the list. If **I** = 3 or 5, control is transferred to statement 50, the *third* and *fifth* numbers in the list. If **I** = 4, control is transferred to statement 60, the *fourth* number in the list. Note that the value of the index (**I**) is really a code that is used to transfer control to any one of the statements whose numbers are listed in the ON...GO TO statement.

In example two, the expression **J−2** is evaluated. If the result is a number that contains a decimal fraction, the decimal part is ignored (that is, the number is truncated), and the integer portion is used as the value of the index. For example, if the evaluation of **J−2** results in 2.85, the .85 (the decimal part) is ignored, and the result of **J−2** is considered to be 2 (the integer part). This means that in the second example, **30 ON J−2 GO TO 60,45,60,80**, control is transferred to statement number 45.

Numbers are represented in a computer as a series of ones and zeros (base two).[3] Due to the conversion of a decimal number to binary format, small inaccuracies may occur in one or several of the low-order digits of the decimal. Here is an example.

```
10 LET A=13.2
20 LET B=13
30 LET C=(A-B)*10
40 PRINT
50 PRINT C
99 END

RUN

  1.99999999
```

Subtracting 13 from 13.2 and multiplying the result by 10 should give the number 2, yet the computer prints out 1.99999999. When this is truncated in an ON...GO TO statement, the index turns out to be 1 instead of 2. You can safeguard the index simply by increasing its value by a small amount. An ON.. GO TO statement may look as follows.

```
20 ON  C+.0001  GO TO 30,50,999
```

RUN the above program to find out what value your computer assigns to **C**. If the result is a decimal number, the digits after the decimal point will give you an idea of how much the index should be increased.

2. Spaces before and after the index have been left only for clarity.
3. This is covered in greater detail in Chapter Twelve.

The value of the index cannot be less than one (negative or zero), nor can it exceed the number of statement numbers shown after the words GO TO. In both cases, the index is considered to be out of the range of the listed numbers. Depending on your computer system, one of the following may occur.
1. Execution stops and the computer gives an error message.
2. The ON...GO TO statement is ignored and the statement following the ON...GO TO is executed.
3. Control is transferred to the last statement number in the list when the value of the index exceeds the number of statement numbers.
4. Control is transferred to the first statement number in the list when the value of the index is less than one.
Check your manual or experiment if you have the time.

Some computer systems may limit the number of branching options offered by an ON...GO TO statement. In example one, there are five choices; in example two, there are four. Also, some computer systems use a different command to accomplish this many-way branch. Here are several other versions of the ON...GO TO statement. Extra spaces are inserted in the statements for clarity only.

```
1. 60  ON  K  THEN  15,120,80

2. 60  ON  K  G.  15,120,80

3. 60  ON  K  GOT  15,120,80

4. 60  GO TO  15,120,80,  ON  K

5. 60  GO TO  K  OF  15,120,80
```

Again, refer to your manual if no version of the ON...GO TO statement mentioned in this section works on your computer system.

You may have realized by now that one ON...GO TO statement can be used instead of several IF/THEN statements. Our first example

```
20 ON  I  GO TO 25,40,50,60,50
```

could have been coded as follows.

```
20 IF I=1 THEN 25
21 IF I=2 THEN 40
22 IF I=3 THEN 50
```

```
23 IF I=4 THEN 60
24 IF I=5 THEN 50
```

Notice that one ON...GO TO statement replaces the five IF/THEN statements.

4.3 THE ON...GO TO STATEMENT—Sample Program

Here is a program that READs in a number and uses an ON...GO TO statement to:

(a) Add 2 to the number if the index is 1.
(b) Subtract 2 from the number if the index is 2.
(c) Multiply the number by 2 if the index is 3.
(d) Divide the number by 2 if the index is 4.
(e) Terminate execution when the index is 5. Use LET statements to initialize the index to one and to generate its remaining values.

Notice how control branches out of the loop to line 999, the END statement, when the index is equal to 5.

```
10 PRINT                            — Leaves a blank line.
20 LET I=1                          — Initializes the index to 1.
30 READ A                           — Reads the value of A from the DATA
                                      statement.
40 DATA 10                          — Supplies the READ statement with data.
50 ON  I  GO TO 60,80,100,120,999   — Branches to a statement whose line
                                      number is in the list. The
                                      branch depends on the value of the index.
60 PRINT A,A+2                       — Prints the values of A and A+2.
70 GO TO 130                         — Transfers control to line 130.
80 PRINT A,A-2                       — Prints the values of A and A−2.
90 GO TO 130                         — Transfers control to line 130.
100 PRINT A,A*2                      — Prints the values of A and A*2.
110 GO TO 130                        — Transfers control to line 130.
120 PRINT A,A/2                      — Prints the values of A and A/2.
130 LET I=I+1                        — Increments the index by 1.
140 GO TO 50                         — Transfers control back to line 50.
999 END                             — Terminates program execution.

RUN

   10          12
   10          8
   10          20
   10          5
```

Note that the output is single spaced. This is your first program that single spaces output when the PRINT statements are inside a loop. To produce a blank line after the word RUN yet keep the rest of the output single spaced, the statement PRINT must be outside the loop. In this program, it has been numbered 10 — the first statement in the program.

4.3 THE ON...GO TO STATEMENT – Your Turn

I. The social fees to a community club are as follows:

1 person	$150
family rate (2 people)	275
family rate (3 people)	400.

Write a program that prints the above fee schedule.
(a) Use the READ/DATA statements to enter the number of people and the fee for each category.
(b) Use an ON...GO TO statement to branch to the statements that print the appropriate fees and to branch to the END statement.
(c) Use the number of people as the index with a code of 4 to terminate the loop.
(d) Fill in the missing lines.

```
01 REM P--NUMBER OF PEOPLE (INDEX)
02 REM F--FEE

10 READ P,F
20 DATA 1,150
30
40
50 DATA 4,85
60 ON  P  GO TO 70,100,120,999
70 PRINT
80
90 GO TO 10
100
110
120
130
999 END

RUN

ONE PERSON: 150
FAMILY--TWO PEOPLE: 275
FAMILY--THREE PEOPLE: 400
```

1. Complete lines 30 and 40 with DATA statements.
2. Complete lines 80 and 100 with PRINT statements.
3. Complete line 110 with a GO TO statement.
4. Complete line 120 with a PRINT statement.
5. Complete line 130 with a GO TO statement.
6. Why does this program require a fourth DATA statement with the value 4 as the first item in the list? What is the purpose of the second number (85)? Must it be a specific number?

II. An article formerly marked at $60 is now advertised at a reduced price in three different stores. Find the amount that a customer would save in each store.

Store	Rate of Reduction
1	25%
2	20%
3	15%

(a) Use two sets of READ/DATA statements, one to enter the marked price and the other to enter the number of each store.
(b) Use the ON…GO TO statement to branch to the statements that multiply the marked price by the appropriate rates of reduction and to branch to the END statement.
(c) Use the number of the store as the index with a code of 4 to terminate your loop.
(d) Amount Saved = Marked Price × Rate of Reduction
(e) The flowchart for this program has four paths coming from the decision symbol. Pairs of connectors (with the same letter inside both connectors of a pair) show where control is transferred depending on the value of **S**. The lines coming from the three process symbols converge to the output figure. Control is then transferred from this figure to the second input symbol.

```
RUN

STORE: 1
AMOUNT SAVED: 15

STORE: 2
AMOUNT SAVED: 12

STORE: 3
AMOUNT SAVED: 9
```

Problem II

M — MARKED PRICE
S — STORE NO. (INDEX)
A — AMOUNT SAVED

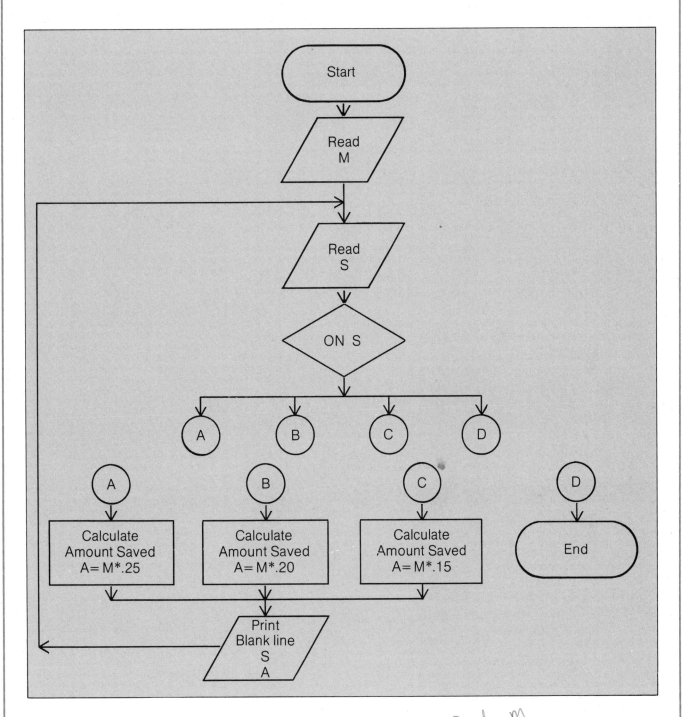

4.3 THE ON...GO TO
STATEMENT—Solutions for "Your Turn"

I.

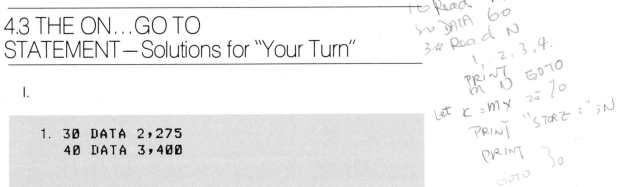

```
1.  30 DATA 2,275
    40 DATA 3,400
```

```
2. 80 PRINT "ONE PERSON:";F
   100 PRINT "FAMILY--TWO PEOPLE:";F
3. 110 GO TO 10
4. 120 PRINT "FAMILY--THREE PEOPLE:";F
5. 130 GO TO 10
```

6. The fourth DATA statement is required in order to assign 4 to the index so that the computer can branch out of the loop. The purpose of the second number is to satisfy the READ statement. Since there are two variables in the READ statement (**P** and **F**), there must be two items of data in the DATA statement. This second number need not be a specific value since the program is stopped before the number can be used.

II.

```
01 REM M--MARKED PRICE
02 REM S--STORE NUMBER (INDEX)
03 REM A--AMOUNT SAVED

10 READ M
20 DATA 60
30 READ S
40 DATA 1,2,3,4
50 ON  S  GO TO 60,80,100,999
60 LET A=M*.25
70 GO TO 110
80 LET A=M*.20
90 GO TO 110
100 LET A=M*.15
110 PRINT
120 PRINT "STORE:";S
130 PRINT "AMOUNT SAVED:";A
140 GO TO 30
999 END
```

4.4 COUNTERS

In some programs, it is necessary to count the number of data items or to count the number of times a computer goes through a loop. The latter is one of the ways by which a loop can be controlled. A counter can also be used in calculations. A loop is controlled by using two LET statements and a test statement. The first LET statement initializes the counter (a variable), the second LET statement increments (increases) or decrements (decreases) the counter within the loop, and the IF/THEN statement tests the counter within the loop.

```
10    --
20 LET K=1
30    ---
40    ---
50    --
60 LET K=K+1
70 IF K>5 THEN 99
80 GO TO 30
99 END
```

Line 20 initializes the counter to 1, line 60 increments the counter by 1, and line 70 tests the current value of the counter. If **K** (the counter) is greater than 5, control is transferred to the END statement. If **K** is not greater than 5, the computer proceeds to the next statement.

Remember, the branch out of the loop does not necessarily have to be to the END statement. Control may be transferred to another statement outside the loop.

4.4 COUNTERS—Sample Programs

I. The following program prints out five numbers (5, 12, 9, 14, 17). A counter controls the loop so that it is performed five times. Along with each number, the current value of the counter is also printed.

```
10 PRINT                  — Leaves a blank line.
20 LET K=1                — Initializes the counter to 1.
30 READ A                 — Reads the values of A one at a time from the DATA
                            statement.
40 DATA 5,12,9,14,17      — Supplies the READ statement with data.
50 PRINT K,A              — Prints the current values of K and A.
60 LET K=K+1              — Increments the counter by 1.
70 IF K>5 THEN 99         — Tests the current value of the counter.
                            (i) If K is greater than 5, control is transferred to the END
                                statement.
                            (ii) If K is not greater than 5, the computer proceeds to the
                                 next statement.
80 GO TO 30               — Transfers control back to line 30.
99 END                    — Terminates program execution.

RUN

1          5
2          12
3          9
4          14
5          17
```

II. Here is another program. This one uses a counter in two ways.
1. It controls a loop.
2. It is used in the program's calculations.

The program multiplies a counter by five after the counter is initialized and each time it is incremented (except the last time).

(a) Use the LET statement to initialize the counter to one.
(b) Inside the loop, multiply the counter by five, print the value of the counter and the product, then increment the counter by one.
(c) Execute the loop four times.

```
01 REM K--COUNTER
02 REM P--PRODUCT

10 PRINT                    — Leaves a blank line.
20 LET K=1                  — Initializes the counter to 5.
30 LET P=K*5                — Reads the values of A one at a time from the DATA
40 PRINT K,P                   statement.
50 LET K=K+1                — Supplies the READ statement with data.
60 IF K>4 THEN 99           — Prints the current values of K and A.
                            — Decrements (decreases) the counter by 1.
                            — Tests the current value of the counter.
                              (i) If K is greater than Ø, control is transferred to line 30 to
70 GO TO 30                     resume READing.
99 END                        (ii) If K is not greater than Ø (that is, equal to Ø), the
                                  computer proceeds to the next statement.
RUN                         — Terminates program execution.

1          5
2          10
3          15
4          20
```

III. Counters may also be negative. For example:

```
10 PRINT                    — Leaves a blank line.
20 LET K=5                  — Initializes the counter to 5.
30 READ A                   — Reads the values of A one at a time from the DATA
                               statement.
40 DATA 5,12,9,14,17        — Supplies the READ statement with data.
50 PRINT K,A                — Prints the current values of K and A.
60 LET K=K-1                — Decrements (decreases) the counter by 1.
70 IF K>Ø THEN 30           — Tests the current value of the counter.
                              (i) If K is greater than Ø, control is transferred to line 30 to
                                  resume READing.
                              (ii) If K is not greater than Ø (that is, equal to Ø), the
                                  computer proceeds to the next statement.
99 END                      — Terminates program execution.
```

```
RUN

5        5
4        12
3        9
2        14
1        17
```

Each time the computer passes through the loop, the counter is decreased by one. Once the counter has been reduced to zero, the computer is out of the loop. The loop, therefore, is performed five times (5, 4, 3, 2, 1).

Counters may be increased or decreased by any number (whole or decimal) or by a variable previously defined in the program. However, care must be taken in choosing the initial value and in choosing the position (that is, the line number) of the initializing statement.

4.4 COUNTERS—Your Turn

I. A retailer purchases three articles from a wholesaler; the first one costs $50, the second one costs $10, and the third one costs $30. Before placing them in the salesroom, the retailer marks up each article by 30%. What is the markup and what is the retail price of each article?

(a) Use the READ/DATA statements to READ in the cost price of each article.
(b) Use a counter to control your loop.
(c) Print out the number of the article (1, 2, 3, which is your counter), the cost price, markup, and retail price.
(d) Markup = Cost Price × .30
(e) Retail Price = Cost Price + Markup

```
01 REM K--COUNTER (ARTICLE NO.)
02 REM C--COST PRICE
03 REM M--MARKUP
04 REM R--RETAIL PRICE

10 PRINT
20 LET K=1
30 READ C
40
50
60
70 PRINT K,C,M,R
80
90
100
999 END
```

```
RUN

1          50        15        65
2          10         3        13
3          30         9        39
```

1. Complete line 40 with a DATA statement.
2. Which statement should be coded in line 50?

```
(a)  LET R=M*.30
(b)  LET C=R*.30
(c)  LET M=C+R
(d)  LET C=M+R
(e)  LET M=C*.30
```

3. Which statement should be coded in line 60?

```
(a)  LET R=C-M
(b)  LET C=R-M
(c)  LET R=C+M
(d)  LET M=C*.30
(e)  LET C=M*.30
```

4. Increment the counter in line 80.
5. Which statement should be coded in line 90?

```
(a)  IF K<3 THEN 999
(b)  IF K=3 THEN 70
(c)  IF K<3 THEN 40
(d)  IF K>3 THEN 999
(e)  IF K>3 THEN 30
```

6. Complete line 100 with a GO TO statement.

II. Suppose a deduction of $600 is allowed on taxable income for each dependent under the age of 18. Find the deductions on three income tax returns — the first with 1 dependent, the second with 2 dependents, and the third with 3 dependents.

   (a) Use a counter
       — to terminate your loop;
       — in your calculations.

(b) Deduction = Dependents (your counter) × 600
(c) Draw a flowchart before you write the program.

```
RUN

DEPENDENTS: 1        DEDUCTION: 600
DEPENDENTS: 2        DEDUCTION: 1200
DEPENDENTS: 3        DEDUCTION: 1800
```

4.4 COUNTERS—Solutions for "Your Turn"

I.

```
1. 40 DATA 50,10,30
2. (e) 50 LET M=C*.30
3. (c) 60 LET R=C+M
4. 80 LET K=K+1
5. (d) 90 IF K>3 THEN 999
6. 100 GO TO 30
```

II.

```
01 REM K--COUNTER (NO. OF DEPENDENTS)
02 REM D--DEDUCTION

10 PRINT
20 LET K=1
30 LET D=K*600
40 PRINT "DEPENDENTS:";K,"DEDUCTION:";D
50 LET K=K+1
60 IF K>3 THEN 99
70 GO TO 30
99 END
```

Notice the two paths leading from the decision symbol. Make sure you understand what they represent. The **Yes** exit means that the IF/THEN test is true. The **No** exit, in this flowchart, is a GO TO statement. The statement is executed when the IF/THEN test is false. Also, a symbol representing only the "blank" PRINT is often not drawn.

Problem II

K — COUNTER
D — DEDUCTION

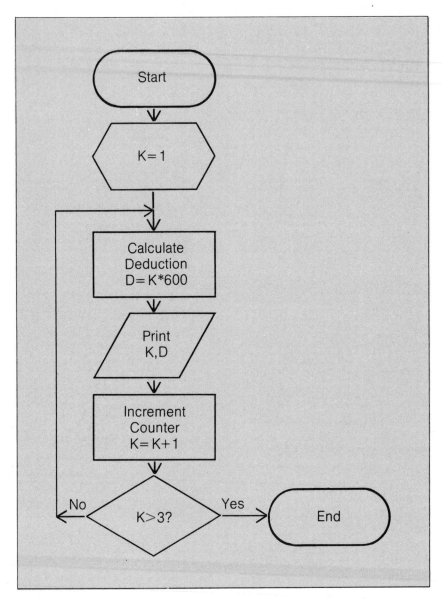

4.5 TERMINOLOGY

Two terms were used in the previous sections to indicate the alternative paths that can be taken during the execution of a program. These were:

1. **A branch** The transfer of control to another statement in a program. On some systems, the transfer may be to a non-executable statement such as a REM statement or a DATA statement.
2. **A loop** The repetition of a series of instructions often caused by a branch to a lower-numbered statement.

A Branch   A Loop

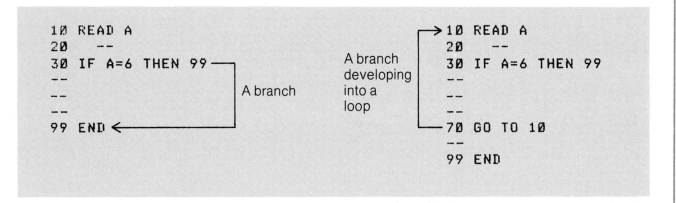

```
    10 READ A                              →10 READ A
    20   --                                 20   --
    30 IF A=6 THEN 99 ─┐    A branch        30 IF A=6 THEN 99
    --                  │    developing      --
    --                  ├ A branch into a    --
    --                  │    loop            --
    99 END ←────────────┘              └─── 70 GO TO 10
                                             --
                                             99 END
```

A Short Summary

The series of instructions that the computer follows can be altered in a number of ways. One method is by using a GO TO statement. This transfers control to another statement in the program. The GO TO is considered an unconditional branch, since there is no other alternative than to GO TO a specific statement. The IF/THEN statement is another method by which control can be transferred. This statement is referred to as a conditional branch because control is transferred only when a certain condition is met. It offers a two-way choice. If the condition is true, control is transferred to the statement specified; if the condition is false, the computer proceeds to the next line.

The third statement that transfers control is the ON...GO TO statement. It offers a many-way choice by allowing the computer to transfer to one of several statements in the program, depending on the current value of a certain variable or expression called the index. The ON...GO TO statement is often used to replace a number of consecutive IF/THEN statements.

Counters are frequently used to control loops. The counter (a variable) is initially set at a specific value, then incremented (or decremented) within the loop. An IF/THEN statement tests the value of the counter. When the counter reaches a particular value, control is transferred out of the loop.

Up to this point, three ways have been shown by which a loop can be controlled. The three methods are listed below with an example for each. The IF/THEN statement terminates a loop two ways.

1. It checks each data item for the final value.

```
    10 LET A=40
    20 IF A>100 THEN 80 ─┐
    --                    │
    60 LET A=A+20         │
                          │
                          │
```

```
70 GO TO 20
80    --  ←
--
999 END
```

2. It checks a counter for a specific value.

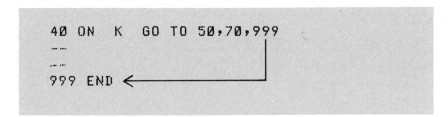

```
10 LET K=1
20    --
--
50 LET K=K+1
60 IF K>3 THEN 80 ──┐
70 GO TO 20         │
80    --  ←─────────┘
--
999 END
```

The third method of controlling a loop is by means of the ON...GO TO statement, which uses its index to transfer control to a particular statement. In the example shown below, control is transferred to the END statement when the value of the index (**K**) becomes 3.

```
40 ON  K  GO TO 50,70,999
--                 │
--                 │
999 END ←──────────┘
```

The decision symbol, a diamond-shaped figure, was introduced in this chapter. It indicates that the computer is about to make a decision. Two outgoing branches from the symbol usually signify an IF/THEN statement, while multiple outgoing branches signify an ON... GO TO statement.

Questions and Exercises

1. Why is a GO TO statement considered an unconditional branch?
2. What happens when a GO TO statement directs control to a statement with a lower line number?
3. Identify the errors, if any, in the GO TO statements shown below. Make the necessary corrections.

```
(a)   80  GO  TO  01
(b)   50  GO  TO  END
(c)   40  GO  TO  B9
(d)   80  GO  TO  99
(e)   30  GO  TO  5*9
```

4. Why is an IF/THEN statement considered a conditional branch?
5. How do the following statements differ in the number of alternatives offered in transferring control?
   (a) The GO TO statement
   (b) The IF/THEN statement
   (c) The ON...GO TO statement
6. List the six BASIC relational operators and their meanings.
7. Write IF/THEN statements for the following.
   (a) Branches to line 30 if the value of **A** is equal to 12.
   (b) Branches to line 50 if the value of **A** is not equal to the value of **C**.
   (c) Branches to line 70 if the value of **A** divided by 10 is less than the value of **B**.
   (d) Branches to line 40 if the value of **A** multiplied by 5 is greater than or equal to the value of **B** multiplied by the value of **C**.
8. Identify the errors, if any, in the IF/THEN statements shown below. Assume that the variables have been assigned values prior to each IF/THEN statement.

```
(a)   50  IF  A  THEN  70
(b)   50  IF  B<>B  THEN  90
(c)   50  IF  A/B  THEN  80
(d)   50  IF  A<=B  THEN  END
(e)   50  IF  A*B>C*D  THEN  80-10
(f)   50  IF  A>=B  THEN  85
```

9. Give the definition of
   (a) A branch.
   (b) A loop.
10. Rewrite the following program so that the test in line 30 determines whether or not the value of **A** is less than or equal to 10 (instead of greater than 10).

```
10  PRINT
20  LET  A=1
30  IF  A>10  THEN  99
40  PRINT  A
```

```
50 LET A=A+1
60 GO TO 30
99 END
```

11. What is wrong with the following program?

```
10 PRINT
20 LET A=4
30 LET B=A*2
40 IF B<10 THEN 60
50 PRINT "A =";A,"B =";B
60 LET B=B+A
70 PRINT "B =";B
80 IF B>10 THEN 30
99 END
```

12. What is the difference in execution between the ON...GO TO statement and the GO TO statement?

13. What happens when the value of the index of an ON...GO TO statement is a number that contains a decimal fraction? Give an example.

14. Identify the errors, if any, in the ON...GO TO statements shown below. How does your computer respond to (a) and (d)?

```
(a) 10 LET K=3
    20 ON K-3 GO TO 30,50,70,999

(b) 10 LET K=12
    20 ON K/6 THEN GO 90,110,80

(c) 10 LET K=10
    20 ON K/4 GO TO 60,55,80

(d) 10 LET K=3
    20 ON K*2 GO TO 120,190,145

(e) 10 LET K=1
    20 ON K+1 GO TO 55,85,95,999

(f) 10 LET K=3
    20 LET J=4
    30 ON K OR J GO TO 40,60,80,999
```

15. Do the following program segments give the same results?

```
(a) 30 LET K=1
    40 ON  K  GO TO 50,70,999
    --
    80 LET K=K+1
    90 GO TO 40

(b) 20 IF K=1 THEN 50
    30 IF K=2 THEN 70
    40 IF K=3 THEN 999
```

16. What is the output of the following program?

```
10 PRINT
20 LET K=1
30 LET A=3
40 PRINT A
50 ON  K  GO TO 60,60,60,99
60 LET A=A+3
70 LET K=K+1
80 GO TO 40
99 END
```

17. (a) State two restrictions that limit the index of an ON...GO TO statement.
    (b) Summarize how your computer responds to an ON...GO TO statement whose index is out of the range.
18. State the purpose of each of the three statements that are required to set up a counter that controls a loop. Code each statement along with your explanation.
19. Rewrite the program shown below so that the counter runs in a negative direction; that is, the counter is decremented rather than incremented in line 60.

```
10 PRINT
20 LET K=1
30 READ A
40 DATA 10,8,12,4,6
50 PRINT A
60 LET K=K+1
70 IF K>5 THEN 99
80 GO TO 30
99 END
```

```
RUN

  10
  8
  12
  4
  6
```

Programming Problems[4]

1. A store is offering a discount of 15% on any article purchased between 5:00 p.m. and 6:00 p.m. each day it is open during the month of August. If you purchased three articles whose regular prices were $40, $60, and $80, what was the amount of discount and what was the reduced price of each article?

   (a) Use LET statements to enter the data. Generate the data by incrementing each regular price by $20.
   (b) Terminate your loop by checking each data item for the final amount.
   (c) Discount = Price × .15
   (d) Reduced Price = Price − Discount

```
RUN

REGULAR PRICE: 40
DISCOUNT: 6
REDUCED PRICE: 34

REGULAR PRICE: 60
DISCOUNT: 9
REDUCED PRICE: 51

REGULAR PRICE: 80
DISCOUNT: 12
REDUCED PRICE: 68
```

2. Suppose the employees of the XYZ Manufacturing Company are paid on the basis of the number of parts produced. If the rate of pay is $2 per part in department 12, find the incomes of three employees using the weekly record shown on page 143.

4. Replace the INPUT statement by the READ/DATA statements in your programs if you are not using an interactive system. This applies to the remaining problems in this book.

Employee	Number of Parts Produced
1	212
2	213
3	209

(a) Use the READ/DATA statements to enter the number of parts produced by each employee.

(b) Use a counter:
  — to keep track of the number of the employee.
  — to terminate your loop after the third employee.

(c) Print the department number (12) along with the rate.

(d) Income = Number of Parts Produced × Rate

Problem 1

P — REGULAR PRICE
D — DISCOUNT
R — REDUCED PRICE

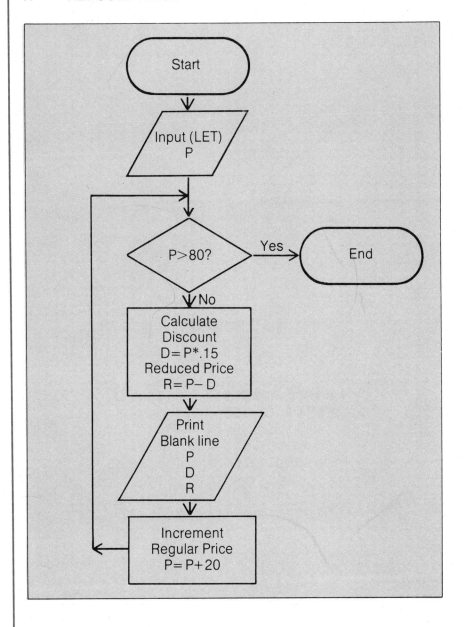

```
RUN

DEPARTMENT: 12      RATE: 2

EMPLOYEE: 1
NO. OF PARTS: 212
INCOME: 424

EMPLOYEE: 2
NO. OF PARTS: 213
INCOME: 426

EMPLOYEE: 3
NO. OF PARTS: 209
INCOME: 418
```

3. Write a program that determines the balance of a customer's account after each of the following transactions. There is no previous balance. Codes are used to indicate whether the transaction is a purchase or a payment.

    Purchase $250
    Payment 150
    Purchase 300
    Payment 200

    (a) Use the INPUT statement to enter the code and the amount of each transaction.
    (b) Use an ON...GO TO statement for multiple branching.
    (c) Use a code of 1 if the transaction is a purchase, a code of 2 if a payment is made, and a code of 3 to indicate the end of the data.
    (d) Depending on your code:
                Balance = Balance + Purchase
                          or
            Balance = Balance − Payment.

Using the INPUT Statement

Using the READ/DATA Statements

```
RUN                           RUN

CODE,AMOUNT? 1,250            CODE,AMOUNT: 1   250
BALANCE: 250                  BALANCE: 250

CODE,AMOUNT? 2,150            CODE,AMOUNT: 2   150
BALANCE: 100                  BALANCE: 100

CODE,AMOUNT? 1,300            CODE,AMOUNT: 1   300
BALANCE: 400                  BALANCE: 400

CODE,AMOUNT? 2,200            CODE,AMOUNT: 2   200
BALANCE: 200                  BALANCE: 200

CODE,AMOUNT? 3,0
```

Problem 3

B — BALANCE
C — CODE (INDEX)
A — AMOUNT

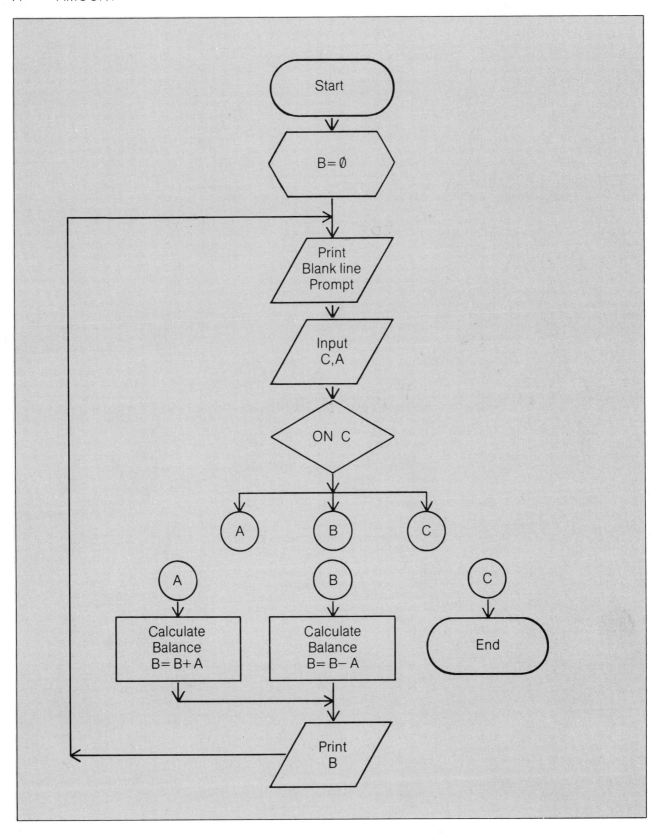

4. Rewrite the program for Problem 3. This time, use IF/THEN statements to check the code, rather than the ON...GO TO statement.
   (a) Use the same method to enter the data.
   (b) Your output should be the same.
   (c) Is there any major difference between your flowchart and the one drawn for the program in Problem 3?

5. Find the semiannual interest and the new principal for each of the following amounts: $2000, $3000, and $4000. The rate of interest is 14%.
   (a) Use LET statements to enter the data (the amounts). Generate the data by incrementing each amount by $1000.
   (b) Terminate your loop by checking each data item for the final amount.
   (c) Time = 6/12
   (d) Interest = Amount × Rate × Time
   (e) New Principal = Amount + Interest

```
RUN

AMOUNT: 2000
INTEREST: 140
NEW PRINCIPAL: 2140

AMOUNT: 3000
INTEREST: 210
NEW PRINCIPAL: 3210

AMOUNT: 4000
INTEREST: 280
NEW PRINCIPAL: 4280
```

6. Programs are often written to find the largest sale, or the highest mark, or the highest number, etc. When writing the program for the problem shown below, set a variable to a value that is lower than any of the data items to be entered, say, **L= −1**, where **L** represents LARGE. Each time an item of data is entered, check to see whether or not this data item is greater than the current value of **L**. If it is, replace the value of **L** by the item just entered. Print the value of **L** after the last data item is checked. The three main statements in such a program are as follows.

```
30 LET L=-1           — Initializes LARGE to − 1.
--
60 IF S>L THEN 80     — Tests to see if the SALE is greater than LARGE. If it is, control is
                         transferred to line 80.
--
80 LET L=S            — Replaces LARGE by the amount of the SALE.
```

Complete the program segment on page 146 so that your program finds the largest sale made by one salesperson whose sales are: $8700, $6300, $9400, $7600, $8500.

(a) Use the INPUT statement to enter the data.
(b) Use a counter to terminate your loop.

Using the INPUT Statement	Using the READ/DATA Statements

```
RUN                              RUN

SALE? 8700                       SALE: 8700
SALE? 6300                       SALE: 6300
SALE? 9400                       SALE: 9400
SALE? 7600                       SALE: 7600
SALE? 8500                       SALE: 8500

THE LARGEST SALE IS: 9400        THE LARGEST SALE IS: 9400
```

Problem 6

K — COUNTER
L — LARGE
S — SALE

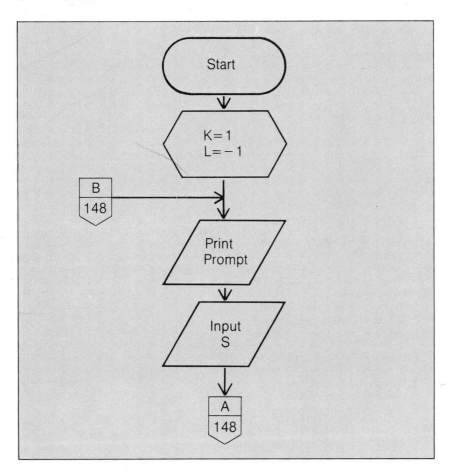

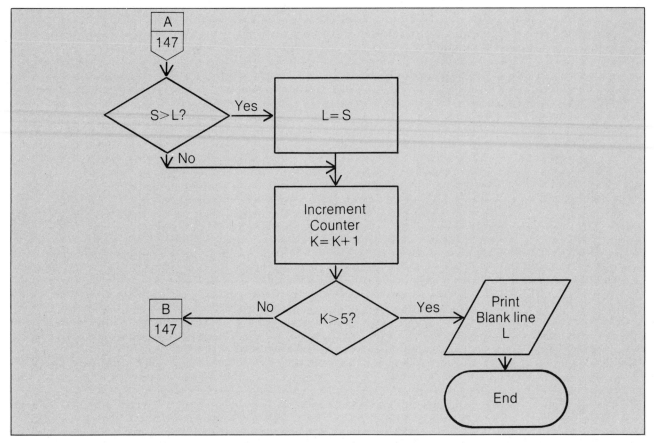

7. Shown below is the formula that finds the area of a rectangle.

Area = Length × Width

Find the areas of 5 rectangles. The first one has a length of 3 units and a width of 2 units.

(a) Use LET statements to enter the dimensions of the first rectangle.
(b) Inside a loop, increase the length of this rectangle by one unit and the width by one unit. Find the dimensions of the remaining rectangles the same way, that is, increase the length and the width of each previous rectangle.
(c) Use a counter to control your loop.
(d) Print headings over the lengths, widths, and areas, as shown in the RUN. Leave a blank line after the headings. Code the headings as strings in a PRINT statement.
(e) Print your output widely spaced.

```
RUN

LENGTH      WIDTH       AREA

3           2           6
4           3           12
5           4           20
6           5           30
7           6           42
```

FIVE BRANCHING AND LOOPING II

A. After completing this chapter, you should be able to write BASIC programs and complete skeletal BASIC programs that use:

1. Trailer values to terminate loops.
2. Special values that represent the number of data items.
3. Sets of data entered during passes through loops.
4. The summation routine.

B. In addition, you should be able to:

1. Explain the purpose of a trailer value.
2. Summarize how a special value terminates a loop.
3. (a) Explain how sets of data are assigned to variables during passes through a loop.
   (b) State the purpose of the last set.
4. Find errors in programs.
5. Produce the output of programs.
6. Differentiate between the various ways of terminating a loop.
   (a) a counter
   (b) a special value
   (c) a trailer value
   (d) a test on each data item
   (e) an ON...GO TO statement

5.1 TERMINATING A LOOP—TRAILER VALUE

The last chapter illustrated three ways by which a loop can be controlled. These are:

1. An IF/THEN statement that checks each data item for the final value.
2. An IF/THEN statement that checks a counter for a particular value.
3. An ON...GO TO statement that uses its index to transfer control to a specific statement.

There are two more ways by which the IF/THEN statement can control a loop. One of them detects the end of input data by the use of a trailer value or a **flag**. This value is usually some illogical number for the program being written and is entered as the last item. Each time a data item is entered, a test is made to determine whether or not this number is the trailer value. If the item is not the trailer value, execution continues; if it is, control is transferred to another routine or to the END statement. Here are two program segments, each using a trailer value to detect the end of input data. One program enters data by means of the INPUT statement; the other program enters data by the use of the READ/DATA statements.

1. Using the INPUT statement

```
10     --
20     --
30  INPUT  A
40  IF  A=99999  THEN  99 ──────┐
50     --                       │
60  GO TO 10                    │
--                             │
99  END ◄───────────────────────┘
```

2. Using the READ/DATA statements

```
10  READ  A
20  DATA  1,2,3,4,99999
30  IF  A=99999  THEN  99 ──────┐
40     --                       │
50     --                       │
60  GO TO 10                    │
--                             │
99  END ◄───────────────────────┘
```

In Program 1, the trailer value is keyed in as the last number in response to the INPUT statement in line 30. Line 40 tests this value, and if the number is the trailer value, control is transferred to the END statement. If the number keyed in is not the trailer value, the computer proceeds to line 50. In Program 2, the flag is listed as the last item in the DATA statement. The test in line 30 is executed in the same manner as in Program 1.

5.1 TERMINATING A LOOP — TRAILER VALUE — Sample Programs

The three sample programs in Section 4.1 of Chapter Four made no provisions for the computer to branch out of the loops. These three programs printed the whole numbers 1, 2, and 3. Two of these programs will now be rewritten — the one using the INPUT statement and the one using the READ/DATA statements. To detect the end of data, a trailer value (a flag) of 99999 will be used.

1. Using the INPUT statement

```
10  PRINT
20  PRINT  "VALUE FOR A";
30  INPUT  A
40  IF  A=99999  THEN  99
```
— Leaves a blank line.
— Identifies value to be entered.
— Requests data. The last value entered will be 99999.
— Tests the current value of **A**.
  (i) If **A** is equal to 99999, control is transferred to the END statement.
  (ii) If **A** is not equal to 99999, the computer proceeds to the next statement.

```
50  PRINT  "A =";A
60  GO TO 10
99  END
```
— Prints the current value of **A**.
— Transfers control back to line 10.
— Terminates program execution.

```
RUN

VALUE FOR A? 1
A = 1
```

```
VALUE FOR A? 2
A = 2

VALUE FOR A? 3
A = 3

VALUE FOR A? 99999
```

In the RUN, notice that a flag of 99999 is entered after the last prompt. In this way, you are able to terminate the computer's request for more data.

2. Using the READ/DATA statements

`10 READ A`	— Reads the values of **A** one at a time from the DATA statement.
`20 DATA 1,2,3,99999`	— Supplies the READ statement with data. The last item in the list is 99999.
`30 IF A=99999 THEN 99`	— Tests the current value of **A**.
	(i) If **A** is equal to 99999, control is transferred to the END statement.
	(ii) If **A** is not equal to 99999, the computer proceeds to the next statement.
`40 PRINT`	— Leaves a blank line.
`50 PRINT 'A =';A`	— Prints the current value of **A**.
`60 GO TO 10`	— Transfers control back to line 10.
`99 END`	— Terminates program execution.

```
RUN

A = 1

A = 2

A = 3
```

In this program, the trailer value is entered as the last item in the DATA statement.

5.1 TERMINATING A LOOP—TRAILER VALUE —Your Turn

Now might be a good time to review some of the problems in the "Your Turn" units of Chapter Four. In each of the following, use a flag of 99999 to terminate input.

1. Problem from Section 4.2, Page 120

A customer buys three watches: the first one priced at $55, the second one priced at $60, and the third one priced at $40. If a sales tax of 5% is added to the retail price, what is the tax and what is the total cost of each watch?

(a) Use the INPUT statement to enter each retail price. Your flowchart should be similar to the one on page 121 in Chapter Four. The only difference is in the decision symbol, where you should check for the trailer value instead of the last data item.

(b) Sales Tax = Retail Price × .05

(c) Total Cost = Retail Price + Sales Tax

Using the INPUT Statement

```
RUN

RETAIL PRICE? 55
SALES TAX: 2.75
TOTAL COST: 57.75

RETAIL PRICE? 60
SALES TAX: 3
TOTAL COST: 63

RETAIL PRICE? 40
SALES TAX: 2
TOTAL COST: 42

RETAIL PRICE? 99999
```

Using the READ/DATA Statements

```
RUN

RETAIL PRICE: 55
SALES TAX: 2.75
TOTAL COST: 57.75

RETAIL PRICE: 60
SALES TAX: 3
TOTAL COST: 63

RETAIL PRICE: 40
SALES TAX: 2
TOTAL COST: 42
```

2. Problem from Section 4.4, Page 133

A retailer purchases three articles from a wholesaler; the first one costs $50, the second one costs $10, and the third one costs $30. Before placing them in the salesroom, the retailer marks up each article by 30%. What is the markup and what is the retail price of each article?

(a) Use the READ/DATA statements to enter the cost price of each article.

(b) Use a counter to keep track of the article currently being marked up (article 1, article 2, article 3).

(c) Print out the number of the article along with its cost, markup, and retail price.

(d) Markup = Cost Price × .30

(e) Retail Price = Cost Price + Markup

```
RUN

1        50       15       65
2        10       3        13
3        30       9        39
```

Problem 2

K — COUNTER (ARTICLE NO.)
C — COST PRICE
M — MARKUP
R — RETAIL PRICE

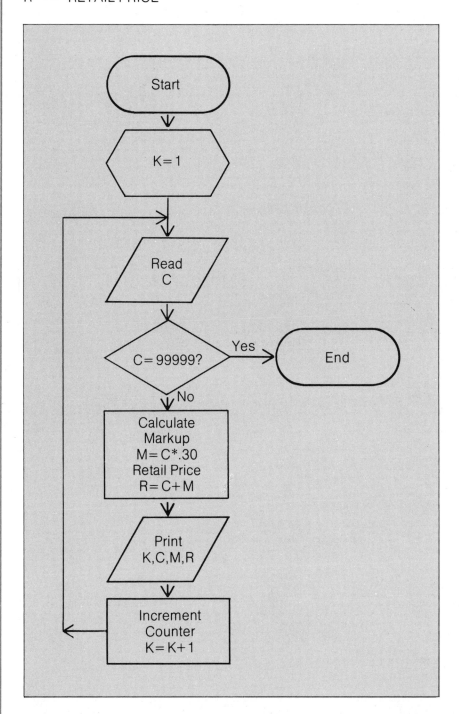

3. Problem from Section 4.4, Page 134

Suppose a deduction of $600 is allowed on taxable income for each dependent under the age of 18. Find the deductions on three income tax returns — the first with 1 dependent, the sec-

ond with 2 dependents, and the third with 3 dependents.
(a) Use the READ/DATA statements to enter the number of dependents on each income tax return.
(b) Deduction = Dependents × 600

```
RUN

NO. OF DEPENDENTS: 1
DEDUCTION: 600

NO. OF DEPENDENTS: 2
DEDUCTION: 1200

NO. OF DEPENDENTS: 3
DEDUCTION: 1800
```

5.1 TERMINATING A LOOP—TRAILER VALUE —Solutions for "Your Turn"

1. Using the INPUT Statement

Using the READ/DATA Statements

```
01 REM R--RETAIL PRICE
02 REM T--TAX
03 REM C--TOTAL COST

10 PRINT
20 PRINT "RETAIL PRICE";
30 INPUT R
40 IF R=99999 THEN 99
50 LET T=R*.05
60 LET C=R+T
70 PRINT "SALES TAX:";T
80 PRINT "TOTAL COST:";C
90 GO TO 10
99 END
```

```
01 REM R--RETAIL PRICE
02 REM T--TAX
03 REM C--TOTAL COST

10 READ R
20 DATA 55,60,40,99999
30 IF R=99999 THEN 999
40 LET T=R*.05
50 LET C=R+T
60 PRINT
70 PRINT "RETAIL PRICE:";R
80 PRINT "SALES TAX:";T
90 PRINT "TOTAL COST:";C
100 GO TO 10
999 END
```

2.

```
01 REM K--COUNTER (ARTICLE NO.)
02 REM C--COST PRICE
03 REM M--MARKUP
04 REM R--RETAIL PRICE
```

```
10 PRINT
20 LET K=1
30 READ C
40 DATA 50,10,30,99999
50 IF C=99999 THEN 999
60 LET M=C*.30
70 LET R=C+M
80 PRINT K,C,M,R
90 LET K=K+1
100 GO TO 30
999 END
```

3.

```
01 REM N--NUMBER OF DEPENDENTS
02 REM D--DEDUCTION

10 READ N
20 DATA 1,2,3,99999
30 IF N=99999 THEN 99
40 LET D=N*600
50 PRINT
60 PRINT "NO. OF DEPENDENTS:";N
70 PRINT "DEDUCTION:";D
80 GO TO 10
99 END
```

5.2 TERMINATING A LOOP—SPECIAL VALUE

Here is one more method that uses the IF/THEN statement to control a loop. This one uses the READ/DATA statements and a counter. First, look at the READ/DATA statements.

```
10 READ N
20 READ A
30 DATA 4,67,85,79,93
40   --
50   --
60 GO TO 20
```

Line 10 assigns 4 to **N** as a special value. Since the statement **READ N** is placed before the loop, this value must be the first item of data and **N** is assigned the value only once. The special number tells the computer how many data items follow. As there are four pieces of data (67,85,79,93), this number must be 4. The remaining values are assigned to **A** one at a time. (One number is assigned each time the computer passes through the loop.)

30 DATA   4,   67,85,79,93

    Value of N   Values of A

How does this work with a counter?

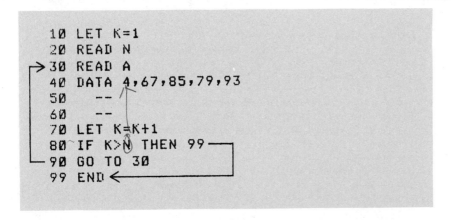

```
10 LET K=1
20 READ N
30 READ A
40 DATA 4,67,85,79,93
50   --
60   --
70 LET K=K+1
80 IF K>N THEN 99
90 GO TO 30
99 END
```

In line 80, the counter is compared to **N**, which has a value of 4 (assigned to it by the READ statement in line 20). The loop is performed repeatedly as long as the value of **K** is not greater than 4 (K = 1, 2, 3, 4). The last time the computer is in the loop, the value of **K** is greater than 4, causing control to transfer out of the loop to the END statement. Notice that while **K** is less than or equal to 4, control is transferred to line 30 — the READ statement that reads in the next item of data, and not to line 20, which reads in the number of data items.

5.2 TERMINATING A LOOP—SPECIAL VALUE—Sample Program

The storage room in a stationery store contains the following items:

10 pen and pencil sets	@	$13.50 each.
10 pads of bond paper	@	1.25 each.
10 pencil erasers	@	.45 each.

The program finds the extended value of each of the above articles.
(a) Use the READ statement to store the number of different articles (3) in a simple variable. The variable is used subsequently with a counter to terminate the loop.
(b) Use another READ statement to enter the unit price of each article.
(c) Use one DATA statement.
(d) Extended Value of each Article = Unit Price × 10

```
10 LET K=1    — Initializes the counter to 1.
20 READ N     — Reads the number of data items.
```

```
30 READ P
40 DATA 3,13.50,1.25,.45

50 LET V=P*10
60 PRINT
70 PRINT "UNIT PRICE:";P
80 PRINT "EXTENDED VALUE:";V
90 LET K=K+1
100 IF K>N THEN 999




110 GO TO 30
999 END

RUN

UNIT PRICE: 13.5
EXTENDED VALUE: 135

UNIT PRICE: 1.25
EXTENDED VALUE: 12.5

UNIT PRICE: .45
EXTENDED VALUE: 4.5
```

— Reads the prices one at a time.
— First number is assigned to **N**; prices are assigned to **P**.
— Calculates the extended value of the article.
— Leaves a blank line.
— Prints the unit price.
— Prints the extended value of the article.
— Increments the counter by 1.
— Tests the current value of the counter.
  (i) If **K** is greater than **N** (the number of data items), control is transferred to the END statement.
  (ii) If **K** is not greater than **N**, the computer proceeds to the next statement.
— Transfers control back to line 30.
— Terminates program execution.

5.2 TERMINATING A LOOP—SPECIAL VALUE—Your Turn

I. Three depositors have the following balances in their personal savings accounts:

Depositor	Balance
1	$4000
2	2500
3	5700

If interest is paid at a rate of 10% once every six months, what interest income does each depositor receive at the end of the first six months? What would be the amount in each account if the interest is deposited and no withdrawals were made?

(a) Use the READ statement to store the number of depositors in a simple variable. The variable is used subsequently with a counter to terminate the loop.
(b) Use another READ statement to enter the balance of each account.
(c) Use one DATA statement.
(d) Print the counter as the number of the depositor.

(e) Interest = Balance × Rate of Interest
(f) Balance = Balance + Interest
(g) Fill in the missing lines.

```
01 REM K--COUNTER (NO. OF DEPOSITOR)
02 REM R--RATE OF INTEREST
03 REM N--NUMBER OF DEPOSITORS
04 REM B--BALANCE IN ACCOUNT

10 LET K=1
20 LET R=.10
30 READ N
40 READ B
50
60 PRINT
70
80
90
100
110
120 LET K=K+1
130
140
999 END

RUN

DEPOSITOR: 1          BALANCE: 4000
INTEREST: 400
NEW BALANCE: 4400

DEPOSITOR: 2          BALANCE: 2500
INTEREST: 250
NEW BALANCE: 2750

DEPOSITOR: 3          BALANCE: 5700
INTEREST: 570
NEW BALANCE: 6270
```

1. Complete line 50 with a DATA statement.
2. Complete line 70 with a PRINT statement.
3. Which statement should be coded in line 80?

```
(a)  LET B=I*R
(b)  LET I=B*R
(c)  LET B=I+R
(d)  LET I=B+R
(e)  LET R=B-I
```

4. Which statement should be coded in line 90?

```
(a)  LET  B=R*I
(b)  LET  B=R+I
(c)  LET  I=B+R
(d)  LET  I=B-R
(e)  LET  B=B+I
```

5. Complete lines 100 and 110 with PRINT statements.
6. Which statement should be coded in line 130?

```
(a)  GO TO 999
(b)  IF K<N THEN 999
(c)  GO TO 30
(d)  IF K>N THEN 999
(e)  IF K>N THEN 30
```

7. Complete line 140 with a GO TO statement.

II. Suppose your consumption of electricity for each of the first three months of the year was as follows.

Month	Kilowatt hours
1	1000
2	950
3	930

If the consumption charge is 3.5 cents per kilowatt hour, what would be the amount of your electrical bill for each of the three months?
(a) Use the READ statement to store the number of months in a simple variable. The variable is used subsequently with a counter to terminate the loop.
(b) Use another READ statement to enter the kilowatt hours.
(c) Use one DATA statement.
(d) Print the counter as the number of the month.
(e) Bill = Kilowatt hours × Rate (.035)

```
RUN

MONTH: 1
KILOWATT HOURS: 1000
ELECTRIC BILL: 35

MONTH: 2
KILOWATT HOURS: 950
ELECTRIC BILL: 33.25
```

```
MONTH: 3
KILOWATT HOURS: 930
ELECTRIC BILL: 32.55
```

Problem II

R — RATE PER KILOWATT HOUR
K — COUNTER (MONTH NO.)
N — NO. OF MONTHS
H — KILOWATT HOURS
B — ELECTRIC BILL

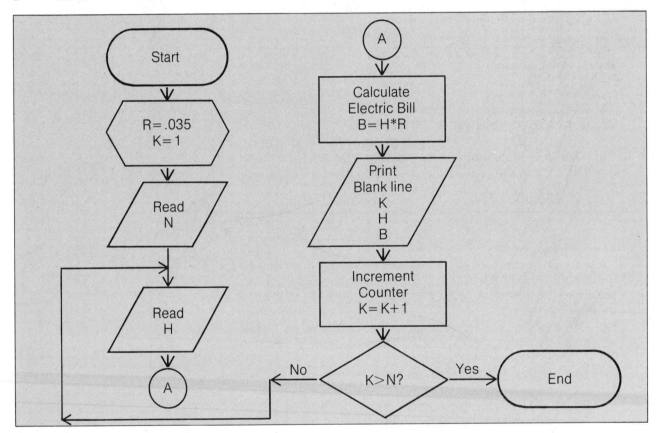

5.2 TERMINATING A LOOP—SPECIAL VALUE—Solutions for "Your Turn"

I.

```
1. 50 DATA 3,4000,2500,5700
```

```
2. 70 PRINT "DEPOSITOR:";K,"BALANCE:";B
3. (b) 80 LET I=B*R
4. (e) 90 LET B=B+I
5. 100 PRINT "INTEREST:";I
   110 PRINT "NEW BALANCE:";B
6. (d) 130 IF K>N THEN 999
7. 140 GO TO 40
```

II.

```
01 REM R--RATE PER KILOWATT HOUR
02 REM K--COUNTER (MONTH NO.)
03 REM N--NO. OF MONTHS
04 REM H--KILOWATT HOURS
05 REM B--ELECTRIC BILL

10 LET R=.035
20 LET K=1
30 READ N
40 READ H
50 DATA 3,1000,950,930
60 LET B=H*R
70 PRINT
80 PRINT "MONTH:";K
90 PRINT "KILOWATT HOURS:";H
100 PRINT "ELECTRIC BILL:";B
110 LET K=K+1
120 IF K>N THEN 999
130 GO TO 40
999 END
```

5.3 SETS OF DATA READ IN A LOOP

One of the problems in the "Your Turn" unit of Section 4.3 in Chapter
Four used four DATA statements to supply one READ statement with
numbers which were read in pairs each time the computer passed
through the loop. The statements looked like this.

```
10 READ P,F
20 DATA 1,150
30 DATA 2,275
40 DATA 3,400
50 DATA 4,85
```

The first number of each pair was assigned to **P** (the number of people) and the second number was assigned to **F** (the social fee). The number 4 in the last DATA statement terminated the loop by causing control to transfer to the END statement by means of an ON . . . GO TO statement.

The number of DATA statements can be reduced by placing as many items as possible in one DATA statement. This is illustrated in the program segment shown below. Notice that the last pair of numbers has been changed from **4,85** to **−1,0**.

```
10 READ P,F
20 DATA 1,150,2,275,3,400,-1,0
30    --
40    --
50    --
60 GO TO 10
99 END
```

How is an item of data assigned to its respective variable? Here is how it is done, using the above program segment as an example.

The first time through the loop

1 is assigned to **P**   READ P,F
150 is assigned to **F**   DATA (1,150),2,275,3,400,-1,0

The next time through the loop

2 is assigned to **P**   READ P,F
275 is assigned to **F**   DATA 1,150,(2,275),3,400,-1,0

The next time through the loop

3 is assigned to **P**   READ P,F
400 is assigned to **F**   DATA 1,150,2,275,(3,400),-1,0

The last time through the loop

−1 is assigned to **P**   READ P,F
0 is assigned to **F**   DATA 1,150,2,275,3,400,(-1,0)

The second question is this: "How does the computer break out of the loop?" Here is the program segment once more, but with an additional statement.

```
10 READ P,F
20 DATA 1,150,2,275,3,400,-1,0
30 IF P=-1 THEN 99 ┐
40    --            |
50    --            |
60 GO TO 10         |
99 END ←────────────┘
```

Notice that the last set of numbers is illogical for this program segment (you cannot have − 1 people apply for membership to a community club). In the above example, the first number of this last set is used in an IF/THEN statement, where a test is made to determine whether or not the number has been assigned to its variable.

```
30 IF P=-1 THEN 99
```

If − 1 has been assigned to **P**, control is transferred to the END statement. Although only one number of the set is used in the IF/THEN statement, there must be two numbers in the set, since the READ statement lists two variables and both variables must be assigned values. This last set of numbers is often called a **dummy** set, as the numbers are never utilized in calculations. In fact, the number used to detect the end of input data is actually the trailer value or flag you learned about in Section 5.1, where a number consisting of a series of nines was used as the flag.

Listed below are a few rules you should remember.

1. You must always satisfy the READ statement. If *two* variables are to be assigned values each time the computer passes through a loop, then you must have sets of data in the DATA statement with *two* numbers in each set.
2. The dummy numbers need not be − 1,∅; they may be any values you wish, *except* data values.
3. Any of the variables in the READ statement may be tested for its dummy value; it does not necessarily have to be the first variable.

5.3 SETS OF DATA READ IN A LOOP— Sample Program

Programs entering sets of data may have their loops controlled by any of the methods shown so far; that is, by a counter, a special value, a trailer value, a test on each data item, or by using an ON...GO TO statement. The last program segment used a trailer value (a flag) of − 1. Here is a program that uses an ON...GO TO statement.

The salespersons of the XYZ Shoe Company are each paid a commission based on the amount of their sales. The company has computerized its payroll and uses codes to identify sales amounts. The program finds the amount of commission for each of three salespersons whose respective sales are $350, $290, and $467. The company uses the following codes:

Amount of Sale	Code	Rate of Commission
Less than $300	1	10%
$300 to $399.99	2	12%
$400 to $499.99	3	15%

(a) Use the READ/DATA statements to enter the amount of the sale and the code for each of the three salespersons.

(b) Use an ON...GO TO statement to branch to the statements that assign the appropriate rates of commission and to branch to the END statement.

(c) Use a code of 4 to terminate the loop.

(d) Commission = Sales × Rate

(e) Trace through the logic then RUN the program. Explanations of important concepts are supplied at the end of the program.

```
01  REM  K--CODE (INDEX)
02  REM  S--SALES
03  REM  R--RATE
04  REM  C--COMMISSION

10  READ S,K
20  DATA 350,2,290,1,467,3,0,4
30  ON  K  GO TO 40,60,80,999
40  LET R=.10
50  GO TO 90
60  LET R=.12
70  GO TO 90
80  LET R=.15
90  LET C=S*R
100 PRINT
110 PRINT "SALES:";S
120 PRINT "RATE:";R
130 PRINT "COMMISSION:";C
140 GO TO 10
999 END

RUN

SALES: 350
RATE: .12
COMMISSION: 42

SALES: 290
RATE: .1
COMMISSION: 29

SALES: 467
RATE: .15
COMMISSION: 70.05
```

Two numbers in each set (the sales and the code) are assigned to the variables **S** and **K** respectively each time the computer passes through the loop. The first time through the loop, 350 and 2 are assigned to **S** and **K**; the second time, 290 and 1; the third time, 467 and 3; and the last time, Ø and 4. The purpose of the last set of numbers is to terminate the program. The number 4 (assigned to the index K) causes control to transfer to the END statement. The zero (or some other non-data value) must be assigned to **S** in order to satisfy the READ statement. The ON…GO TO statement results in multiple branching as follows.

When the code (**K**) is 1, control is transferred to line 40, which assigns .10 to **R**.
When the code (**K**) is 2, control is transferred to line 60, which assigns .12 to **R**.
When the code (**K**) is 3, control is transferred to line 80, which assigns .15 to **R**.
When the code (**K**) is 4, control is transferred to line 999, the END statement.

Notice that immediately after **R** is assigned a rate, the computer goes to line 90, which calculates the commission. This is followed by the required PRINT statements.

5.3 SETS OF DATA READ IN A LOOP — Your Turn

1. A retailer receives a discount from a wholesaler, depending upon the number of articles purchased. The retailer's Accounts Payable has been computerized and codes have been assigned as follows.

Number of Articles	Code	Rate of Discount
Less than 100	1	6%
100 to 199	2	8%
200 to 299	3	10%

The program shown below prints the number of articles and the rate of discount for each of the following purchases: 250 articles, 60 articles, and 140 articles.

(a) Use the READ/DATA statements to enter the number of articles and the code for each purchase.
(b) Use an ON…GO TO statement to branch to the statements that assign the appropriate rates of discount and to branch to the END statement.

```
01 REM N--NUMBER OF ARTICLES
02 REM K--CODE (INDEX)
03 REM R--RATE
```

```
10 READ N,K
20 DATA 250,3,60,1,140,2,0,4
30 ON  K  GO TO 40,60,80,999
40 LET R=.06
50 GO TO 90
60 LET R=.08
70 GO TO 90
80 LET R=.10
90 PRINT
100 PRINT "NO. OF ARTICLES:";N
110 PRINT "RATE OF DISCOUNT:";R
120 GO TO 10
999 END

RUN

NO. OF ARTICLES: 250
RATE OF DISCOUNT: .1

NO. OF ARTICLES: 60
RATE OF DISCOUNT: .06

NO. OF ARTICLES: 140
RATE OF DISCOUNT: .08
```

Refer to the preceding program to answer the following questions.
(a) What values are assigned to the variable **K** during execution of the program?
(b) Explain how the various rates are assigned to **R**.
(c) What would be the output if lines 50 and 70 were omitted?
(d) How is the program terminated?
(e) What is wrong with the following DATA statement, if this statement is used instead of the one shown in the program? How does it affect execution of the program on your computer?

```
20 DATA 3,250,60,1,140,2,0,4
```

2. What is wrong with the following program? Make the necessary corrections.

```
10 PRINT
20 READ K,A
30 DATA 1,10,2,20,3,30
```

```
40 ON   K   GO TO 70,90,999
50 LET B=A+1
60 GO TO 100
70 LET B=A+2
80 GO TO 100
90 LET B=A+3
100 PRINT 'A ='iA,'B ='iB
110 GO TO 20
999 END

RUN

A = 10      B = 11
A = 20      B = 22
A = 30      B = 33
```

3. What is the output of the following program?

```
10 PRINT
20 READ K,A
30 DATA 1,6,2,8,3,0
40 ON   K   GO TO 50,70,99
50 LET B=A*2
60 GO TO 80
70 LET B=A*3
80 PRINT K,'A ='iA,'B ='iB
90 GO TO 20
99 END
```

4. Rewrite the program for Problem 1 so that your modified program calculates the amount of discount and the net cost of each purchase. The gross costs are recorded below.

Number of Articles Purchased	Gross Cost
250	$500
60	120
140	280

(a) Use the READ/DATA statements to enter the number of articles, the gross cost, and the code for each purchase. Do not use more than two DATA statements.
(b) Use an ON…GO TO statement to branch to the statements that assign the appropriate rates of discount and to branch to the END statement.
(c) Use a code of 4 to terminate your loop.
(d) Discount = Gross Cost × Rate of Discount
(e) Net Cost = Gross Cost − Discount

(f) Remember to draw a flowchart for your program. Your flowchart should be similar to the one in Chapter Four on page 129. The following changes are required:

(i) You should have only one READ statement.
(ii) Each branch, except the one to the END, should lead to a different process symbol to assign a different rate of discount to the same variable. Logic then converges from these symbols to one process symbol which depicts the calculation of the discount and the calculation of the net cost. This is followed by the output figure.

```
RUN

NO. OF ARTICLES: 250
GROSS COST: 500
RATE OF DISCOUNT: .1
AMOUNT OF DISCOUNT: 50
NET COST: 450

NO. OF ARTICLES: 60
GROSS COST: 120
RATE OF DISCOUNT: .06
AMOUNT OF DISCOUNT: 7.2
NET COST: 112.8

NO. OF ARTICLES: 140
GROSS COST: 280
RATE OF DISCOUNT: .08
AMOUNT OF DISCOUNT: 22.4
NET COST: 257.6
```

5.3 SETS OF DATA READ IN A LOOP – Solutions for "Your Turn"

1. (a) K = 3, 1, 2, 4
   (b) In the ON...GO TO statement:
   When **K** is equal to 3, control is transferred to statement number 80, which assigns .10 to **R**.
   When **K** is equal to 1, control is transferred to statement number 40, which assigns .06 to **R**.
   When **K** is equal to 2, control is transferred to statement number 60, which assigns .08 to **R**.
   When **K** is equal to 4, control is transferred to line 999, which is the END statement.

```
(c) RUN

    NO. OF ARTICLES: 250
    RATE OF DISCOUNT: .1

    NO. OF ARTICLES: 60
    RATE OF DISCOUNT: .1

    NO. OF ARTICLES: 140
    RATE OF DISCOUNT: .1
```

(d) The program terminates when the READ statement assigns 4 to **K** and control is transferred to the fourth number listed in the ON...GO TO statement. This is line number 999, which is the END statement.

(e) The first two numbers in the DATA statement are in reverse order. The value of the index is 250, which is out of the range of the numbers listed in the ON...GO TO statement. Depending on your computer system, one of the following may occur.

    1. Execution stops and the computer gives an error message.

    2. The ON...GO TO statement is ignored and the statement following the ON...GO TO is executed.

    3. Control is transferred to the last number in the list.

2. Line 50 is never executed as this statement number is not listed in the ON...GO TO statement. There should be four statement numbers in the ON...GO TO statement and four sets of data in the DATA statement (two numbers in each set). The two statements should be changed to the following.

```
30 DATA 1,10,2,20,3,30,4,555    — Last item may be any number, since the program
                                   ends before it can be used.
40 ON  K  GO TO 50,70,90,999
```

3.

```
RUN

    1          A = 6      B = 12
    2          A = 8      B = 24
```

4.

```
01 REM N--NUMBER OF ARTICLES
02 REM G--GROSS COST
03 REM K--CODE (INDEX)
04 REM R--RATE
05 REM D--DISCOUNT
06 REM C--NET COST

10 READ N,G,K
20 DATA 250,500,3,60,120,1,140,280,2
30 DATA 0,0,4
40 ON  K  GO TO 50,70,90,999
50 LET R=.06
60 GO TO 100
70 LET R=.08
80 GO TO 100
90 LET R=.10
100 LET D=G*R
110 LET C=G-D
120 PRINT
130 PRINT "NO. OF ARTICLES:";N
140 PRINT "GROSS COST:";G
150 PRINT "RATE OF DISCOUNT:";R
160 PRINT "AMOUNT OF DISCOUNT:";D
170 PRINT "NET COST:";C
180 GO TO 10
999 END
```

5.4 SUMMATION

How does a computer add a number of values and print subtotals? Computers can add only two numbers at a time. If you want to add the numbers 67, 85, 79, 93, the computer would add them in the following manner.

Subtotal	0
	+ 67
Subtotal	67
	+ 85
Subtotal	152
	+ 79
Subtotal	231
	+ 93
Sum	324

A variable, say **S**, should first be initialized to zero outside a loop.[1] It is used subsequently inside the loop to accumulate the sum.

1. Some computers automatically set all numeric variables to zero when programs are cleared from memory.

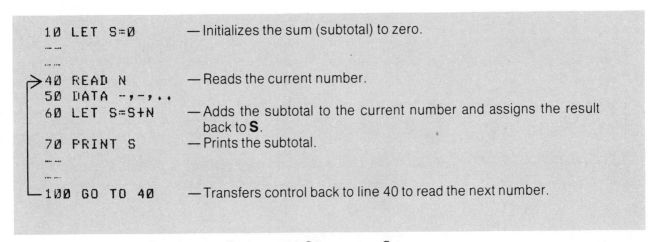

10 LET S=0	— Initializes the sum (subtotal) to zero.
→40 READ N	— Reads the current number.
50 DATA -,-,..	
60 LET S=S+N	— Adds the subtotal to the current number and assigns the result back to **S**.
70 PRINT S	— Prints the subtotal.
└─100 GO TO 40	— Transfers control back to line 40 to read the next number.

Once you get a sum, many things can be done with it. The simplest thing is to print it out. One of the most frequently used routines is the one that finds an average.

5.4 SUMMATION — Sample Program

As mentioned in Chapter Four on page 118, a loop may be terminated by transferring control to a statement that starts a new routine. This feature will now be combined with the summation concept you have just learned. The program shown below finds the average of the four numbers 67, 85, 79, and 93.[2] Instead of transferring control to the END statement (when summation is complete), the computer branches to the statement that finds the average. Two PRINT statements and the END statement complete the program. Its output includes the numbers and the subtotals.

(a) Use the READ statement to store the number of numbers in a simple variable. The variable is used subsequently with a counter to branch to the statement that finds the average.

(b) Use another READ statement to enter the numbers.

(c) Use one DATA statement.

(d) Average = $\dfrac{\text{Sum of Numbers}}{\text{''Number'' of Numbers}}$

```
01 REM K--COUNTER
02 REM S--SUM
03 REM N1--'NUMBER' OF NUMBERS
04 REM N--NUMBERS TO BE AVERAGED
05 REM A--AVERAGE
```

2. This is the program that was shown to you in Chapter Two where BASIC rules were first discussed.

```
10 PRINT              — Leaves a blank line.
20 LET K=1            — Initializes the counter to 1.
30 LET S=0            — Initializes the sum (subtotal) to zero.
40 READ N1            — Reads the number of values (4).
50 READ N             — Reads the numbers one at a time.
60 DATA 4,67,85,79,93 — Supplies the READ statements with the number
                        of values and the numbers themselves.
70 LET S=S+N          — Adds the subtotal to the current number and
                        assigns the result back to S.
80 PRINT N,S          — Prints the current number and the subtotal.
90 LET K=K+1          — Increments the counter by 1.
100 IF K>N1 THEN 120  — Tests the current value of the counter.
                        (i) If K is greater than N1 (4), control is
                            transferred to line 120 to find the average.
                        (ii) If K is not greater than N1, the computer
                            proceeds to the next statement to resume
                            the reading of numbers.
110 GO TO 50          — Transfers control back to line 50.
120 LET A=S/N1        — Finds the average.
130 PRINT             — Leaves a blank line.
140 PRINT "THE AVERAGE IS:";A  — Prints the average.
999 END               — Terminates program execution.

RUN

   67          67
   85          152
   79          231
   93          324

THE AVERAGE IS: 81
```

5.4 SUMMATION—Your Turn

1. Identify the errors in the program segments shown below. Make
   the necessary corrections.

```
(a) --
    --
    50 LET S=0
    60 READ D
    70 DATA 10,20,30
    80 LET S=S+D
    --
    110 GO TO 50  60
    --
    999 END
```

(b)
```
30 LET K=1
40 READ N
50 READ D
60 DATA 6,69,82,46
--
90 LET K=K+1
100 IF K>N THEN 999
110 GO TO 50
--
999 END
```
not enough data

(c)
```
01 REM A--AVERAGE
--
20 LET S=0
30 READ D
40 DATA 10,20,30,3
50 IF D=3 THEN 80
60 LET S=S+D
70 GO TO 30
80 LET A=D/S
--
99 END
```
A=3/
S=S+10
10
30
60

2. What is the output of each of the following programs?

blank line
10, 10, 20, 30,

(a)
```
10 PRINT
20 LET S=0
30 READ D
40 DATA 10,20,30,99999
50 IF D=99999 THEN 99
60 LET S=S+D
70 PRINT D,S
80 GO TO 30
99 END
```
10

(b)
```
10 PRINT
20 READ D
30 DATA 10,20,30,99999
40 LET S=0
50 IF D=99999 THEN 99
60 LET S=S+D
70 PRINT D,S
80 GO TO 20
99 END
```

3. Write a program that finds your total sales for the first four weeks of this year then calculates your commission based on this total. The rate of commission is 15% and your sales are as follows.

| Week 1 | $4000 | Week 3 | 4400 |
| Week 2 | 3800 | Week 4 | 4600 |

(a) Use the READ statement to store the number of weeks in a simple variable. The variable is used subsequently with a counter to branch to the statement that calculates the commission.
(b) Use another READ statement to enter the sales.
(c) Use one DATA statement.
(d) Print the number of the week along with your sales and the subtotal.
(e) Commission = Total Sales × .15
(f) Leave a blank line, then print your total sales and your commission.

2, Let T=0
5, Let K=1
10 Read N
20 Read S
30 DATA 4,4000,3800,4400,4600
40 let K=K+S
50 let T=T+1
55 GOTO 20
60 if T>N THEN C=K.15*
*70 PRINT C=K**

```
RUN

WEEK 1      4000      4000
WEEK 2      3800      7800
WEEK 3      4400     12200
WEEK 4      4600     16800

TOTAL SALES: 16800
COMMISSION: 2520
```

Problem 3

K — COUNTER
T — TOTAL SALES   S — SALES
N — NUMBER OF WEEKS   C — COMMISSION

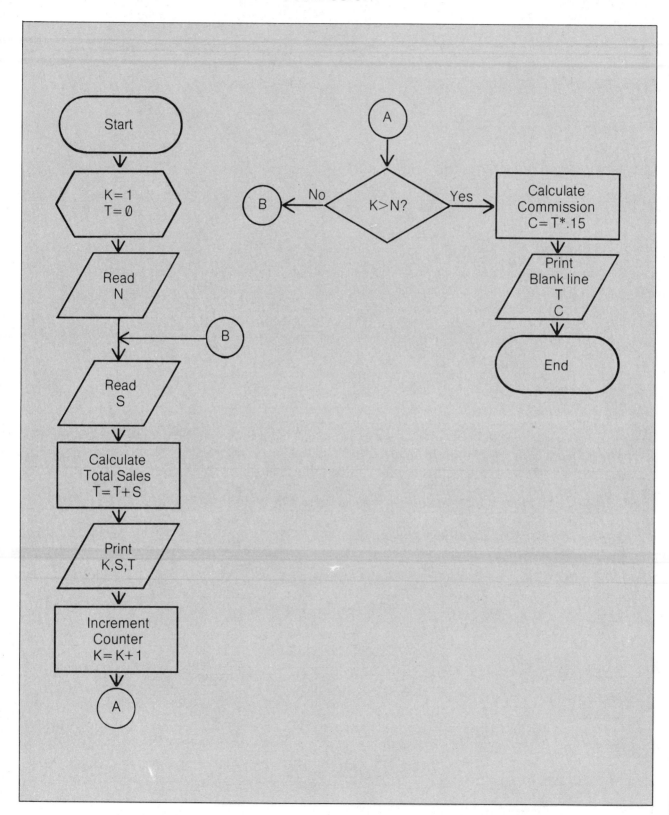

5.4 SUMMATION—Solutions for "Your Turn"

1. (a) **S** reverts to zero each time the computer executes the loop, since **S** is initialized inside the loop. The GO TO statement should transfer control to line 60 rather than to line 50. **S** would now be initialized outside the loop.

```
  --  --
   -- --
  50 LET S=0
→ 60 READ D
  70 DATA 10,20,30
  80 LET S=S+D
   -- --
  110 GO TO 60
  --  --
  999 END
```

(b) There is insufficient data in the DATA statement. **READ N** assigns the number 6 to the variable **N**, which means that there should be six items of data following the number 6. Either change the first number in the DATA statement to three or add three more items in the DATA statement.

```
60 DATA 3,69,82,46    or    60 DATA 6,69,82,46,58,93,87
```

(c) To find an average, you must divide the sum by the number of data items; not the last data item by the sum.

```
80 LET A=S/D
```

2.

```
(a) RUN              (b) RUN

     10       10         10       10
     20       30         20       20
     30       60         30       30
```

3.

```
01 REM K--COUNTER
02 REM T--TOTAL SALES
03 REM N--NUMBER OF WEEKS
04 REM S--SALES
05 REM C--COMMISSION

10 PRINT
20 LET K=1
30 LET T=0
40 READ N
50 READ S
60 DATA 4,4000,3800,4400,4600
70 LET T=T+S
80 PRINT "WEEK";K,S,T
90 LET K=K+1
100 IF K>N THEN 120
110 GO TO 50
120 LET C=T*.15
130 PRINT
140 PRINT "TOTAL SALES:";T
150 PRINT "COMMISSION:";C
999 END
```

5.5 A WAGE PROGRAM

The program in Chapter Three calculated an employee's earnings based on the number of hours worked and the hourly rate of pay. Deductions were made for income tax, union dues, and a registered pension plan. In order to incorporate some of the concepts that you learned in this chapter and the last, the program below is written for three employees whose regular work week is 39 hours. They are paid time-and-a-half for overtime. Here is the data you will need for the program.

Employee No.	Hrs. Worked	Rate	Income Tax Ded.	Union Dues	Pension Ded.
1	44	10.24	80	2	3.00
2	37	11.54	75	2	2.50
3	39	12.34	90	2	4.00

(a) The READ/DATA statements are used:
  —To assign a special number to a variable that represents the number of employees. This variable is used subsequently with a counter to terminate the loop.
  —To input data (hours, rates, and deductions).
(b) Remarks are placed in strategic spots to help you understand the program.

(c) Blank lines have been inserted only for clarity.

(d) *Calculations*

1. Gross Pay (no overtime) = Regular Hours × Regular Rate
2. Gross Pay with overtime:
   — Overtime Hours = Regular Hours − 39
   — Overtime Rate = Regular Rate × 1.5
   — Overtime Pay = Overtime Hours × Overtime Rate
   — Gross Pay (with overtime) = 39 × Regular Rate + Overtime Pay
3. Net Pay:
   — Total Deductions = Income Tax Deduction + Union Dues + Pension Deduction
   — Net Pay = Gross Pay − Total Deductions

```
01  REM  K--COUNTER
02  REM  N1--NUMBER OF EMPLOYEES
03  REM  H--REGULAR HOURS
04  REM  R--REGULAR RATE
05  REM  I--INCOME TAX DED.
06  REM  U--UNION DUES
07  REM  P--PENSION FUND DED.
08  REM  H1--OVERTIME HOURS
09  REM  R1--OVERTIME RATE
10  REM  V--OVERTIME
11  REM  G--GROSS PAY
12  REM  D--DEDUCTIONS
13  REM  N--NET PAY

100 REM  SET UP A COUNTER
105 LET  K=1

200 REM  READ/DATA STATEMENTS
205 REM  READ NO. OF EMPLOYEES
210 READ N1
215 DATA 3
220 REM  READ HOURS, RATE, DEDUCTIONS
225 READ H,R,I,U,P
230 DATA 44,10.24,80,2,3
235 DATA 37,11.54,75,2,2.50
240 DATA 39,12.34,90,2,4

300 REM  CHECK FOR OVERTIME
305 IF H>39 THEN 500

400 REM  GROSS PAY--NO OVERTIME
405 LET  H1=0
410 LET  R1=0
415 LET  V=0
420 LET  G=H*R
425 GO TO 600
```

Handwritten notes in right margin:

```
10  Let K = 1
20  Read N
30  DATA 3
40  Read H, H, R, I, U, P
50  DATA 1, 44, 10.24, 80, 2, 3
60  Let G = H * R
70  Let U = H - 39
    Let P = U *
80  Let R₁ = R * 1.5
90  Let P₁ = U * R₁
100 Let G₁ = 39 * R + P₁
110 Let T = I + U + P
120 Let N = G - T
130 print

Let K = K + 1
If K > N THEN
GoTo 40
End
```

```
500 REM GROSS PAY--WITH OVERTIME
505 LET H1=H-39
510 LET R1=R*1.5
515 LET V=H1*R1
520 LET G=39*R+V

600 REM NET PAY
605 LET D=I+U+P
610 LET N=G-D

700 REM PRINT STATEMENTS
705 PRINT
710 PRINT "EMPLOYEE";K,"HRS";H,"RATE";R
715 PRINT "OVERTIME HOURS";H1
720 PRINT "OVERTIME RATE";R1
725 PRINT "OVERTIME PAY";V
730 PRINT "GROSS PAY";G
735 PRINT "INCOME TAX";I
740 PRINT "UNION DUES";U
745 PRINT "PENSION";P
750 PRINT "TOTAL DEDUCTIONS";D
755 PRINT "NET PAY";N

800 REM CHECK FOR LAST DATA ITEM
805 LET K=K+1
810 IF K>N1 THEN 999
815 GO TO 225

999 END

RUN

EMPLOYEE 1            HRS 44      RATE 10.24
OVERTIME HOURS 5
OVERTIME RATE 15.36
OVERTIME PAY 76.8
GROSS PAY 476.16
INCOME TAX 80
UNION DUES 2
PENSION 3
TOTAL DEDUCTIONS 85
NET PAY 391.16

EMPLOYEE 2            HRS 37      RATE 11.54
OVERTIME HOURS 0
OVERTIME RATE 0
OVERTIME PAY 0
GROSS PAY 426.98
INCOME TAX 75
```

```
UNION DUES 2
PENSION 2.5
TOTAL DEDUCTIONS 79.5
NET PAY 347.48

EMPLOYEE 3           HRS 39     RATE 12.34
OVERTIME HOURS 0
OVERTIME RATE 0
OVERTIME PAY 0
GROSS PAY 481.26
INCOME TAX 90
UNION DUES 2
PENSION 4
TOTAL DEDUCTIONS 96
NET PAY 385.26
```

Wage Program

K — COUNTER
N1 — NUMBER OF EMPLOYEES
H — REGULAR HOURS
R — REGULAR RATE
I — INCOME TAX DEDUCTION
U — UNION DUES
P — PENSION FUND DEDUCTION

H1 — OVERTIME HOURS
R1 — OVERTIME RATE
V — OVERTIME
G — GROSS PAY
D — DEDUCTIONS
N — NET PAY

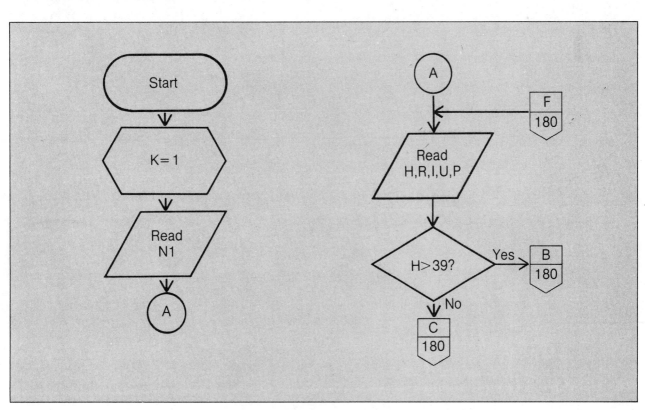

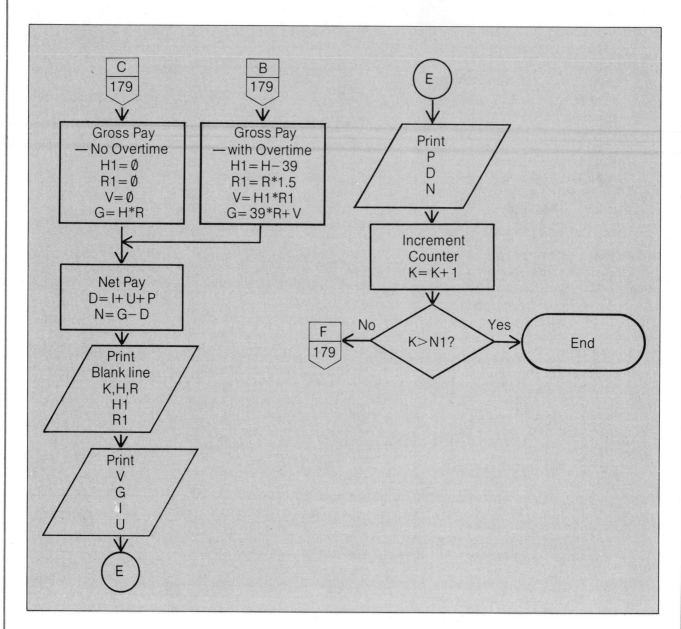

1. Which two statements enter the number of employees into the computer?

```
*******************************************
210 READ N1
215 DATA 3
```

2. Which statement compares the above variable with a counter?

```
*******************************************
810 IF K>N1 THEN 999
```

3. Which statement checks for overtime?

```
*****************************************
305 IF H>39 THEN 500
```

4. If the above statement is true, which routine calculates the overtime?

```
*****************************************
```

Several statements in the 500 range.

5. Which statement finds the overtime rate?

```
*****************************************
510 LET R1=R*1.5
```

6. Which statement finds the gross pay without overtime? With overtime?

```
*****************************************
420 LET G=H*R
520 LET G=39*R+V
```

7. Which statement transfers control back to the READ statement to read more data?

```
*****************************************
815 GO TO 225
```

A SHORT SUMMARY

Shown in this summary are five methods by which a loop may be controlled. These include the three that were discussed in Chapter Four. The first four programs print and read four data items. The last program calculates three simple arithmetic expressions.

1. A counter

```
  10 PRINT
  20 LET K=1
→ 30 READ A
  40 DATA 10,20,30,40
```

```
50 PRINT A
60 LET K=K+1
70 IF K>4 THEN 99
80 GO TO 30
99 END
```

A counter (**K**) keeps track of the data items. The counter is first initialized to 1 outside the loop, and then incremented (or decremented) by 1 each time the computer passes through the loop. In the above program, as long as the value of the counter is less than or equal to the number of data items (4), the computer continues to execute the loop. Once the counter reaches a value greater than the number of data items, the loop terminates.

2. A special value

```
10 PRINT
20 LET K=1
30 READ N
40 READ A
50 DATA 4,10,20,30,40
60 PRINT A
70 LET K=K+1
80 IF K>N THEN 99
90 GO TO 40
99 END
```

A special number which denotes the number of data items is assigned to a variable (**N**). As in Program 1, a counter keeps track of the data. As long as the value of the counter is less than or equal to that of the variable storing the number of items (4), execution of the loop continues. The loop ends once the value of the counter is greater than that of the variable (**N**).

3. A trailer value

```
10 PRINT
20 READ A
30 DATA 10,20,30,40,99999
40 IF A=99999 THEN 99
50 PRINT A
60 GO TO 20
99 END
```

A trailer value (some illogical number in relation to the program) is entered as the last item of data. Each time a data item is entered, it is checked to determine whether or not the item is the trailer value. If it is not the trailer value, looping continues; if it is, the loop terminates.

4. A test on data

```
   10 PRINT
   20 LET A=10
 ┌→30 IF A>40 THEN 99─┐
 │ 40 PRINT A         │
 │ 50 LET A=A+10      │
 └─60 GO TO 30        │
   99 END←────────────┘
```

Data that increases (or decreases) by equal amounts can be checked to determine whether or not the final value has been reached. In the above program, execution continues until the increment causes a result that is greater than the final value required in the program. At this point, looping terminates.

5. A code

```
    10  PRINT
  ┌→20 READ C,A
  │ 30 DATA 1,10,2,20,3,30,4,0
  │ 40 ON  C  GO TO 50,70,90,999
  │ 50 PRINT A,A+2            │
  │←60 GO TO 20               │
  │ 70 PRINT A,A-2            │
  │←80 GO TO 20               │
  │ 90 PRINT A,A/2            │
  │←100 GO TO 20              │
    999 END←─────────────────┘
```

The ON...GO TO statement uses an index as a code to transfer control to one of several statements in its list. One of the values of the index causes control to transfer to a statement outside the loop, thereby terminating the loop. In the above program, a code of 4 transfers control to the END statement.

Sets of data items, consisting of two or more values in a set, may be coded in one DATA statement. Each time the computer passes through the loop, consecutive sets of data are assigned to the same variables.

The summation of numbers can be accomplished by accumulating the sum in a variable. The addition is performed within a loop. With each pass through the loop, another number is added to the subtotal. The variable that accumulates this sum should first be initialized to zero outside the loop.

Questions and Exercises

1. What is the purpose of a trailer value (a flag)?
2. Complete lines 30 and 40 so that the program terminates by means of a trailer value.

```
10 PRINT
20 READ A
30 DATA
40
50 PRINT A
60 GO TO 20
99 END

RUN

   2
   4
   6
```

3. The following program counts the number of data items (excluding the trailer value). Fill in the missing lines.

```
10
20 READ A
30 DATA 40,50,60,-1
40
50 LET K=K+1
60
70 PRINT
80
99 END

RUN

   3
```

(i) Which statement should be coded in line 10?

```
(a) LET K=0
(b) LET K=1
(c) LET K=2
(d) LET K=-1
(e) LET A=-1
```

(ii) Which statement should be coded in line 40?

```
(a) GO TO 50
(b) GO TO 70
(c) IF A=40 THEN 70
(d) IF A=-1 THEN 70
(e) IF A=-1 THEN 99
```

(iii) Complete line 60 with a GO TO statement.

(iv) Complete line 80 with a PRINT statement.

4. (a) Summarize the procedure followed by the computer during execution of the READ/DATA statements in the program segment shown below.

```
10    --
20 READ N
30 READ A
40 DATA 5,11,22,33,44,55
50    --
60    --
70    --
80 GO TO 30
99 END
```

(b) A counter is often incorporated in a program in order to terminate a loop. What three statements must be added to the above program segment so that the loop will be terminated? Explain how these statements are executed.

5. Refer to the program shown below to answer the following questions.

   (a) Explain how data is assigned to variables **A** and **B** each time the computer goes through the loop.

   (b) What is the purpose of the last set of numbers? Why must there be two numbers in this set?

   (c) What is the output of the program?

```
10 PRINT
20 READ A,B
30 DATA 1,10,2,20,3,30,888,999
40 IF A=888 THEN 99
50 PRINT B
60 GO TO 20
99 END
```

6. Write a program that adds the numbers 10, 20, 30, 40 and prints subtotals after each addition. Use the READ/DATA statements to

enter the numbers and a trailer value to terminate the loop.
Explain each step the computer takes during summation.

```
RUN

10        10
20        30
30        60
40        100
```

7. What is wrong with each of the following program segments?
Make the necessary corrections.

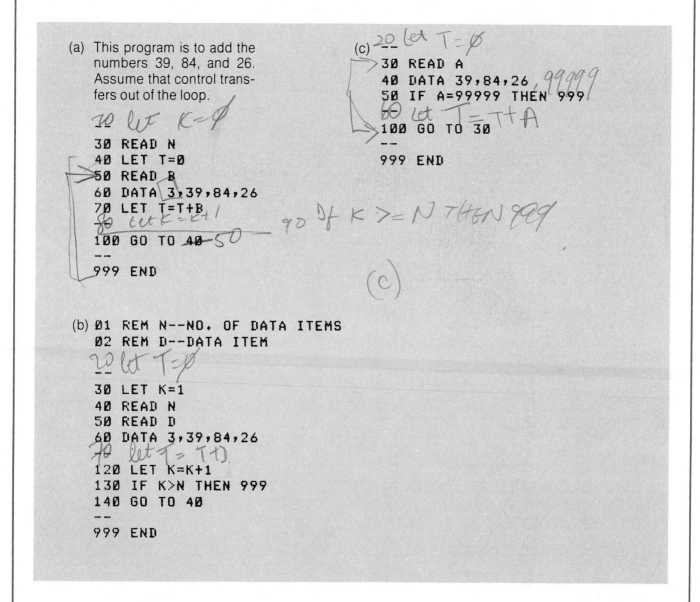

(a) This program is to add the numbers 39, 84, and 26. Assume that control transfers out of the loop.

10 let K=∅

```
30 READ N
40 LET T=0
50 READ B
60 DATA 3,39,84,26
70 LET T=T+B    1
80  let K=K+1
100 GO TO 40  50
--
999 END
```

90 If K >= N THEN 999

(c) *20 let T=∅*

```
--
30 READ A
40 DATA 39,84,26, 99999
50 IF A=99999 THEN 999
60 let T=T+A
100 GO TO 30
--
999 END
```

(c)

(b)
```
01 REM N--NO. OF DATA ITEMS
02 REM D--DATA ITEM
```
20 let T=∅
```
--
30 LET K=1
40 READ N
50 READ D
60 DATA 3,39,84,26
```
70 let T = T+D
```
120 LET K=K+1
130 IF K>N THEN 999
140 GO TO 40
--
999 END
```

8. What is the output of each of the following programs?

```
(a) 10  PRINT
    20  READ A
    30  DATA 1,2,3,-1
    40  LET T=0
    50  IF A=-1 THEN 99
    60  LET T=T+A
    70  PRINT A,T
    80  GO TO 20
    99  END
```

```
(c) 10  PRINT
    20  READ A,B
    30  DATA 1,100,2,200,3,300,4,99999
    40  IF B=99999 THEN 99
    50  LET C=B/A
    60  PRINT B,C
    70  GO TO 20
    99  END
```

```
(b) 10  PRINT
    20  LET T=0
    30  READ A
    40  DATA 1,2,3,-1
    50  IF A=-1 THEN 99
    60  LET T=T+A
    70  PRINT A,T
    80  GO TO 30
    99  END
```

9. During execution of the following program, the computer informs you that there is insufficient data. Rewrite this program in four different ways, each version using one of the methods listed below to terminate input.

```
       5 let K=0
10  PRINT
20  READ A
30  DATA 10,20,30,40,50
40  PRINT A    if K=5 then 99
50  GO TO 20
99  END
       let K=K+1
```

(a) A counter.
(b) A special number assigned to a variable by means of a READ statement. This variable is used subsequently with a counter to terminate input.
(c) A trailer value (a flag).
(d) A test on each increased (or decreased) amount to determine whether or not the final value has been reached. Use LET statements in this program.

Programming Problems

1. Suppose you are one of the three employees of the XYZ Manufacturing Company mentioned in Problem 2 on page 142 of Chapter Four. If your production of machine parts last week was 43, 42, 45, 43, and 40 for the five days of work, what total number of parts did you produce? If the rate paid for each part produced is $2, what was your income for the week?
    (a) Use the READ statement to store the number of days in a simple variable. The variable is used subsequently with a counter to terminate the loop.
    (b) Use another READ statement to enter the number of parts.
    (c) Use one DATA statement.
    (d) Print subtotals along with the number of parts produced.
    (e) Income = Total Number of Parts × Rate

```
RUN

NO. OF PARTS 43        SUBTOTAL 43
NO. OF PARTS 42        SUBTOTAL 85
NO. OF PARTS 45        SUBTOTAL 130
NO. OF PARTS 43        SUBTOTAL 173
NO. OF PARTS 40        SUBTOTAL 213

TOTAL NO. OF PARTS: 213
RATE: 2
INCOME: 426
```

Problem 1

K — COUNTER   N — NUMBER OF DAYS
R — RATE   P — PARTS
S — SUBTOTAL   I — INCOME

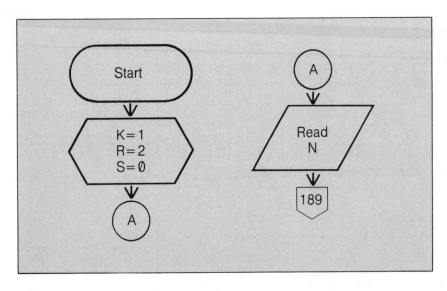

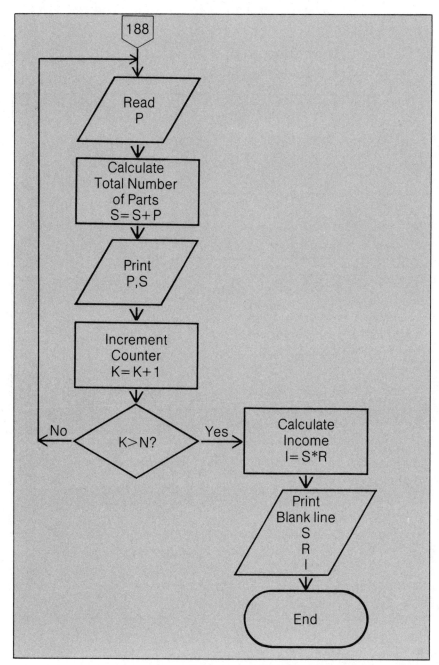

2. Using a code of 1 to indicate TRUE and a code of 2 to indicate FALSE, write a program that finds the number of TRUE answers and the number of FALSE answers on a questionnaire that consists of 20 questions. Initialize a variable, say **T**, to zero. If an answer is TRUE, increment this variable by 1.

```
xx  LET  T=0³
    --
    --
xx  LET  T=T+1
```

3. "xx" denotes a statement number.

Problem 2

K — COUNTER
T — TRUE
F — FALSE

N — NUMBER OF ANSWERS
A — ANSWER (INDEX)

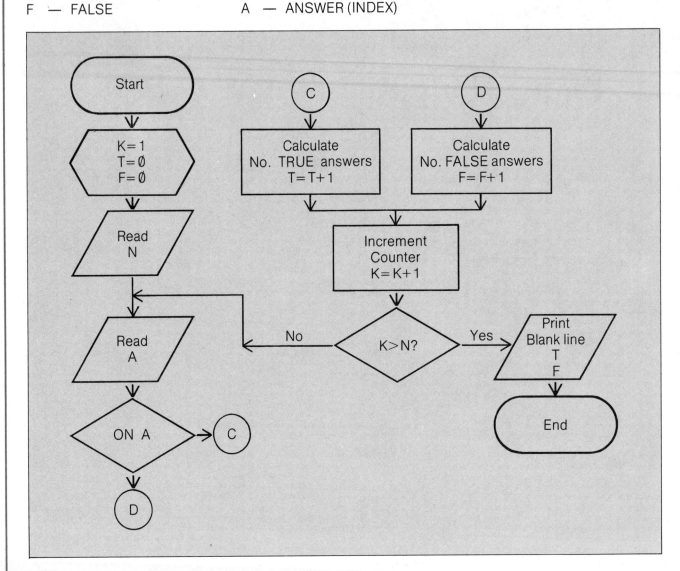

Do the same for a variable, say **F**, for a FALSE answer. Use the DATA statements shown below.

```
xx DATA 20,1,1,2,1,2,2,1,1,1,2
xx DATA 1,2,1,1,2,1,2,1,1,2
```

(a) Use the READ statement to store the number of answers in a simple variable. The variable is used subsequently with a counter to terminate the loop.

(b) Use another READ statement to enter the data.

(c) Use an ON...GO TO statement for branching.

```
RUN

NO. OF TRUE ANSWERS: 12
NO. OF FALSE ANSWERS: 8
```

3. From the information recorded below, find:

   (i) The extended cost of each item.
   (ii) The total cost of all the items.

Item	Quantity	Unit Price
1	2	$4.50
2	4	3.00
3	5	2.25
4	3	5.15

(a) Use the INPUT statement to enter the quantity and the unit price of each item.
(b) Use a trailer value to terminate your loop.
(c) Extended Cost of Each Item = Quantity × Unit Price
(d) Total Cost = Total Cost + Extended Cost of Each Item

Using the INPUT Statement

```
RUN

QUANTITY,UNIT PRICE? 2,4.50
EXTENDED COST: 9

QUANTITY,UNIT PRICE? 4,3.00
EXTENDED COST: 12

QUANTITY,UNIT PRICE? 5,2.25
EXTENDED COST: 11.25

QUANTITY,UNIT PRICE? 3,5.15
EXTENDED COST: 15.45

QUANTITY,UNIT PRICE? 99999,0

TOTAL COST: 47.7
```

Using the READ/DATA Statements

```
RUN

QUANTITY,UNIT PRICE: 2    4.5
EXTENDED COST: 9

QUANTITY,UNIT PRICE: 4    3
EXTENDED COST: 12

QUANTITY,UNIT PRICE: 5    2.25
EXTENDED COST: 11.25

QUANTITY,UNIT PRICE: 3    5.15
EXTENDED COST: 15.45

TOTAL COST: 47.7
```

4. Write a program that counts the number of one-dollar bills, five-dollar bills, and ten-dollar bills deposited in a bank account. The bills deposited are:
5,10,1,5,1,10,5,1,10,1,1,5,10,1,1,10,20,5,1,5,1.
(a) Use the READ/DATA statements to enter the data.
(b) Use a trailer value to terminate your loop.
(c) Use IF/THEN statements to determine the denomination of each bill.

(d) Your program should check for the deposit of a different denomination of bill. This is shown in the flowchart. If the results of all the IF/THEN tests are false (because a bill other than a 1, a 5, or a 10 is deposited), control should be transferred to the READ statement.

```
RUN

NO. OF ONE-DOLLAR BILLS: 9
NO. OF FIVE-DOLLAR BILLS: 6
NO. OF TEN-DOLLAR BILLS: 5
```

Problem 4

N — ONE-DOLLAR BILL   T — TEN-DOLLAR BILL
F — FIVE-DOLLAR BILL   B — BILL DEPOSITED

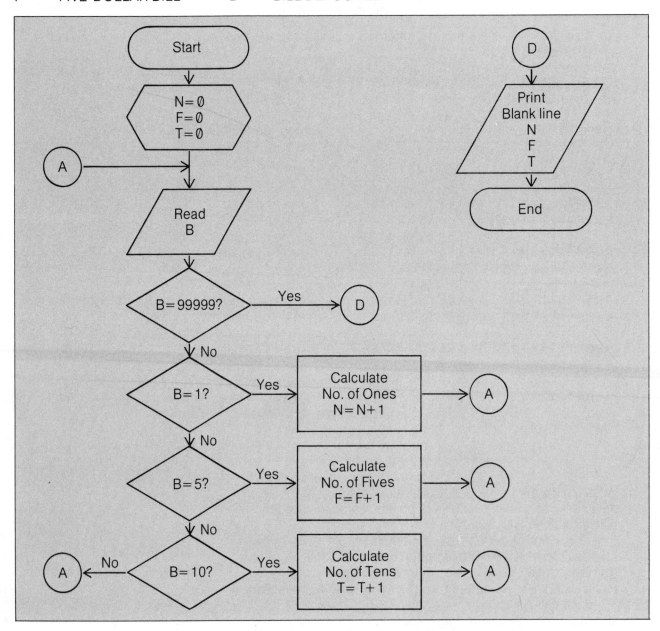

5. Write a program that enters the numbers 1, −2, 3, −4, and 5, then finds the following:

(i) The number of positive numbers entered.
(ii) The sum of these positive numbers.
   (a) Use the INPUT statement to enter the numbers.
   (b) Use a counter to terminate your loop.
   (c) If the number entered is less than or equal to zero, transfer control to the statement that increments your counter; if it is greater than zero, find the number of positive numbers and the sum of the positive numbers.
   (d) If the counter is greater than 5, print the results; if it is not greater than 5, input another number.

Using the INPUT Statement

```
RUN

VALUE FOR N? 1
VALUE FOR N? -2
VALUE FOR N? 3
VALUE FOR N? -4
VALUE FOR N? 5


NO. OF POSITIVE NUMBERS: 3
SUM OF POSITIVE NUMBERS: 9
```

Using the READ/DATA Statements

```
RUN

NO. OF POSITIVE NUMBERS: 3
SUM OF POSITIVE NUMBERS: 9
```

6. In Chapter Three (Page 106), you were asked to write a program to convert a Fahrenheit degree to a Celsius degree. Write a program that converts the following five Fahrenheit degrees to Celsius degrees.

$$50°, 59°, 68°, 77°, 86°$$

(a) Use LET statements to enter your data. Generate the data by incrementing each degree by 9.
(b) Terminate your loop by checking each data item for the final degree.
(c) The conversion formula is: $C = \frac{5}{9}(F - 32)$

```
RUN

FAHRENHEIT: 50      CELSIUS: 10
FAHRENHEIT: 59      CELSIUS: 15
FAHRENHEIT: 68      CELSIUS: 20
FAHRENHEIT: 77      CELSIUS: 25
FAHRENHEIT: 86      CELSIUS: 30
```

7. On July 1, your bank account showed a balance of $1000. During the month you made the following deposits and withdrawals:

July 1	balance	$1000
10	withdrawal	80
15	deposit	450
23	withdrawal	100
31	deposit	450

Write a program that calculates the balance of your bank account after each transaction.

(a) Initialize a variable to the July 1 balance.

(b) Use a code of 1 for a deposit, a code of 2 for a withdrawal, and a code of 3 to terminate your loop.

(c) Use the READ/DATA statements to enter the code and the amount of each transaction. Use one DATA statement.

(d) Use an ON...GO TO statement for multiple branching.

(e) Depending on your code:

$$Balance = Balance + Deposit$$

or

$$Balance = Balance - Withdrawal$$

```
RUN

AMOUNT: 80       BALANCE: 920
AMOUNT: 450      BALANCE: 1370
AMOUNT: 100      BALANCE: 1270
AMOUNT: 450      BALANCE: 1720
```

```
5 Let M=1000
10 Let K=1
20 Read N
30 Read C, B
40 on C GOTO 50, 80, 120
50 Rem WITH DRAWAL
60 Let m=m-B
70 GOTO 30
80 Rem deposit
90 Let m=m+B
100 GOTO 30
110 DATA
120 END
```

SIX FOR/NEXT LOOPS

A. After completing this chapter, you should be able to write BASIC programs and complete skeletal BASIC programs that use:

1. Single FOR/NEXT loops.
2. Nested FOR/NEXT loops.
3. PRINT statements to counteract commas or semicolons at the end of previous PRINT statements.
4. PRINT statements that leave blank lines between specific rows of output.

B. In addition, you should be able to:

1. Display and label a FOR statement.
2. State the purpose of each part of a FOR statement.
3. State the purpose of the NEXT statement.
4. Explain the execution of a FOR/NEXT loop.
5. Make corrections to:
   (a) Invalid FOR statements.
   (b) Invalid program segments using FOR/NEXT loops.
   (c) Invalid program segments using nested FOR/NEXT loops.
6. Determine how many times a FOR/NEXT loop is executed when:
   (a) The initial value and the test value are the same, and the step value is any number.
   (b) The test value is greater than the initial value and the step value is zero or negative.
   (c) The test value is less than the initial value and the step value is zero or positive.
7. Determine the value of the index after a FOR/NEXT loop is complete.
8. Calculate the number of times
   (a) A FOR/NEXT loop is executed.
   (b) An inner FOR/NEXT loop is executed.
9. State the values the index takes on in a FOR statement.
10. Complete a FOR statement.
11. Explain what is meant by a nested loop.
12. Determine the output of programs.

6.1 GENERAL FORM

In Chapter Four, a loop was set up and controlled by the use of a counter. There is another way to generate and control a loop, one that is powerful and flexible yet simple and convenient to use. It is called a **FOR/NEXT** loop and its general form looks like this.

```
10    --
20 FOR I=1 TO 3 STEP 1
```

Two statements control a FOR/NEXT loop. The FOR statement sets up the loop and the NEXT statement marks the end of the loop. The two statements always work together. All statements between these two are said to be inside the loop. This means that statements 30 and 40 are executed each time the computer passes through the loop. When looping is complete, control transfers to the statement immediately following the NEXT statement.

The FOR Statement

		Index		Initial Value		Test Value		Step Value
		↓		↓		↓		↓
20	FOR	I	=	1	TO	3	STEP	1

The above FOR statement consists of an index (**I**), an initial value (1), a test value (3), and a step value (the 1 in the STEP clause).

Index Keeps track of the number of times the loop is performed. It is similar to a counter.

Initial value The first value assigned to the index.

Test value The limiting value of the index. When the initial value and the step value are 1, the test value indicates the number of times the loop will be performed.

Step value Indicates the number of units the index is incremented (increased) or decremented (decreased) each time the computer passes through the loop. Some computer systems use the word BY. STEP will be used in the programs throughout this book.

The NEXT Statement

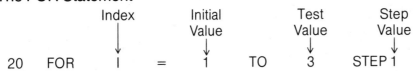

The NEXT statement instructs the computer to increment or decrement the index (I) by the value indicated in the STEP clause, and then to branch back to the beginning of the loop. This makes it essential that the variable in the NEXT statement be the same as the index in the corresponding FOR statement.

Here are the steps the computer takes when executing a FOR/NEXT loop. The program segment on pages 195-96 will be used in the discussion. As you read the steps listed below, try and trace the computer's path by following the arrows drawn in the program segment. Do this several times to make sure you understand the procedure.

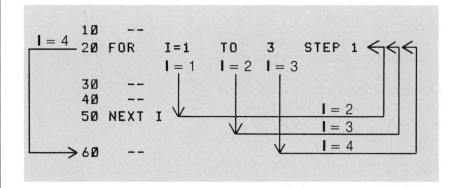

1. In line 20, **I** is assigned a value of 1. **I** = 1.
2. Statements 30 and 40 are executed.
3. The statement **NEXT I** in line 50 instructs the computer to increment **I** by 1 (**STEP 1**). **I** = 2. Control is transferred back to line 20.
4. The computer checks to see if **I** is greater than 3. Since **I** = 2 and 2 is not greater than 3, statements 30 and 40 are executed.
5. The statement **NEXT I** in line 50 instructs the computer to increment **I** by 1 (**STEP 1**). **I** = 3. Control is transferred back to line 20.
6. The computer checks to see if **I** is greater than 3. Since **I** = 3 and 3 is not greater than 3, statements 30 and 40 are executed.
7. The statement **NEXT I** in line 50 instructs the computer to increment **I** by 1 (**STEP 1**). **I** = 4. Control is transferred back to line 20.
8. The computer checks to see if **I** is greater than 3. Since **I** = 4 and 4 is greater than 3, control is transferred to the statement immediately after the NEXT statement, skipping those instructions inside the loop. The FOR/NEXT loop is now terminated.

Shown below is a comparison of a program segment that controls a loop by the use of a FOR/NEXT loop with one that uses a counter.

(a) Using a Counter

(b) Using a FOR/NEXT Loop

```
110    --                      10    --
120 LET K=1                    20 FOR I=1 TO 3 STEP 1
130    --                      30    --
140    --                      40    --
150 LET K=K+1                  50 NEXT I
160 IF K>3 THEN 180            60    --
170 GO TO 130
180    --
```

Line 20 in program (b) replaces lines 120 and 160 in program (a). The index **I** is initially set at 1 (this replaces line 120) and the test value (3) limits the number of times the loop is performed. (This replaces line 160.)

The NEXT statement, in conjunction with the STEP value, increments (increases) I by 1. (This replaces line 150.)

The NEXT statement replaces line 170. The result is a program that not only has fewer statements but clearly defines the beginning and the ending of a loop.

There are a number of rules that must be observed when using FOR/NEXT statements. They are not difficult to learn, and once mastered, they are very easy to follow. Examples will be used to make sure you understand each rule as it is presented.

1. The index must be a simple numeric variable which takes on a number of numeric values.

```
20 FOR I=1 TO 3 STEP 1
```

I takes on the value 1, then 2, then 3, and finally 4. Once I is set at 4, its value is greater than the test value and control is transferred to the statement immediately after the loop. This means that the loop is executed three times — when I = 1, 2, and 3. There is a formula to calculate the number of times a loop is performed. Its general form is as follows.

$$\left(\frac{n_2 - n_1}{n_3}\right) + 1$$

Where n_1 = the initial value
n_2 = the test value
n_3 = the step value

Applying the formula to the FOR statement above gives 3 as the result.

```
20 FOR I=1 TO 3 STEP 1
         ↑      ↑      ↑
         n₁     n₂     n₃
```

$$\left(\frac{n_2 - n_1}{n_3}\right) + 1 = \left(\frac{3-1}{1}\right) + 1 = \left(\frac{2}{1}\right) + 1 = 2+1 = 3.$$

2. The NEXT statement must always have a higher line number than its corresponding FOR statement, and its variable must be the same as the one that is used as the index in the FOR statement.

```
      →20 FOR I=1 TO 3 STEP 1
       30    --
Higher line  40    --        Same variable
number →50 NEXT I
```

3. There may be any number of statements inside the loop with a minimum of one. In the above example, there are two statements — lines 30 and 40.
4. If the step clause is omitted, the computer uses 1 as the step value. In other words, the step value is assigned the number 1 by default.

```
20 FOR I=1 TO 3
```

5. The index may be used in a statement inside the loop. However, some versions of BASIC explicitly disallow the index to be altered within the loop, regardless whether it's done by a READ statement, an INPUT statement, or a LET statement. Others allow the index to be changed, but this change may interfere with the automatic incrementing (or decrementing) as specified in the STEP clause. What does your computer print when you RUN the following program?

```
10 FOR I=1 TO 7 STEP 1
20    PRINT I
30    LET I=I+2 ←————————— Index altered
40    PRINT "ALTERED I =";I
50 NEXT I
99 END
```

6. It is possible to transfer out of a FOR/NEXT loop before it has reached its limit by using a GO TO, an IF/THEN, or an ON...GO TO, but it is not possible to transfer to a statement within a FOR/NEXT loop. In other words, the only entry into a FOR/NEXT loop is by means of the FOR statement.

```
10 GO TO 30 ←————————————— Invalid
20 FOR I=1 TO 3 STEP 1
30    --
40    --
50 NEXT I
```

Programs are given for rules 7, 8, and 9. RUN each one to see how your computer system executes the FOR/NEXT loop. Does each RUN produce a result, or do you get an error message? If you do get a result, how many values of **I** are printed and what are the values?

7. If the initial value and the test value are the same and the step value is any number, most computer systems will execute the loop once.

(a) Step value is positive

```
10 FOR I=1 TO 1 STEP 1
20 PRINT I
30 NEXT I
99 END
```

(c) Step value is negative

```
10 FOR I=1 TO 1 STEP -1
20 PRINT I
30 NEXT I
99 END
```

(b) Step value is zero

```
10 FOR I=1 TO 1 STEP 0
20 PRINT I
30 NEXT I
99 END
```

8. If the test value is greater than the initial value and the step value is zero or negative, the loop may be executed once, not at all, or continuously.

(a) Step value is zero

```
10 FOR I=1 TO 10 STEP 0
20 PRINT I
30 NEXT I
99 END
```

(b) Step value is negative

```
10 FOR I=1 TO 10 STEP -1
20 PRINT I
30 NEXT I
99 END
```

9. If the test value is less than the initial value and the step value is zero or positive, the loop may be executed once, not at all, or continuously.

(a) Step value is zero

```
10 FOR I=10 TO 1 STEP 0
20 PRINT I
30 NEXT I
99 END
```

(b) Step value is positive

```
10 FOR I=10 TO 1 STEP 1
20 PRINT I
30 NEXT I
99 END
```

10. When looping is complete, the value of the index is greater than the test value. On some computer systems, it remains at this number; on others, the value of the index reverts to the test value (or the closest number to it when the step value is not one). Here is an example.

```
10    --
20 FOR I=1 TO 3 STEP 1
```

```
30    --
40    --
50 NEXT I
60    --
```

I has a value of 4 when the FOR/NEXT loop is complete. On some computers, the value of **I** remains at 4; on others it reverts to 3. In the event that you may want to use the index after a loop, you should know what value the index takes on in your computer system when a loop is complete. RUN the following program. What is the value of **I** when it is printed outside the loop?

```
10 FOR I=1 TO 3 STEP 1
20 PRINT I
30 NEXT I
40 PRINT "VALUE OF I OUTSIDE LOOP:";I
99 END
```

11. On some systems, you may omit the variable after the key word NEXT. However, this is not advisable, as it may confuse you (and your computer) if there is more than one FOR/NEXT loop in the program.
12. This is not really a rule — it's merely a suggestion. Some programmers highlight the statements within a FOR/NEXT loop by indenting them several spaces.

```
10 FOR I=1 TO 10 STEP 1
20    LET J=I↑2  ⎤
30    PRINT I,J  ⎦ ←— Indented
40 NEXT I
99 END
```

6.1 GENERAL FORM—Sample Program

A sample program in Chapter Five on page 171 found the average of four numbers. A special value was read to indicate the number of numbers that were to be averaged. This special value was then compared with a counter to terminate input. In this program, a FOR/NEXT loop will be used to control the entering of data. Here is the problem once more.

Find the average of the four numbers 67, 85, 79, 93. Print each number currently added along with a subtotal.

(a) Use a FOR/NEXT loop to keep track of the input (the four numbers).

(b) Use the READ/DATA statements to enter the numbers (one at a time).

(c) Average $= \dfrac{\text{Sum of the Numbers}}{\text{''Number'' of Numbers}}$

```
10 PRINT                          —Leaves a blank line.
20 LET S=0                        —Initializes the sum to 0.
30 FOR I=1 TO 4 STEP 1            —Sets up a loop.
40    READ N                      —Reads the numbers one at a time.
50    DATA 67,85,79,93            —Supplies the READ statement with the numbers.
60    LET S=S+N                   —Accumulates the sum of the numbers.
70    PRINT N,S                   —Prints the number and the accumulated sum.
80 NEXT I                         —Transfers control to line 30.
90 LET A=S/4                      —Finds the average.
100 PRINT                         —Leaves a blank line.
110 PRINT "THE AVERAGE IS:";A     —Prints the average.
999 END                           —Terminates program execution.

RUN

   67          67
   85          152
   79          231
   93          324

THE AVERAGE IS: 81
```

6.1 GENERAL FORM—Your Turn

I. A retailer is allowed a cash discount of 2% if the store's accounts are paid within 10 days. Suppose the retailer takes advantage of this cash discount when three accounts with balances of $450, $600, and $240 are cleared. Find the discount and the amount remitted (paid) on each account.

(a) Use a FOR/NEXT loop to keep track of the accounts.

(b) Use the READ/DATA statements to enter the balance of each account.

(c) Discount = Balance × .02

(d) Amount Remitted = Balance − Discount

(e) Fill in the missing lines.

```
01 REM I--INDEX (NO. OF ACCOUNT)
02 REM B--BALANCE IN ACCOUNT
03 REM D--DISCOUNT
04 REM R--AMOUNT REMITTED
```

```
10
20     READ B
30
40     LET D=B*.02
50
60     PRINT
70
80
90
100
110
999 END

RUN

ACCOUNT: 1
BALANCE: 450
DISCOUNT: 9
AMOUNT REMITTED: 441

ACCOUNT: 2
BALANCE: 600
DISCOUNT: 12
AMOUNT REMITTED: 588

ACCOUNT: 3
BALANCE: 240
DISCOUNT: 4.8
AMOUNT REMITTED: 235.2
```

1. Which statement should be coded in line 10?

```
(a) FOR I=B TO D STEP R
(b) FOR I=R TO D
(c) FOR I=1 TO 3 STEP 2
(d) FOR I=1 TO 3
(e) FOR I=3 TO 1
```

2. Complete line 30 with a DATA statement.
3. Which statement should be coded in line 50?

```
(a) LET B=R-D
(b) LET R=B-D
(c) LET D=B-R
(d) LET R=B+D
(e) LET B=D+R
```

Problem II

Using the INPUT Statement	Using the READ/DATA Statements
I — INDEX (NO. OF THE EQUIPMENT)	I — INDEX (NO. OF THE EQUIPMENT)
S — SALES PRICE	S — SALES PRICE
C — COMMISSION	C — COMMISSION

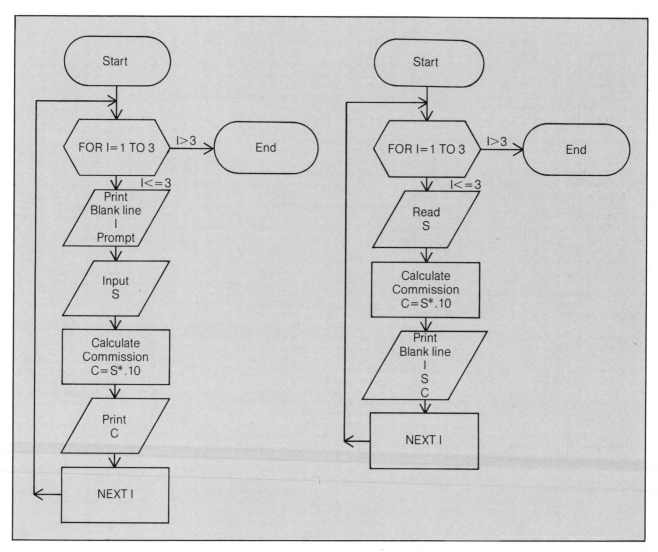

4. Which statement should be coded in line 70?

```
(a) PRINT "ACCOUNT:";A
(b) PRINT "ACCOUNT:";B
(c) PRINT "ACCOUNT";I
(d) PRINT "ACCOUNT:";R
(e) PRINT "ACCOUNT:";I
```

5. Complete lines 80, 90, and 100 with PRINT statements.
6. Which statement should be coded in line 110?

```
(a) NEXT K
(b) NEXT=I
(c) NEXT 3
(d) NEXT I
(e) GO TO 10
```

II. A salesperson sold three pieces of equipment, the first for
$1200, the second for $1500, and the third for $1300. If 10%
commission based on sales is received, what commission does
the salesperson receive on each piece of equipment sold?
   (a) Use a FOR/NEXT loop to keep track of the input (each piece of
       equipment).
   (b) Use an INPUT statement to enter the sales price. If you are
       not using an interactive system, use the READ/DATA state-
       ments.
   (c) Print the number of the equipment (first, second, or third).
   (d) Commission = Sales Price × .10
   (e) No standardized symbols mark the beginning and the end-
       ing of a FOR/NEXT loop. In the flowcharts shown, the prepara-
       tion symbol is used to represent the FOR statement and the
       process symbol is used to represent the NEXT statement. In
       both flowcharts, logic flows from the FOR statement to the
       NEXT statement and then back to the FOR, as long as I is less
       than or equal to 3. When I is greater than 3, control is
       transferred to the END statement.

Using the INPUT Statement

Using the READ/DATA Statements

```
RUN

EQUIPMENT: 1
SALES PRICE? 1200
COMMISSION: 120

EQUIPMENT: 2
SALES PRICE? 1500
COMMISSION: 150
```

```
RUN

EQUIPMENT: 1
SALES PRICE: 1200
COMMISSION: 120

EQUIPMENT: 2
SALES PRICE: 1500
COMMISSION: 150
```

```
EQUIPMENT: 3                    EQUIPMENT: 3
SALES PRICE? 1300               SALES PRICE: 1300
COMMISSION: 130                 COMMISSION: 130
```

6.1 GENERAL FORM—Solutions for "Your Turn"

I.

```
1. (d) 10 FOR I=1 TO 3
2.    30 DATA 450,600,240
3. (b) 50 LET R=B-D
4. (e) 70 PRINT "ACCOUNT:";I
5.    80 PRINT "BALANCE:";B
      90 PRINT "DISCOUNT:";D
     100 PRINT "AMOUNT REMITTED:";R
6. (d) 110 NEXT I
```

II. Using the INPUT Statement

```
01 REM I--INDEX (NO. OF THE EQUIPMENT)
02 REM S--SALES PRICE
03 REM C--COMMISSION

10 FOR I=1 TO 3 STEP 1
20    PRINT
30    PRINT "EQUIPMENT:";I
40    PRINT "SALES PRICE";
50    INPUT S
60    LET C=S*.10
70    PRINT "COMMISSION:";C
80 NEXT I
99 END
```

Using the READ/DATA Statements

```
01 REM I--INDEX (NO. OF THE EQUIPMENT)
02 REM S--SALES PRICE
03 REM C--COMMISSION
```

```
10 FOR I=1 TO 3 STEP 1
20    READ S
30    DATA 1200,1500,1300
40    LET C=S*.10
50    PRINT
60    PRINT "EQUIPMENT:";I
70    PRINT "SALES PRICE:";S
80    PRINT "COMMISSION:";C
90 NEXT I
99 END
```

6.2 VARIATIONS—INITIAL VALUE AND TEST VALUE

The initial value and the test value need not always be written as in Section 6.1. There are a number of variations in their codings which give greater flexibility to the writing of programs.

I. The initial value and the test value may be represented by variables that have been assigned values prior to their use in the FOR statement. On many computer systems, these variables must be different than the index. Some versions of BASIC do not allow the initial value and/or the test value to be altered inside the loop. What does your computer print when you RUN the following programs?

1. Initial value changed within the loop

```
10 LET A=1
20 LET B=10
30 FOR I=A TO B STEP 1
40    LET A=A+3
50    PRINT I,A
60 NEXT I
99 END
```

2. Test value changed within the loop

```
10 LET A=1
20 LET B=10
30 FOR I=A TO B STEP 1
40    LET B=B+2
50    PRINT I,B
60 NEXT I
99 END
```

II. On many computer systems, the initial value and the test value may be negative, zero, or fractional (decimal values). Here are some examples.

```
10 FOR I=5 TO 8 STEP 1
40 FOR I=.5 TO 8.5 STEP 1
30 FOR I=0 TO 10 STEP 1
60 FOR I=-4 TO 0 STEP 1
50 FOR I=-8.5 TO -1.5 STEP 1
```

Some versions of BASIC will truncate a decimal value to the next lower integer. For example, .5 becomes 0, 8.5 becomes 8, and − 8.5 becomes − 9. When all the parts of the FOR statement have been discussed, a sample program will show you how the desired results can be obtained if your computer system truncates the decimal numbers in a FOR statement.

III. An expression may be used as the initial value and/or test value. Any variable in the expression must be assigned a value prior to its use in the FOR statement, and on many computer systems it must be different than the index. The following FOR statements have the same initial value and the same test value.

(a) `20 FOR I=1 TO 3`

    Initial value = 1
    Test value = 3

(b) `10 LET A=2`
    `20 FOR I=A/2 TO A+1`

    Initial value = A/2 = 2/2 = 1
    Test value = A + 1 = 2 + 1 = 3

6.2 VARIATIONS—INITIAL VALUE AND TEST VALUE—Sample Programs

The following programs demonstrate the three variations discussed in this section. Each program prints the numbers 0, 1, 2, 3, 4 and the squares of these numbers (0, 1, 4, 9, 16), as shown in the RUN below.

```
RUN

0        0
1        1
2        4
3        9
4        16
```

1. Variables used as initial and test values

```
10 PRINT                    — Leaves a blank line.
20 LET A=0                  — Initializes A to 0.
30 LET B=4                  — Initializes B to 4.
40 FOR I=A TO B STEP 1      — Sets up a loop, using A as the initial value and B as the
                              test value.
50    LET Y=I↑2             — Squares the index and stores the result in Y.
60    PRINT I,Y             — Prints the value of the index and its square.
70 NEXT I                   — Transfers control to line 40.
99 END                      — Terminates program execution.
```

2. Initial value different than one

```
10 PRINT                    — Leaves a blank line.
20 FOR I=0 TO 4 STEP 1      — Sets up a loop with the initial value set to 0.
30    LET Y=I↑2             — Squares the index and stores the result in Y.
40    PRINT I,Y             — Prints the value of the index and its square.
50 NEXT I                   — Transfers control to line 20.
99 END                      — Terminates program execution.
```

3. Expressions used as initial and test values

```
10 PRINT                    — Leaves a blank line.
20 LET A=5                  — Initializes A to 5.
30 FOR I=A-5 TO A-1 STEP 1  — Sets up a loop using expressions to set the initial
                              and test values to 0 and 4 respectively.
40    LET Y=I↑2             — Squares the index and stores the result in Y.
50    PRINT I,Y             — Prints the value of the index and its square.
60 NEXT I                   — Transfers control to line 30.
99 END                      — Terminates program execution.
```

6.2 VARIATIONS—INITIAL VALUE AND TEST VALUE—Your Turn

1. State the error in the program shown below.

```
10 PRINT
20 READ A,B
30 DATA 6,10
```

```
40 FOR I=A/3-1 TO C/2+1
50    LET J=I↑2
60    PRINT I,J
70 NEXT I
99 END
```

2. What is the RUN of the following program?

```
10 PRINT
20 FOR I=1 TO 3
30    READ A
40    DATA 7,8,9
50    LET B=A-I↑2
60    PRINT I,A,B
70 NEXT I
99 END
```

3. Trace through the logic of the program shown below, then answer the following questions.

    (a) How many times will the loop be performed?
    (b) What is the output of the program?
    (c) Suppose the data statement is changed to **3O DATA 8,12**. What value will be assigned to **J** the last time the loop is executed?

```
10 PRINT
20 READ X,Y
30 DATA 16,20
40 FOR I=X TO Y STEP 1
50    LET J=I-1
60    LET K=I-2
70    PRINT I,J,K
80 NEXT I
99 END
```

4. What RUN does the following program produce?

```
10 PRINT
20 FOR I=-6.5 TO -4.5 STEP 1
30    LET J=I*2
40    PRINT J
50 NEXT I
99 END
```

5. A clothier is offering a 20% discount on all items in the store. If you purchased a coat, a jacket, and a pair of gloves regularly priced at $190, $80, and $12.50 respectively, what amount did you save on each item? What was the reduced price of each item and what was the total amount of your bill?

(a) Use a FOR/NEXT loop to keep track of the input (the three articles).
(b) Use variables to represent the initial value and the test value.
(c) Use the index to print the number of the article.
(d) Use the READ/DATA statements to enter the marked price of each article.
(e) Amount Saved = Marked Price × .20
(f) Reduced Price = Marked Price − Amount Saved
(g) Total Bill = Total Bill + Reduced Price

```
RUN

ARTICLE 1              MARKED PRICE 190
AMOUNT SAVED 38
REDUCED PRICE 152

ARTICLE 2              MARKED PRICE 80
AMOUNT SAVED 16
REDUCED PRICE 64

ARTICLE 3              MARKED PRICE 12.5
AMOUNT SAVED 2.5
REDUCED PRICE 10

TOTAL BILL 226
```

Problem 5

T	— TOTAL BILL		
I	— INDEX (NO. OF THE ARTICLE)	S	— AMOUNT SAVED
M	— MARKED PRICE	R	— REDUCED PRICE

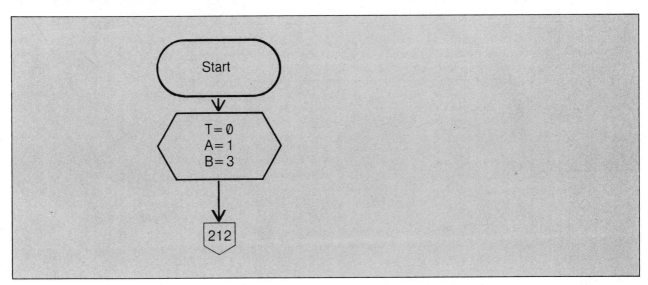

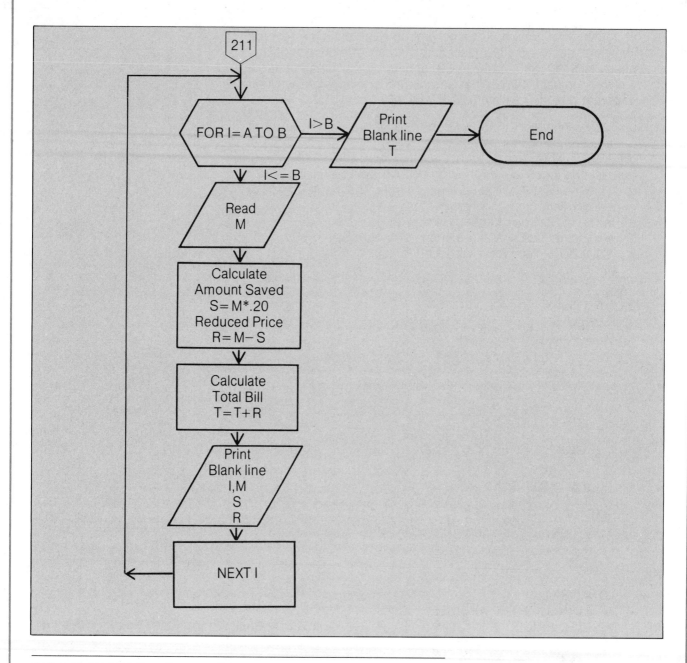

6.2 VARIATIONS—INITIAL VALUE AND TEST VALUE—Solutions for "Your Turn"

1. Variable **C** has not been assigned a value prior to the FOR statement.

2.

```
RUN

1        7        6
2        8        4
3        9        0
```

3. (a) $\left(\dfrac{20-16}{1}\right) + 1 = \left(\dfrac{4}{1}\right) + 1 = 4+1 = 5$

(b) RUN

```
16          15          14
17          16          15
18          17          16
19          18          17
20          19          18
```

(c) 11

4. Answers will vary depending on whether or not the decimal numbers for the initial value and the test value are truncated.

(a) **Decimal Numbers Not Truncated**   (b) **Decimal Numbers Truncated to Next Lower Integer**

```
RUN                      RUN

-13                       -14
-11                       -12
-9                        -10
```

5.

```
01 REM T--TOTAL BILL
02 REM I--INDEX (NO. OF THE ARTICLE)
03 REM M--MARKED PRICE
04 REM S--AMOUNT SAVED
05 REM R--REDUCED PRICE

10 LET T=0
20 LET A=1
30 LET B=3
40 FOR I=A TO B STEP 1
50    READ M
60    DATA 190,80,12.50
70    LET S=M*.20
80    LET R=M-S
90    LET T=T+R
100   PRINT
110   PRINT "ARTICLE";I,"MARKED PRICE";M
120   PRINT "AMOUNT SAVED";S
130   PRINT "REDUCED PRICE";R
140 NEXT I
150 PRINT
160 PRINT "TOTAL BILL";T
999 END
```

6.3 VARIATIONS—STEP CLAUSE

To provide even greater flexibility in programming, the value in the STEP clause is not always restricted to 1. It may be a multiple of 1, a decimal fraction, or a negative number. It may also be a variable or an expression. If the value is not 1, the STEP clause must be coded in the FOR statement.

1. The step value may be a variable or an expression

(a) The step value as a variable.

```
10 LET C=1
20 FOR I=1 TO 3 STEP C
```

(b) The step value as an expression.

```
10 LET C=4
20 FOR I=1 TO 3 STEP C/4
```

Notice in the above examples that the variable is assigned a value prior to its use in the STEP clause and that the variable is different than the one representing the index. As with the index, the initial value, and the test value, the step value should not be changed within the loop.

2. The step value may be a multiple of one

```
10 FOR I=1 TO 6 STEP 2
```

In this example, the index is increased by 2 each time the computer passes through the loop. When the value of the index becomes 7 (1,3,5,7), this value exceeds the test value and looping terminates.

3. The step value may be a decimal fraction

```
10 FOR I=1 TO 3 STEP .5
```

The index, in this example, is incremented by .5 each time the loop is executed (1,1.5,2,2.5,3,3.5). When the value of the index reaches 3.5, its value is greater than the test value, and the loop terminates. Note that this example may cause problems if the computer truncates the step value of .5 to zero and zero increments are not accepted.

4. The step value may be negative

```
10 FOR I=6 TO 3 STEP -1
```

In this FOR statement, the initial value is greater than the test value. The index is set to 6, then decreases by 1 each time the computer passes through the loop. When the value of the index is less than 3 (6,5,4,3,2), the value is less than the test value and looping terminates. It should be mentioned that going backward from 6 to 3 results in the same number of executions as going forward from 3 to 6. The loop is performed four times in each case.

```
10 FOR I=6 TO 3 STEP -1  ⎱
50 FOR I=3 TO 6 STEP 1   ⎰ ←—— Loop performed
                              four times
```

5. The following calculates the number of times a loop is executed when the step value is different than one

```
10 FOR I=1 TO 10 STEP 2
```

I takes on the values 1,3,5,7,9,11. The loop is not performed when **I** = 11, since 11 is greater than the test value. This means that the loop is executed five times (when I= 1,3,5,7,9). The formula is used below to determine the number of times the loop is performed.

$$\left(\frac{n_2 - n_1}{n_3}\right) + 1 = \left(\frac{10-1}{2}\right) + 1 = \left(\frac{9}{2}\right) + 1 = 4+1 = 5$$

Notice that the division operation does not give an integer result (9÷2= 4.5). In a case such as this, the decimal portion is dropped (.5 of 4.5) and the integer part (4) is retained.

6.3 VARIATIONS—STEP CLAUSE—Sample Programs

Step clauses with values that are multiples of one and those with variables or expressions are relatively easy to understand. The ones with fractional values and negative values may be a little more difficult. The sample programs shown below use the last two features.

1. Suppose you wish to borrow $4000 and would like to know the amounts of interest at rates of 12%, 13%, and 14%. Here is the program.

(a) Use the LET statement to enter the amount to be borrowed.
(b) Use a FOR/NEXT loop to generate the interest rates.
(c) Use a fractional value in the STEP clause.
(d) Interest = Amount × Rate (index)

```
10 LET A=4000              — Initializes A to 4000.
20 PRINT                   — Leaves a blank line.
30 PRINT "AMOUNT:";A       — Prints the amount to be borrowed.
40 FOR R=.12 TO .14 STEP .01  — Sets up a loop which initializes the rate to .12
                             then increments the rate by .01.
50    LET I=A*R            — Calculates the interest.
60    PRINT                — Leaves a blank line.
70    PRINT "RATE:";R      — Prints the rate of interest.
80    PRINT "INTEREST:";I  — Prints the amount of interest.
90 NEXT R                  — Transfers control to line 40.
99 END                     — Terminates program execution.

RUN

AMOUNT: 4000

RATE: .12
INTEREST: 480

RATE: .13
INTEREST: 520

RATE: .14
INTEREST: 560
```

For computer systems that truncate the decimal numbers in the FOR statement, the above program can be modified as follows.

```
(a) Change line 40 to  40 FOR J=12 TO 14 STEP 1
(b) Add line 45        45 LET R=J/100
(c) Change line 90 to  90 NEXT J
```

With each pass through the loop, the required interest rate is obtained in line 45 by the division of 100 into the current value of **J**.

The first time through the loop J = 12.   R = J/100 = 12/100 = .12
The second time through the loop J = 13.   = 13/100 = .13
The third time through the loop J = 14.   = 14/100 = .14

2. This program prints numbers in a decreasing sequence from 25 to 10 in steps of 5.

```
10 PRINT
20 FOR I=25 TO 10 STEP -5

30    PRINT I,  ◄────── Remember the comma and the semicolon in Chapter Two?
40 NEXT I                When either one is placed at the end of a PRINT statement, the
99 END                   numbers are printed on the same line.

RUN

  25          20          15          10
```

If the PRINT statement had ended with a semicolon, the output would have been:

```
RUN

 25  20  15  10
```

6.3 VARIATIONS—STEP CLAUSE—Your Turn[1]

1. How many times will the loop be performed for each of the following FOR statements?

   (a) 10 FOR I=1 TO 8 STEP 2
   (b) 30 FOR I=8 TO 1 STEP -2
   (c) 50 FOR I=.10 TO .15 STEP .01

2. What values will the index take on in each of the following FOR statements? Do not include the value that terminates the loop.

   (a) FOR I=450 TO 600 STEP 50
   (b) FOR I=7 TO 15 STEP 3
   (c) FOR I=.5 TO 3 STEP .5
   (d) FOR I=-8 TO 8 STEP 3
   (e) FOR I=14 TO 0 STEP -2

1. Exercises that use decimal numbers in the FOR statement may be omitted if your computer system truncates these numbers.

3. Fill in the blanks in the following program.

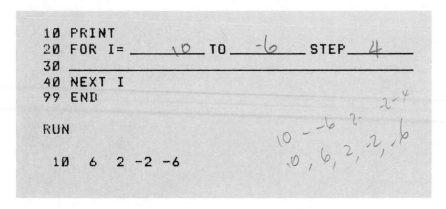

```
10 PRINT
20 FOR I = ____10____ TO ____-6____ STEP____4____
30 _____
40 NEXT I
99 END

RUN

   10   6   2  -2  -6
```

4. State the error in the program shown below.

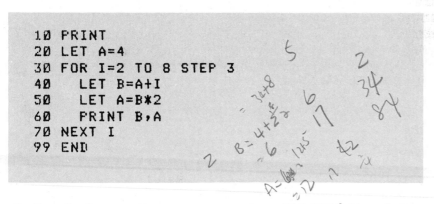

```
10 PRINT
20 READ A,B
30 DATA 20,10
40 FOR I=A TO B STEP 2
50    PRINT I
60 NEXT I
99 END
```

5. What is the RUN of the following program?

```
10 PRINT
20 LET A=4
30 FOR I=2 TO 8 STEP 3
40    LET B=A+I
50    LET A=B*2
60    PRINT B,A
70 NEXT I
99 END
```

6. Rewrite the sample program on pages 215-216.[2] Here is the problem once more, but with different interest rates.

Suppose you wish to borrow $4000 and would like to know the amounts of interest at rates of 10%, 12%, and 14%.

(a) Use the LET statement to enter the amount to be borrowed.
(b) Use variables to represent the initial, test, and step values. Enter these values into the computer by means of the READ/DATA statements.

2. Use whole numbers in the FOR statements of your programs if your computer system truncates the decimal values, then convert the index to the required decimal numbers as shown on page 216.

(c) Use a FOR/NEXT loop to generate the interest rates.
(d) Use a fractional value in the STEP clause.
(e) Interest = Amount × Rate (index)
(f) Draw a flowchart before you write the program.

```
RUN

AMOUNT: 4000

RATE: .1
INTEREST: 400

RATE: .12
INTEREST: 480

RATE: .14
INTEREST: 560
```

7. Write a program that prints the numbers 30, 28, 26, 24, 22, and 20 in a column as shown below. Use a FOR/NEXT loop.

```
RUN

30
28
26
24
22
20
```

6.3 VARIATIONS—STEP CLAUSE—Solutions for "Your Turn"

1. (a) $\left(\dfrac{8-1}{2}\right) + 1 = \left(\dfrac{7}{2}\right) + 1 = 3 + 1 = 4$

   (b) $\left(\dfrac{1-8}{-2}\right) + 1 = \left(\dfrac{-7}{-2}\right) + 1 = 3 + 1 = 4$

   (c) $\left(\dfrac{.15-.10}{.01}\right) + 1 = \left(\dfrac{15-10}{01}\right) + 1 = \left(\dfrac{5}{1}\right) + 1 = 5 + 1 = 6$

2. (a) I = 450,500,550,600
   (b) I = 7,10,13
   (c) I = .5,1,1.5,2,2.5,3
   (d) I = −8,−5,−2,1,4,7
   (e) I = 14,12,10,8,6,4,2,0

3.

```
20 FOR I=10 TO -6 STEP -4
30    PRINT I;
```

4. The step value should be −2.

5.

```
RUN

   6          12
  17          34
  42          84
```

6.

```
01 REM A--AMOUNT
02 REM X--INITIAL VALUE
03 REM Y--TEST VALUE
04 REM Z--STEP VALUE              Decimal numbers truncated
05 REM R--RATE (INDEX)           in the FOR statement.
06 REM I--INTEREST

10 LET A=4000
20 READ X,Y,Z
30 DATA .10,.14,.02 ──────────→ 30 DATA 10,14,2
40 PRINT
50 PRINT "AMOUNT:";A
60 FOR R=X TO Y STEP Z ─────→  60 FOR J=X TO Y STEP Z
70    LET I=A*R                 65    LET R=J/100
80    PRINT
90    PRINT "RATE:";R
100   PRINT "INTEREST:";I
110 NEXT R ──────────────────→ 110 NEXT J
999 END
```

Problem 6

A — AMOUNT
X — INITIAL VALUE
Y — TEST VALUE
Z — STEP VALUE
R — RATE (INDEX)
I — INTEREST

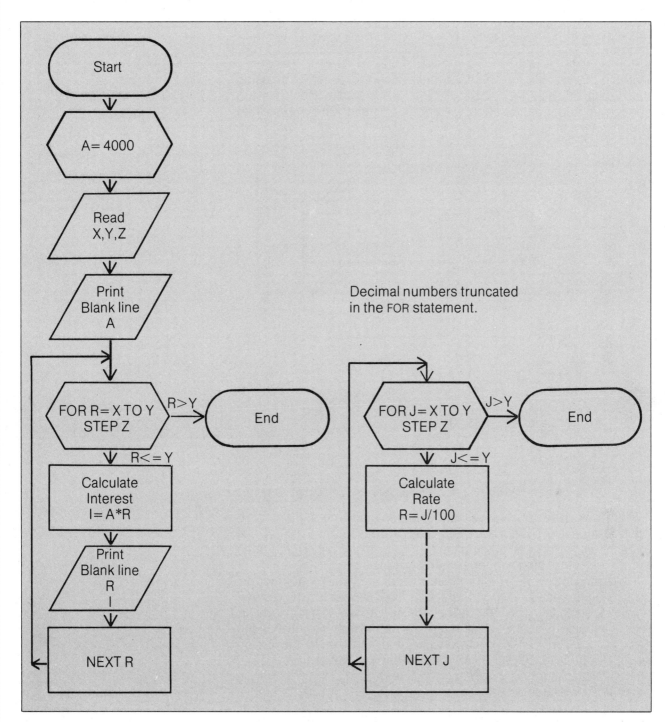

Decimal numbers truncated in the FOR statement.

7.

```
.10 PRINT
20 FOR I=30 TO 20 STEP -2
30   PRINT I
40 NEXT I
99 END
```

6.4 NESTED LOOPS

In some programs it may be necessary to control routines by using more than one FOR/NEXT loop. Here is an example. Don't be too concerned about all the PRINT statements. These will be explained later on in the section.

```
 10  FOR I=1 TO 3
 20    PRINT
 30    PRINT 'I =';I
 40    FOR J=1 TO 4
 50      PRINT 'J =';J;
 60    NEXT J
 70    PRINT
 80  NEXT I
 99  END

RUN

I = 1
J = 1 J = 2 J = 3 J = 4

I = 2
J = 1 J = 2 J = 3 J = 4

I = 3
J = 1 J = 2 J = 3 J = 4
```

First, look at the RUN. Notice that **J** changes much more often than **I**. While **I** is equal to 1, **J** changes four times (from 1 to 2 to 3 to 4). Once **J** reaches 4, **I** changes to 2 and the four values of **J** are printed once more. The same thing happens when **I** is equal to 3.

How does this work in the program? There are two FOR/NEXT loops, one inside the other. In computer terms they are **nested**. The slow-moving loop (in this case, **I**) is on the outside; the fast-moving loop (**J**) is on the inside. The first time through the outer loop, **I** is initialized to 1 in line 10. While **I** remains at this value, **J** is initialized to 1 in line 40 and its loop (lines 40, 50, and 60) causes **J** to change from 1 to 4. Once **J** has reached its limit, control is transferred to line 70 and the computer proceeds to line 80. Now it's **I**'s turn to change. **I** is increased to 2 and the computer goes back to line 10. While **I** is equal to 2, **J** reverts to 1 (line 40) and goes through its cycle once more (**J** = 1,2,3,4). Again, when **J**'s limit is reached, control is transferred to line 70 and the computer proceeds to line 80. **I** is increased to 3 and control is transferred to the top of the **I** loop (line 10). **J** reverts to 1 (line 40) and goes through its loop for the third time. When **J** has reached its limit, **I** is increased to 4 and the computer branches back to line 10. This time, the value of **I** is greater than the test value and control is transferred to the statement following **NEXT I**, which is the END statement.

The program segments below are labelled to show you what happens each time the computer goes through the **I** loop.

```
 10  FOR I=1 TO 3
 20     --
 30     --
 40     FOR J=1 TO 4                    I = 1
 50     --
 60     NEXT J                 J = 1,2,3,4
 70     --
 80  NEXT I
 99  END
```

```
 10  FOR I=1 TO 3
 20     --
 30     --
 40     FOR J=1 TO 4                    I = 2
 50     --
 60     NEXT J                 J = 1,2,3,4
 70     --
 80  NEXT I
 99  END
```

```
 10  FOR I=1 TO 3
 20     --
 30     --
 40     FOR J=1 TO 4                    I = 3
 50     --
 60     NEXT J                 J = 1,2,3,4
 70     --
 80  NEXT I
 99  END
```

The program on page 222 has two loops, one nested inside the other. It is possible to have several levels of loops. There is usually a limit to the number of levels, the number depending on the version of BASIC being used. Check your manual to see how many levels your computer allows.

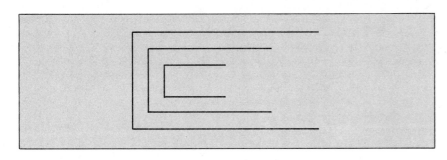

It is also possible to have several inner loops nested inside one outer loop.

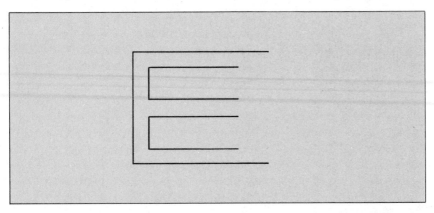

In addition to the rules for single loops, there are a number of restrictions that must be observed when using nested loops.

1. Each FOR/NEXT pair of statements must have its own index variable. On some computer systems, the variable after the key word **NEXT** may be left out. However, this may cause some confusion, particularly when there are several loops in a program. Therefore, it's probably well worth the effort to type it in.
2. A loop may not cross over (overlap) another loop.

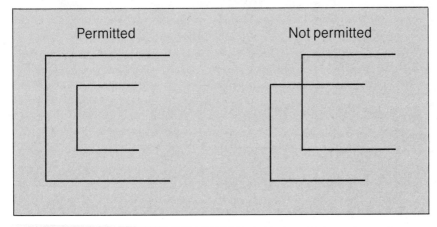

3. It is possible to transfer control from a point within an inner loop to a statement outside the loop. However, the reverse is not possible. You may not transfer control from a point outside the inner loop to a statement inside.

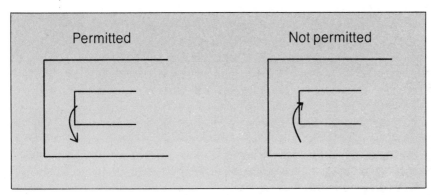

How does one calculate the number of times an inner loop is performed? Use the program segment shown below.

```
10 FOR I=1 TO 3
20    FOR J=1 TO 4
--
70    NEXT J
80 NEXT I
99 END
```

Each time the outer loop is executed, the inner loop is performed four times. Since the outer loop is executed three times, the inner loop will be performed $3 \times 4 = 12$ times. Using the formula:

Outer loop: $\left(\dfrac{n_2 - n_1}{n_3}\right) + 1 = \left(\dfrac{3-1}{1}\right) + 1 = \left(\dfrac{2}{1}\right) + 1 = 2+1 = 3$

$$3 \times 4 = 12$$

Inner loop: $\left(\dfrac{n_2 - n_1}{n_3}\right) + 1 = \left(\dfrac{4-1}{1}\right) + 1 = \left(\dfrac{3}{1}\right) + 1 = 3+1 = 4$

Sometimes calculations within the inner loop accumulate. An example is the addition of the monthly salaries of each of several employees to get a yearly salary. This total should not be carried over into another employee's calculations. If the outer loop keeps track of the employees, then initialization of each employee's total salary to zero should be done right after the outer loop is set up, that is, between the two FOR statements. Part of the program for the above problem might look something like this:

```
01 REM N--EMPLOYEE NUMBER
02 REM T--TOTAL SALARY
03 REM S--MONTHLY SALARY

10 FOR N=1 TO 3
20    LET T=0          —Initializes each employee's total yearly salary to zero before the
30    --                  total is calculated.
40    FOR M=1 TO 12
--
100      LET T=T+S —Calculates the total yearly salary of each employee.
```

6.4 NESTED LOOPS—Sample Programs

Nested loops are often used to print tables such as multiplication tables or interest tables. Here is a program that prints the multiplication table for the numbers 1, 2, and 3. It also gives you an opportunity to apply what you learned in Chapter Two about commas and sem-icolons placed at the end of PRINT statements. Statements are explained after the RUN.

```
01 REM R--ROW (ROWS GO ACROSS)
02 REM C--COLUMN (COLUMNS GO DOWN)
03 REM P--PRODUCT

10 PRINT
20 PRINT "           1   2   3"
30 PRINT
40 FOR R=1 TO 3
50    PRINT R,
60    FOR C=1 TO 3
70       LET P=R*C
80       PRINT P;
90    NEXT C
100   PRINT
110 NEXT R
999 END

RUN

           1   2   3

   1       1   2   3
   2       2   4   6
   3       3   6   9
```

Line 10 — Leaves a blank line after the word RUN.
Line 20 — Prints the heading **1 2 3**. Notice the eleven spaces before the numbers. This causes the numbers **1 2 3** to be centred over their appropriate columns.
Line 30 — Leaves a blank line after the heading.
Line 40 — Sets up a loop for the three rows.
Line 50 — Prints the number of the row. This statement is placed between the two FOR statements so that the only time the row number is printed is when **R** changes. The comma causes the next PRINT statement to print values on the same line as the row number.
Line 60 — Sets up the loop for the three columns.
Line 70 — Multiplies the row number by the column number. Since the values of both **R** and **C** are 1, the result is 1 (Row **1** × Column **1**). This is stored in **P**.
Line 80 — Prints the value of **P**. The semicolon causes the values of **P** to be printed on the same line. The output so far is:

                    1   1

Line 90 — The column number changes from 1 to 2. Control is transferred back to line 60 and the **C** loop is executed a second time.

The result of line 70 is 2 (Row **1** × Column **2**). The output so far is:

$$1 \qquad 1\ 2$$

Line 90 is reached once more, and the column number changes from 2 to 3. Control is transferred back to line 60 and the **C** loop is executed for the third and last time. The result of line 70 is 3 (Row **1** × Column **3**). The output so far is:

$$1 \qquad 1\ 2\ 3$$

C is increased to 4. Since this is higher than the test value, control is transferred to line 100.

Line 100 — This PRINT statement counteracts the semicolon in **PRINT P;**. The next value will be printed on a new line.

Line 110 — The row number now changes to 2 and **C** reverts to 1. The whole cycle is repeated, starting with the printing of the new row number on the next line. Looping continues until **R** is greater than 3. Control is then transferred to the END statement, which terminates the program.

PRINT statements in a program that contains nested loops are often confusing. Here are two programs that add the numbers 2, 3, and 4 to each of the numbers 1, 2, 3, and 4. The first one single spaces its output; the second one double spaces the output.

1. Output single spaced

```
10  PRINT
20  FOR I=2 TO 4
30     FOR J=1 TO 4
40        LET K=I+J
50        PRINT K;
60     NEXT J
70     PRINT — Counteracts the semicolon in PRINT K;
80  NEXT I
99  END

RUN

   3   4   5   6
   4   5   6   7
   5   6   7   8
```

2. Output double spaced

```
10  FOR I=2 TO 4
20     PRINT — Leaves a blank line before each row.
30     FOR J=1 TO 4
```

```
40      LET K=I+J
50      PRINT K;
60    NEXT J
70      PRINT —Counteracts the semicolon in PRINT K;
80  NEXT I
99  END

RUN

  3   4   5   6

  4   5   6   7

  5   6   7   8
```

In both programs, the statement **50 PRINT K;** causes items to be printed on the same line. The **PRINT** in line 70 counteracts the semicolon in **PRINT K;** and forces the computer off the line so that the next item (which starts a new row) is printed on a new line. Program 2 has a PRINT statement between the two FOR statements, and the one at the beginning of the program is eliminated. This **PRINT** leaves a blank line before each row. To be consistent, the **PRINT** that counteracts the semicolon will be kept between the NEXT statements. The one that leaves a blank line before each row will be placed between the FOR statements. If output is to be single spaced, the first **PRINT** will be placed at the beginning of the program rather than between the FOR statements. Also, most of the remaining flowcharts will include symbols for "blank" **PRINT**s.

6.4 NESTED LOOPS—Your Turn

I. Problem 2 on page 142 in Chapter Four gave the total number of parts produced by each of three employees for the XYZ Manufacturing Company. In this problem, you are to find these totals as well as the income for each employee. The rate paid is $2 for each part produced.

Employee	Parts Produced Per Day
1	42,41,44,45,40
2	43,42,45,43,40
3	43,39,44,42,41

(a) Use an outer FOR/NEXT loop to keep track of the three employees.
(b) Use an inner FOR/NEXT loop to keep track of the days.
(c) Between the two FOR statements, initialize to zero a variable that represents the total number of parts produced by each employee.

(d) Use the READ/DATA statements to enter the number of parts produced by each employee.

(e) Total Number of Parts = Total Number of Parts + Parts Produced in One Day

(f) Income = Total Number of Parts × Rate

(g) Fill in the missing lines.

```
01 REM R--RATE
02 REM T--TOTAL NO. OF PARTS
03 REM N--EMPLOYEE NUMBER
04 REM D--DAY
05 REM P--PARTS PRODUCED PER DAY
06 REM I--INCOME

10 LET R=2
20
30    LET T=0
40
50       READ P
60
70
80
90
100   NEXT D
110
120   PRINT
130
140
150
160
999 END

RUN

EMPLOYEE: 1
PARTS: 212
INCOME: 424

EMPLOYEE: 2
PARTS: 213
INCOME: 426

EMPLOYEE: 3
PARTS: 209
INCOME: 418
```

1. Which statement should be coded in line 20?

```
(a) FOR D=1 TO 5
(b) FOR R=1 TO 3
```

```
(c) FOR N=1 TO 5
(d) FOR D=1 TO 3
(e) FOR N=1 TO 3
```

2. Which statement should be coded in line 40?

```
(a) FOR N=1 TO 5
(b) FOR D=1 TO 3
(c) FOR T=1 TO 5
(d) FOR D=1 TO 5
(e) FOR N=1 TO 3
```

3. Complete lines 60, 70, and 80 with DATA statements (one DATA statement for each employee).
4. Which statement should be coded in line 90?

```
(a) LET T=T+P
(b) LET T=T*P
(c) LET T=T*R
(d) LET I=T+P
(e) LET I=T*P
```

5. Which statement should be coded in line 110?

```
(a) LET I=T+R
(b) LET I=T+I
(c) LET I=T*R
(d) LET I=I*R
(e) LET I=I*T
```

6. Complete lines 130, 140, and 150 with PRINT statements.

7. Which statement should be coded in line 160?

```
(a) GO TO 20
(b) IF N>3 THEN 20
(c) NEXT N
(d) NEXT,N
(e) NEXT N+3
```

II. Two salespersons receive a commission of 20% on their sales. Based on the sales shown below, what commission does each salesperson receive each month? What total commission does each salesperson earn for the three months?

Salesperson	Sales Each Month
1	7000,6000,6500
2	8000,7500,6000

(a) Use an outer FOR/NEXT loop to keep track of the salespersons.
(b) Use an inner FOR/NEXT loop to keep track of the months.
(c) Between the two FOR statements, initialize to zero a variable that represents each salesperson's total commission. Also code the PRINT statement that prints the number of a salesperson.
(d) Use the READ/DATA statements to enter the sales.
(e) Commission = Sales × .20
(f) Print the number of the month alongside the commission.
(g) Total Commission = Total Commission + Commission Per Month
(h) The flowchart on page 232 illustrates how the two loops are nested. The inner loop goes through its cycle as long as **M** is less than or equal to 3. Once **M** is greater than 3, control re-enters the outer loop. This loop terminates when **N** is greater than 2.

```
RUN

SALESPERSON: 1
COMMISSION 1          1400
COMMISSION 2          1200
COMMISSION 3          1300
TOTAL COMMISSION: 3900

SALESPERSON: 2
COMMISSION 1          1600
COMMISSION 2          1500
COMMISSION 3          1200
TOTAL COMMISSION: 4300
```

6.4 NESTED LOOPS—Solutions for "Your Turn"

I.

```
1. (e) 20 FOR N=1 TO 3
2. (d) 40 FOR D=1 TO 5
3.     60 DATA 42,41,44,45,40
       70 DATA 43,42,45,43,40
       80 DATA 43,39,44,42,41
4. (a) 90 LET T=T+P
5. (c) 110 LET I=T*R
```

Problem II

N — NO. OF SALESPERSON   S — SALES
T — TOTAL COMMISSION   C — COMMISSION
M — MONTH

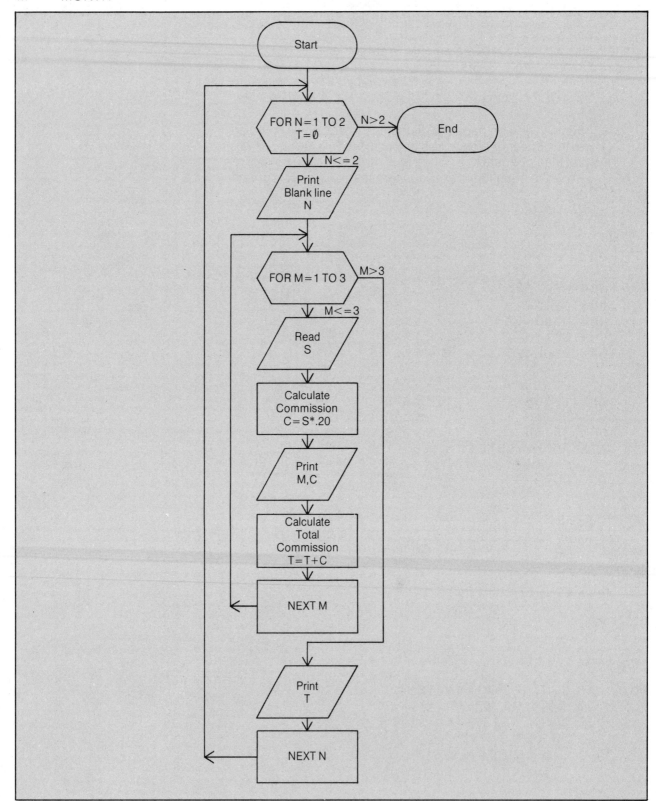

```
6. 130 PRINT "EMPLOYEE:";N
   140 PRINT "PARTS:";T
   150 PRINT "INCOME:";I
7. (c) 160 NEXT N
```

II.

```
01 REM N--NO. OF SALESPERSON
02 REM T--TOTAL COMMISSION
03 REM M--MONTH
04 REM S--SALES
05 REM C--COMMISSION

10 FOR N=1 TO 2
20    LET T=0
30    PRINT
40    PRINT "SALESPERSON:";N
50    FOR M=1 TO 3
60       READ S
70       DATA 7000,6000,6500
80       DATA 8000,7500,6000
90       LET C=S*.20
100      PRINT "COMMISSION";M,C
110      LET T=T+C
120   NEXT M
130   PRINT "TOTAL COMMISSION:";T
140 NEXT N
999 END
```

6.5 A WAGE PROGRAM

Here is the wage program once more. The data shown in Chapter Five on page 176 will be used. A FOR/NEXT loop terminates input rather than a counter. The index of the FOR statement represents the number of the employee.

Employee No.	Hrs. Worked	Rate	Income Tax Ded.	Union Dues	Pension Ded.
1	44	10.24	80	2	3.00
2	37	11.54	75	2	2.50
3	39	12.34	90	2	4.00

(a) Use a FOR/NEXT loop to keep track of the employees.
(b) Use the READ/DATA statements to enter the hours, rates, and deductions.
(c) Remarks are placed in strategic spots to help you understand the program.

(d) Blank lines have been inserted for clarity only.

(e) *Calculations*

    1. Gross Pay (no overtime) = Regular Hours × Regular Rate

    2. Gross Pay with overtime:

       — Overtime Hours = Regular Hours − 39

       — Overtime Rate = Regular Rate × 1.5

       — Overtime Pay = Overtime Hours × Overtime Rate

       — Gross Pay (with overtime) = 39 × Regular Rate + Overtime Pay

    3. Net Pay:

       — Total Deductions = Income Tax Deduction + Union Dues + Pension Deduction

       — Net Pay = Gross Pay − Total Deductions

```
01 REM E--INDEX (EMPLOYEE NUMBER)
02 REM H--REGULAR HOURS
03 REM R--REGULAR RATE
04 REM I--INCOME TAX DED.
05 REM U--UNION DUES
06 REM P--PENSION FUND DED.
07 REM H1--OVERTIME HOURS
08 REM R1--OVERTIME RATE
09 REM V--OVERTIME
10 REM G--GROSS PAY
11 REM D--DEDUCTIONS
12 REM N--NET PAY

100 REM SET UP A FOR/NEXT LOOP
105 FOR E=1 TO 3

200 REM READ HOURS,RATES,DEDUCTIONS
205 READ H,R,I,U,P
210 DATA 44,10.24,80,2,3
215 DATA 37,11.54,75,2,2.50
220 DATA 39,12.34,90,2,4

300 REM CHECK FOR OVERTIME
305 IF H>39 THEN 500

400 REM GROSS PAY--NO OVERTIME
405 LET H1=0
410 LET R1=0
415 LET V=0
420 LET G=H*R
425 GO TO 600

500 REM GROSS PAY--WITH OVERTIME
505 LET H1=H-39
510 LET R1=R*1.5
515 LET V=H1*R1
520 LET G=39*R+V

600 REM NET PAY
```

```
605 LET D=I+U+P
610 LET N=G-D

700 REM PRINT STATEMENTS
705 PRINT
710 PRINT "EMPLOYEE";E,"HRS";H,"RATE";R
715 PRINT "OVERTIME HOURS";H1
720 PRINT "OVERTIME RATE";R1
725 PRINT "OVERTIME PAY";V
730 PRINT "GROSS PAY";G
735 PRINT "INCOME TAX";I
740 PRINT "UNION DUES";U
745 PRINT "PENSION";P
750 PRINT "TOTAL DEDUCTIONS";D
755 PRINT "NET PAY";N

800 REM TRANSFER TO BEGINNING OF LOOP
805 NEXT E

999 END

RUN

EMPLOYEE 1            HRS 44     RATE 10.24
OVERTIME HOURS 5
OVERTIME RATE 15.36
OVERTIME PAY 76.8
GROSS PAY 476.16
INCOME TAX 80
UNION DUES 2
PENSION 3
TOTAL DEDUCTIONS 85
NET PAY 391.16

EMPLOYEE 2            HRS 37     RATE 11.54
OVERTIME HOURS 0
OVERTIME RATE 0
OVERTIME PAY 0
GROSS PAY 426.98
INCOME TAX 75
UNION DUES 2
PENSION 2.5
TOTAL DEDUCTIONS 79.5
NET PAY 347.48

EMPLOYEE 3            HRS 39     RATE 12.34
OVERTIME HOURS 0
OVERTIME RATE 0
OVERTIME PAY 0
GROSS PAY 481.26
INCOME TAX 90
UNION DUES 2
PENSION 4
```

```
TOTAL DEDUCTIONS 96
NET PAY 385.26
```

Wage Program

E	— INDEX (EMPLOYEE NUMBER)	H1	— OVERTIME HOURS
H	— REGULAR HOURS	R1	— OVERTIME RATE
R	— REGULAR RATE	V	— OVERTIME
I	— INCOME TAX DEDUCTED	G	— GROSS PAY
U	— UNION DUES	D	— DEDUCTIONS
P	— PENSION FUND DED.	N	— NET PAY

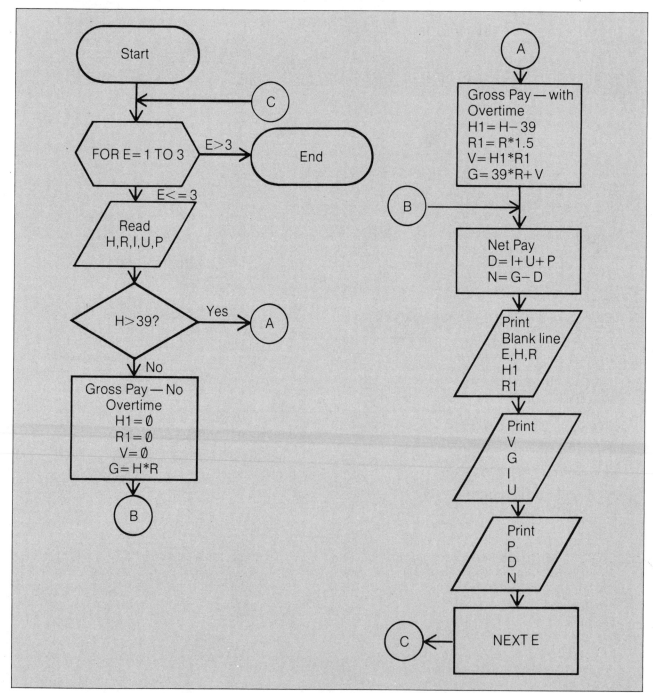

1. In the above program, what two statements control the loop?

```
**********************************
105 FOR E=1 TO 3
805 NEXT E
```

2. In the wage program in Chapter Five, page 177
   (a) What five statements are replaced by **105 FOR E=1 TO 3**?

```
**********************************
105 LET K=1
210 READ N1
215 DATA 3
805 LET K=K+1
810 IF K>N1 THEN 999
```

   (b) What statement is replaced by **805 NEXT E**?

```
**********************************
815 GO TO 225
```

A SHORT SUMMARY

FOR/NEXT statements provide another method of controlling loops. The general form of a FOR/NEXT loop is as follows.

```
            Index        Initial        Test        Step
                          value        value        value
             ↓             ↓            ↓            ↓
10 FOR       I    =       1    TO      3    STEP     1
20    --
30    --
40 NEXT I
50    --
```

The initial value, test value, and step value may also be written as variables or expressions. They may be positive, negative, fractional, and, except for the step value, may also be zero. However, some computers truncate a decimal value in the FOR statement. If the STEP clause is omitted, the increment is assumed to be one. The test value should be less than the initial value when the step value is negative. Although the index can be used inside a loop, some versions of BASIC do not allow its value to be altered within the loop. The same rule may apply to the initial, test, and step values. Control can be transferred from a point within the loop to a statement outside. However, the reverse is not permitted. Control must not be transferred from a point outside the loop to a statement inside.

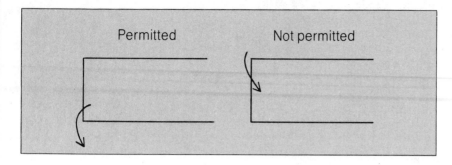

A FOR/NEXT loop can be nested inside another as long as the loops do not cross over (overlap).

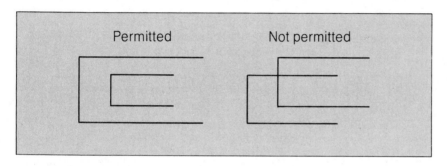

It is possible to have several inner loops nested inside one outer loop and to have several levels of looping, although there may be a limit as to the number of levels.

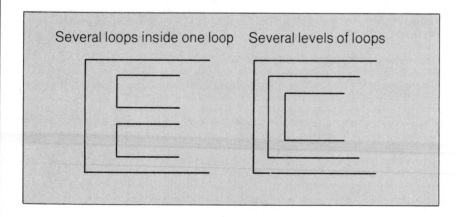

Questions and Exercises[3]

1. Display and label the general form of a FOR statement. State the purpose of each part of the statement.
2. What is the purpose of the NEXT statement?

3. Questions and exercises that use decimal numbers in the FOR statement may be omitted if your computer system truncates these numbers.

3. Using a simple program segment, explain how the computer executes a FOR/NEXT loop.

4. Identify the errors, if any, in the program segments shown below. Make the necessary corrections.

```
(a) 10  NEXT I              (d) 10  FOR L=1 TO 5
    20     --                   20     --
    30 FOR I=1 TO 10            30 NEXT L
                                40 GO TO 20

(b) 10 FOR J=1 TO 3         (e) 10 FOR M>10 TO 50
    20    READ K                20     --
    30    DATA 10,20,30         30 NEXT M
    40     --
    50 NEXT K

(c) 10 LET I=0              (f) 10 FOR N=10 STEP 1
    20 FOR J=1 TO 3             20     --
    30    LET K=I+JT4           30 NEXT N
    40     --
    50 NEXT J
```

5. How many times does your computer system execute a FOR/NEXT loop for each of the following FOR statements?

```
(a) 10 FOR A=1 TO 1 STEP 1
(b) 20 FOR B=1 TO 1 STEP -1
(c) 30 FOR C=1 TO 1 STEP 0
(d) 40 FOR D=1 TO 10 STEP 0
(e) 50 FOR E=10 TO 1 STEP 1
```

6. On your computer system, what value does the index take on *after* a FOR/NEXT loop is complete?

7. How many times will the FOR/NEXT loop be executed in each of the following program segments?

```
(a) 10 FOR P=1 TO 10 STEP 1   (d) 10 FOR S=10 TO 2 STEP -2
    20     --                     20     --
    30 NEXT P                     30 NEXT S

(b) 10 FOR Q=4 TO 26 STEP 2   (e) 10 FOR T=-9 TO 9 STEP 3
    20     --                     20     --
    30 NEXT Q                     30 NEXT T

(c) 10 FOR R=3 TO 21 STEP 4   (f) 10 FOR U=.5 TO 5 STEP .5
    20     --                     20     --
    30 NEXT R                     30 NEXT U
```

8. Identify the errors, if any, in the FOR statements shown below. Assume that the loop is to be executed more than once. Make the necessary corrections.

```
(a) 10 FOR I=3 TO 6 STEP -1       (f) 10 LET A=-6
                                      20 LET B=-12
                                      30 FOR N=A TO B

(b) 10 LET A=5                     (g) 10 FOR P=.1 TO 1 STEP .1
    20 FOR J=A TO B STEP 2

(c) 10 FOR K=5 TO 25               (h) 10 FOR Q=Q TO 10 STEP 5

(d) 10 FOR L=10 TO STEP 3          (i) 10 LET A=-1
                                      20 LET B=-20
                                      30 FOR R=A TO B-1 STEP -1

(e) 10 LET A=4                     (j) 10 LET A=36
    20 LET B=16                       20 FOR S=A/3 TO A/6
    30 FOR M=A TO M STEP 2
```

9. What is meant by a nested loop?
10. Identify the errors, if any, in the program segments shown below. Make the necessary corrections.

```
(a) 10 FOR I=5 TO 14 STEP 3       (d) 10 FOR I=1 TO 4
    20    FOR J=1 TO K STEP 1         20    FOR J=1 TO 5
    --                                30    --
    60    NEXT J                      40    NEXT J
    70 NEXT I                         50    GO TO 30
                                      60 NEXT I

(b) 10 FOR I=3 TO 7 STEP 2         (e) 10 FOR I=1 TO 10
    20    FOR J=1 TO 4                 20    FOR J=1 TO 14
    --                                --
    60    NEXT I                       60       LET K=J+I
    70 NEXT J                          70       IF K>20 THEN 140
                                       80    NEXT J
                                       90    --
                                       --
                                       130 NEXT I
                                       140 --

(c) 10 FOR I=3 TO 12 STEP 3        (f) 10 FOR I=.02 TO .08 STEP .02
    20    FOR J=5 TO 20 STEP 5         20    FOR J=.01 TO .04 STEP .01
    --                                --
    50    NEXT J                       60    IF J<=.04 THEN 20
    60    FOR K=1 TO 6                 70 NEXT I
    --
    90    NEXT K
    100 NEXT I
```

11. What values will the index take on in each of the following FOR statements? Do not include the value that terminates the loop.

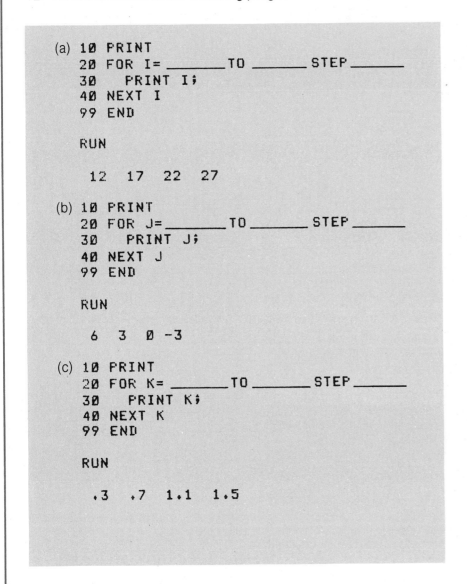

(a) 10 FOR A=3 TO 13 STEP 2
    --
    60 NEXT A

(b) 10 FOR B=15 TO 29 STEP 3
    --
    60 NEXT B

(c) 10 FOR C=32 TO 16 STEP -4
    --
    60 NEXT C

(d) 10 FOR D=10 TO -20 STEP -5
    --
    60 NEXT D

(e) 10 FOR E=-21 TO 9 STEP 6
    --
    60 NEXT E

(f) 10 FOR F=.2 TO .9 STEP .2
    --
    60 NEXT F

12. Fill in the blanks in the following programs.

```
(a) 10 PRINT
    20 FOR I= _____ TO _____ STEP _____
    30    PRINT I;
    40 NEXT I
    99 END

    RUN

     12   17   22   27
```

```
(b) 10 PRINT
    20 FOR J= _____ TO _____ STEP _____
    30    PRINT J;
    40 NEXT J
    99 END

    RUN

     6   3   0  -3
```

```
(c) 10 PRINT
    20 FOR K= _____ TO _____ STEP _____
    30    PRINT K;
    40 NEXT K
    99 END

    RUN

     .3   .7   1.1   1.5
```

13. How many times is the inner loop executed in the following program segment?

```
10 FOR I=1 TO 9 STEP 2
20    FOR J=1 TO 13 STEP 3
--
60    NEXT J
70 NEXT I
```

14. What is the output of each of the following programs?

```
(a) 10 FOR I=1 TO 3
    20    PRINT
    30    PRINT 'I ='¡I
    40    FOR J=2 TO 6 STEP 2
    50      PRINT 'J ='¡J,
    60    NEXT J
    70    PRINT
    80 NEXT I
    99 END
```

```
(b) 10 PRINT
    20 LET N=12
    30 FOR I=N TO 1 STEP -1
    40    FOR J=1 TO I STEP 1
    50      PRINT '*';
    60    NEXT J
    70    PRINT
    80 NEXT I
    99 END
```

Programming Problems[4]

1. Write a program that converts weekly wages of $350, $400, $450, and $500 to hourly rates based on a 40-hour week.
   (a) Use a FOR/NEXT loop to generate the weekly wages.
   (b) Hourly Rate $= \dfrac{\text{Weekly Wages (Index)}}{40}$

```
RUN

WEEKLY WAGES: 350
HOURLY RATE: 8.75
```

4. If your computer system truncates the decimal values in the FOR statement, use whole numbers then convert the index to the required decimal numbers as shown on page 216.

```
WEEKLY WAGES: 400
HOURLY RATE: 10

WEEKLY WAGES: 450
HOURLY RATE: 11.25

WEEKLY WAGES: 500
HOURLY RATE: 12.5
```

Problem 1

W — WEEKLY WAGES (INDEX)
H — HOURLY RATE

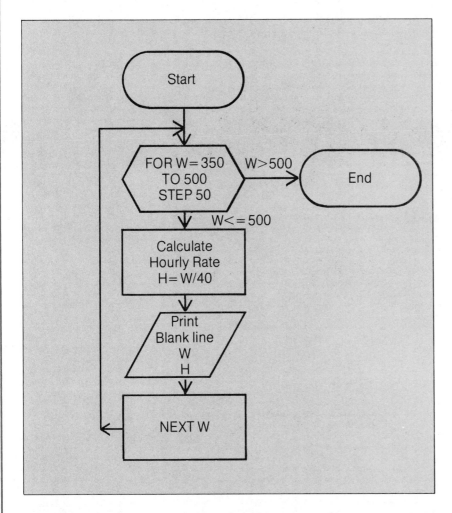

2. Companies A, B, and C, selling farm equipment, pay their salespersons commissions of $2000, $2200, and $2400 respectively on sales amounting to $10 000. What rate of commission is each company offering?
   (a) Use a LET statement to enter the sales.
   (b) Use a FOR/NEXT loop to generate the commissions paid.
   (c) Rate of Commission = $\dfrac{\text{Commission (Index)}}{\text{Sales}}$

```
RUN

SALES: 10000

COMMISSION: 2000
RATE OF COMMISSION: .2

COMMISSION: 2200
RATE OF COMMISSION: .22

COMMISSION: 2400
RATE OF COMMISSION: .24
```

3. Suppose your yearly salary is $19 000 and that at the end of every year your salary will be increased by $1000. What will your salary be after the sixth increase?
   (a) Use the LET statement to enter the initial salary.
   (b) Use a FOR/NEXT loop to keep track of the increases.
   (c) Salary = Salary + 1000

```
RUN

INITIAL SALARY: 19000

INCREASE: 1        SALARY: 20000
INCREASE: 2        SALARY: 21000
INCREASE: 3        SALARY: 22000
INCREASE: 4        SALARY: 23000
INCREASE: 5        SALARY: 24000
INCREASE: 6        SALARY: 25000
```

4. To each of the numbers 3, 4, and 5, add each of the numbers 1, 2, 3, and 4.
   (a) Use an outer FOR/NEXT loop to generate the numbers 3, 4, and 5.
   (b) Use an inner FOR/NEXT loop to generate the numbers 1, 2, 3, and 4.
   (c) Add the indexes of the two FOR statements and store the result in another variable.

```
RUN

    4   5   6   7
    5   6   7   8
    6   7   8   9
```

5. Find the total sales for each of the three stores shown below.

Store Number	Sales Per Month
1	2000,2200,1700,2300
2	1800,2100,2200,2400
3	1900,2000,1800,2200

(a) Use an outer FOR/NEXT loop to keep track of the stores.
(b) Use an inner FOR/NEXT loop to keep track of the months.
(c) Between the two FOR statements, initialize to zero a variable that represents each store's total sales. Also code the PRINT statement that prints the number of a store.
(d) Use the READ/DATA statements to enter the sales.
(e) Total Sales = Total Sales + Sales Per Month
(f) Your flowchart should be similar to the one for Problem II on page 232. In addition to changing the descriptions within some of the symbols, omit the two figures that represent the calculation and the printing of the commission.

```
RUN

STORE: 1
TOTAL SALES: 8200

STORE: 2
TOTAL SALES: 8500

STORE: 3
TOTAL SALES: 7900
```

6. Discounts are often offered by manufacturers to encourage retailers to purchase merchandise in large quantities. What amount of discount would a clothier receive from each of three manufacturers on a shipment of suits if the quoted price is $4000 and a discount of 4% is offered by one manufacturer, 6% by another, and 8% by a third? What would be the net price in each case?
(a) Use the READ/DATA statements to enter the quoted price.
(b) Use a FOR/NEXT loop to generate the rates of discount.
(c) Discount = Quoted Price × Rate of Discount
(d) Net Price = Quoted Price − Discount

```
RUN

QUOTED PRICE: 4000

RATE: .04
DISCOUNT: 160
NET PRICE: 3840
```

```
RATE: .06
DISCOUNT: 240
NET PRICE: 3760

RATE: .08
DISCOUNT: 320
NET PRICE: 3680
```

Problem 6

Q — QUOTED PRICE   D — DISCOUNT
R — RATE OF DISCOUNT (INDEX)   N — NET PRICE

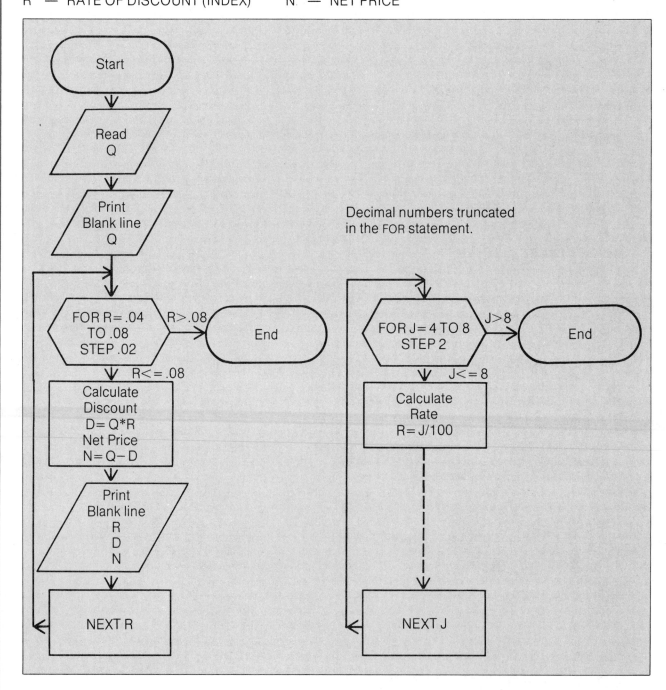

Decimal numbers truncated in the FOR statement.

7. As an extension to Problem 6, suppose the clothier wishes to know what discounts would be received from each of the three manufacturers if two separate purchases are to be made priced at $3000 and $4000 respectively. Do not find the net prices.
   (a) Use an outer FOR/NEXT loop to generate the quoted prices.
   (b) Use an inner FOR/NEXT loop to generate the rates of discount.
   (c) Between the two FOR statements, code the PRINT statement that prints a quoted price.
   (d) Discount = Quoted Price × Rate of Discount

```
RUN

QUOTED PRICE: 3000
RATE: .04          DISCOUNT: 120
RATE: .06          DISCOUNT: 180
RATE: .08          DISCOUNT: 240

QUOTED PRICE: 4000
RATE: .04          DISCOUNT: 160
RATE: .06          DISCOUNT: 240
RATE: .08          DISCOUNT: 320
```

Problem 7

Q — QUOTED PRICE (OUTER INDEX)
R — DISCOUNT RATE (INNER INDEX)
D — DISCOUNT

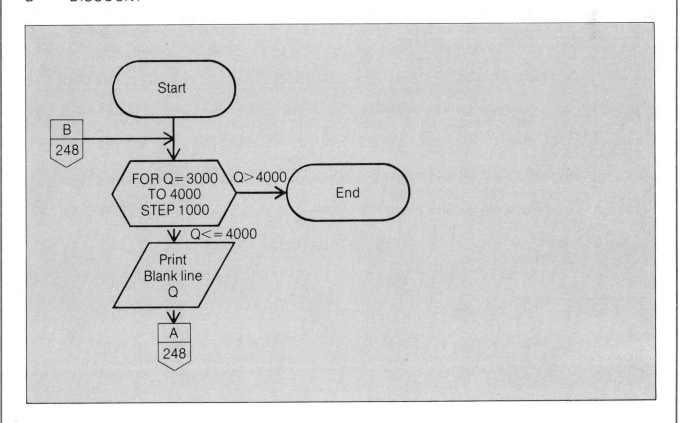

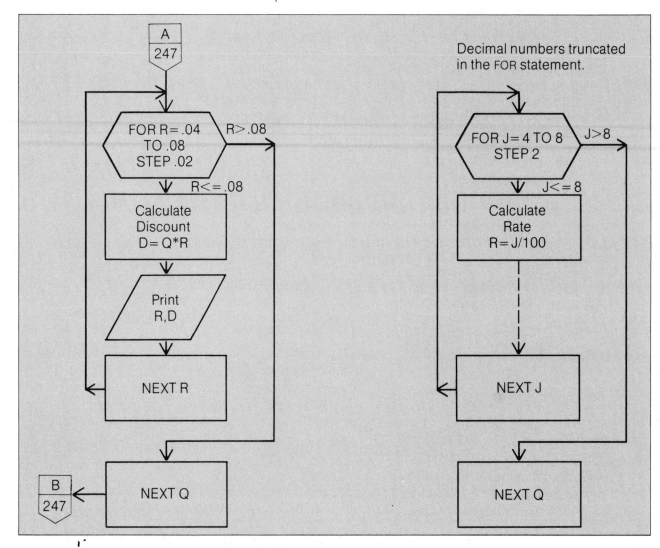

Decimal numbers truncated in the FOR statement.

8. Interest is often added to its principal. Suppose the next time the interest is calculated it is based on the new (increased) principal so that one is actually getting interest on interest. Interest worked out this way is called **compound interest**, and the final principal is known as the **compound amount**. There is a formula that can be used to find the compound amount which greatly reduces the work involved.

Compound Amount = Principal $(1+ \text{Rate of Interest})^{\text{Period of Time}}$

Using an initial principal of $1000, find the compound amounts at the end of 4 years at interest rates of 13%, 14%, and 15%.

(a) Use a FOR/NEXT loop to generate the interest rates.
(b) Compound Amount = $1000 (1+R)^4$
(c) Notice that each amount is not rounded off to the nearest cent. Rounding off numbers will be discussed in later chapters.

```
RUN

RATE: .13 AMOUNT: 1630.47361
RATE: .14 AMOUNT: 1688.96017
RATE: .15 AMOUNT: 1749.00625
```

9. Rewrite the previous program so that the compound amounts are calculated each year. Use each of the three rates each year.
   (a) Use nested FOR/NEXT loops:
      (i) The outer loop keeps track of the years (period of time in the formula). Use the index of the FOR statement to print the number of the year at the beginning of each output line. Place this PRINT statement between the FOR statements.
      (ii) The inner loop generates the interest rates.
   (b) Compound Amount $= 1000(1+R)^{\text{Year Number}}$
   (c) Print the first year's compound amounts across the first line of output (for each rate of interest), the second year's compound amounts across the second line of output (for each rate of interest), etc. To do this, your PRINT statement that prints the number of the year and the PRINT statement that prints the compound amount should each end with a semicolon.
   (d) Compound amounts will not be rounded off to the nearest cent.

```
RUN

1   1130   1140   1150
2   1276.9   1299.6   1322.5
3   1442.897   1481.544   1520.875
4   1630.47361   1688.96017   1749.00625
```

Problem 9

Y — YEAR NO. (OUTER INDEX)
R — INTEREST RATE (INNER INDEX)   C — COMPOUND AMOUNT

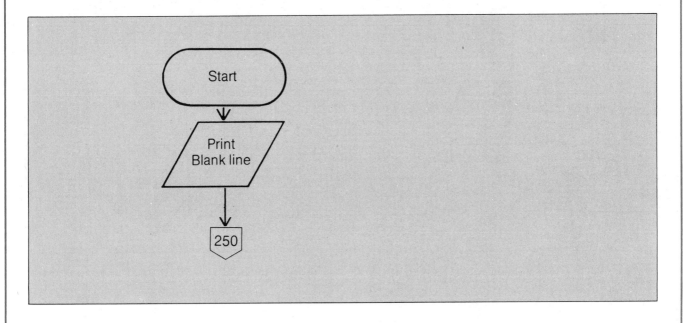

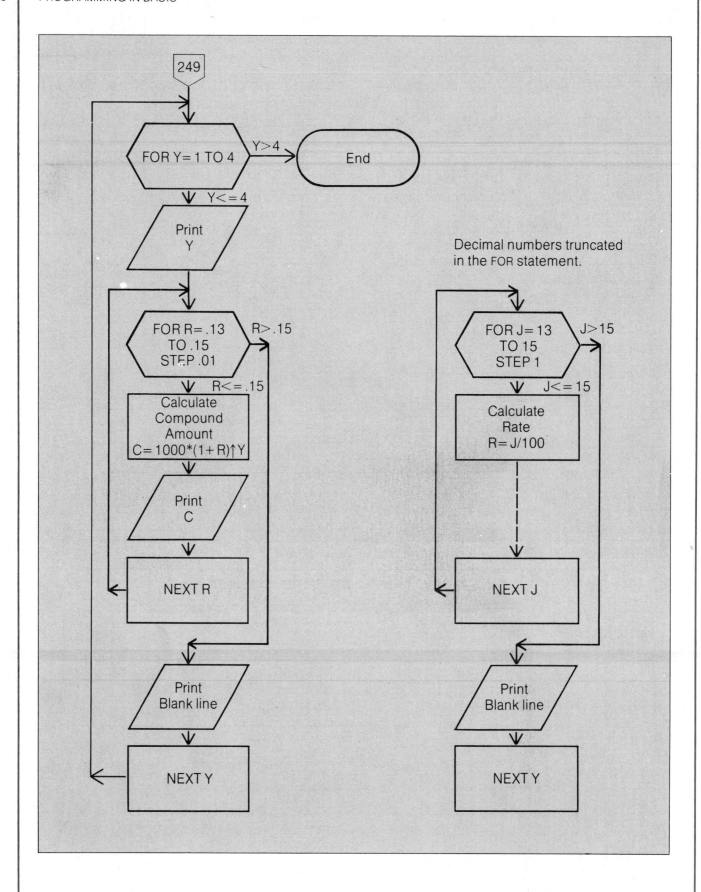

249

FOR Y = 1 TO 4 → Y > 4 → End

Y <= 4

Print Y

Decimal numbers truncated in the FOR statement.

FOR R = .13 TO .15 STEP .01 → R > .15

R <= .15

Calculate Compound Amount C = 1000*(1+R)↑Y

FOR J = 13 TO 15 STEP 1 → J > 15

J <= 15

Calculate Rate R = J/100

Print C

NEXT R

NEXT J

Print Blank line

Print Blank line

NEXT Y

NEXT Y

SEVEN ONE-DIMENSIONAL ARRAYS

A. After completing this chapter, you should be able to write BASIC programs and complete skeletal BASIC programs that:
   1. Store data in one-dimensional arrays.
   2. Print information from one-dimensional arrays.
   3. Perform calculations on data stored in one-dimensional arrays.
   4. Combine the above operations in a variety of ways within FOR/NEXT loops.
B. In addition, you should be able to:
   1. Define
      (a) A one-dimensional array.
      (b) A subscripted variable.
   2. Differentiate between a simple numeric variable and a subscripted numeric variable.
   3. Display and name the different parts of the DIM statement.
   4. State the purpose of the DIM statement and the restrictions imposed upon the DIM statement.
   5. Write program segments that:
      (a) Print specific elements of an array.
      (b) Perform calculations on specific elements of an array.
   6. List data items various ways in DATA statements to produce the same output.
   7. State what is stored in each variable of an array.
   8. Find errors in programs.
   9. Produce the output of programs.

7.1 STORING DATA IN ARRAYS

Until now, you have been using simple numeric variables, such as **A**, **K**, **N1**, **A9**, etc., to store your numbers. Each variable is capable of storing only one number at a time. If a different number is assigned to the same variable, the previously stored value is replaced by the new one. To store two numbers, two variables must be used; three numbers require three variables, etc. Using the LET statement, the numbers are entered as follows.

```
10 LET A=1
20 LET B=2
30 LET C=3
```

The values can also be entered by the INPUT statement or by the READ/DATA statements. However, no matter which way they are entered, you still need three different variables — one variable for each number. This means that if you want to keep all the numbers in storage so that they can be referenced later on in the program, each number must have its own storage location with an address that is unique. Note that a number is always referenced by a variable, which is considered to be its address. When there are only a few numbers to store, it is fairly simple for the programmer to supply these variables. But if you want to store 10, 50, or 100 different numbers, you will need 10, 50, or 100 different variables. Not only is the process of storing the numbers cumbersome and time-consuming, but referencing them may cause some confusion. However, there is a way by which the computer can store and retrieve numbers automatically.

What the programmer does is inform the computer that it must set aside enough locations in memory to store all the data. These locations are adjacent to one another in a block of storage called an **array** to which the programmer assigns a name. Each storage location within the block must be given an address that is unique. The address is created by having the computer assign a number to a location and attaching this number to the name of the array. In this chapter, one-dimensional arrays will be discussed. This type of an array, also referred to as a vector or a list, consists of only one row or one column of numbers.

An analogy is a one-storied apartment block. Suppose you live in the Parkview Apartments. There are four apartments and you live in apartment number 3. If you want to direct some friends over for a visit, you would probably give them the name of the apartment block (Parkview) and the number of your apartment (3). If you used an abbreviated version for Parkview, say **P**, your address could be written as **P(3)** in BASIC. The address of the people who live in the first apartment would be written **P(1)**. This system of notation gives each apartment a unique address since the apartment numbers differ: **P(1)**, **P(2)**, **P(3)**, and **P(4)**; spoken as **"P sub 1"**, **"P sub 2"**, **"P sub 3"**, **"P sub 4"**. The **P** is the name of the array; the number is called the **subscript**. **P(1)**, **P(2)**, **P(3)**, and **P(4)** are referred to as subscripted variables. They store elements of the array **P**. In this particular array, there are four subscripted variables. Depending on your computer system, the subscript of a subscripted variable may range from zero[1] to 255, or to a maximum number that is dependent on available memory.

To reference a specific data item, you must use the name of the array of which it is a member, along with its location within the array. This location, or subscript, must follow the array name and must be in parentheses. The subscripts must be whole numbers, not decimal numbers, and on most systems they cannot be negative. A subscript may also be a variable or an expression. Any variable used as a subscript must be assigned a value previous to its use. For example, if **N=1**, **P(N)** refers to the first location in the array; if **N=5**, **P(N-3)** refers to the second location in the array. On most computer systems, an array name may be any valid variable name (some computers insist that it be a single letter). It must be unique; that is, no two array names may be the same. Some systems allow the name of a numeric array to be the same as that of a simple numeric variable. (It would be

1. In this book, one will be used as the smallest subscript.

wise to check your manual.) You should understand that **P(3)** is not the same as **P3**. The former is a subscripted numeric variable; the latter is a simple numeric variable.

How is a number assigned to each location in the array? It is usually done by using a FOR/NEXT loop. Suppose that you want to store, in array **P**, the *number* of people living in each apartment. Shown below is the information you will need.

Apartment Number	Number of People
1	4
2	3
3	1
4	2

You can use either an INPUT statement or the READ/DATA statements to enter the data. The following program uses the READ/DATA statements.

```
10 DIM P(4)
20 FOR I=1 TO 4
30    READ P(I)
40    DATA 4,3,1,2
50 NEXT I
99 END
```

Here is the way each data item (the number of people living in each apartment) is entered into the computer as an element of array **P**. The first time through the loop I = 1. In line 30, **P(I)** is actually **P(1)**. The number 4 is stored in **P(1)**.

30 READ P(I) means READ P(1)
40 DATA④,3,1,2

P(1)	P(2)	P(3)	P(4)
4			

The second time through the loop I = 2. **P(I)** is actually **P(2)**. The number 3 is stored in **P(2)**.

30 READ P(I) means READ P(2)
40 DATA 4,③,1,2

P(1)	P(2)	P(3)	P(4)
4	3		

The third time through the loop I = 3. **P(I)** is now **P(3)**. The number 1 is stored in **P(3)**.

30 READ P(I) means READ P(3)
40 DATA 4,3,①,2

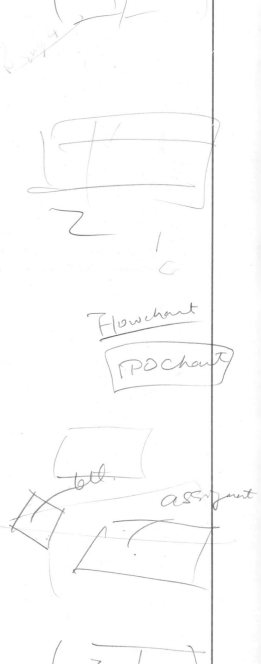

P(1)	P(2)	P(3)	P(4)
4	3	1	

The fourth time through the loop **I** = 4. **P(I)** is now **P(4)**. The number 2 is stored in **P(4)**.

---

30 READ P(I) means READ P(4)
40 DATA 4,3,1,②

P(1)	P(2)	P(3)	P(4)
4	3	1	2

Did you notice that no data item was destroyed as the numbers were being stored? This is because each location has a unique address — **P(1)**, **P(2)**, **P(3)**, **P(4)** — which, in effect, is the same as four different variables. However, this time the computer, not the programmer, named the variables by attaching a number to the array name to identify a specific storage location. This was done each time the computer passed through the loop. What you must remember is that anytime you reference an item in the array, the number of the storage location must be used along with the array name. In other words, you must use a subscripted variable, such as **P(3)**. A simple variable, that is, one without a subscript, may not be used with arrays.

Here is a precautionary note. Try not to have the variable that represents an array name the same as the variable that represents the index of a FOR statement. Not only may it confuse a reader of your program, it may also confuse your computer.

```
10 DIM I(4)
20 FOR I=1 TO 4
30    READ I(I)   —Array name and index the same.
40    DATA -,-,.,.
50 NEXT I
```

Refer to the first statement in the program that stored the number of people living in each apartment.

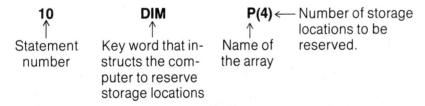

10	**DIM**	**P(4)** ← Number of storage
↑	↑	↑ locations to be
Statement number	Key word that instructs the computer to reserve storage locations	Name of the array reserved.

What is the purpose of this statement? The computer must know in advance the maximum number of storage locations needed to store all the data. The **DIMENSION** statement (usually abbreviated to **DIM**) performs this function. It consists of a statement number; the key word DIM; the name of the array; and, in parentheses, the number of locations to be reserved. This number can be misleading. Depending on your computer system **DIM A(10)** may mean:

— Locations Ø to 9, which gives 10 locations.
— Locations 1 to 10, which gives 10 locations.
— Or locations Ø to 10, which gives 11 locations.

On many systems, the DIM statement is not needed for arrays with 11 or fewer elements. The computer will automatically reserve these locations for you. However, it's best to dimension every array yourself. This way *you* determine the maximum size of the array. If there are more than 10 or 11 elements in your array, space must be reserved by using the DIM statement. It should also be noted that some computer systems allow a variable (which has previously been assigned a value) in the DIM statement to indicate the number of storage locations to be reserved.

Here are a few more rules concerning the DIMENSION statement. The same DIM statement must not be executed more than once. This is why most programmers place it at the beginning of a program, although some computer systems insist that it be the first statement. Also, the DIM statement must precede statements that enter data into the arrays. The number of reserved locations does not necessarily have to be the same as the number of data items stored. You may reserve more locations than you need; however, you may not reserve less than you need. If your program uses more than one array, both may be dimensioned in one statement with a comma between the names of the arrays.

```
10 DIM P(4),R(20)
```

7.1 STORING DATA IN ARRAYS — Sample Programs

Now trace through some sample programs. There is no output (except for the prompt in the second program), since all that the programs do is store data.

I. In this program, the READ/DATA statements are used to store four values in an array named A. The values are 25, 50, 75, 100.

`10 DIM A(4)`	—Reserves four storage locations.
`20 FOR I=1 TO 4`	—Sets up a loop.
`30   READ A(I)`	—Reads values from the data statement one at a time and stores each item as an element of array A.
`40   DATA 25,50,75,100`	—Supplies the READ statement with data.
`50 NEXT I`	—Transfers control to line 20.
`99 END`	—Terminates program execution.

II. This program uses the INPUT statement to enter the data into array A.

```
10 DIM A(4)              — Reserves four storage locations.
20 FOR I=1 TO 4          — Sets up a loop.
30   PRINT "VALUE FOR A(I)";  — Identifies the value to be entered
                              (a prompt).
40   INPUT A(I)          — Requests data, user enters the value for A(I).
50 NEXT I                — Transfers control to line 20.
99 END                   — Terminates program execution.
```

III. Shown below is a problem that appeared in Chapter Five (Review Problem 3, page 191). This time arrays are used to store the data. The program will be developed in four stages:

1. In Section 7.1, the data is stored.
2. In Section 7.2, the data is stored and printed.
3. In Section 7.3, the data is stored and printed and the extended cost of each item is calculated.
4. Finally, in the review problems, you will be asked to program all of the above and calculate the total cost of all the items.

Here is the data.

Item	Quantity	Unit Price
1	2	$4.50
2	4	3.00
3	5	2.25
4	3	5.15

(a) READ/DATA statements are used to enter the quantity and the unit price of each item. The information is stored in two arrays. Array Q stores the quantities; array U stores the unit prices.

(b) Three programs are written:

1. The first program uses two FOR/NEXT loops and two DATA statements.
2. The second program uses two FOR/NEXT loops and one DATA statement.
3. The third program uses one FOR/NEXT loop and one DATA statement.

1. Using two FOR/NEXT loops and two DATA statements

```
10 DIM Q(4),U(4)

100 REM STORE QUANTITIES IN ARRAY Q
110 FOR I=1 TO 4
120   READ Q(I)
```

```
130    DATA 2,4,5,3
140 NEXT I

200 REM STORE UNIT PRICES IN ARRAY U
210 FOR J=1 TO 4
220    READ U(J)
230    DATA 4.50,3.00,2.25,5.15
240 NEXT J

999 END
```

Notice how the data is stored. Each array is filled by means of a separate routine. The first loop stores the quantities. When this loop is complete, the second loop stores the unit prices.

First Loop Stores the Quantities		Second Loop Stores the Unit Prices	
Q(1)	2	U(1)	4.50
Q(2)	4	U(2)	3.00
Q(3)	5	U(3)	2.25
Q(4)	3	U(4)	5.15

Data does not necessarily have to be listed in two DATA statements. One DATA statement may be used. On some computer systems, the statement may be placed anywhere in the program.[2] The program might look like this:

2. Using two FOR/NEXT loops and one DATA statement

```
10 DIM Q(4),U(4)

100 REM STORE QUANTITIES IN ARRAY Q
110 FOR I=1 TO 4
120    READ Q(I)
130 NEXT I

200 REM STORE UNIT PRICES IN ARRAY U
210 FOR J=1 TO 4
220    READ U(J)
230 NEXT J

300 REM DATA STATEMENT
310 DATA 2,4,5,3,4.50,3.00,2.25,5.15

999 END
```

Note that the first four values in the DATA statement are stored in array Q; the next four values are stored in array U.

2. Some systems insist that the DIM statement be the first statement in the program; some insist that the END statement be the last statement in the program. Thus, on these computers, care must be taken in the placement of the DATA statement.

3. Using one FOR/NEXT loop and one DATA statement

```
10 DIM Q(4),U(4)

100 FOR I=1 TO 4
110    READ Q(I),U(I)
120    DATA 2,4.50,4,3.00,5,2.25,3,5.15
130 NEXT I

999 END
```

In this program, data is stored in pairs (See Chapter Five, "Sets of Data Read in a Loop," page 161.) This is an example of how sub-scripted variables act like ordinary variables — they're just named differently. Instead of using variables **P** and **F** as you did in Chapter Five, the subscripted variables **Q(I)** and **U(I)** are used. Below is an explanation of how the numbers are assigned to the subscripted variables in pairs.

The first time through the loop **I=1**.

2 is assigned to Q(1)   110   READ Q(1),U(1)
4.50 is assigned to U(1)   120   DATA (2,4.50)4,3.00,5,2.25,3,5.15

Q(1) $\boxed{2}$ U(1) $\boxed{4.50}$

The second time through the loop **I=2**
4 is assigned to Q(2)   110   READ Q(2),U(2)
3.00 is assigned to U(2)   120   DATA 2,4.50,(4,3.00)5,2.25,3,5.15

Q(1) $\boxed{2}$ U(1) $\boxed{4.50}$
Q(2) $\boxed{4}$ U(2) $\boxed{3.00}$

The third time through the loop **I=3**

5 is assigned to Q(3)   110   READ Q(3),U(3)
2.25 is assigned to U(3)   120   DATA 2,4.50,4,3.00,(5,2.25)3,5.15

Q(1) $\boxed{2}$ U(1) $\boxed{4.50}$
Q(2) $\boxed{4}$ U(2) $\boxed{3.00}$
Q(3) $\boxed{5}$ U(3) $\boxed{2.25}$

The fourth time through the loop **I=4**

3 is assigned to Q(4)   110   READ Q(4),U(4)
5.15 is assigned to U(4)   120   DATA 2,4.50,4,3.00,5,2.25,(3,5.15)

Q(1) $\boxed{2}$ U(1) $\boxed{4.50}$
Q(2) $\boxed{4}$ U(2) $\boxed{3.00}$
Q(3) $\boxed{5}$ U(3) $\boxed{2.25}$
Q(4) $\boxed{3}$ U(4) $\boxed{5.15}$

Now to summarize the programming of Problem III: The program using one loop requires fewer statements; however, care must be taken in listing the data. The data must be listed in pairs, of which the first value is stored in array Q and the second value is stored in array U. The items are listed in this order because the READ statement lists array Q before array U.

```
110 READ Q(I),U(I)
          ↑      ↑
120 DATA  2  , 4.50, -, -,....
```

The DATA statement in Program 2, which uses two loops, lists the quantities first, then the unit prices. This is because the storing of quantities is completed before the storing of unit prices begins.

Something else that should be noted: When there is one loop, as in Program 3, the number of elements in both arrays is the same, since the subscript of each array (the **I** in **Q(I)** and **U(I)**) is the index of the FOR statement **FOR I = 1 TO 4**. The test value indicates the number of elements in the arrays. When there are two loops, as in Programs 1 and 2, the indexes may differ and so may the test values. As a result, the number of elements in array Q may be different than the number of elements in array U.

7.1 STORING DATA IN ARRAYS—Your Turn

1. Identify the errors, if any, in the program segments shown below. Make the necessary corrections.

```
(a) 10 DIM A(5)
    20 FOR I=1 TO 10
    30   READ A(I)
    40   DATA 2,4,6,8,10,12,14,16,18,20
    50 NEXT I
    --
    99 END
```

Too many data in the data statement.

```
(b) 10 DIM B(10)
    20 FOR K=1 TO 10
    30   READ K(B)
    40   DATA 2,4,6,8,10,12,14,16,18,20
    50 NEXT K
    --
    99 END
```

B should be the array
K should be the subscript.

```
(c) 10 DIM 45
    20 FOR J=1 TO 45
    30   READ A(J)
    40   DATA -,-,-,.....(45 data items)
    50 NEXT J
    --
    99 END
```

We need an array A array

(d)
```
10 DIM R(15)
20 PRINT
30 FOR S=1 TO 5
40    PRINT "VALUE FOR R(S)";
50    INPUT R(S)
60 NEXT S
--
99 END
```

(e) In this program segment, the data items are to be stored as follows.

Array A	Array B
3	9
6	18
9	27
12	36
15	45

```
10 DIM A(5),B(5)
20 FOR K=1 TO 5
30    READ A(K),B(K)
40    DATA 3,6,9,12,15,9,18,27,36,45
50 NEXT K
--
99 END
```

(f) In the program segment shown below, the data items are to be stored as follows.

Array C	Array D
2	12
4	14
6	16
8	18
10	20

```
10 DIM C(5),D(5)
20 FOR I=1 TO 5
30    READ C(I)
40 NEXT I
50 FOR J=1 TO 5
60    READ D(J)
70 NEXT J
80 DATA 2,4,6,8,10,12,14,16,18,20
--
999 END
```

2. What will be stored in each variable of the array(s) after execution of each of the following program segments? Show the name of

the variable and its content. For example, if there are two arrays, you could show the contents in the following manner.

Array A		Array B	
A(1)	1	B(1)	10
A(2)	2	B(2)	20
A(3)	3	B(3)	30

```
(a) 10 DIM A(5)
    20 FOR I=1 TO 5
    30    READ A(I)
    40    DATA 11,22,33,44,55
    50 NEXT I
    --
    99 END


(b) 10 DIM M(3),N(3)
    20 FOR I=1 TO 3
    30    READ M(I),N(I)
    40    DATA 11,22,33,44,55,66
    50 NEXT I
    --
    99 END


(c) 10 DIM M(2),N(2)
    20 FOR I=1 TO 2
    30    READ M(I),N(I),C
    40    DATA 11,33,55,22,44,66
    50 NEXT I
    --
    99 END
```

3. Suppose a savings and loan company offers varying rates of interest on investments depending on the length of time the money is invested. The data is as follows.

No. of Years	Rate of Interest
10	12%
15	13%
20	15%

(a) Write two programs, each one READing the above information into two arrays. One program uses two FOR/NEXT loops and two DATA statements; the other program uses one FOR/NEXT loop and one DATA statement.

(b) In the program that uses one loop, explain why the data items in the DATA statement must be listed in a specific order.

(c) The DIM statement in the flowchart is represented by the process symbol. Subsequent to the DIM statement, notice that the variables **Y** and **R** in the flowchart are subscripted whenever they are used.

Problem 3

Using Two FOR/NEXT Loops

Y — YEARS
R — RATE

Using One FOR/NEXT Loop

Y — YEARS
R — RATE

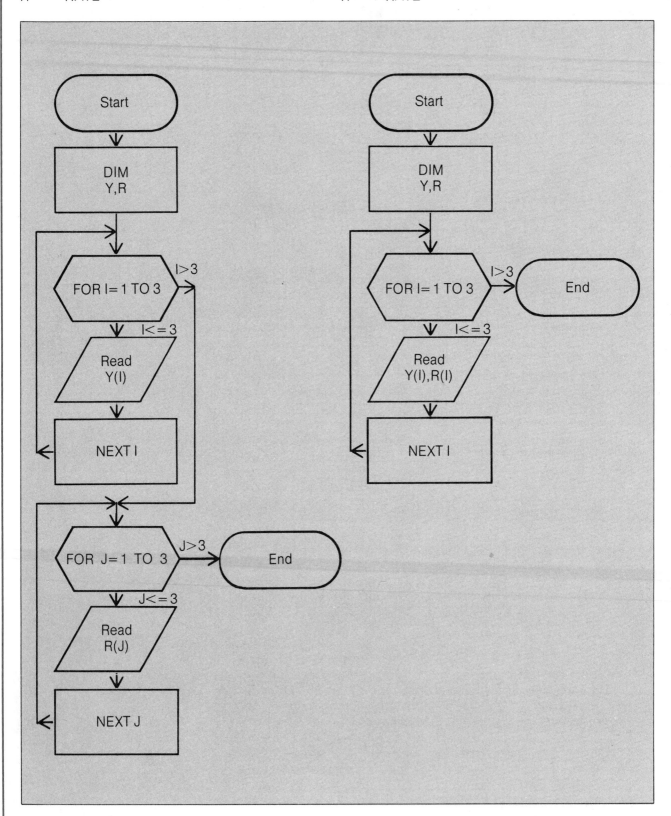

7.1 STORING DATA IN ARRAYS—
Solutions for "Your Turn"

1. (a) There are not enough storage locations reserved for array A. Either increase the dimension of A to 10 or change the test value in the FOR statement to 5. In the second alternative, the data statement may remain unchanged since, on most computer systems, excess data is ignored.

```
10 DIM A(10)       or          --
                            20 FOR I=1 TO 5
```

(b) In line 30, the index and the name of the array are interchanged. The index should be the subscript of the array name.

```
30 READ B(K)
```

(c) The DIM statement must include the name of the array. Also, the number 45 must be enclosed in parentheses and must follow the name of the array.

```
10 DIM A(45)
```

(d) Nothing is wrong.
(e) The data items in the DATA statement are not listed in their proper order. Since they are being read in as pairs, the first item of each pair must be assigned to a variable of array A, the second item of each pair must be assigned to a variable of array B.

```
30 READ A(K),B(K)
40 DATA 3,9,6,18,9,27,12,36,15,45
        ↑ ↑ ↑ ↑              ↑   ↑
array   A B A B  .   .   .   A   B
```

(f) Nothing is wrong.

2. (a)

Array A

A(1)	11
A(2)	22
A(3)	33
A(4)	44
A(5)	55

(b)

Array M		Array N	
M(1)	11	N(1)	22
M(2)	33	N(2)	44
M(3)	55	N(3)	66

(c)

Array M		Array N		Variable C		
M(1)	11	N(1)	33	C	55	(replaced by 66)
M(2)	22	N(2)	44	C	66	

Notice that the value 55, entered in the simple variable C, is lost, since it is replaced by the number 66. The other values are retained as each is stored in its own subscripted variable.

3. (a)

Using Two FOR/NEXT Loops

```
01 REM Y--YEARS
02 REM R--RATE

10 DIM Y(3),R(3)

100 REM STORE YEARS IN ARRAY Y
110 FOR I=1 TO 3
120    READ Y(I)
130    DATA 10,15,20
140 NEXT I

200 REM STORE RATES IN ARRAY R
210 FOR J=1 TO 3
220    READ R(J)
230    DATA .12,.13,.15
240 NEXT J

999 END
```

Using One FOR/NEXT Loop

```
01 REM Y--YEARS
02 REM R--RATE

10 DIM Y(3),R(3)
20 FOR I=1 TO 3
30    READ Y(I),R(I)
40    DATA 10,.12,15,.13,20,.15
50 NEXT I
99 END
```

(b) The data must be listed in pairs, so that the first item of each pair is assigned to a variable of array Y and the second item of each pair is assigned to a variable of array R.

7.2 PRINTING FROM ARRAYS

In the last section, you learned how numbers can be stored in an array. A sufficient number of storage locations was reserved by the DIM statement. As each value was stored, the computer attached a number to the array name to identify a specific location in storage. In this section, you will learn how to print the contents of each location.

Again, the Parkview Apartments will be used as an analogy. The block has 4 apartments, and in Section One a program was written that stored the number of people living in each apartment.

```
10 DIM P(4)
20 FOR I=1 TO 4
30   READ P(I)
40   DATA 4,3,1,2
50 NEXT I
99 END
```

P(1)	P(2)	P(3)	P(4)
4	3	1	2

The following examples will show you how information can be printed from this array. Suppose you want the computer to print the number of people living in your apartment (apartment 3). You simply ask the computer to print the contents of **P(3)**.

```
--
50 PRINT P(3)
--
99 END

RUN

 1
```

The computer prints the *contents* of **P(3)** just as it PRINTed the contents of a simple numeric variable. How would you ask the computer to print the contents of the first storage location?

```
--
50 PRINT P(1)
--
99 END

RUN

 4
```

How would you code the PRINT statement if you wanted the computer to print the contents of the first and the fourth storage locations on the same line widely spaced?

```
--
50 PRINT P(1),P(4)
```

```
--
99 END

RUN

    4         2
```

What would the PRINT statement and the RUN look like if you wanted the contents of all the storage locations printed on the same line closely spaced?

```
--
50 PRINT P(1);P(2);P(3);P(4)
--
99 END

RUN

    4  3  1  2
```

This isn't too onerous if you have only a few numbers in the array. It's just the same as printing the contents of four simple numeric variables, such as **A**, **B**, **C**, and **D**. But what would you do if the array contained 100 items and you wanted the computer to print them all? As in the storage of data items in an array, the FOR/NEXT loop can be used to make the computer look after the job of referencing each storage location. Here is a program segment that prints the number of people living in each apartment of the Parkview Apartments. Although it is written to print four items, it can just as easily print more or less. Simply change the subscript in the DIM statement, the test value in the FOR statement, and the number of data items in the DATA statement.

```
10 DIM P(4)
--
40 FOR I=1 TO 4
50    PRINT P(I);
60 NEXT I
--
99 END

RUN

    4  3  1  2
```

Notice the semicolon at the end of the PRINT statement. This causes the items to be printed on the same line closely spaced.

In the above examples, it was assumed that the data items had been stored by previous statements. The programs below show how the operations of storing and printing are combined in one program. One or two FOR/NEXT loops can be used. The first program uses two loops. It stores the data items in the first loop and prints them in the second loop. The second program does both in one loop.

1. Using two FOR/NEXT loops

```
10 DIM P(4)

100 REM STORE ITEMS IN AN ARRAY
110 FOR I=1 TO 4
120    READ P(I)
130    DATA 4,3,1,2
140 NEXT I

200 REM PRINT ITEMS FROM AN ARRAY
210 PRINT
220 FOR J=1 TO 4
230    PRINT P(J);
240 NEXT J

999 END

RUN

   4  3  1  2
```

Note that a different index is used for printing the items. If there are two loops in a program, it is better to use different indexes. Notice as well that the numeric subscripts of array P are the same in both loops, regardless of whether **I** or **J** is used, since the range of both indexes is the same. In the first loop, the values are stored in **P(1)**, **P(2)**, **P(3)**, and **P(4)** because **I** ranges from 1 to 4. In the second loop, the values are referenced by the same subscripts because **J** also ranges from 1 to 4. One more thing. Note that the array is DIMENSIONed only once — at the beginning of the program.

An easier and more efficient way to write this program is to use just one FOR/NEXT loop.

2. Using one FOR/NEXT loop

```
10 DIM P(4)
20 PRINT
30 FOR I=1 TO 4
40    READ P(I)
50    DATA 4,3,1,2
```

```
60    PRINT P(I);
70 NEXT I
99 END

RUN

   4   3   1   2
```

Make sure you understand the difference in the execution of these two programs. The one using two FOR/NEXT loops reads in *all* the data items. After they have all been entered, the computer then prints them. It completes one operation at a time (the READing of data) before going on to the next operation (the PRINTing of data). Each operation uses a different FOR/NEXT loop. The program using one FOR/NEXT loop reads one item of data and prints it right away. It then reads the second item of data and prints that one. The operations of READ and PRINT alternate within the one loop. Which program do you prefer?

Here is a challenge. How would you instruct the computer to print the items backwards (that is, a program that prints the number of people in each apartment but starts with apartment 4 and ends with apartment 1)?

P(1)	P(2)	P(3)	P(4)
4	3	1	2

Your statements should look something like this.

```
10 DIM P(4)
--
40 FOR I=4 TO 1 STEP -1
50    PRINT P(I);
60 NEXT I
--
99 END

RUN

   2   1   3   4
```

One last comment before going on to some sample programs. The placement of blank PRINT statements is often confusing. Examine where they are coded in the following two program segments.

1. Output single spaced

```
10 DIM Q(4),U(4)
--
50 PRINT    —Placed just before the loop that prints the results.
```

```
60 FOR J=1 TO 4
70   PRINT Q(J),U(J)
80 NEXT J
99 END

RUN
                    —Blank line before the results.
   2         4.5
   4         3
   5         2.25
   3         5.15
```

2. Blocks of output double spaced

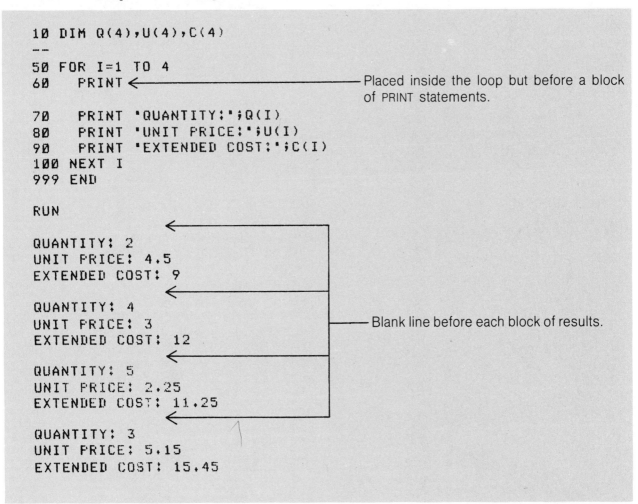

```
10 DIM Q(4),U(4),C(4)
--
50 FOR I=1 TO 4
60   PRINT  ←─────────────────────  Placed inside the loop but before a block
                                     of PRINT statements.
70   PRINT "QUANTITY:";Q(I)
80   PRINT "UNIT PRICE:";U(I)
90   PRINT "EXTENDED COST:";C(I)
100 NEXT I
999 END

RUN

QUANTITY: 2      ←
UNIT PRICE: 4.5
EXTENDED COST: 9

QUANTITY: 4      ←
UNIT PRICE: 3                          —Blank line before each block of results.
EXTENDED COST: 12

QUANTITY: 5      ←
UNIT PRICE: 2.25
EXTENDED COST: 11.25

QUANTITY: 3      ←
UNIT PRICE: 5.15
EXTENDED COST: 15.45
```

7.2 PRINTING FROM ARRAYS—Sample Programs

The following programs print what was stored in the sample programs in Section 7.1.

I. This program stores and prints the four values 25, 50, 75, 100. It uses the READ/DATA statements to enter the values into an array named A.

```
10 DIM A(4)              —Reserves four storage locations.
20 PRINT                 —Leaves a blank line.
30 FOR I=1 TO 4          —Sets up a loop.
40    READ A(I)          —Reads values from the data statement one at a time and
                          stores each item as an element of array A.
50    DATA 25,50,75,100   —Supplies the READ statement with data.
60    PRINT A(I),        —Prints the items widely spaced on one line.
70 NEXT I                —Transfers control to line 30.
99 END                   —Terminates program execution.

RUN

 25           50          75          100
```

II. This program uses the INPUT statement to enter the data into array A. It uses a separate loop to print the data so that the output is apart from the prompts.

```
10 DIM A(4)                    —Reserves four storage locations.
20 PRINT                       —Leaves a blank line.
30 FOR I=1 TO 4                —Sets up a loop to enter the data.
40    PRINT "VALUE FOR A(I)";  —Identifies the value to be entered
                                (a prompt).
50    INPUT A(I)               —Requests data, user enters the value for A(I).
60 NEXT I                      —Transfers control to line 30.
70 PRINT                       —Leaves a blank line after the prompts.
80 FOR J=1 TO 4                —Sets up a loop to print the data.
90    PRINT A(J),              —Prints the data widely spaced on one line.
100 NEXT J                     —Transfers control to line 80.
999 END                        —Terminates program execution.

RUN

VALUE FOR A(I)? 25
VALUE FOR A(I)? 50
VALUE FOR A(I)? 75
VALUE FOR A(I)? 100

 25           50          75          100
```

III. Here is the second stage of the program that was started in Section 7.1, page 256.

Item	Quantity	Unit Price
1	2	$4.50
2	4	3.00
3	5	2.25
4	3	5.15

(a) READ/DATA statements are used to enter the quantity and the unit price of each item. The information is stored in two arrays. Array Q stores the quantities; array U stores the unit prices.

(b) Two programs are written:

1. The first program uses two FOR/NEXT loops — one loop to store the data, the other loop to print the data.
2. The second program uses one FOR/NEXT loop to store and print the data.

1. Using two FOR/NEXT loops

```
10 DIM Q(4),U(4)

100 REM STORE THE DATA
110 FOR I=1 TO 4
120    READ Q(I),U(I)
130    DATA 2,4.50,4,3.00,5,2.25,3,5.15
140 NEXT I

200 REM PRINT THE DATA
210 PRINT
220 FOR J=1 TO 4
230    PRINT Q(J),U(J)
240 NEXT J

999 END

RUN

2          4.5
4          3
5          2.25
3          5.15
```

The data is stored in the first loop. After this operation is complete, the data is printed in the second loop.

2. Using one FOR/NEXT loop

```
10 DIM Q(4),U(4)
20 PRINT
```

```
30 FOR I=1 TO 4
40   READ Q(I),U(I)
50   DATA 2,4.50,4,3.00,5,2.25,3,5.15
60   PRINT Q(I),U(I)
70 NEXT I
99 END

RUN

2           4.5
4           3
5           2.25
3           5.15
```

In line 40, two data items are read. They are then printed before the next two items are read and printed. The operations of READ and PRINT alternate within the one loop.

7.2 PRINTING FROM ARRAYS—Your Turn

1. Write one or more statements to perform the following. Assume the data has already been stored.
   (a) Write a PRINT statement that prints the first element of the array A.
   (b) Write a PRINT statement that prints the first and tenth elements of the array A widely spaced on the same line.
   (c) Write a program segment that prints the first four elements of array A. Use a FOR/NEXT loop.

```
RUN

2       4       6       8
```

   (d) Do the same as in question (c), but this time print the items backwards.

```
RUN

8       6       4       2
```

   (e) Write a program segment that prints the first four elements of array A and the first four elements of array B, using one FOR/NEXT loop.

```
RUN

   2            4
   4           16
   6           36
   8           64
```

2. Is there anything wrong with each of the following programs? If there is no error, show the output; if there is an error, state what is wrong and make the necessary corrections.

```
(a) 10 DIM A(4)              (c) 10 DIM A(3),B(4)
    20 PRINT                     20 PRINT
    30 FOR I=1 TO 4              30 FOR I=1 TO 4
    40    READ A(I)              40    READ A(I),B(I)
    50    DATA 5,10,15,20        50    DATA 1,15,2,46,3,23,58
    60    PRINT A                60    PRINT A(I),B(I)
    70 NEXT I                    70 NEXT I
    99 END                       99 END
```

It shud be 60 PRINT A(I)

```
(b) 10 DIM A(3),B(3),C(3)
    20 PRINT
    30 FOR I=1 TO 3
    40    READ A(I),B(I),C(I)
    50    DATA 1,10,100,2,20,200,3,30,300
    60    PRINT A(I),B(I),C(I)
    70 NEXT I
    99 END
```

1   10   100
2   20   200
3   30   300

3. This is an extension of the "Your Turn" problem in Section 7.1. In this section, you are to print the data in addition to storing it.
   Suppose a savings and loan company offers varying rates of interest on investments depending on the length of time the money is invested. The data is as follows.

No. of Years	Rate of Interest
10	12%
15	13%
20	15%

10 DIM N(3), R(3)
20 FOR I=1 TO 3
30 Read N(I), R(I)
35 PRINT "Year #"; N(I), Rate; R(I)
40 Next
50 DATA
60 End

(a) Use the READ statement with one DATA statement to store the above information in two arrays.

(b) Use one FOR/NEXT loop to read and print the above information.

```
RUN

YEARS: 10          RATE: .12
YEARS: 15          RATE: .13
YEARS: 20          RATE: .15
```

Problem 3

Y — YEARS
R — RATE

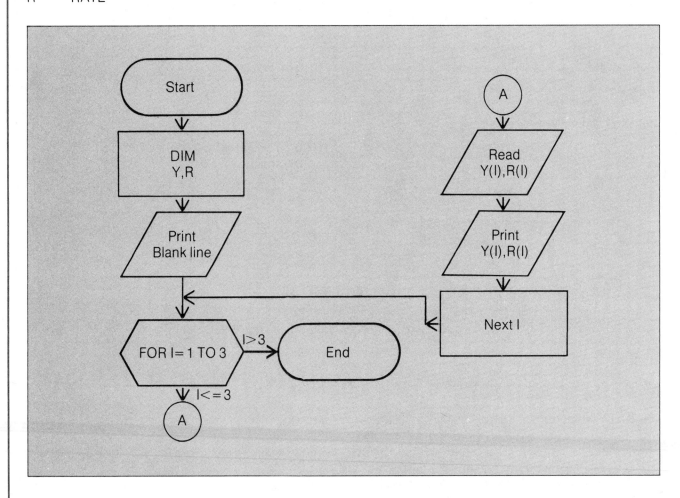

7.2 PRINTING FROM ARRAYS—Solutions for "Your Turn"

1.

```
(a)  60 PRINT A(1)
```

```
(b)  80 PRINT A(1),A(10)
(c)  ---
     60 FOR I=1 TO 4
     70   PRINT A(I),
     80 NEXT I
     ---
     999 END

(d)  ---
     60 FOR I=4 TO 1 STEP -1
     70   PRINT A(I),
     80 NEXT I
     ---
     999 END

(e)  ---
     60 FOR I=1 TO 4
     70   PRINT A(I),B(I)
     80 NEXT I
     ---
     999 END
```

2. (a) In line 60, the variable **A** in the PRINT statement must be a subscripted variable.

```
60 PRINT A(I)
```

(b) Nothing is wrong.

```
RUN

1          10         100
2          20         200
3          30         300
```

(c) There is insufficient data for the array A. Since the test value in the FOR statement is 4 and the data pattern for A is 1,2,3, it appears that A should have one more value and that this value should be 4. This means that the DIM statement and the DATA statement should be changed.

```
10 DIM A(4),B(4)
50 DATA 1,15,2,46,3,23,4,58
```

3.

```
01 REM Y--YEARS
02 REM R--RATE

10 DIM Y(3),R(3)
20 PRINT
30 FOR I=1 TO 3
40    READ Y(I),R(I)
50    DATA 10,.12,15,.13,20,.15
60    PRINT "YEARS:";Y(I),"RATE:";R(I)
70 NEXT I
99 END
```

7.3 CALCULATING WITH ARRAYS

Section 7.1 entered data into an array; Section 7.2 printed the data. In this section, calculations are performed using this data. Again, the number of people living in each apartment of the Parkview Apartments will be used as data items. The first few examples are program segments in which it is assumed that the data has already been stored in an array called P.

P(1)	P(2)	P(3)	P(4)
4	3	1	2

I. Suppose you want to know the total number of people living in apartments one and two. Here is a statement that performs this calculation.

```
--
50 LET T=P(1)+P(2)
60 PRINT T
--
99 END

RUN

7
```

Line 50 is executed as follows:

```
50 LET T=P(1)+P(2)
        = 4 + 3
        = 7
```

II. If you want to know the total number of people living in the apartment block, the statement will look like the following.

```
--
50 LET T=P(1)+P(2)+P(3)+P(4)
60 PRINT T
--
99 END

RUN

   10
```

III. The previous statement is relatively simple if there are only a few elements to add. But what if there are 100 elements? The task becomes quite onerous. In the examples shown below, FOR/NEXT loops are used to find the total number of people living in the Parkview Apartments. As mentioned in the previous section, the programs can just as easily manipulate 100 elements of an array. Simply change the subscript in the DIM statement, the test value in the FOR statement, and increase the number of data items. Here are two versions of the same program.

1. This version stores and prints the data in one loop, then calculates and prints the total in a separate loop.

```
10 DIM P(4)
20 LET T=0

100 REM STORE AND PRINT THE DATA
110 PRINT
120 FOR I=1 TO 4
130    READ P(I)
140    DATA 4,3,1,2
150    PRINT P(I),
160 NEXT I

200 REM CALCULATE AND PRINT THE TOTAL
210 FOR J=1 TO 4
220    LET T=T+P(J)
230    PRINT T   —Placed inside the loop.
240 NEXT J

999 END

RUN

   4          3          1          2
   4
   7
   8
   10
```

Notice in this program that the statement **PRINT T** is inside the loop. This gives a subtotal after each calculation. Here is how the computer accumulates the total.

P(1)	P(2)	P(3)	P(4)
4	3	1	2

Before the loop starts, **T** is initialized to zero. $T=\emptyset$.

The first time through the loop **J=1**. The computer adds whatever is currently stored in **T** to whatever is stored in **P(1)**. The result is stored back into **T**.

$$220 \text{ LET } T = T + P(J)$$
$$= T + P(1)$$
$$= \emptyset + 4$$
$$= 4$$

The second time through the loop **J=2**. The current value of **T** is 4.

$$220 \text{ LET } T = T + P(J)$$
$$= T + P(2)$$
$$= 4 + 3$$
$$= 7$$

The third time through the loop **J=3**. The current value of **T** is 7.

$$220 \text{ LET } T = T + P(J)$$
$$= T + P(3)$$
$$= 7 + 1$$
$$= 8$$

The fourth time through the loop **J=4**. The current value of **T** is 8.

$$220 \text{ LET } T = T + P(J)$$
$$= T + P(4)$$
$$= 8 + 2$$
$$= 10$$

To print just the total without subtotals, the routine will look as follows.

```
200 REM CALCULATE AND PRINT THE TOTAL
210 FOR J=1 TO 4
220    LET T=T+P(J)
230 NEXT J
240 PRINT T    —Placed outside the loop.
999 END

RUN

4            3           1           2
10
```

2. The storing and printing of data and the summation of numbers can be combined in one loop.

```
10  DIM P(4)
20  PRINT
30  LET T=0
40  FOR I=1 TO 4
50     READ P(I)
60     DATA 4,3,1,2
70     PRINT P(I),
80     LET T=T+P(I)
90  NEXT I
100 PRINT T   —Placed outside the loop.
999 END

RUN

  4            3           1           2
  10
```

The above program gives no subtotals since the statement **PRINT T** is outside the loop. To obtain subtotals, place the **PRINT T** statement inside the loop as follows.

```
--
40  FOR I=1 TO 4
50     READ P(I)
60     DATA 4,3,1,2
70     PRINT P(I),
80     LET T=T+P(I)
90     PRINT T   —Placed inside the loop.
100 NEXT I
999 END

RUN
                Subtotal

  4            4
  3            7
  1            8
  2            10
```

The comma after **PRINT P(I),** causes the subtotal to be printed on the same line as the data item. Since the statement **PRINT T** does not end with a comma, the next data item and subtotal are printed on a new line.

IV. Let us now assume that the four people who live in Apartment 1 move out and that the family moving in has six members. Here is the statement that makes this change.

```
80 LET P(1)=6
```

	P(1)	P(2)	P(3)	P(4)
	6	3	1	2

V. Here is another change. Suppose the family in Apartment 4 moves out and the new family has the same number of people as the family now living in Apartment 2. Instead of coding

```
80 LET P(4)=3
```

you can write

```
80 LET P(4)=P(2)
```

A copy of the number stored in **P(2)** is placed in **P(4)**. Both storage locations now contain the number 3. The statement is similar to one that was discussed in Chapter Three, page 56, where simple variables were used: **40 LET B=A**. Here subscripted variables are used, but they act just the same. Each apartment now contains the following number of people.

	P(1)	P(2)	P(3)	P(4)
	6	3	1	3

VI. The family in Apartment 2 has an additional member. The statement that makes this change is:

```
80 LET P(2)=P(2)+1
```

One is added to the number already stored in **P(2)**.

$$P(2) = P(2)+1$$
$$= 3 + 1$$
$$= 4$$

VII. Suppose everyone moves out of the apartment block because of renovations. Zero must now be stored in each variable of the array. This can be accomplished by the following statements.

```
--
40 LET P(1)=0
50 LET P(2)=0
60 LET P(3)=0
70 LET P(4)=0
```

However, an easier method is to use a FOR/NEXT loop, particularly when zero (or any other number) must be assigned to many variables of the array.

```
--
40 FOR I=1 TO 4
50    LET P(I)=0
60 NEXT I
```

As the index **I** changes from 1 to 4, the subscript of array P also changes from 1 to 4. Each time the computer passes through the loop, a subscripted variable is assigned a value of zero; first **P(1)**, then **P(2)**, then **P(3)**, and finally **P(4)**.

VIII. This is the third stage of the program that was started in Section 7.1, page 256.

Item	Quantity	Unit Price
1	2	$4.50
2	4	3.00
3	5	2.25
4	3	5.15

Again the READ/DATA statements will be used to store the quantities in array Q and the unit prices in array U. Here are several programs that calculate the extended cost of each item.

1. This program uses two FOR/NEXT loops:

   (a) The first loop reads and prints the data.
   (b) The second loop calculates and prints the extended cost of each item.
       Extended Cost of Each Item = Quantity × Unit Price

```
10 DIM Q(4),U(4)

100 REM READ AND PRINT THE DATA
110 PRINT
120 FOR I=1 TO 4
130    READ Q(I),U(I)
140    DATA 2,4.50,4,3.00,5,2.25,3,5.15
150    PRINT Q(I),U(I)
160 NEXT I

200 REM CALCULATE AND PRINT THE
201 REM EXTENDED COST OF EACH ITEM
210 PRINT
220 FOR J=1 TO 4
230    LET C=Q(J)*U(J)
240    PRINT C
250 NEXT J

999 END
```

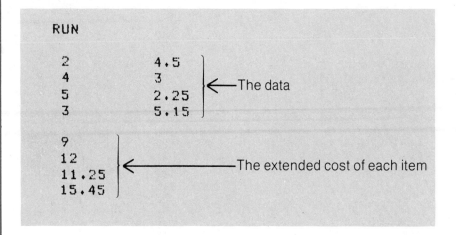

```
RUN

    2            4.5  ⎫
    4            3    ⎪  ← The data
    5            2.25 ⎪
    3            5.15 ⎭

    9            ⎫
   12            ⎪  ← The extended cost of each item
   11.25         ⎪
   15.45         ⎭
```

The following programs are quite different from Program 1. They place the extended costs of the items in a separate array. First you will be shown two versions of a program. The differences between the first three programs will then be reviewed.

2. This version uses two FOR/NEXT loops:
   (a) The first loop reads and prints the data and calculates the extended cost of each item.
   (b) The second loop prints the costs.

```
10 DIM Q(4),U(4),C(4)

100 REM READ AND PRINT THE DATA
101 REM CALCULATE THE COSTS
110 PRINT
120 FOR I=1 TO 4
130   READ Q(I),U(I)
140   DATA 2,4.50,4,3.00,5,2.25,3,5.15
150   PRINT Q(I),U(I)
160   LET C(I)=Q(I)*U(I)
170 NEXT I

200 REM PRINT THE COSTS
210 PRINT
220 FOR J=1 TO 4
230   PRINT C(J),
240 NEXT J

999 END

RUN

    2            4.5
    4            3
    5            2.25
    3            5.15
```

```
   9              12           11.25        15.45
```

The DIM statement sets aside four storage locations for array C in which the results are stored. Here is how line 160 is executed.

The first time through the loop $I = 1$

$$C(1) = Q(1) * U(1)$$
$$= 2 * 4.5$$
$$= 9$$

C(1)	C(2)	C(3)	C(4)
9			

The second time through the loop $I = 2$

$$C(2) = Q(2) * U(2)$$
$$= 4 * 3$$
$$= 12$$

C(1)	C(2)	C(3)	C(4)
9	12		

The third time through the loop $I = 3$

$$C(3) = Q(3) * U(3)$$
$$= 5 * 2.25$$
$$= 11.25$$

C(1)	C(2)	C(3)	C(4)
9	12	11.25	

The fourth time through the loop $I = 4$

$$C(4) = Q(4) * U(4)$$
$$= 3 * 5.15$$
$$= 15.45$$

C(1)	C(2)	C(3)	C(4)
9	12	11.25	15.45

3. This version uses one FOR/NEXT loop to do everything — read, calculate, and print.

```
10 DIM Q(4),U(4),C(4)
20 PRINT
30 FOR I=1 TO 4
40   READ Q(I),U(I)
50   DATA 2,4.50,4,3.00,5,2.25,3,5.15
60   LET C(I)=Q(I)*U(I)
```

```
70    PRINT Q(I),U(I),C(I)
80 NEXT I
99 END

RUN

  2         4.5       9
  4         3         12
  5         2.25      11.25
  3         5.15      15.45
```

Now look at the differences. Program 2 prints the extended costs after they have all been calculated. This is possible, since each cost is stored in its own location and may be referenced any time after it is calculated (before the END statement). Using the four subscripted variables **C(1)**, **C(2)**, **C(3)**, and **C(4)** gives four different storage locations. It is impossible to print the costs this way in Program 1, where each result was stored in variable **C**. In Program 1, the contents of **C** had to be printed immediately after the cost was calculated, since each stored cost (except the last one) was replaced by a new one.

Program 3 is something like Program 1, in that the extended costs are printed right after each one is calculated. However, there is a difference. When the loop is complete in Program 3, all the costs are retained because each is stored in its own subscripted variable. In Program 1, all that is left in variable **C** at the end of the second loop is the last cost, since the previous values in **C** were continually replaced by new ones.

4. The output of Programs 2 and 3 may cause some confusion as to the meaning of the numbers. Shown below is a different version of Program 3. Strings are printed to indicate what the various numbers represent.

```
10 DIM Q(4),U(4),C(4)
20 FOR I=1 TO 4
30    READ Q(I),U(I)
40    DATA 2,4.50,4,3.00,5,2.25,3,5.15
50    LET C(I)=Q(I)*U(I)
60    PRINT
70    PRINT "QUANTITY";Q(I)
80    PRINT "UNIT PRICE";U(I)
90    PRINT "EXTENDED COST OF ITEM";C(I)
100 NEXT I
999 END

RUN
```

```
QUANTITY 2
UNIT PRICE 4.5
EXTENDED COST OF ITEM 9

QUANTITY 4
UNIT PRICE 3
EXTENDED COST OF ITEM 12

QUANTITY 5
UNIT PRICE 2.25
EXTENDED COST OF ITEM 11.25

QUANTITY 3
UNIT PRICE 5.15
EXTENDED COST OF ITEM 15.45
```

Problem I

Y — YEARS   I — INTEREST
R — RATE   A — AMOUNT OF INVESTMENT

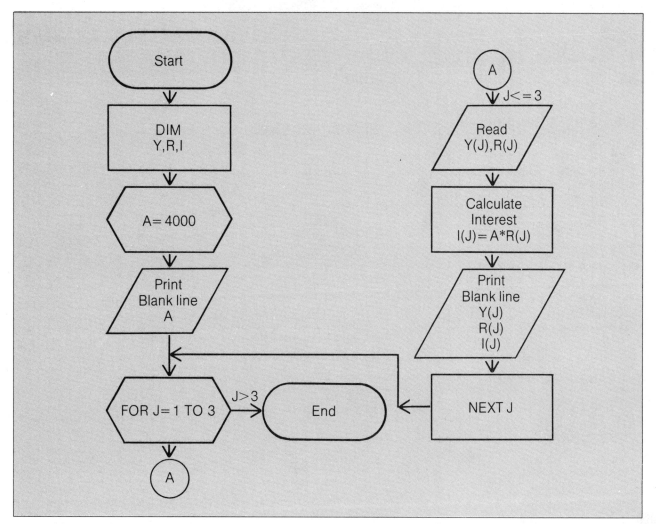

7.3 CALCULATING WITH ARRAYS—Your Turn

I. This is a further extension of the problem that appeared in Sections 7.1 and 7.2. In this section, you are to calculate the yearly interest on an investment of $4000, using the rates shown below.

No. of Years	Rate of Interest
10	12%
15	13%
20	15%

(a) Use two arrays to store the data (years and rates).
(b) Store each calculated interest in a third array.
(c) Use one FOR/NEXT loop to read, calculate, and print. Print the amount of the investment before the loop.
(d) Interest = Amount Invested × Rate of Interest
(e) Fill in the missing lines.

```
01 REM  Y--YEARS
02 REM  R--RATE
03 REM  I--INTEREST
04 REM  A--AMOUNT OF INVESTMENT

10 DIM Y(3),R(3),I(3)
20 LET A=4000
30 PRINT
40
50 FOR J=1 TO 3
60
70
80
90    PRINT
100
110
120
130
999 END

RUN

AMOUNT: 4000

YEARS: 10
RATE: .12
INTEREST: 480
```

```
YEARS: 15
RATE: .13
INTEREST: 520

YEARS: 20
RATE: .15
INTEREST: 600
```

1. Complete line 40 with a PRINT statement.
2. Which statement should be coded in line 60?

```
(a)   READ  Y(I),R(I)   ✓
(b)   READ  I(J),Y(J)
(c)   READ  I(J),R(J)
(d)   READ  I(I),Y(I)
(e)   READ  Y(J),R(J)
```

3. Complete line 70 with a DATA statement.
4. Which statement should be coded in line 80?

```
(a)   LET  I(J)=A*Y(J)
(b)   LET  I(J)=A*R(J)   ✓
(c)   LET  Y(J)=I(J)*A
(d)   LET  A=Y(J)*R(J)
(e)   LET  A=I(J)*Y(J)
```

5. Complete lines 100, 110, and 120 with PRINT statements.
6. Complete line 130 with a NEXT statement.

II. A retailer is allowed a 3% discount on accounts that are paid within 10 days, 2% if they are paid within 20 days, and no discount if they are paid on the due date. Find the amount of discount for each of the three conditions on an account that has a balance of $2000.

(a) Use two arrays — one for the rates of discount and the other to store the amounts of discount as they are being calculated.
(b) Use a LET statement to enter the balance of the account.
(c) Use the READ/DATA statements to enter the rates of discount.
(d) Read, calculate, and print in one FOR/NEXT loop. Print the account balance before the loop.
(e) Discount = Rate of Discount × Account Balance

[Handwritten notes in right margin:]

```
10  DIM R(3), A(3)
20  Let B = 2000
30  PRINT "Account balance"; B
40  FOR I = 1 TO 3
50  Read R(I)
60  Let A(I) = B × R(I)
70  PRINT "Rate "; R(I)
80  PRINT "Discount"; A(I)
90  NEXT I
100 DATA — — —
110 End
```

```
RUN

ACCOUNT BALANCE: 2000

RATE OF DISCOUNT: .03
AMOUNT OF DISCOUNT: 60

RATE OF DISCOUNT: .02
AMOUNT OF DISCOUNT: 40

RATE OF DISCOUNT: 0
AMOUNT OF DISCOUNT: 0
```

III. Rewrite the above program. This time use the INPUT statement to enter the rates.[3]

```
RUN

ACCOUNT BALANCE: 2000

RATE OF DISCOUNT? .03
AMOUNT OF DISCOUNT: 60

RATE OF DISCOUNT? .02
AMOUNT OF DISCOUNT: 40

RATE OF DISCOUNT? 0
AMOUNT OF DISCOUNT: 0
```

7.3 CALCULATING WITH ARRAYS—Solutions for "Your Turn"

I.

```
1.   40 PRINT "AMOUNT:";A
2. (e) 60 READ Y(J),R(J)
3.   70 DATA 10,.12,15,.13,20,.15
4. (b) 80 LET I(J)=A*R(J)
5.   100 PRINT "YEARS:";Y(J)
```

3. You may omit this problem if you are not using an interactive computer system.

```
      110 PRINT 'RATE:';R(J)
      120 PRINT 'INTEREST:';I(J)
   6. 130 NEXT J
```

II. Using the READ/DATA statements

```
01 REM R--RATE OF DISCOUNT
02 REM D--DISCOUNT
03 REM B--ACCOUNT BALANCE

10 DIM R(3),D(3)
20 LET B=2000
30 PRINT
40 PRINT 'ACCOUNT BALANCE:';B
50 FOR I=1 TO 3
60    READ R(I)
70    DATA .03,.02,0
80    LET D(I)=R(I)*B
90    PRINT
100   PRINT 'RATE OF DISCOUNT:';R(I)
110   PRINT 'AMOUNT OF DISCOUNT:';D(I)
120 NEXT I
999 END
```

III. Using the INPUT statement

```
01 REM R--RATE OF DISCOUNT
02 REM D--DISCOUNT
03 REM B--ACCOUNT BALANCE

10 DIM R(3),D(3)
20 LET B=2000
30 PRINT
40 PRINT 'ACCOUNT BALANCE:';B
50 FOR I=1 TO 3
60    PRINT
70    PRINT 'RATE OF DISCOUNT';
80    INPUT R(I)
90    LET D(I)=R(I)*B
100   PRINT 'AMOUNT OF DISCOUNT:';D(I)
110 NEXT I
999 END
```

7.4 A SORTING PROGRAM

A different version of a wage program was listed in each of Chapters
Three, Five, and Six. The calculation of payroll is usually computerized in many business firms that have computers, particularly if the
payroll is large. Another program that is often used is one that sorts
numbers or names. Shown below is a program that sorts numbers in
ascending order. In Chapter Twelve, you will be asked to write a
program that sorts names alphabetically.

```
01 REM A--ARRAY THAT STORES THE DATA
02 REM T--TEMPORARY STORAGE

10 DIM A(6)

100 REM READ THE NUMBERS
110 FOR I=1 TO 6
120    READ A(I)
130    DATA 4,2,1,5,6,3
140 NEXT I

200 REM SORT THE NUMBERS
210 FOR L=1 TO 6
220    FOR J=1 TO 5
230      IF A(J)<=A(J+1) THEN 270
240      LET T=A(J)
250      LET A(J)=A(J+1)
260      LET A(J+1)=T
270    NEXT J
280 NEXT L

300 REM PRINT THE SORTED NUMBERS
310 PRINT
320 FOR K=1 TO 6
330    PRINT A(K)
340 NEXT K

999 END

RUN

1
2
3
4
5
6
```

Sorting Program

A — ARRAY THAT STORES THE NUMBERS
T — TEMPORARY STORAGE OF A NUMBER

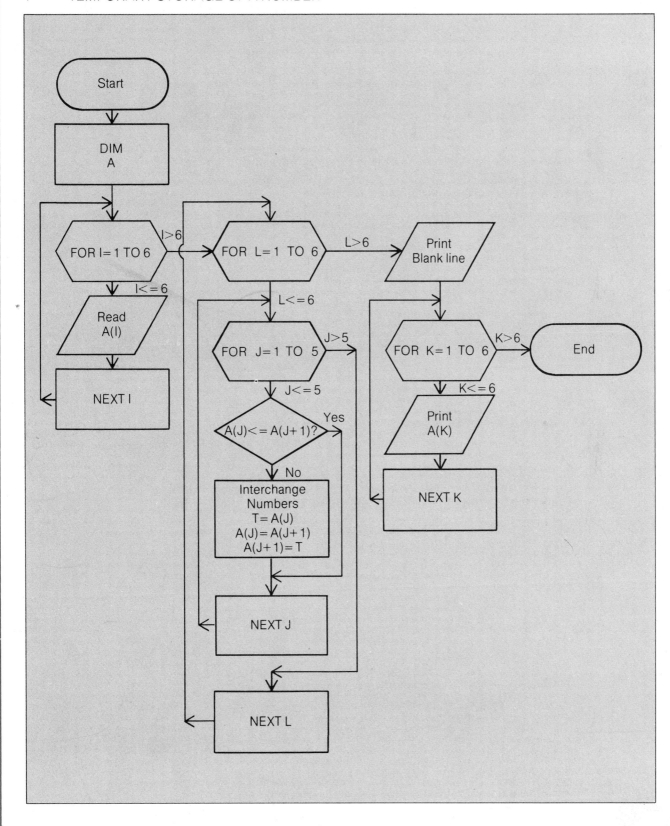

Line 210 — Sets up a loop to sort through the numbers 6 times. *Line 220* — Sets up a loop to sort two adjacent numbers each time the computer passes through the loop. The test value must be one number less than the number of data items, since the number stored in **A(J)** will be compared with the number stored in **A(J+1)**. If the numbers are already in order, no exchange is made; if they are not in order, the two numbers must be interchanged. To perform this, the concept of copying the content of a storage location and placing the value in another location is used. The exchange of two numbers must be done in three stages. At this point **L**, the index of the outer loop, is 1. The numbers are currently stored in this order: 4 2 1 5 6 3. The following is an explanation of one entire **J** cycle.

I. The first time through the loop **J=1**. **A(J)** is actually **A(1)** and **A(J+1)** is actually **A(2)**. Line 230 is false since 4 is not less than 2. Therefore, 4 and 2 must be interchanged.

  1. Place the 4 in temporary storage.   LET $T = A(1)$

T	A(1)	A(2)
4	4	2

  2. Place the 2 in location **A(1)**.   LET $A(1) = A(2)$

T	A(1)	A(2)
4	2	2

  3. Place the 4 in location **A(2)**.   LET $A(2) = T$

T	A(1)	A(2)
4	2	4

The 4 and 2 are interchanged and the order is now:

2 4 1 5 6 3

II. The second time through the loop **J=2**. **A(J)** is actually **A(2)** and **A(J+1)** is actually **A(3)**. Line 230 is false, since 4 is not less than 1. Therefore, 4 and 1 must be interchanged.

  1. Place the 4 in temporary storage.   LET $T = A(2)$

T	A(2)	A(3)
4	4	1

  2. Place the 1 in location **A(2)**.   LET $A(2) = A(3)$

T	A(2)	A(3)
4	1	1

  3. Place the 4 in location **A(3)**.   LET $A(3) = T$

T	A(2)	A(3)
4	1	4

The 4 and 1 are interchanged and the order is now:

2 1 4 5 6 3

III. The third time through the loop **J=3**. **A(J)** is actually **A(3)** and **A(J+1)** is actually **A(4)**. Line 230 is true, since 4 is less than 5. Therefore, no interchange is made and control is transferred back to line 220 by branching first to line 270 (**NEXT J**). The order of the numbers remains

2 1 4↓ 5↓ 6 3.

IV. The fourth time through the loop **J=4**. **A(J)** is actually **A(4)** and **A(J+1)** is actually **A(5)**. Line 230 is true, since 5 is less than 6. Therefore, no interchange is made and control is transferred back to line 220 by branching first to line 270 (**NEXT J**). The order of the numbers remains

2 1 4 5↓ 6↓ 3.

V. The fifth time through the loop **J=5**. **A(J)** is actually **A(5)** and **A(J+1)** is actually **A(6)**. Line 230 is false, since 6 is not less than 3. Therefore, 6 and 3 must be interchanged.

   1. Place the 6 in temporary storage.   LET T = A(5)

T	A(5)	A(6)
6	6	3

   2. Place the 3 in location **A(5)**.   LET A(5) = A(6)

T	A(5)	A(6)
6	3	3

   3. Place the 6 in location **A(6)**.   LET A(6) = T

T	A(5)	A(6)
6	3	6

   The 6 and 3 are interchanged and the order is now

   2 1 4 5 3↓ 6↓.

The **J** loop is complete and control enters the **L** loop. The value of **L** becomes 2 and the **J** cycle is repeated. The **L** and **J** loops continue until the value of **L** is greater than 6. At this point, looping terminates. The numbers are now sorted in ascending order: 1 2 3 4 5 6.

A SHORT SUMMARY

In many applications of programming, the computer must retain all the data that is used in the program. One example is in the sorting of names or numbers; all must be in memory in order to compare one with another to see which one comes first. Some business applications use the same data items several times in a program. This makes it essential that the items be stored in their own locations so that no values are lost when new ones are entered. Although simple variables may perform the same functions, what makes subscripted variables so convenient is the fact that the computer, not the programmer, sets up explicit storage locations to store all the data. These locations are adjacent to one another in a block of storage called an array, to which the programmer assigns a name. In order to give every location a different address, the programmer tells the computer to assign a number to each location along with the name of the array. Thus, each address is unique, since the number assigned to a location is different from any other. An example of a subscripted variable is **P(3)**.

The **P** is the name of the array; the **3** is the subscript. This particular variable represents the third storage location in array **P**.

Usually, a number is assigned to each location of an array by the use of a FOR/NEXT loop as the data items are being stored. The operations of storing, printing, and calculating may be combined in various ways.

1. All three operations may be performed in one loop.
2. Each of the three operations may be performed in its own loop.
3. The data may be read and printed in one loop, while results are obtained and printed in another loop.
4. The data may be read in one loop, while all other operations are performed in a second loop.

By now, you have probably thought of other combinations.

Perhaps the best way to illustrate the difference between the use of subscripted variables and simple variables is by looking at sample programs. The two programs below are actually quite similar; the difference is in the retention of values. Trace through the logic of each program. The problem is one you had in Chapter Four (Review Problem 6, page 146).

Find the largest sale made by one salesperson whose sales are: $8700, $6300, $9400, $7600, $8500.

(a) Use the READ/DATA statements to enter the sales.

(b) In a FOR/NEXT loop, enter and print the data and find the largest sale.

1. Using a Simple Variable

```
01 REM L--LARGE
02 REM S--SALE

10 LET L=-1
20 PRINT
30 FOR I=1 TO 5
40    READ S
50    DATA 8700,6300,9400,7600,8500
60    PRINT "SALE:";S
70    IF S>L THEN 90
80    GO TO 100
90    LET L=S
100 NEXT I
110 PRINT
120 PRINT "THE LARGEST SALE IS:";L
999 END


RUN

SALE: 8700
```

```
SALE: 6300
SALE: 9400
SALE: 7600
SALE: 8500

THE LARGEST SALE IS: 9400
```

2. Using Subscripted Variables

```
01 REM S--SALE
02 REM L--LARGE

10 DIM S(5)
20 LET L=-1
30 PRINT
40 FOR I=1 TO 5
50    READ S(I)
60    DATA 8700,6300,9400,7600,8500
70    PRINT "SALE:";S(I)
80    IF S(I)>L THEN 100
90    GO TO 110
100   LET L=S(I)
110 NEXT I
120 PRINT
130 PRINT "THE LARGEST SALE IS:";L
999 END

RUN
```

One - dimensional.

```
SALE: 8700
SALE: 6300
SALE: 9400
SALE: 7600
SALE: 8500

THE LARGEST SALE IS: 9400
```

Program 1 assigns each sale to one variable — the variable **S**. Each
time a value is read, the sale currently in storage is replaced by the
new one. This means that the contents of **S** *must* be printed before a
new item is entered. Printing the contents of **S** after all sales have
been entered will give you only the last value, since all previous
values have been continually replaced by new ones. As there is only
one storage location for all the sales, a value is referenced by using
just the simple variable **S**.

Program 2 stores each sale in its own storage location: **S(1)**, **S(2)**,
S(3), **S(4)**, **S(5)**. To reference a particular value, the array name must
be used along with its subscript. Since no value is lost as each new
one is entered, there is no need to print each item of data as it is
stored (although Program 2 does it in this way just to show you how

similar the two programs are). This means that data stored in subscripted variables may be printed after all the items are entered.

One final comment. The computer must know in advance the maximum number of storage locations needed, particularly (in most versions of BASIC) when the number of elements in the array is more than 10 or 11. The statement that instructs the computer to reserve a specific number of storage locations is the DIM (DIMENSION) statement.

Questions and Exercises

1. What is a one-dimensional array? How are the items of an array arranged in the computer's memory?
2. What is a subscripted variable?
3. What is the difference between the variable **P3** and the variable **P(3)**?
4. (a) Display and name the different parts of the DIM statement.
   (b) What is the purpose of the DIM statement?
   (c) What three restrictions must be observed when using the DIM statement?
5. Why is it not necessary to dimension an array of less than ten or eleven elements on some computer systems?
6. Write two BASIC programs, each storing ten data items (numbers 1 to 10 inclusive) in the array A.
   (a) Use the INPUT statement in one program to enter the data.
   (b) Use the READ/DATA statements in the other program.
7. Write two BASIC programs, each reading the following data into two arrays.

Array A	Array B
4	16
7	49
2	4

   (a) Use two FOR/NEXT loops and two DATA statements in one program.
   (b) Use one FOR/NEXT loop and one DATA statement in the other program.
   (c) In the program that uses one loop, explain how the data items must be listed in the DATA statement.
8. Write program segments that print the following elements of array A which consists of ten elements.
   (a) The first element.
   (b) The first and tenth elements on the same line widely spaced.
   (c) All ten elements. Use a FOR/NEXT loop. Output is to be printed on one line closely spaced.
   (d) Repeat (c), but have the program print the elements backwards, that is, from last to first.
9. (a) Explain the difference in execution between the following two programs.
   (b) Show the output of each.

I.

```
10 DIM A(4)
20 FOR I=1 TO 4
30   READ A(I)
40   DATA 3,6,9,12
50 NEXT I
60 PRINT
70 FOR J=1 TO 4
80   PRINT A(J);
90 NEXT J
99 END
```

II.

```
10 DIM A(4)
20 PRINT
30 FOR I=1 TO 4
40   READ A(I)
50   DATA 3,6,9,12
60   PRINT A(I);
70 NEXT I
99 END
```

10. Show the RUN of each of the following program segments. Assume that the data items 2, 5, 1, 4 have already been entered into the computer.

(a)

```
10 DIM C(4)
20 LET T=0
--
100 PRINT
110 FOR J=1 TO 4
120   LET T=T+C(J)
130   PRINT T;
140 NEXT J
999 END
```

(b)

```
10 DIM C(4)
20 LET T=0
--
100 PRINT
```

```
110 FOR J=1 TO 4
120    LET T=T+C(J)
130 NEXT J
140 PRINT T
999 END
```

11. Code one or more statements to perform the following operations on array D that consists of six elements. Assume that the data items have already been entered.

(a) Replace the third element by the number 7.
(b) Copy the element in the first storage location by placing the value in the fifth location of the array.
(c) Subtract the first element from the fourth. Store the result in the first location of the array.
(d) Increase the sixth element by 2.
(e) Find the sum of all six elements of the array. Use a FOR/NEXT loop. Store the result in a simple numeric variable.
(f) Multiply each of the six elements of the array by 2 and place each product in the array E. Use a FOR/NEXT loop.
(g) Print the contents of the even-numbered locations of the array on one line closely spaced. Use a FOR/NEXT loop.
(h) Initialize all six elements to zero. Use a FOR/NEXT loop.

12. What is the output of each of the following programs?

```
(a) 10 DIM A(3),B(3)
    20 PRINT
    30 FOR I=1 TO 3
    40    READ A(I),B(I)
    50    DATA 2,8,3,27,4,64
    60    PRINT A(I),B(I)
    70 NEXT I
    99 END
```

```
(b) 10 DIM A(3),B(3)
    20 PRINT
    30 FOR I=1 TO 3
    40    READ A(I)
    50    PRINT A(I),
    60 NEXT I
    70 PRINT
    80 FOR J=1 TO 3
    90    READ B(J)
    100   PRINT B(J),
    110 NEXT J
    120 DATA 2,3,4,8,27,64
    999 END
```

```
(c) 10 DIM A(3),B(3),C(3)
    20 PRINT
    30 FOR I=1 TO 3
    40    READ A(I),B(I)
    50    DATA 3,5,6,4,2,20
    60    PRINT A(I),B(I)
    70 NEXT I
    80 PRINT
    90 FOR J=1 TO 3
    100   LET C(J)=A(J)*B(J)
    110   PRINT C(J)
    120 NEXT J
    999 END
```

```
(d) 10 DIM A(3),B(3),C(3)
    20 PRINT
    30 FOR I=1 TO 3
    40    READ A(I),B(I)
    50    DATA 3,5,6,4,2,20
    60    LET C(I)=A(I)*B(I)
    70    PRINT A(I),B(I),C(I)
    80 NEXT I
    99 END
```

13. Identify the errors, if any, in the program segments shown below. Assume that the required number of items are listed in the DATA statement. Make the necessary corrections.

```
(a) 10 DIM A(10)
    20 FOR J=1 TO 10
    30    READ J(A)
    40    DATA -,-,-,.......
    50 NEXT J
    --
    99 END
```

```
(b) 10 DIM M(16),N(20)
    20 FOR I=1 TO 16
    30    READ M(I)
    40    DATA -,-,-,.......
    50 NEXT I
    --
    100 FOR J=1 TO 14
    110   READ N(J)
    120   DATA -,-,-,.......
    130 NEXT J
    --
    999 END
```

```
(c) 10 DIM X(3),Y(3)
    20 PRINT
    30 FOR K=1 TO 3
    40    READ X(K),Y(K)
    50    DATA -,-,-,.......
    60    PRINT X,Y
    70 NEXT K
    --
    999 END

(d) 10 DIM A(4),B(5)
    20 FOR I=1 TO 5
    30    READ A(I),B(I)
    40    DATA 1,6,2,7,3,8,4,9,5,10
    50 NEXT I
    --
    99 END
```

14. What will be stored in each variable of the array(s) after execution of each of the following program segments? Show the name of the variable and its content. For example, if there are two arrays, you could show the contents in the following manner.

Array A		Array B	
A(1)	1	B(1)	10
A(2)	2	B(2)	20
A(3)	3	B(3)	30

```
(a) 10 DIM A(5)
    20 FOR I=1 TO 5
    30    READ A(I)
    40    DATA 4,8,12,16,20
    50 NEXT I
    --
    99 END

(b) 10 DIM X(3),Y(3)
    20 FOR I=1 TO 3
    30    READ X(I),Y(I)
    40    DATA 4,8,12,16,20,24
    50 NEXT I
    --
    99 END

(c) 10 DIM X(3),Y(3)
    20 FOR I=1 TO 3
    30    READ X(I)
    40 NEXT I
```

```
50 FOR J=1 TO 3
60    READ Y(J)
70 NEXT J
80 DATA 4,8,12,16,20,24
--
99 END
```

(d) Notice that the data statements are the same in Programs (b) and (c). Is there any change in the order of the data items in arrays X and Y after execution of Program (c) in comparison to the way the items were stored in Program (b)? If the order has changed, state the reason.

Problem 1

Q — QUANTITY   C — EXTENDED COST
U — UNIT PRICE   T — TOTAL COST

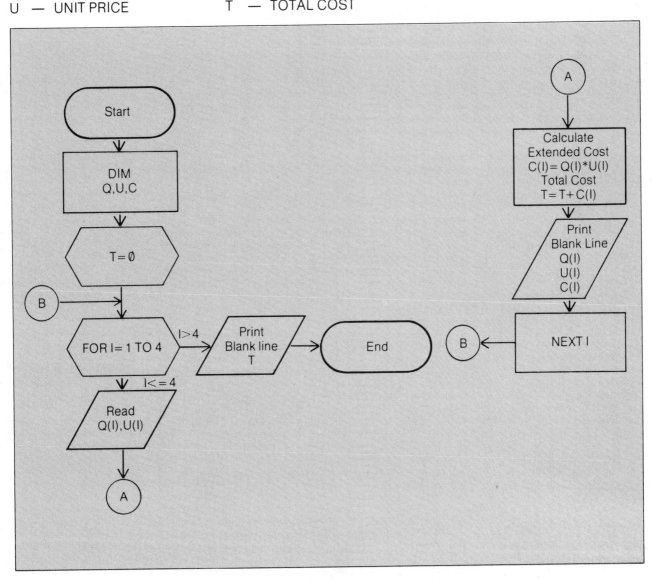

PROGRAMMING PROBLEMS

1. This is the final stage of the program that was started in Section 7.1, page 256. Find the extended costs of the following items and the total cost of all the items.

Item	Quantity	Unit Price
1	2	$4.50
2	4	3.00
3	5	2.25
4	3	5.15

(a) Use the READ/DATA statements to store the above information in two arrays. Array Q stores the quantities, array U stores the unit prices.

(b) Store the extended cost of each item in a third array.

(c) Accumulate the total cost of all the items in a simple numeric variable.

(d) In one FOR/NEXT loop have the computer perform the following:
   (i) Read the data using one DATA statement.
   (ii) Calculate the extended cost of each item.
   (iii) Accumulate the total cost of all the items.
   (iv) Print the data and extended costs as shown in the RUN.

(e) Place the PRINT statement that prints the total cost outside the loop.

(f) Extended Cost of Each Item = Quantity × Unit Price

(g) Total Cost = Total Cost + Extended Cost of Each Item

```
RUN

QUANTITY 2
UNIT PRICE 4.5
EXTENDED COST OF ITEM 9

QUANTITY 4
UNIT PRICE 3
EXTENDED COST OF ITEM 12

QUANTITY 5
UNIT PRICE 2.25
EXTENDED COST OF ITEM 11.25

QUANTITY 3
UNIT PRICE 5.15
EXTENDED COST OF ITEM 15.45

TOTAL COST 47.7
```

Programming Problems 2 to 6 are problems you had in previous chapters. This time you will be using subscripted variables instead of simple numeric variables.

2. Chapter 5, Section 5.4, Page 171

Find the average of the four numbers 67, 85, 79, 93.

(a) Use the READ statement to store the number of numbers in a simple variable. Use this variable as the test value in your FOR statement.

(b) Use another READ statement to store the numbers in an array.

(c) Use one DATA statement.

(d) Use one FOR/NEXT loop to perform the following:
 (i) Read the numbers.
 (ii) Accumulate the sum in a simple numeric variable.
 (iii) Print each number along with a subtotal.

(e) Average = $\dfrac{\text{Sum of Numbers}}{\text{“Number” of Numbers}}$

```
RUN

   67         67
   85        152
   79        231
   93        324

THE AVERAGE IS: 81
```

3. Chapter 6, Section 6.1, Page 202

A retailer is allowed a cash discount of 2% if the store's accounts are paid within 10 days. Suppose the retailer takes advantage of this cash discount when three accounts are cleared with balances of $450, $600, and $240. Find the discount and the amount remitted (paid) on each account.

(a) Use the INPUT statement to store the account balances in an array.

(b) Store the discounts and the amounts remitted in two separate arrays.

(c) Use one FOR/NEXT loop to:
 (i) Enter the data.
 (ii) Calculate the discount and the amount remitted on each account.
 (iii) Print the information as shown in the RUN. (Hint: Use the index as your account number.)

(d) Discount = Balance × .02

(e) Amount Remitted = Balance − Discount

Using the INPUT Statement

```
RUN

ACCOUNT: 1
BALANCE? 450
DISCOUNT: 9
AMOUNT REMITTED: 441
```

Using the READ/DATA Statements

```
RUN

ACCOUNT: 1
BALANCE: 450
DISCOUNT: 9
AMOUNT REMITTED: 441
```

```
ACCOUNT: 2                        ACCOUNT: 2
BALANCE? 600                      BALANCE: 600
DISCOUNT: 12                      DISCOUNT: 12
AMOUNT REMITTED: 588              AMOUNT REMITTED: 588

ACCOUNT: 3                        ACCOUNT: 3
BALANCE? 240                      BALANCE: 240
DISCOUNT: 4.8                     DISCOUNT: 4.8
AMOUNT REMITTED: 235.2            AMOUNT REMITTED: 235.2
```

4. Chapter 6, Review Problem 1, Page 242

Write a program that converts weekly wages of $350, $400, $450, and $500 to hourly rates based on a 40-hour week.

(a) Use the READ/DATA statements to store the weekly wages in an array.

(b) Store the hourly rates in another array.

(c) Use two FOR/NEXT loops:

    (i) One to read and print the data and to calculate the hourly rates.

    (ii) The other to print the hourly rates.

(d) Hourly Rate $= \dfrac{\text{Weekly Wages}}{40}$

```
RUN

WEEKLY WAGES:
   350        400        450        500

HOURLY RATES:
   8.75        10       11.25       12.5
```

5. Chapter 4, Review Problem 3, Page 144

Write a program that determines the balance of a customer's account after each of the following transactions. There is no previous balance. Codes are used to indicate whether the transaction is a purchase or a payment.

```
Purchase . . . . . . . . . . $250
Payment  . . . . . . . . . .  150
Purchase . . . . . . . . . .  300
Payment  . . . . . . . . . .  200
```

(a) Use the READ/DATA statements to enter the code and the amount of each transaction. Store the information in two arrays.

(b) Store the balance in a simple numeric variable. Initialize this variable to zero outside the FOR/NEXT loop.

(c) Use one FOR/NEXT loop to
   (i) Read the data.
   (ii) Calculate the balance.
   (iii) Print the information as shown in the RUN.
(d) Use an ON...GO TO statement for multiple branching.
(e) Use a code of 1 if the transaction is a purchase, a code of 2 if a
    payment is made.
(f) Depending on your code:
    Balance = Balance + Purchase
         or
    Balance = Balance − Payment

```
RUN

CODE, AMOUNT: 1   250
BALANCE: 250


CODE, AMOUNT: 2   150
BALANCE: 100


CODE, AMOUNT: 1   300
BALANCE: 400


CODE, AMOUNT: 2   200
BALANCE: 200
```

Problem 5

C — CODE (INDEX)
A — AMOUNT OF TRANSACTION
B — BALANCE

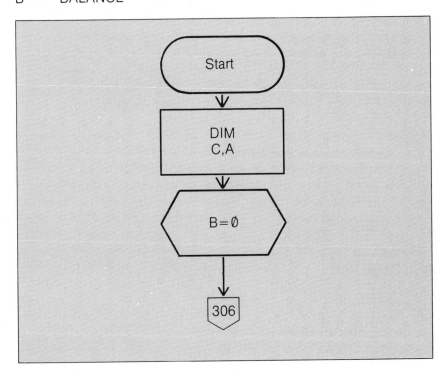

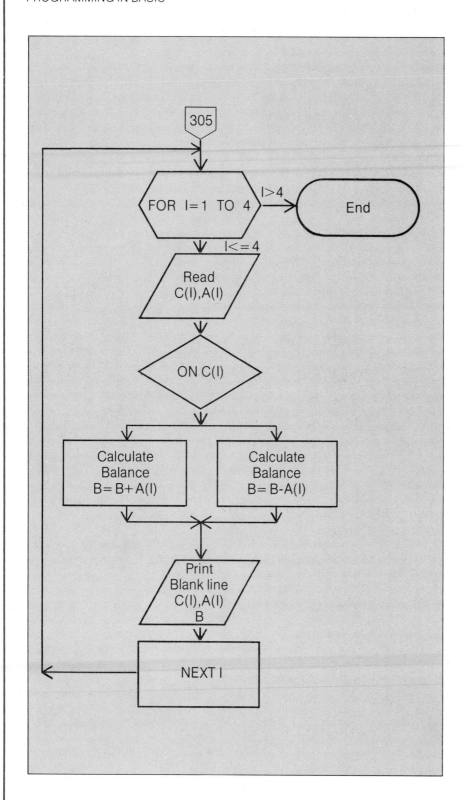

6. Chapter 4, Review Problem 2, Page 142

Employees working for the XYZ Manufacturing Company are paid on the basis of the number of parts produced. If the rate is $2 per part, find the incomes of the following three employees using the weekly record given below.

Employee Number	Number of Parts Produced
49	160
67	158
52	162

(a) Use the INPUT statement to enter the number of the employee and the number of parts produced. Store the information in two arrays.
(b) Store an income in a simple numeric variable.
(c) Use one FOR/NEXT loop to enter the data, to calculate an income, and to print the output.
(d) Income = Number of Parts Produced × Rate

Using the INPUT Statement

```
RUN

EMPLOYEE, PARTS? 49,160
INCOME: 320

EMPLOYEE, PARTS? 67,158
INCOME: 316

EMPLOYEE, PARTS? 52,162
INCOME: 324
```

Using the READ/DATA Statements

```
RUN

EMPLOYEE, PARTS: 49   160
INCOME: 320

EMPLOYEE, PARTS: 67   158
INCOME: 316

EMPLOYEE, PARTS: 52   162
INCOME: 324
```

The remaining four problems are new.

7. Write a program that squares the even numbers from 12 to 20 inclusive.

(a) Use one FOR/NEXT loop to
   (i) Generate the numbers in the FOR statement. (Hint: You will need a STEP clause.)
   (ii) Square the even numbers (the values of the index) and store the results in an array.
   (iii) Print the original (even) numbers.
(b) Use another FOR/NEXT loop with the same initial, test, and step values to print the contents of the array.
(c) Note: Although you will be using only five storage locations in the array, 20 locations must be dimensioned. This is because the DIM statement reserves *adjacent* storage locations starting at location number one (or zero, depending on the computer system being used). Each location is numbered *one* higher than the previous location. When the value of the index is 20, the square of 20 is stored in the twentieth storage location of the array.

Problem 8 conserves memory by reading in the numbers, rather than using the values in the FOR statement as data.

```
RUN

 12   14   16   18   20
144   196  256  324  400
```

8. Write a program that prints the multiplication table for the even numbers 12 to 20 inclusive.

   (a) Use one FOR/NEXT loop to read the five numbers into an array, say N.

   (b) Use nested FOR/NEXT loops to produce the table. The outer loop retains a value, while the inner loop multiplies this value by all the numbers in the array. Your main statement should be

$$\text{xx LET P(J)=N(I)*N(J)}$$

assuming that the index of the outer loop is **I** and the one for the inner loop is **J**. The first time through the **I** loop, 12 is multiplied by each of the numbers in the array. This is performed (and the results printed) during the **J** cycles to produce the following.

        144   168   192   216   240

Control enters the **I** loop and the second number (14) is multiplied by all the numbers in the array during the passes through the **J** loop. The output produced so far is as follows.

        144   168   192   216   240
        168   196   224   252   280

This continues until **I** is greater than 5, at which time looping terminates.

   (c) Print each product immediately after it is calculated. Remember to code a semicolon after the PRINT statement and to place a blank PRINT between the NEXT statements in order to produce the output shown below.

```
RUN

 144   168   192   216   240
 168   196   224   252   280
 192   224   256   288   320
 216   252   288   324   360
 240   280   320   360   400
```

Problem 8

N — DATA NUMBER
P — PRODUCT

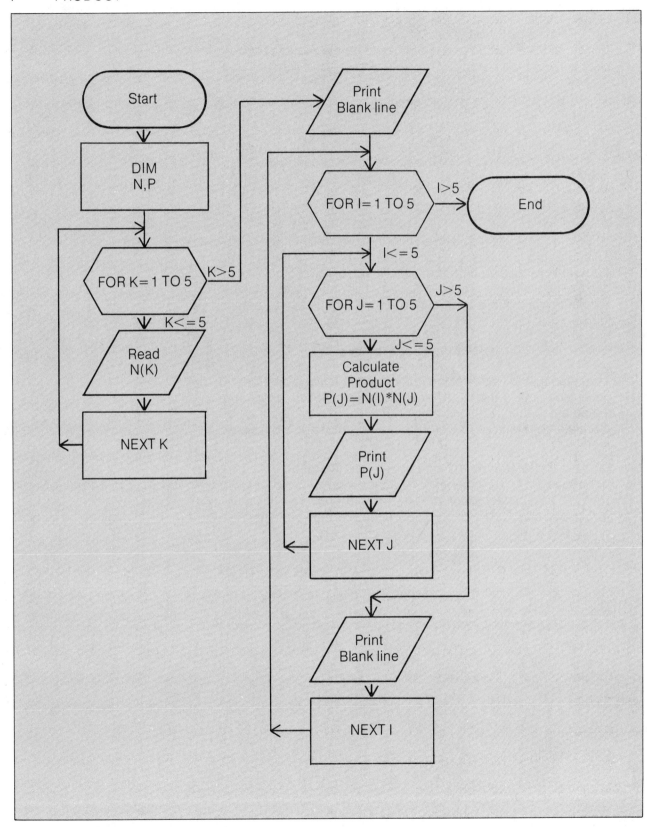

9. Write a program that checks the contents of two arrays to see whether or not a common number is stored in both arrays. If it is, print the number.

Array A contains the numbers 1,3,4,5,7,8.
Array B contains the numbers 9,7,6,5,3,2.
(Hint: Have the computer compare *each* number in array A with *all* of the numbers in array B. The first comparison is when A = 1.)

$$A = 1$$
$$B = 9,7,6,5,3,2$$

If a 1 is found in array B, have the computer print it, otherwise, no printing takes place. Now do the same for the second number in array A.

$$A = 3$$
$$B = 9,7,6,5,3,2$$

This time a 3 is found in array B. The number 3 is printed. To perform the above routine, you need two loops — an outer one to access the elements of array A and an inner one to access all the elements of array B for each one of array A. Your main statement will be

xx IF A(I) = B(J) THEN xx

assuming that the index of the outer loop is **I** and the one for the inner loop is **J**. If the statement is true, transfer control to the statement that prints the common number (from either array). If the statement is false, transfer control to the inner NEXT statement.

(a) Use the READ/DATA statements to store the numbers in two arrays.
(b) Use a separate FOR/NEXT loop to read and print the data.
(c) Use nested FOR/NEXT loops to find the common numbers and to print them.

```
RUN

ARRAY A 1          ARRAY B 9
ARRAY A 3          ARRAY B 7
ARRAY A 4          ARRAY B 6
ARRAY A 5          ARRAY B 5
ARRAY A 7          ARRAY B 3
ARRAY A 8          ARRAY B 2

NO. IN BOTH ARRAYS: 3
NO. IN BOTH ARRAYS: 5
NO. IN BOTH ARRAYS: 7
```

Problem 9

A — ARRAY A
B — ARRAY B

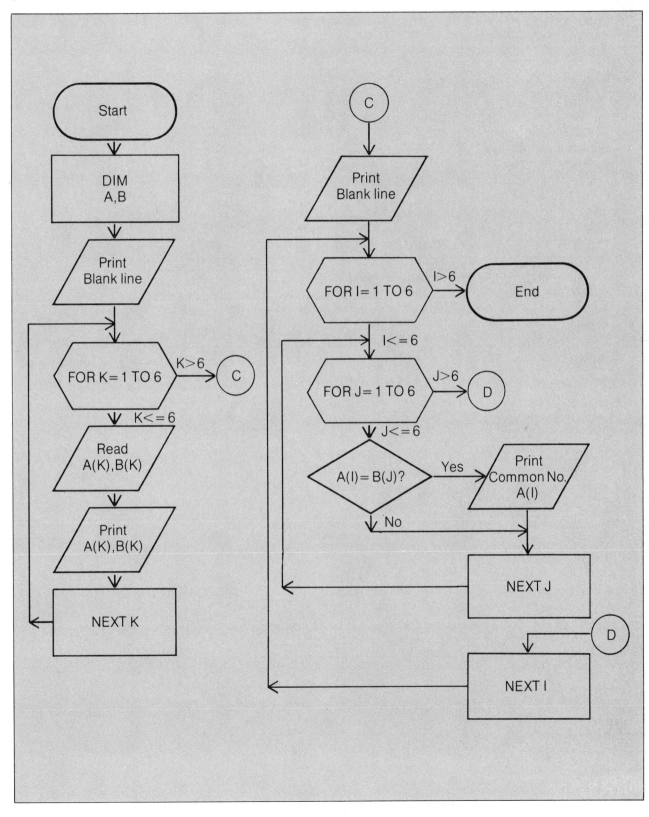

10. Using the data from Problem 9, have the computer add the corresponding elements of arrays A and B. Store the results in array C. Your calculations should be as follows.

Array A	1	3	4	5	7	8
Array B	9	7	6	5	3	2
Array C	10	10	10	10	10	10

Array C now contains a series of tens.

(a) Use the READ/DATA statements to store the data in two arrays (array A and array B).
(b) Use two FOR/NEXT loops:
  (i) One to read the data.
  (ii) The other to perform the additions, print the data, and print the results.
(c) Your statement to add should be

$$\textbf{xx LET C(I)=A(I)+B(I)}$$

assuming that the index for this loop is **I**.

```
RUN

ARRAY A     ARRAY B     ARRAY C
  1           9           10
  3           7           10
  4           6           10
  5           5           10
  7           3           10
  8           2           10
```

EIGHT TWO-DIMENSIONAL ARRAYS

A. After completing this chapter, you should be able to write BASIC programs and complete skeletal BASIC programs that:

1. Store data in two-dimensional arrays by rows or by columns.
2. Print information from two-dimensional arrays by rows or by columns.
3. Perform calculations on data stored in two-dimensional arrays by rows or by columns.
4. Combine the above operations in a variety of ways within FOR/NEXT loops.

B. In addition, you should be able to:

1. Differentiate between:
   (a) A one-dimensional array and a two-dimensional array.
   (b) The DIM statements that reserve storage locations for the two types of arrays.
2. Display and label a doubly subscripted variable.
3. Find errors in programs.
4. Given program segments:
   (a) Indicate how the data is stored, by rows or by columns.
   (b) State what is stored in each variable of the array(s).
5. Write program segments that:
   (a) Print specific elements of an array.
   (b) Perform calculations on specific elements of an array.
6. Produce the output of programs.

8.1 STORING DATA IN ARRAYS

Chapter Seven introduced you to a one-dimensional array. This type of an array can be thought of as a list of numbers arranged either horizontally (in a row) or vertically (in a column).

$$\begin{array}{llll} 1 & 2 & 3 & 4 \end{array} \longleftarrow \text{One row} \qquad \begin{array}{l} \downarrow \\ 1 \\ 2 \\ 3 \\ 4 \end{array} \quad \text{One column}$$

One-dimensional arrays are suitable for a variety of applications, such as storing lists of numbers or names, but they may not be adequate if a large number of data items is required as in statistical programs and various business programs. These are more conveniently handled by two-dimensional arrays, each of which consists of two or more rows (or two or more columns). This arrangement of numbers is also referred to as a matrix.

```
1   2   3   4 ◄── Two rows          1   5
5   6   7   8      Four columns      2   6 ◄── Four rows
                                     3   7      Two columns
                                     4   8
```

As in Chapter Seven, something tangible will be used as an analogy. Suppose a library is located not far from where you live. Books are stored on long shelves and the shelves are partitioned into sections. Although there are many more bookshelves in the library than the number used in this illustration, assume that there are three shelves and that the shelves are partitioned into four sections, giving a total of twelve storage areas. Each storage area holds a different type of book; for example, history books may be stored on the top shelf in the first section, science-fiction books may be stored on the top shelf in the second section, autobiographies may be stored on the top shelf in the third section, etc. In keeping an inventory of the books, the librarian records the number of the shelf and the number of the section where a specific type of book is kept. A two-digit number is used; the first digit denotes the number of the shelf (the row) and the second digit represents the number of the section (the column). The storage areas are numbered as follows.

The storage areas on the first shelf (row) are numbered 11, 12, 13, 14.

	Column 1	Column 2	Column 3	Column 4
Row 1				
	11	12	13	14

Notice that the row is listed first, then the column.

```
1  ,  1        1  ,  2        1  ,  3        1  ,  4
↑     ↑        ↑     ↑        ↑     ↑        ↑     ↑
Row  Column   Row  Column   Row  Column   Row  Column
```

The storage areas on the second shelf (row) are numbered 21, 22, 23, 24.

	Column 1	Column 2	Column 3	Column 4
Row 2				
	21	22	23	24

The storage areas on the third shelf (row) are numbered 31, 32, 33, 34.

	Column 1	Column 2	Column 3	Column 4
Row 3				
	31	32	33	34

Shown below are the twelve storage areas in the library. The library is named the Roxvale Park Library.

ROXVALE PARK LIBRARY

	Column 1	Column 2	Column 3	Column 4
Row 1				
Row 2				
Row 3				

Suppose that mystery books are stored on the third shelf (row 3) in the first section (column 1). This would be recorded as storage area 31. If an abbreviated version of the library's name (say, **R**) is used along with the location of a book, the inventory records would indicate that mystery books are stored in **R**(31); that is, Roxvale Park Library, storage area 31. The location of the history books would be **R**(11), while that of autobiographies would be **R**(13). In BASIC these locations are written as **R(3,1)**, **R(1,1)**, and **R(1,3)**, where **R** is the name of the array and the digits within the parentheses are the subscripts. The two subscripts give the terms **doubly subscripted variable** and **two-dimensional array**. The array is two-dimensional because you work in two directions — across the rows and down the columns. The subscripted variables store the elements of the array. In this case, they store the elements of array **R** and there are 12 such elements (3 rows × 4 columns = 12 elements). As in one-dimensional arrays, a particular item of data is referenced by using the name of the array and the location of the stored value. Unlike one-dimensional arrays, the location must consist of two numbers (subscripts) enclosed in parentheses. The first subscript is the number of the row; the second subscript is the number of the column. These subscripts must be separated by a comma.

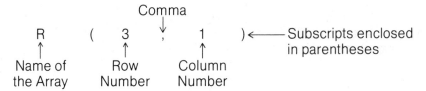

The array name must be unique — no two-dimensional arrays may have the same name. Moreover, it is best not to name a two-dimensional array and a one-dimensional array the same, although some systems allow this. The rule may also apply to a two-dimensional array and a simple variable. Again, check your manual.

The current number of books in each storage area is as follows.

ROXVALE PARK LIBRARY

	Column 1	Column 2	Column 3	Column 4
Row 1	3	2	0	1
Row 2	1	0	2	3
Row 3	2	4	1	0

Make sure you understand that the numbers in the areas shown above represent the *number* of books, just as the array in Chapter Seven showed the *number* of people living in each apartment. There are two mystery books, since a number 2 is shown in row 3, column 1. In BASIC, variable **R(3,1)** is said to contain the number 2. What does **R(1,1)** contain? the number 3.

How does the computer store these numbers in a two-dimensional array? This time nested FOR/NEXT loops are used — one loop for the rows and one loop for the columns. Here is a program that stores the numbers in the computer as elements of array **R**.

```
10 DIM R(3,4)
20 FOR I=1 TO 3          — Row loop on the outside.
30    FOR J=1 TO 4
40       READ R(I,J)
50       DATA 3,2,0,1
60       DATA 1,0,2,3    — Items listed by rows.
70       DATA 2,4,1,0
80    NEXT J
90 NEXT I
99 END
```

Before going through the program, you should know the difference between the variables **I** and **J** in the subscripted variable **R(I,J)**. Because **I** is listed first, this variable represents the number of the row; **J**, then, represents the number of the column. Since **I** denotes rows and there are three rows, the test value in **20 FOR I=1 TO 3** is three. **J** denotes columns, and since there are four columns, the test value in **30 FOR J=1 TO 4** is four. Illustrated below is how the data is stored.

The first time through the loops, **I**=1 and **J**=1. In line 40, **R(I,J)** is actually **R(1,1)**. The number 3 is stored in the first row, first column.

> **40 READ R(I,J) means READ R(1,1)**
> **50 DATA③,2,0,1**

	Column 1	Column 2	Column 3	Column 4
Row 1	3			
Row 2				
Row 3				

I now remains constant, while **J** goes through its cycles. This means that the row number stays the same, while the column number changes.

The second time through the **J** (column) loop, **I**=1 and **J**=2. In line 40, **R(I,J)** is actually **R(1,2)**. The number 2 is stored in the first row, second column.

> **40 READ R(I,J) means READ R(1,2)**
> **50 DATA 3,②,0,1**

	Column 1	Column 2	Column 3	Column 4
Row 1	3	2		
Row 2				
Row 3				

The third time through the **J** loop, **I** = 1 and **J** = 3. In line 40, **R(I,J)** is actually **R(1,3)**. The number 0 is stored in the first row, third column.

```
40 READ R(I,J) means READ R(1,3)
50 DATA 3,2,0,1
```

	Column 1	Column 2	Column 3	Column 4
Row 1	3	2	0	
Row 2				
Row 3				

The fourth time through the **J** loop, **I** = 1 and **J** = 4. In line 40, **R(I,J)** is actually **R(1,4)**. The number 1 is stored in the first row, fourth column.

```
40 READ R(I,J) means READ R(1,4)
50 DATA 3,2,0,1
```

	Column 1	Column 2	Column 3	Column 4
Row 1	3	2	0	1
Row 2				
Row 3				

The **J** (column) loop is now complete and control enters the **I** (row) loop. The value of **I** changes to 2, while the value of **J** reverts to 1. All four columns of the second row will be filled as **J** goes through its cycles. In the READ statements shown below, the number of the row (**I**) remains at 2, while the number of the column (**J**) varies from 1 to 4. The numbers, 1,0,2,3 are stored in the second row.

```
40 READ R(I,J) means READ R(2,1)
                READ R(2,2)
```

```
                        READ R(2,3)
                        READ R(2,4)
60 DATA 1,0,2,3
```

	Column 1	Column 2	Column 3	Column 4
Row 1	3	2	0	1
Row 2	1	0	2	3
Row 3				

The **J** (column) loop is again complete and control enters the **I** (row) loop. The value of **I** changes to 3, while the value of **J** reverts to 1. All four columns of the third row will be filled as **J** goes through its cycles. In the READ statements shown below, the number of the row (**I**) remains at 3, while the number of the column (**J**) varies from 1 to 4. The numbers 2,4,1,0 are stored in the third row.

```
40 READ R(I,J) means READ R(3,1)
                     READ R(3,2)
                     READ R(3,3)
                     READ R(3,4)
70 DATA 2,4,1,0
```

	Column 1	Column 2	Column 3	Column 4
Row 1	3	2	0	1
Row 2	1	0	2	3
Row 3	2	4	1	0

The **I** cycle is now complete and control is transferred to the END statement.

Did you notice that the numbers are stored by rows? The first row is filled, then the second row, and finally the third row. This is because the **I** loop (which represents rows) is placed on the outside, while the **J** loop (which represents columns) is placed on the inside.

```
20 FOR I=1 TO 3      —Row loop on the outside.
30    FOR J=1 TO 4   —Column loop on the inside.
--
80    NEXT J
90 NEXT I
```

While the value of **I** remains one (in the first row), the value of **J** changes from the first column to the second, third, and fourth columns. After the **J** loop is satisfied, **I** changes to 2, which means that the second row is filled as **J** goes through its loops once more. The third row is filled when **I** is equal to 3 and **J** has gone through all its cycles. When **I** is equal to 4, looping terminates.

Care must be taken in listing the numbers in the DATA statement. Because the data is stored by rows, the numbers in the DATA statement must be listed by rows. This is why three DATA statements are used (one for each row), so you can readily see that the data items are listed by rows. The three statements can be combined into one as follows.

1st row   2nd row   3rd row
↓   ↓   ↓

50 DATA | 3,2,0,1, | 1,0,2,3, | 2,4,1,0 |

However, multiple DATA statements will be used in most of the programs in this book so that you can easily distinguish each row (or column).

An alternative method for storing the numbers is by columns.

```
10 DIM R(3,4)
20 FOR J=1 TO 4        — Column loop on the outside.
30    FOR I=1 TO 3
40       READ R(I,J)
50       DATA 3,1,2
60       DATA 2,0,4    — Items listed by columns.
70       DATA 0,2,1
80       DATA 1,3,0
90    NEXT I
100 NEXT J
999 END
```

This program differs from the previous one in two ways:
1. The loops are interchanged. The **J** (column) loop is on the outside, while the **I** (row) loop is on the inside.
2. The data items in the DATA statement are listed by columns rather than by rows.

Illustrated below is a trace through the cycles that fill the first column. The first time through the loops **I**= 1 and **J**= 1. In line 40, **R(I,J)** is actually **R(1,1)**. The number 3 is stored in the first row, first column.

> **40 READ R(I,J) means READ R(1,1)**
> **50 DATA ③,1,2**

	Column 1	Column 2	Column 3	Column 4
Row 1	3			
Row 2				
Row 3				

J now remains constant while **I** goes through its cycles. This means that the column number stays the same while the row number changes. The second time through the **I** (row) loop, **I** = 2 and **J** = 1. In line 40, **R(I,J)** is actually **R(2,1)**. The number 1 is stored in the second row, first column.

40 READ R(I,J) means READ R(2,1)
50 DATA 3①2

	Column 1	Column 2	Column 3	Column 4
Row 1	3			
Row 2	1			
Row 3				

The third time through the **I** (row) loop, **I** = 3 and **J** = 1. In line 40, **R(I,J)** is actually **R(3,1)**. The number 2 is stored in the third row, first column.

40 READ R(I,J) means READ R(3,1)
50 DATA 3,1②

	Column 1	Column 2	Column 3	Column 4
Row 1	3			
Row 2	1			
Row 3	2			

The **I** (row) loop is now complete and control enters the **J** (column) loop. The value of **J** changes to 2, while the value of **I** reverts to 1. The second column will be filled as **I** goes through its cycles.

	Column 1	Column 2	Column 3	Column 4
Row 1	3	2		
Row 2	1	0		
Row 3	2	4		

The process continues for columns 3 and 4. Notice that the order of the variables **I** and **J** was not changed in the subscripted variable **R(I,J)**. The first subscript is *always* the number of the row, regardless of the letter of the alphabet; the second subscript is *always* the number of the column. However, the **I** and **J** loops were interchanged which placed the **J** (column) loop on the outside and in the DATA statement, the data items were listed by columns rather than by rows. As with the DATA statements in the program that stores the items by rows, the DATA statements in this program may also be combined.

$$\text{Col 1} \quad \text{Col 2} \quad \text{Col 3} \quad \text{Col 4}$$
$$\downarrow \qquad\quad \downarrow \qquad\quad \downarrow \qquad\quad \downarrow$$
$$50\ \text{DATA}\ \boxed{\ 3,1,2,\ |\ 2,0,4,\ |\ 0,2,1,\ |\ 1,3,0\ }$$

Shown below are the number of books in each storage area, this time in the form of a matrix without headings or marginal information.

$$R$$

$$
\begin{array}{cccc}
3 & 2 & 0 & 1 \\
1 & 0 & 2 & 3 \\
2 & 4 & 1 & 0
\end{array}
$$

Here is the way to determine the order of the data items in the DATA statement if you want to store the matrix as shown above, that is, **R(1,1)=3, R(1,2)=2, R(1,3)=0, R(1,4)=1, R(2,1)=1**, etc. The loop you place on the outside indicates the way the values are to be listed in the DATA statement. If you have the row loop on the outside, the data items should be listed by rows; if you have the column loop on the outside, the data items should be listed by columns. It doesn't matter how the items are stored (by rows or by columns); if the loop on the outside corresponds with the way the data items are listed, the end result will be the same.

By Rows	By Columns	Final Result
3 2 0 1	3 2 0 1	3 2 0 1
1 0 2 3	1 0 2 ↓	1 0 2 3
2 4 ⟶	2 4 1 ↓	2 4 1 0

Suppose you had the row loop on the outside but listed the data items by columns.

```
--
20 FOR I=1 TO 3
30    FOR J=1 TO 4
--
50        DATA 3,1,2,2,0,4,0,2,1,1,3,0
```

What will now be stored in the array?

$$R$$

$$
\begin{array}{cccc}
3 & 1 & 2 & 2 \\
0 & 4 & 0 & 2 \\
1 & 1 & 3 & 0
\end{array}
$$

In the above matrix **R(1,1)=3, R(1,2)=1, R(1,3)=2, R(1,4)=2, R(2,1)=0**, etc. This is not the same as the original matrix.

Perhaps it should be pointed out that matrices are not actually organized as such in the computer. They are stored as lists. However, users find matrices the most convenient way to think of and to manipulate large amounts of data.

Now look at the DIM statement. Notice that it has two subscripts which are separated by a comma. The first subscript reserves a sufficient number of storage locations for the rows; the second subscript reserves a sufficient number of locations for the columns.

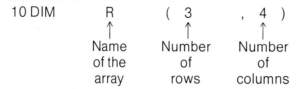

```
10 DIM        R        ( 3      ,  4 )
              ↑          ↑         ↑
            Name       Number   Number
           of the       of       of
            array       rows    columns
```

In this DIM statement, twelve storage locations have been reserved (**3×4=12**). You may reserve more locations than you need for either the rows or the columns, but you may not reserve less. On some computer systems, the DIM statement is not required if each subscript is less than 11. The computer will automatically reserve these locations. However, if one of the subscripts is greater than 10, the DIM statement must be used. As mentioned in Chapter Seven, it is best to dimension every array yourself. You should also note, as you go over the various programs presented in this chapter, that doubly subscripted variables are used the same way as simple variables — they're just named differently. One more comment before going on to some sample programs. In many versions of BASIC, the numbering of the rows and the numbering of the columns start at zero.

Array A

	Column Ø	Column 1	Column 2	Column 3	
Row Ø					← Row Zero
Row 1					
Row 2					

↑
Column Zero

The elements of this matrix are referenced in the same manner as the elements of a matrix that does not have a row zero and a column zero. For example, the top row gives variables A(Ø,Ø), A(Ø,1), A(Ø,2) and A(Ø,3). The variable in the next row, left-most column, is A(1,Ø).

Throughout this book, the top row of a matrix is considered as row one and the first column on the left is considered as column one.

8.1 STORING DATA IN ARRAYS—Sample Programs

As in the first section in Chapter Seven, these sample programs will not give you any output (except for the prompts in the second program), since the programs just store the data and do not print it.

I. In this program, the READ/DATA statements are used to store values in a 2×3 array by rows. Here is the data to be stored in array A.

A

```
10  20  30
40  50  60
```

```
10 DIM A(2,3)
20 FOR I=1 TO 2        — Row loop on the outside.
30    FOR J=1 TO 3
40      READ A(I,J)
50      DATA 10,20,30   — Items listed by rows.
60      DATA 40,50,60
70    NEXT J
80 NEXT I
99 END
```

II. This program uses the INPUT statement to enter the same data, this time by columns.

```
10 DIM A(2,3)
20 PRINT
30 FOR J=1 TO 3   — Column loop on the outside.
40    FOR I=1 TO 2
50      PRINT "VALUE FOR A(I,J)";
60      INPUT A(I,J)
70    NEXT I
80 NEXT J
99 END

RUN

VALUE FOR A(I,J)? 10
VALUE FOR A(I,J)? 40
VALUE FOR A(I,J)? 20   — Values entered by columns.
VALUE FOR A(I,J)? 50
VALUE FOR A(I,J)? 30
VALUE FOR A(I,J)? 60
```

III. Here is a problem that will be completed in three stages:

1. In Section 8.1, the data is stored.
2. In Section 8.2, the data is stored and printed.
3. In Section 8.3, the data is stored and printed and a summation routine is performed.

A department store has two storerooms in which it keeps various styles of shoes. Suppose each room has three shelves with the shelves partitioned into three sections, giving a total of nine storage locations. The storerooms contain identical stock in corresponding locations. For example, in both storerooms, style **A** of shoe is stored on the top shelf, first section; style **B** is stored on the top shelf, second section; style **C** is stored on the top shelf, third section, etc. An inventory is taken and the following number of pairs of each style of shoe is recorded.

Storeroom A	Sec 1	Sec 2	Sec 3
Shelf 1	1	2	3
Shelf 2	4	5	6
Shelf 3	7	8	9

Storeroom B	Sec 1	Sec 2	Sec 3
Shelf 1	9	8	7
Shelf 2	6	5	4
Shelf 3	3	2	1

(a) READ/DATA statements are used to enter the data by rows.
(b) Two programs are written:
   1. The first program stores the data in arrays A and B, using a separate set of nested FOR/NEXT loops for each array.
   2. The second program uses one set of nested FOR/NEXT loops to store the data into both arrays.

1. Using two sets of nested FOR/NEXT loops

```
10 DIM A(3,3),B(3,3)

100 REM STORE DATA IN ARRAY A
110 FOR I=1 TO 3          — Row loop on the outside.
120    FOR J=1 TO 3
130       READ A(I,J)
140       DATA 1,2,3
150       DATA 4,5,6      — Items listed by rows.
160       DATA 7,8,9
170    NEXT J
180 NEXT I

200 REM STORE DATA IN ARRAY B
210 FOR K=1 TO 3          — Row loop on the outside.
220    FOR L=1 TO 3
230       READ B(K,L)
240       DATA 9,8,7
250       DATA 6,5,4      — Items listed by rows.
260       DATA 3,2,1
270    NEXT L
280 NEXT K

999 END
```

In this program, each array is filled by means of a separate routine. The first set of loops stores data in array A. When this is complete, the second set of loops stores data in array B. It is possible to combine all DATA statements, provided the ''combined'' statement is not too long. The listing of the data, however, must be in proper order. All of the data for A must be listed first, followed by the data for B. As mentioned in the previous chapter, some computer systems allow this statement to be placed anywhere in the program, while others insist that it be placed after the DIM statement and/or before the END statement.

290 DATA |1,2,3,4,5,6,7,8,9| , |9,8,7,6,5,4,3,2,1|

Data for Array A   Data for Array B

2. Using one set of nested FOR/NEXT loops

```
10  DIM A(3,3),B(3,3)
20  FOR I=1 TO 3          — Row loop on the
30    FOR J=1 TO 3          outside.
40      READ A(I,J),B(I,J)
50      DATA 1,9,2,8,3,7
60      DATA 4,6,5,5,6,4    — Items listed by rows.
70      DATA 7,3,8,2,9,1
80    NEXT J
90  NEXT I
99  END
```

In this program, the data items are read into the computer in pairs; the first member of each pair is read into array A, the second member of each pair is read into array B. The first time through the **J** cycles, **I**=1 (row 1) and **J**=1, then 2, and 3 (columns 1, 2, and 3). The statements

```
40  READ A(I,J),B(I,J)
50  DATA 1,9,2,8,3,7
```

result in

A(1,1)	1	B(1,1)	9
A(1,2)	2	B(1,2)	8
A(1,3)	3	B(1,3)	7

This is shown below in matrix form.

Storeroom A

	Sec 1	Sec 2	Sec 3
Shelf 1	1	2	3

Storeroom B

	Sec 1	Sec 2	Sec 3
Shelf 1	9	8	7

The second time through the **J** cycles, **I** = 2 (row 2) and **J** = 1, then 2, and 3 (columns 1, 2, and 3). The statements

```
40 READ A(I,J),B(I,J)
60 DATA 4,6,5,5,6,4
```

result in

A(2,1) | 4 | B(2,1) | 6 |
A(2,2) | 5 | B(2,2) | 5 |
A(2,3) | 6 | B(2,3) | 4 |

This is shown below in matrix form.

| | Storeroom A | | | | Storeroom B | | |
	Sec 1	Sec 2	Sec 3		Sec 1	Sec 2	Sec 3
Shelf 1	1	2	3	Shelf 1	9	8	7
Shelf 2	4	5	6	Shelf 2	6	5	4

The third time through the **J** cycles **I** = 3 (row 3) and **J** = 1, then 2, and 3 (columns 1, 2, and 3). The statements

```
40 READ A(I,J),B(I,J)
70 DATA 7,3,8,2,9,1
```

result in

A(3,1) | 7 | B(3,1) | 3 |
A(3,2) | 8 | B(3,2) | 2 |
A(3,3) | 9 | B(3,3) | 1 |

This is shown below in matrix form.

| | Storeroom A | | | | Storeroom B | | |
	Sec 1	Sec 2	Sec 3		Sec 1	Sec 2	Sec 3
Shelf 1	1	2	3	Shelf 1	9	8	7
Shelf 2	4	5	6	Shelf 2	6	5	4
Shelf 3	7	8	9	Shelf 3	3	2	1

Compare the DATA statements in the first program with those in the second. In Program 1, all of the data for array A is listed first, followed by all of the data for array B. This is because each array is filled by a separate set of nested FOR/NEXT loops.

Data for Array A

```
140 DATA 1,2,3
150 DATA 4,5,6
160 DATA 7,8,9
```

Data for Array B

```
240 DATA 9,8,7
250 DATA 6,5,4
260 DATA 3,2,1
```

The second program has only one set of nested FOR/NEXT loops and only one READ statement. The data items are listed in pairs. The first member of each pair is stored in array A; the second member of each pair is stored in array B.

Data for Arrays A and B

```
50 DATA 1,9,2,8,3,7
60 DATA 4,6,5,5,6,4
70 DATA 7,3,8,2,9,1
```

Data is stored in pairs because the READ statement lists both arrays. In this program, array A is listed before array B.

```
40 READ A(I,J),B(I,J)
                ↑       ↑
50 DATA         1,      9  -,-,-,-
```

8.1 STORING DATA IN ARRAYS—Your Turn

I. Identify the errors, if any, in the program segments shown below. Make the necessary corrections.

```
1. 10 DIM A(4,5)
   20 FOR I=1 TO 5
   30   FOR J=1 TO 4
   40     READ A(I,J)
   50     DATA -,-,-,....... (20 items of data)
   --
   100  NEXT J
   110 NEXT I
   999 END

2. 10 DIM B(3,3)
```

for J=1 to 5
for I=1 to 4

```
   20 FOR J=1 TO 3
   30    FOR I=1 TO 3
   40       READ B(J,I)
   50       DATA -,-,-,...... (9 items of data)
   ---
   100   NEXT I
   110 NEXT J
   999 END
```

3.
```
   10 DIM C(3,2),D(3,2)
   20 FOR J=1 TO 2
   30    FOR I=1 TO 3
   40       READ C(I,J),D(I,J)
   50       DATA -,-,-,...... (6 items of data)
   ---
   100   NEXT I
   110 NEXT J
   999 END
```

4.
```
   10 DIM M(4),N(3,4)
   20 FOR I=1 TO 3
   30    FOR J=1 TO 4
   40       READ M(I,J),N(I,J)
   50       DATA -,-,-,...... (24 items of data)
   ---
   100   NEXT J
   110 NEXT I
   999 END
```

5.
```
   10 DIM P(7,8),R(8,7)
   20 FOR J=1 TO 7
   30    FOR I=1 TO 7
   40       READ P(I,J),R(I,J)
   50       DATA -,-,-,...... (98 items of data)
   ---
   100   NEXT I
   110 NEXT J
   999 END
```

6. In the following program segment, the data items are to be stored in their respective arrays by rows.

A				B		
1	2	3		1	4	9
4	5	6		16	25	36
7	8	9		49	64	81

```
10 DIM A(3,3),B(3,3)
20 FOR I=1 TO 3
30    FOR J=1 TO 3
40      READ A(I,J),B(I,J)
50      DATA 1,2,3,4,5,6,7,8,9
60      DATA 1,4,9,16,25,36,49,64,81
--
100   NEXT J
110 NEXT I
999 END
```

II. Answer the following questions for each program shown below.

1. How is the data read, by rows or by columns?
2. What will be stored in the array(s) after execution of each program? You may show the contents in matrix form. For example, if there are two 2×3 arrays, you may display the contents in the following manner.

	A			B	
1	2	3	10	20	30
4	5	6	40	50	60

```
(a) 10 DIM A(3,4)
    20 FOR I=1 TO 3
    30    FOR J=1 TO 4
    40      READ A(I,J)
    50      DATA 10,12,14,16,18,20
    60      DATA 22,24,26,28,30,32
    70    NEXT J
    80 NEXT I
    99 END

(b) 10 DIM M(2,3),N(2,3)
    20 FOR I=1 TO 2
    30    FOR J=1 TO 3
    40      READ M(I,J)
    50    NEXT J
    60 NEXT I
    70 FOR K=1 TO 2
    80    FOR L=1 TO 3
    90      READ N(K,L)
```

```
100   NEXT L
110  NEXT K
120  DATA 10,20,30,40,50,60
130  DATA 15,25,35,45,55,65
999  END

(c) 10  DIM M(2,3),N(2,3)
    20  FOR I=1 TO 2
    30    FOR J=1 TO 3
    40      READ M(I,J),N(I,J)
    50      DATA 10,20,30,40,50,60
    60      DATA 15,25,35,45,55,65
    70    NEXT J
    80  NEXT I
    99  END

(d) 10  DIM M(2,3),N(2,3)
    20  FOR J=1 TO 3
    30    FOR I=1 TO 2
    40      READ M(I,J),N(I,J)
    50      DATA 10,20,30,40,50,60
    60      DATA 15,25,35,45,55,65
    70    NEXT I
    80  NEXT J
    99  END
```

(e) Notice that the data statements are the same in Programs (c) and (d). Is there any change in the order of the data items in arrays M and N after execution of Program (d) in comparison to the way the items were stored in Program (c)? If the order has changed, state the reason.

III. This problem is similar to a problem in the "Your Turn" units of Chapter Seven. Instead of storing information in two one-dimensional arrays, you are to store the data in two 2×3 arrays.

Suppose a savings and loan company offers varying rates of interest on investments, depending on the length of time the money is invested. The data is shown below in matrix form.

No. of Years			Rate of Interest		
Y			R		
10	12	14	.10	.11	.12
16	18	20	.13	.14	.15

(a) Write two programs to enter the above data items into the arrays by rows.

(i) The first program uses two sets of nested FOR/NEXT loops. One set reads the years into array Y; the other reads the rates into array R.

(ii) The second program uses one set of nested loops to read the data into arrays Y and R. Use one READ statement.

(b) In the program that uses one set of nested FOR/NEXT loops, explain why the data items in the DATA statement must be listed in a specific order.

Problem III—Using Two Sets of Nested FOR/NEXT Loops

Y — YEARS
R — RATE

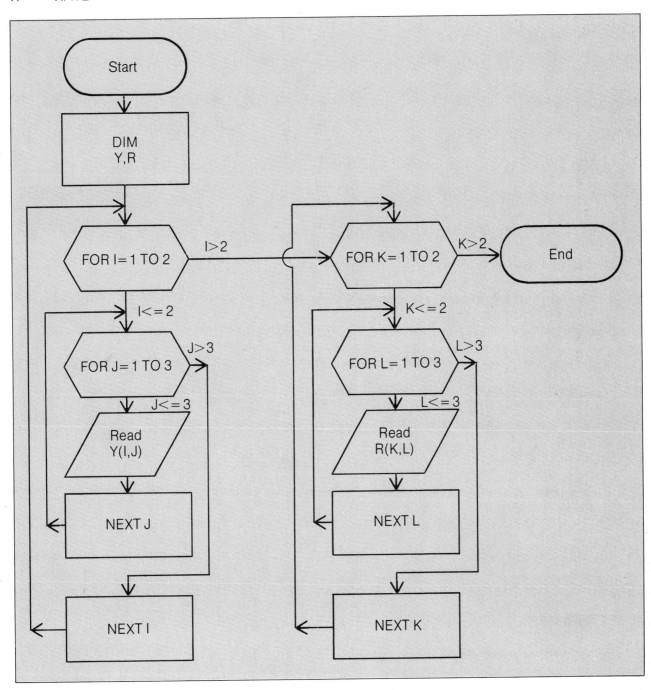

8.1 STORING DATA IN ARRAYS—Solutions for "Your Turn"

I. 1. There is an insufficient number of storage locations reserved for the rows. Depending on the program, this may be corrected in one of two ways.
   (a) Exchange the subscripts of the subscripted variable **A** in the DIM statement.

```
10 DIM A(5,4)
```

   (b) Interchange the test values in the two FOR statements.

```
10 DIM A(4,5)
20 FOR I=1 TO 4
30   FOR J=1 TO 5
```

2. Nothing is wrong. Notice that the subscripts of **B** are **B(J,I)**. In this case, **J** represents the number of the row, since **J** is the first subscript and the first subscript always indicates the number of the row. **I** represents the number of the column. The data is read in by rows because **J** (the row subscript) is the index of the outer loop.

3. The program runs out of data. There should be twelve items of data—six values for array C and six values for array D.

```
50 DATA -,-,-,...... (12 items of data)
```

4. In the DIM statement, the array M must have storage locations reserved for the rows as well as for the columns. Because the row (**I**) loop has a test value of 3, the number of reserved locations for the rows must be at least 3.

```
10 DIM M(3,4),N(3,4)
```

5. Nothing is wrong.

6. Since the READ statement lists two arrays (A and B) and since array A is coded before array B, the DATA statement must list the data items in pairs, so that the first member of

each pair is stored in array A, and the second member is stored in array B.

```
40 READ A(I,J),B(I,J)
50 DATA 1,1,2,4,3,9
60 DATA 4,16,5,25,6,36
70 DATA 7,49,8,64,9,81
```

II. (a) 1. The data items are read in by rows because the index of the outer loop is the first subscript of array A. The first subscript of a doubly subscripted variable represents the number of the row.

2.
```
            A
     10  12  14  16
     18  20  22  24
     26  28  30  32
```

(b) 1. The data items are read in by rows.

2.
```
        M                N
  10  20  30       15  25  35
  40  50  60       45  55  65
```

(c) 1. The data items are read in by rows.

2.
```
        M                N
  10  30  50       20  40  60
  15  35  55       25  45  65
```

(d) 1. The data items are read in by columns since the index of the outer loop is the second subscript of arrays M and N. The second subscript of a doubly subscripted variable represents the number of the column.

2.
```
        M                N
  10  50  35       20  60  45
  30  15  55       40  25  65
```

(e) The order of the data items in arrays M and N is changed after execution of Program (d). This is because Program (c) reads the data by rows, while Program (d) reads the data by columns.

III. (a) **Using Two Sets of Nested FOR/NEXT Loops**

```
01 REM Y--YEARS
02 REM R--RATE
```

```
10 DIM Y(2,3),R(2,3)

100 REM STORE YEARS IN ARRAY Y
110 FOR I=1 TO 2            — Row loop on the outside.
120    FOR J=1 TO 3
130       READ Y(I,J)
140       DATA 10,12,14     — Items listed by rows.
150       DATA 16,18,20
160    NEXT J
170 NEXT I

200 REM STORE RATES IN ARRAY R
210 FOR K=1 TO 2            — Row loop on the outside.
220    FOR L=1 TO 3
230       READ R(K,L)
240       DATA .10,.11,.12  — Items listed by rows.
250       DATA .13,.14,.15
260    NEXT L
270 NEXT K

999 END
```

Using One Set of Nested FOR/NEXT Loops

```
01 REM Y--YEARS
02 REM R--RATE

10 DIM Y(2,3),R(2,3)
20 FOR I=1 TO 2                        — Row loop on the outside.
30    FOR J=1 TO 3
40       READ Y(I,J),R(I,J)
50       DATA 10,.10,12,.11,14,.12     — Items listed by rows.
60       DATA 16,.13,18,.14,20,.15
70    NEXT J
80 NEXT I
99 END
```

(b) The data items must be listed in a specific order because the
     READ statement reads the values into two arrays — Y and R.
     This means that the data items must be listed in pairs, with
     the first item of each pair assigned to a variable of array Y
     (since Y is the first array listed in the READ statement) and the
     second item of each pair assigned to a variable of array R.

```
40 READ Y(I,J),R(I,J)
          ↑        ↑
50 DATA   10  ,  .10  ,12,.11,14,.12
```

8.2 PRINTING FROM ARRAYS

This section explains how the contents of a two-dimensional array can be printed out on a screen or on paper. Below is the program that stored the number of each type of library book in an array called R.

```
10 DIM R(3,4)
20 FOR I=1 TO 3
30   FOR J=1 TO 4
40     READ R(I,J)
50     DATA 3,2,0,1
60     DATA 1,0,2,3
70     DATA 2,4,1,0
80   NEXT J
90 NEXT I
99 END
```

Here are the contents of the array.

Array R

	Column 1	Column 2	Column 3	Column 4
Row 1	3	2	0	1
Row 2	1	0	2	3
Row 3	2	4	1	0

Suppose you want the computer to print the number of mystery books. Since mystery books are stored on the third shelf (row) in the first section (column), simply ask the computer to print the contents of **R(3,1)**.

```
--
50 PRINT R(3,1)
--
99 END

RUN

 2
```

How would you ask the computer to print the element in row 1, column 1, of the array shown above?

```
--
50 PRINT R(1,1)
--
99 END

RUN

 3
```

How would you code the PRINT statement if you wanted to have two elements printed on the same line widely spaced — the element in row 1, column 1, and the element in row 3, column 4?

```
-- --
50 PRINT R(1,1),R(3,4)
--
99 END

RUN

 3          0
```

What would the PRINT statements and the RUN look like if you wanted to have all the elements printed by rows on one line closely spaced?

```
--
40 PRINT R(1,1);R(1,2);R(1,3);R(1,4);
50 PRINT R(2,1);R(2,2);R(2,3);R(2,4);
60 PRINT R(3,1);R(3,2);R(3,3);R(3,4)
--
99 END

RUN

 3  2  0  1  1  0  2  3  2  4  1  0
```

The coding becomes burdensome with so many elements in the array. It would be especially onerous if there were, say, 100 items in the array and you wanted to print them all. As in storing, you can make use of nested FOR/NEXT loops and make the computer look after the job of referencing each storage location. Here is another program segment that prints the number of books in each storage area. This one uses nested FOR/NEXT loops. Although it is written to print 12 items, it can just as easily print more or less. Simply change the subscripts in the DIM statement, the test values in the FOR statements, and the number of data items in the DATA statement.

```
10 DIM R(3,4)
--
100 PRINT
110 FOR I=1 TO 3
120    FOR J=1 TO 4
130       PRINT R(I,J);        ← This PRINT statement counteracts the semicolon.
140    NEXT J                    The next item is printed on a new line.
150    PRINT  ←
160 NEXT I
--
999 END

RUN

   3   2   0   1
   1   0   2   3
   2   4   1   0
```

How did the computer print the numbers as a matrix? It's very similar to what was done in Chapter Six, page 227. The semicolon at the end of **130 PRINT R(I,J);** prints the items on the same line while the computer is in the **J** (column) cycles. Before the computer enters another **I** (row) loop, it is forced off the line by the PRINT statement in line 150. The next item, which is the first item of a new row, is printed on a new line.

In the previous program segments, it was assumed that the data items had already been entered. Two programs that include both the entering and the printing of data are shown below. The first program reads and prints the data items using separate sets of nested FOR/NEXT loops; the second program does both in one set of loops.

1. Using two sets of nested FOR/NEXT loops

```
10 DIM R(3,4)

100 REM STORE ITEMS IN AN ARRAY
110 FOR I=1 TO 3         —Row loop on the outside.
120    FOR J=1 TO 4
130       READ R(I,J)
140       DATA 3,2,0,1
150       DATA 1,0,2,3   —Items listed by rows.
160       DATA 2,4,1,0
```

```
170    NEXT J
180 NEXT I

200 REM PRINT ITEMS FROM AN ARRAY
210 PRINT
220 FOR K=1 TO 3        — Row loop on the outside.
230    FOR L=1 TO 4
240       PRINT R(K,L);
250    NEXT L
260    PRINT
270 NEXT K

999 END

RUN

   3  2  0  1
   1  0  2  3
   2  4  1  0
```

2. Using one set of nested FOR/NEXT loops

```
10 DIM R(3,4)
20 PRINT
30 FOR I=1 TO 3        — Row loop on the outside.
40    FOR J=1 TO 4
50       READ R(I,J)
60       DATA 3,2,0,1
70       DATA 1,0,2,3   — Items listed by rows.
80       DATA 2,4,1,0
90       PRINT R(I,J);
100   NEXT J
110   PRINT
120 NEXT I

999 END

RUN

   3  2  0  1
   1  0  2  3
   2  4  1  0
```

What is the difference in the execution of these two programs? As in the programs in Chapter Seven, pages 267 and 268, the program using two sets of nested FOR/NEXT loops reads in all the data in the first set of loops, then prints the data in the second set. It completes the

READing operation before it starts the PRINTing operation. The program using one set of nested FOR/NEXT loops reads one item of data and prints it right away. It then reads the second item of data and prints that one. The operations of READ and PRINT alternate within the inner loop.

Both programs read and print the data items by rows. The READing and PRINTing of items do not necessarily have to be done this way. They can be read and printed by columns. In fact, the program that uses two sets of loops can read the items one way and print them the other way. The program that uses one set of loops will print the data items the same way as they are read, since the READ and PRINT statements are within the same set of loops. Here are two more variations of the program that uses two sets of nested FOR/NEXT loops. Both read the data by rows, however, the first version prints by rows; the second one prints by columns. Output for both programs is printed on one line closely spaced so you can readily see the difference in the order of the printed items.

1. Prints by rows

```
10 DIM R(3,4)

100 REM STORE ITEMS BY ROWS
110 FOR I=1 TO 3          — Row loop on the outside.
120    FOR J=1 TO 4
130       READ R(I,J)
140       DATA 3,2,0,1
150       DATA 1,0,2,3    — Items listed by rows.
160       DATA 2,4,1,0
170    NEXT J
180 NEXT I

200 REM PRINT ITEMS BY ROWS
210 PRINT
220 FOR K=1 TO 3          — Row loop on the outside.
230    FOR L=1 TO 4
240       PRINT R(K,L);
250    NEXT L
260 NEXT K

999 END

RUN

   3  2  0  1  1  0  2  3  2  4  1  0
```

2. Prints by columns

```
10 DIM R(3,4)
```

```
100 REM STORE ITEMS BY ROWS
110 FOR I=1 TO 3          — Row loop on the outside.
120    FOR J=1 TO 4
130       READ R(I,J)
140       DATA 3,2,0,1
150       DATA 1,0,2,3    — Items listed by rows.
160       DATA 2,4,1,0
170    NEXT J
180 NEXT I

200 REM PRINT ITEMS BY COLUMNS
210 PRINT
220 FOR L=1 TO 4          — Column loop on the outside.
230    FOR K=1 TO 3
240       PRINT R(K,L);
250    NEXT K
260 NEXT L

999 END

RUN

    3  1  2  2  0  4  0  2  1  1  3  0
```

8.2 PRINTING FROM ARRAYS — Sample Programs

What was stored in the sample programs in Section 8.1 will now be printed.

I. This program uses the READ/DATA statements to enter values into a 2×3 array. It uses one set of nested FOR/NEXT loops to store and print by rows. Here is the data.

$$A$$

$$
\begin{array}{ccc}
10 & 20 & 30 \\
40 & 50 & 60
\end{array}
$$

```
10 DIM A(2,3)            — Reserves six storage locations.
20 PRINT                 — Leaves a blank line.
30 FOR I=1 TO 2          — Sets up a loop for the rows.
40    FOR J=1 TO 3       — Sets up a loop for the columns.
50       READ A(I,J)     — Reads items from the data statement one at a time and stores
                           the items in array A by rows.
60       DATA 10,20,30   — Data items listed by rows.
```

```
70      DATA 40,50,60
80      PRINT A(I,J);          — Prints the data by rows on one line.
90    NEXT J                   — Indicates the end of the column loop.
100 NEXT I                     — Indicates the end of the row loop.
999 END                        — Terminates program execution.

RUN

   10   20   30   40   50   60
```

II. The program shown below uses the INPUT statement to enter the
same data. This time the items are entered and printed by
columns. The program uses separate sets of nested loops to
store and print the data so that the output is apart from the
prompts. Compare the output with that of Program I, which
prints the items by rows.

```
10 DIM A(2,3)                      — Reserves six storage locations.
20 PRINT                           — Leaves a blank line after the word RUN.
30 FOR J=1 TO 3                    — Sets up a loop for the columns.
40    FOR I=1 TO 2                 — Sets up a loop for the rows.
50       PRINT "VALUE FOR A(I,J)"; — Identifies the value to be entered.
                                     I varies from 1 to 2 and J varies from 1 to 3.
60       INPUT A(I,J)              — Requests data. User enters the values by
                                     columns.
70    NEXT I                       — Indicates the end of the row loop.
80 NEXT J                          — Indicates the end of the column loop.
90 PRINT                           — Leaves a blank line after the prompts.
100 FOR L=1 TO 3                   — Sets up a loop for the columns.
110    FOR K=1 TO 2                — Sets up a loop for the rows.
120       PRINT A(K,L);            — Prints the data by columns on one line.
130    NEXT K                      — Indicates the end of the row loop.
140 NEXT L                         — Indicates the end of the column loop.
999 END                            — Terminates program execution.

RUN

VALUE FOR A(I,J)? 10
VALUE FOR A(I,J)? 40
VALUE FOR A(I,J)? 20
VALUE FOR A(I,J)? 50
VALUE FOR A(I,J)? 30
VALUE FOR A(I,J)? 60

   10   40   20   50   30   60
```

III. Here is the second stage of the program that was started in Section 8.1, page 324.

Storeroom A				Storeroom B		
	Sec 1	Sec 2	Sec 3		Sec 1	Sec 2	Sec 3

	Sec 1	Sec 2	Sec 3		Sec 1	Sec 2	Sec 3
Shelf 1	1	2	3	Shelf 1	9	8	7
Shelf 2	4	5	6	Shelf 2	6	5	4
Shelf 3	7	8	9	Shelf 3	3	2	1

(a) READ/DATA statements are used to store the data in arrays A and B.

(b) Two programs are written.

  1. The first program reads and prints by rows. It prints the contents of the arrays in separate sets of nested FOR/NEXT loops so that the output of each array is in matrix form.

  2. The second program reads and prints by columns, using one set of nested FOR/NEXT loops.

1. Reads and prints by rows

```
10 DIM A(3,3),B(3,3)

100 REM READ THE DATA
110 FOR I=1 TO 3            — Row loop on the
                             outside.
120    FOR J=1 TO 3
130       READ A(I,J),B(I,J)
140       DATA 1,9,2,8,3,7
150       DATA 4,6,5,5,6,4   — Items listed by rows.
160       DATA 7,3,8,2,9,1
170    NEXT J
180 NEXT I

200 REM PRINT NO. OF PAIRS
201 REM IN STOREROOM A
210 PRINT
220 PRINT "STOREROOM A"
230 FOR K=1 TO 3            — Row loop on the
                             outside.
240    FOR L=1 TO 3
250       PRINT A(K,L);
260    NEXT L
270    PRINT
280 NEXT K

300 REM PRINT NO. OF PAIRS
301 REM IN STOREROOM B
310 PRINT
320 PRINT "STOREROOM B"
330 FOR M=1 TO 3           — Row loop on the
                             outside.
```

```
340    FOR N=1 TO 3
350      PRINT B(M,N);
360    NEXT N
370    PRINT
380 NEXT M

999 END

RUN

STOREROOM A
   1   2   3
   4   5   6
   7   8   9

STOREROOM B
   9   8   7
   6   5   4
   3   2   1
```

Notice that the data items are listed in pairs and by rows. The first member of each pair is stored in array A, the second in array B. Three DATA statements are used, one for each row so that you can readily see how the data is listed. Also, the PRINT routines use different indexes. Array A uses **K** and **L** in its FOR statements, while array B uses **M** and **N**. Even with different indexes, each routine prints by rows, since the first subscript (that is, the row subscript) of each array is used as the index of the outer loop.

2. Reads and prints by columns

```
10 DIM A(3,3),B(3,3)
20 PRINT
30 FOR J=1 TO 3          —Column loop on the outside.
40   FOR I=1 TO 3
50     READ A(I,J),B(I,J)
60     DATA 1,9,4,6,7,3
70     DATA 2,8,5,5,8,2   —Items listed by columns.
80     DATA 3,7,6,4,9,1
90     PRINT A(I,J),B(I,J)
100  NEXT I
110  PRINT
120 NEXT J
999 END

RUN

   1           9
```

```
    4        6
    7        3

    2        8
    5        5
    8        2

    3        7
    6        4
    9        1
```

Note the difference in the data statements between this program and the previous one. This time the data items are listed by columns. Also notice that the column loop is on the outside. A PRINT statement is placed between the NEXT statements so that the blank line it produces will help you distinguish one column from another.

8.2 PRINTING FROM ARRAYS—Your Turn

1. The following questions ask for specific elements to be printed. Assume that the data has already been entered in a 4×4 array named A.

```
            A
        1   2   3   4
        5   6   7   8
        9   8   7   6
        5   4   3   2
```

(a) Write a PRINT statement that prints the last element of the array (fourth row, fourth column).

```
RUN

  2
```

10 print A(4,4).

(b) Write a PRINT statement that prints the first and last elements of the array widely spaced.

```
RUN

  1        2
```

10 PRINT A(1,1), A(4,4).

(c) Write a program segment that prints the elements in the second row of the array closely spaced. (Hint: Use a FOR/NEXT loop for the columns and 2 as the subscript for the row.)

RUN

```
5  6  7  8
```

Handwritten: FOR I = 2   P(I) = 2.
FOR J = 1 TO 4.
PRINT A(I,J),

(d) Write a program segment that prints the elements in the second column of the array one item per line. (Hint: Use a FOR/NEXT loop for the rows and 2 as the subscript for the column.)

RUN

```
2
6
8
4
```

Handwritten: FOR I = 1 TO 4
PRINT A(I,2)
NEXT I.

(e) Write a program segment that prints the elements in the principal diagonal of the array on one line closely spaced. The diagonal is shown below.

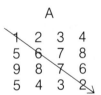

A

```
1  2  3  4
5  6  7  8
9  8  7  6
5  4  3  2
```

Notice that the diagonal falls on those elements whose row numbers and column numbers are the same — that is, where **I=J**. Thus, if **I=J**, the element is to be printed. Use nested FOR/NEXT loops that perform by rows.

RUN

```
1  6  7  2
```

2. Is there anything wrong with the following programs? If there is no error, show the output; if there is an error, state what is wrong and make the necessary corrections. The data is shown below in matrix form.

	A			B	
1	2	3	9	8	7
4	5	6	6	5	4

2.

(a)
```
10 DIM A(2,3)
20 PRINT
30 FOR I=1 TO 3
40    FOR J=1 TO 2
50       READ A(I,J)
60       DATA 1,2,3
70       DATA 4,5,6
80       PRINT A(I,J);
90    NEXT J
100   PRINT
110 NEXT I
999 END
```

(b)
```
10 DIM A(2,3),B(2,3)
20 PRINT
30 FOR I=1 TO 2
40    FOR J=1 TO 3
50       READ A(I,J),B(I,J)
60       DATA 1,2,3,4,5,6
70       DATA 9,8,7,6,5,4
80       PRINT B(I,J);
90    NEXT J
100   PRINT
110 NEXT I
999 END
```

(c)
```
10 DIM A(2,3),B(2,3)
20 PRINT
30 FOR I=1 TO 2
40    FOR J=1 TO 3
50       READ A(I,J),B(I,J)
60       DATA 1,9,2,8,3,7
70       DATA 4,6,5,5,6,4
80       PRINT B(I,J);
90    NEXT J
100   PRINT
110 NEXT I
120 PRINT
130 FOR K=1 TO 2
140   FOR L=1 TO 3
150      PRINT A(K,L);
160   NEXT L
170   PRINT
180 NEXT K
999 END
```

3. This is an extension of the "Your Turn" problem in Section 8.1, page 330. In this section, you are to print the data in addition to storing it.

Suppose a savings and loan company offers varying rates of interest on investments, depending on the length of time the money is invested. The data is shown below in matrix form.

No. of Years			Rate of Interest		
Y			R		
10	12	14	.10	.11	.12
16	18	20	.13	.14	.15

Write two programs, each using the READ/DATA statements to enter the data.

(a) The first program reads and prints the data by rows in one set of nested FOR/NEXT loops.

(b) The second program reads the data by columns but prints it by rows. Use two sets of nested FOR/NEXT loops — one to read the data, the other to print the data. Here is the RUN for both programs.

```
RUN

YEARS 10   RATE .1
YEARS 12   RATE .11
YEARS 14   RATE .12
YEARS 16   RATE .13
YEARS 18   RATE .14
YEARS 20   RATE .15
```

Problem 3 (b)

Y — YEARS   R — RATE

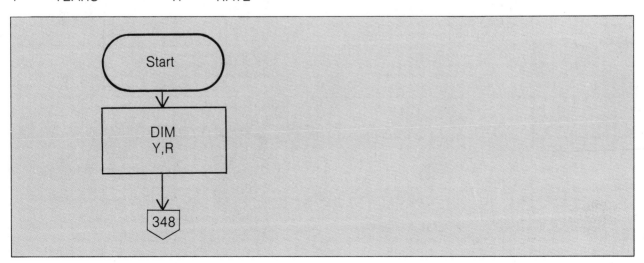

Handwritten notes in margin:

a) 10 DIM Y(2,3), R(2,3).
20 FOR I=1TO 2
30 FOR J=1TO 3
40 Read Y(I,J), R(I,J)
80 PRINT

10 FOR J
FOR I = 1 TO 3
FOR I = 1 TO 2
Read Y(I,J), R(I,J)

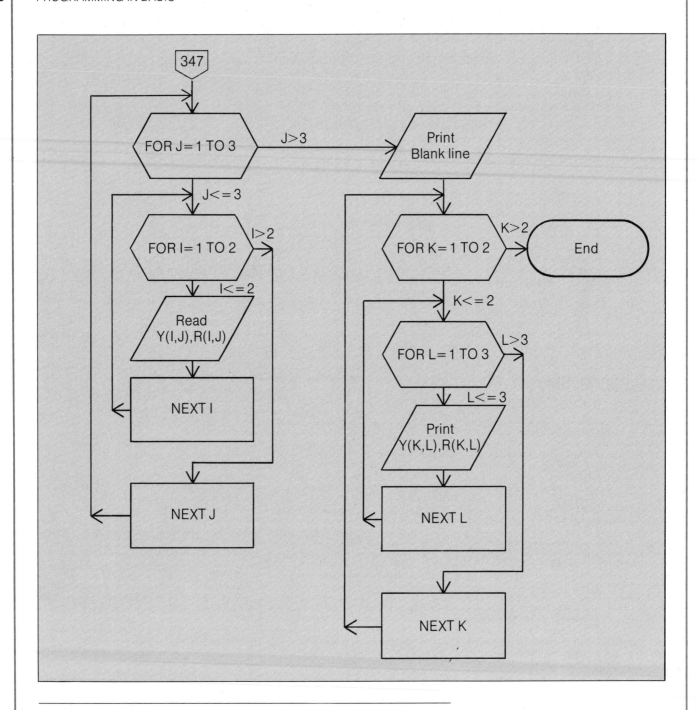

8.2 PRINTING FROM ARRAYS—Solutions for "Your Turn"

1.

(a) `60 PRINT A(4,4)`

(b) `70 PRINT A(1,1),A(4,4)`

(c)
```
30 PRINT
40 FOR J=1 TO 4
50   PRINT A(2,J);
60 NEXT J
--
999 END
```

(d)
```
30 PRINT
40 FOR I=1 TO 4
50   PRINT A(I,2)
60 NEXT I
--
999 END
```

(e)
```
30 PRINT
40 FOR I=1 TO 4
50   FOR J=1 TO 4
60     IF I=J THEN 80
70     GO TO 90
80     PRINT A(I,J);
90   NEXT J
100 NEXT I
--
999 END
```

2. (a) The test values in the FOR statements should be interchanged. Because there are two rows and three columns, the test value for the **I** loop should be 2 and the test value for the **J** loop should be 3.

```
30 FOR I=1 TO 2
40   FOR J=1 TO 3
```

(b) The items in the DATA statement must be listed in pairs so that the first member of each pair is stored in array A, and the second member of each pair is stored in array B.

```
60 DATA 1,9,2,8,3,7
70 DATA 4,6,5,5,6,4
```

(c) Nothing is wrong.

```
RUN

 9  8  7
 6  5  4

 1  2  3
 4  5  6
```

3. (a) Reads and Prints by Rows

```
01 REM Y--YEARS
02 REM R--RATE

10 DIM Y(2,3),R(2,3)
20 REM READ AND PRINT BY ROWS
30 PRINT
40 FOR I=1 TO 2              —Row loop on the outside.
50 FOR J=1 TO 3
60 READ Y(I,J),R(I,J)
70 DATA 10,.10,12,.11,14,.12  —Items listed by rows.
80 DATA 16,.13,18,.14,20,.15
90 PRINT "YEARS";Y(I,J),"RATE";R(I,J)
100 NEXT J
110 NEXT I
999 END
```

(b) Reads by Columns, Prints by Rows

```
01 REM Y--YEARS
02 REM R--RATE

10 DIM Y(2,3),R(2,3)

100 REM READ BY COLUMNS
110 FOR J=1 TO 3            —Column loop on the outside.
120 FOR I=1 TO 2
130 READ Y(I,J),R(I,J)
140 DATA 10,.10,16,.13
150 DATA 12,.11,18,.14       —Items listed by columns.
160 DATA 14,.12,20,.15
170 NEXT I
180 NEXT J

200 REM PRINT BY ROWS
210 PRINT
220 FOR K=1 TO 2            —Row loop on the outside.
230 FOR L=1 TO 3
240 PRINT "YEARS";Y(K,L),"RATE";R(K,L)
250 NEXT L
260 NEXT K

999 END
```

8.3 CALCULATING WITH ARRAYS

How does the computer process data that has been stored in a two-dimensional array? A number of programs and program segments concerning the library books in the Roxvale Park Library are listed in this section to show you how various calculations may be performed. Recorded below, in matrix form, are the number of books in each storage area of the library.

R

	Column 1	Column 2	Column 3	Column 4
Row 1	3	2	0	1
Row 2	1	0	2	3
Row 3	2	4	1	0

I. Suppose you want to know the total number of books in the first two storage areas (row 1, columns 1 and 2). Here is a statement that performs this calculation.

```
--
50 LET T=R(1,1)+R(1,2)
60 PRINT T
--
99 END

RUN

 5
```

Line 50 is executed as follows.

```
50 LET T=R(1,1)+R(1,2)
        = 3 + 2
        = 5
```

II. If you want to know the total number of books on the first shelf (row), the statement will look as follows.

```
--
50 LET T=R(1,1)+R(1,2)+R(1,3)+R(1,4)
60 PRINT T
--
```

```
99 END

RUN

  6
```

III. The previous statement is not too difficult to code since there are only four sections to a shelf. But what if you wanted to know the total number of books in all the storage areas? The statement gets to be quite long. In fact, if there were 100 or 1000 storage areas, it would be almost impossible to code the statement in this fashion. As in storing and printing, FOR/NEXT loops will be used so that the computer references each storage location in the array. Here are two versions of the same program. Both programs store, print, and calculate by rows.

1. This version stores and prints the data in one set of nested FOR/NEXT loops and calculates the total in another set. Notice that the variable **T**, in this program, is initialized just before its use in the calculation routine. Initialization may take place prior to this; for example, right after the DIM statement.

```
10 DIM R(3,4)

100 REM STORE AND PRINT THE DATA
110 PRINT
120 FOR M=1 TO 3          — Row loop on the outside.
130    FOR N=1 TO 4
140       READ R(M,N)
150       DATA 3,2,0,1
160       DATA 1,0,2,3     — Items listed by rows.
170       DATA 2,4,1,0
180       PRINT R(M,N);
190    NEXT N
200    PRINT
210 NEXT M

300 REM CALCULATE AND PRINT THE TOTAL
310 LET T=0
320 FOR I=1 TO 3          — Row loop on the outside.
330    FOR J=1 TO 4
340       LET T=T+R(I,J)
350    NEXT J
360 NEXT I
370 PRINT T

999 END
```

```
RUN

3   2   0   1
1   0   2   3
2   4   1   0
19
```

Here is how the computer accumulates the total.
The first time through the **J** loop, **I**=1, **J**=1, **T**=0, and **R(1,1)**=3. The computer adds whatever is currently stored in **T** to whatever is stored in **R(1,1)**. The result is stored back into **T**.

$$340 \ LET \ T = T + R(I,J)$$
$$= T + R(1,1)$$
$$= 0 + 3$$
$$= 3$$

The second time through the **J** loop, **I**=1, **J**=2, **T**=3, and **R(1,2)**=2.

$$340 \ LET \ T = T + R(I,J)$$
$$= T + R(1,2)$$
$$= 3 + 2$$
$$= 5$$

The third time through the **J** loop, **I**=1, **J**=3, **T**=5, and **R(1,3)**=0.

$$340 \ LET \ T = T + R(I,J)$$
$$= T + R(1,3)$$
$$= 5 + 0$$
$$= 5$$

The fourth time through the **J** loop, **I**=1, **J**=4, **T**=5, and **R(1,4)**=1.

$$340 \ LET \ T = T + R(I,J)$$
$$= T + R(1,4)$$
$$= 5 + 1$$
$$= 6$$

The **J** loop is complete. Control enters the **I** loop and the value of **I** changes to 2 (row 2). The value of **J** reverts to 1. The element in the second row, first column, will now be added. **R(2,1)**=1.

$$340 \ LET \ T = T + R(I,J)$$
$$= T + R(2,1)$$
$$= 6 + 1$$
$$= 7$$

The inside (**J**) loop continues until **J**=4. At this point **T**=12. Control enters the **I** loop (row 3) and **J** goes through its cycles for the last time. The total eventually reaches 19.

Notice that no subtotals are printed, just the final total after all calculations have taken place. If you want subtotals, the statement **PRINT T** must be placed inside both loops (usually right after the summation).

```
300 REM CALCULATE AND PRINT THE TOTAL
310 LET T=0
320 FOR I=1 TO 3
330    FOR J=1 TO 4
340       LET T=T+R(I,J)
350       PRINT T;  —Placed inside both loops.
360    NEXT J
370 NEXT I
```

Output for the subtotals only will look like this:

3   5   5   6   7   7   9   12   14   18   19   19

2. This version combines all operations (except the printing of the total) in one set of nested FOR/NEXT loops.

```
10 DIM R(3,4)
20 LET T=0
30 PRINT
40 FOR I=1 TO 3
50    FOR J=1 TO 4
60       READ R(I,J)
70       DATA 3,2,0,1
80       DATA 1,0,2,3
90       DATA 2,4,1,0
100      PRINT R(I,J);
110      LET T=T+R(I,J)
120    NEXT J
130    PRINT
140 NEXT I
150 PRINT T
999 END

RUN

3   2   0   1
1   0   2   3
2   4   1   0
19
```

The next two program segments perform summations — one adds a row of numbers, the other adds a column of numbers. Assume that the data has already been stored.

IV. Program segment II on page 351 added the number of books on the first shelf (row). It used explicit numbers as subscripts — **R(1,1)**, **R(1,2)**, etc. The program segment is rewritten, this time using a variable to denote the column number.

```
--
40 FOR J=1 TO 4
50    LET T=T+R(1,J)
60 NEXT J          ↑
70 PRINT           Variable used for the number
80 PRINT T         of the column.
--
999 END

RUN

 6
```

Notice that there is no need to use a variable as the subscript for the number of the row since you remain in row one throughout the summation. A variable for the column number is needed because you move from the first column, to the second, third, and fourth. Thus, a loop is required for the columns only.

V. The program segment shown below finds the total number of books in the last section (column). This time the column number remains constant while the row number changes. $J=4$ but a variable is needed for the number of the row. The routine requires a loop for the changing row numbers.

```
--
40 FOR I=1 TO 3
50    LET T=T+R(I,4)
60 NEXT I          ↑
70 PRINT           Variable used for the number
80 PRINT T         of the row.
--
999 END

RUN

 4
```

VI. Assume that the librarian places another book in the storage area located in row 2, column 3. Here is the statement that makes this change.

```
80 LET R(2,3)=R(2,3)+1
```

One is added to the number already stored in **R(2,3)**.

$$R(2,3) = R(2,3)+1$$
$$= 2+1$$
$$= 3$$

VII. Here is another change. The number of books in the first row, first column, is now the same as the number of books in the third row, second column. The statement for this change is as follows.

```
80 LET R(1,1)=R(3,2)
```

This means that whatever is stored in **R(3,2)** is copied and stored in **R(1,1)**. Both storage locations now contain the number 4.

VIII. The program segment below prints out the storage areas (the row numbers and the column numbers) that have no books. It performs by rows.

```
40 PRINT
50 FOR I=1 TO 3
60   FOR J=1 TO 4
70     IF R(I,J)=0 THEN 90
80       GO TO 100
90       PRINT "ROW:";I,"COLUMN:";J
100  NEXT J
110 NEXT I
999 END

RUN

ROW: 1      COLUMN: 3
ROW: 2      COLUMN: 2
ROW: 3      COLUMN: 4
```

Line 70 is executed in the following manner. If an element in the array is the number zero, control is transferred to line 90 and the computer prints the number of the row and the number of the column. The element in the next column of the same row is then checked for zero. If it is not zero, control is transferred to line 100 to check the element in the next column. Once all the elements in the row are checked (the **J** loop is complete), the computer re-enters the **I** loop and each element in the next row is checked for zero as **J** goes through its cycles. Finally, when the elements in all the rows have been checked (in other words, when the **I** loop is satisfied), execution terminates.

IX. Suppose all the books have been signed out. The easiest way to assign zero to each variable of the array is by using nested FOR/NEXT loops.[1]

```
40 FOR I=1 TO 3
50   FOR J=1 TO 4
```

1. It should be noted that some of the elements of the array are already zero. The program segment does not check for this and assigns zero to these variables as well.

```
60      LET R(I,J)=0
70    NEXT J
80 NEXT I
```

The first time through the **I** loop the value of **J** changes from 1 to 4 and each element in row 1 becomes zero. Control re-enters the **I** loop. The value of **I** is now 2 and each element in the second row becomes zero, as **J** goes through its cycles once more. The last time through the **I** loop (the value of **I** is now 3), each element in the third row becomes zero.

X. Here is the last stage of the program that was started in Section 8.1, page 324.

Storeroom A

	Sec 1	Sec 2	Sec 3
Shelf 1	1	2	3
Shelf 2	4	5	6
Shelf 3	7	8	9

Storeroom B

	Sec 1	Sec 2	Sec 3
Shelf 1	9	8	7
Shelf 2	6	5	4
Shelf 3	3	2	1

The supervisor of the shoe department wants to know the total number of each style of shoe. Since each style is stored on the same numbered shelf and section in storeroom A as in storeroom B, all that needs to be done is to add the number of pairs in the corresponding storage areas. For example, in the first row of the matrices shown above, the program adds 1+9, 2+8, 3+7. The corresponding numbers in the remaining rows are then added. The sum of each calculation will equal 10.

(a) All operations are performed by rows.
(b) One set of nested FOR/NEXT loops is used to read the data and to perform the calculations. The sums are stored in a third (two-dimensional) array.
(c) A second set of nested loops is used to print the information shown below.

```
10 DIM A(3,3),B(3,3),C(3,3)

100 REM READ THE DATA
101 REM CALCULATE THE SUMS
110 FOR I=1 TO 3
120    FOR J=1 TO 3
130       READ A(I,J),B(I,J)
140       DATA 1,9,2,8,3,7
150       DATA 4,6,5,5,6,4
160       DATA 7,3,8,2,9,1
170       LET C(I,J)=A(I,J)+B(I,J)
180    NEXT J
190 NEXT I
```

```
200 REM PRINT STATEMENTS
210 FOR K=1 TO 3
220   FOR L=1 TO 3
230     PRINT
240     PRINT "A";A(K,L),"B";B(K,L)
250     PRINT "TOTAL";C(K,L)
260   NEXT L
270 NEXT K
999 END

RUN

A 1        B 9
TOTAL 10

A 2        B 8
TOTAL 10

A 3        B 7
TOTAL 10

A 4        B 6
TOTAL 10

A 5        B 5
TOTAL 10

A 6        B 4
TOTAL 10

A 7        B 3
TOTAL 10

A 8        B 2
TOTAL 10

A 9        B 1
TOTAL 10
```

8.3 CALCULATING WITH ARRAYS— Your Turn

I. This is the final extension of the problem presented in Sections 8.1 and 8.2. In this section, you are to calculate the yearly interest on an investment of $4000 using the rates shown below. The rates are dependent on the number of years the money is invested.

No. of Years			Rate of Interest		
	Y			R	
10	12	14	.10	.11	.12
16	18	20	.13	.14	.15

(a) Perform all operations by rows.

(b) Use one set of nested FOR/NEXT loops to read the data and calculate the interest. Store the interest in a third (two-dimensional) array.

(c) Use another set of nested loops to print the years, rates, and interest amounts as shown in the RUN.

(d) Interest = Amount Invested × Rate of Interest

(e) Fill in the missing lines.

```
01 REM Y--YEARS
02 REM R--RATE
03 REM I--INTEREST
04 REM A--AMOUNT INVESTED

10 DIM Y(2,3),R(2,3),I(2,3)
20 LET A=4000

100 REM READ THE DATA
110 FOR M=1 TO 2
120 FOR N=1 TO 3
130              Read Y(M,N), R(M,N).
140 DATA 10,.10,12,.11,14,.12
150 NEXT N
160 REM CALCULATE THE INTEREST  Y(M,N)*R(M,N).
170 Let I(M,N) = A*R(M,N)
180
190 NEXT M
200 REM PRINT AMOUNT INVESTED
210 PRINT
220

300 REM PRINT YEARS, RATE, INTEREST
310 FOR K=1 TO 2
320 FOR L=1 TO 3
330 PRINT
340
350
360 NEXT L
370

999 END

RUN

AMOUNT INVESTED 4000
```

```
YEARS 10   RATE .1
INTEREST 400

YEARS 12   RATE .11
INTEREST 440

YEARS 14   RATE .12
INTEREST 480

YEARS 16   RATE .13
INTEREST 520

YEARS 18   RATE .14
INTEREST 560

YEARS 20   RATE .15
INTEREST 600
```

1. Which statement should be coded in line 130?

```
(a) READ Y(N,M),R(N,M)
(b) READ Y(M,N),R(M,N)  ✓
(c) READ R(M,N),Y(M,N)
(d) READ Y(N,M),R(M,N)
(e) READ R(N,M),Y(M,N)
```

2. Complete line 150 with a DATA statement.

3. Which statement should be coded in line 170?

```
(a) LET A(M,N)=I(M,N)*R(M,N)
(b) LET R(M,N)=A*I(M,N)
(c) LET I(M,N)=A(M,N)*R(M,N)
(d) LET I(M,N)=A*R(M,N)
(e) LET I=A*R(M,N)
```

4. Complete line 180 with a NEXT statement.

5. Complete line 220 with a PRINT statement.

6. Complete lines 340 and 350 with PRINT statements.

7. Complete line 370 with a NEXT statement.

II. Shown on page 361 is the number of each type of book originally stored in the Roxvale Park Library.

R

	Column 1	Column 2	Column 3	Column 4
Row 1	3	2	0	1
Row 2	1	0	2	3
Row 3	2	4	1	0

Assume that the librarian places two more books in each storage area. Write a program that prints the original number of books and the increased number of books in each storage area.

(a) Perform all operations by rows.
(b) Use one set of nested FOR/NEXT loops to read and print the data.
(c) Use another set of nested loops to increase each element of the array by two, and print these increased amounts.
(d) Draw a flowchart before you write the program.

```
RUN

3   2   0   1
1   0   2   3
2   4   1   0

5   4   2   3
3   2   4   5
4   6   3   2
```

8.3 CALCULATING WITH ARRAYS—Solutions for "Your Turn"

I.

```
1. (b) 130 READ Y(M,N),R(M,N)
2. 150 DATA 16,.13,18,.14,20,.15
3. (d) 170 LET I(M,N)=A*R(M,N)
4. 180 NEXT N
5. 220 PRINT "AMOUNT INVESTED";A
6. 340 PRINT "YEARS";Y(K,L),"RATE";R(K,L)
   350 PRINT "INTEREST";I(K,L)
7. 370 NEXT K
```

II.

```
10 DIM R(3,4)

100 REM READ AND PRINT THE DATA
110 PRINT
120 FOR I=1 TO 3
130    FOR J=1 TO 4
140       READ R(I,J)
150       DATA 3,2,0,1
160       DATA 1,0,2,3
170       DATA 2,4,1,0
180       PRINT R(I,J);
190    NEXT J
200    PRINT
210 NEXT I

300 REM INCREASE THE ELEMENTS
301 REM PRINT THE INCREASED AMOUNTS
310 PRINT
320 FOR K=1 TO 3
330    FOR L=1 TO 4
340       LET R(K,L)=R(K,L)+2
350       PRINT R(K,L);
360    NEXT L
370    PRINT
380 NEXT K

999 END
```

Problem II

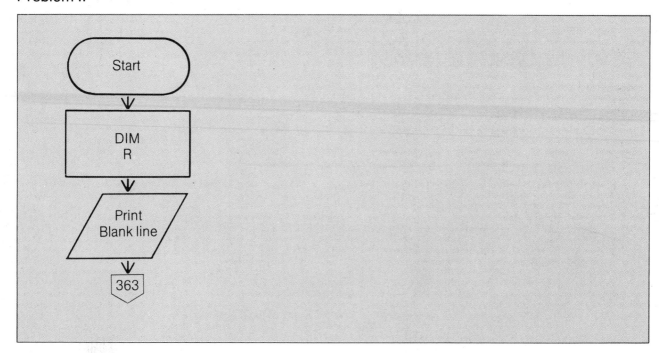

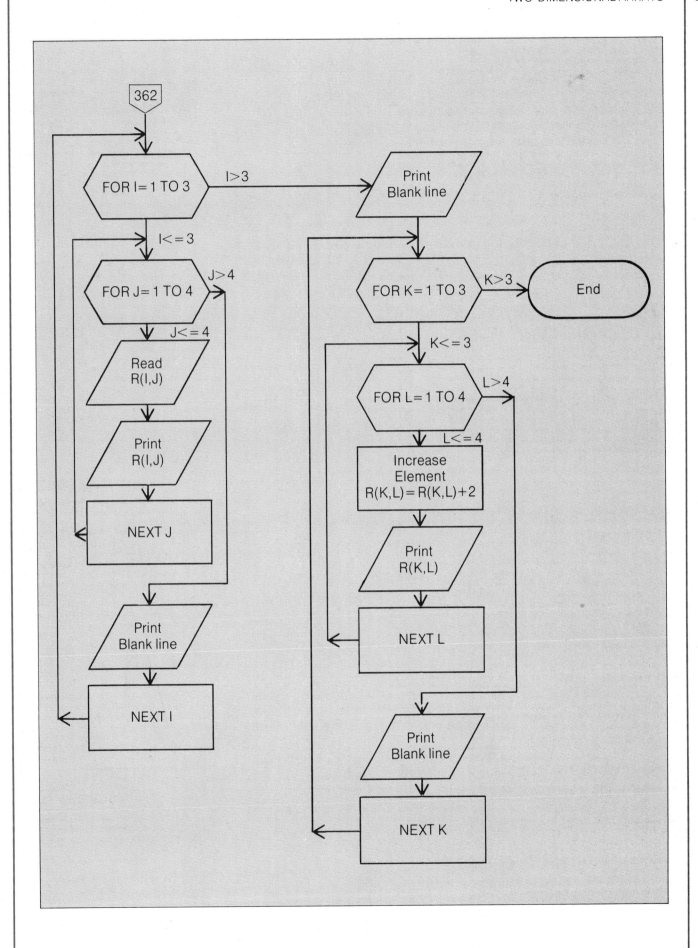

A SHORT SUMMARY

One-dimensional arrays are often inadequate when large quantities of data are to be entered into the computer. These are more conveniently handled by two-dimensional arrays, which are often referred to as matrices. Here is an example of a matrix.

$$A$$

$$\begin{array}{cccc} 2 & 3 & 1 & 2 \\ 4 & 0 & 3 & 1 \\ 0 & 1 & 4 & 2 \end{array}$$

This matrix has three rows and four columns. To reference a particular item of data, the array name must be used and must be followed by two subscripts enclosed in parentheses. The first subscript is *always* the number of the row; the second subscript is *always* the number of the column. These subscripts must be separated by a comma.

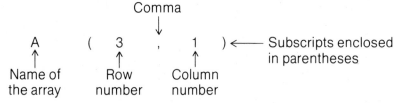

In order to reserve a sufficient number of storage locations, the subscripted variable in the DIM statement must also have two subscripts. The first subscript reserves storage locations for the rows; the second subscript reserves storage locations for the columns.

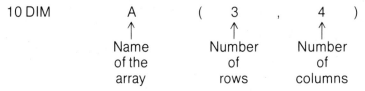

In this DIM statement, twelve storage locations are reserved ($3 \times 4 = 12$).

Whereas a one-dimensional array requires one FOR/NEXT loop, a two-dimensional array usually requires nested FOR/NEXT loops — one loop for the rows and the other loop for the columns. Data may be manipulated either by rows or by columns, depending on the subscript used as the index of the outer loop and on the order of the data items in the DATA statement. If the row subscript is used as the index of the outer loop and the data items are listed by rows, the data will be manipulated by rows.

The storing, printing, and processing of data may be performed in one set of nested FOR/NEXT loops or in several. If one set of loops is used, all operations are performed the same way — either by row or by column. If several sets are used, operations may be performed differently among the sets of nested FOR/NEXT loops.

Questions and Exercises

1. What is the difference between a one-dimensional array and a two-dimensional array?

2. Display and label a doubly subscripted variable.
3. State the difference between a DIM statement that reserves storage locations for a two-dimensional array and one that reserves storage locations for a one-dimensional array.
4. Write two programs that store the following data items in array A by rows.

$$A$$

2	4	6	8
10	12	14	16
18	20	22	24

(a) One program uses the INPUT statement to enter the data.
(b) The other program uses the READ/DATA statements.

5. Write two programs, each reading the following data into two arrays. Use one READ statement in each program.

X	Y
20 22 24	60 66 72
26 28 30	78 84 90

(a) One program reads the data by rows.
(b) The other program reads the data by columns.

6. Identify the errors, if any, in the program segments shown below. Assume that a sufficient number of data items has been supplied. Make the necessary corrections.

```
(a) 10 DIM B(5,4)
    20 FOR I=1 TO 5
    30    FOR J=1 TO 5
    40       READ B(I,J)
    50       DATA -,-,-,...... (25 items of data)
    60    NEXT J
    70 NEXT I
    --
    999 END
```

```
(b) 10 DIM C(3,4)
    20 FOR M=1 TO 4
    30    FOR N=1 TO 3
    40       READ C(N,M)
    50       DATA -,-,-,...... (12 items of data)
    60    NEXT N
    70 NEXT M
    --
    999 END
```

```
(c) 10 DIM X(6,7),Y(7,6)
    20 FOR I=1 TO 6
    30    FOR J=1 TO 6
    40       READ X(I,J),Y(I,J)
    50       DATA -,-,-,...... (72 items of data)
```

```
60    NEXT J
70 NEXT I
--
999 END
```

(d) In the program segment shown below, the data items are to be stored in their respective arrays by columns.

	A			B	
1	2	3	3	6	9
4	5	6	12	15	18
7	8	9	21	24	27

```
10 DIM A(3,3),B(3,3)
20 FOR J=1 TO 3
30    FOR I=1 TO 3
40       READ A(I,J),B(I,J)
50       DATA 1,3,2,6,3,9
60       DATA 4,12,5,15,6,18
70       DATA 7,21,8,24,9,27
80    NEXT I
90 NEXT J
--
999 END
```

7. (i) In each of the following programs, is the data read in by rows or by columns?
   (ii) What will be stored in the array(s) after execution of each program? You may show the contents in matrix form. For example, if there are two 2×3 arrays, you may display the contents in the following manner.

	A			B	
4	5	6	16	20	24
7	8	9	28	32	36

```
(a) 10 DIM A(3,2)
    20 FOR J=1 TO 2
    30    FOR I=1 TO 3
    40       READ A(I,J)
    50       DATA 10,20,30,40,50,60
    60    NEXT I
    70 NEXT J
    99 END
```

```
(b) 10 DIM A(2,3),B(2,3)
    20 FOR I=1 TO 2
    30   FOR J=1 TO 3
    40     READ A(I,J),B(I,J)
    50     DATA 10,100,20,200,30,300
    60     DATA 40,400,50,500,60,600
    70   NEXT J
    80 NEXT I
    99 END

(c) 10 DIM A(2,3),B(2,3)
    20 FOR J=1 TO 3
    30   FOR I=1 TO 2
    40     READ A(I,J),B(I,J)
    50     DATA 10,100,20,200,30,300
    60     DATA 40,400,50,500,60,600
    70   NEXT I
    80 NEXT J
    99 END
```

8. Write one or more statements that print the following elements of a 4×5 array named A.

   (a) The first element (first row, first column).
   (b) The first and last elements on one line widely spaced. (The last element is in the fourth row, fifth column.)
   (c) All 20 elements by rows. Use nested FOR/NEXT loops. Output is to be printed in matrix form.

9. Show the RUN for each of the following program segments. Assume that the data shown below has already been entered.

$$R$$

```
4 7 8 5
8 6 9 7
```

```
(a) 10 DIM R(2,4),P(2,4)
    --
    100 PRINT
    110 FOR I=1 TO 2
    120   FOR J=1 TO 4
    130     LET P(I,J)=R(I,J)*3
    140     PRINT P(I,J);
    150   NEXT J
    160   PRINT
    170 NEXT I
    999 END
```

```
(b) 10 DIM R(2,4)
    20 LET T=0
    --
    100 PRINT
    110 FOR I=1 TO 2
    120    FOR J=1 TO 4
    130       LET T=T+R(I,J)
    140       PRINT T;
    150    NEXT J
    160 NEXT I
    999 END

(c) 10 DIM R(2,4)
    20 LET T=0
    --
    100 PRINT
    110 FOR I=1 TO 2
    120    FOR J=1 TO 4
    130       LET T=T+R(I,J)
    140    NEXT J
    150 NEXT I
    160 PRINT T
    999 END
```

10. Code one or more statements to perform the following operations on a 3× 4 array named R. Assume that the data has already been entered.

$$
\begin{array}{cccc}
& & R & \\
12 & 10 & 16 & 14 \\
20 & 18 & 30 & 22 \\
26 & 24 & 10 & 32
\end{array}
$$

Let R(2,4) = 34

(a) Replace the element in row 2, column 4, by 34.
(b) Copy the element in row 1, column 3, by storing the value in row 2, column 3.
(c) Subtract the element in row 1, column 1, from the element in row 3, column 4. Store the result in row 1, column 1.
(d) Increase the element in row 3, column 1, by 10.
(e) Find the sum of the elements in the second row. Use one FOR/NEXT loop. Store the result in a simple variable.
(f) Find the sum of the elements in the second column. Use one FOR/NEXT loop. Store the result in a simple variable.
(g) Print the number of the row and the number of the column where the element is a 10. Use nested FOR/NEXT loops and perform the routine by rows.
(h) Square each element of the array and store the results in a two-dimensional array named S. Use nested FOR/NEXT loops. Perform the routine by rows.
(i) Initialize all 12 elements to zero. Use nested FOR/NEXT loops and perform the routine by columns.

11. What is the output of each of the following programs?

(a)
```
10 DIM A(2,3),B(2,3)
20 PRINT
30 FOR I=1 TO 2
40   FOR J=1 TO 3
50     READ A(I,J),B(I,J)
60     DATA 1,10,2,20,3,30
70     DATA 4,40,5,50,6,60
80     PRINT A(I,J);
90   NEXT J
100  PRINT
110 NEXT I
120 PRINT
130 FOR K=1 TO 2
140   FOR L=1 TO 3
150     PRINT B(K,L);
160   NEXT L
170   PRINT
180 NEXT K
999 END
```

(b)
```
10 DIM A(4,4)
20 PRINT
30 FOR I=1 TO 4
40   FOR J=1 TO 4
50     READ A(I,J)
60     DATA 1,2,3,4,5,6,7,8
70     DATA 9,10,11,12,13,14,15,16
80     IF I=J THEN 110
90     LET A(I,J)=0
100    GO TO 120
110    LET A(I,J)=1
120    PRINT A(I,J);
130  NEXT J
140  PRINT
150 NEXT I
999 END
```

(c)
```
10 DIM A(2,2),B(2,2),C(2,2)
20 PRINT
30 FOR I=1 TO 2
40   FOR J=1 TO 2
50     READ A(I,J),B(I,J)
60     DATA 7,6,1,0
70     DATA 9,8,5,4
80     LET C(I,J)=A(I,J)-B(I,J)
90     PRINT C(I,J);
100  NEXT J
110  PRINT
120 NEXT I
999 END
```

```
(d) 10 DIM X(3,2)
    20 FOR I=1 TO 3
    30   FOR J=1 TO 2
    40     READ X(I,J)
    50     DATA 5,10,15,20,25,30
    60   NEXT J
    70 NEXT I
    80 PRINT
    90 FOR L=1 TO 2
    100  FOR K=1 TO 3
    110    PRINT X(K,L);
    120  NEXT K
    130 NEXT L
    999 END
```

12. The following program squares each element of array A, stores the results in array B, then sums the squared values. The program, however, has a number of errors. Make the necessary corrections so that it produces the RUN as shown. Here is the data.

A

5	8	6
4	5	4
8	4	5

```
10 DIM A(3,3),B(3,3)
20 FOR I=1 TO 3
30   FOR J=1 TO 3
40     READ A(I,J)
50     DATA 5,4,8,8,5,4,6,4,5
60   NEXT I
70 NEXT J
80 PRINT
90 FOR K=1 TO 3
100  FOR L=1 TO 3
110    LET S=0
120    LET B(K,L)=A(K,L)↑2
130    LET S=S+A(K,L)
140    PRINT B(K,L);
150  NEXT L
160 NEXT K
170 PRINT S
999 END

RUN

25   64   36
16   25   16
64   16   25
287
```

(handwritten annotation near line 30/50: `5,8,6,4,5,4,8,4,5`)

PROGRAMMING PROBLEMS

The first two problems involve the number of library books in the Roxvale Park Library first discussed in Section 8.1. Shown below is the current number of each type of book in each storage area of the library.

	R			
	Column 1	Column 2	Column 3	Column 4
Row 1	2	4	3	2
Row 2	4	2	4	3
Row 3	2	5	3	2

1. Write a program that finds the average number of books in each storage area.

    (a) Use one set of nested FOR/NEXT loops to read and print the data.
    (b) Use another set of nested loops to accumulate the total in a simple variable, say **T**. Keep a running counter to count the number of storage areas as the total number of books is being accumulated.
    (c) Total = Total + Number of books in each storage area
    (d) Average $= \dfrac{\text{Total}}{\text{Counter}}$
    (e) Print the total and the average.

```
RUN

   2   4   3   2
   4   2   4   3
   2   5   3   2

TOTAL: 36              AVERAGE: 3
```

2. This problem is similar to one you had in Chapter Four (Review Problem 6, page 146.) This time you will be using a doubly subscripted variable instead of a simple variable.

    Write a program that finds the storage area that has the greatest number of books. Print the number of books it contains and its location.

    (a) Except for printing the results, perform all operations in one set of nested FOR/NEXT loops.
    (b) Find the greatest number of books as follows. Assign a number, such as − 1, to a simple variable, say **L**. Compare each item of data with the value of **L** and replace **L** with the data item if the item is larger. Your main statement should be **IF R(I,J) > L THEN xx**, where xx is the number of the statement that replaces **L** with the data item.
    (c) Each time a data item is larger than **L**, store the number of the row and the number of the column in simple variables, such as **R1** and **C1**.

```
RUN

GREATEST NO. OF BOOKS: 5
ROW: 3    COLUMN: 2
```

Problem 2

L — LARGE
R1 — ROW NUMBER   C1 — COLUMN NUMBER

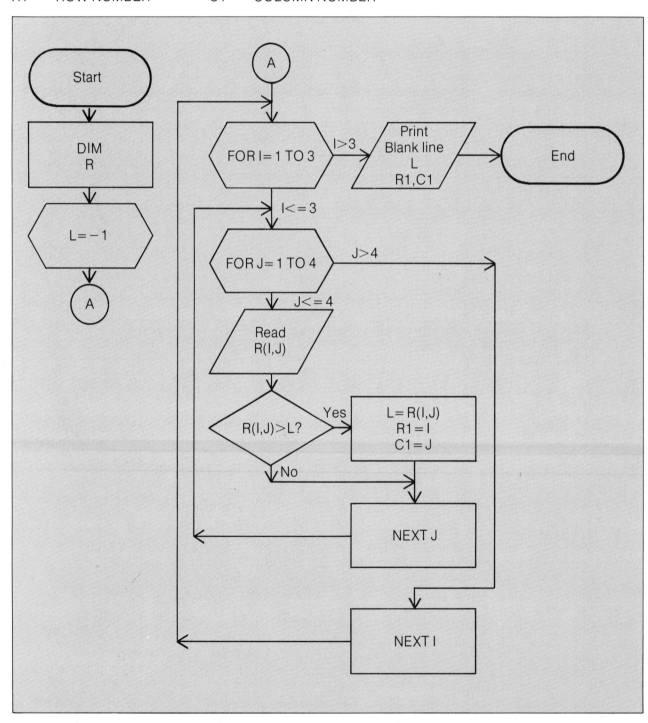

The next five questions are problems concerning the two store-rooms that contain various styles of shoes. Here is the information once more.

	Storeroom A		
	Sec 1	Sec 2	Sec 3
Shelf 1	1	2	3
Shelf 2	4	5	6
Shelf 3	7	8	9

	Storeroom B		
	Sec 1	Sec 2	Sec 3
Shelf 1	9	8	7
Shelf 2	6	5	4
Shelf 3	3	2	1

3. Write a program that finds the following:

— The total number of pairs of shoes in storeroom A.
— The total number of pairs of shoes in storeroom B.
— The total number of pairs of shoes in both storerooms.

Refer to page 352.
Program III (1)

Use four sets of nested FOR/NEXT loops:

— The first set reads the data.
— The second set prints (in matrix form) the number of pairs of shoes in storeroom A.
— The third set prints (in matrix form) the number of pairs of shoes in storeroom B.
— The fourth set finds the total number of pairs of shoes in each storeroom.

(a) Use simple variables to store the totals — for example, **T1, T2, T3**.
(b) Total in Both Storerooms = Total in Storeroom A + Total in Storeroom B

```
RUN

STOREROOM A
   1   2   3
   4   5   6
   7   8   9

STOREROOM B
   9   8   7
   6   5   4
   3   2   1

TOTAL IN STOREROOM A 45
TOTAL IN STOREROOM B 45
TOTAL IN BOTH STOREROOMS 90
```

4. Suppose the supervisor asks the stock clerk to move some of the shoes from one storeroom to the other so that the corresponding storage locations in each storeroom have the same number of pairs of shoes.

   (a) In one set of nested FOR/NEXT loops, read the data and perform the calculations.
   (b) To obtain the same number of pairs in the corresponding storage locations, you must:
   — add the number of pairs in the corresponding locations and store the sums in a third array. (See page 357, Program X.) Your statement should be something like the following.

   $$\text{xx LET } C(I,J) = A(I,J) + B(I,J)$$

   — divide the numbers stored in the third array by 2 and store the results in both array A and array B. One of your statements should be as follows:

   $$\text{xx LET } A(I,J) = C(I,J)/2$$

   You should have a similar statement for array B.
   (c) Use two sets of nested FOR/NEXT loops to print the new numbers from both arrays.

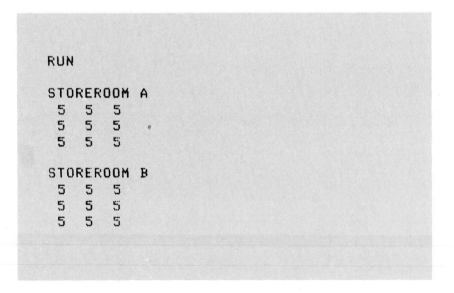

```
RUN

STOREROOM A
   5   5   5
   5   5   5
   5   5   5

STOREROOM B
   5   5   5
   5   5   5
   5   5   5
```

5. Suppose that several pairs of shoes have been sold and that the following numbers of pairs remain in each storeroom.

Storeroom A				Storeroom B		
	Sec 1	Sec 2	Sec 3		Sec 1	Sec 2	Sec 3
Shelf 1	1	3	2	Shelf 1	4	0	3
Shelf 2	5	4	0	Shelf 2	3	1	2
Shelf 3	2	3	5	Shelf 3	5	4	3

Calculate the value of the shoes in each storage location in storeroom A. Shown below are the prices for each style of shoe.

	Prices		
	Sec 1	Sec 2	Sec 3
Shelf 1	$50	$48	$52
Shelf 2	45	53	46
Shelf 3	62	58	64

Use three sets of nested FOR/NEXT loops:

(a) The first set reads the prices into a two-dimensional array, say **P**.

(b) The second set reads the number of pairs of shoes in each storage location of storeroom A and calculates the values. Your statement that calculates the value of each style of shoe should look something like the following.

xx LET V(I,J)=A(I,J)*P(I,J)

(c) The third set prints the values as shown in the RUN.

```
RUN

VALUE OF SHOES IN EACH
LOCATION OF STOREROOM A
  50   144   104
 225   212     0
 124   174   320
```

Problem 5

A — STOREROOM A
V — VALUE OF SHOES   P — PRICE

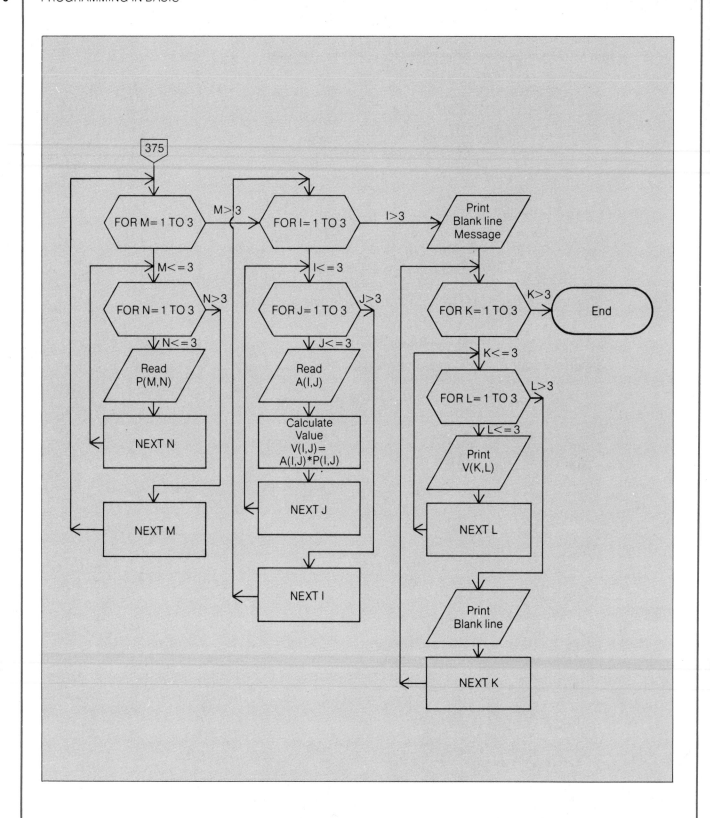

6. Write a program that finds the total value of the shoes in store-room A.

   (a) Use one set of nested FOR/NEXT loops to read the prices.

(b) Use another set of nested FOR/NEXT loops to read the number of pairs of shoes in each storage location of storeroom A, and to calculate the total value. Store the total value in a simple variable, say **T**.

(c) Total Value = Total Value + Number of Pairs in Each Location × Price for Each Location

```
RUN

  1353
```

7. Here is the last problem concerning the storerooms. The supervisor wants to know which styles (that is, which storage locations) in each storeroom have two pairs of shoes or less so that an order may be placed to replenish the existing stock.

(a) Use one set of nested FOR/NEXT loops to perform the following:

— Read the data into both arrays.
— Find each storage location in storeroom A that has two pairs of shoes or less. Your statement to find such a location should look something like the following.

_____IF A(I,J)<=2 THEN xx

where **xx** is the number of the statement that prints the shelf number and the section number of the storage location that has two pairs of shoes or less.

(b) Use another set of nested loops to find the required storage locations in storeroom B and to print these shelf and section numbers.

```
RUN

STOREROOM A
SHELF 1    SECTION 1
SHELF 1    SECTION 3
SHELF 2    SECTION 3
SHELF 3    SECTION 1

STOREROOM B
SHELF 1    SECTION 2
SHELF 2    SECTION 2
SHELF 2    SECTION 3
```

Problem 7

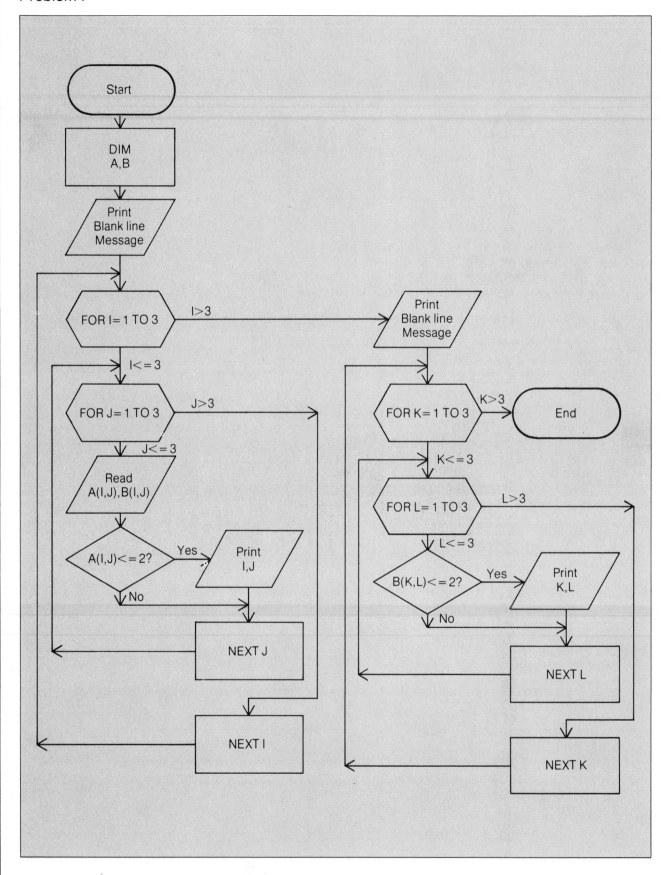

The last three problems will use one or both of the following matrices.

A

1 2 3
4 5 6
7 8 9

B

5 2 7
4 9 6
3 8 1

8. Find the sum of the elements in the principal diagonal of matrix A. Do you remember what is meant by the principal diagonal of a matrix? This is the line that falls on those elements whose row numbers and column numbers are the same. (See page 345, "Your Turn," Problem 1(e).)

Check each element to see if it is located in a row and a column that are numbered the same; that is, if **I**=**J**. If it is, perform the addition and store the sum in a simple variable. Print the element. If **I** is not equal to **J**, print the element just checked, then check the next element. When all the elements have been checked and printed, print the sum of the diagonal as shown in the RUN. Perform all operations in one set of nested FOR/NEXT loops (except the last PRINT). Note: Other than different descriptions within the symbols and a few more PRINT figures, your flowchart should be similar to the one for Problem 2.

```
RUN

   1   2   3
   4   5   6
   7   8   9


THE SUM OF THE ELEMENTS
OF THE DIAGONAL IS: 15
```

9. Write a program that answers the following question. Which numbers stored in array A are also stored in the respective positions of array B? For example, the number 2 in row 1, column 2, of array A is also in row 1, column 2, of array B. When you find such a number, store it in a simple variable, say **C**. Your main statement should be

_____IF A(I,J)=B(I,J) THEN xx

where **xx** is the number of the statement that stores the common number in variable **C**. Use one set of nested FOR/NEXT loops.

```
RUN

   2   4   6   8
```

Problem 9

C — COMMON NUMBER

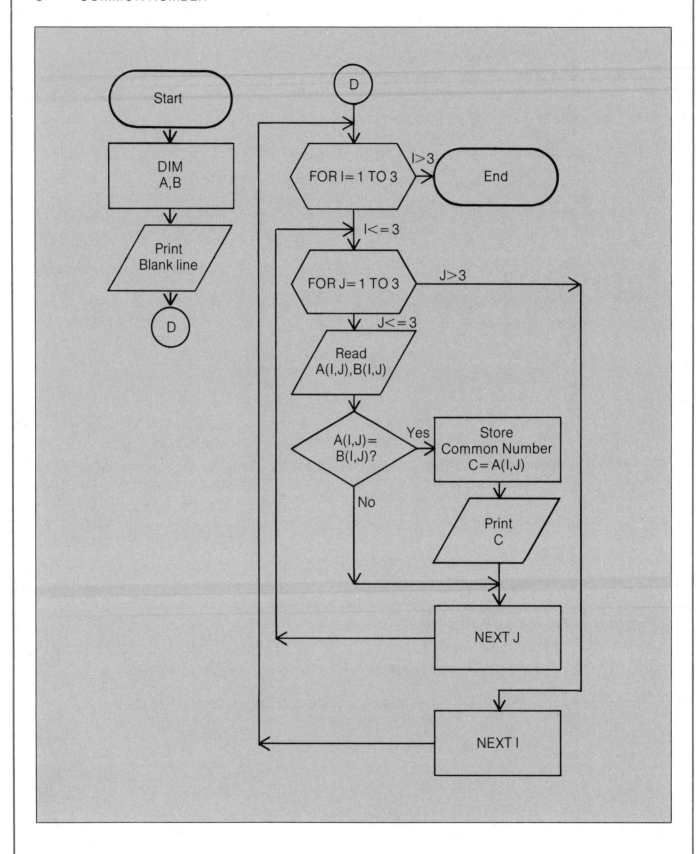

10. Write separate programs to perform the following on matrix A:

    (a) Find the sum of the elements in each row.
    (b) Find the sum of the elements in each column.
    To find the sum of the elements in each row:
    — Place the row loop on the outside.
    — Initialize **S** (SUM) to zero between the FOR statements.
    — Place the column loop on the inside.
    To find the sum of the elements in each column:
    — Place the column loop on the outside.
    — Initialize **S** (SUM) to zero between the FOR statements.
    — Place the row loop on the inside.
       Use separate sets of nested FOR/NEXT loops in each program to read the data and find the sums. To print the row numbers and the column numbers as shown in the RUNS, print the values of **I** and **J**.

Program (a)

```
RUN

SUM OF ROW 1 IS: 6
SUM OF ROW 2 IS: 15
SUM OF ROW 3 IS: 24
```

Program (b)

```
RUN

SUM OF COLUMN 1 IS: 12
SUM OF COLUMN 2 IS: 15
SUM OF COLUMN 3 IS: 18
```

NINE MATRIX STATEMENTS AND LIBRARY FUNCTIONS

A. Depending on the support given by your computer system, the completion of this chapter should enable you to write BASIC programs and complete skeletal BASIC programs that:
1. Use MAT statements to manipulate data in arrays.
2. Use the INT function to:
   (a) Separate digits from numbers and break down amounts into components.
   (b) Check the exactness of division.
   (c) Round off numbers.
3. Use the RND function to:
   (a) Generate random decimal numbers.
   (b) Generate random whole numbers.
4. Use the ABS, SGN, and SQR library functions.

B. In addition, you should be able to:
1. Convert a program that uses FOR/NEXT loops to manipulate data in arrays to one that uses MAT statements.
2. State how data is entered by a MAT READ and a MAT INPUT.
3. Write MAT statements that perform specific functions.
4. (a) State which MAT statements may be used to redimension arrays.
   (b) Code these statements in a program segment.
5. Produce the output of programs.
6. Find errors in program segments.
7. (a) Define the term library function.
   (b) State two other terms that name this function.
   (c) Explain how library functions are "called."
8. State the purpose of:
   (a) A library function.
   (b) The INT function.
   (c) The RND function.
   (d) The ABS, SGN, and SQR functions.
9. Recognize other library functions.
10. (a) Define the term argument.
    (b) State how an argument may be expressed.
11. Evaluate expressions that use the INT function.
12. (a) State two reasons why numbers generated by the RND function are not truly random.
    (b) Summarize the meaning of the statement "numbers generated by the RND function are evenly distributed between 0 and 1."

9.1 MATRIX STATEMENTS

The last two chapters introduced you to one-dimensional and two-dimensional arrays. To be able to read data, print items, and perform calculations, FOR/NEXT loops were used. However, a number of operations involving arrays can be handled more conveniently by **MATrix** statements. Not all versions of BASIC include these instructions, so check your manual or experiment with some of the ones shown below. If your computer system does not support MATrix statements, you may skip this section.

MAT statements instruct the computer to perform operations on an entire array rather than on one element at a time. Thus, programs are much shorter, since operations performed by these instructions do not require FOR/NEXT loops. The general form of a MAT statement looks like the following.

20	MAT	READ	A
↑	↑	↑	↑
Statement Number	Key word	Function to be performed	Name of the Array

Here is a list of some of the functions performed by MAT statements.

Input/Output

MAT READ A	— Reads the data into array A.
MAT INPUT A	— Allows the user to key the data into array A.
MAT PRINT A	— Prints items from array A.

Assignment[1]

MAT B = A	— Copies the elements of array A and stores them in array B.
MAT A = ZER	— Assigns zero to each variable of array A.
MAT A = CON	— Assigns the number one to each variable of array A.
MAT A = IDN	— Assigns the identity matrix to matrix A.

Mathematical

MAT C = A + B	— Adds the elements of array A to the corresponding elements of array B and stores the sums in the corresponding locations of array C.
MAT C = A − B	— Subtracts the elements of array B from the corresponding elements of array A and stores the differences in the corresponding locations of array C.
MAT B = (2)*A	— Multiplies each element of array A by 2 (a scalar) and stores the products in array B.
MAT C = A*B	— Using **matrix** multiplication, multiplies matrix A by matrix B and stores the products in matrix C.

Special

MAT B = TRN(A)	— Transposes the rows and columns of matrix A and stores the result in matrix B.
MAT B = INV(A)	— Determines the inverse of matrix A and stores the result in matrix B.

---

1. As with an array created in a FOR/NEXT loop, subscripted variables will be used to refer to storage locations in an array created by a MAT statement. The term matrix refers strictly to a two-dimensional array.

Before these statements are explained, compare a program that uses MAT statements with one that uses FOR/NEXT loops.

Using FOR/NEXT Loops   ## Using MAT Statements

```
10 DIM A(2,3)                10 DIM A(2,3)
20 PRINT                     20 MAT READ A
30 FOR I=1 TO 2              30 DATA -,-,-,  (6 items of data)
40    FOR J=1 TO 3           40 PRINT
50       READ A(I,J)         50 MAT PRINT A
60       DATA -,-,-, (6 items of data)   99 END
70       PRINT A(I,J);
80    NEXT J
90    PRINT
100 NEXT I
999 END
```

The program using FOR/NEXT loops requires at least eleven statements to read and print the data; more would be needed if the PRINT routine had its own nest of loops. The program using MAT statements requires only six statements, yet data is entered and printed the same way — that is, by rows.

It was mentioned in the previous chapter that some computer systems support matrices with zero subscripts.[2] On these systems, MAT statements may not manipulate variables with zero subscripts; they assume that the subscripts start at 1. This means that **DIM A(3,4)** reserves 20 storage locations (0 to 3 for the first subscript, and 0 to 4 for the second subscript), but a MAT statement will use only 12 of these locations (1 to 3 for the first subscript, and 1 to 4 for the second subscript). If the DIM statement is omitted, matrix A will automatically have 121 storage locations reserved for its elements (0 to 10 for each subscript). It may be necessary to supply 100 values (1 to 10 for each subscript, since the zero subscripts may be ignored). If only 12 data items are supplied, an error message may occur when an attempt is made to use a MAT statement. It is therefore recommended that all matrices referenced by MAT statements have their dimensions defined.

It should also be mentioned that each MAT statement works independently of another. For example, if data is read by a **MAT READ**, it is not necessary that the data be printed by a **MAT PRINT**. Furthermore, a specific element of the array must still be accessed by a subscripted variable. And, on many computer systems, the same array name may not be coded on both sides of the equals sign. Examples of invalid statements are as follows.

```
30 MAT A=A+B
40 MAT B=A*B
50 MAT C=INV(C)
```

2. As mentioned in Chapter Eight, zero subscripts are not used in this book.

Each of the MAT statements listed earlier in this section will now be briefly explained.

The following program segment stores data in a one-dimensional array (a vector).

```
10 DIM A(4)
20 MAT READ A
30 DATA 1,2,3,4
---
99 END
```

Some computer systems allow one subscript in the DIM statement of a one-dimensional array, such as **DIM A(4);** followed by a MAT READ statement or a **MAT INPUT** statement. Others insist on two sub-scripts — **A(1,4)** if the list is thought of as a row of numbers, or **A(4,1)** if the list is thought of as a column of numbers.

The MAT READ statement may also be used to store values in a two-dimensional array (a matrix).

```
10 DIM A(3,4)
20 MAT READ A
30 DATA 1,2,3,4,5,6,7,8,9,10,11,12
---
99 END
```

Values that are stored in a matrix by a MAT READ statement must be entered by rows, which means that the items in the DATA statement must be listed by rows.

Most versions of BASIC allow several matrices and vectors to be listed in one MAT READ statement.

```
10 DIM A(3,4),B(2,3),C(4)
20 MAT READ A,B,C
30 DATA 1,2,3,4,5,6,7,8,9,10,11,12
40 DATA 6,5,4,3,2,1
50 DATA 4,3,2,1
---
99 END
```

The first 12 data items are stored in matrix A, the next 6 are stored in matrix B, and the last 4 are stored in vector C. On the majority of systems, there must be sufficient data to fill all the positions reserved by the DIM statement.

The MAT INPUT statement is another MAT instruction that enters values into an array.

```
10 DIM A(4)
20 MAT INPUT A
99 END

RUN

?
```

When the above program is executed, the computer displays a question mark. Numbers may be typed on separate lines by pressing the RETURN key after each value is entered. A comma must separate the numbers if more than one value is typed on a line. If there are too many entries for one line, some systems allow an ampersand to be typed at the end of the unfinished line. Another question mark, generated by the ampersand, is displayed at the beginning of the next line and the remaining data items are then keyed in. The process may be repeated for additional lines of input. Many systems automatically display a question mark on a new line when the RETURN key is pressed and not enough values have been entered to satisfy the MAT INPUT statement.

On some computer systems, the MAT INPUT statement allows fewer values to be entered into a one-dimensional array than there are locations reserved by the DIM statement. Consider the following program.

```
10 DIM A(12)
20 MAT INPUT A
99 END

RUN

?
```

If only four numbers are typed in response to the question mark, the variable A(Ø) and the variables A(5) to A(12) inclusive will not be used.

The MAT INPUT instruction also stores values in a two-dimensional array.

```
10 DIM A(2,3)
20 MAT INPUT A
99 END

RUN

?
```

As with the MAT READ statement, the values must be entered by rows and, on most computer systems, the number of values entered is determined by the dimensions specified in the DIM statement. In the above program, six values must be keyed in, since the dimension statement has reserved six storage locations. First A(1,1) is filled, then A(1,2), A(1,3), A(2,1), A(2,2), and finally A(2,3). It should be noted that some versions of BASIC do not allow more than one vector and/or matrix to be filled by one MAT INPUT statement.

The MAT PRINT statement prints elements from either a one-dimensional array or from a two-dimensional array. The statement outputs all positions, including blank ones, which are printed as zeros. First consider the output from a one-dimensional array (a vector).

III. MAT PRINT

```
10 DIM A(4)
-- --
40 MAT PRINT A
-- --
99 END
```

Output from a vector differs greatly among computer systems. If the computer considers the list as a row vector, output is printed in row form. Spacing between items may or may not depend on the punctuation placed after the name of the vector. On some systems, a comma produces wide spacing, a semicolon produces closely spaced output. Other computers make no distinction between a comma and a semicolon. If the computer considers the list as a column of numbers, output is printed in columnar form, either single spaced or double spaced. Whether in row form or columnar form, output from two vectors may or may not have an extra blank line between each vector's output.

Try the following program several times, first with no punctuation after the array name in the MAT PRINT statement, then with a comma, and finally with a semicolon after the name. What kind of output does your computer system produce? Does punctuation make any difference? Does one of the punctuation marks produce an error message? In the programs that follow, the output from a one-dimensional array will be double spaced and in columnar form, regardless of the type of punctuation (if any) placed after the name of the vector in the MAT PRINT statement.

```
10 DIM A(4)
20 MAT READ A
30 DATA 1,2,3,4
40 PRINT
50 MAT PRINT A
99 END
```

```
RUN

1

2

3

4
```

Now, consider the output from a two-dimensional array (a matrix). The output of the program shown below is from a computer that has four print zones.

```
10 DIM A(2,3),B(2,7),C(4)
20 MAT READ A,B,C
30 DATA 10,20,30,40,50,60
40 DATA 1,2,3,4,5,6,7
50 DATA 8,9,10,11,12,13,14
60 DATA 100,200,300,400
70 PRINT
80 MAT PRINT A,B,C
99 END
```

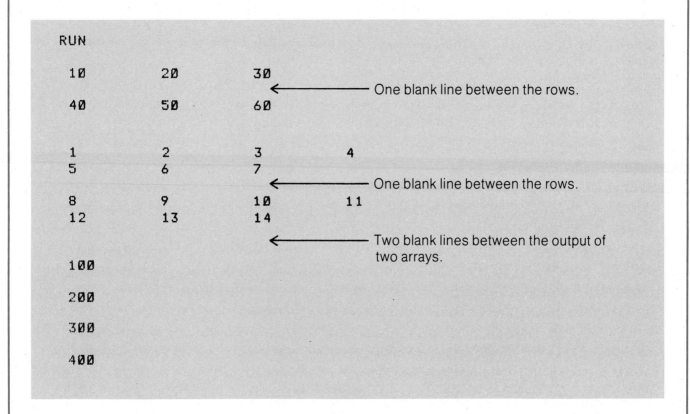

```
RUN

    10        20        30
                                    ← —————— One blank line between the rows.
    40        50        60


    1         2         3         4
    5         6         7
                                    ← —————— One blank line between the rows.
    8         9         10        11
    12        13        14
                                    ← —————— Two blank lines between the output of
                                             two arrays.

    100

    200

    300

    400
```

Most computer systems print the values of a matrix by rows. Since A is dimensioned as a 2x3 matrix, its output has two rows and three columns. A blank line is left between the rows. Matrix B is dimensioned as a 2x7 matrix. Since the computer used for the programs in this book does not print more than four items on one line, each row for matrix B requires two lines in order to print out seven columns of numbers. A blank line is left between the two rows. The last item in the dimension statement is a vector. As already explained, the computer prints the values of a vector double spaced and in columnar form, regardless of the type of punctuation following the vector's name in the MAT PRINT statement. Notice that this computer leaves an extra blank line (two blank lines) between the output of matrix A and that of matrix B, and between the output of matrix B and the output of vector C. It should also be mentioned that on some systems, a comma placed after the last matrix name in a MAT PRINT statement produces the same spacing between the items of the matrix as coding no punctuation at all. Both cause the items of the matrix to be widely spaced.

If the MAT PRINT statement in the previous program is changed to

```
80 MAT PRINT A;B;C;
```

the output will be as follows.

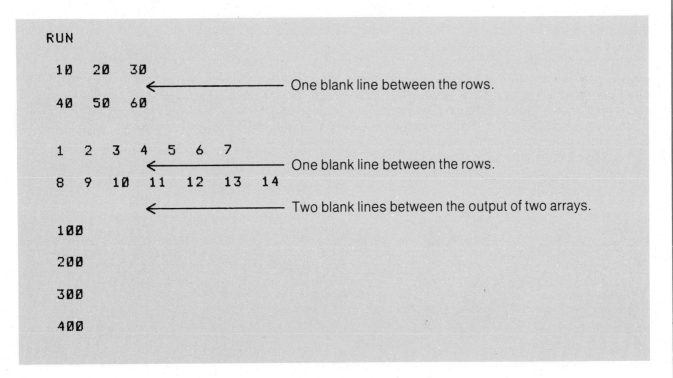

The semicolons after A and B cause the output to be closely spaced. Each row of matrix B is now printed on one line, since there are enough print positions for the seven columns. A blank line is left between the rows. The items of vector C continue to be in columnar form, double spaced. Again, two blank lines are left between the output of two arrays. Remember, the output shown on page 389 is a sample of how one computer system prints the values of arrays. Try the program on page 388. How does your computer print the numbers? Compare your output with the output shown on the same page. Now, replace the MAT PRINT statement with one that uses semicolons. Again, examine your output and compare it with the one shown on page 389.

For the remaining MAT statements, RUNs will be displayed only for concepts that may be unfamiliar to you. Keep in mind that these RUNs might not be exactly the same form as the ones produced by your computer system.

Assignment

I. MAT B＝A

Arrays (either one-dimensional or two-dimensional) may be duplicated by this statement. Each element of array A is copied by assigning it to a corresponding variable of array B. Two identical arrays are now stored in memory.

One-dimensional Array

```
10 DIM A(3),B(3)
20 MAT READ A
30 DATA 1,2,3
40 MAT B=A
50 PRINT
60 MAT PRINT A,B
99 END
```

Two-dimensional Array

```
10 DIM A(2,3),B(2,3)
20 MAT READ A
30 DATA 1,2,3,4,5,6
40 MAT B=A
50 PRINT
60 MAT PRINT A;B;
99 END
```

II. MAT A＝ZER

This statement assigns zero to each variable of array A. Thus, **MAT ZER** is often considered an initialization statement. If the array is two-dimensional and your computer system supports variables with zero subscripts, these variables may be ignored and you may have to set them to zero by using the LET statement, the READ/DATA statements, or the INPUT statement. Some computer systems do not allow MAT ZER to be used on one-dimensional arrays.

One-dimensional Array

```
10 DIM A(3)
20 MAT A=ZER
30 PRINT
40 MAT PRINT A
99 END
```

Two-dimensional Array

```
10 DIM A(2,3)
20 MAT A=ZER
30 PRINT
40 MAT PRINT A;
99 END
```

III. MAT A＝CON

The **MAT CON** statement may also be considered an initialization statement. The only difference between this statement and the MAT ZER statement is that MAT CON assigns the number one instead of zero to each variable of an array. The statement may not work on a one-dimensional array.

One-dimensional Array

```
10 DIM A(3)
20 MAT A=CON
30 PRINT
40 MAT PRINT A
99 END
```

Two-dimensional Array

```
10 DIM A(2,3)
20 MAT A=CON
30 PRINT
40 MAT PRINT A;
99 END
```

This statement assigns the identity matrix to A. The identity matrix is a square matrix whose principal diagonal consists of ones and whose remaining elements are zeros.

IV. MAT A = IDN

```
10 DIM A(3,3)
20 MAT A=IDN
30 PRINT
40 MAT PRINT A;
99 END

RUN

 1   0   0

 0   1   0

 0   0   1
```

This statement adds the elements of array A to the corresponding elements of array B and stores the sums in the corresponding locations of array C. All three arrays must have the same dimensions. The statement may be used on both one-dimensional and two-dimensional arrays.

Mathematical[3]
I. MAT C = A+B

One-dimensional Array

```
10 DIM A(3),B(3),C(3)
20 MAT READ A,B
```

Two-dimensional Array

```
10 DIM A(2,3),B(2,3),C(2,3)
20 MAT READ A,B
```

3. The intent of this section is to explain the various MAT functions. If you wish to become more familiar with matrix mathematics, read any Algebra text that includes operations on matrices.

Small inaccuracies in the storage of some numbers may produce results that are approximations when the numbers are used in calculations. For example, the numbers representing zeros in the identity matrix (found by multiplying the original matrix by its inverse) may be near zero, such as 8.52463E-09. These approximations apply to non-zero numbers as well.

```
30 DATA 1,2,3              30 DATA 1,2,3,4,5,6
40 DATA 9,8,7              40 DATA 9,8,7,6,5,4
50 MAT C=A+B               50 MAT C=A+B
60 PRINT                   60 PRINT
70 MAT PRINT A,B,C         70 MAT PRINT A;B;C;
99 END                     99 END
```

II. MAT C=A-B

This statement is similar to the previous one, except that **MAT C=A-B** subtracts the elements of array B from the corresponding elements of array A. The differences are stored in the corresponding locations of array C. All three arrays must have the same dimensions. The statement may be used on both one-dimensional and two-dimensional arrays.

III. MAT B=(2)*A

This MAT statement multiplies each element of array A by 2 (a scalar) and stores the products in the corresponding locations of array B. Arrays A and B must have the same dimensions. On most computer systems, the parentheses around the scalar are required, and on some systems the scalar must be to the left of the array name. The scalar may be a number, a variable, an expression, a subscripted variable, or a library function, as long as it represents a single value. The statement may be used on both one-dimensional and two-dimensional arrays.

One-dimensional Array	Two-dimensional Array

```
10 DIM A(3),B(3)           10 DIM A(2,3),B(2,3)
20 MAT READ A              20 MAT READ A
30 DATA 1,2,3              30 DATA 1,2,3,4,5,6
40 MAT B=(2)*A             40 MAT B=(2)*A
50 PRINT                   50 PRINT
60 MAT PRINT A,B           60 MAT PRINT A;B;
99 END                     99 END
```

IV. MAT C=A*B

MAT C=A*B multiplies matrix A by matrix B, using matrix multiplication and stores the products in matrix C. In this type of multiplication, the number of columns in matrix A must be the same as the number of rows in matrix B.

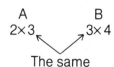

The result is a 2x4 matrix that has the same number of rows as matrix A and the same number of columns as matrix B.

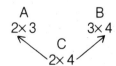

```
10  DIM A(2,3),B(3,4),C(2,4)
20  MAT READ A,B
30  DATA 1,2,3,4,5,6
40  DATA 9,8,7,6,5,4,3,2,1,0,1,2
50  MAT C=A*B
60  PRINT
70  MAT PRINT A;B;C;
99  END

RUN

 1   2   3

 4   5   6


 9   8   7   6

 5   4   3   2

 1   0   1   2


22  16  16  16

67  52  49  46
```

After execution of this statement, the rows and columns of matrix A are transposed (interchanged) and the result is stored in matrix B. If matrix A has 2 rows and 3 columns, matrix B will have 3 rows and 2 columns.

Special Functions
I. MAT B = TRN(A)

```
10  DIM A(2,3),B(3,2)
20  MAT READ A
30  DATA 1,2,3,4,5,6
40  MAT B=TRN(A)
50  PRINT
60  MAT PRINT A;B;
99  END

RUN

 1   2   3

 4   5   6


 1   4
```

```
2   5

3   6
```

The **MAT INV** statement finds the inverse of a matrix, if its inverse exists. The inverse is a particular matrix which, when multiplied by the original matrix, yields the identity matrix. That is,

II. MAT B=INV(A)

$$A*B = B*A = I$$

where **I** is the identity matrix. All three matrices must be square. Some of the elements of the inverse may be close approximations. (See Footnote 3 on page 391.)

```
10 DIM A(2,2),B(2,2)
20 MAT READ A
30 DATA 1,2,3,4
40 MAT B=INV(A)
50 PRINT
60 MAT PRINT A;B;
99 END

RUN

  1   2

  3   4


 -2   1

  1.5 -.5
```

On some systems, you may check for the existence of an inverse by using the **DET** function. If the DET function, performed on the original matrix, returns a non-zero value, the matrix has an inverse. Some systems that recognize the DET function insist that the function be used after the **MAT INV** statement. It may or may not require an argument.

```
10 DIM A(2,2),B(2,2),C(2,2)
20 MAT READ A
30 DATA 1,2,3,4
40 MAT B=INV(A)
50 PRINT
60 MAT PRINT A;B;
70 PRINT "THE DETERMINANT OF A IS:";DET
99 END
```

```
RUN

  1   2

  3   4


 -2   1

  1.5 -.5

THE DETERMINANT OF A IS:-2
```

If your computer does not support the DET function, multiply the original matrix by its inverse. The result should be the identity matrix (or a close approximation).

```
10 DIM A(2,2),B(2,2),C(2,2)
20 MAT READ A
30 DATA 1,2,3,4
40 MAT B=INV(A)
50 PRINT
60 MAT PRINT A;B;
70 MAT C=A*B
80 MAT PRINT C
99 END

RUN

  1   2

  3   4


 -2   1

  1.5 -.5

  1         0

  0         1
```

Changing the Dimensions of an Array

It was mentioned that on some computer systems, the MAT INPUT statement allows any number of data items to be entered into the computer, provided the number does not exceed the dimensions of the array. Several other MAT statements may be used to redimension arrays during execution of a program. These include MAT READ, MAT ZER, MAT CON, and MAT IDN. On many systems, MAT PRINT may not be used to redimension an array. The new dimensions must not exceed the original dimensions as specified in the DIM statement. Dimensions may be changed on both one-dimensional and two-dimensional arrays. Here are some examples.

```
1. 10 DIM A(4)           2. 10 DIM B(3,4)
   20 MAT READ A(3)         20 MAT READ B(2,3)
   30 DATA 1,2,3            30 DATA 1,2,3,4,5,6
   40 PRINT                 40 PRINT
   50 MAT PRINT A           50 MAT PRINT B;
   99 END                   99 END
```

In Program 1, vector A has been redimensioned so that it is now a three-element vector. In Program 2, matrix B has been redimensioned so that it is now a 2x3 matrix. The MAT READ statement in both programs stores values in the redimensioned arrays.

```
3. 10 DIM A(3,4),B(5,7),C(6,4)
   --
   40 MAT A=ZER(2,3)
   50 MAT B=CON(3,4)
   60 MAT C=IDN(3,3)
   70 PRINT
   80 MAT PRINT A;B;C;
   99 END
```

Statement 40 redimensions A as a 2x3 matrix, then assigns zero to each variable of the redimensioned matrix. Statement 50 redimensions B as a 3x4 matrix, then assigns 1 to each variable of the redimensioned matrix. Statement 60 redimensions C as a 3x3 matrix, then assigns the identity matrix to the redimensioned matrix. The MAT ZER and MAT CON statements may also redimension vectors. MAT IDN may redimension only matrices.

The dimensions in the MAT statements may be expressed as variables. However, positive integers must be assigned to these variables prior to their use in the statements. And, as with constants, the values of the variables may not be greater than the dimensions originally specified in the DIM statement.

9.1 MATRIX STATEMENTS – Your Turn

Many sample programs were listed in this section. For the following questions, page numbers are given so that you can quickly refer to a program if you need some help.

1. Define the errors, if any, in the program segments shown below.

   Make the necessary corrections.

   (a) `10 DIM A(3,2)`
       `20 MAT INPUT` . . . .(Page 386)

   (b) This MAT statement is to make a duplicate copy
       of matrix A.
       `10 DIM A(4,3),B(4,3)`
       `--`
       `25 MAT A=B` . . . .(Page 390)

   (c) `10 DIM A(2,3)`
       `--`
       `30 MAT A=ZER(3,4)` . . . .(Page 395)

   (d) `10 DIM A(3,4)`
       `--`
       `35 MAT A=IDN` . . . .(Page 391)

   (e) `10 DIM A(2,3),B(2,3),C(2,3)`
       `--`
       `40 MAT C=A+B` . . . .(Page 391)

   (f) `10 DIM A(5,7),B(5,7)`
       `--`
       `45 LET C=4`
       `50 MAT B=C*A` . . . .(Page 392)

   (g) `10 DIM A(4,5),B(5,3),C(4,3)`
       `--`
       `55 MAT C=A*B` . . . .(Page 392)

   (h) `10 DIM A(3,4),B(3,4)`
       `--`
       `60 MAT B=TRN(A)` . . . .(Page 393)

   (i) `10 DIM A(8,7),B(8,7)`
       `--`
       `65 MAT B=INV(A)` . . . .(Page 394)

2. Write a program that reads data into 2 two-dimensional arrays
   and performs the following operations using MAT statements.
   The data is shown below in matrix form.

	A			B	
1	2	3	4	5	6
4	5	6	7	8	9

   (a) Read the data using one MAT statement.
   (b) Subtract the elements of matrix A from the corresponding
       elements of matrix B and store the differences in matrix C.

(c) Multiply the elements of matrix B by the scalar 3 and store the products in matrix D.
(d) Transpose the rows and columns of matrix A and store the result in matrix E.
(e) Set all the elements of matrix B to 1.
(f) Print matrices C, D, E, and the new B matrix with headings as shown in the following RUN. Remember, the output produced by your computer system may not be exactly the same as the one shown below.

```
RUN

SUBTRACTION
   3   3   3

   3   3   3


SCALAR MULTIPLICATION
  12   15   18

  21   24   27


TRANSPOSITION
   1   4

   2   5

   3   6


INITIALIZATION
   1   1   1

   1   1   1
```

9.1 MATRIX STATEMENTS — Solutions for "Your Turn"

1. (a) The MAT INPUT statement must include the name of the matrix.

```
20 MAT INPUT A
```

(b) To make a duplicate copy of matrix A, the values of matrix A must be assigned to matrix B. Therefore, A must be on the right-hand side of the equals sign and B must be on the left-hand side.

```
25 MAT B=A
```

(c) The size of the redimensioned matrix must not be greater than the size of the original matrix as specified in the DIM statement. Either increase the dimensions in the DIM statement or decrease the dimensions in the MAT ZER statement.

```
10 DIM A(4,5)        or    10 DIM A(2,3)
--                         --
30 MAT A=ZER(3,4)          30 MAT A=ZER(2,2)
```

(d) The identity matrix is a square matrix. Since it is being assigned to A, A must also be a square matrix.

```
10 DIM A(3,3)        or    10 DIM A(4,4)
```

(e) Nothing is wrong.
(f) Most computer systems require parentheses around the scalar.

```
50 MAT B=(C)*A
```

(g) Nothing is wrong.
(h) Transposing a matrix interchanges its rows and columns. If a matrix has three rows and four columns, its transposed form will have four rows and three columns. In this program segment, the dimensions of B should be four rows and three columns.

```
10 DIM A(3,4),B(4,3)
```

(i) A matrix multiplied by its inverse produces the identity matrix. Since the identity matrix is a square matrix, the matrices involved in the calculations must also be square.

Matrices A and B in this program segment must be square matrices.

```
10 DIM A(8,8),B(8,8) or 10 DIM A(7,7),B(7,7)
```

2.

```
10 DIM A(2,3),B(2,3),C(2,3)
20 DIM D(2,3),E(3,2)
30 MAT READ A,B
40 DATA 1,2,3,4,5,6
50 DATA 4,5,6,7,8,9
60 MAT C=B-A
70 MAT D=(3)*B
80 MAT E=TRN(A)
90 MAT B=CON
100 PRINT
110 PRINT "SUBTRACTION"
120 MAT PRINT C;
130 PRINT "SCALAR MULTIPLICATION"
140 MAT PRINT D;
150 PRINT "TRANSPOSITION"
160 MAT PRINT E;
170 PRINT "INITIALIZATION"
180 MAT PRINT B;
999 END
```

9.2 THE INT FUNCTION

BASIC has a number of library (standard or built-in) functions that are written directly into the language. These are prewritten routines that may be called upon to perform certain operations, such as finding the square root of a number. To call a library function, its name (which consists of three letters) must be coded along with the value upon which the computer is to operate. This value, called the argument, must follow the function name and must be in parentheses. It may be expressed as a constant, a variable, a library function, an arithmetic expression, or as a string.[4] For example, the square root function is accessed by **SQR(X)**, where X has previously been assigned a number. The function may be called by coding it in a LET statement, such as **xx LET B=SQR(25)**, or by placing the function in a PRINT statement, such as **xx PRINT SQR(25)**. The LET statement assigns the result of the function to the variable that is to the left of the equals sign; the PRINT statement prints the result. A library function may also be placed in an IF/THEN statement. One or more library functions may

4. Functions that operate on strings are covered in a later chapter.

form an expression such as **SQR(25)+INT(6.85)-2**, which is placed in a LET statement, in a PRINT statement, or in an IF/THEN statement. In this expression, the result of the SQR function is added to the result of the INT function to give another answer from which 2 is subtracted.

The function to be discussed in this section is the INT function. Remember in Chapter Four it was mentioned that a decimal number is made up of two parts — the integer portion and the decimal portion. An example is the number 5.17 which has 5 as the integer part and .17 as the decimal part.

Suppose you want to retain only the integer part of a number. The INT function will perform this operation for you. Here is a program that keeps the integer part of 5.17.

```
10 LET X=5.17
20 PRINT
30 PRINT X,INT(X)
99 END

RUN

 5.17         5
```

Notice that the decimal part is removed. Generally, the rules are as follows.

1. If the argument is positive, the decimal part is discarded and the resultant number is smaller than the argument. In the above example, 5 is smaller than 5.17.
2. If the argument is negative, the computer may do one of two things:
   (a) Remove the decimal part. The number − 5.17 becomes − 5.
   (b) Change the number to the next lower integer. The number − 5.17 now becomes − 6.

Here are some more examples.

X	INT(X)
642	642
7.094	7
0	0
.025	0
− 934	− 934
− 49.321	− 49 or − 50
− .067	0 or − 1

RUN the following program and see what your computer produces when the argument is negative.

```
10 LET X=-49.321
20 LET Y=-.067
30 PRINT
40 PRINT X,INT(X)
```

```
50 PRINT Y,INT(Y)
99 END
```

What value does your computer print for INT(X), −49 or −50?
What value does your computer print for INT(Y), Ø or −1?

The INT function can be used to isolate digits from numbers. The idea   Isolating digits
is to get the digit you want in the position that is immediately to the left
of the decimal point (in the units position), then discard the decimal
part. First a digit will be separated from a whole number and then
digits will be separated from two decimal numbers.

   1. This example separates the digit 3 from the whole number 349.

```
10 LET N=349
20 LET H=INT(N/100)
30 PRINT
40 PRINT H
99 END

RUN

   3
```

Line 20 isolates the 3 as follows:

```
20 LET H=INT(N/100)
      = INT(349/100)
      = INT(3.49)
      = 3
```

   2. This program separates the digit 4 from .23456.

```
10 LET N=.23456
20 LET M=N*100
30 LET T=INT((M-INT(M))*10)
40 PRINT
50 PRINT T
99 END

RUN

   4
```

Line 20 moves the decimal two places to the right so that the
decimal point is just before the 4.

```
20 LET M=N*100
      =.23456*100
      =23.456
```

Line 30 isolates the 4 as follows:

```
30 LET T=INT((M-INT(M))*10)
      =INT((23.456-INT(23.456))*10)
      =INT((23.456-23)*10)
      =INT(.456*10)
      =INT(4.56)
      =4
```

3. Digits may be separated from decimal numbers greater than one in the same manner as in Program 2. The program below separates the digit 5 from the number 1.23456.

```
10 LET N=1.23456
20 LET M=N*1000
30 LET T=INT((M-INT(M))*10)
40 PRINT
50 PRINT T
99 END

RUN

   5
```

Line 20 moves the decimal three places to the right so that the decimal point is just before the 5.

```
20 LET M=N*1000
      =1.23456*1000
      =1234.56
```

Line 30 isolates the 5 as follows:

```
30 LET T=INT((M-INT(M))*10)
      =INT((1234.56-INT(1234.56))*10)
      =INT((1234.56-1234)*10)
      =INT(.56*10)
      =INT(5.6)
      =5
```

A note of warning is in order. It was mentioned in Chapter Four that small inaccuracies in the storage of some numbers may cause problems. Here is an example of what could happen. The program is to isolate the digit 4.

```
10 LET N=.264
20 LET M=N*100
30 LET T=INT((M-INT(M))*10)
40 PRINT
50 PRINT T
99 END

RUN

   3
```

Notice that the computer gives an output of 3. The error occurs when the INT of **M** (which is 26) is subtracted from **M** (which is 26.4). The computer arrives at a difference of .399999999 which, when multiplied by 10 and truncated by the INT function, results in 3. You can safeguard the desired result by increasing the difference by a small amount. If you add, for example, .00001 to .399999999 you get:

$$\begin{array}{r} .399999999 \\ + .00001 \\ \hline .400009999 \end{array}$$

Multiplying .400009999 by 10 and then using the INT function on the product gives 4. Statement 30 should now look as follows.

```
30 LET T=INT((M-INT(M)+.00001)*10)
```

Note that the amount added to .399999999 need not be .00001. It can be as large as .1 or as small as .000000001 on some computers.

The INT function can check to see if one integer will divide evenly into another (in other words, there will be no remainder). The statement that performs this operation is:

Checking division

$$\textbf{xx IF I/J=INT(I/J) THEN xx}$$

where **I** is the integer to be tested and **J** is the divisor. Here are a few examples.

1. $I = 8$
   $J = 2$

$$\begin{array}{rcl} \text{xx IF I/J} &=& \text{INT(I/J) THEN xx} \\ 8/2 &=& \text{INT(8/2)} \\ 4 &=& \text{INT(4)} \\ 4 &=& 4 \end{array}$$

Since the statement is true, 2 divides evenly into 8.

2. I=9
   J=2

$$xx \ IF \ I/J = INT(I/J) \ THEN \ xx$$
$$9/2 = INT(9/2)$$
$$4.5 = INT(4.5)$$
$$4.5 = 4$$

This statement is not true; therefore, 2 does not divide evenly into 9.

Care must be taken when one of the numbers is negative, since this will give the INT function a negative argument. If your computer changes a negative decimal number to the next lower integer when it uses the INT function (-5.17 becomes -6), you must add 1 to the result of the INT function. The example shown below divides 2 into -9 and increases the result of the INT function by 1.

3. I=-9
   J=2

$$xx \ IF \ I/J = INT(I/J) + 1 \ THEN \ xx$$
$$-9/2 = INT(-9/2) + 1$$
$$-4.5 = INT(-4.5) + 1$$
$$-4.5 = -5 + 1$$
$$-4.5 = -4$$

The results, without the negative signs, are the same as the results in example two, where positive numbers were used.

In Chapter Six (page 248), you wrote a program for a review problem that involved compound interest. The program produced numbers with more than two decimal places. At that time, it was mentioned that these figures could be rounded off to the nearest cent and that the methods for rounding off would be shown in later chapters.[5] Here is the formula that performs the rounding off function.

Rounding off numbers

$$INT(N*10\uparrow D + .5)/10\uparrow D$$

N is the number to be rounded and **D** is the desired number of decimal places. Shown below are examples of rounding off the number 4.5678 to various decimal places—to the nearest tenth, hundredth, thousandth, and to the nearest whole number.

1. Rounding off 4.5678 to the nearest tenth

Rounding off a number to the nearest tenth means that the rounded number has one digit to the right of the decimal point. D=1.

R= INT(N*10↑D+.5)/10↑D
 = INT(4.5678*10↑1+.5)/10↑1
 = INT(4.5678*10+.5)/10↑1
 = INT(45.678+.5)/10↑1
 = INT(46.178)/10↑1
 = 46/10↑1
 = 46/10
 = 4.6

4.5678 has been rounded off to 4.6

5. Output can also be rounded by the **PRINT USING** statement. This is covered in the next chapter.

2. Rounding off 4.5678 to the nearest hundredth

Rounding off a number to the nearest hundredth means that the rounded number has two digits to the right of the decimal point. $D = 2$.

$R = INT(N*10\uparrow D + .5)/10\uparrow D$
$= INT(4.5678*10\uparrow 2 + .5)/10\uparrow 2$
$= INT(4.5678*100 + .5)/10\uparrow 2$
$= INT(456.78 + .5)/10\uparrow 2$
$= INT(457.28)/10\uparrow 2$
$= 457/10\uparrow 2$
$= 457/100$
$= 4.57$

4.5678 has been rounded off to 4.57

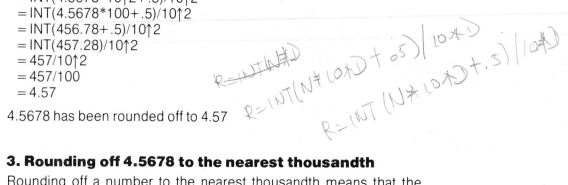

3. Rounding off 4.5678 to the nearest thousandth

Rounding off a number to the nearest thousandth means that the rounded number has three digits to the right of the decimal point. $D = 3$.

$R = INT(N*10\uparrow D + .5)/10\uparrow D$
$= INT(4.5678*10\uparrow 3 + .5)/10\uparrow 3$
$= INT(4.5678*1000 + .5)/10\uparrow 3$
$= INT(4567.8 + .5)/10\uparrow 3$
$= INT(4568.3)/10\uparrow 3$
$= 4568/10\uparrow 3$
$= 4568/1000$
$= 4.568$

4.5678 has been rounded off to 4.568

4. Rounding off 4.5678 to the nearest whole number

Rounding off a number to the nearest whole number means that the rounded number has no digits to the right of the decimal point. $D = 0$.[6]

$R = INT(N*10\uparrow D + .5)/10\uparrow D$
$= INT(4.5678*10\uparrow 0 + .5)/10\uparrow 0$
$= INT(4.5678*1 + .5)/10\uparrow 0$
$= INT(4.5678 + .5)/10\uparrow 0$
$= INT(5.0678)/10\uparrow 0$
$= 5/10\uparrow 0$
$= 5/1$
$= 5$

4.5678 has been rounded off to 5

9.2 THE INT FUNCTION – Sample Program

On page 402, you were shown how a digit can be separated from a whole number. Do you remember how this is done? First, the

6. Raising a number to the power of zero results in one.

required digit is moved to the position immediately to the left of the decimal point (the units position) by dividing the number by a power of 10. The decimal part is then removed by the INT function. For example, to separate the 3 from 349, the following calculations are performed.

$$
\begin{aligned}
H &= INT(N/100) \\
&= INT(349/100) \\
&= INT(3.49) \\
&= 3
\end{aligned}
$$

Here is an extension of this principle. The following program isolates each of the three digits in the numbers 853, 267, and 913.

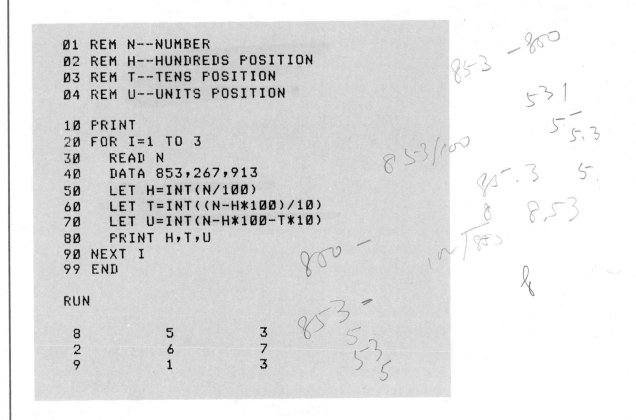

```
01 REM N--NUMBER
02 REM H--HUNDREDS POSITION
03 REM T--TENS POSITION
04 REM U--UNITS POSITION

10 PRINT
20 FOR I=1 TO 3
30    READ N
40    DATA 853,267,913
50    LET H=INT(N/100)
60    LET T=INT((N-H*100)/10)
70    LET U=INT(N-H*100-T*10)
80    PRINT H,T,U
90 NEXT I
99 END

RUN

8          5          3
2          6          7
9          1          3
```

This is how the computer executes lines 50, 60, and 70 using the value 853. Move the 8 to the units position.

```
50 LET H=INT(N/100)
      = INT(853/100)
      = INT(8.53)
      = 8
```

Algebraically

$$\frac{853}{100} = 8.53 = 8$$

Remove the hundreds and move the 5 to the units position.

```
60 LET T=INT((N-H*100)/10)
   =INT((853-8*100)/10)
   =INT((853-800)/10)
   =INT(53/10)
   =INT(5.3)
   =5
```

$$
\begin{array}{r}
853 \\
-\ 800 \\
\hline
53 \\
\hline
10
\end{array} = 5.3 = 5
$$

Remove the hundreds and the tens.

```
70 LET U=INT(N-H*100-T*10)
   =INT(853-8*100-5*10)
   =INT(853-800-5*10)
   =INT(853-800-50)
   =INT(53-50)
   =INT(3)
   =3
```

$$
\begin{array}{r}
853 \\
-\ 800 \\
\hline
53 \\
-\ 50 \\
\hline
3
\end{array}
$$

9.2 THE INT FUNCTION—Your Turn

1. Given that **I** = 6, what value does your computer assign to **J** in each of the following statements?

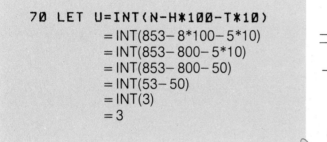

(a) `30 LET J=INT(I+3.2)`

(b) `40 LET J=INT(I-I)`

(c) `50 LET J=INT(I-10.99)`

(d) `60 LET J=INT(I-INT(I+1.54))`

(e) `70 LET J=INT(I+INT(I-4.85))`

(f) `80 LET J=INT(I-INT(I-8.63))`

2. **Isolating Digits from Numbers**
   (a) Write a program that separates the digit 6 from 63.
   (b) Write a program that separates the digit 7 from 789.
   (c) Write a program that separates the digit 8 from 285.
   (d) Write a program that separates the digit 1 from 37.51.

3. **Checking Division**
   Write a program that checks whether or not 2 divides evenly into 468. Print **DOES NOT DIVIDE EVENLY** if the division is not exact; print **DIVIDES EVENLY** if the division is exact.

4. **Rounding Off Numbers**
   (a) Write a program that rounds off 45.16 to the nearest tenth.
   (b) Write a program that rounds off 45.168 to the nearest hundredth.
   (c) Write a program that rounds off 45.1687 to the nearest thousandth.
   (d) Write a program that rounds off 24.68 to the nearest whole number.
5. The sample program on page 407 isolated the digits of three different numbers. Modify the program so that it prints a number whose digits are in reverse order. For example, the reverse of 853 is 358. The numbers you are to reverse are 853, 267, and 913.
   (a) Isolate each digit as in the sample program.
   (b) Change the position of the digits by multiplying the former units digit by 100, the former tens digit by 10, and leaving the former hundreds digit unaltered. Using 853 as our example, the digits are changed as follows:
   3 (the former units digit) becomes 300. (3×100)
   5 (the former tens digit) again becomes 50. (5×10)
   8 (the former hundreds digit) remains 8.
   (c) Add the repositioned digits.
   (d) Print the original number and its reverse.
   Note: Perform (b) and (c) in one statement. Your program should be very similar to the sample program on page 407.

```
RUN

853        358
267        762
913        319
```

9.2 THE INT FUNCTION – Solutions for "Your Turn"

The answers for Problem 1 will vary depending on whether your computer truncates a negative value or changes the value to the next lower integer.

1.

```
(a) 30 LET J=INT(I+3.2)
        = INT(6+3.2)
        = INT(9.2)
        = 9
```

(b) `40 LET J=INT(I-I)`
$$= INT(6-6)$$
$$= INT(0)$$
$$= 0$$

(c) `50 LET J=INT(I-10.99)`
$$= INT(6-10.99)$$
$$= INT(-4.99)$$
$$= -4 \, or -5$$

(d) `60 LET J=INT(I-INT(I+1.54))`
$$= INT(6- INT(6+1.54))$$
$$= INT(6- INT(7.54))$$
$$= INT(6-7)$$
$$= INT(-1)$$
$$= -1$$

(e) `70 LET J=INT(I+INT(I-4.85))`
$$= INT(6+INT(6-4.85))$$
$$= INT(6+INT(1.15))$$
$$= INT(6+1)$$
$$= INT(7)$$
$$= 7$$

(f) `80 LET J=INT(I-INT(I-8.63))`
$$= INT(6-INT(6-8.63))$$
$$= INT(6-INT(-2.63))$$
$$= INT(6-(-2)) \quad or \quad = INT(6-(-3))$$
$$= INT(6+2) \qquad\qquad = INT(6+3)$$
$$= INT(8) \qquad\qquad\;\; = INT(9)$$
$$= 8 \qquad\qquad\qquad = 9$$

2. Isolating Digits from Numbers

Result

(a)
```
10 LET N=63
20 LET T=INT(N/10)
30 PRINT
40 PRINT T
99 END
```
63
INT(63/10) = INT(6.3) = 6

6

(b)
```
10 LET N=789
20 LET H=INT(N/100)
30 PRINT
40 PRINT H
99 END
```
789
INT(789/100) = INT(7.89) = 7

7

(c)
```
10 LET N=285
20 LET H=INT(N/100)
30 LET T=INT((N-H*100)/10)
40 PRINT
50 PRINT T
99 END
```
285
INT(285/100) = INT(2.85) = 2
INT((285−2*100)/10) =
INT((285−200)/10) =
INT(85/10) = INT(8.5) = 8
8

(d)
```
10 LET N=37.51
20 LET M=N*10
30 LET T=INT((M-INT(M))*10)
40 PRINT
50 PRINT T
99 END
```
37.51
37.51*10 = 375.1
INT((375.1−INT(375.1))*10) =
INT((375.1−375)*10) =
INT(.1*10) = INT(1) = 1
1

3. Checking Division

```
10 PRINT
20 LET N=468
30 LET J=2
40 IF N/J=INT(N/J) THEN 70
50 PRINT "DOES NOT DIVIDE EVENLY"
60 GO TO 99
70 PRINT "DIVIDES EVENLY"
99 END

RUN

DIVIDES EVENLY
```

4. Rounding Off Numbers

	Result

(a)
```
10 LET N=45.16
20 LET D=1
30 LET R=INT(N*10↑D+.5)/10↑D

40 PRINT
50 PRINT R
99 END
```
45.16
1
$INT(45.16*10↑1+.5)/10↑1 = INT(452.1)/10 = 452/10 = 45.2$

45.2

(b)
```
10 LET N=45.168
20 LET D=2
30 LET R=INT(N*10↑D+.5)/10↑D

40 PRINT
50 PRINT R
99 END
```
45.168
2
$INT(45.168*10↑2+.5)/10↑2 = INT(4517.3)/100 = 4517/100 = 45.17$

45.17

(c)
```
10 LET N=45.1687
20 LET D=3
30 LET R=INT(N*10↑D+.5)/10↑D

40 PRINT
50 PRINT R
99 END
```
45.1687
3
$INT(45.1687*10↑3+.5)/10↑3 = INT(45169.2)/1000 = 45169/1000 = 45.169$

45.169

(d)
```
10 LET N=24.68
20 LET D=0
30 LET R=INT(N*10↑D+.5)/10↑D

40 PRINT
50 PRINT R
99 END
```
24.68
0
$INT(24.68*10↑0+.5)/10↑0 = INT(25.18)/1 = 25/1 = 25$

25

5.

```
01 REM N--NUMBER
02 REM H--HUNDREDS POSITION
03 REM T--TENS POSITION
04 REM U--UNITS POSITION
05 REM R--REVERSED NUMBER

10 PRINT
20 FOR I=1 TO 3
30    READ N
40    DATA 853,267,913
50    LET H=INT(N/100)
60    LET T=INT((N-H*100)/10)
70    LET U=INT(N-H*100-T*10)
80    LET R=U*100+T*10+H
90    PRINT N,R
100 NEXT I
999 END
```

9.3 THE RND FUNCTION

One of the more interesting library functions is the **RND(X)** function. RND is the abbreviation for random number. Each time it is referenced, a different decimal number is generated (produced), consisting of at least six digits and whose value ranges between 0 and 1. This means that the RND(X) function generates numbers from .000001 to .999999 inclusive. Not all computers produce numbers with six digits. Some generate a random number that contains as many digits as will fit into one zone. For example, if a computer allows ten characters per zone, the random number may consist of nine digits if the first position is reserved for the assumed plus sign and trailing zeros are printed. When the number is too small (that is, too close to zero), most versions of BASIC convert it to scientific notation.

The RND function varies greatly among computer systems. Some require initialization, such as **LET R=RND(−1)**, to activate the random number generator. This is followed later on in the program by other statements that contain the RND function. Other systems require no initialization.

For those systems that require initialization, the sign of the argument determines whether the seed (the starting point of a sequence of random numbers) is always the same or different. Generally, the RND(X) function used in statements after initialization has an argument that is different from that used in initialization.

```
10 LET R=RND(-1)  ◄──────── Initialization
--
30 LET A=INT(N*RND(1)+I)
                  ▲──────── Different argument
```

The argument in line 30 may be (1) on some computer systems.

The versions of BASIC that require no initialization may produce random numbers, regardless of whether the argument is positive, negative, or zero. Some versions that require no initialization insist that the argument be non-zero while others are much more restrictive and produce random numbers only when the argument is positive or only when it is negative or only when the argument is zero. In addition, some computer systems insist that the argument be an integer, and some systems require no argument at all. Because of these variations, check your manual or try some programs yourself to see what version suits your computer.

Suppose your computer system requires no initialization and that it accepts a positive integer (1) as the argument of the RND function. Here is a program that prints six random numbers.

```
10 PRINT              — Leaves a blank line.
20 FOR I=1 TO 6       — Sets up a loop.
30   LET R=RND(1)     — Generates a random number and assigns it to R.
40   PRINT R          — Prints the random number.[7]
50 NEXT I             — Transfers control to line 20.
99 END                — Terminates program execution.

RUN

 .681657766
 .128694532
 .31534812
 .715774119
3.22490736E-03
 .855953187
```

Notice that the random numbers in the above RUN each have nine digits, except for a number that ends with a zero (insignificant zeros are not printed). Also, numbers that are too small are converted to **E** format. Here is another RUN from the same program. Is the output the same?

```
RUN

 .937648934
 .027785757
 .180831534
 .377229542
 .759118247
 .443307551
```

7. Note that lines 30 and 40 could have been combined into one statement: **30 PRINT RND(1)**.

Although the numbers in the above two RUNs may appear to be random, they are not truly random and are often called **pseudo-random numbers**. They are not truly random because they are generated by a fixed numerical algorithm (procedure) and because of the predictability of the relationship of time after the first random number is generated. In order to start with a different seed (a different starting point), some systems require a **RANDOM** statement or a **RANDOMIZE** statement before the statement that includes the RND function. Some *randomize* the seed by using a negative argument in the RND function, while others (as mentioned above) use an initialization statement in which the RND function has a negative argument. To resolve the time relationship problem, some of the computers that have a real-time clock use the time (**RND(−TI)** or something similar) to produce the random seed. A different argument is then used in subsequent RND functions to generate random numbers. You should check your manual for the following points to see what your computer system requires to produce random numbers.

(a) Do you need an initialization statement? If so, what argument does the RND function require in the initialization statement?
(b) Do RND functions in other statements require arguments? If so, what kind?
(c) Do you need a RANDOM or a RANDOMIZE statement?
(d) If your computer has a real-time clock, what argument do you use to produce random seed?

RUN the program on page 413 several times and check your output for the following:
(a) How many digits does each random number have?
(b) Is a zero printed at the end of a number?
(c) Is any number expressed in E format?

To keep calculations clear, the random numbers displayed in this book will consist of six digits.

At this point, it should be mentioned that the RND function produces numbers that are evenly distributed between 0 and 1. This means that in a long RUN, the probability of a number falling between 0 and .5 is about the same as the probability of one falling between .5 and 1.[8] Looking at it in a different perspective, the chance of a number being less than 1 is 100% (every number will be less than 1), of a number being less than .9 is 90% (about 9 out of 10 numbers will be less than .9), of a number being less than .333 is $33\frac{1}{3}$% (about 333 out of 1000 numbers will be less than .333) and of a number being less than 0 is 0% (no numbers will be less than 0).

Now that you know how to generate random numbers, what can you do with them? You can use them to simulate (imitate) a procedure or use them to test a new program. Random numbers are often used in programs to test the outcome of events that take place in a random fashion. Of course, many games are based on random numbers, such as those that use spinners or dice. The numbers generated in the program on page 413 are not too useful in the form shown. Whole numbers, say from 1 to 10 or from 1 to 100, may be more appropriate for some of the above applications. How are these numbers converted to the more convenient whole numbers?

8. The midpoint .5 can be included in either ''between 0 and .5'' or ''between .5 and 1''.

This can be accomplished by using the following conversion formula:

INT(N*RND(1)+I)

N is the "number" of numbers in the range, and **I** is the first endpoint (the lowest number wanted). Finding the "number" of numbers involves a basic principle in counting. If you want to know how many numbers there are between 2 and 7 inclusive, simply use the formula

(J−I)+1

where **J** is the second endpoint and **I** is the first endpoint. One is added to the difference because you want to include both endpoints. Therefore, the "number" of numbers between 2 and 7 inclusive is $(7-2)+1 = 6$.

The result obtained within the parentheses of the conversion formula is usually a decimal number. The INT function is used to change this random decimal number to a random whole number. Here are some examples. In each one, the lowest random number (.000001) and the highest random number (.999999) are used in the formula as numbers that have been generated by the RND function. The purpose is to see if the statement produces the two endpoints given in each example. If it does, all the other random whole numbers produced by the formula should fall between these two endpoints. RUN the program for each example several times to verify that the numbers generated are in the required range.

"Number" of numbers: $(J-I)+1 = (10-1)+1 = 9+1 = 10$
First endpoint: 1

Generating whole numbers between 1 and 10 inclusive

```
10 LET N=10
20 LET I=1
30 LET R=INT(N*RND(1)+I)
40 PRINT
50 PRINT R
99 END
```

Lowest Random Number

$R = INT(N*RND(1)+I)$
$= INT(10*.000001+1)$
$= INT(.00001+1)$
$= INT(1.00001)$
$= 1$

Highest Random Number

$R = INT(N*RND(1)+I)$
$= INT(10*.999999+1)$
$= INT(9.99999+1)$
$= INT(10.99999)$
$= 10$

"Number" of numbers: $(J-I)+1 = (100-1)+1 = 99+1 = 100$
First endpoint: 1

Generating whole numbers between 1 and 100 inclusive

```
10 LET N=100
20 LET I=1
30 LET R=INT(N*RND(1)+I)
40 PRINT
50 PRINT R
99 END
```

Lowest Random Number

$R = INT(N*RND(1)+I)$
$\quad = INT(100*.000001+1)$
$\quad = INT(.0001+1)$
$\quad = INT(1.0001)$
$\quad = 1$

Highest Random Number

$R = INT(N*RND(1)+I)$
$\quad = INT(100*.999999+1)$
$\quad = INT(99.9999+1)$
$\quad = INT(100.9999)$
$\quad = 100$

"Number" of numbers: $(J-I)+1 = (6-1)+1 = 5+1 = 6$
First endpoint: 1

Generating whole numbers between 1 and 6 inclusive

```
10 LET N=6
20 LET I=1
30 LET R=INT(N*RND(1)+I)
40 PRINT
50 PRINT R
99 END
```

Lowest Random Number

$R = INT(N*RND(1)+I)$
$\quad = INT(6*.000001+1)$
$\quad = INT(.000006+1)$
$\quad = INT(1.000006)$
$\quad = 1$

Highest Random Number

$R = INT(N*RND(1)+I)$
$\quad = INT(6*.999999+1)$
$\quad = INT(5.999994+1)$
$\quad = INT(6.999994)$
$\quad = 6$

"Number" of numbers: $(J-I)+1 = (26-7)+1 = 19+1 = 20$
First endpoint: 7

Generating whole numbers between 7 and 26 inclusive

```
10 LET N=20
20 LET I=7
30 LET R=INT(N*RND(1)+I)
40 PRINT
50 PRINT R
99 END
```

Lowest Random Number

$R = INT(N*RND(1)+I)$
$\quad = INT(20*.000001+7)$
$\quad = INT(.00002+7)$
$\quad = INT(7.00002)$
$\quad = 7$

Highest Random Number

$R = INT(N*RND(1)+I)$
$\quad = INT(20*.999999+7)$
$\quad = INT(19.99998+7)$
$\quad = INT(26.99998)$
$\quad = 26$

Finally, instead of generating just one random whole number, the following program generates ten random whole numbers. The numbers range from 5 to 12 inclusive. RUN the program several times.

"Number" of numbers: $(J-I)+1 = (12-5)+1 = 7+1 = 8$
First endpoint: 5

```
10 LET N=8
20 LET I=5
30 PRINT
40 FOR K=1 TO 10
50   LET R=INT(N*RND(1)+I)
60   PRINT R
70 NEXT K
99 END
```

9.3 THE RND FUNCTION—Sample Program

Here is a program that simulates the roll of a pair of dice. It prints out the number rolled on the first die, the number rolled on the second die, and the total rolled on both dice. The pair of dice are rolled three times. (Note: The roll of one die results in a number that ranges from 1 to 6 inclusive.)

```
01 REM D1--DIE NUMBER ONE
02 REM D2--DIE NUMBER TWO
03 REM D--TOTAL OF BOTH DICE

10 LET N=6                          —"Number" of numbers in the range.
20 LET I=1                          — First endpoint in the range.
30 FOR K=1 TO 3                     — Sets up a loop.
40   LET D1=INT(N*RND(1)+I)         — Generates a whole number between
                                      1 and 6 inclusive.
50   LET D2=INT(N*RND(1)+I)         — Generates a whole number between
                                      1 and 6 inclusive.
60   LET D=D1+D2                    — Adds the two random whole numbers.
70   PRINT                          — Leaves a blank line.
80   PRINT "DIE 1:";D1,"DIE 2:";D2  — Prints the number rolled on each die.
90   PRINT "BOTH DICE:";D           — Prints the total rolled on both dice.
100 NEXT K                          — Transfers control to line 30.
999 END                             — Terminates program execution.

RUN  (Sample RUN)

DIE 1: 6  DIE 2: 4
BOTH DICE: 10

DIE 1: 5  DIE 2: 2
BOTH DICE: 7

DIE 1: 4  DIE 2: 3
BOTH DICE: 7
```

9.3 THE RND FUNCTION—Your Turn

1. For each of the following, code a program that generates a random number.
   (a) A decimal number between Ø and 1.
   (b) A whole number between 1 and 10 inclusive.
   (c) A whole number between 1 and 1000 inclusive.
   (d) A whole number between 1 and 8 inclusive.
   (e) A whole number between 5 and 25 inclusive.
   (f) A whole number between 20 and 36 inclusive.

2. Random numbers can simulate the tossing of a coin. Since there are only two possibilities (heads or tails), you can assign, say, 1 to heads and 2 to tails. The range of random numbers will be from 1 to 2 inclusive. Write a program that counts the number of heads and the number of tails that are "flipped" out of ten tosses. Draw a flowchart before you write the program.

   (a) If the random whole number is 1, increase the number of heads by one.
   (b) If the random whole number is 2, increase the number of tails by one.

```
RUN       (Sample RUN)

HEADS: 6
TAILS: 4
```

9.3 THE RND FUNCTION—Solutions for "Your Turn"9

1.

```
(a) 10 LET R=RND(1)
    20 PRINT
    30 PRINT R
    99 END

(b) 10 LET N=10
    20 LET I=1
    30 LET R=INT(N*RND(1)+I)
    40 PRINT
    50 PRINT R
    99 END
```

9. Your computer may require a different argument for the RND function.

```
(c) 10 LET N=1000        (e) 10 LET N=21
    20 LET I=1               20 LET I=5
    30 LET R=INT(N*RND(1)+I)  30 LET R=INT(N*RND(1)+I)
    40 PRINT                 40 PRINT
    50 PRINT R               50 PRINT R
    99 END                  99 END

(d) 10 LET N=8           (f) 10 LET N=17
    20 LET I=1               20 LET I=20
    30 LET R=INT(N*RND(1)+I)  30 LET R=INT(N*RND(1)+I)
    40 PRINT                 40 PRINT
    50 PRINT R               50 PRINT R
    99 END                  99 END
```

2.

```
01 REM H--HEADS
02 REM T--TAILS
03 REM R--RANDOM NUMBER

10 LET N=2
20 LET I=1
30 LET H=0
40 LET T=0
50 PRINT
60 FOR K=1 TO 10
70    LET R=INT(N*RND(1)+I)
80    IF R=2 THEN 110
90    LET H=H+1
100   GO TO 120
110   LET T=T+1
120 NEXT K
130 PRINT 'HEADS:';H
140 PRINT 'TAILS:';T

999 END
```

Problem 2

H — HEADS
T — TAILS   R — RANDOM NUMBER

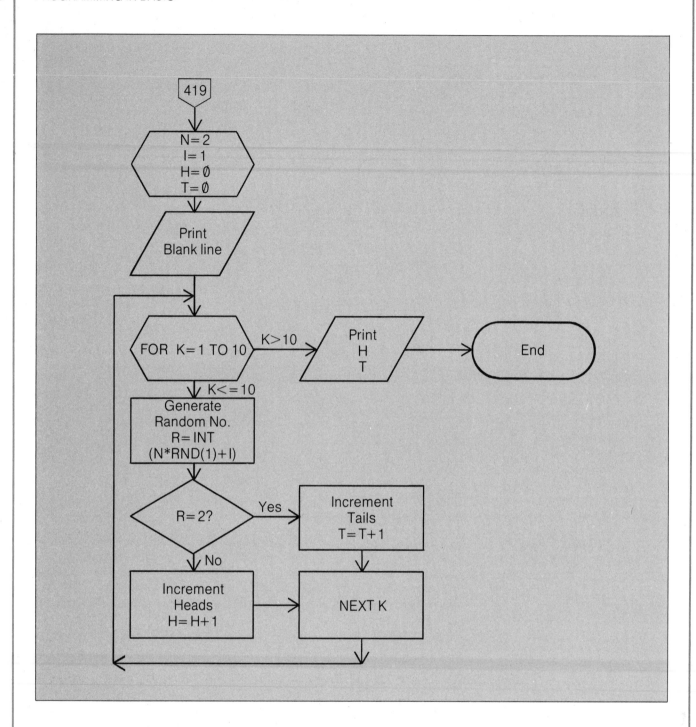

9.4 OTHER LIBRARY FUNCTIONS

A number of other library functions are included in the BASIC language. Here is a list of the most common functions available with a brief description of each.

Function Description

ABS(X)   Calculates the absolute value of X.
ATN(X)   Calculates the arctangent of X*.
COS(X)   Calculates the cosine of X*.
EXP(X)   Raises e to the power of X**.
INT(X)   Retains the integer part of X.
LOG(X)   Calculates the natural logarithm of X (X must be positive).
RND(X)   Generates random numbers.
SGN(X)   Determines the sign of X.
SIN(X)   Calculates the sine of X*.
SQR(X)   Calculates the square root of absolute X.
TAB(X)   Tabulates to the appropriate column.
TAN(X)   Calculates the tangent of X*.

ATN, **COS**, **SIN**, and **TAN** are trigonometric functions; **EXP** and **LOG** are algebraic functions; **ABS**, **SGN**, and **SQR** are primarily mathematical functions but may occasionally be used in business applications. In this section the ABS, SGN, and SQR functions will be explained. The INT and RND functions have already been discussed; the **TAB** function will be covered in the next chapter.

This function calculates the absolute value of a number, which is the number without a sign regardless of whether the number is positive or negative.

ABS(X)

Thus: ABS(12) = 12
      ABS(0) = 0
      ABS(−12) = 12

```
10 READ X,Y,Z
20 DATA 12,0,-12
30 PRINT
40 PRINT ABS(X),ABS(Y),ABS(Z)
99 END

RUN

   12          0          12
```

The SGN function determines the sign of a number. The function returns a 1 if the number is positive, a 0 if the number is zero, and a −1 if the number is negative.

SGN(X)

Thus: SGN(12)= 1
      SGN(0)= 0
      SGN(−12)= −1

*On most computer systems, **X** must be in radians. However, on some systems, radians (**R**), degrees (**D**), or gradians (**G**) may be entered into a trigonometric function by means of a **SELECT** statement.
**The letter e represents an irrational number whose numerical value is 2.7183 when rounded off to 4 decimal places.

```
10 READ X,Y,Z
20 DATA 12,0,-12
30 PRINT
40 PRINT SGN(X),SGN(Y),SGN(Z)
99 END

RUN

  1         0        -1
```

This function calculates the square root of a number. The square root SQR(X)
of a number is a value that yields a given quantity when the value is
multiplied by itself. For example, 5 is the square root of 25 because
5×5=25. The argument of this function must be positive.

```
10 LET X=25
20 PRINT
30 PRINT X,SQR(X)
99 END

RUN

  25        5
```

9.4 OTHER LIBRARY FUNCTIONS—Sample Program

This problem reads in two values at a time, determines the sign of the
first one, then solves an equation in which the functions ABS and SQR
are used.

```
01 REM A--FIRST VALUE
02 REM B--SECOND VALUE
03 REM S--SIGN OF THE FIRST VALUE
04 REM R--RESULT OF THE EQUATION

10 FOR I=1 TO 3              —Sets up a loop.
20    READ A,B              —Reads in the values of **A** and **B**.
30    DATA 2,9,-3,25,-21,49 —Supplies the READ statement with data.
40    LET S=SGN(A)          —Determines the sign of **A**.
```

```
50    LET R=ABS(A)+SQR(B)
```
— Adds the absolute value of **A** to the square root of **B**.
```
60    PRINT
```
— Leaves a blank line.
```
70    PRINT "THE SIGN OF A IS:";S
```
— Prints the sign of **A**.
```
80    PRINT "THE RESULT IS:";R
```
— Prints the result of the equation.
```
90 NEXT I
```
— Transfers control to line 10.
```
99 END
```
— Terminates program execution.

```
RUN

THE SIGN OF A IS: 1
THE RESULT IS: 5

THE SIGN OF A IS:-1
THE RESULT IS: 8

THE SIGN OF A IS:-1
THE RESULT IS: 28
```

9.4 OTHER LIBRARY FUNCTIONS—Your Turn

I. Write a program that calculates the square roots of numbers. Read in the data, then check each item to see if it is negative (use the SGN function). If it is, change the value of the number to its absolute value and store the result in the same variable. Calculate the square roots of all the numbers.

    (a) Print each value and its square root on one line widely spaced.
    (b) Use the following data: 4,−9,16,−25,36,−49.
    (c) Fill in the missing lines.

```
01 REM N--NUMBER READ IN
02 REM S--SQUARE ROOT OF THE NUMBER

10 PRINT
20 FOR I=1 TO 6
30    READ N
40    DATA 4,-9,16,-25,36,-49
50    IF SGN(N)=-1 THEN 70
60    GO TO 80
70
80
90
100
999 END
```

```
RUN

4          2
9          3
16         4
25         5
36         6
49         7
```

1. Which statement should be coded in line 70?

```
(a) LET N=ABS(I)
(b) LET N=ABS(N)
(c) GO TO 100
(d) GO TO 30
(e) LET N=SQR(I)
```

2. Which statement should be coded in line 80?

```
(a) LET N=SQR(N)
(b) LET N=SQR(S)
(c) LET S=SQR(N)
(d) LET S=SQR(I)
(e) LET N=SQR(I)
```

3. Complete line 90 with a PRINT statement.
4. Complete line 100 with a NEXT statement.

II. Write a program that reads in six non-zero numbers and adds only the positive values. Use the library function SGN to check the sign of the number. If it is positive, add the number; if it is negative, skip the number.

    (a) Use a FOR/NEXT loop to control input.
    (b) Use the following data: 2, − 3, 4, − 5, 6, − 7.
    (c) Print the positive numbers and their cumulative totals.

```
RUN

2          2
4          6
6          12
```

(Handwritten annotations:)
```
5 Let T=0
10 FOR I=1 To 6
20 Read N
30 IF SGN(N) = -1 THEN
40 Let T = T+N
50 PRINT N, T
60 ~~GO TO 20~~
70 NEXT I
```

Problem II

T — TOTAL
N — NUMBER READ IN
S — SIGN OF THE NUMBER

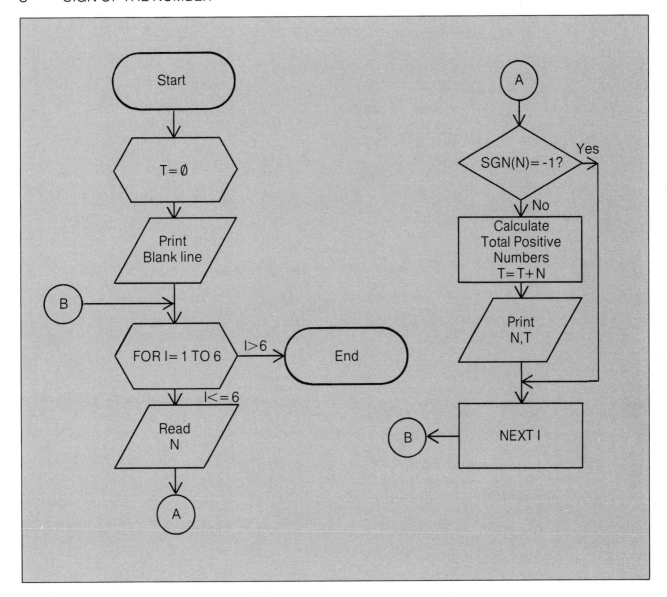

9.4 OTHER LIBRARY FUNCTIONS—Solutions for "Your Turn"

I.

```
1. (b) 70 LET N=ABS(N)
2. (c) 80 LET S=SQR(N)
```

```
3. 90 PRINT N,S
4. 100 NEXT I
```

II.

```
01 REM T--TOTAL
02 REM N--NUMBER READ IN
03 REM S--SIGN OF THE NUMBER

10 LET T=0
20 PRINT
30 FOR I=1 TO 6
40   READ N
50   DATA 2,-3,4,-5,6,-7
60   IF SGN(N)=-1 THEN 90
70   LET T=T+N
80   PRINT N,T
90 NEXT I
99 END
```

A SHORT SUMMARY

BASIC provides a number of features that greatly facilitate the writing of programs. One of these features, although not supported by all computer systems, is the handling of arrays by the use of MAT statements. These special statements instruct the computer to perform operations on an entire array, rather than on one element at a time. Thus, programs are much shorter, since FOR/NEXT loops are not required. Section 9.1 introduced the following MAT instructions.

Input/Output

MAT READ A, MAT INPUT A, MAT PRINT A

Assignment

MAT B= A, MAT A= ZER, MAT A= CON, MAT A= IDN

Mathematical

MAT C= A+B, MAT C= A− B, MAT B= (2)*A, MAT C= A*B

Special

MAT B= TRN(A), MAT B= INV(A)

BASIC also offers a number of library (standard or built-in) functions. These are prewritten routines that may be "called" upon to perform certain operations. One of the functions available on most computer systems is the INT function. This library function retains the integer part of a number and discards the decimal part. Three uses of the INT function were discussed in Section 9.2. Each is listed below along with a sample statement.

1. Separating Digits from Numbers

This statement separates a digit from the hundreds position of a number.

xx LET H=INT(N/100)

2. Checking Division

This statement checks whether or not one integer divides exactly into another.

xx IF I/J=INT(I/J) THEN xx

3. Rounding Off Numbers

The general formula for rounding off numbers is:

$$INT(N*10\uparrow D+.5)/10\uparrow D$$

where **N** is the number to be rounded and **D** is the number of desired decimal places.

Another library function available in the BASIC language is the RND function. This built-in function, discussed in Section 9.3, generates a pseudo-random number. Random numbers are frequently used to simulate procedures or to test new programs. Since the numbers generated by the RND function fall between 0 and 1, they are usually converted to whole numbers so that they are in a more acceptable form. The formula for this conversion is:

$$INT(N*RND(1)+I)$$

where **I** is the first endpoint (the lowest number wanted) and **N** is the "number" of numbers in the range. The latter value is calculated by subtracting the first endpoint from the second and adding 1: **(J−I)+1**. The argument of the RND function varies greatly among computer systems. It's best to check your manual to find out what your computer requires.

A number of other library functions are available in the BASIC language. These include the trigonometric functions ATN, COS, SIN, and TAN; the algebraic functions EXP and LOG; and the mathematical functions ABS, SGN, and SQR. The last three functions were discussed in Section 9.4. The ABS function calculates the absolute value of a number; the SGN function determines the sign of a number; and the SQR function finds the square root of a positive number.

Questions and Exercises[10]

1. Modify the program shown below so that the reading and printing of data items are performed by MATRIX statements.

```
10 DIM A(3,2)
20 PRINT
30 FOR I=1 TO 3
```

10. Unless an alternative method is specified, any question or problem that involves a BASIC feature not supported by your computer system may be omitted.

```
40    FOR J=1 TO 2
50      READ A(I,J)
60      DATA -,-,-,.... (6 items of data)
70      PRINT A(I,J);
80    NEXT J
90    PRINT
100 NEXT I
999 END
```

2. (a) When a MAT READ statement is used to store data in a two-dimensional array, are the items entered by rows or by columns?

(b) Complete the two DATA statements in the following program. The data is shown below in matrix form.

```
10 DIM A(3,4),B(3,2)
20 MAT READ A,B
30 DATA -,-,-,....
40 DATA -,-,-,....
--
99 END
```

	A				B	
9	8	7	6		1	2
5	4	3	2		3	4
1	0	9	8		5	6

3. Suppose the MAT INPUT statement is used to store the data items 1,2,3,4,5,6 in the 2x3 matrix A. To which variable of A is each item assigned? (Hint: $A(1,1)=1$; $A(1,2)=2$; etc.)

4. (a) What output does your computer system produce for the following program?

```
10 DIM A(2,3),B(2,6),C(3)
20 MAT READ A,B,C
30 DATA 15,25,35,45,55,65
40 DATA 1,2,3,4,5,6,7,8,9,0,1,2
50 DATA 10,20,30
60 PRINT
70 MAT PRINT A,B,C
99 END
```

(b) What would the output look like if the items in the MAT PRINT statement were separated by semicolons instead of by commas with a semicolon following the last item?

```
70 MAT PRINT A;B;C;
```

5. Write MATRIX statements that perform the following operations.

   (a) Make a duplicate copy of array A and store it in array B.
   (b) Assign zero to each variable of array C.
   (c) Assign one to each variable of array D.
   (d) Assign the identity matrix to matrix E.
   (e) Add the elements of array F to the corresponding elements of array G and store the sums in the corresponding locations of array H.
   (f) Subtract the elements of array I from the corresponding elements of array J and store the differences in the corresponding locations of array K.
   (g) Multiply each element of matrix L by the scalar 4 and store the products in matrix M.
   (h) Multiply matrix N by matrix P using matrix multiplication and store the products in matrix Q.
   (i) Transpose the rows and columns of matrix R and store the transposed matrix in matrix S.
   (j) Calculate the inverse of matrix T and store the inverse in matrix V.

6. (a) Which MATRIX statements allow changes in the dimensions of one-dimensional and two-dimensional arrays?
   (b) Code three different MATRIX statements, each one redimensioning one of the matrices listed in the following DIM statement.

```
10 DIM A(4,5),B(7,8),C(6,5)
```

7. Identify the errors, if any, in the program segments shown below. Make the necessary corrections.

   (a) The following MAT statement is to make a duplicate copy of matrix A.

   ```
   10 DIM A(3,4),B(4,3)
   --
   40 MAT B=A
   ```

   (b)
   ```
   10 DIM A(4,3)
   --
   40 MAT A=CON(5,4)
   ```

   (c)
   ```
   10 DIM A(4,3)
   --
   40 MAT A=IDN
   ```

```
(d) 10  DIM  A(3,2),B(3,2),C(3,2)     (g) 10  DIM  A(2,3),B(2,3)
    --                                    --
    40  MAT  C=B-A                         40  MAT  B=TRN(A)

(e) 10  DIM  A(3,4),B(3,4)            (h) 10  DIM  A(6,6),B(6,6)
    --                                    --
    40  MAT  B=3*A                         40  MAT  B=INV(A)

(f) 10  DIM  A(4,5),B(5,3),C(4,5)
    --
    40  MAT  C=A*B
```

8. (a) What is a library function?
   (b) What two other terms name these functions?
   (c) How is a library function called and where is this "call" usually placed in a program?
   (d) What is an *argument*? How may it be expressed?

9. (a) What is the purpose of the INT function?
   (b) What output does your computer produce for the following program?

```
10  PRINT
20  FOR I=1 TO 7
30    READ X
40    DATA 493,6.714,0,,039
50    DATA -582,-36.123,-,042
60    PRINT X,INT(X)
70  NEXT I
99  END
```

10. If M = 7, what value does your computer assign to N in each of the following statements?

```
(a) 10  LET  N=INT(M+5.9)        (d) 40  LET  N=INT(M-INT(M+3.2))

(b) 20  LET  N=INT(M/M-1)        (e) 50  LET  N=INT(M+INT(M-4.5))

(c) 30  LET  N=INT(M-16.5)       (f) 60  LET  N=INT(M-INT(M-16.5))
```

11. **Isolating Digits from Numbers**
    (a) Write a program that separates the digit 8 from 85.
    (b) Write a program that separates the digit 2 from 268.
    (c) Write a program that separates the digit 9 from 591.
    (d) Write a program that separates the digit 6 from 31.62.

12. **Checking Division**
Write a program that checks whether or not 3 divides evenly into 367. Print **DIVIDES EVENLY** if the division is exact; print **DOES NOT DIVIDE EVENLY** if the division is not exact.

13. **Rounding Off Numbers**
    (a) Write a program that rounds off 27.15 to the nearest tenth (27.2).
    (b) Write a program that rounds off 27.156 to the nearest hundredth (27.16).
    (c) Write a program that rounds off 27.1567 to the nearest thousandth (27.157).
    (d) Write a program that rounds off 19.85 to the nearest whole number (20).

14. What is the purpose of the RND function?

15. State two reasons why random numbers generated by the RND function are not truly random.

16. The RND function produces numbers that are evenly distributed between 0 and 1. Explain the meaning of this statement.

17. For each of the following, code a program that generates a random number.
    (a) A decimal number between 0 and 1.
    (b) A whole number between 1 and 100 inclusive.
    (c) A whole number between 1 and 9 inclusive.
    (d) A whole number between 8 and 24 inclusive.
    (e) A whole number between 23 and 36 inclusive.

18. What output will the following programs produce?

```
(a) 10 PRINT
    20 FOR I=1 TO 3
    30    READ X
    40    DATA 14,0,-14
    50    PRINT X,ABS(X)
    60 NEXT I
    99 END

(b) 10 PRINT
    20 FOR I=1 TO 3
    30    READ X
    40    DATA 14,0,-14
    50    PRINT X,SGN(X)
    60 NEXT I
    99 END

(c) 10 LET X=49
    20 PRINT
    30 PRINT X,SQR(X)
    99 END
```

Programming Problems

1. Chapter Eight presented a number of review problems that involved two storerooms in which various styles of shoes were stored. Each room had three shelves with the shelves partitioned into three sections so that it was possible to treat each storeroom as a matrix. In Problem 7, page 377, the supervisor wanted to replenish the stock in the storage locations that had two pairs of shoes or less. Suppose an order has been filled and that these locations now have eight pairs of shoes each. Write a program that will show this change for both storerooms.

   (a) Check each storage location (element of the matrix) to see whether or not it has two pairs of shoes or less. If it has, change the quantity to 8. Do this for both storerooms.
   (b) Use two sets of nested FOR/NEXT loops; one to check the stock in storeroom A and the other to check the stock in storeroom B.
   (c) Use MAT statements to read the old quantities and to print the new quantities. Here is the data before the order was filled.

Storeroom A

	Sec 1	Sec 2	Sec 3
Shelf 1	1	3	2
Shelf 2	5	4	0
Shelf 3	2	3	5

Storeroom B

	Sec 1	Sec 2	Sec 3
Shelf 1	4	0	3
Shelf 2	3	1	2
Shelf 3	5	4	3

```
RUN

STOREROOM  A
   8   3   8

   5   4   8

   8   3   5


STOREROOM  B
   4   8   3

   3   8   8

   5   4   3
```

Problem 1

A — STOREROOM A
B — STOREROOM B

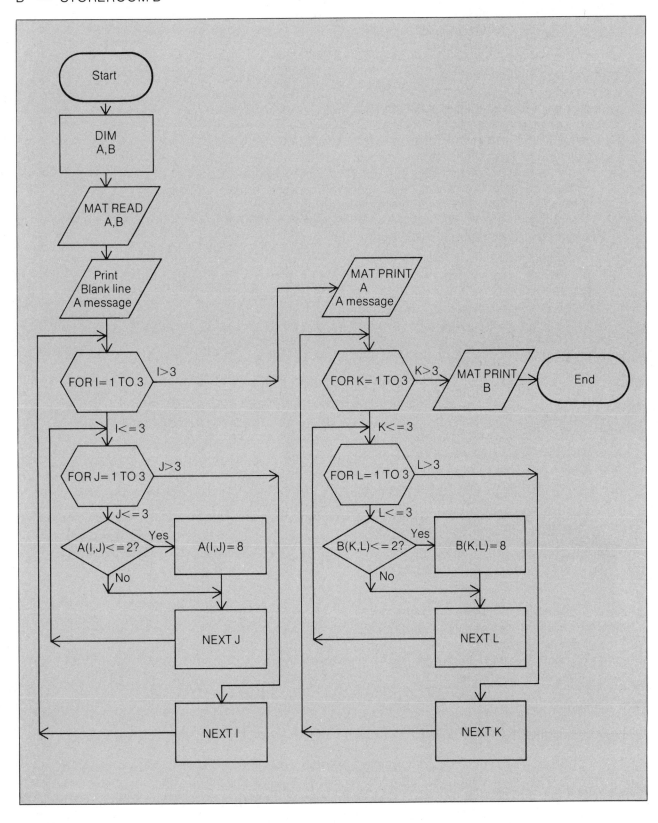

2. This is a review problem from Chapter Six (Problem 9, page 249) in which compound amounts were calculated but not rounded off to the nearest cent. This time you are to round off the amounts to dollars and cents. Here is the problem once more.

Using an initial principal of $1000, find the amount of an investment at the end of each year for four years, using interest rates of 13%, 14%, and 15%. The amount of the investment after interest has been added is called the compound amount. The formula to calculate this amount is as follows.

Compound Amount = Principal$(1+$Rate of Interest$)^{\text{Period of Time}}$

(a) Use nested FOR/NEXT loops:

    (i) The outer loop keeps track of the years (period of time in the formula). Use the index of the FOR statement to print the number of the year at the beginning of each output line. Place this PRINT statement between the FOR statements.

    (ii) The inner loop generates the interest rates.

(b) Compound Amount $= 1000(1+$R$)^{\text{Year Number}}$

(c) Print the first year's compound amounts across the first line of output (for each rate of interest), the second year's compound amounts across the second line of output (for each rate of interest), etc. To do this, your PRINT statement that prints the number of the year and the PRINT statement that prints the compound amount should each end with a semicolon.

(d) After each compound amount has been calculated, use the INT function to round off the amount to the nearest cent. (See page 406.)

```
RUN

1    1130    1140    1150
2    1276.9   1299.6   1322.5
3    1442.9   1481.54  1520.88
4    1630.47  1688.96  1749.01
```

3. A prime number is an integer greater than one that cannot be divided exactly by any positive integer except by one and itself. To determine whether or not an integer is prime, divide the integer by all the whole numbers between 2 and n−1 inclusive, where n is the number (integer) to be tested. If the divisions are not exact, the number is prime; if a division is exact, the number is not prime.

(a) In an outer FOR/NEXT loop, read in the numbers 17, 25, and 29.

(b) In an inner FOR/NEXT loop, determine whether or not the integer is prime. In your FOR statement, set the initial value at 2 and the test value at n−1. The index will be your divisor.

(c) Your main statement should be

xx IF N/J = INT(N/J) THEN xx

where **N** is the number read in and **J** is the index. For example, if 9 is the integer to be tested, then

$$9/2 = INT(9/2)$$
$$4.5 = INT(4.5)$$
$$4.5 = 4$$

This statement is not true when 9 is divided by 2. Therefore, 9 is prime at this point in the program. Your program should now divide 9 by 3.

$$9/3 = INT(9/3)$$
$$3 = INT(3)$$
$$3 = 3$$

Since this statement is true, 9 is not a prime number. To test a prime number such as 17, your program should divide 17 by all the integers between 2 and 16 inclusive.

(d) If the main statement is true, transfer control to a statement that prints the number being tested and the message **IS NOT A PRIME NUMBER**. Otherwise, divide the number by the next divisor. If the statement is false for every division, print the number being tested and the message **IS A PRIME NUMBER**.

(e) Do the same for the next two data numbers.

```
RUN

17        IS A PRIME NUMBER
25        IS NOT A PRIME NUMBER
29        IS A PRIME NUMBER
```

4. There are two ways by which the efficiency of your program on prime numbers can be improved.

   (i) After dividing by 2, only odd integers need to be used as divisors.

   (ii) It is not necessary to try all odd integer divisors between 2 and n− 1. The number of divisors can be greatly reduced if your program uses only those divisors that do not exceed the square root of the number being tested.

   (a) In an outer FOR/NEXT loop, read in the numbers 17, 25, and 29.

   (b) In an inner FOR/NEXT loop, determine whether or not the integer is prime. Use 3 as the initial value and **SQR(N)** as the test value in the FOR statement of this loop. Use a step value of 2. The index will be your divisor.

   (c) Between the two FOR statements, test each data item by dividing the number by 2.

```
RUN

    17          IS A PRIME NUMBER
    25          IS NOT A PRIME NUMBER
    29          IS A PRIME NUMBER
```

5. This will be your last problem on prime numbers. Instead of reading in three numbers, have the computer generate 15 random whole numbers between 2 and 100 inclusive. Check these numbers to see whether or not they are prime. Your program for Problem 4 should be modified as follows:

(a) Change the test value of the outer loop to 15.
(b) Code initialization statements that supply the statement that generates a random number with the "number" of numbers and the first endpoint. Remember, the definition of a prime number does not include the number 1, therefore the first endpoint must be 2.
(c) Replace the READ/DATA statements by a statement that generates a random whole number between 2 and 100 inclusive. This statement should be placed immediately following the FOR statement of the outer loop.
(d) Following the statement that generates a random number, insert a statement that checks whether or not the random number is 3 or less. If it is, transfer control to the statement that prints the number and the message **IS A PRIME NUMBER**.

Since output differs with each RUN, none is shown below. Instead, all the prime numbers between 2 and 100 inclusive have been listed. Your RUNs should include some of these numbers as prime numbers.

2,3,5,7,11,13,17,19,23,29,31,37,41,43,47,53,59,61,67,71,73,
79,83,89,97

Problem 4

N — NUMBER TO BE TESTED   J — INDEX USED AS THE DIVISOR

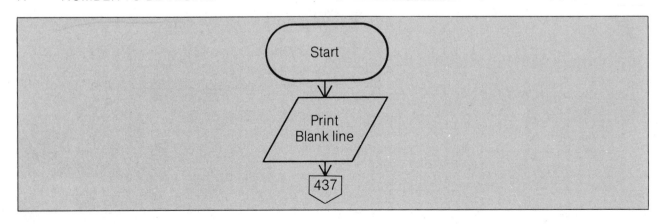

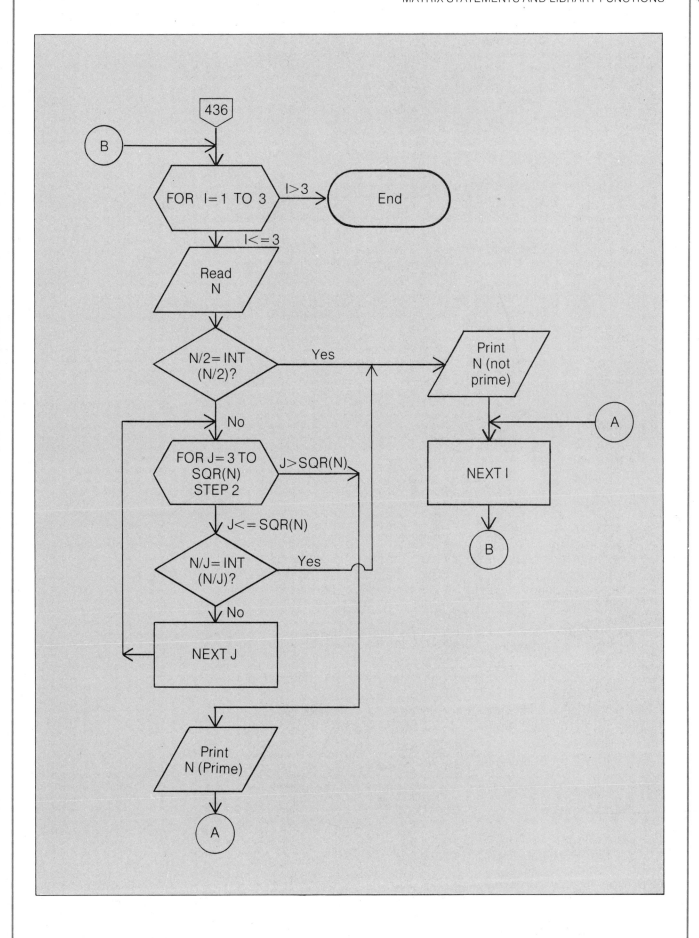

6. This problem is similar to the sample program (Page 407) that separates digits from a number. Write a program that converts 1 000 000 seconds to days, hours, minutes, and seconds.

1 day	= 86 400 seconds
1 hour	= 3600 seconds
1 minute	= 60 seconds

(a) Assign the one million seconds to a variable, say I, by using a LET statement.
(b) Use the INT function on all calculations that include division.
(c) Days: Divide I by 86 400.
(d) Hours: Subtract the days (in seconds) from I and divide the result by 3600.
(e) Minutes: Subtract the days (in seconds) and the hours (in seconds) from I, then divide the result by 60.
(f) Seconds: Subtract the days (in seconds), the hours (in seconds), and the minutes (in seconds) from I.
(g) Print the number of days, hours, minutes, and seconds as in the RUN shown below.

```
RUN

DAYS: 11
HOURS: 13
MINUTES: 46
SECONDS: 40
```

7. Suppose two players are playing a game in which each one moves his/her chip a certain number of times, depending on where the dial stops on a spinner. The dial may stop at any number from 1 to 9 inclusive. Write a program that determines which player made the greatest number of moves after each one had 10 plays.

(a) Use a FOR/NEXT loop to control the number of plays.
(b) Generate a random number from 1 to 9 inclusive for the first player. This represents the number of moves he/she can make. Immediately following this statement, accumulate the player's moves.
(c) Do the same for the second player.
(d) After 10 plays, find the winner by comparing the accumulated moves of the two players.
(e) Print the winner as shown in the sample RUN.

```
RUN            (Sample RUN)

PLAYER 1 IS THE WINNER
WITH A TOTAL OF 52 MOVES
```

Problem 7

N — NUMBER OF POSSIBLE MOVES
I — FIRST ENDPOINT
P1 — FIRST PLAYER
P2 — SECOND PLAYER
R1 — RANDOM NO. FOR 1ST PLAYER
R2 — RANDOM NO. FOR 2ND PLAYER

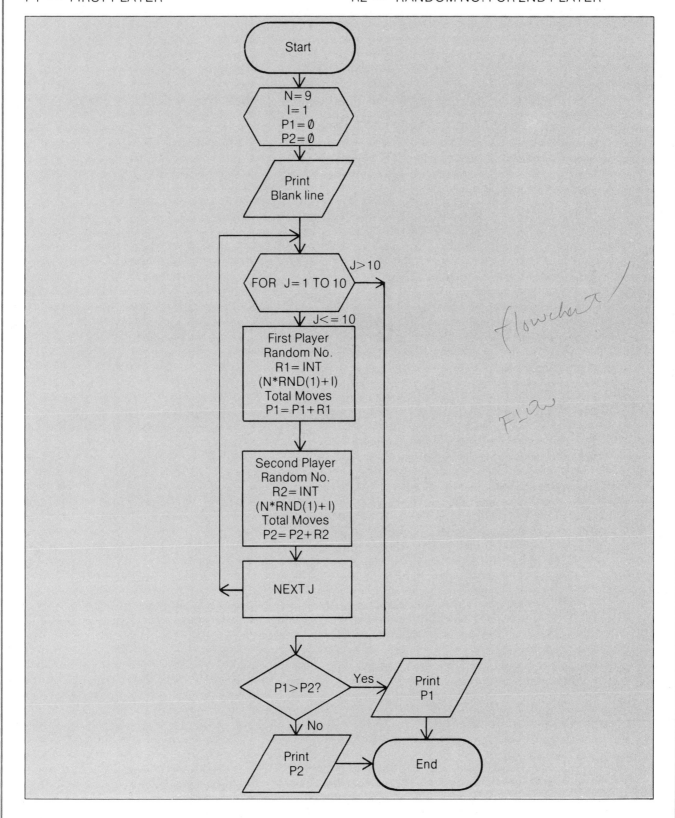

8. Using the index of a FOR statement as your data, find the square roots of the numbers from 1 to 10 inclusive. Round off each square root to:

(a) The nearest tenth.
(b) The nearest hundredth.
(c) The nearest thousandth.

Use nested FOR/NEXT loops:

(i) The outer loop generates the data.
(ii) The inner loop uses the index of its FOR statement as the number of required decimal places. Code this variable in the statement that finds the square root and rounds off the result. Your statement should look as follows.

$$xx \text{ LET } S = INT(SQR(N)*10 \uparrow D + .5)/10 \uparrow D$$

where **S** is the square root rounded off to the required number of decimal places, **N** is the data (the index of the outer FOR/NEXT loop), and **D** is the number of decimal places (the index of the inner FOR/NEXT loop).

Print the number and the three versions of its square root on one line widely spaced.

```
RUN

1        1          1         1
2        1.4        1.41      1.414
3        1.7        1.73      1.732
4        2          2         2
5        2.2        2.24      2.236
6        2.4        2.45      2.449
7        2.6        2.65      2.646
8        2.8        2.83      2.828
9        3          3         3
10       3.2        3.16      3.162
```

9. It was demonstrated in a sample program on page 417 that the random number generator can be used to simulate the roll of a pair of dice. Write a program that finds out how many times a roll of dice adds to 7 if the pair are rolled 50 times. Remember, the random numbers must be converted to whole numbers between 1 and 6 inclusive.

(a) Use a FOR/NEXT loop to control the number of times the pair of dice are rolled.
(b) Keep a running counter to accumulate the number of times the number 7 is rolled.

```
RUN               (Sample RUN)

THE NUMBER 7 WAS ROLLED
 12 TIMES OUT OF 50 ROLLS
```

Problem 9

N — "NUMBER" OF NUMBERS IN THE RANGE
I — FIRST ENDPOINT
C — COUNTER
D1 — DIE NUMBER ONE
D2 — DIE NUMBER TWO
D — TOTAL OF BOTH DICE

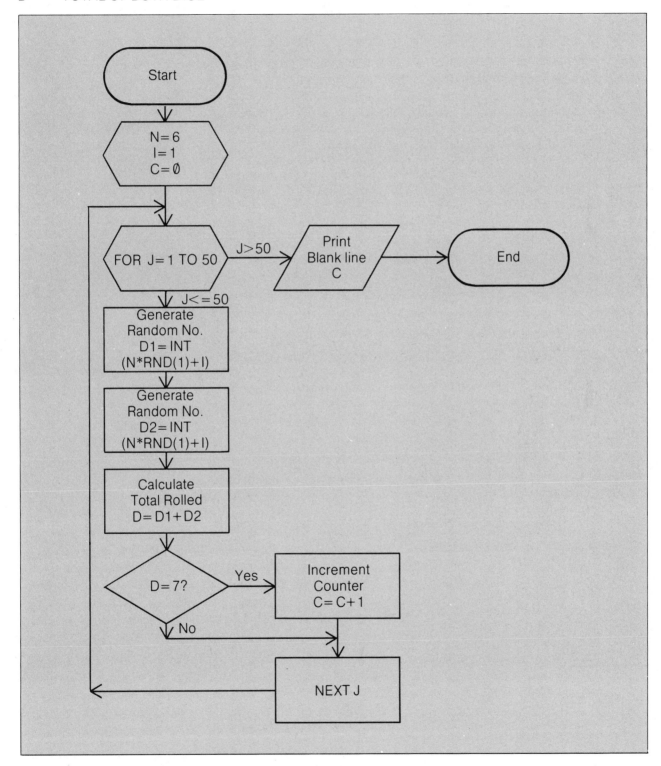

10. In Chapter Six, you were asked to write a program to convert weekly wages to hourly rates based on a 40-hour week. (See Review Problem 1 on page 242.) Write a new program, this time using wages of $455, $493, and $525, and incorporating the following changes:

(a) Store the data and the hourly rates in 2 one-dimensional arrays.

(b) $$\text{Hourly Rate} = \frac{\text{Weekly Wage}}{40}$$

(c) Use the INT function to round off each hourly rate to the nearest cent. (The number of decimal places is 2.) Use one statement to find the hourly rate and to round it off.

(d) Use the MAT READ statement to read the data and MAT PRINT statements to print the weekly wages and the hourly rates.

(e) If your computer system does not support MAT statements, read and print the data in a FOR/NEXT loop. Use another FOR/NEXT loop to print the hourly rates. Don't forget to place an extra blank PRINT statement before the statement that prints HOURLY RATES so that this heading is printed on a new line.

Using MAT Statements

```
RUN

WEEKLY WAGES
 455

 493

 525


HOURLY RATES
 11.38

 12.33

 13.13
```

Without MAT Statements

```
RUN

WEEKLY WAGES
 455   493   525
HOURLY RATES
 11.38  12.33  13.13
```

TEN ADVANCED OUTPUT FEATURES

A. After completing this chapter, you should be able to write BASIC programs to format output by means of:
1. The TAB function.
2. The PRINT USING and IMAGE statements.

B. In addition, you should be able to:
1. Display and label a PRINT statement that uses the TAB function.
2. Write short BASIC programs using the TAB function to produce the following:
   (a) Positive and negative signs before numbers.
   (b) Strings and numbers on one output line.
   (c) Dollar signs before amounts.
   (d) Centred headings.
   (e) Numbers centred under headings.
3. Produce the output of programs.
4. (a) State the purpose of the PRINT USING statement.
   (b) Display and label a PRINT USING statement.
5. (a) State the purpose of the IMAGE statement.
   (b) Display and label an IMAGE statement.
6. Write short BASIC programs using the PRINT USING and IMAGE statements to produce the following:
   (a) Centred headings.
   (b) Numbers centred under headings.
   (c) Positive and negative signs before numbers.
   (d) Dollar signs before amounts.
   (e) Whole numbers aligned in a column.
   (f) Numbers aligned by decimal points.
   (g) Numbers rounded off to a specific number of decimal places.
   (h) Numbers expressed in scientific notation.
7. (a) Summarize what happens when more positions are reserved in a field of an IMAGE than are needed for:
      (i) A string.
      (ii) A number that contains a decimal point.
   (b) Produce the output of a program involving (i) and (ii).
8. (a) Summarize what happens when a field specification is too narrow for:
      (i) A string.
      (ii) A number.
   (b) Produce the output of a program involving (i) and (ii).
9. (a) Summarize what happens when there is an insufficient number of field specifications for the number of items to be printed.
   (b) Produce the output of a program involving (a).

10. (a) Summarize what happens when there are more field specifications than items to be printed.
    (b) Produce the output of a program involving (a).

10.1 THE TAB FUNCTION

Until now, the output of a program was formatted (arranged) by the computer. This type of output is known as format-free output. Your only control was in the horizontal spacing of items by the use of commas or semicolons in a PRINT statement. The **TAB** function is a feature that gives greater flexibility in the positioning of items. Used only in PRINT statements (and available in most versions of BASIC), it instructs the computer to override a print zone and skip to a specific column to display an item. It is similar to the setting of tab stops on a typewriter. Here is the general form.

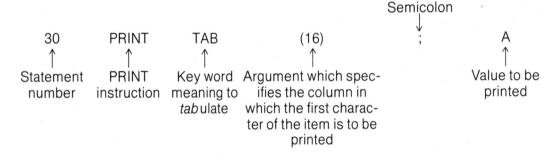

The TAB instruction must precede the item to be printed and must consist of the key word TAB followed by an argument (in parentheses) which specifies the column in which the displayed item is to begin. The argument may be expressed as a constant, a variable, or an arithmetic expression. Its value must not be negative. The argument is usually followed by a semicolon,[1] which is followed by the item to be printed. Each tabulated position is counted from the current line's left-most column, which is considered to be the zero column on the majority of computers. For the programs in this book, the left-most column is numbered zero.

In the previous chapters, statements consisted of 40 characters or less. When a statement contains more than 40 characters, the extra characters can be coded on the next line starting in the left-most column. Thus, the number of PRINT statements can be reduced by using one long PRINT statement rather than several short ones to obtain the same line of output. Compare the following.

```
(a) 30 PRINT TAB(3);"NAME";TAB(11);
    40 PRINT "ADDRESS";TAB(22);"ACCOUNT ";
    50 PRINT "NUMBER"
```

1. Some systems accept a comma after the argument, others require no punctuation. In this book, the argument will be followed by a semicolon.

```
(b) 30 PRINT TAB(3);"NAME";TAB(11);"ADDRESS"
    ;TAB(22);"ACCOUNT NUMBER"
```

Both examples print the heading

```
NAME      ADDRESS      ACCOUNT NUMBER
```

By eliminating line numbers 40 and 50 and the two PRINTs, the number of coded lines can be reduced to two.

Care must be taken when reaching the last print position in a line. On an interactive system, the cursor automatically shifts to the first position in the next line and waits for the statement to be completed. If there are no other characters to enter, the RETURN key must be pressed to transmit the typed statement to memory, even though the cursor is positioned on a new line.

Shown below are a number of PRINT statements that use the TAB function to format output.

1.

```
30 PRINT TAB(0);"HI"
```

HI starts in the left-most column.

2.

```
30 PRINT TAB(12);"HI"
```

This time **HI** starts in column 12, which is actually the thirteenth column, since the left-most column is numbered 0.

3.

```
30 PRINT TAB(0);"HI";TAB(3);"THERE"
```

This statement has two TAB functions. Notice that the column number in the second function specifies the position counted from the left-most column, not from the item just printed. A semicolon must be coded before each TAB function (except for the first function) so that items are printed on the same line. In the statement above, the semicolon referred to is the one before **TAB(3)**. If a comma is used, some systems ignore the TAB command and **THERE** would be printed in the next available print zone. Thus, a computer that allows 10 characters to a zone would print **THERE** starting in column 10.

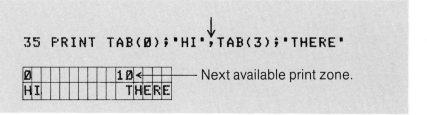

4.

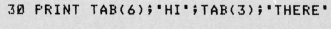

The first TAB command prints the first character of the string **HI** in column 6. The second TAB command instructs the computer to print the string **THERE** starting in column 3. Since the carrier has already passed column 3, the instruction **TAB(3)** is ignored and **THERE** is printed immediately after **HI**. On some computer systems **THERE** is printed on the next line. In other words, the print mechanism cannot move from right to left (it cannot backspace).

5.

```
10 LET A=12
20 PRINT TAB(4);A
```

Tabulates to the column set aside for the space that precedes a positive number.

Tabulates to the column set aside for the first digit of a positive number.

These examples print a positive number. As mentioned in a previous chapter, some computer systems leave a space before a positive number for the assumed plus sign. This means that the space is considered as the first character of the number and a column is set aside for this space. When you tabulate for the number, you must tabulate to the column reserved for this space. Other computers leave no space before a positive number. In this case, you tabulate to the column reserved for the first digit of the number. In this book, a positive number is preceded by a space and you must tabulate to the column set aside for this space.

6.

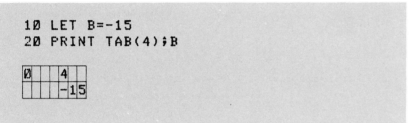

```
10 LET B=-15
20 PRINT TAB(4);B
```

This example prints a negative number. When the number is negative, you must tabulate to the column set aside for the sign, since the minus sign is the first character of the number.

7.

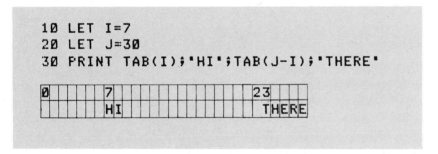

```
10 LET I=7
20 LET J=30
30 PRINT TAB(I);"HI";TAB(J-I);"THERE"
```

Arguments may be variables or arithmetic expressions as well as constants (numbers). The argument of the first TAB function in line 30 instructs the computer to print **HI** starting in column 7. In the second TAB function, the expression is evaluated (30− 7= 23), and the string **THERE** is printed starting in column 23.

8.

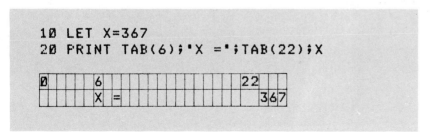

```
10 LET X=367
20 PRINT TAB(6);"X =";TAB(22);X
```

The PRINT statement in this program prints the string **X** = and the value **367** on one line.

9.

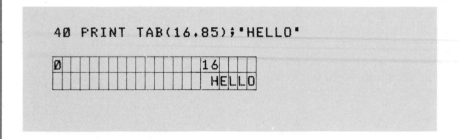

The INT function is automatically applied to the argument 16.85. This means that the number is truncated and the integer part (16) is retained. The string **HELLO** starts in column 16.

10.

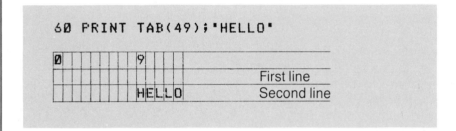

HELLO is to be printed starting in column 49, which is the fiftieth column when you consider the left-most column as column 1. Since the computer allows only 40 columns on one print line, the string **HELLO** will be printed on the next line starting in column 9. This is because 50 − 40 = 10, which is the tenth column when you consider the left-most column as column 1, but the nineth column when you consider the left-most column as column zero.

11. The TAB function is often used in the spacing of headings.

```
10 PRINT TAB(2);"RETAIL PRICE";TAB(19);"
TAX";TAB(27);"TOTAL COST"
```

0	2											19				27						
	RETAIL	PRICE			TAX			TOTAL	COST													

Notice that the PRINT statement takes up two lines, since it contains more than 40 characters. Also, headings should be placed outside a loop so that they are printed only once.

12. The headings in Example 11 can be printed on two lines.

```
10 PRINT TAB(7);"RETAIL";TAB(27);"TOTAL"
20 PRINT TAB(7);"PRICE";TAB(18);"TAX";TA
B(27);"COST"
```

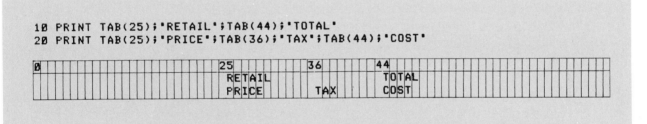

Line 10 prints the word **RETAIL** starting in column 7 and the word **TOTAL** starting in column 27. This statement ends in the fortieth position of the line. If you are using an interactive system with a 40-character line, your cursor will have dropped to the first position in the next line. As already mentioned, you must press the RETURN key to transmit the statement to the computer's memory, even though the cursor is positioned on a new line. Line 20 prints **PRICE** starting in column 7, **TAX** starting in column 18, and **COST** starting in column 27. Because this statement consists of more than 40 characters, it is continued on the next line.

Remember, the computer used for these programs has only 40 columns to one print line. If your system allows more characters on one line, your centring will be different. For example, if you are using a computer that has 75 columns to a line, the headings could be centred as follows.

```
10 PRINT TAB(25);"RETAIL";TAB(44);"TOTAL"
20 PRINT TAB(25);"PRICE";TAB(36);"TAX";TAB(44);"COST"
```

Notice that more spacing is left on both sides of the headings, since there are 75 columns to a print line instead of 40.

To centre the headings, you must determine the number of spaces that must be left on either side of the headings. To do this, subtract the total number of print positions that will be used (including the spaces between columnar headings) from the number of positions on a print line and divide the result by 2. Using the second output in Example 12, the first line will be centred, since it is the longer of the two. This line has 24 characters including the 13 spaces between the words **RETAIL** and **TOTAL**. Because the computer, in this example, has 75 print positions, 24 is subtracted from 75 and the difference (51) is divided by 2. The result is 25 (the fraction is dropped) so that there are 25 spaces to the left of the headings and 26 spaces to the right of the headings.

In this chapter and in the remaining chapters of this book, all programs and problems are written for a computer that has a 40-

character line, that considers the left-most column as the zero column, and that leaves a space before a positive number. The space before a positive number and the minus sign before a negative number are considered part of the respective number.

13. The TAB function can also be used to print dollar signs before amounts.

```
40 LET S=150.45
50 LET C=22.57
60 PRINT "SALES";TAB(7);"$";TAB(8);S;TAB
(21);"COMMISSION";TAB(33);"$";TAB(34);C
```

0							7	8									21									33	34				
S	A	L	E	S			$		1	5	0	.	4	5			C	O	M	M	I	S	S	I	O	N		$		2	2	.	5	7

Notice that there is no need to tabulate for **SALES** since it begins in column zero. The computer is instructed to tabulate to column 7 for the first dollar sign and to column 8 for the amount 150.45. Because the computer leaves a space for the sign of a positive number, column 8 is left blank. It is not possible to eliminate this space, even if you tabulate to column 7 for the amount 150.45, since the carrier is already past this column after printing the dollar sign and you cannot tabulate backwards. If you are using a computer that leaves no space for a positive sign, column 8 will be filled in with the 1 of 150.45 and the amount will be printed as follows.

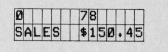

0							7	8						
S	A	L	E	S			$	1	5	0	.	4	5	

Completing the PRINT statement, the computer tabulates to column 21 before printing **COMMISSION**, then tabulates to column 33 for the second dollar sign, and finally tabulates to column 34 for the amount 22.57.

10.1 THE TAB FUNCTION—Sample Programs

I. Here is one of the "Your Turn" problems that was presented in Chapter Five on page 152. This time the headings shown in Example 12, page 449, will be printed and the data and results centred under these headings. The price of the second watch has been changed to $50.

A customer buys three watches, the first one priced at $55, the second one priced at $50, and the third one priced at $40. If a sales tax of 5% is added to the retail price, what is the sales tax and what is the total cost for each watch?

(a) Use the READ/DATA statements to enter the retail price of each watch.
(b) Use a trailer value to terminate input.
(c) Sales Tax = Retail Price × .05
(d) Total Cost = Retail Price + Sales Tax

```
01 REM R--RETAIL PRICE
02 REM T--TAX
03 REM C--TOTAL COST

10 REM PRINT THE HEADINGS
20 PRINT                                        —Leaves a blank line.
30 PRINT TAB(7);"RETAIL";TAB(27);"TOTAL"        —Prints the first line of the
                                                  heading using the TAB
                                                  function for centring.
40 PRINT TAB(7);"PRICE";TAB(18);"TAX";TA         —Prints the second line of the
B(27);"COST"                                      heading using the TAB
                                                  function for centring.
50 PRINT                                         —Leaves a blank line.

100 REM CALCULATE THE TOTAL COST
101 REM PRINT THE AMOUNTS
110 READ R                                       —Reads the values of R one at
                                                  a time.
120 DATA 55,50,40,99999                          —Provides the READ statement
                                                  with data.
130 IF R=99999 THEN 999                          —Checks for the trailer value.
140 LET T=R*.05                                  —Calculates the sales tax.
150 LET C=R+T                                    —Calculates the total cost of a
                                                  watch.
160 PRINT TAB(8);R;TAB(17);T;TAB(26);C           —Prints the retail price, sales
                                                  tax, and total cost using the
                                                  TAB function for centring.
170 GO TO 110                                    —Transfers control back to the
                                                  READ statement.
999 END                                          —Terminates program
                                                  execution.
```

Your output should be as follows.

```
0       7           1718        27
        RETAIL              TOTAL
        PRICE       TAX     COST
            55        2.75      57.75
            50        2.5       52.5
            40        2         42
```

Since the space for an assumed plus sign is considered to be part of a positive number, this space must be taken into consideration when centring the number under its heading. Examine the TAX column. The **T** in the heading **TAX** is printed in column 18 (the argument of the TAB function is 18).

TAB(18);"TAX"

The space before the number 2.75 is printed in column 17 (the argument of the TAB function is 17).

TAB(17);T

This gives the following output.

```
1718
    TAX
    2.75
↑
Blank column
```

If the arguments had been the same, the output would be as follows.

```
18
 TAX
 2.75
↑
Blank column
```

The amount 2.75 is no longer centred under **TAX**.

II. It was mentioned on page 447 that the argument of the TAB function may be a variable. This allows pictures or graphs to be drawn under programmer control, since the value of the argument may vary. Here are some examples.

1. A Letter of the Alphabet

This program prints the letter **T**. Notice that the symbols used to print the letter are also **T**'s.

```
10 PRINT
20 FOR I=1 TO 7
30    PRINT TAB(5+I);"T";
40 NEXT I
50 PRINT
60 FOR J=1 TO 6
70    PRINT TAB(9);"T"
80 NEXT J
99 END

RUN

     TTTTTTT
        T
        T
        T
        T
        T
        T
```

Lines 20 to 40 — These lines form a loop in which seven **T**'s are printed on one line (the PRINT statement ends with a semicolon). The line of **T**'s starts in column 6 (5+**I** = 5+1 = 6) and ends in column 12 (5+**I** = 5+7 = 12).

Line 50 — Counteracts the semicolon after PRINT statement 30, causing the next **T** symbol to be printed on a new line.

Lines 60 to 80 — These lines form a loop, in which six **T** symbols are printed. Each **T** is printed on a new line (the PRINT statement ends with no punctuation) and each symbol is printed in column 9.

2. A Bar Graph (Histogram)

Suppose you want to compare the sales of six stores. This can be done graphically by means of a histogram. In the following program, each column of a bar represents $1000 worth of sales. Store 1 has sales of $6000 since it has 6 columns of asterisks; store 2 has sales of $9000 since it has 9 columns of asterisks, etc. Notice that each bar has two lines of asterisks. A blank line separates the bars of two stores.

```
10 PRINT
20 FOR I=1 TO 6
```

```
30    READ A,B
40    DATA 1,6,2,9,3,2,4,10,5,13,6,4
50    PRINT A;
60    FOR J=1 TO 2
70      FOR K=1 TO B
80        PRINT TAB(3+K);"*";
90      NEXT K
100     PRINT
110   NEXT J
120 PRINT
130 NEXT I
999 END

RUN

1    ******
     ******

2    ********
     ********

3    **
     **

4    *********
     *********

5    ************
     ************

6    ****
     ****
```

Line 30 — Assigns data to variables **A** and **B**. **A** represents the number of the store and **B** represents the number of asterisks to be printed (the amount of sales).

Line 50 — Prints the store number in column one opposite the first line of each bar.

Line 60 — Sets up a loop to print two lines of asterisks for each bar.

Line 70 — Sets up a loop to print a number of asterisks on one line, the number depending on the value of **B**.

Line 80 — Prints the asterisks starting in column 4 ($3+K = 3+1 = 4$) and ending in column $3+B$ ($3+K = 3+B$, where **B** has been assigned a value by the READ/DATA statements).

Line 100 — Counteracts the semicolon at the end of PRINT statement 80 in order to print the second row of asterisks of each bar on a new line.

Line 120 — Leaves a blank line between two bars.

3. The Graph of an Equation

This program draws the graph of the equation $x = y^2$, where y ranges from 6 to −6 inclusive. Thus, when y=6, x=36 and an asterisk is printed in column 36. When y=∅, x=∅ and an asterisk is printed in column zero. When y=−6, x=36 and an asterisk is printed in column 36. These values of x are used in the TAB function to give the horizontal placement for the asterisks. For vertical placement, the PRINT statement that prints an asterisk ends without a comma or a semicolon, which causes each asterisk to be printed on a new line.

```
10 PRINT
20 FOR Y=6 TO -6 STEP -1
30   LET X=YT2
40   PRINT TAB(X);"*"
50 NEXT Y
99 END

RUN

                                    *
                              *
                        *
                    *
                *
            *
          *
        *
          *
            *
                *
                    *
                        *
```

Line 20 — Sets up a loop with the value of the index ranging from 6 to −6.

Line 30 — Squares the value of the index and assigns the result to X.

Line 40 — Prints an asterisk in column X of a new line each time through the loop.

— The first time through the loop, an asterisk is printed in column 36 ($x = y^2 = 6^2 = 36$).

— The second time through the loop, an asterisk is printed in column 25 of a new line ($x = y^2 = 5^2 = 25$).

— The seventh time through the loop, an asterisk is printed in column ∅ of a new line ($x = y^2 = ∅^2 = ∅$).

— The last time through the loop an asterisk is printed in column 36 of a new line ($x = y^2 = (−6)^2 = 36$).

10.1 THE TAB FUNCTION—Your Turn

I. Code PRINT statements with TAB functions to produce the following. Numbers are to be coded directly into the PRINT statements; do not assign them to variables.

1.

```
TAB(0); 24 ; TAB (15); -49.
```

```
0                 16
 24               -49
```

2.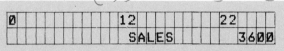

```
TAB (12); "SALES"; TAB (21); 3600.
```

```
0           12          22
            SALES       3600
```

3.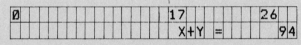

```
TAB(17); "X+Y ="; TAB(25); 94
```

```
0                  17        26
                   X+Y =     94
```

4.

```
TAB(3); "NAME"; TAB(14); "ADDRESS"; TAB(28); "TELEPHONES"
```

```
0   3          14            28
    NAME       ADDRESS       TELEPHONE
```

5.

```
TAB(8); "Amount"
TAB(8); "OF LOAN"; TAB(24); "Interest.
```

```
0       8               24
        AMOUNT
        OF LOAN         INTEREST
```

6.

```
0       8               25
        DEPOSIT         BALANCE
        1400            12695
```

II. Show the output of each of the following program segments. Indicate the column in which the first character of each item is printed. Remember, the computer used for the programs in this book considers the space for the assumed plus sign of a positive number as the first character of the number.

```
1. 40 PRINT TAB(0);"HOURS";TAB(12);"RATE"
```

```
0                        12
HOURS                    Rate
```

```
2. 40 PRINT TAB(10);"NUMBER";TAB(23);"RATE
   PER"
   50 PRINT TAB(9);"OF HOURS";TAB(25);"HOUR
   "

3. 20 LET H=40
   30 LET R=19.55
   40 PRINT TAB(12);"HOURS";TAB(23);"RATE"
   50 PRINT TAB(12);H;TAB(22);R

4. 40 PRINT TAB(12);"HOW";TAB(5);"ARE";TAB(
   26);"YOU?"

5. 30 LET C=31
   40 PRINT TAB(9);"A+B =";TAB(20);C

6. 10 LET I=4
   20 LET J=26
   30 LET A=24
   40 LET B=-8
   50 PRINT TAB(I);A;TAB(J-I);B

7. 30 LET I=17.64
   40 PRINT TAB(I);"NAME"

8. 40 PRINT TAB(52);"BYE"
```

III. This problem appeared in Chapter Five, page 159. Suppose your consumption of electricity for each of the first three months of the year was as follows.

Month	Kilowatt hours
1	1000
2	950
3	930

If the consumption charge is 3.5 cents per kilowatt hour, what would be the amount of your electric bill for each of the three months?

(a) Use a FOR/NEXT loop to keep track of the months.
(b) Use the READ/DATA statements to enter the data (kilowatt hours).
(c) Bill = Kilowatt hours × Rate (.035)
(d) Centre the headings, data, and results, as shown in the output below.

```
0       6           16              29
        MONTH       K HOURS         BILL

        1           1000            35
        2           950             33.25
        3           930             32.55
```

IV. Write a program that prints the letter **Z** six characters wide and whose left-most characters are in column 9.

(a) Use three FOR/NEXT loops:
  (i) The first loop prints the top line of the **Z**.
  (ii) The second loop prints the diagonal of the **Z**. The index in the FOR statement should run in a negative direction; that is, the test value should be less than the initial value and the step value should be −1.
  (iii) The third loop prints the bottom line of the **Z**. This loop is similar to the one that prints the top line.

(b) The argument of the TAB function in each of the three loops should be 8 plus the index of the loop. This places the left-most characters of the **Z** in column 9. (Hint: You will need a semicolon at the end of some of the PRINT statements to produce characters on the same line.)

```
RUN

        ZZZZZZ
             Z
            Z
           Z
          Z
         Z
        Z
        ZZZZZZ
```

10.1 THE TAB FUNCTION – Solutions for "Your Turn"

I.

```
1. 40  PRINT  TAB(0);24;TAB(16);-49

2. 40  PRINT  TAB(12);"SALES";TAB(22);3600

3. 40  PRINT  TAB(17);"X+Y =";TAB(26);94

4. 40  PRINT  TAB(3);"NAME";TAB(14);"ADDRESS"
   ;TAB(28);"TELEPHONE"

5. 40  PRINT  TAB(8);"AMOUNT"
   50  PRINT  TAB(8);"OF LOAN";TAB(24);"INTER
   EST"

6. 40  PRINT  TAB(8);"DEPOSIT";TAB(25);"BALAN
   CE"
   50  PRINT  TAB(9);1400;TAB(25);12695
```

Problem IV

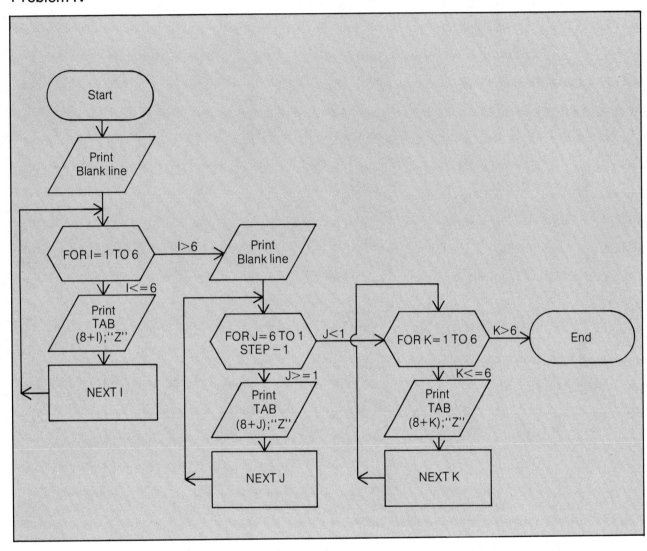

II.

1.

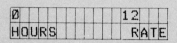

0												12							
H	O	U	R	S								R	A	T	E				

HOURS: Column 0
RATE: Column 12

2.

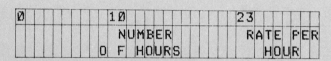

0										10												23				
										N	U	M	B	E	R							R	A	T	E	PER
								O	F		H	O	U	R	S								H	O	U	R

NUMBER: Column 10
RATE PER: Column 23
OF HOURS: Column 9
HOUR: Column 25

3.

0												12							23			
												H	O	U	R	S			R	A	T	E
													4	0					1	9	.	55

HOURS: Column 12
RATE: Column 23
 40:        Column 12
 19.55:   Column 22

4.

0												12		15							26		
												H	O	W		A	R	E				Y	O	U?

HOW: Column 12
ARE: Column 15
YOU?:   Column 26

5.

0									9							20		
								A	+	B		=						31

A+B =:   Column 9
  31:     Column 20

6.

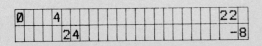

  24:     Column 4
−8:   Column 22

7.

NAME: Column 17

8.

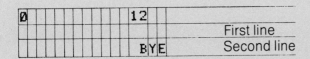

BYE: Column 12 on the second line.

III.

```
01 REM R--RATE PER KILOWATT-HOUR
02 REM H--KILOWATT HOURS
03 REM B--BILL

10 REM PRINT THE HEADINGS
20 PRINT
30 PRINT TAB(6);"MONTH";TAB(16);"K HOURS
";TAB(29);"BILL"
40 PRINT

100 REM CALCULATE THE BILL AND
101 REM PRINT THE DATA AND AMOUNTS
110 LET R=.035
120 FOR I=1 TO 3
130    READ H
```

```
140    DATA 1000,950,930
150    LET B=H*R
160    PRINT TAB(7);I;TAB(17);H;TAB(28);B
170 NEXT I

999 END
```

IV.

```
10 PRINT
20 FOR I=1 TO 6
30    PRINT TAB(8+I);"Z";
40 NEXT I
50 PRINT
60 FOR J=6 TO 1 STEP -1
70    PRINT TAB(8+J);"Z"
80 NEXT J
90 FOR K=1 TO 6
100    PRINT TAB(8+K);"Z";
110 NEXT K
999 END
```

10.2 THE PRINT USING AND IMAGE STATEMENTS[2]

Another method to format output is by means of the **PRINT USING** and **IMAGE** statements. Until now, the printed numbers either had too many decimal places (and had to be rounded off by the INT function) or they had an insufficient number of decimal places, since insignificant zeros were not printed (e.g., 2.40 was printed as 2.4). The PRINT USING and IMAGE statements can also be used to align decimal points and print dollar signs. You no longer need to code lengthy and cumbersome PRINT statements such as

```
60 PRINT "SALES";TAB(7);"$";TAB(8);S;TAB
(21);"COMMISSION";TAB(33);"$";TAB(34);C
```

2. If your computer system does not use an IMAGE statement but instead references a string variable to which a formatted string (an image) has been assigned, refer to the examples on page 474. You should first read the material in this section to become familiar with the terminology. If the PRINT USING statement is not available on your computer system, you may skip this section.

in order to print the following.

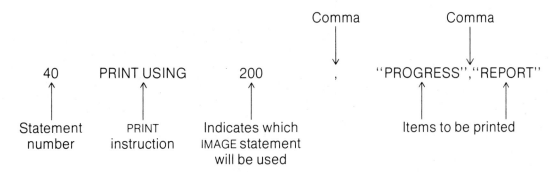

The PRINT USING and IMAGE statements always work together. The PRINT USING statement instructs the computer what to print and which IMAGE statement it must use; the IMAGE statement provides the format (the pattern). Here is the general form of the PRINT USING statement.

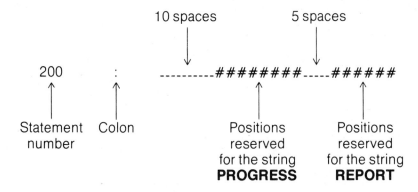

When the computer executes the above statement, it will use IMAGE statement numbered 200 to print the two strings **PROGRESS** and **REPORT**. This IMAGE statement may be coded as in the example shown below. The hyphens in the statement represent spaces.

When the computer executes the above statement, it will use IMAGE statement numbered 200 to print the two strings **PROGRESS** and **REPORT**. This IMAGE statement may be coded as in the example shown below. The hyphens in the statement represent spaces.

Notice that the line number of the IMAGE statement is the same as the one that follows PRINT USING. A colon must immediately follow this line number.[3] A series of number signs (#) designates the location of an item and is referred to as a field specification. The output for the above PRINT USING and IMAGE statements will be printed as follows.

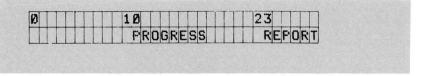

3. Some computer systems use a percent symbol (%) instead of a colon (:).

More than one PRINT USING statement may reference the same IMAGE statement. Shown below are a number of PRINT USING and IMAGE statements and their output. Coding and output may differ on your computer system and some of the features may not be available. Check your manual to find out which ones you can use and how they are coded. The computer used for the programs in this book considers the left-most column as the zero column. This means that if there are 10 spaces before an item, the printed item starts in column 10. (This is actually the eleventh column when the left-most column is considered column 1.)

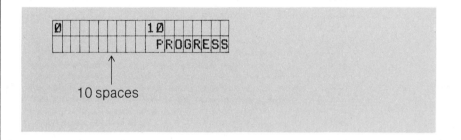

10 spaces

1. The PRINT USING and IMAGE statements may be used to set up headings.

```
10 PRINT USING 100,"RETAIL","TOTAL"
15 PRINT USING 110,"PRICE","TAX","COST"
--
100:_____######_____#####
110:_____######_____###_____####
```

Reserved Locations

```
100:_____######_____#####
               RETAIL               TOTAL
110:_____######_____###_____####
               PRICE       TAX      COST
```

Output

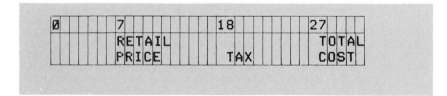

Line 10 instructs the computer to print the strings **RETAIL** and **TOTAL** using IMAGE statement 100 as follows.

(a) Leave 7 spaces.
(b) Print the string **RETAIL** starting in column 7. Strings are left-justified, which means that they start in the left-most column of a field.[4]
(c) Leave 14 spaces.
(d) Print the string **TOTAL** starting in column 27.

Line 15 instructs the computer to print the strings **PRICE, TAX,** and **COST**, using IMAGE statement 110 as follows.
(a) Leave 7 spaces.
(b) Print the string **PRICE** starting in column 7. Notice that 6 positions have been reserved for only 5 letters. Excess columns to the right of the string are left blank.

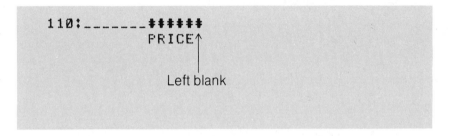

```
110:_____######
         PRICE↑
             |
        Left blank
```

(c) Leave 5 spaces.
(d) Print the string **TAX** starting in column 18.
(e) Leave 6 spaces.
(f) Print the string **COST** starting in column 27.

2. Instead of coding strings in a PRINT USING statement, they may be placed directly into an IMAGE statement. The PRINT USING and IMAGE statements for the above headings will now look as follows.

```
10 PRINT USING 100
15 PRINT USING 110
--
100:_____RETAIL_____TOTAL
110:_____PRICE_____TAX_____COST
```

3. This example prints a positive integer.

```
20 PRINT USING 120,158
--
120:____#####
```

4. A field is a sequence of positions set aside for a specific item of information, such as a name or an address or an account number.

Reserved Locations

Output

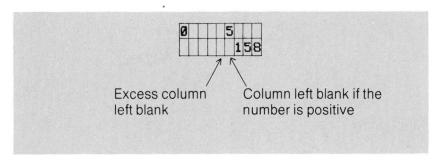

Excess column
left blank

Column left blank if the
number is positive

Line 20 instructs the computer to print the number 158 using
IMAGE statement 120 as follows:

(a) Leave 4 spaces.
(b) Print the number 158 right-justified. This means that the last
digit is printed in the right-most column of the field and the
remaining digits are printed consecutively to the left of this
digit. The column reserved for the sign is left blank if the
number is positive. Excess columns to the left of the column
for the assumed plus sign are also filled with blanks.
Remember, the computer being used leaves a space for an
assumed plus sign and this space is considered to be part of
the number. Thus, the field specification for any number
(positive or negative) must include a column for the sign.

4. This example prints a negative integer.

```
25 PRINT USING 130,-159
--
130:____#####
```

Reserved Locations   Output

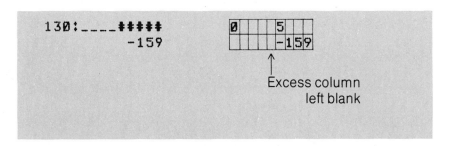

Excess column
left blank

Line 25 instructs the computer to print the number −159 using
IMAGE statement 130 as follows.

(a) Leave 4 spaces.
(b) Print the number − 159 right-justified. Since the number is negative, the column reserved for the sign is filled with a minus sign. Again, excess columns to the left of the number are filled with blanks.

5. This example shows how a decimal number can be printed.

```
30 PRINT USING 140,94.6
--                    -
140:____####.##
```

Reserved Locations   **Output**

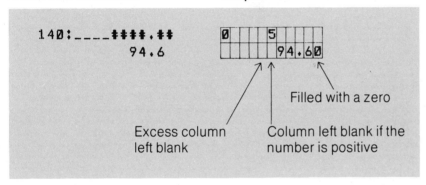

Line 30 instructs the computer to print the number 94.6 using IMAGE statement 140 as follows.

(a) Leave 4 spaces.
(b) Print the number 94.6. Notice that a decimal point is coded within the number symbols. Excess columns to the left of the decimal point are filled with blanks; excess columns to the right of the decimal point are filled with zeros.

6. Both the PRINT USING and IMAGE statements combine numbers with strings in this example.

```
35 LET K=1000
40 LET B=33
45 PRINT USING 150,K,'BILL',B
--
150:__K HOURS########_____#####__###.##
```

Reserved Locations

```
150:__K HOURS########_____#####__###.##
                1000        BILL     33
```

Output

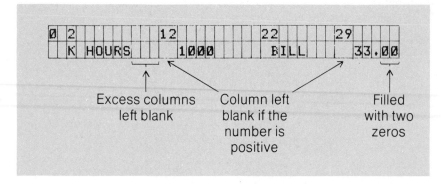

Line 45 instructs the computer to print the values of **K** and **B** and the string **BILL**, using IMAGE statement 150 as follows.

(a) Leave 2 spaces.
(b) The IMAGE statement supplies the string **K HOURS**.
(c) Print the number 1000 right-justified. Eight positions are reserved for the number. Four positions are for the digits; one position is for the assumed plus sign and is left blank; three positions are extra. These three extra positions are also filled with blanks.
(d) Leave 5 spaces.
(e) Print the string **BILL** left-justified. Five positions are reserved for the word; 4 positions are for the four letters; the fifth position is extra and is filled with a blank.
(f) Leave 2 spaces.
(g) Print the number 33 right-justified with the decimal point. Three positions are reserved to the left of the decimal point. Two positions are for the digits, the third position is for the assumed plus sign and is left blank. The two reserved positions to the right of the decimal point are filled with zeros.

7. Here is an example of what happens when field specifications are too small.

```
50 LET S=1500
55 LET C=185
60 PRINT USING 160,S,"COMMISSION",C
-- --
160:____SALES___###___########___####
```

Reserved Locations

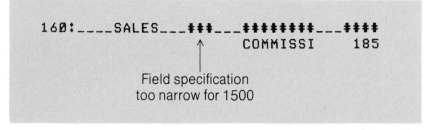

Output

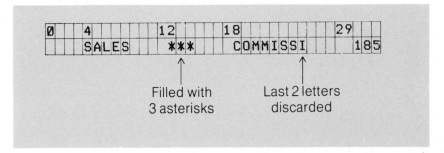

In this example, the field specification is too small for the number 1500. Three positions have been reserved instead of five for the four-digit number and its sign. Most computers will fill the three available positions with three asterisks or with three number symbols. Other computers will print the number with one asterisk (*), or one number symbol (#), or one percent symbol (%) to the left of the number. The field specification for the string **COMMIS-SION** is also too narrow (eight positions have been reserved for a ten-character string). This time, the computer prints as many characters as possible in the positions available, with the result that the two right-most characters are discarded.

8. This is what happens when there are not enough field specifications in an IMAGE statement.

```
65 PRINT USING 170,"COST","TAX","TOTAL"
--
170:____#####_____###
```

Reserved Locations

```
170:____#####_____###
     COST      TAX
     TOTAL
```

Output

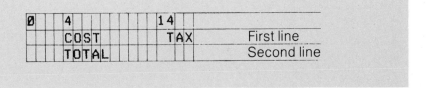

In this example, three items are to be printed, yet only two fields have been designated. In this situation, the computer reuses the IMAGE statement and prints the unformatted items on additional lines. Some computer systems print the unformatted items on the same line.

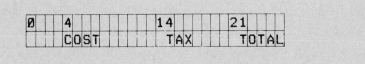

9. When there are more field specifications than items to be printed, the extra fields are ignored.

Reserved Locations

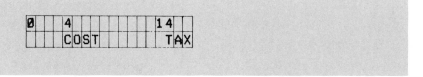

Output

The remaining programs illustrate additional features available in most versions of BASIC that support the PRINT USING and IMAGE statements.

10. Whole numbers can be aligned in a column and decimal points can be aligned one under the other.

```
10 READ A,B,C
20 DATA 325,32,3
30 READ A1,B1,C1
40 DATA 325,32.5,3.25
50 PRINT
60 PRINT USING 90,A,A1
70 PRINT USING 90,B,B1
80 PRINT USING 90,C,C1
90:___#####_____####.##
99 END

RUN

      325       325.00
       32        32.50
        3         3.25
```

11. Numbers can be rounded (some computers truncate) and dollar signs can be printed.

```
10 READ A,B,C
20 DATA 5.93852,67.4628,853.9254
30 PRINT
40 PRINT USING 70,A
50 PRINT USING 70,B
60 PRINT USING 70,C
70:___$###.##
99 END

RUN

    $   5.94
    $  67.46
    $853.93
```

If your computer truncates a decimal number, increase the number by a small amount (the amount depends on the number of desired decimal places). For example, to round 853.9254 to two decimal places, the following PRINT USING and IMAGE statements may be used.

```
40 PRINT USING 70,C+.005
--
70:___$###.##
99 END
```

After adding .005 to 853.9254, the result is 853.9304. This number is truncated to two decimal places, since there are two number symbols after the decimal point in the IMAGE statement. The output is $853.93.

12. The PRINT USING and IMAGE statements may be used to convert ordinary numbers to scientific notation. To inform the computer of the conversion, four exclamation marks must follow the number's field specification (##.###!!!!). The symbol E, a sign, and a two-digit exponent will replace these explanation marks.

```
10 LET A=1234.567
20 PRINT
30 PRINT USING 40,A
40:___##.######!!!!
99 END

RUN

    1.234567E+03
```

13. The PRINT USING and IMAGE statements can be used to print the sign of a number. Here are three examples.

   (a) When a plus sign is placed before a number's field specification, most computers print a sign before the number. The sign that is printed depends upon the number. If the number is positive, the computer prints "+"; if the number is negative, the computer prints "−"

```
10 LET A=52.64
20 LET B=-63.89
30 PRINT
40 PRINT USING 50,A,B
50:___+##.##_____+##.##
99 END

RUN

    +52.64      -63.89
```

   (b) When a minus sign is placed before a number's field specification, some computers print a minus sign before a negative number and leave a space before a positive number. Other systems print a minus sign before a positive number and indicate an error for the negative number.

```
10 LET C=52.64
20 LET D=-63.89
30 PRINT
40 PRINT USING 50,C,D
50:___-##.##_____-##.##
99 END

RUN

     52.64      -63.89
```

   (c) When there is no sign before a number's field specification and no position has been reserved for the sign, some computers print a negative number without its sign, causing the number to appear positive. Other systems consider the field specification to be too small and indicate an error by printing one or several asterisks or number symbols, or a percent symbol as explained on page 469.

```
10 LET E=-42.53
20 PRINT
```

```
30 PRINT USING 40,E
40:____##.##
99 END

RUN

    42.53
```

14. With the exception of the number symbol (#) which is used to designate a field, PRINT USING statements will print any character that appears in an IMAGE statement. This includes periods, commas, and dollar signs within a field, and exclamation marks that do not form the set that converts numbers to scientific notation. Some computer systems will not print a row of asterisks. The following example prints a colon after the word **SALES**, a dollar sign before the number 69413.87, and a comma and a decimal point within the number.

```
10 LET S=69413.87
20 PRINT
30 PRINT USING 40,S
40:___SALES:_____$##,###.##
99 END

RUN

    SALES:       $69,413.87
```

Some computers offer a number of specialized features. Several are mentioned below. Check your manual for features offered by your computer system.

1. Amounts can be protected by printing asterisks to the left of the number.
2. Dollar signs can float so that a dollar sign is always printed just before any number regardless of the length of the number.
3. Asterisks can fill unused positions to the left of a number with a floating dollar sign printed just before the number.
4. Commas can be automatically inserted in any number to segregate digits in groups of three, working from right to left.

Some computer systems do not require an IMAGE statement. Instead, the image is assigned as a string to a string variable.[5] The computer "calls" the image by referencing the string variable in a PRINT USING statement. The programs shown below were written for a computer that requires a semicolon after this string variable. One or several variables, whose values are to be printed, follow the semicolon. The

5. A string variable is represented by a letter of the alphabet followed by a dollar sign ($). A string must be enclosed in quotation marks when it is assigned to a string variable by the LET statement. Strings and string variables are discussed in detail in Chapter 12.

computer used designates locations for numeric values in the image by number signs (#), while the locations for string values are delimited by percent signs (%). The computer leaves a space before a positive number. There are other variations in the coding of the PRINT USING statement and the LET statement that contains the image. For example, in the PRINT USING statement some systems require a comma instead of a semicolon after the string variable that stores the image. In the image, some computers require a series of number signs (#) to designate a string instead of percent signs (%) that delimit the string. You should refer to your manual to find out how to code these two statements for your computer system. The following examples are taken from this section. Your output for some may be slightly different than what is shown on the referenced page. The hyphens indicate spaces.

1. Example 3, page 465   (Prints a positive integer.)

```
10 LET N=158
20 LET F$='____#####'
30 PRINT
40 PRINT USING F$;N
99 END
```

2. Example 4, page 466   (Prints a negative integer.)

```
10 LET N=-159
20 LET F$='____#####'
30 PRINT
40 PRINT USING F$;N
99 END
```

3. Example 5, page 467   (Prints a decimal number.)

```
10 LET N=94.6
20 LET F$='____####.##'
30 PRINT
40 PRINT USING F$;N
99 END
```

4. Example 6, page 467   (Prints numbers and strings.)

```
10 LET K=1000
20 LET B=33
30 LET B$='BILL'
40 LET F$='__K HOURS#########_____%___%__###.##'
50 PRINT
60 PRINT USING F$;K,B$,B
99 END
```

The string **BILL** is assigned to the string variable **B$**. The reserved location is delimited by percent signs and consists of five positions (the percent signs are included in the count). **BILL** is left-justified, which results in one space after the printed word.

5. Example 7, page 468 (Field specifications too small.)

```
10 LET S=1500
20 LET C=185
30 LET C$="COMMISSION"
40 LET F$="____SALES___###___%_____%___####"
50 PRINT
60 PRINT USING F$;S,C$,C
99 END

RUN

     SALES  %1500   COMMISSI   185
```

Since the field specification for the number 1500 is too small, the computer being used prints a percent symbol to the left of the number. The word **COMMISSION** has as many characters printed as there are positions reserved.

6. Page 469 (Insufficient number of field specifications.)

```
10 LET S=1500
20 LET C=185
30 LET C$="COMMISSION"
40 LET F$="____SALES___#####___%_____%"
50 PRINT
60 PRINT USING F$;S,C$,C
99 END

RUN

     SALES   1500   COMMISSION   SALES   185
```

No location has been reserved for the value of C (185). The computer reuses the image and prints the remaining item on the same line. The first location reserved for a number will be used to print 185. Notice that **SALES** is printed again. This is because **SALES** is coded as the first item in the image.

7. Example 10, page 470 (Aligns numbers and decimal points.)

```
10 READ A,B,C
20 DATA 325,32,3
```

```
30 READ A1,B1,C1
40 DATA 325,32.5,3.25
50 LET F$="___####_____####.##"
60 PRINT
70 PRINT USING F$;A,A1
80 PRINT USING F$;B,B1
90 PRINT USING F$;C,C1
99 END
```

8. Examples 11 and 14, pages 471 and 473

(Rounds off numbers and prints special characters.)

```
10 READ A,B,C,D
20 DATA 5.93852,67.4628,853.9254,69413
30 LET F$="___$##,###.##"
40 PRINT
50 PRINT USING F$;A
60 PRINT USING F$;B
70 PRINT USING F$;C
80 PRINT USING F$;D
99 END

RUN

    $       5.94
    $      67.46
    $     853.93
    $69,413.00
```

9. Examples 13 (a) and 13 (b), page 472

(Prints plus and minus signs before numbers.)

```
10 LET A=52.64
20 LET B=-63.89
30 LET F$="___+##.##_____+##.##"
40 LET G$="___-##.##_____-##.##"
50 PRINT
60 PRINT USING F$;A,B
70 PRINT USING G$;A,B
99 END

RUN

    +52.64      -63.89
    -52.64      -%-63.89
```

The computer being used prints a plus sign before a positive number and a minus sign before a negative number when a plus sign is coded before a number's field specification. When a minus sign is coded before a number's field specification, a minus sign is printed before a positive number and two minus signs separated by a percent symbol are printed before a negative number.

10. Sample Program, page 478   (Modify statements as follows.)

```
30 PRINT "_____RETAIL_____TOTAL"
40 PRINT "_____PRICE_____TAX_____COST"
--
160 LET F$="_____$##_____$#.##____$###.##"
170 PRINT USING F$;R,T,C
```

It should be noted that on some computer systems, the PRINT USING statement must have at least one variable following the string variable that stores the image. If only headings are to be centred, it is simpler to code the headings in regular PRINT statements, as in lines 30 and 40 above, rather than to assign the images to string variables.

10.2 THE PRINT USING AND IMAGE STATEMENTS — Sample Programs

1. The following program was listed in Section 10.1 on page 451. Instead of using the TAB function to format the output, this program uses the PRINT USING and IMAGE statements. Here is the problem once more.

   A customer buys three watches, the first one priced at $55, the second one priced at $50, and the third one priced at $40. If a sales tax of 5% is added to the retail price, what is the sales tax and what is the total cost for each watch?

   (a) Use the READ/DATA statements to enter the retail price of each watch.
   (b) Use a trailer value to terminate input.
   (c) Sales Tax = Retail Price × .05
   (d) Total Cost = Retail Price + Sales Tax

```
01 REM R--RETAIL PRICE
02 REM T--TAX
03 REM C--TOTAL COST

10 REM PRINT HEADINGS
20 PRINT            — Leaves a blank line.
30 PRINT USING 50   — Prints the first line of the heading using
                      IMAGE statement 50.
```

```
40 PRINT USING 60
```
— Prints the second line of the heading using IMAGE statement 60.
```
50:_____RETAIL_____TOTAL
```
— IMAGE statement that provides the format for the first line of the heading.
```
60:_____PRICE_____TAX_____COST
```
— IMAGE statement that provides the format for the second line of the heading.
```
70 PRINT
```
— Leaves a blank line.

```
100 REM CALCULATE THE TOTAL COST
101 REM PRINT THE AMOUNTS
110 READ R
```
— Reads the values of **R** one at a time.
```
120 DATA 55,50,40,99999
```
— Provides the READ statement with data.
```
130 IF R=99999 THEN 999
```
— Checks for the trailer value.
```
140 LET T=R*.05
```
— Calculates the sales tax.
```
150 LET C=R+T
```
— Calculates the total cost of a watch.
```
160 PRINT USING 170,R,T,C
```
— Prints the retail price, sales tax, and total cost, using IMAGE statement 170.
```
170:_____$##_____$#.##____$###.##
```
— IMAGE statement that provides the format for PRINT USING statement 160.
```
180 GO TO 110
```
— Transfers control back to the READ statement.
```
999 END
```
— Terminates program execution.

The output should be as shown below.

```
0       7               18          27
        RETAIL                      TOTAL
        PRICE           TAX         COST

        $55        $  2.75     $   57.75
        $50        $  2.50     $   52.50
        $40        $  2.00     $   42.00
```

2. The PRINT USING and IMAGE statements can be used to print letters of the alphabet. On page 453, the letter **T** was printed by means of the TAB function. The following program uses the PRINT USING and IMAGE statements to print the same letter.[6]

```
10 PRINT
20 PRINT USING 30
```

6. For computers that do not use an IMAGE statement, it may be simpler to use regular PRINT statements to format the T.

```
20 PRINT '_____TTTTTT'
  --
50 PRINT '_____T'
```

```
30:_____TTTTTT
40 FOR I=1 TO 6
50    PRINT USING 60
60:_____T
70 NEXT I
99 END

RUN

        TTTTTT
           T
           T
           T
           T
           T
           T
```

Line 20 — Prints the horizontal bar of the **T** using IMAGE statement 30 to format. The left-most character is positioned in column 6.

Lines 40 to 70 — These lines form a loop in which a column of T's is printed in print position 9.

10.2 THE PRINT USING AND IMAGE STATEMENTS — Your Turn[7]

Many sample programs and lines of output were shown in this section. A page number is written opposite each question so that you may quickly refer to a particular example if you need help. Keep in mind that the computer being used has a 40-character line, considers the left-most column as the zero column, and leaves a space before a positive number.

I. Write programs that produce the following outputs. Use one or several PRINT USING statements but only one IMAGE statement.

   1. Write two programs for the output shown below.
      (a) In one program, code the strings in the PRINT USING statement.
      (b) In the other program, code the strings in the IMAGE statement.

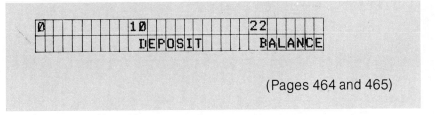

(Pages 464 and 465)

7. If your computer references a string variable for an image rather than an IMAGE statement, refer to pages 473 through to 478.

2. Code the numbers shown below in the PRINT USING statement. Use the IMAGE statement simply to format.

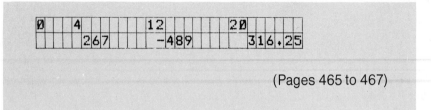

(Pages 465 to 467)

3. Use LET statements to assign the amounts to variables. Code the strings as well as the dollar signs, the comma, and the decimal points in the IMAGE statement.

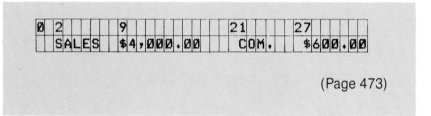

(Page 473)

4. Use the READ/DATA statements to enter the numbers into the computer. Print the numbers aligned in a column as shown below.

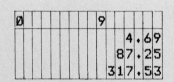

(Page 470)

5. Use the READ/DATA statements to enter the numbers 4.68945, 87.25391, and 317.52849 into the computer. Align the decimal points and round off the numbers to two decimal places by means of the PRINT USING and IMAGE statements.

(Pages 470 and 471)

6. Rewrite the program for Problem 5. This time place a dollar sign before each number.

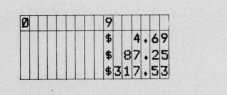

(Page 471)

7. Use the LET statement to assign 98765.432 to a variable. Convert the number to scientific notation.

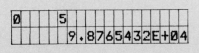

(Page 471)

8. Use LET statements to assign the numbers shown below to two variables. Code an IMAGE statement that produces a plus sign before the positive number, and a minus sign before the negative number.

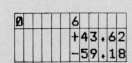

(Page 472)

9. Rewrite the program for Problem 8. This time, code an IMAGE statement that produces a minus sign before the negative number, but no sign before the positive number. Reserve only two print positions for the digits to the left of the decimal point.

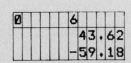

(Page 472)

10. (a) What happens when a field specification is too narrow for:
       (i) A string?
       (ii) A number?

(b) What is the output of the following program? Indicate the columnar position of each item.

```
10 LET S=46327
20 PRINT
30 PRINT USING 40,"TOTAL SALES",S
40:_____########_____###
99 END
```

(Page 468)

11. (a) What happens when there is an insufficient number of field specifications for the number of items to be printed?
    (b) What is the output of the following program? Indicate the columnar position of each item.

```
10 LET S=46327
20 LET C=925
30 PRINT
40 PRINT USING 50,"SALES",S,"COM.",C
50:_____#####_____$#####
99 END
```

(Page 469)

12. (a) What happens when there are more field specifications than items to be printed?
    (b) Show the output of the following program. Indicate the columnar position of each item.

```
10 PRINT
20 PRINT USING 30,"NAME","ADDRESS"
30:_____####_____#######_____######
99 END
```

(Page 470)

II. Rewrite the program you wrote in the "Your Turn" unit of Section 10.1 on page 457. Use PRINT USING and IMAGE statements rather than the TAB function to centre headings and amounts. Here is the problem.

Suppose your consumption of electricity for each of the first three months of the year was as follows.

Month	Kilowatt hours
1	1000
2	950
3	930

If the consumption charge is 3.5 cents per kilowatt hour, what would be the amount of your electric bill for each of the three months?

(a) Use a FOR/NEXT loop to keep track of the months.
(b) Use the READ/DATA statements to enter the data (kilowatt hours).
(c) Bill = Kilowatt hours × Rate (.035)
(d) Use the PRINT USING and IMAGE statements to print the headings, the data, and the results as shown in the output below. Code the headings in the IMAGE statement.

```
0      6          16           29
       MONTH      K HOURS       BILL

       1          1000       $  35.00
       2           950       $  33.25
       3           930       $  32.55
```

III. In Section 10.1 (Page 453), a sample program was listed that drew a bar graph (a histogram) that showed the sales amounts of six stores. Each bar had two lines of asterisks with each column of asterisks in a bar representing $1000 worth of sales. The sales represented on the graph were $6000, $9000, $2000, $10 000, $13 000, and $4000. Rewrite the program to include the following changes.

(a) Do not print the number of the store.
(b) Start each bar in column zero.
(c) If your computer does not print a row of asterisks, use another symbol.
(d) Replace the PRINT statement that contains the TAB function with a PRINT USING statement and code the symbol of your choice in an IMAGE statement.[8] Code a semicolon at the end of the PRINT USING statement in order to print symbols consecutively on the same line. A following blank PRINT will counteract the semicolon so that a new line of symbols can be printed. Another blank PRINT will produce a blank line between two bars. See the program on pages 453-454 if you need help.

```
RUN

XXXXXX
XXXXXX

XXXXXXXXX
XXXXXXXXX
```

8. Code the symbol as a string in a regular PRINT statement if your computer does not use an IMAGE statement. (Notice that the program does not print a value.)

```
XX
XX

XXXXXXXXX
XXXXXXXXX

XXXXXXXXXXXX
XXXXXXXXXXXX

XXXX
XXXX
```

10.2 THE PRINT USING AND IMAGE STATEMENTS—Solutions for "Your Turn"[9]

I. 1. (a) Strings Coded in the PRINT USING Statement

```
10 PRINT
20 PRINT USING 30,"DEPOSIT","BALANCE"
30:_____#######_____#######
99 END
```

9. If your computer does not use an IMAGE statement, assign images to string variables and reference the string variables in the PRINT USING statements. The following two programs show how output can be formatted for computers that do not reference an IMAGE statement. Other examples are given on pages 474 through to 477. Your manual should show you how to code the programs if your computer requires something different. The remaining programs for Problem I would be coded in a similar manner.

Using a String Variable (Problem 3)

```
10 LET S=4000
20 LET C=600
30 LET F$="__SALES__$#,###.##___COM.__$###.##"
40 PRINT
50 PRINT USING F$;S,C
99 END
```

Using a Regular PRINT Statement (Problem 1)

```
10 PRINT
20 PRINT "_____DEPOSIT_____BALANCE"
99 END
```

(b) Strings Coded in the IMAGE Statement

```
10 PRINT
20 PRINT USING 30
30:_____DEPOSIT_____BALANCE
99 END
```

2.

```
10 PRINT
20 PRINT USING 30,267,-489,316.25
30:____####____####____####.##
99 END
```

3.

```
10 LET S=4000
20 LET C=600
30 PRINT
40 PRINT USING 50,S,C
50:__SALES__$#,###.##___COM.__$###.##
99 END
```

4.

```
10 READ A,B,C
20 DATA 689,94,5
30 PRINT
40 PRINT USING 70,A
50 PRINT USING 70,B
60 PRINT USING 70,C
70:___####
99 END
```

5.

Systems That Truncate a Number

```
10 READ A,B,C
20 DATA 4.68945,87.25391,317.52849
30 PRINT
40 PRINT USING 70,A          40 PRINT USING 70,A+.005
50 PRINT USING 70,B          50 PRINT USING 70,B+.005
60 PRINT USING 70,C          60 PRINT USING 70,C+.005
70:_____####.##
99 END
```

6.

Systems That Truncate a Number

```
10 READ A,B,C
20 DATA 4.68945,87.25391,317.52849
30 PRINT
40 PRINT USING 70,A          40 PRINT USING 70,A+.005
50 PRINT USING 70,B          50 PRINT USING 70,B+.005
60 PRINT USING 70,C          60 PRINT USING 70,C+.005
70:_____$###.##
99 END
```

7.

```
10 LET A=98765.432
20 PRINT
30 PRINT USING 40,A
40:_____##.#######!!!!
99 END
```

8.

```
10 LET A=43.62
20 LET B=-59.18
30 PRINT
40 PRINT USING 60,A
50 PRINT USING 60,B
60:_____+##.##
99 END
```

9.

```
10 LET A=43.62
20 LET B=-59.18
30 PRINT
40 PRINT USING 60,A
50 PRINT USING 60,B
60:_____-##.##
99 END
```

10. (a) When a field specification is too narrow for a string, the computer prints as many characters as possible in the

positions that are available. Since a string is left-justified, the right-most characters that have no reserved locations are discarded.

When a field specification is too narrow for a number, some computers fill the available positions with asterisks or with number symbols (#). Other computers print the number with one asterisk (*), or one number symbol (#), or one percent symbol (%) to the left of the number.

(b)

```
0      5              18
       TOTAL SA       ***
```
or
```
0      5              18
       TOTAL SA       *46327
```

11. (a) When there is an insufficient number of field specifications for the number of items to be printed, the computer reuses the IMAGE statement and prints the unformatted items on additional lines. Some computer systems print the unformatted items on the same line.

(b)

```
0      5          15
       SALES      $46327        First line
       COM.       $   925       Second line
```

or

```
0      5          15          26          36
       SALES      $46327       COM.        $   925
```

12. (a) When there are more field specifications than items to be printed, the extra fields are ignored.

(b)

```
0      5          14
       NAME       ADDRESS
```

II.

```
01 REM R--RATE PER KILOWATT HOUR
```

```
02 REM H--KILOWATT HOURS
03 REM B--BILL

10 REM PRINT THE HEADINGS
20 PRINT
30 PRINT USING 40
40:_____MONTH_____K HOURS_____BILL
50 PRINT

100 REM CALCULATE THE BILL AND
101 REM PRINT THE DATA AND AMOUNTS
110 LET R=.035
120 FOR I=1 TO 3
130 READ H
140 DATA 1000,950,930
150 LET B=H*R
160 PRINT USING 170,I,H,B
170:_____##_____#####_____$##.##
180 NEXT I

999 END
```

Using a String Variable

```
160 LET F$="_____##_____#####_____$##.##"
170 PRINT USING F$;I,H,B
```

III.

Using a Regular PRINT Statement

```
10 PRINT
20 FOR I=1 TO 6
30    READ B
40    DATA 6,9,2,10,13,4
50    FOR J=1 TO 2              --
60      FOR K=1 TO B                60 FOR K=1 TO B
70        PRINT USING 80;           70    PRINT "X";
80:X                                90 NEXT K
90      NEXT K                      --
100     PRINT
110   NEXT J
120   PRINT
130 NEXT I
999 END
```

A SHORT SUMMARY

Two features that have been added to the original BASIC language (although not available on all computer systems) are the TAB function and the PRINT USING and IMAGE statements. Both provide a programmer with greater flexibility in the spacing of output items. The general form of a TAB function is as follows.

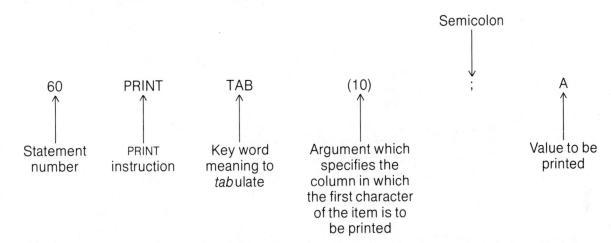

60	PRINT	TAB	(10)	;	A
Statement number	PRINT instruction	Key word meaning to *tab*ulate	Argument which specifies the column in which the first character of the item is to be printed		Value to be printed

The TAB command instructs the computer to override a print zone and to tabulate to a specific column before printing an item. Similar to the setting of tab stops on a typewriter, it is often used to centre headings and to centre items beneath the headings. It is also used to draw pictures and graphs. Each tabulated position is counted from the current line's left-most column, which is considered to be the zero column on the majority of computers. Care must be taken when tabulating, since forgotten items may not be inserted by tabulating backwards.

The PRINT USING and IMAGE statements always work together. The PRINT USING statement instructs the computer what to print and which IMAGE statement to use; the IMAGE statement provides the format. The general form of each statement is as follows.

The PRINT USING Statement

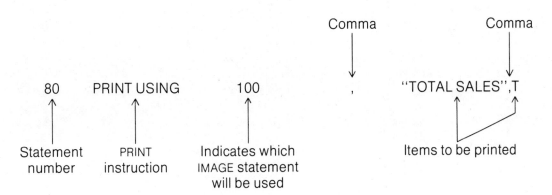

80	PRINT USING	100	,	"TOTAL SALES",T
Statement number	PRINT instruction	Indicates which IMAGE statement will be used		Items to be printed

The IMAGE Statement

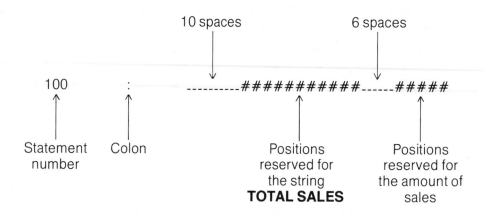

These two statements greatly simplify the centring of headings and numbers. Some computer systems do not use an IMAGE statement. Instead, a PRINT USING statement references a string variable to which a formatted string (an image) has been assigned. Several additional features are offered by the PRINT USING statement. They include the following.

— Align whole numbers in a column.
— Align decimal points.
— Round off or truncate numbers and print insignificant zeros to the right of the decimal point.
— Print dollar signs before amounts.
— Print commas within numbers to group digits.
— Print signs before numbers.
— Print special characters other than those used in formatting.
— Convert numbers to scientific notation.

QUESTIONS AND EXERCISES

1. What is the purpose of the TAB function?
2. Display and label a PRINT statement that uses the TAB function to print an item that starts in column 12.
3. Write programs that produce the following outputs. Use the TAB function to position items in specific columns. Assign all constants to variables.

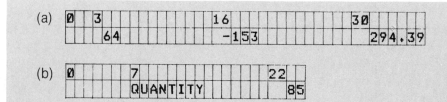

a) Print TAB(3); 64; TAB(16); -153; TAB(30); 294.39

b) Print TAB(7); "Quantity"; TAB(22); 85.

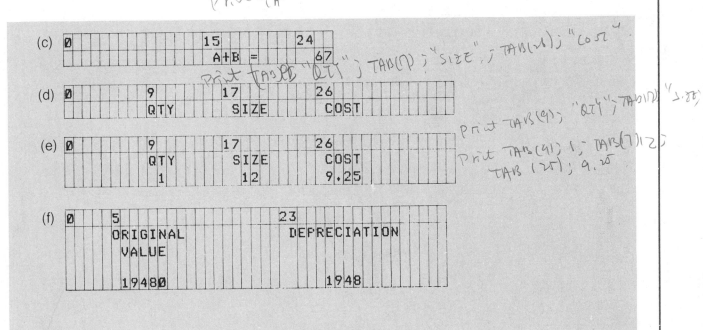

(Handwritten notes in margins:)
Print TAB (15) 3 "A+b"; TAB (24); 67
Print TAB(8 "QTY"; TAB(17); "SIZE"; TAB(26); "COST".
Print TAB(9); "QTY"; TAB(17);
Print TAB (9); 1; TAB(7)12;
TAB (25); 9.25

4. Show the output of each of the following programs. Indicate the starting position of each item as in the outputs shown in Problem 3.

(a)

```
10 PRINT
20 PRINT TAB(6);"FAHRENHEIT"
99 END
```

(b)

```
10 PRINT
20 PRINT TAB(6);"FAHRENHEIT";TAB(26);"CE
LSIUS"
99 END
```

(c)

```
10 LET F=68
20 LET C=20
30 PRINT
```

```
40 PRINT TAB(6);"FAHRENHEIT";TAB(26);"CE
LSIUS"
50 PRINT
60 PRINT TAB(9);F;TAB(28);C
99 END
```

(d)

```
10 PRINT
20 PRINT TAB(15);"NAME";TAB(6);"DEPT."
99 END
```

NAMEDEPT.

(e)

```
10 LET I=10
20 LET C=245
30 LET D=-63
40 PRINT
50 PRINT TAB(I);C;TAB(I+12);D
99 END
```

(f)

```
10 LET J=14.93
20 PRINT
30 PRINT TAB(J);"DISCOUNT"
99 END
```

(g)

```
10 LET C=-243
20 PRINT
30 PRINT TAB(5);"A-B =";TAB(15);C
99 END
```

(h)

```
10 PRINT TAB(47);"DEPARTMENT NUMBER"
99 END
```

5. (a) What is the purpose of the PRINT USING statement?
   (b) Display and label a PRINT USING statement.

6. (a) What is the purpose of the IMAGE statement?
   (b) Display and label an IMAGE statement.

7. Write programs that produce the following outputs. Use one or several PRINT USING statements but only one IMAGE statement.[10] Assign all constants to variables by the READ/DATA statements.

   (a) Write two programs for the output shown below.
      (i) In one program, code the strings in the PRINT USING statement.
      (ii) In the other program, code the strings in the IMAGE statement.

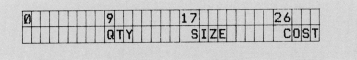

   (b) Place the numbers in the columns as specified.

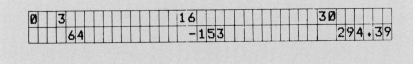

   (c) Code the strings in the IMAGE statement.

   (d) Align the numbers 248, 48, and 8 as shown below.

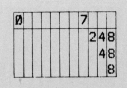

10. Instead of referencing an IMAGE statement, your computer may require a string variable to which an image has been assigned. For Problem 7(a), use the regular PRINT statement to format the output on this computer.

(e) Round off each of the numbers 4.89457, 96.00587, and 352.66823 to three decimal places by means of the PRINT USING and IMAGE statements.

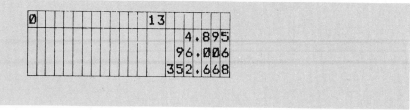

(f) Round off each of the amounts 1234.567, 23456.782, and 345678.926 to the nearest cent by means of the PRINT USING and IMAGE statements.

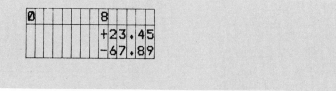

(g) In your program, code an IMAGE statement that produces a plus sign before the positive number and a minus sign before the negative number.

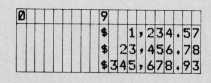

(h) Rewrite the program for Problem (g). This time, code an IMAGE statement that produces a minus sign when the number is negative but no sign when the number is positive. Reserve only two print positions for the digits to the left of the decimal point.

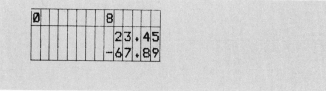

(i) Enter the number .00812345, then convert the number to scientific notation.

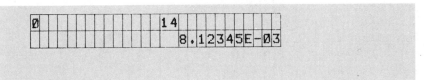

Indicate the starting position of each item when you show the output of the following programs.

8. (a) What happens when more positions are reserved in a field than are needed:
    (i) For a string?
    (ii) For a number that contains a decimal point?
   (b) What is the output of the following program?

```
10 LET T=25.673
20 PRINT
30 PRINT USING 50,"TOTAL"
40 PRINT USING 60,T
50:____########
60:____######.#####
99 END
```

9. (a) What happens when a field specification is too narrow for:
    (i) A string?
    (ii) A number?
   (b) What is the output of the following program?

```
10 LET U=24936
20 PRINT
30 PRINT USING 40,"UNIT PRICE",U
40:_____#######_____####
99 END
```

10. (a) What happens when there is an insufficient number of field specifications for the number of items to be printed?
    (b) What is the output of the following program?

```
10 LET Q=843
20 PRINT
30 PRINT USING 40,"QUANTITY",Q,"PRICE"
40:_____########_____####
99 END
```

11. (a) What happens when there are more field specifications than items to be printed?

(b) What is the output of the following program?

```
10 LET U=63.95
20 PRINT
30 PRINT USING 40,"UNIT PRICE",U
40:___##########___$##.##___$###.##
99 END
```

PROGRAMMING PROBLEMS[11]

For each of the first seven problems, write two programs:

(i) One program that uses the TAB function to format output.

(ii) The other program that uses the PRINT USING and IMAGE statements to format output.

Insert commas within numbers only in those programs that use the PRINT USING statement. Except for Problem 4, code all strings in the image. A statement may require more than one line. If you are using an interactive system, you must press the RETURN key after each typed statement, even when the cursor has automatically dropped to the beginning of a new line. The RETURN key transmits the statement to the computer's memory.

1. Write programs that print the initials of your name. You may use any symbol you wish to print the letters. In the example below, an **E** was used for the letter **E**; a **B** was used for the letter **B**, and an **L** was used for the letter **L**.

```
RUN

    EEEEEEE     BBBBBB      L
    E           B     B     L
    E           B     B     L
    EEEEE       BBBBBB      L
    E           B     B     L
    E           B     B     L
    EEEEEEE     BBBBBB      LLLLLLL
```

11. Remember, instead of referencing an IMAGE statement, your computer may require a string variable to which an image has been assigned. Furthermore, it may be simpler, on these computers, to format headings by using regular PRINT statements. If your computer system does not support the PRINT USING statement, use just the TAB function to format output.

2. Write programs that will draw pictures. You may use the one displayed below or any other drawing you wish to select.

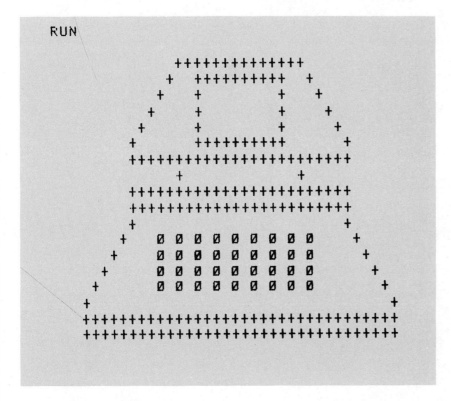

3. On November 1 your checking account showed a balance of $2000. During the month you made the following deposits and withdrawals:

November 10	Withdrawal	$ 100
15	Deposit	450
24	Withdrawal	120
30	Deposit	450

Write programs that calculate the balance in your bank account after each transaction.

(a) Use the LET statement to assign the initial balance to a variable, say **B**.

(b) Use the READ/DATA statements to enter the code and the amount of each transaction.

(c) Use a code of 1 if the transaction is a deposit, a code of 2 if the transaction is a withdrawal, and a code of 3 to terminate the input.

(d) Use the ON...GO TO statement to branch to the appropriate statements.

(e) Depending upon your code,

Balance = Balance + Deposit

or

Balance = Balance − Withdrawal

Using the TAB Function

```
0    5          15          28
     DEPOSIT    WITHDRAWAL   BALANCE

                            $  2000
                $  100      $  1900
     $  450                 $  2350
                $  120      $  2230
     $  450                 $  2680
```

Using the PRINT USING and IMAGE Statements

```
0    5          15          28
     DEPOSIT    WITHDRAWAL   BALANCE

                            $  2,000
                $  100      $  1,900
     $  450                 $  2,350
                $  120      $  2,230
     $  450                 $  2,680
```

Problem 3

B — BALANCE
C — CODE
A — AMOUNT

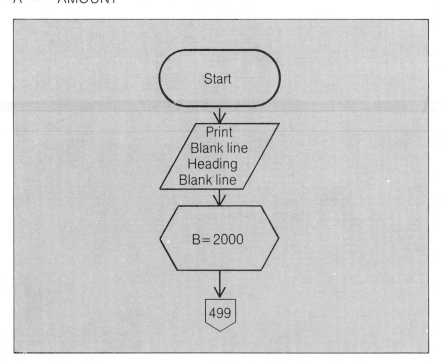

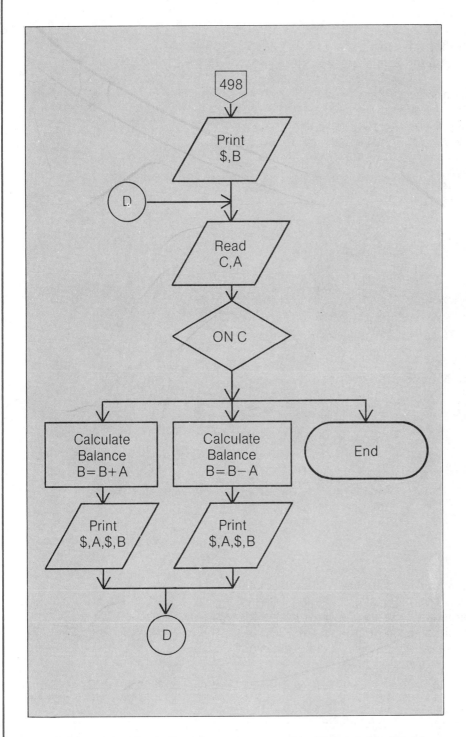

4. This problem is similar to one presented in Chapter Six (Problem 5, page 245). Find the total sales for each of the three stores shown below.

Store Number	Sales per Month
1	2367.25, 1985.60, 2249.05, 1857
2	1952.30, 2149.15, 1767.80, 2364
3	2284.10, 1849.55, 1987.85, 2193

(a) Use an outer FOR/NEXT loop to keep track of the stores.
(b) Use an inner FOR/NEXT loop to keep track of the months.
(c) Between the two FOR statements, initialize each store's total sales to zero.
(d) Use the READ/DATA statements to enter the sales.
(e) Total Sales = Total Sales + Sales per Month
(f) In the program that uses the PRINT USING and IMAGE statements, code the headings in the PRINT USING statement.

Using the TAB Function

```
0       7               22
        STORE           TOTAL SALES

          1             $  8458.9
          2             $  8233.25
          3             $  8314.5
```

Using the PRINT USING and IMAGE Statements

```
0       7               22
        STORE           TOTAL SALES

          1             $  8,458.90
          2             $  8,233.25
          3             $  8,314.50
```

5. Here is a problem from the "Your Turn" units of Chapter Eight. Suppose a savings and loan company offers varying rates of interest on investments depending on the length of time the money is invested. The amount of the investment is $4000. Find the yearly interest for each rate shown below. The interest is not added to the investment each year it is calculated.

No. of Years	Rate of Interest
Y	R
10 12 14	.10 .11 .12
16 18 20	.13 .14 .15

(a) Store the numbers of years and the rates in 2 two-dimensional arrays.
(b) Use one set of nested FOR/NEXT loops to read, calculate, and print by rows.
(c) Store the calculated interests in a two-dimensional array.
(d) Interest = Amount Invested × Rate of Interest

Using the TAB Function

```
0    4      11       20       28
          INVESTMENT :  $  4000

    NO. OF  YEARS       RATE      INTEREST

            10          .1        $  400
            12          .11       $  440
            14          .12       $  480
            16          .13       $  520
            18          .14       $  560
            20          .15       $  600
```

Using the PRINT USING and IMAGE Statements

```
0    4      11       20       28
          INVESTMENT :  $  4,000

    NO. OF  YEARS       RATE      INTEREST

            10          .10       $  400.00
            12          .11       $  440.00
            14          .12       $  480.00
            16          .13       $  520.00
            18          .14       $  560.00
            20          .15       $  600.00
```

6. This problem is an extension of Problem 9, Chapter Nine, page 440. This time you are to find out how many 7's and how many 11's are rolled out of 50 rolls of the dice. Use the random number generator to simulate the roll of a pair of dice. Remember, the random numbers must be converted to whole numbers between 1 and 6 inclusive. See Chapter Nine, page 416 if you need any help.

(a) Use a FOR/NEXT loop to control the number of times the pair of dice are rolled.
(b) Keep two running counters, say **S** for *seven* and **E** for *eleven*, to accumulate the number of times the numbers 7 and 11 are rolled.
(c) The output will be different for each RUN.

Using the TAB Function

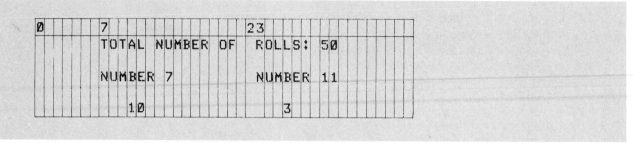

Using the PRINT USING and IMAGE Statements

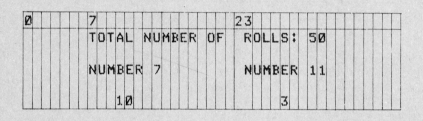

Problem 6

N — "NUMBER" OF NUMBERS IN RANGE   D1 — DIE NUMBER ONE
I — FIRST ENDPOINT   D2 — DIE NUMBER TWO
S — NUMBER OF SEVENS   D — TOTAL OF BOTH DICE
E — NUMBER OF ELEVENS

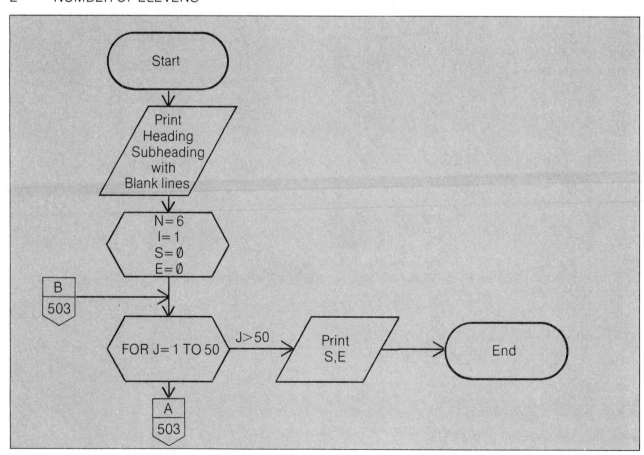

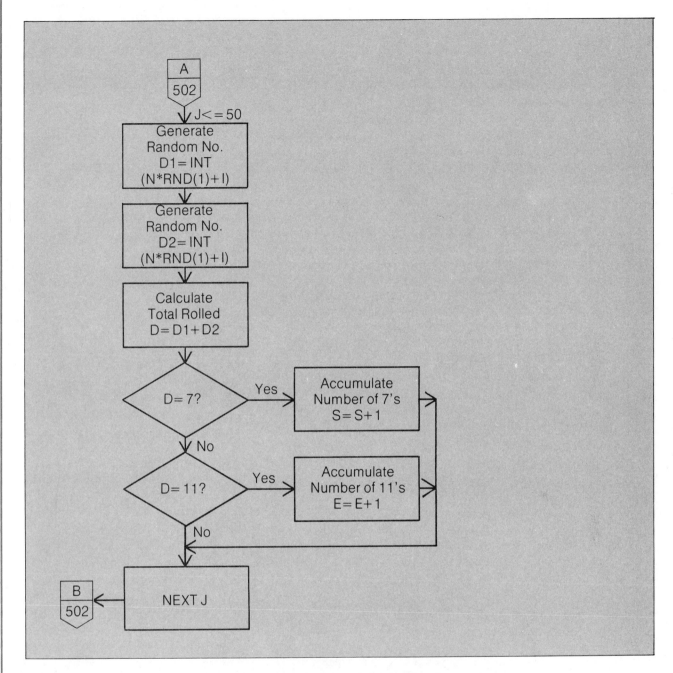

7. A furniture store is offering a 12½% discount on television sets at its end-of-the-year sale. Calculate the discounts and the reduced prices for six TV sets regularly priced at $853, $894, $842, $925, $987, and $961.

(a) Use a FOR/NEXT loop to read the data, to perform the calculations, and to print the data and the results.
(b) Discount = Regular Price × .125
(c) Reduced Price = Regular Price − Discount
(d) In the program that uses the TAB function, use the INT function to round off each discount to the nearest cent. In the program that uses the PRINT USING and IMAGE statements, use these two statements to round off each discount and each reduced price to the nearest cent. Output for the latter program may be slightly different than the one following.

0	4		16			29		
	REGULAR					REDUCED		
	PRICE		DISCOUNT			PRICE		
	853		106.63			746.37		
	894		111.75			782.25		
	842		105.25			736.75		
	925		115.63			809.37		
	987		123.38			863.62		
	961		120.13			840.87		

8. Write a program that uses the TAB function to draw the figure shown below.
   (a) Print an asterisk in column 15.
   (b) Use two FOR/NEXT loops:
       (i) The first loop prints the remaining asterisks of the upper part of the figure. Your PRINT statement should contain two TAB functions. The first function has the argument **15−I** and the second function has the argument **15+I**, where **I** is the index of the loop.
       (ii) The second loop prints all but the last asterisk of the lower part of the figure. The index of this loop should run in a negative direction. The PRINT statement should have two TAB functions with arguments that are the same as those in the first loop (the index may be different).
   (c) Following the NEXT statement of the second loop, print an asterisk in column 15.

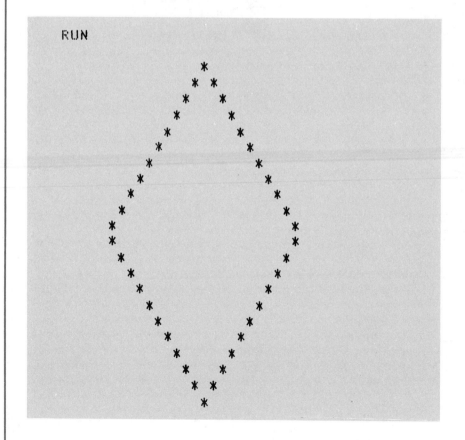

9. In Section 10.1 (page 455), a program was listed that used the TAB function to draw the graph of the equation $x = y^2$. Rewrite the program. This time have the computer draw the x and y axis as well as the curve of the equation.

Use three FOR/NEXT loops:

(a) The first loop draws the upper part of the curve:
   — The value of the index should range from 6 to 1 inclusive.
   — Square the value of the index.
   — In one PRINT statement, print the symbol for the y axis in column zero and the asterisk (which represents the squared value) in column X.
   — Between the first and second loops, code the statement that prints an asterisk in column zero.

(b) The second loop prints the x axis.
   — The value of the index should range from 1 to 36 inclusive.
   — Between the second and third loops, code a "blank" PRINT so that the symbol for the y axis and the next asterisk are printed on a new line.

(c) The third loop prints the lower part of the curve.
   — The value of the index should range from −1 to −6 inclusive.
   — The statements within this loop should be the same as those within the first loop.

Note: Two PRINT statements each require a semicolon at the end of the statement. Check your program carefully to determine which PRINT statements need this punctuation mark.

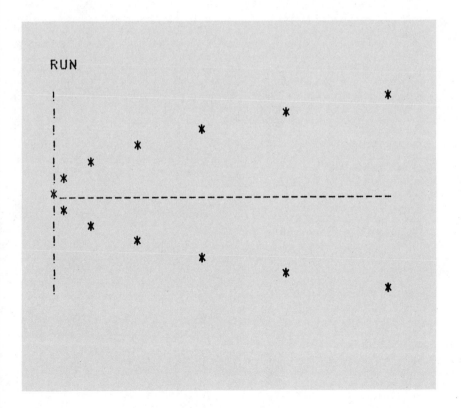

Problem 9

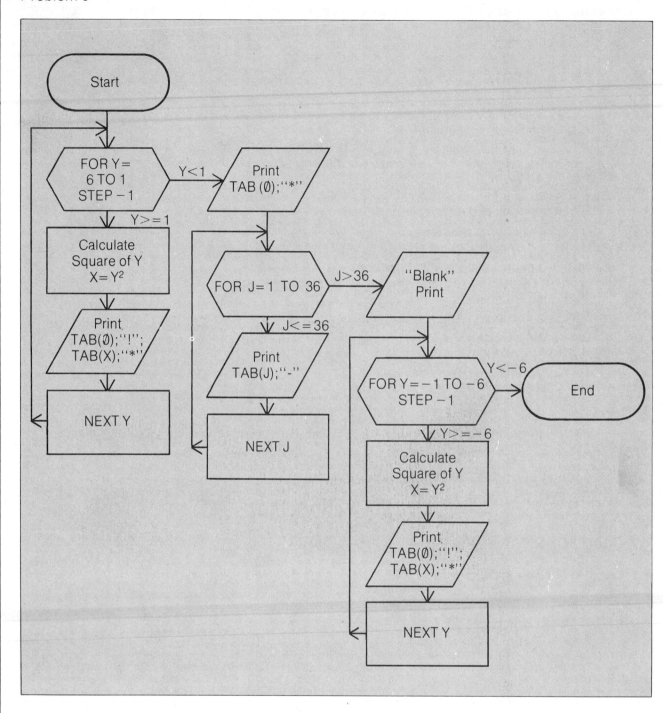

ELEVEN SUBPROGRAMS

A. After completing this chapter, you should be able to write BASIC programs and complete skeletal BASIC programs that reference:

1. (a) One subroutine.
   (b) Several subroutines.
   (c) Nested subroutines.
   (d) Several subroutines by use of the ON...GOSUB statement.
2. (a) Single-line, user-defined functions.
   (b) Multiline, user-defined functions.

B. In addition, you should be able to:

1. Define a subroutine.
2. State the advantages of subroutines and user-defined functions.
3. Explain how GOSUB and RETURN statements are executed.
4. Produce the output of programs.
5. Find errors in programs:
   (a) Make corrections if there are errors.
   (b) Show RUNs if there are no errors.
6. Define a user-defined function.
7. State the purpose of a DEF statement.
8. Explain where DEF statements and function references may be placed in programs.
9. Display and label a DEF statement.
10. State the rules that must be observed when naming user-defined functions.
11. Differentiate between a function definition and a function reference.
12. Define a dummy argument and state its purpose.
13. Define an actual argument and state its purpose.
14. (a) State how the argument in a function definition may be expressed.
    (b) State the various ways by which the argument in a function reference may be expressed.
    (c) State the restriction placed on the argument in the function definition and on the argument in the function reference.
15. Summarize three rules that must be observed when more than one argument is allowed in the function definition and in the function reference.
16. (a) Describe the composition of a multiline user-defined function.
    (b) Explain when a multiline user-defined function should be used.
    (c) Explain how a value is passed from a function reference to a statement in a multiline user-defined function.
17. State the number of values returned from a user-defined function.
18. Determine the results of user-defined functions.

11.1 SUBROUTINES

Some procedures are used so frequently that it is more efficient to write the routine only once and then call the routine from various points within a program whenever the routine is needed. The sequence of instructions is called a subprogram. One example is the standard (library or built-in) function that was discussed in Chapter Nine. This prewritten set of instructions forms part of the BASIC language and may be called upon to perform a particular computation, such as finding the square root of a number. Another example of a subprogram is the subroutine. The routine is not an integral part of BASIC but is written by a programmer as a separate module or section of the whole program. Thus, subroutines provide a method by which a very long program can be broken down into a number of parts. One of these parts must be the main program capable of communicating with the various subroutines. The main program and the subroutines make it possible for more than one programmer to be assigned to a program, thereby reducing the amount of time it takes to write the program and quite often reducing the number of errors in the first RUN. Once these subroutines are RUNning, they can be saved on a disk or on a cassette tape and loaded into the computer's memory whenever they are required. In this way, subroutines that perform specific tasks need to be written only once. Some of these tasks may be the sorting or merging of names or numbers, the setting up of frequently used headings, or the calculations of recurrent arithmetic problems. To explain how subroutines are executed, the following examples will be used. Each one is slightly different, yet each one processes a main program and its subroutine (or subroutines) the same way.

1. A main program that calls one subroutine once

```
10 REM THIS IS THE MAIN PROGRAM
20 LET A=5
30 LET B=3
40 REM CALL THE SUBROUTINE THAT ADDS
50 GOSUB 200
60 PRINT
70 PRINT "THE SUM IS:";S
80 END

200 REM THIS SUBROUTINE ADDS
210 LET S=A+B
220 RETURN

RUN

THE SUM IS: 8
```

Line 50 calls the subroutine that starts at line 200. The coding of the calling statement varies, depending on the computer being used.

Some systems require **GOSUB**; some insist on **GO SUB**; others accept an abbreviation (such as **GOS.**). Notice that the statement referenced by the GOSUB is a REM statement. In some versions of BASIC, the referenced statement must be an executable statement.

After control is transferred to the subroutine, the statements in the subroutine are executed until a RETURN statement is reached. This transfers control back to the main program, specifically to the statement immediately after the GOSUB that referenced the subroutine. In the above program, this is statement 60.

Execution continues in the main program until the END statement is encountered. This statement is required at the end of a main program to prevent execution from dropping through to the first subroutine. Some versions of BASIC allow a **STOP** statement. In this case, the last statement in the program may have to be an END statement. Experiment or check your manual to find out what your computer system requires. The STOP and END statements are explained in greater detail a little further on in this section.

2. A main program that calls one subroutine several times

```
10 REM THIS IS THE MAIN PROGRAM
20 LET A=5
30 LET B=3
40 REM CALL THE SUBROUTINE THAT ADDS
50 GOSUB 200
60 PRINT
70 PRINT "THE SUM IS:";S
80 LET A=15
90 LET B=13
100 GOSUB 200
110 PRINT "THE SUM IS:";S
120 LET A=25
130 LET B=23
140 GOSUB 200
150 PRINT "THE SUM IS:";S
160 END

200 REM THIS SUBROUTINE ADDS
210 LET S=A+B
220 RETURN

RUN

THE SUM IS: 8
THE SUM IS: 28
THE SUM IS: 48
```

In this program, subroutine 200[1] is called three times — in lines 50, 100, and 140. The RETURN statement transfers control to line 60, line 110, or line 150, depending on which GOSUB statement called the subroutine.

---

1. Subroutine 200 means the subroutine that starts at line 200.

3. A subroutine that returns more than one value

```
10 REM THIS IS THE MAIN PROGRAM
20 LET A=5
30 LET B=3
40 REM CALL THE SUBROUTINE THAT
41 REM PERFORMS SEVERAL CALCULATIONS
50 GOSUB 200
60 PRINT
70 PRINT "THE SUM IS:";S
80 PRINT "THE DIFFERENCE IS:";D
90 PRINT "THE PRODUCT IS:";P
100 END

200 REM THIS SUBROUTINE PERFORMS
201 REM SEVERAL CALCULATIONS
210 LET S=A+B
220 LET D=A-B
230 LET P=A*B
240 RETURN

RUN

THE SUM IS: 8
THE DIFFERENCE IS: 2
THE PRODUCT IS: 15
```

Several calculations are performed in the subroutine before control is transferred back to line 60 in the main program.

4. A main program that calls more than one subroutine

```
10 REM THIS IS THE MAIN PROGRAM
20 LET A=5
30 LET B=3
40 REM CALL THE SUBROUTINE THAT ADDS
50 GOSUB 200
60 PRINT
70 PRINT "THE SUM IS:";S
80 REM CALL THE SUBROUTINE THAT
81 REM SUBTRACTS
90 GOSUB 300
100 PRINT "THE DIFFERENCE IS:";D
110 REM CALL THE SUBROUTINE THAT
111 REM MULTIPLIES
120 GOSUB 400
130 PRINT "THE PRODUCT IS:";P
140 END
```

```
      200 REM THIS SUBROUTINE ADDS
      210 LET S=A+B
      220 RETURN

      300 REM THIS SUBROUTINE SUBTRACTS
      310 LET D=A-B
      320 RETURN

      400 REM THIS SUBROUTINE MULTIPLIES
      410 LET P=A*B
      420 RETURN

      RUN

      THE SUM IS: 8
      THE DIFFERENCE IS: 2
      THE PRODUCT IS: 15
```

Line 50 calls subroutine 200; line 90 calls subroutine 300; and line 120 calls subroutine 400. After execution of one of the subroutines, control is transferred to the statement immediately following the GOSUB that referenced the subroutine.

5. A subroutine that calls another subroutine (nested subroutines)

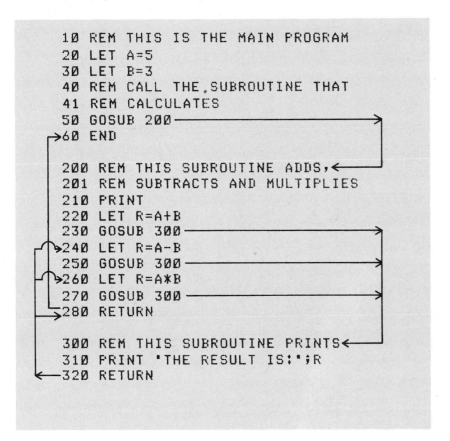

```
      10 REM THIS IS THE MAIN PROGRAM
      20 LET A=5
      30 LET B=3
      40 REM CALL THE SUBROUTINE THAT
      41 REM CALCULATES
      50 GOSUB 200
      60 END

      200 REM THIS SUBROUTINE ADDS,
      201 REM SUBTRACTS AND MULTIPLIES
      210 PRINT
      220 LET R=A+B
      230 GOSUB 300
      240 LET R=A-B
      250 GOSUB 300
      260 LET R=A*B
      270 GOSUB 300
      280 RETURN

      300 REM THIS SUBROUTINE PRINTS
      310 PRINT "THE RESULT IS:";R
      320 RETURN
```

```
RUN

THE RESULT IS: 8
THE RESULT IS: 2
THE RESULT IS: 15
```

Line 50 in the main program calls subroutine 200 to perform various calculations. After each calculation, subroutine 300 is called to print the result. The RETURN statement in the second subroutine transfers control back to the first subroutine to line 240, line 260, or line 280, depending on which GOSUB called the subroutine. Thus, in the first subroutine, calculations are performed and the PRINT subroutine is called until the RETURN statement is encountered. Control is then transferred to line 60 in the main program.

6. A subroutine with multiple RETURNs

```
10 REM THIS IS THE MAIN PROGRAM
20 READ A,B
30 DATA 5,3
40 PRINT
50 FOR I=1 TO 3
60    READ C
70    DATA 1,2,3
80    REM CALL THE SUBROUTINE
81    REM THAT CALCULATES
90    GOSUB 200
100   PRINT "THE RESULT IS:";R
110 NEXT I
120 END

200 REM THIS SUBROUTINE ADDS, SUBTRACTS
201 REM AND MULTIPLIES DEPENDING ON
202 REM THE VALUE OF THE CODE
210 ON  C  GO TO 220,240,260
220 LET R=A+B
230 RETURN
240 LET R=A-B
250 RETURN
260 LET R=A*B
270 RETURN

RUN

THE RESULT IS: 8
THE RESULT IS: 2
THE RESULT IS: 15
```

Line 60 reads in a code. A code of one denotes addition, a code of two means subtraction, and a code of three represents multiplication.

Line 90 calls the subroutine, which performs a particular arithmetic operation depending on the value of C (the code). After each calculation, control RETURNs to statement 100 in the main program.

7. Subroutines with one-dimensional arrays

(a) Using Two FOR/NEXT Loops

```
   10 REM THIS IS THE MAIN PROGRAM
   20 DIM P(4)
   30 FOR I=1 TO 4
   40    READ P(I)
   50    DATA 4,3,1,2
   60 NEXT I
   70 REM CALL THE SUBROUTINE
   71 REM THAT PRINTS
   80 GOSUB 200
   90 END

  200 REM THIS SUBROUTINE PRINTS
  210 PRINT
  220 FOR J=1 TO 4
  230    PRINT P(J);
  240 NEXT J
  250 RETURN

  RUN

    4   3   1   2
```

(b) Using One FOR/NEXT Loop

```
   10 REM THIS IS THE MAIN PROGRAM
   20 DIM P(4)
   30 PRINT
   40 FOR I=1 TO 4
   50    READ P(I)
   60    DATA 4,3,1,2
   70    REM CALL THE SUBROUTINE
   71    REM THAT PRINTS
   80    GOSUB 200
   90 NEXT I
  100 END

  200 REM THIS SUBROUTINE PRINTS
  210 PRINT P(I);
  220 RETURN

  RUN

    4   3   1   2
```

Both programs read and print data using a one-dimensional array for storage. In Program (a), the statement that calls the subroutine is *outside* the FOR/NEXT loop in the main program. This means that the data items are printed after all have been read into the array. The subroutine requires its own FOR/NEXT loop to print the data. In Program (b), the statement that calls the subroutine is *inside* the FOR/NEXT loop. This time each item of data is printed immediately after it is read and the subroutine no longer requires a FOR/NEXT loop.

8. Subroutines with two-dimensional arrays

(a) Using Two Sets of Nested FOR/NEXT Loops

```
 10 REM THIS IS THE MAIN PROGRAM
 20 DIM R(3,4)
 30 FOR I=1 TO 3
 40   FOR J=1 TO 4
 50     READ R(I,J)
 60     DATA 3,2,0,1
 70     DATA 1,0,2,3
 80     DATA 2,4,1,0
 90   NEXT J
100 NEXT I
110 REM CALL THE SUBROUTINE
111 REM THAT PRINTS
120 GOSUB 200
130 END

200 REM THIS SUBROUTINE PRINTS
210 PRINT
220 FOR K=1 TO 3
230   FOR L=1 TO 4
240     PRINT R(K,L);
250   NEXT L
260   PRINT
270 NEXT K
280 RETURN

RUN

   3   2   0   1
   1   0   2   3
   2   4   1   0
```

(b) Using One Set of Nested FOR/NEXT Loops

```
 10 REM THIS IS THE MAIN PROGRAM
 20 DIM R(3,4)
 30 PRINT
 40 FOR I=1 TO 3
```

```
 50    FOR J=1 TO 4
 60      READ R(I,J)
 70      DATA 3,2,0,1
 80      DATA 1,0,2,3
 90      DATA 2,4,1,0
100      REM CALL THE SUBROUTINE
101      REM THAT PRINTS
110      GOSUB 200
120    NEXT J
130  PRINT
140  NEXT I
150  END

200  REM THIS SUBROUTINE PRINTS
210  PRINT R(I,J);
220  RETURN

RUN

   3   2   0   1
   1   0   2   3
   2   4   1   0
```

Both programs read and print data using a two-dimensional array for storage. In Program (a), the statement that calls the subroutine is *outside* the set of nested FOR/NEXT loops in the main program. This means that the data items are printed after all have been read into the array. The subroutine requires its own set of nested FOR/NEXT loops to print the data. In Program (b), the statement that calls the subroutine is *inside* the set of nested FOR/NEXT loops. This time each item of data is printed immediately after it is read and the subroutine no longer requires FOR/NEXT loops.

Some of the statements that have been introduced in this section will now be explained in greater detail.

The STOP and END statements

Depending on the computer system being used, either an END statement or a STOP statement must be placed at the end of the main program, otherwise execution continues into the first subroutine. If the system requires an END statement, another such statement is probably not needed at the end of the program. The STOP statement is treated differently among computer systems. Some consider it as a GO TO statement that causes control to branch to the END statement. Others execute the program but print the message **BREAK AT xx** or something similar (**xx** represents the number of the STOP statement). Still others stop execution entirely and print the **break** message. On some systems, execution of the program may be resumed by typing **CONT** or **CONTINUE**. If the STOP statement is accepted, any number of STOP statements may be used, however, a STOP may not be placed at the end of a program. Also, several END statements may be allowed in a program, but execution ENDs when the statement is encountered. When using either a STOP or an END, care should be taken to branch around the statement when a particular routine is to be continued.

The GOSUB statement is an unconditional branch which transfers control to a subroutine. Reference to a subroutine may not be made by any other branching statement, such as a GO TO, an IF/THEN, or an ON...GO TO, when the routine that is called ends with a RETURN. Although each statement appears to perform a similar operation, only the GOSUB remembers the point of reference so that control can be automatically transferred to the appropriate statement of the calling program when a RETURN is encountered. Some computer systems insist that the first statement of the subroutine be an executable statement; others are not so particular. Line numbers in a subroutine must be different from those in the calling program. However, the GOSUB statement need not have a line number that is lower than the number of the statement it is calling.

The GOSUB statement

Nested subroutines must be in a hierarchical order. The first subroutine may call the second subroutine but the second one may not call the first. In other words, a subroutine may not reference its calling program. The following program segment is invalid.

```
→100 REM THIS IS THE FIRST SUBROUTINE
 --
 --
 140 GOSUB 200 ─────────────────────────────
 --                                          │
 180 RETURN                                  │
                                             │
 200 REM THIS IS THE SECOND SUBROUTINE ←─────┘
 --
 --
─250 GOSUB 100
 --
 290 RETURN
```

A RETURN statement must be placed at the end of each subroutine in order to transfer control automatically back to the calling program. The point of return is the statement immediately following the GOSUB that referenced the subroutine. In some versions of BASIC, this statement must be executable.

The RETURN statement

Some computer systems support an ON...GOSUB statement which is similar to the ON...GO TO statement. The ON...GOSUB allows the computer to select a subroutine from several incorporated in a program. Here is an example of a program that uses an ON...GOSUB statement.

The ON...GOSUB statement[2]

```
10 REM THIS IS THE MAIN PROGRAM
20 PRINT
```

2. Try the above program. If your computer system does not support the ON...GOSUB statement, you may omit this part of the chapter.

```
30 FOR I=1 TO 3
40    READ C
50    DATA 1,2,3
60    REM CALL ONE OF THE SUBROUTINES
61    REM DEPENDING ON THE VALUE OF C
70    ON C  GOSUB 100,200,300
80 NEXT I
90 END

100 REM THIS IS THE FIRST SUBROUTINE
110 PRINT "SUBROUTINE 1"
120 RETURN

200 REM THIS IS THE SECOND SUBROUTINE
210 PRINT "SUBROUTINE 2"
220 RETURN

300 REM THIS IS THE THIRD SUBROUTINE
310 PRINT "SUBROUTINE 3"
320 RETURN

RUN

SUBROUTINE 1
SUBROUTINE 2
SUBROUTINE 3
```

The ON...GOSUB in line 70 transfers control to one of the subroutines, depending on the value of **C**. If the value of **C** is 1, control is transferred to subroutine 100. If the value of **C** is 2, control is transferred to subroutine 200. And if the value of **C** is 3, control is transferred to subroutine 300. The RETURN statement in each of the three subroutines transfers control back to line 80, which is the statement immediately following the ON...GOSUB.

As with the ON...GO TO statement, the value of the index cannot be less than 1 (negative or zero), nor can it be greater than the number of statement numbers in the list. Depending on your computer system, one of the following may occur:

(a) Execution stops and the computer gives an error message.
(b) The ON...GOSUB statement is ignored and the statement following the ON...GOSUB is executed.
(c) Control is transferred to the last statement number in the list when the value of the index exceeds the number of statement numbers.
(d) Control is transferred to the first statement number in the list when the value of the index is less than one.

11.1 SUBROUTINES—Sample Programs

1. Here is a problem that appeared in Chapter Five on page 156. The program shown on page 518 reviews the method by which a

loop can be terminated by using a special value and a counter. It
also incorporates some of the concepts most recently covered,
such as the INT function, the TAB function, and the subroutines.

A storage room in a stationery store contains the following
items.

9 pen and pencil sets	@	$23.85	each
8.5 boxes bond paper	@	19.49	each
8.5 boxes carbon paper	@	15.67	each

The program finds the extended value of each of the above
articles.

(a) Use the READ statement to store the number of different
    articles (3) in a simple variable. The variable is used subse-
    quently with a counter to terminate the loop.
(b) Use the READ/DATA statements to enter the quantity and the
    unit price of each article.
(c) Use the INT function to round off the extended value of each
    article to the nearest cent.
(d) Use the TAB function to format the output.
(e) Use one subroutine to calculate the extended value of each
    article.
(f) Use a second subroutine (called by the first subroutine) to
    print the information as shown.
(g) Extended Value = Quantity x Unit Price

```
01 REM K--COUNTER
02 REM D--NUMBER OF DECIMAL PLACES
03 REM N--NUMBER OF ARTICLES
04 REM Q--QUANTITY
05 REM P--UNIT PRICE
06 REM V--EXTENDED VALUE

10 REM THIS IS THE MAIN PROGRAM
20 PRINT                                    — Leaves a blank line.
30 PRINT TAB(2);"QUANTITY";TAB(15);"UNIT    — Prints the heading.
   PRICE";TAB(31);"VALUE"
40 PRINT                                    — Leaves a blank line.
50 LET D=2                                  — Two decimal places.
60 LET K=1                                  — Initializes the counter to 1.
70 READ N                                   — Reads the number of articles.
80 DATA 3                                   — Supplies the number of articles.
90 READ Q,P                                 — Reads the quantity and price
                                              of each article.
100 DATA 9,23.85,8.5,19.49,8.5,15.67        — Supplies the quantity and price
                                              of each article.
110 GOSUB 200 ────────────────────────────→ — Calls the subroutine that
                                              calculates the extended
                                              value of each article.
```

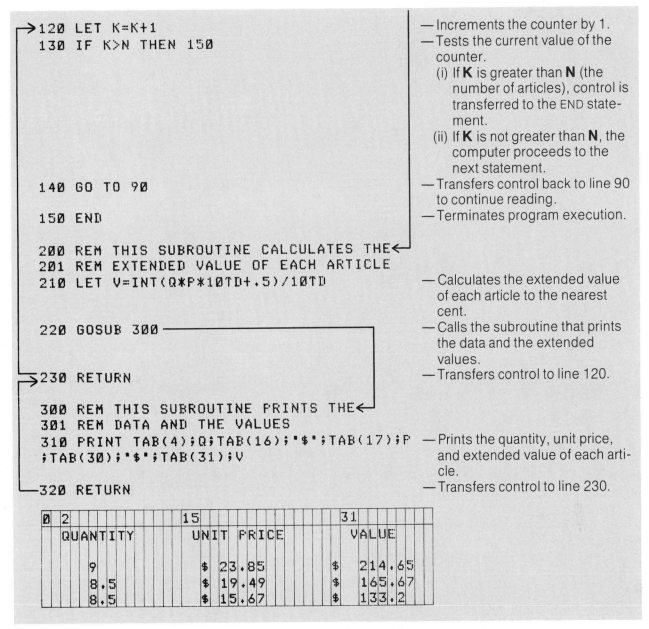

```
120 LET K=K+1
130 IF K>N THEN 150




140 GO TO 90

150 END

200 REM THIS SUBROUTINE CALCULATES THE
201 REM EXTENDED VALUE OF EACH ARTICLE
210 LET V=INT(Q*P*10TD+.5)/10TD


220 GOSUB 300


230 RETURN

300 REM THIS SUBROUTINE PRINTS THE
301 REM DATA AND THE VALUES
310 PRINT TAB(4);Q;TAB(16);"$";TAB(17);P
;TAB(30);"$";TAB(31);V

320 RETURN
```

— Increments the counter by 1.
— Tests the current value of the counter.
  (i) If **K** is greater than **N** (the number of articles), control is transferred to the END statement.
  (ii) If **K** is not greater than **N**, the computer proceeds to the next statement.
— Transfers control back to line 90 to continue reading.
— Terminates program execution.

— Calculates the extended value of each article to the nearest cent.
— Calls the subroutine that prints the data and the extended values.
— Transfers control to line 120.

— Prints the quantity, unit price, and extended value of each article.
— Transfers control to line 230.

0	2					15						31			
QUANTITY						UNIT PRICE						VALUE			
	9						$	23.85				$		214.65	
	8.5						$	19.49				$		165.67	
	8.5						$	15.67				$		133.2	

2. Subroutines are often used to draw pictures or letters of the alphabet when several of the lines are the same. Here is a program that prints the letter **B**. The left-most symbols are printed in print position one when using the TAB function.

(a) Using the TAB Function

```
10 REM SET UP A LOOP FOR
11 REM EACH HALF OF THE 'B'
20 LET M=6

30 PRINT
40 FOR K=1 TO 2
50     GOSUB 200
60     GOSUB 300
```

— **M** represents the number of symbols in a row. It is also used to position a symbol.

— Calls subroutine 200 to print a row of symbols.
— Calls subroutine 300 to print the left-most and right-most symbols of a row.

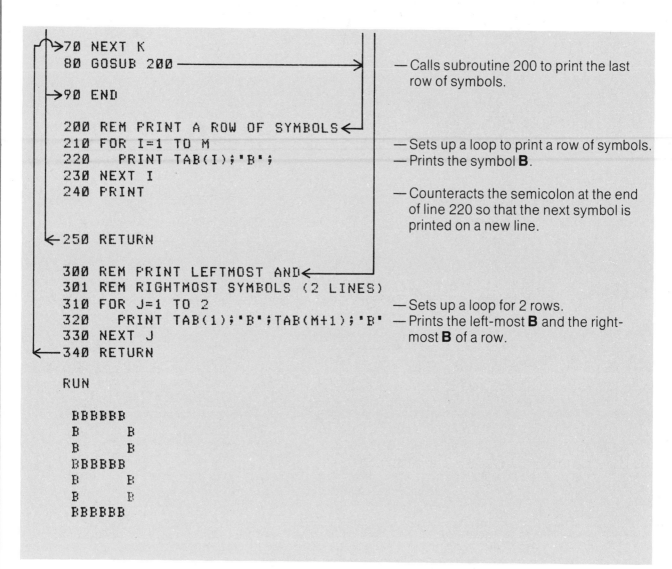

```
  70 NEXT K
  80 GOSUB 200 ─────────────────────►  — Calls subroutine 200 to print the last
                                          row of symbols.
→ 90 END

  200 REM PRINT A ROW OF SYMBOLS◄─
  210 FOR I=1 TO M                     — Sets up a loop to print a row of symbols.
  220     PRINT TAB(I);"B";            — Prints the symbol B.
  230 NEXT I
  240 PRINT                            — Counteracts the semicolon at the end
                                          of line 220 so that the next symbol is
                                          printed on a new line.
← 250 RETURN

  300 REM PRINT LEFTMOST AND◄─
  301 REM RIGHTMOST SYMBOLS (2 LINES)
  310 FOR J=1 TO 2                     — Sets up a loop for 2 rows.
  320     PRINT TAB(1);"B";TAB(M+1);"B" — Prints the left-most B and the right-
  330 NEXT J                             most B of a row.
← 340 RETURN

  RUN

    BBBBBB
    B    B
    B    B
    BBBBBB
    B    B
    B    B
    BBBBBB
```

(b) Using the PRINT USING and IMAGE Statements

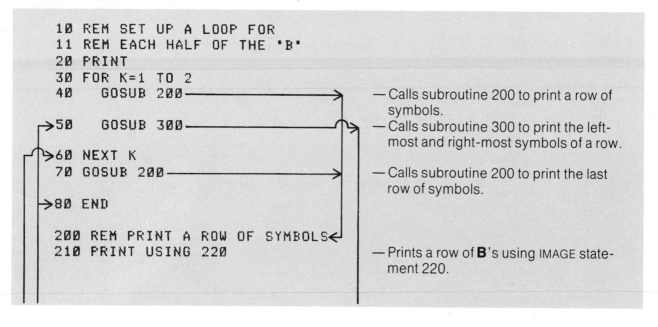

```
  10 REM SET UP A LOOP FOR
  11 REM EACH HALF OF THE "B"
  20 PRINT
  30 FOR K=1 TO 2
  40     GOSUB 200 ───────────────►   — Calls subroutine 200 to print a row of
                                          symbols.
→ 50     GOSUB 300 ───────────────►   — Calls subroutine 300 to print the left-
                                          most and right-most symbols of a row.
→ 60 NEXT K
  70 GOSUB 200 ───────────────────►   — Calls subroutine 200 to print the last
                                          row of symbols.
→ 80 END

  200 REM PRINT A ROW OF SYMBOLS◄─
  210 PRINT USING 220                  — Prints a row of B's using IMAGE state-
                                          ment 220.
```

```
   220:BBBBBB
←  230 RETURN

   300 REM PRINT LEFTMOST AND ←
   301 REM RIGHTMOST SYMBOLS (2 LINES)
   310 FOR J=1 TO 2                    — Sets up a loop for 2 rows.
   320    PRINT USING 330              — Prints the left-most B and the right-most B
                                          of a row using IMAGE statement 330.
   330:B_____B
   340 NEXT J
←  350 RETURN

   RUN

   BBBBBB
   B    B
   B    B
   BBBBBB
   B    B
   B    B
   BBBBBB
```

11.1 SUBROUTINES—Your Turn

1. Write a subroutine for the following main program to calculate the
   amount of cash a grocer has at the end of a day if he received
   $431 and paid out $16.50.
   Balance = Receipts − Payments

```
01 REM R--RECEIPTS
02 REM P--PAYMENTS
03 REM B--BALANCE

10 REM THIS IS THE MAIN PROGRAM
20 READ R,P
30 DATA 431,16.50
40 GOSUB 200
50 PRINT
60 PRINT "RECEIPTS:";R
70 PRINT "PAYMENTS:";P
80 PRINT "BALANCE:";B
90 END

RUN

RECEIPTS: 431
```

(handwritten)
200 Rem Subroutine.
210 Let B = R−P
220 Return

```
PAYMENTS: 16.5
BALANCE: 414.5
```

2. Modify the program in Problem 1 so that there are two subroutines; the first one is called by the main program, the second one is called by the first subroutine.

   (a) The first subroutine calculates the balance.
   (b) The second subroutine formats the headings and amounts as shown in the output below. Use the TAB function.

```
01 REM R--RECEIPTS
02 REM P--PAYMENTS
03 REM B--BALANCE

10 REM THIS IS THE MAIN PROGRAM
20 READ R,P
30 DATA 431,16.50
40 GOSUB 200
50 END
```

(handwritten annotations:)

```
200 Rem First subroutine
210 Let B = R-P
220 GOSUB 300
230 Return

300 Rem 2nd subroutine
305 PRINT
310 Print TAB(3); "Recpts"; R
320 PRINT
330 PRINT TAB(4); "B";
340 Return
```

0	3							16							29						
	RECEIPTS							PAYMENTS							BALANCE						
		$	431							$	16.5						$	414.5			

3. Rewrite the sample program on page 518 but with the following changes.

   (a) Use a FOR/NEXT loop to control input rather than a counter tested against the number of data items read in.
   (b) Have the main program call both subroutines.
   (c) In the flowchart, the process symbol is used to indicate the GOSUB statement. The oval denotes the RETURN statement since this symbol represents a terminal point.

0	2							15							31					
	QUANTITY							UNIT PRICE							VALUE					
		9						$	23.85						$	214.65				
		8.5						$	19.49						$	165.67				
		8.5						$	15.67						$	133.2				

Problem 3

Q — QUANTITY   D — NUMBER OF DECIMAL PLACES
P — UNIT PRICE   V — EXTENDED VALUE

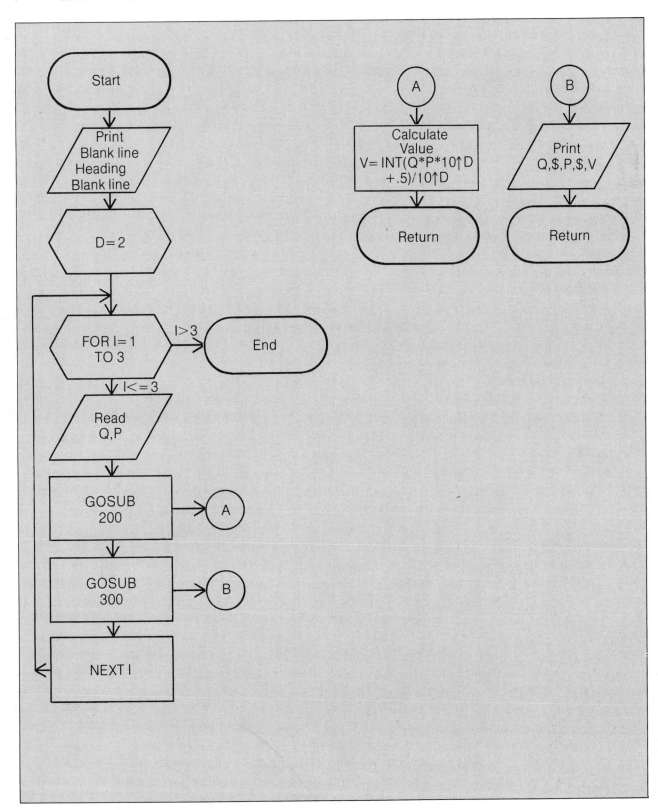

11.1 SUBROUTINES—Solutions for "Your Turn"

1.

```
200 REM THIS SUBROUTINE CALCULATES
201 REM THE BALANCE
210 LET B=R-P
220 RETURN
```

2.

```
200 REM THIS SUBROUTINE CALCULATES
201 REM THE BALANCE
210 LET B=R-P
220 GOSUB 300
230 RETURN

300 REM THIS SUBROUTINE PRINTS
310 PRINT
320 PRINT TAB(3);"RECEIPTS";TAB(16);"PAY
MENTS";TAB(29);"BALANCE"
330 PRINT
340 PRINT TAB(4);"$";TAB(5);R;TAB(17);"$
";TAB(18);P;TAB(29);"$";TAB(30);B
350 RETURN
```

3.

```
01 REM Q--QUANTITY
02 REM P--UNIT PRICE
03 REM D--NUMBER OF DECIMAL PLACES
04 REM V--EXTENDED VALUE

10 REM THIS IS THE MAIN PROGRAM
20 PRINT
30 PRINT TAB(2);"QUANTITY";TAB(15);"UNIT
 PRICE";TAB(31);"VALUE"
40 PRINT
50 LET D=2
60 FOR I=1 TO 3
70    READ Q,P
80    DATA 9,23.85,8.5,19.49,8.5,15.67
90    GOSUB 200
100   GOSUB 300
```

```
110 NEXT I
120 END

200 REM THIS SUBROUTINE CALCULATES THE
201 REM EXTENDED VALUE OF EACH ARTICLE
210 LET V=INT(Q*P*10TD+.5)/10TD
220 RETURN

300 REM THIS SUBROUTINE PRINTS THE
301 REM DATA AND THE VALUES
310 PRINT TAB(4);Q;TAB(16);"$";TAB(17);P
;TAB(30);"$";TAB(31);V
320 RETURN
```

11.2 USER-DEFINED FUNCTIONS

It was mentioned at the beginning of this chapter that standard or built-in functions are a particular type of subprogram. These routines are written by someone else and may be called upon to perform specific operations. BASIC gives you the opportunity to write your own functions (mathematical expressions). Referred to as user-defined functions, they are incorporated in a program when the same calculations must be performed several times. Different values may be used for each calculation. Here is a program that calls a user-defined function to convert miles to kilometres.

```
01 REM M1--DUMMY VARIABLE
02 REM M--MILES
03 REM K--KILOMETRES

10 DEF FNM(M1)=M1*1.609
20 LET M=5
30 LET K=FNM(M)
40 PRINT
50 PRINT M;"MILES =";K;"KILOMETRES"
99 END

RUN

 5 MILES = 8.045 KILOMETRES
```

Line 10 contains a user-defined function. Notice that the function must be named and defined in a DEF statement. If there is more than one user-defined function in the program, each one must be described in its own DEF statement. The position of this statement in the program depends on the computer system being used. On some systems the function must be defined before it is called; on others the DEF statement may be placed anywhere in the program. Usually, all DEF statements are placed together at the beginning of a program.

The general form of a DEF statement is as follows.

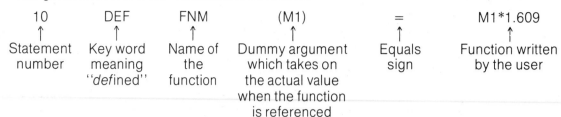

10	DEF	FNM	(M1)	=	M1*1.609
↑	↑	↑	↑	↑	↑
Statement number	Key word meaning "*def*ined"	Name of the function	Dummy argument which takes on the actual value when the function is referenced	Equals sign	Function written by the user

The statement begins with a line number followed by the key word DEF, which is an abbreviation for "*def*ined." This is followed by the function definition which consists of the name of the function, its argument (in parentheses), an equals sign, and a mathematical expression. The function name requires three letters of the alphabet. The first two letters must be **FN**; the third is supplied by the user and may be any letter of the alphabet. This means that there may be as many as twenty-six different user-defined functions in one program. Examples of function names are: **FNA**, **FNR**, **FNZ**. Usually, the user supplies a letter that is appropriate for the function. In the name FNM shown above, the letter **M** was chosen because the function converts miles to kilometres.

The variable immediately after the function name is called the function's argument. It must be enclosed in parentheses and must be a simple variable; it may not be a subscripted variable. Usually, but not always, it appears in the mathematical expression on the right-hand side of the equals sign. Some versions of BASIC allow several arguments within the parentheses. These arguments must be separated by commas. An example is shown below.

```
10 DEF FNQ(A,B,C)=B↑2-4*A*C
            ↖↗
           Commas
```

A function name may also be coded without an argument on some computer systems.

The argument in the function definition is referred to as the *dummy* argument, since it plays no significant role, other than to act as a place-holder for the value that will be operated on when the function is called. The mathematical expression on the right-hand side of the equals sign is the function that has been constructed by the user.

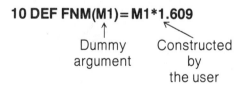

10 DEF FNM(M1)=M1*1.609

Dummy argument	Constructed by the user

Besides the dummy variable, the function may contain constants, library functions, other previously defined functions, and simple or subscripted numeric variables. Most versions of BASIC do not permit self-referencing of user-defined functions.

10 DEF FNS(A1)＝A1＊FNS(A1+2)

↑

May not be allowed

The values of the variables in the function are the ones most recently assigned. In the conversion program shown below, the value for **C** is 1.609.

```
10 DEF FNM(M1)=M1*C
15 LET C=1.609
20 LET M=5
30 LET K=FNM(M)
--
```

FNM(M) in line 30 is called the function reference, since it makes a reference to a function definition. It consists of the name of the function and its argument in parentheses. It is similar to a library function that calls a routine already written. The function reference is usually coded in a LET statement or in a PRINT statement to call a user-defined function. The value of its argument is passed to the dummy argument in the function definition. On most computer systems, the function reference may appear within an algebraic expression, in another user-defined function, in another function reference and, on some systems, nested in its own function reference. This last method of coding a function reference is discussed in further detail on page 529.

While the argument of a function definition must be a simple variable, the argument of a function reference may be a constant, a simple variable, a subscripted variable, an expression, or a library function. As already mentioned, some computers may allow the argument to be a function reference. Remember, it is the *value* of the argument that is passed to the function definition. Shown below are some examples of function references.

```
10 DEF FNR(A1)=A1+FNM(M)    — In another user-defined function, argument is a
                              simple variable.
20 IF FNM(6)+2>10 THEN 160  — In an arithmetic expression, argument is a constant.

30 LET K=FNM(M(I))          — In a LET statement, argument is a subscripted variable.

40 PRINT FNM(4+A/2)         — In a PRINT statement, argument is an expression.

50 PRINT FNM(SQR(M))        — In a PRINT statement, argument is a library function.

60 LET K=FNR(FNM(M))        — In another function reference, arguments are a
                              function reference and a simple variable.
```

To distinguish the argument in the function definition from the one in the function reference, the argument in the function reference is called the **actual** argument. Remember, the one in the function definition was referred to as the **dummy** argument.

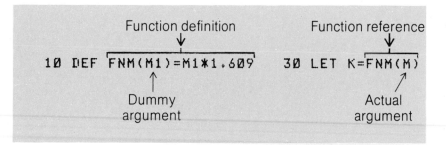

The logic of the program that converts miles to kilometres will now be traced. Here is the program once more.

```
01 REM M1--DUMMY VARIABLE
02 REM M--MILES
03 REM K--KILOMETRES

10 DEF FNM(M1)=M1*1.609
20 LET M=5
30 LET K=FNM(M)
40 PRINT
50 PRINT M;"MILES =";K;"KILOMETRES"
99 END

RUN

 5 MILES = 8.045 KILOMETRES
```

1. The computer obtains a value for the actual argument.

```
20 LET M=5
30 LET K=FNM(M)
```

The value of the actual argument (**M**) is 5.

2. The computer looks for the function named FNM and passes the value of **M** from the actual argument to the dummy argument.

```
10 DEF FNM(M1)=M1*1.609
--
30 LET K=FNM(M)
```

The dummy argument (**M1**) is replaced by 5.

3. The computer passes the 5 from the argument on the left-hand side of the equals sign to the variable on the right-hand side of the equals sign.

```
10 DEF FNM(M1)=M1*1.609
```

The value of **M1** in the equation is 5.

4. The computer evaluates the equation (function). The function name serves as a temporary storage location for the result 8.045, which cannot be accessed until it is assigned to the variable **K**. Other methods of calling the user-defined function and obtaining the result are listed on page 527.

Passes the result 8.045 to **K**.

```
10 DEF FNM(M1)=M1*1.609
--
30 LET K=FNM(M)
```

5. The computer prints the values of **M** and **K**.

```
50 PRINT M;"MILES =";K;"KILOMETRES"
```

As mentioned on page 527, some versions of BASIC allow nested function references. Here is an example.

```
10 DEF FNC(N1)=N1+2
20 LET N=3
30 LET C=FNC(FNC(N))
40 PRINT
50 PRINT C
99 END

RUN

7
```

The inner function reference passes 3 to the dummy argument in the function definition and 5 is returned as the argument of the outer function reference. The outer function reference then passes 5 to the dummy argument and the result of the calculation (7) is returned and assigned to **C**.

On the following page are a number of statements that call a user-defined function. In each problem, the value for **K** will be found using the function definition and the value for **M** given before the statements.

```
      10 DEF FNM(M1)=M1*1.609
      20 LET M=10
```

(a)
```
      30 LET K=FNM(M)
```
$$= FNM(10)$$
$$FNM(M1) = M1*1.609$$
$$FNM(10) = 10*1.609$$
$$= 16.09$$

```
      30 LET K=FNM(M)
```
$$= 16.09$$

(b)
```
      30 LET K=FNM(M+1)
```
$$= FNM(10+1)$$
$$= FNM(11)$$

$$FNM(M1) = M1*1.609$$
$$FNM(11) = 11*1.609$$
$$= 17.699$$

```
      30 LET K=FNM(M+1)
```
$$= 17.699$$

(c)
```
      30 LET K=FNM(M)+1
```
$$= FNM(10)+1$$

$$FNM(M1) = M1*1.609$$
$$FNM(10) = 10*1.609$$
$$= 16.09$$

```
      30 LET K=FNM(M)+1
```
$$= 16.09+1$$
$$= 17.09$$

(d)
```
      30 LET K=FNM(M)+SQR(64)-.09
```
$$= FNM(10)+SQR(64)-.09$$

$$FNM(M1) = M1*1.609$$
$$FNM(10) = 10*1.609$$
$$= 16.09$$

```
      30 LET K=FNM(M)+SQR(64)-.09
```
$$= 16.09+SQR(64)-.09$$
$$= 16.09+8-.09$$
$$= 24.09-.09$$
$$= 24$$

(e)
```
      30 PRINT "K =";SQR(FNM(M)+84-.09)
```
$$SQR(FNM(10)+84-.09)$$

$$FNM(M1) = M1*1.609$$
$$FNM(10) = 10*1.609$$
$$= 16.09$$

```
30 PRINT "K =";SQR(FNM(M)+84-.09)
```
$$\begin{aligned}
&\text{SQR}(16.09+84-.09)\\
&\text{SQR}(100.09-.09)\\
&\text{SQR}(100)\\
&10
\end{aligned}$$

Output: K = 10

The following user-defined function rounds off the result in Problem (b) on page 530 to two decimal places.

```
10 DEF FNM(M1)=INT(M1*1.609*10↑D+.5)/10↑D
20 LET D=2
30 LET M=10

40 LET K=FNM(M+1)
```
$$\begin{aligned}
&=\text{FNM}(10+1)\\
&=\text{FNM}(11)
\end{aligned}$$

$$\begin{aligned}
\text{FNM}(M1) &= \text{INT}(M1*1.609*10{\uparrow}D+.5)/10{\uparrow}D\\
\text{FNM}(11) &= \text{INT}(11*1.609*10{\uparrow}2+.5)/10{\uparrow}2\\
&= \text{INT}(11*1.609*100+.5)/10{\uparrow}2\\
&= \text{INT}(17.699*100+.5)/10{\uparrow}2\\
&= \text{INT}(1769.9+.5)/10{\uparrow}2\\
&= \text{INT}(1770.4)/10{\uparrow}2\\
&= 1770/10{\uparrow}2\\
&= 1770/100\\
&= 17.70
\end{aligned}$$

```
40 LET K=FNM(M+1)
```
$$= 17.70$$

There are several rules that must be observed concerning the relationship between the function definition and the function reference.

1. The name of the function in the function definition and the name in the function reference must be the same. This lets the computer know which user-defined function is being called. In the conversion program, the name of the function is **FNM**. It appears in statement 10 (in the function definition) and in statement 30 (in the function reference).

```
10 DEF FNM(M1)=M1*1.609
--
30 LET K=FNM(M)
```

2. The actual argument must correspond in type to the dummy argument (either numeric or string). It is not necessary that the argument names be the same.

```
10 DEF FNM(M1)=M1*1.609
--                                      — Both represent a
30 LET K=FNM(M)                           numeric value.
```

3. Some versions of BASIC allow several dummy arguments in the function definition and several actual arguments in the function reference. In this situation, the dummy arguments must correspond to the actual arguments in number, order, and type.

```
10 DEF FNQ(A,B,C)=......   — Same number.
--                         — Same order.
50 LET Q=FNQ(X,Y,Z)        — Same type.
```

Here is another example.

```
10 DEF FNQ(A,B,C)=BT2-4*A*C
--
--
50 LET Q=FNQ(4*X-Y,Z(I),SQR(W))
```

The arguments in the function definition are simple numeric variables. The arguments in the function reference are a numeric expression, a subscripted variable, and a library function. Although expressed differently, they correspond to those in the function definition in number, order, and type. The value of **4*X−Y** is passed to **A**; the value of **Z(I)** is passed to **B**; and the value of **SQR(W)** is passed to **C**.

4. When a function definition and a function reference have one argument each, just one value is passed from the actual argument to the dummy argument. Computer systems that allow several arguments are able to pass more than one value from the function reference to the function definition. In the program segment

```
10 DEF FNQ(A,B,C)=......
--
50 LET Q=FNQ(X,Y,Z)
```

three values are passed to the function definition. The three dummy arguments, **A**, **B**, and **C**, are replaced by the values of **X**, **Y**, and **Z**. However, in every program, only one numeric value results from the evaluation of a user-defined function and, therefore, only one value is returned to the calling statement. In the above program segment, the returned value is assigned to the variable **Q**.

As already mentioned, each user-defined function must have its own DEF statement with a function name that is unique (different from the other user-defined functions).

Some versions of BASIC allow multiline user-defined functions.[3] These define complex functions that often require branching and looping. The function must be preceded by a DEF statement which consists of a line number, the key word DEF followed by the name of the function, and its argument in parentheses. As in single-line functions, some computer systems allow more than one dummy argument in the function's argument list. Just one value is returned to the calling statement after the function is evaluated. Unlike single-line functions, the DEF statement must not include an arithmetic equation. To define the function, several statements must follow the DEF statement. The result of the multiline function is returned to the calling statement by assigning the value to the name of the function in one of its statements. The entire definition ends with the statement **FNEND**.[4]

The rules observed for single-line functions must also be observed for multiline functions. However, there are several additional restrictions. Control may not be transferred *to* a statement within the function from a point outside or *from* a statement within the function to a point outside. Also, some versions of BASIC do not allow INPUT statements or PRINT statements inside the user-defined function. Here is an example of a program that uses a multiline user-defined function.

Multiline user-defined function

```
10  DEF FNB(A1)
20     IF A1<=10 THEN 50
30     LET FNB=A1-2
40     GO TO 60
50     LET FNB=A1+2
60  FNEND
70  LET A=4
80  LET B=FNB(A)
90  PRINT
100 PRINT A;B
999 END

RUN

   4    6
```

The function **FNB** adds 2 to a number if the number is less than or equal to 10; otherwise, it subtracts 2 from the number, that is, if the number is greater than 10.

Line 10 — The DEF statement is comprised of a statement number, the key word DEF, followed by the name of the function and its

---

3. Check your manual or try the above program to see if your computer system supports multiline user-defined functions. If not, you may omit this part of the chapter.

4. Some systems require a RETURN statement instead of FNEND, since these computers treat the function as a subroutine.

argument in parentheses. Some computer systems allow more than one argument, in which case the arguments must correspond to those in the function reference. The argument **A1** acts as a placeholder for the value of the actual argument **A**. When the function reference calls the user-defined function, the dummy argument is replaced by the value of the actual argument. This value (4) is passed to the dummy variable that may appear in one or more of the statements in the user-defined function.

Line 20 — Checks the number that has been passed to the user-defined function:

(i) If the number is less than or equal to 10, control is transferred to line 50.

(ii) If the number is greater than 10, the computer proceeds to the next line.

Line 30 — Subtracts 2 from the number if the number is greater than 10, and assigns the result to the function name **FNB**.

Line 40 — Transfers control to line 60, which is the end statement of the user-defined function.

Line 50 — Adds 2 to the number if the number is less than or equal to 10, and assigns the result to the function name **FNB**.

Line 60 — Marks the end of the user-defined function.

Line 70 — Assigns 4 to the variable **A**.

Line 80 — Contains the function reference that calls the user-defined function **FNB**. It passes the value of **A** to the dummy argument in the function definition. The result (only one value) is returned to the calling statement and assigned to **B**.

Line 100 — Prints the value of **A** (the data) and the value of **B** (the result).

Line 999 — Terminates program execution.

11.2 USER-DEFINED FUNCTIONS — Sample Program

Suppose that the price of an article has been reduced from $15 for one article to $22.95 for two, and that you would like to know the cost of three articles, the cost of five articles, and the cost of seven articles. Here is a program that performs these calculations using a user-defined function.

(a) Use the READ/DATA statements to enter the price.

(b) Use a FOR/NEXT loop to control the number of times the function is evaluated. Use the value of the index as the number of articles.

(c) Cost of the articles $= \dfrac{\text{Price}}{2} \times$ Number of Articles (the index)

```
01 REM P1--DUMMY VARIABLE
02 REM P--ACTUAL PRICE
03 REM N--NUMBER OF ARTICLES (INDEX)
04 REM C--COST OF THE ARTICLES

10 DEF FNC(P1)=P1/2*N          — Defines the function.
20 READ P                     — Reads in the price.
30 DATA 22.95                 — Supplies the READ statement with the price.
```

```
40 PRINT                              — Leaves a blank line.
50 FOR N=3 TO 7 STEP 2               — Sets up a loop.
60    LET C=FNC(P)                   — Calls the user-defined function and
                                       passes the price to the dummy
                                       argument P1. After the function is
                                       evaluated, the result is assigned
                                       to C.
70    PRINT "COST OF";N;"ARTICLES IS:";C  — Prints the cost of a specific
                                             number of articles.
80 NEXT N                            — Transfers control to line 50.
99 END                               — Terminates program execution.

RUN

COST OF 3 ARTICLES IS: 34.425
COST OF 5 ARTICLES IS: 57.375
COST OF 7 ARTICLES IS: 80.325
```

11.2 USER-DEFINED FUNCTIONS — Your Turn

In the first four problems perform all calculations by hand.
1. Find the value of B in each of the following program segments.
   The function in the function definition is the one that rounds off
   dollars and cents to the nearest cent.

```
      10 DEF FNR(A1)=INT(A1*10↑D+.5)/10↑D
      20 LET D=2

(a)   30 LET A=13.485
      40 LET B=FNR(A)

(b)   30 LET A=14.163
      40 LET B=FNR(A)*2

(c)   30 LET A=14.163
      40 LET B=FNR(A*2)

(d)   30 LET A=16.398
      40 LET B=SQR(FNR(A)+32.60)
```

[handwritten:] $13.485 = INT(13.485 \times 100 + .5)/100$
13.5

[handwritten:] 1428.3

2. In the program shown below, find the net wages of an employee
   who has no overtime hours. The first user-defined function in the
   program gives the value of **W** (wages not rounded). The second
   user-defined function rounds off the wages to the nearest cent.
   This gives the value of **N**.

```
01 REM H1--DUMMY VARIABLE
02 REM H--HOURS WORKED
```

```
03 REM R--RATE PER HOUR
04 REM D--DEDUCTIONS
05 REM D2--NUMBER OF DECIMAL PLACES
06 REM W--NET WAGES (NOT ROUNDED)
07 REM N--NET WAGES (ROUNDED)

10 DEF FNN(H1)=R*H1-D
20 DEF FNR(W1)=INT(W1*10TD2+.5)/10TD2
30 LET D2=2
40 READ H,R,D
50 DATA 37,11.543,79.50
60 LET W=FNN(H)
70 LET N=FNR(W)
80 PRINT N
99 END
```

3. Suppose an employee's regular weekly hours are 39 hours and that the company offers time-and-a-half for overtime. The following function finds the employee's net wages, including overtime.

$$R*39+(H-39)*R*1.5-D$$

R denotes **R**ate per hour, **H** stands for **H**ours worked, and **D** means **D**eductions.

(a) **R * 39** — rate times regular hours gives regular pay.
(b) **H − 39** — hours worked minus regular hours gives overtime hours.
(c) **R * 1.5** — rate times 1.5 gives overtime rate.
(d) **(H−39) * R*1.5** — overtime hours times overtime rate gives overtime pay.
(e) **R*39 + (H−39)*R*1.5** — regular pay plus overtime pay gives gross wages.
(f) **R*39+(H−39)*R*1.5 − D** — gross wages minus deductions gives net wages.

The following program uses the above formula as a user-defined function to find the wages of an employee who has worked overtime. The wages are then rounded off to the nearest cent by the second user-defined function. Find the value of **N**.

```
01 REM H1--DUMMY VARIABLE
02 REM H--HOURS WORKED
03 REM R--RATE PER HOUR
04 REM D--DEDUCTIONS
05 REM D2--NUMBER OF DECIMAL PLACES
06 REM W--NET WAGES (NOT ROUNDED)
07 REM N--NET WAGES (ROUNDED)

10 DEF FNV(H1)=R*39+(H1-39)*R*1.5-D
20 DEF FNR(W1)=INT(W1*10TD2+.5)/10TD2
30 LET D2=2
40 READ H,R,D
50 DATA 44,10.241,85
60 LET W=FNV(H)
```

```
70 LET N=FNR(W)
80 PRINT N
99 END
```

4. Find the value of **Q** in each of the statements shown below using the following function definition and the values given for **A**, **B**, and **C**.[5]

```
10 DEF FNQ(A1,B1,C1)=B1↑2-(4*A1*C1)
20 READ A,B,C
30 DATA 2,6,3
```
(a) `40 LET Q=FNQ(A,B,C)`

(b) `40 LET Q=FNQ(A,B,C)+10`

(c) `40 LET Q=FNQ(A,B+1,C)`

(d) `40 LET Q=SQR(FNQ(A,B+1,C))`

5. Fill in the missing lines for the following programs.
   (a) Calculate the sales tax of an article.
      (i) Sales Tax = Price × Rate
      (ii) Complete line 10 with a DEF statement.

```
01 REM P1--DUMMY VARIABLE
02 REM P--PRICE
03 REM R--RATE
04 REM T--TAX

10 DEF FN(P1) = P1 * R
20 READ P,R
30 DATA 37,.05
40 LET T=FNT(P)
50 PRINT
60 PRINT P,T
99 END

RUN

   37            1.85
```

   (b) Calculate the amount of an investment by adding the yearly interest to the investment. Use $1000 as the initial investment for each of the rates 17%, 18%, and 19%.
      (i) Amount = Investment + (Investment × Rate)
      (ii) Complete line 60 with a function reference coded in a LET statement.

5. You may omit Problem 4 if your computer does not allow several variables in the argument list.

```
01 REM R1--DUMMY VARIABLE
02 REM R--RATE
03 REM I--INITIAL INVESTMENT
04 REM A--AMOUNT

10 DEF FNA(R1)=I+(I*R1)
20 PRINT
30 LET I=1000
40 LET R=.17
50 FOR N=1 TO 3
60 LET FNA(B)=          [let A = FNA(R)]
70    PRINT A
80    LET R=R+.01
90 NEXT N
99 END

RUN

   1170
   1180          16
   1190
```

(c) Calculate the squares of the numbers from 1 to 5 inclusive.
  (i) Complete line 10 with a DEF statement.
  (ii) Complete line 40 with a function reference coded in a LET statement.

```
01 REM N1--DUMMY VARIABLE
02 REM N--NUMBER
03 REM S--NUMBER SQUARED

10 DEF
20 PRINT
30 FOR N=1 TO 5
40 let S = FN
50    PRINT N,S
60 NEXT N
99 END

RUN

   1              1
   2              4
   3              9
   4              16
   5              25
```

(d) The following program uses a multiline user-defined function.[6] It cubes a number if the number is less than or equal to 5, otherwise it squares the number; that is, if the number is greater than 5.

 (i) Complete line 30 with a statement that squares the number.

 (ii) Complete line 50 with a statement that cubes the number.

```
10 DEF FNB(A1)
20    IF A1<=5 THEN 50
30
40    GO TO 60
50
60 FNEND
70 LET A=3
80 PRINT
90 PRINT A,FNB(A)
99 END

RUN

  3         27
```

6. Rewrite the sample program on page 534. This time, code a user-defined function that not only calculates the cost of each article but also rounds off the result to the nearest cent. Here is the problem once more.

  Suppose that the price of an article has been reduced from $15 for one article to $22.95 for two and that you would like to know the cost of three articles, the cost of five articles, and the cost of seven articles.

(a) Use the READ/DATA statements to enter the price.
(b) Use a FOR/NEXT loop to control the number of times the function is evaluated. Use the value of the index as the number of articles.
(c) Cost of the articles $= \dfrac{\text{Price}}{2} \times$ Number of Articles (the index)
(d) In the flowchart, the DEF statement and the LET statement that calls the user-defined function are represented by process symbols.

```
RUN

COST OF 3 ARTICLES IS: 34.43
COST OF 5 ARTICLES IS: 57.38
COST OF 7 ARTICLES IS: 80.33
```

6. You may skip question 5(d) if your computer system does not support multiline user-defined functions.

Problem 6

P1 — DUMMY VARIABLE   N — NUMBER OF ARTICLES (INDEX)
P — ACTUAL PRICE   C — COST OF THE ARTICLES

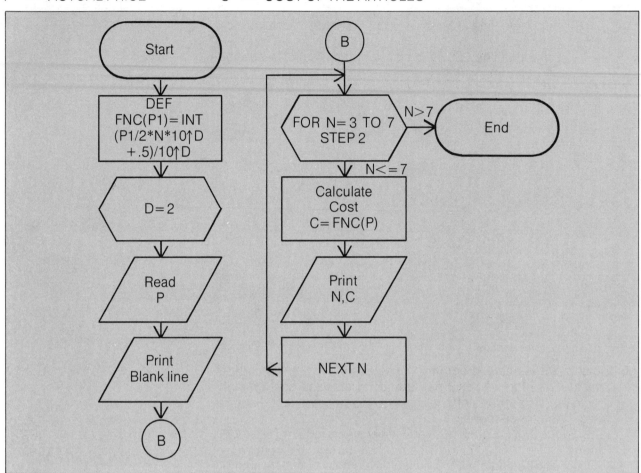

11.2 USER-DEFINED FUNCTIONS – Solutions for "Your Turn"[7]

1.

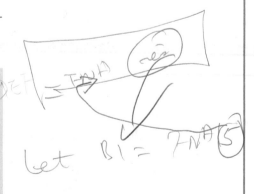

```
(a)  40 LET B=FNR(A)
              = FNR(13.485)
     FNR(A1)= INT(A1*10↑D+.5)/10↑D
     FNR(13.485)= INT(13.485*10↑2+.5)/10↑2
               = INT(1348.5+.5)/10↑2
               = INT(1349.0)/10↑2
               = 1349/100
               = 13.49
     40 LET B=FNR(A)
              = 13.49
```

(b) `40 LET B=FNR(A)*2`
$$= FNR(14.163)*2$$
$$FNR(A1) = INT(A1*10\uparrow D + .5)/10\uparrow D$$
$$FNR(14.163) = INT(14.163*10\uparrow 2 + .5)/10\uparrow 2$$
$$= INT(1416.3 + .5)/10\uparrow 2$$
$$= INT(1416.8)/10\uparrow 2$$
$$= 1416/100$$
$$= 14.16$$
`40 LET B=FNR(A)*2`
$$= 14.16*2$$
$$= 28.32$$

(c) `40 LET B=FNR(A*2)`
$$= FNR(14.163*2)$$
$$= FNR(28.326)$$
$$FNR(A1) = INT(A1*10\uparrow D + .5)/10\uparrow D$$
$$FNR(28.326) = INT(28.326*10\uparrow 2 + .5)/10\uparrow 2$$
$$= INT(2832.6 + .5)/10\uparrow 2$$
$$= INT(2833.1)/10\uparrow 2$$
$$= 2833/100$$
$$= 28.33$$
`40 LET B=FNR(A*2)`
$$= 28.33$$

(d) `40 LET B=SQR(FNR(A)+32.60)`
$$= SQR(FNR(16.398)+32.60)$$
$$FNR(A1) = INT(A1*10\uparrow D + .5)/10\uparrow D$$
$$FNR(16.398) = INT(16.398*10\uparrow 2 + .5)/10\uparrow 2$$
$$= INT(1639.8 + .5)/10\uparrow 2$$
$$= INT(1640.3)/10\uparrow 2$$
$$= 1640/100$$
$$= 16.40$$
`40 LET B=SQR(FNR(A)+32.60)`
$$= SQR(16.40+32.60)$$
$$= SQR(49)$$
$$= 7$$

2.

`60 LET W=FNN(H)`
$$= FNN(37)$$

$$FNN(H1) = R*H1 - D$$
$$FNN(37) = 11.543*37 - 79.50$$
$$= 427.091 - 79.50$$
$$= 347.591$$

`60 LET W=FNN(H)`
$$= 347.591$$

```
70 LET N=FNR(W)
        =FNR(347.591)

   FNR(W1)=INT(W1*10↑D2+.5)/10↑D2
   FNR(347.591)=INT(347.591*10↑2+.5)/10↑2
            =INT(34759.1+.5)/10↑2
            =INT(34759.6)/10↑2
            =34759/100
            =347.59

70 LET N=FNR(W)
        =347.59
```

3.

```
60 LET W=FNV(H)
        =FNV(44)

   FNV(H1)=R*39+(H1-39)*R*1.5-D
   FNV(44)=10.241*39+(44-39)*10.241*1.5-85
          =10.241*39+5*10.241*1.5-85
          =399.399+5*10.241*1.5-85
          =399.399+51.205*1.5-85
          =399.399+76.8075-85
          =476.2065-85
          =391.2065

60 LET W=FNV(H)
        =391.2065

70 LET N=FNR(W)
        =FNR(391.2065)

   FNR(W1)=INT(W1*10↑D2+.5)/10↑D2
   FNR(391.2065)=INT(391.2065*10↑2+.5)/10↑2
            =INT(39120.65+.5)/10↑2
            =INT(39121.15)/10↑2
            =39121/100
            =391.21

70 LET N=FNR(W)
        =391.21
```

4.

```
(a) 40 LET Q=FNQ(A,B,C)
          =FNQ(2,6,3)
```

FNQ(A1,B1,C1)=B1↑2−4*A1*C1
FNQ(2,6,3)=6↑2−4*2*3
          =36−4*2*3
          =36−8*3
          =36−24
          =12
```
40 LET Q=FNQ(A,B,C)
```
          =12

(b)
```
40 LET Q=FNQ(A,B,C)+10
```
          =FNQ(2,6,3)+10
FNQ(A1,B1,C1)=B1↑2−4*A1*C1
FNQ(2,6,3)=6↑2−4*2*3
          =36−4*2*3
          =36−8*3
          =36−24
          =12
```
40 LET Q=FNQ(A,B,C)+10
```
          =12+10
          =22

(c)
```
40 LET Q=FNQ(A,B+1,C)
```
          =FNQ(2,6+1,3)
          =FNQ(2,7,3)
FNQ(A1,B1,C1)=B1↑2−4*A1*C1
FNQ(2,7,3)=7↑2−4*2*3
          =49−4*2*3
          =49−8*3
          =49−24
          =25
```
40 LET Q=FNQ(A,B+1,C)
```
          =25

(d)
```
40 LET Q=SQR(FNQ(A,B+1,C))
```
          =SQR(FNQ(2,6+1,3))
          =SQR(FNQ(2,7,3))
FNQ(A1,B1,C1)=B1↑2−4*A1*C1
FNQ(2,7,3)=7↑2−4*2*3
          =49−4*2*3
          =49−8*3
          =49−24
          =25
```
40 LET Q=SQR(FNQ(A,B+1,C))
```
          =SQR(25)
          =5

5.

(a)
```
10 DEF FNT(P1)=P1*R
```

(b)
```
60 LET A=FNA(R)
```

```
(c) 10 DEF FNS(N1)=N1T2
    40 LET S=FNS(N)

(d) 30 LET FNB=A1T2
    50 LET FNB=A1T3
```

6.

```
01 REM P1--DUMMY VARIABLE
02 REM P--ACTUAL PRICE
03 REM N--NUMBER OF ARTICLES (INDEX)
04 REM C--COST OF THE ARTICLES

10 DEF FNC(P1)=INT(P1/2*N*10TD+.5)/10TD
20 LET D=2
30 READ P
40 DATA 22.95
50 PRINT
60 FOR N=3 TO 7 STEP 2
70   LET C=FNC(P)
80   PRINT "COST OF";N;"ARTICLES IS:";C
90 NEXT N
99 END
```

A SHORT SUMMARY

Subroutines and user-defined functions allow a programmer to write often-used routines or calculations just once. These may be called upon from various points within a program whenever they are needed. The computer branches to the routine or function and after processing the statement(s), returns to the point of reference where execution resumes. A subroutine is called by a GOSUB statement, which gives the number of the line where control is to be directed. The instructions in the subroutine are executed until a RETURN statement is encountered. This statement RETURNs control to the main program—specifically, to the statement immediately after the GOSUB that referenced the subroutine. The main program must end with an END statement or a STOP statement, depending upon the computer system being used.

```
40 GOSUB 200 ⟶
 ⟶ --
 160 END
```

```
200 LET C=A+B
--
280 RETURN
```

More than one value may be sent to the subroutine and more than one value may be returned to the main program. A main program may call several different subroutines or it may call the same subroutine more than once. Subroutines may be nested (one calling another), however, they must be in a hierarchical order. Thus, a program utilizing subroutines must be comprised of a main program and at least one subroutine.

A user-defined function is a mathematical equation (function) named and defined in a DEF statement. The function is called by the function reference which includes the name of the function and an argument. It is usually coded in a PRINT statement or in a LET statement. A value is passed from the actual argument in the function reference to the dummy argument in the function definition.

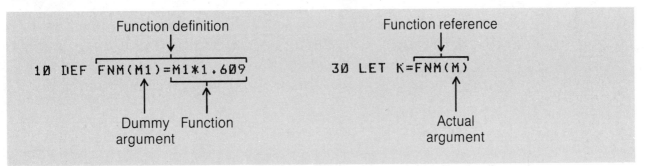

Some computer systems allow more than one argument in the function definition and in the function reference, making it possible to pass more than one value to the function definition. However, on all systems, only one value is returned to the calling statement. Some systems support multiline user-defined functions. These are used to define complex functions that often require branching and looping.

Questions and Exercises[8]

1. What is a subroutine?
2. State two advantages in the use of subroutines.
3. Explain how the GOSUB and RETURN statements work together.
4. What is the output of each of the following programs?

```
(a) 10 PRINT
    20 LET P=0
```

8. You may skip questions concerning multiline user-defined functions, ON...GOSUB statements, and user-defined functions with more than one argument if your computer system does not support these.

```
30 LET N=0
40 FOR I=1 TO 6
50    READ A
60    DATA 5,-2,9,-4,3,-6
70    GOSUB 200
80 NEXT I
90 PRINT P,N
100 END

200 IF A<0 THEN 230
210 LET P=P+A
220 RETURN
230 LET N=N+A
240 RETURN
```

(b)
```
10 PRINT
20 LET E=0
30 LET D=0
40 FOR I=1 TO 6
50    READ A
60    DATA 5,-2,9,-4,3,-6
70    IF A/2=INT(A/2) THEN 100
80    GOSUB 300
90    GO TO 110
100   GOSUB 200
110 NEXT I
120 PRINT E,D
130 END

200 LET E=E+1
210 RETURN

300 LET D=D+1
310 RETURN
```

(c)
```
10 DIM P(4),R(4)
20 PRINT
30 FOR I=1 TO 4
40    READ P(I)
50    DATA 4,3,1,2
60    PRINT P(I);
70 NEXT I
80 GOSUB 200
90 END

200 PRINT
210 FOR J=1 TO 4
220    LET P(J)=P(J)*2
230    PRINT P(J);
240 NEXT J
250 RETURN
```

```
(d) 10 DIM R(3,4)
    20 PRINT
    30 FOR I=1 TO 3
    40    FOR J=1 TO 4
    50    READ R(I,J)
    60    DATA 3,2,0,1
    70    DATA 1,0,2,3
    80    DATA 2,4,1,0
    90    GOSUB 200
    100 NEXT J
    110 PRINT
    120 NEXT I
    130 GOSUB 300
    140 PRINT
    150 PRINT S
    160 END

    200 PRINT R(I,J);
    210 RETURN

    300 LET S=0
    310 FOR L=1 TO 4
    320    LET S=S+R(1,L)
    330 NEXT L
    340 RETURN

(e) 10 PRINT
    20 FOR I=1 TO 3
    30    READ C
    40    DATA 1,2,3
    50    ON  C  GOSUB 100,200,300
    60 NEXT I
    70 END

    100 PRINT
    110 PRINT I,IT1
    120 RETURN

    200 PRINT
    210 PRINT I,IT2
    220 RETURN

    300 PRINT
    310 PRINT I,IT3
    320 RETURN
```

5. For the main program shown on page 548, write a subroutine that finds the average of four numbers.

   (a) Use a FOR/NEXT loop in your subroutine.
   (b) Use a counter to keep track of the "number" of numbers.
   (c) Don't forget to initialize to zero the counter, and the variable that accumulates the sum.

```
01 REM N--NUMBERS TO BE AVERAGED
02 REM S--SUM
03 REM A--AVERAGE

10 REM THIS IS THE MAIN PROGRAM
20 PRINT
30 FOR I=1 TO 4
40    READ N(I)
50    DATA 67,85,79,93
60    PRINT N(I)
70 NEXT I
80 GOSUB 200
90 PRINT
100 PRINT "THE SUM IS:";S
110 PRINT "THE AVERAGE IS:";A
120 END

RUN

   67
   85
   79
   93

THE SUM IS: 324
THE AVERAGE IS: 81
```

6. Modify the program in Problem 5 so that there are two subroutines; the first one is called by the main program and the second one is called by the first subroutine.

   (a) The first subroutine finds the sum and the average.
   (b) The second subroutine prints the sum and the average with headings as shown on page 549. Use the TAB function.

```
01 REM N--NUMBERS TO BE AVERAGED
02 REM S--SUM
03 REM A--AVERAGE

10 REM THIS IS THE MAIN PROGRAM
20 PRINT
30 FOR I=1 TO 4
40    READ N(I)
50    DATA 67,85,79,93
60    PRINT N(I)
70 NEXT I
80 GOSUB 200
90 END
```

```
RUN

    67
    85
    79
    93
```

```
0            10              23
             SUM             AVERAGE

             324             81
```

7. What is wrong with each of the following programs?

(a)
```
10 LET A=8
20 LET B=4
30 GOSUB 200
40 LET S=A+B
50 PRINT S
60 END

200 PRINT
210 PRINT A,B
```

(b)
```
10 LET S=0
20 LET A=8
30 LET B=4
40 GOSUB 200
50 END

200 LET S=A+B
210 PRINT
220 PRINT A,B,S
230 LET A=AT2
240 GOSUB 30
250 RETURN
```

(c) This program is to find the square of **A** after its
initial value has been added to **B**.

```
10 LET S=0
20 LET A=8
30 LET B=4
40 GOSUB 200
50 END

200 LET S=A+B
210 PRINT
```

```
        220 PRINT A,B,S
        230 RETURN
        240 LET A=AT2
        250 RETURN

(d) 10 LET S=0
    20 LET A=8
    30 GOSUB 200
    40 END

    200 LET S=S+A
    210 PRINT
    220 PRINT A,S
    230 LET A=A+1
    240 IF S<20 THEN 10
    250 RETURN
```

8. (a) What is a user-defined function?
   (b) State an advantage in its use.
9. (a) What is the purpose of the DEF statement?
   (b) Where are DEF statements usually placed in a program?
   (c) Display and label a DEF statement.
10. (a) How are user-defined functions named? Give three examples of function names.
    (b) What restriction is placed on the name of a user-defined function if there is more than one such function in a program?
11. (a) State the difference between a function definition and a function reference.
    (b) Where may a function reference appear in a program?
12. (a) Where is a *dummy* argument coded in a program? What is its purpose?
    (b) Where is an *actual* argument coded in a program? What is its purpose?
13. (a) How may the argument in a function reference be expressed? Give four examples.
    (b) State one restriction placed on this argument in its relation to the dummy argument in a function definition.
    (c) How must the argument in a function definition be expressed?
14. What three rules must be observed when a computer system allows more than one argument in the function definition and in the function reference?
15. How many values are returned from the function definition to the statement that contains the function reference?
16. (a) Summarize the composition of a multiline user-defined function.
    (b) When is this type of function used?
    (c) How is a value passed from a function reference to a variable in a multiline user-defined function?
    (d) How many values are returned from the multiline user-defined function?

17. Find, by hand, the value of **R** in each of the following program segments. The user-defined function is the expression that rounds off a decimal number to the nearest whole number.

```
10 DEF FNR(N1)=INT(N1*10↑D+.5)/10↑D
20 LET D=0
```

(a)
```
30 LET N=2.68
40 LET R=FNR(N)
```

(b)
```
30 LET N=6.32
40 LET R=FNR(N)*2
```

(c)
```
30 LET N=6.32
40 LET R=FNR(N*2)
```

18. What is the output of each of the following programs?

(a)
```
10 DEF FNR(N1)=INT(N1*10↑D+.5)/10↑D
20 DEF FNS(R1)=SQR(R1)
30 LET D=0
40 LET N=63.85
50 LET R=FNR(N)
60 LET S=FNS(R)
70 PRINT
80 PRINT N,R,S
99 END
```

(b)
```
10 DEF FNR(B)=INT(B*10↑D+.5)/10↑D
20 DEF FNW(A1)=A1*14.3
30 LET D=0
40 LET A=5
50 LET W=FNR(FNW(A))
60 PRINT
70 PRINT W
99 END
```

19. Find, by hand, the value of **Y** in each of the following statements, using the function definition and the values for **A** and **B** as shown below.

```
10 DEF FNY(A1,B1)=A1↑2+B1↑2
20 READ A,B
30 DATA 3,4
```

(a)
```
40 LET Y=FNY(A,B)
```

(b) 40 LET Y=FNY(A,B)+2

(c) 40 LET Y=FNY(A,B+2)

(d) 40 LET Y=SQR(FNY(A,B))

20. Indicate the errors, if any, in the programs shown below. If there is an error, make the necessary correction. If there is no error, show the result of a RUN.

```
(a)  10 DEF FNB(A1)=A1+2
     20 LET A=5
     30 LET B=FNA(A)
     40 PRINT
     50 PRINT A,B
     99 END

(b)  10 DEF FNB(A1)=A1+2
     20 PRINT
     30 FOR I=1 TO 5
     40    READ A(I)
     50    DATA 10,20,30,40,50
     60    LET B=FNB(A(I))
     70    PRINT A(I),B
     80 NEXT I
     99 END

(c)  10 DEF FNB(A1)=A1+B+C
     20 READ B,C
     30 DATA 4,8
     40 LET D=FNB(A)
     50 PRINT
     60 PRINT D
     99 END

     RUN

      18

(d)  10 DEF FNB(A1)=SQR((BT2+A1)/2)
     20 READ A,B
     30 DATA 2,4
     40 LET C=FNB(A)
     50 PRINT
     60 PRINT A,B,C
     99 END
```

21. Fill in the missing lines for the following program. The program calculates a table of cubes for the numbers from 1 to 5 inclusive.

    (i) Complete line 10 with a DEF statement.
    (ii) Complete line 40 with a function reference coded in a LET statement.

```
01 REM N1--DUMMY VARIABLE
02 REM N--NUMBER
03 REM C--NUMBER CUBED

10
20 PRINT
30 FOR N=1 TO 5
40
50    PRINT N,C
60 NEXT N
99 END

RUN

1          1
2          8
3          27
4          64
5          125
```

22. Complete the program below with a multiline user-defined function. The program checks a number to see if it is odd or even. A code of 1 is printed if the number is even; a code of 0 is printed if the number is odd. Use the INT function to check divisibility. Refer to Chapter 9, page 404, if you need help.

```
10 DEF FNB(A1)
20
30
40
50
60 FNEND
70 LET A=9
80 PRINT
90 PRINT A,FNB(A)
99 END

RUN

9          0
```

Programming Problems[9]

Subprograms provide an excellent opportunity to review concepts learned in earlier chapters, since all that needs to be done is to divide previous programs into two or more parts (main program and subroutines) or to call a user-defined function several times to perform a calculation more than once. The concept being reviewed and the page number where it was first introduced is given for each problem to enable you to refer to a particular page should you need some help. Some problems are slightly modified so that the latest techniques are utilized along with the ones being reviewed.

1. ON...GO TO statement — Chapter Four, page 123
Programming problem — Chapter Four, page 144

Write a program that determines the balance of a customer's account after each of the following transactions. There is no previous balance. Codes are used to indicate whether the transaction is a purchase or a payment.

```
Purchase ........................$250
Payment ........................ 150
Purchase ........................ 300
Payment ........................ 200
```

(a) Use two subroutines. Call each subroutine from the main program.

   (i) One subroutine adds the amount of a purchase to the balance.
   (ii) The other subroutine subtracts the amount of a payment from the balance.

(b) Use the PRINT USING and IMAGE statements to format the output. Code the headings in the PRINT USING statement.
(c) Use the READ/DATA statements to enter the code and the amount of each transaction.
(d) Use an ON...GO TO statement to branch to the statement that calls the appropriate subroutine or to branch to the end of the main program. A code of 1 indicates a purchase, a code of 2 denotes a payment, and a code of 3 terminates input.
(e) Depending on your code:

$$\text{Balance} = \text{Balance} + \text{Purchase}$$
$$or$$
$$\text{Balance} = \text{Balance} - \text{Payment}$$

9. If your computer system does not support the PRINT USING statement, use the TAB function to format your output. Also, instead of an IMAGE statement, some systems reference a string variable to which an image has been assigned.

Using the PRINT USING and IMAGE Statements

```
0       8                24
        AMOUNT           BALANCE

        $250             $250
        $150             $100
        $300             $400
        $200             $200
```

Using the TAB Function

```
0       8                24
        AMOUNT           BALANCE

        $  250           $  250
        $  150           $  100
        $  300           $  400
        $  200           $  200
```

2. RESTORE statement—Chapter Three, page 89
Programming problem—Chapter Three, page 92

A customer is shopping for two items—a chair and a table lamp. These items were originally marked at $80 and $60 respectively at two different stores. The first store is offering a discount of $10 on each item, while the second store is offering a discount of $20 on each item. Write a program that finds the reduced price of each item in each store.

(a) Use two subroutines:
   (i) The first subroutine calculates the reduced prices offered by the first store.
   (ii) The second subroutine calculates the reduced prices offered by the second store.
(b) Print the information for each store in the appropriate subroutine. Use format-free output.
(c) Remember to print the original value of each item before making any change in its value.
(d) In the main program, perform the following:
   (i) Use the READ/DATA statements to assign the original prices to **C1** (chair in first store) and **L1** (lamp in first store).
   (ii) Call the first subroutine to change the values of **C1** and **L1**.
   (iii) Use a RESTORE statement to reassign the original prices to variables **C2** (chair in second store) and **L2** (lamp in second store).
   (iv) Call the second subroutine to change the values of **C2** and **L2**.

```
RUN

FIRST STORE
CHAIR: 80            LAMP: 60
REDUCED: 70          REDUCED: 50

SECOND STORE
CHAIR: 80            LAMP: 60
REDUCED: 60          REDUCED: 40
```

3. ON...GOSUB statement[10]—Chapter Eleven, page 516
Programming problem—Chapter Five, page 189

Write a program that finds the number of TRUE answers and the number of FALSE answers on a questionnaire that consists of 20 questions.

(a) Use two subroutines:
   (i) One subroutine calculates the number of TRUE answers.
   (ii) The other subroutine calculates the number of FALSE answers.

   Remember to initialize two variables to zero in the main program before accumulating the number of TRUE answers and the number of FALSE answers.

(b) Use the PRINT USING and IMAGE statements to format the output. Code the headings in the PRINT USING statement.

(c) Use a FOR/NEXT loop to control input.

(d) Use the READ/DATA statements to enter the data shown below.

```
xx DATA 2,1,2,1,2,2,1,2,1,2
xx DATA 1,2,1,1,2,1,2,1,1,2
```

(e) Use the ON...GOSUB statement to branch to the appropriate subroutine. A code of 1 indicates a TRUE answer and a code of 2 indicates a FALSE answer.

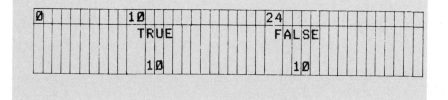

10. If your computer system does not allow the use of the ON...GOSUB statement, use the ON...GO TO statement to branch to a statement that calls the appropriate subroutine.

Problem 3

T — TRUE
F — FALSE
A — ANSWER

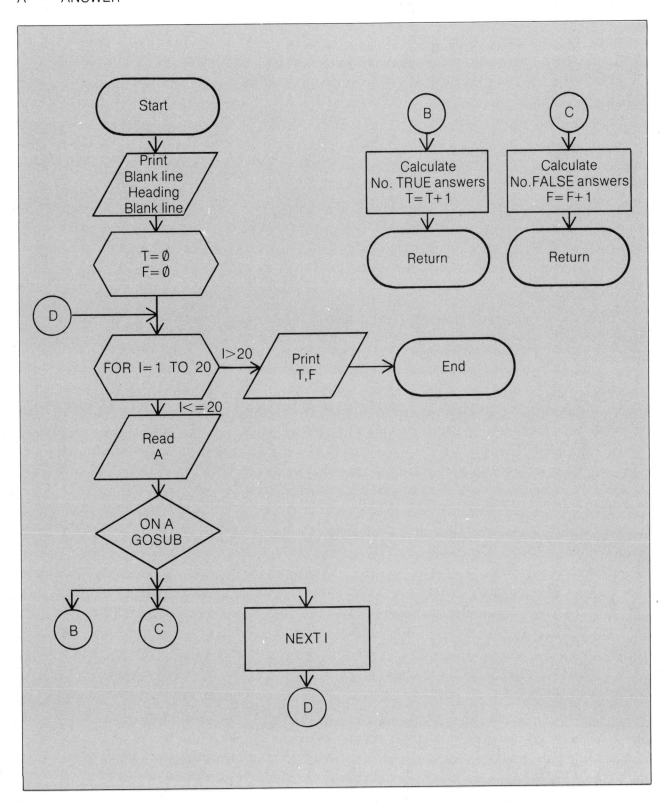

4. INT function—Chapter Nine, page 400
Programming problem—Chapter Six, page 233

A wage program was written in Chapter Three and modified in Chapters Five and Six. Rewrite the program so that it is divided into several subroutines. Shown below is the problem with the information you need.

Find the wages for three employees who are paid on the basis of a 39-hour week and who receive time-and-a-half for overtime. Deductions are made for income tax, union dues, and a registered pension plan.

Employee No.	Hrs. Worked	Rate	Income Tax Ded.	Union Dues	Pension Ded.
1	44	10.241	80	2	3.00
2	37	11.543	75	2	2.50
3	39	12.349	90	2	4.00

(a) Use four subroutines:

   (i) One subroutine calculates the gross pay with overtime. This subroutine calls the subroutine that calculates the net pay.

   (ii) A second subroutine calculates the gross pay with no overtime. This subroutine also calls the subroutine that calculates the net pay.

   (iii) A third subroutine calculates the net pay. This subroutine calls the subroutine that prints.

   (iv) A fourth subroutine prints the information as shown below, using format-free output.

(b) Use a FOR/NEXT loop to keep track of the employees, with the index of the FOR statement denoting the number of the employee.

(c) Use the READ/DATA statements to enter the hours, rate, and deductions.

(d) *Calculations*

   (i) Gross Pay with overtime:
     — Overtime Hours = Regular Hours − 39
     — Overtime Rate = Regular Rate × 1.5
     — Overtime Pay = Overtime Hours × Overtime Rate
     — Gross Pay (with overtime) = 39 × Regular Rate + Overtime Pay. Use the INT function to round off the gross pay to the nearest cent.

   (ii) Gross Pay (no overtime) = Regular Hours × Regular Rate Use the INT function to round off the gross pay to the nearest cent.

   (iii) Net Pay:
     — Total Deductions = Income Tax Deduction + Union Dues + Pension Deduction
     — Net Pay = Gross Pay − Total Deductions

Problem 4

D2 —	NUMBER OF DECIMAL PLACES	H1 —	OVERTIME HOURS
E —	INDEX (EMPLOYEE NUMBER)	R1 —	OVERTIME RATE
H —	REGULAR HOURS	V —	OVERTIME
R —	REGULAR RATE	G —	GROSS PAY
I —	INCOME TAX DED.	D —	DEDUCTIONS
U —	UNION DUES	N —	NET PAY
P —	PENSION FUND DED.		

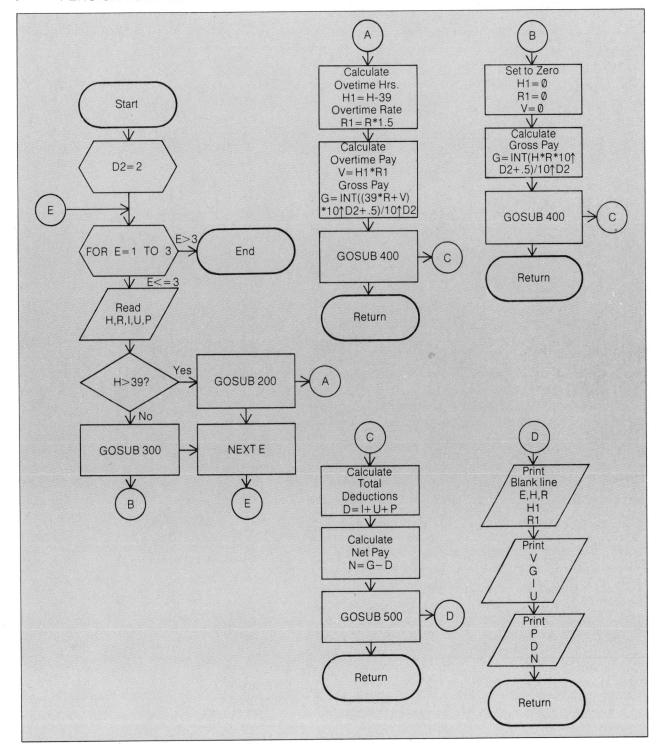

```
RUN

EMPL. 1    HRS 44     RATE 10.241
OVERTIME HOURS 5
OVERTIME RATE 15.3615
OVERTIME PAY 76.8075
GROSS PAY 476.21
INCOME TAX 80
UNION DUES 2
PENSION 3
TOTAL DEDUCTIONS 85
NET PAY 391.21

EMPL. 2    HRS 37     RATE 11.543
OVERTIME HOURS 0
OVERTIME RATE 0
OVERTIME PAY 0
GROSS PAY 427.09
INCOME TAX 75
UNION DUES 2
PENSION 2.5
TOTAL DEDUCTIONS 79.5
NET PAY 347.59

EMPL. 3    HRS 39     RATE 12.349
OVERTIME HOURS 0
OVERTIME RATE 0
OVERTIME PAY 0
GROSS PAY 481.61
INCOME TAX 90
UNION DUES 2
PENSION 4
TOTAL DEDUCTIONS 96
NET PAY 385.61
```

5. INT function — Chapter Nine, page 400
User-defined functions — Chapter Eleven, page 525
Programming problem — Chapter Six, page 233

The number of statements in the wage program in Problem 4 can be greatly reduced if only the net wages are calculated and the remaining information is not required. Two functions that calculate the net wages are shown on page 561. The first one finds the wages of an employee who works more than 39 hours; the second one finds the wages of an employee who works 39 hours or less. Deductions are subtracted in both functions. **R** represents **RATE**, **H1** is the dummy argument for **HOURS**, and **D** denotes **DEDUCTIONS**.

With overtime	`R*39+(H1-39)*R*1.5-D`			
With no overtime	`R*H1-D`			

You should use three user-defined functions:

 (i) One finds the wages that include overtime.
(ii) Another finds the wages that do not include overtime.
(iii) The third rounds off either one of the above wages to the nearest cent.

Code the function references in LET statements. Pass the hours of work to the user-defined functions that calculate the wages and pass the wages to the user-defined function that rounds off the wages to the nearest cent. If you need some help, refer to page 535 of this chapter, where the wage functions were introduced as "Your Turn" problems.

(a) Use a FOR/NEXT loop to keep track of the employees. Use the index of the FOR statement to represent the number of the employee.
(b) Use the TAB function to format your output. Print the headings outside the FOR/NEXT loop.
(c) Use the READ/DATA statements to enter the hours, rate, and deductions.
(d) Check the hours for overtime. If the employee worked more than 39 hours, call the user-defined function that calculates wages with overtime; otherwise, call the user-defined function that calculates wages with no overtime.
(e) After finding the employee's wages, call the user-defined function that rounds off the wages to the nearest cent.

```
0       7                27
        EMPLOYEE         WAGES
               1      $   391.21
               2      $   347.59
               3      $   385.61
```

Problem 5

FNV	— FUNCTION WITH OVERTIME		H1,W1	— DUMMY VARIABLES
FNN	— FUNCTION WITH NO OVERTIME		H	— HOURS
FNR	— FUNCTION THAT ROUNDS OFF AN AMOUNT		R	— RATE
			D	— DEDUCTIONS
D2	— NUMBER OF DECIMAL PLACES		W	— WAGES (NOT ROUNDED)
E	— INDEX (EMPLOYEE NUMBER)		N	— NET WAGES (ROUNDED)

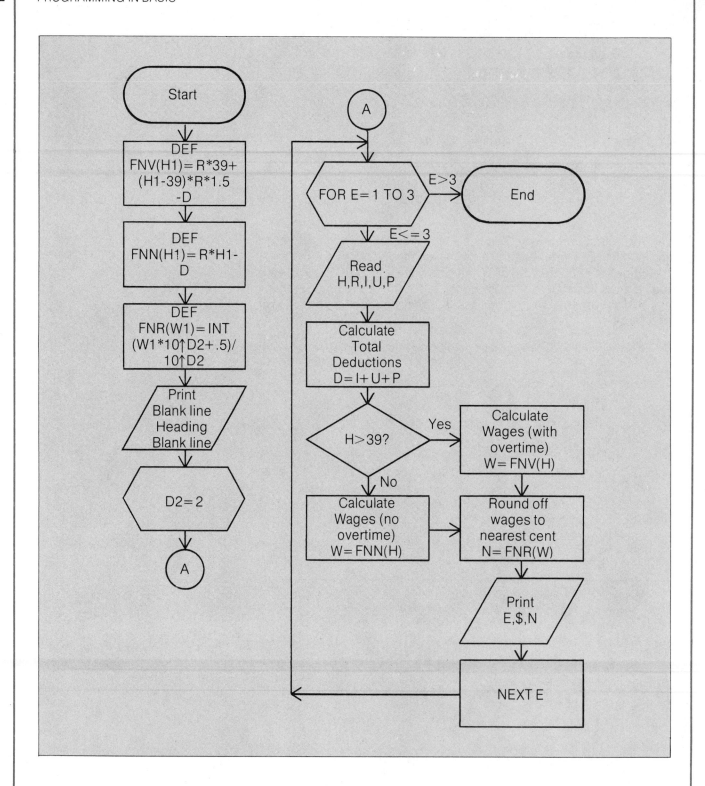

6. RND function — Chapter Nine, page 412
Programming problem — Chapter Nine, page 438

Suppose two players are playing a game in which each one moves
his/her chip a certain number of times, depending on where the dial
stops on a spinner. The dial may stop at any number from 1 to 9
inclusive. Write a program that determines which player makes the
greater number of moves after each one has had 10 plays.

(a) Use two subroutines. Call each subroutine from the main program.
   (i) One subroutine accumulates the total number of moves of each player (see (e)).
   (ii) The other subroutine finds the winner by comparing the two totals, then prints the number of the winner and his/her total number of moves (see (f)).

(b) Use the PRINT USING and IMAGE statements to format your output. Code the headings in the IMAGE statement.

(c) Initialize two variables to zero. These variables accumulate each player's moves. Also set one variable to the "number" of numbers on the dial (9) and another variable to the first endpoint (1).

(d) Use a FOR/NEXT loop to control the number of plays. The loop should contain the statement that calls the first subroutine.

(e) In the first subroutine, generate a random number from 1 to 9 inclusive for the first player. The random number represents the number of moves that can be made. Immediately following this statement, accumulate the player's moves. Do the same for the second player.

(f) In the second subroutine, find the winner by comparing the accumulated moves of the two players. Print the winner and his/her total number of moves as shown below. Print the number of the player (the winner) as a string. Be careful when formatting this number. A space is not left automatically before the number when it is coded as a string.

Note: The output changes with each RUN, since the program uses random numbers.

Sample RUN

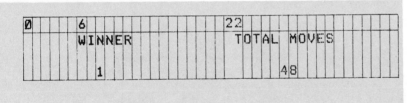

Problem 6

```
P1 — FIRST PLAYER
P2 — SECOND PLAYER
N  — "NO." OF NUMBERS IN RANGE
I  — FIRST ENDPOINT
R1 — RANDOM NO. FOR FIRST PLAYER
R2 — RANDOM NO. FOR SECOND PLAYER
```

```
                    563

                   Print
                 Blank line
                  Heading
                 Blank line

                  P1 = 0
                  P2 = 0
                   N = 9
                   I = 1
```

FOR J = 1 TO 10 ──── J > 10 ──── GOSUB 300 ──── B

│ J <= 10

GOSUB 200 ──── A

End

NEXT J

A

First Player
Random No.
R1 = INT
(N*RND(1)+I)
Total Moves
P1 = P1+R1

Second Player
Random No.
R2 = INT
(N*RND(1)+I)
Total Moves
P2 = P2+R2

Return

B

P1 > P2? ──── Yes ──── Print "1",P1

│ No

Print "2",P2

Return

Return

7. Two-dimensional arrays — Chapter Eight, pages 357, 361, and 362

Write a program that multiplies each element of the matrix shown below by 3 (a scalar), stores the results in matrix B, then adds the two matrices (A and B) to produce a third matrix, C.

(a) Read the data in the main program.

(b) Use nested FOR/NEXT loops in the main program and in each of the subroutines.

(c) Use four subroutines. The main program calls the first subroutine and the first subroutine calls the others to print the three matrices. Reference all subroutines outside the FOR/NEXT loops.

  (i) The first subroutine multiplies matrix A by the scalar to produce matrix B, then adds the two matrices to produce matrix C. Your statement to add should be

xx LET C(K,L)=A(K,L)+B(K,L)

    providing your indexes are K and L.

  (ii) The second subroutine prints matrix A.

  (iii) The third subroutine prints matrix B.

  (iv) The fourth subroutine prints matrix C.

(d) Print the arrays in matrix form as shown in the RUN. Do not use the PRINT USING and IMAGE statements or the TAB function to format your output. Here is the data.

```
        A
   4  5  6
   8  9  4
   7  8  9
```

```
RUN

MATRIX A
   4    5    6
   8    9    4
   7    8    9

MATRIX B
   12   15   18
   24   27   12
   21   24   27

MATRIX C
   16   20   24
   32   36   16
   28   32   36
```

8. MAT statements[11] — Chapter Nine, pages 383, 398, and 400

Rewrite the program in Problem 7, this time using MAT statements to read, multiply, add, and print.

11. You may skip this problem if your computer system does not support MAT statements.

Use two subroutines:
 (i) The first subroutine is called by the main program to multiply and
     add.
(ii) The second subroutine is called by the first subroutine to print the
     three matrices.

```
RUN

MATRIX A
   4   5   6

   8   9   4

   7   8   9


MATRIX B
  12   15   18

  24   27   12

  21   24   27


MATRIX C
  16   20   24

  32   36   16

  28   32   36
```

9. INT function—Chapter Nine, page 400
Programming problem—Chapter Nine, page 434

Using an initial principal of $1000, find the amount of an investment at
the end of each year for four years when interest is added each year to
the investment. Use interest rates of 13%, 14%, and 15%. The
amount of the investment after interest has been added is called the
compound amount. The formula to calculate this amount is as shown
below.

Compound Amount = Principal$(1+$Rate of Interest$)^{\text{Period of Time}}$

(a) Call a user-defined function to calculate the compound amount.
    Use the INT function in this statement to round off the amount to
    the nearest cent.
(b) Use a LET statement to assign the principal ($1000) to a variable.
    Code a function reference in another LET statement and pass the
    $1000 to the user-defined function.
(c) Use nested FOR/NEXT loops:
    (i) The outer loop keeps track of the years (period of time in the
        formula). Use the index of the FOR statement to print the
        number of the year at the beginning of each output line. Place
        this PRINT statement between the FOR statements.
   (ii) The inner loop generates the interest rates.

(d) Print the first year's compound amounts across the first line of output (for each rate of interest), the second year's compound amounts across the second line of output (for each rate of interest), etc. To do this, the PRINT statement that prints the number of the year and the PRINT statement that prints the compound amount should each end with a semicolon. Do not use the PRINT USING and IMAGE statements or the TAB function to format your output.

```
RUN

1   1130   1140   1150
2   1276.9   1299.6   1322.5
3   1442.9   1481.54   1520.88
4   1630.47   1688.96   1749.01
```

10. INPUT statement[12] — Chapter Three, page 66
Trailer value — Chapter Five, page 149
INT function — Chapter Nine, page 400
Programming problem — Chapter Four, page 142

Employees of the XYZ Manufacturing Company are paid on the basis of the number of parts they produce. Find the weekly wages of three employees who are paid $2.343 for each part they produce. Use the following information.

Employee	No. of Parts Produced	Deductions
1	212	105
2	213	110
3	209	102

(a) Use a user-defined function to calculate the wages. Include the INT function to round off the wages to the nearest cent.
Wages = Number of Parts Produced × Rate − Deductions
(b) Use a LET statement to assign the rate to a variable.
(c) Use the INPUT statement to enter the employee number, the number of parts produced, and the employee's deductions. Use a trailer value of 99999 to terminate input.
(d) Code the function reference in a LET statement and pass the number of parts produced to the user-defined function.
(e) Use format-free output.

Using the INPUT Statement

```
RUN

EMPLOYEE,PARTS,DEDUCTIONS? 1,212,105
WAGES: 391.72
```

12. Use the READ/DATA statements to enter the data if you are not using an interactive system.

```
EMPLOYEE,PARTS,DEDUCTIONS? 2,213,110
WAGES: 389.06

EMPLOYEE,PARTS,DEDUCTIONS? 3,209,102
WAGES: 387.69

EMPLOYEE,PARTS,DEDUCTIONS? 99999,0,0
```

Using the READ/DATA Statements

```
RUN

EMPLOYEE: 1
PARTS, DEDUCTIONS: 212   105
WAGES: 391.72

EMPLOYEE: 2
PARTS, DEDUCTIONS: 213   110
WAGES: 389.06

EMPLOYEE: 3
PARTS, DEDUCTIONS: 209   102
WAGES: 387.69
```

11. Special value—Chapter Five, page 155
INT function—Chapter Nine, page 400
Programming problem—Chapter Ten, page 503

A furniture store is offering a 12$\frac{1}{2}$% discount on television sets at its end-of-the-year sale. Calculate the discounts and the reduced prices of six TV sets regularly priced at $853, $894, $842, $925, $987, and $961.

(a) Use two user-defined functions:
   (i) One calculates the discount. Use the INT function in this statement to round off the discount to the nearest cent.
   Discount = Regular Price × .125
   Code the function reference that calls this user-defined function in a LET statement. Pass the regular price to the function and assign the returned value (the discount) to a variable, say **D**.
   (ii) The second user-defined function calculates the reduced price.
   Reduced Price = Regular Price − Discount
   Code the function reference that calls this user-defined function in the PRINT statement that prints the amounts as shown on the following page. Pass the regular price to the user-defined function.
(b) Use the READ statement to store the number of TV sets in a

simple variable. The variable is used subsequently with a counter
to terminate the loop. The counter should be set initially to one
and incremented after each reduced price is calculated.

(c) Use the READ/DATA statements to enter the regular prices.

(d) Use the TAB function to format your output.

```
0    4             16            30
     REGULAR                     REDUCED
     PRICE         DISCOUNT       PRICE

     $  853        $  106.63     $  746.37
     $  894        $  111.75     $  782.25
     $  842        $  105.25     $  736.75
     $  925        $  115.63     $  809.37
     $  987        $  123.38     $  863.62
     $  961        $  120.13     $  840.87
```

12. RND function — Chapter Nine, page 412
Programming problem — Chapter Ten, page 501

Write a program that finds how many 7's and how many 11's are rolled
out of 50 rolls of a pair of dice. Use the random number generator to
simulate the roll of the dice.

(a) Use a user-defined function to generate a random whole number
between 1 and 6 inclusive.

(b) Use the TAB function to format the headings and the results.

(c) Use a LET statement to assign the "number" of numbers (6) to a
variable.

(d) Code a function reference in each of two LET statements — one
for each die. In both statements pass the "number" of numbers
to the user-defined function. Assign the returned random number to the variable representing the die; say **D1** for die number 1
and **D2** for die number 2.

(e) Find the total of a roll and check for a 7 or an 11. Keep two running
counters — one to accumulate the number of times a 7 is rolled,
and the other to accumulate the number of times an 11 is rolled.

```
0    7                 23
     TOTAL NUMBER OF  ROLLS: 50

     NUMBER 7          NUMBER 11

           10                3
```

(f) Except for the following changes, your flowchart should be similar to the one for Problem 6 in Chapter Ten on page 502.

   (i) Draw a symbol for the DEF statement before the symbol that
   represents the printing of the headings.

   (ii) The material in two of the symbols should describe statements that use function references rather than statements that generate random numbers.

Note: Output will differ for each RUN.

13. Multiline user-defined function[13] — Chapter Eleven, page 533

Write a program that uses a multiline user-defined function to find the square root of $B\uparrow 2 - 4*A*C$. Find the square root only if the equation results in a positive or zero value, then assign the square root to the function name. If the result of the equation is a negative value, assign -1 to the function name.

(a)   Use a FOR/NEXT loop to control input.

(b)   Use the READ/DATA statements to assign data to the three variables, **A**, **B**, and **C**, respectively. Use the following data statements.

```
xx DATA 2,6,4
xx DATA 1,8,16
xx DATA 3,4,2
```

(c)   Code the function reference in a LET statement. Pass the value of **A** to the user-defined function.

(d)   Use the TAB function to format your output as shown.

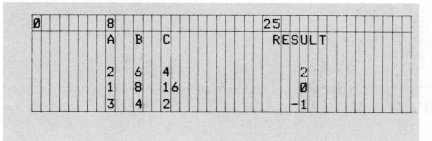

```
0       8           25
        A   B   C    RESULT

        2   6   4         2
        1   8   16        0
        3   4   2        -1
```

Problem 13

Start

DEF
FND(A1)

571

---

13. You may omit Problem 13 if you cannot use multiline user-defined functions on your computer.

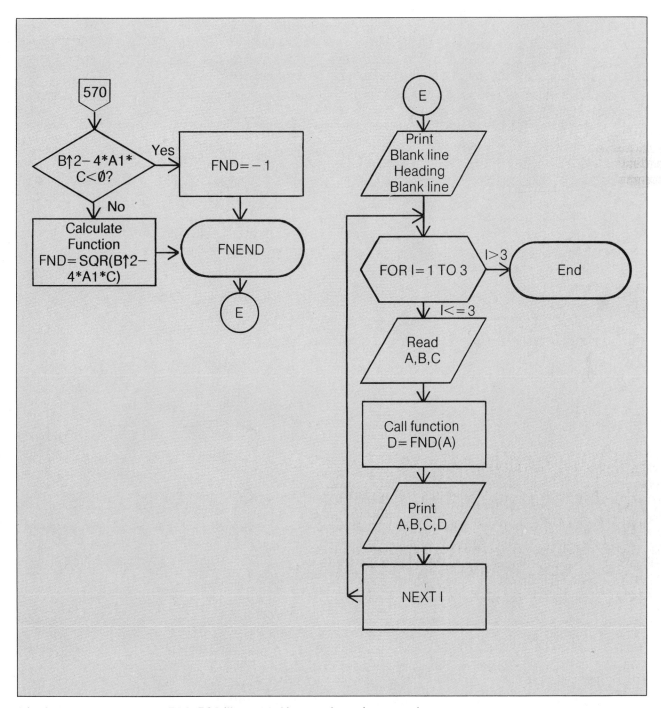

14. A program on **pages** 519-520 illustrated how subroutines can be
    called upon to **draw common** lines of letters of the alphabet. Use
    subroutines **to draw your** initials one under the other such as
    E *or* ⊓
    B   ⊔
    L   ⌐
    The second type **of display is** often used when letters are printed
    on paper.

    (a) Use the TAB function and the same symbol throughout
        (perhaps an asterisk) to draw the letters.

(b) Use one variable to represent the number of symbols to be printed. Change the value of this variable (when necessary) before calling a subroutine. The variable can also be used to position a symbol by coding the variable in the argument of the TAB function.

15. Use subroutines to draw a picture of your choice. You may use either the TAB function or the PRINT USING and IMAGE statements to draw the picture.

TWELVE STRINGS

A. After completing this chapter, you should be able to write BASIC programs that:

1. Store strings in the computer by means of
   (a) The INPUT statement.
   (b) The READ/DATA statements.
   (c) The LET statement.
2. Store strings in
   (a) A simple string variable.
   (b) A one-dimensional array.
   (c) A two-dimensional array.
3. Compare strings.
4. Concatenate strings.
5. Extract
   (a) Any number of left-most characters from a string.
   (b) Any number of right-most characters from a string.
   (c) Any series of characters from a string.
   (d) One character from a string.
6. Sort strings.
7. Use special functions to
   (a) Find the length of a string.
   (b) Convert a string that consists of digits to its numeric value.
   (c) Convert a number to its string equivalent.
   (d) Convert an ASCII code to its ASCII character.
   (e) Convert a single character to its ASCII code.

B. In addition, you should be able to:

1. Define a string variable.
2. Explain how a character is stored in a computer and summarize the reason for this method of storage.
3. State what the letters ASCII represent.
4. Summarize the hierarchical ordering of ASCII codes.
5. Evaluate relational string expressions.
6. Find errors in programs.
7. Produce the output of programs.

12.1 STRING VARIABLES

The programs in the preceding chapters manipulated only numeric data. The use of alphanumeric data (a mixture of numeric, alphabetic, and special characters) was restricted to the PRINT statement. The characters were enclosed within quotation marks and printed as a string. Other than printing a heading or a message a string was not manipulated in any other way.

A string may be assigned to a variable. This type of variable is called a string variable and, like a numeric variable, must begin with a letter of the alphabet. To differentiate between the two types, a string variable on most systems must end with a dollar sign ($). **A$** is a string variable, while **A** is a numeric variable. Some computers accept **A1$**, **N9$**, etc., as string variables. Others allow a double letter, such as **AA**, **NN**. It is a good idea to construct a string variable so that it indicates the kind of information assigned to it. **N$** might represent a person's **N**ame, while **C$** could stand for the name of a **C**ity. The series of characters assigned to a string variable is often considered the **value** of the variable.

Some computer systems require the dimensioning of a string variable when the string contains more than one character. Others require no dimensioning unless the variable represents an array. The undimensioned string variable is allowed a maximum number of characters, the number depending on the computer. If dimensioning is required, the parameter following the string variable represents the maximum number of characters in the string. For example, **10 DIM A$(8)** designates **A$** as a string variable, with a maximum of 8 characters in its string.[1]

Some systems allow two parameters to dimension both the number of elements in an array and the number of characters in each string of the array. The DIM statement

10 DIM A$(6)9, B$(8), C$4

dimensions the variables as follows.

The string variable **A$** is dimensioned as an array of six elements, with each element (string) having a maximum of nine characters.

The string variable **B$** is an array of eight elements, with each element (string) having a default[2] length of one character.

The string variable **C$** is a simple string variable whose string may consist of a maximum of four characters.

The length of a string varies among different computers — from zero characters (the null string) to a specific maximum, which may be as low as 6 characters and as high as 255 characters (72 and 255 are the more common maximums). Check your manual to find out the maximum number of characters allowed in a string by your computer system.

12.2 ENTERING STRINGS INTO THE COMPUTER

The three methods by which strings may be entered into the computer will now be discussed. (Note that they are the same methods that were introduced in Chapter Three.) Strings that are assigned to variables must often be enclosed in quotation marks, particularly when more than one string is entered on the same line in response to an INPUT request or listed in the same DATA statement. These quotes may be double or single, depending on the computer system being used. Some systems require quotes around a string when the string

---

1. In this book, DIM statements are not used to specify string capacity but are used to dimension arrays.
2. In the absence of a parameter, the computer assumes that the value is a specific number.

consists of a number or when one of its characters is a comma or a colon. Quotes may also be necessary when a string contains a leading space or a trailing space. The majority of computers requires quotes when a string is entered by means of a LET statement or when the string is coded in an IF/THEN statement.

```
10 LET A$='HELLO'        30 IF B$='HI' THEN 90
```

Check your computer manual or experiment to find out when you need quotation marks around strings. The strings in this chapter are enclosed in quotes when:

1. The string consists of a number.
2. The string contains a comma or a colon.
3. The string contains a leading space.
4. The string contains a trailing space and the string is the last item in the second line of a DATA statement.
5. The string is in a LET statement, an IF/THEN statement, or a PRINT statement.

It should also be mentioned that a quote is usually not allowed within a string when the quote is the same type (double or single) as the one that delimits the string. Also, a string comprised of numbers may not be used in arithmetic computations.

   As with numeric data, strings must be separated by commas when more than one string is typed in response to an INPUT statement or listed in the same DATA statement. The data must correspond in number, order, and type to the variables listed in the INPUT statement or in the READ statement.

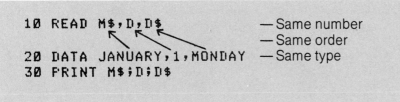

```
10 READ M$,D,D$        — Same number
                       — Same order
20 DATA JANUARY,1,MONDAY   — Same type
30 PRINT M$;D;D$
```

The string **JANUARY** is assigned to the string variable **M$**, the number 1 is assigned to the numeric variable **D**, and the string **MONDAY** is assigned to the string variable **D$**.

   Just a few words concerning the printing of strings. If your computer distinguishes a comma from a semicolon, a comma in the PRINT statement produces wide spacing between two strings; a semicolon leaves no space unless a leading space or a trailing space is coded as part of a string.

```
10 DATA JOHN SMITH ,ROXVALE
```

Trailing space in the string **JOHN SMITH**

A string that includes a leading space must be enclosed in quotation marks.

```
10 DATA JOHN SMITH," ROXVALE"
                           ↑
         Leading space in the string ROXVALE
```

Numbers are printed differently among computer systems. The computer used for this book leaves one space before a positive number for the assumed plus sign and fills this space in with a minus sign when the number is negative. It leaves one space after any number regardless of the number's sign. If your computer leaves no space before a number and no space after a number, a space must be coded in the string that comes before the number and in the string that comes after the number or the space may be coded as a separate string in the PRINT statement. Here are two examples.

```
20 DATA JANUARY ,1," MONDAY"
                ↑     ↑
30 PRINT M$;D;D$             —— A space in each string.
```

or

```
20 DATA JANUARY,1,MONDAY
30 PRINT M$;" ";D;" ";D$
              ↑       ↑
                           —— Spaces coded as strings.
```

Use the various DATA and PRINT statements shown above, along with the READ statement, to find out how your computer prints strings.

12.2 ENTERING STRINGS INTO THE COMPUTER — Sample Programs

A number of programs are shown below to illustrate the three methods of entering strings. Semicolons, rather than commas, are coded in the PRINT statements since differences in spacing are more readily apparent by their use. Each of the programs assigns the name of a person to **N$**, the name of a city to **C$**, and a number to **N**.

1. Using the INPUT statement[3]

```
10 PRINT          — Leaves a blank line.
20 PRINT "DATA";  — A prompt.
```

---

3. If you are not using an interactive system, you may omit programs that use INPUT statements or questions that refer to these statements.

```
30 INPUT N$,C$,N      — Requests data, user enters the name of a person, the name of a
                        city, and a number.
40 PRINT N$;C$;N      — Prints the name of the person, the name of the city, and the
                        number closely spaced.
99 END                — Terminates program execution.

RUN

DATA? JOHN SMITH ,ROXVALE,123456
JOHN SMITH ROXVALE 123456
```

To obtain the space after **SMITH** in the output line, a space must be
left after **JOHN SMITH** when the name is keyed into the computer.
No space needs to be left after **ROXVALE**, since the computer prints
a space before a positive number.

```
DATA? JOHN SMITH ,ROXVALE,123456
                 ↑          ↑
               Space     No space
```

2. Using the READ/DATA statements

```
10 READ N$,C$,N                          — Reads the name, city, and number
                                           from the DATA statement.
20 DATA JOHN SMITH ,ROXVALE,123456       — Supplies the READ statement with data.
30 PRINT                                 — Leaves a blank line.
40 PRINT N$;C$;N                         — Prints the name, city, and number
                                           closely spaced.
99 END                                   — Terminates program execution.

RUN

JOHN SMITH ROXVALE 123456
```

To obtain the space after **SMITH** in the output, a space must be coded
after **SMITH** in the **DATA** statement. As in Program 1, no space
needs to be coded after **ROXVALE**, since the computer leaves a
space before a positive number.

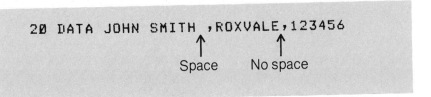

```
20 DATA JOHN SMITH ,ROXVALE,123456
                  ↑          ↑
                Space     No space
```

3. Using LET statements

```
10 LET N$="JOHN SMITH "    — Assigns JOHN SMITHƀ4 to N$.
20 LET C$="ROXVALE"        — Assigns ROXVALE to C$.
30 LET N=123456            — Assigns 123456 to N.
40 PRINT                   — Leaves a blank line.
50 PRINT N$;C$;N           — Prints the name, city, and number closely spaced.
99 END                     — Terminates program execution.

RUN

JOHN SMITH ROXVALE 123456
```

Notice that the computer requires quotes around a string when a LET statement is used to assign the string to a string variable. The space after **JOHN SMITH** in the output is obtained by leaving a trailing space in the string **"JOHN SMITH "** in line 10. An alternative method is to code the space before **ROXVALE**. As in the other programs, no space is needed after **ROXVALE**.

```
10 LET N$="JOHN SMITH "    or    10 LET N$="JOHN SMITH"
20 LET C$="ROXVALE"              20 LET C$=" ROXVALE"
                 ↑                              ↑
               Space                          Space
```

Some versions of BASIC allow multiple assignment statements to assign strings to string variables. For example, the statement

```
10 LET A$=B$=C$="ROXVALE"
```

assigns **ROXVALE** to each of the variables **A$**, **B$**, and **C$**.

String variables can also store arrays. The following program reads the names of the nine planets into a one-dimensional array, then prints the names closely spaced.

```
10 DIM P$(9)
20 PRINT
30 FOR I=1 TO 9
40    READ P$(I)
50    DATA MERCURY ,VENUS ,EARTH ,MARS ,J
UPITER ,SATURN ,URANUS ,NEPTUNE ,PLUTO
60    PRINT P$(I);
```

4. The symbol ƀ represents a space.

```
70 NEXT I
99 END

RUN

MERCURY VENUS EARTH MARS JUPITER SATURN
URANUS NEPTUNE PLUTO
```

The variable in lines 40 and 60 is a subscripted string variable. On most computers, the array needs to be dimensioned when there are more than 10 or 11 elements (strings) in the array. Notice that the data statement requires two lines. This is permitted since the computer being used allows 79 characters in a statement. Each string contains a trailing space. Without this space, the names of the planets would run together when they are printed.

The name of a specific planet can be printed by referencing the appropriate element of the array. For example, if you want to print the name of the planet on which you live, the PRINT statement would be **xx PRINT P$(3)**. The statement must be coded out of the loop, otherwise the name will be printed more than once.

The program below stores the names of the planets as elements of a two-dimensional array, then prints the names in matrix form. Here are the names arranged as a matrix.

P$

	Column 1	Column 2	Column 3
Row 1	MERCURY	VENUS	EARTH
Row 2	MARS	JUPITER	SATURN
Row 3	URANUS	NEPTUNE	PLUTO

```
10 DIM P$(3,3)
20 PRINT
30 FOR I=1 TO 3
40   FOR J=1 TO 3
50     READ P$(I,J)
60     DATA MERCURY ,VENUS ,EARTH ,MARS
,JUPITER ,SATURN ,URANUS ,"NEPTUNE "
70     DATA PLUTO
80     PRINT P$(I,J);
90   NEXT J
100  PRINT
110 NEXT I
999 END
```

```
RUN

MERCURY VENUS EARTH
MARS JUPITER SATURN
URANUS NEPTUNE PLUTO
```

In this program, the string variable is a doubly subscripted string variable. On most systems, the array needs dimensioning only if one of its subscripts is greater than 10 or 11. The names of the planets in the DATA statement are listed by rows since the row loop is on the outside. Again, each string must contain a trailing space. Notice that **NEPTUNE** is enclosed in quotes. These quotes are necessary, as the string must end with a space. Without the quotes, the next planet's name (**PLUTO**) would be printed immediately after **NEP-TUNE**, since **PLUTO** is coded in a new DATA statement.

Specific elements may be referenced by coding explicit subscripts for the row and column. For example, if you want to print **MARS**, your PRINT statement would be **xx PRINT P$(2,1)**.

12.2 ENTERING STRINGS INTO THE COMPUTER — Your Turn

1. What is wrong with each of the following programs? Make the necessary corrections.

```
(a) 10  PRINT
    20  PRINT "NAME,TELEPHONE NUMBER";
    30  INPUT N,T
    40  PRINT N;T
    99  END

(b) 10  PRINT
    20  FOR I=1 TO 3
    30     READ M$
    40     DATA JANUARY,MAY,SEPTEMBER
    50     PRINT M$;
    60  NEXT I
    99  END

(c) 10  LET B$="BLACK"
    20  LET W$="WHITE"
    30  PRINT
    40  PRINT B$;"AND";W$
    99  END
```

2. Write three programs, each one producing the following output.

```
MONDAY JANUARY 1
```

(a) Assign **MONDAY** and **JANUARY** to separate string variables.
(b) Assign the number 1 to a numeric variable.
(c) To enter the data:
— The first program uses the INPUT statement. Show how the data is entered in response to this statement.
— The second program uses the READ/DATA statements.
— The third program uses LET statements.
(d) Use semicolons to separate the items in the PRINT statements.

3. Write three programs, each one producing the output shown below. Replace the score with your own number of points.

```
I SCORED 24 POINTS
```

(a) Assign **I SCORED** to a string variable, the number of points to a numeric variable, and **POINTS** to a second string variable.
(b) To enter the data:
— The first program uses the INPUT statement. Show how the data is entered in response to this statement.
— The second program uses the READ/DATA statements.
— The third program uses LET statements.
(c) Use semicolons to separate the items in the PRINT statements.

4. Write a program that enters the following six names into the computer and prints only the first, third, and fifth names widely spaced.

Anne, Craig, Barry, Roger, Laurie, Tracy

(a) Use a FOR/NEXT loop to control input.
(b) Use the READ/DATA statements to enter the names. Leave a trailing space after each name in the DATA statement.
(c) Store the names in a one-dimensional array.
(d) Use explicit subscripts to print the appropriate elements of the array.
(e) Notice that there is no extra space between the names in the output. Each name starts in the first print position of a zone. The trailing space in each string in the DATA statement is part of the name.

```
RUN

ANNE       BARRY       LAURIE
```

5. Rewrite the program for Problem 4. This time, read the names into a two-dimensional array that has two rows and three columns. Here is the data in matrix form.

Anne	Craig	Barry
Roger	Laurie	Tracy

(a) Use nested FOR/NEXT loops to control input.
(b) Read the names by rows.
(c) Print only the first, third, and fifth names closely spaced. Use explicit subscripts to denote the row and the column of each element of the array.

```
RUN

ANNE BARRY LAURIE
```

12.2 ENTERING STRINGS INTO THE COMPUTER—Solutions for "Your Turn"[5]

1. (a) The variable **N** in lines 30 and 40 should be a string variable, since a person's name will be assigned to this variable.

```
30 INPUT N$,T
40 PRINT N$;T
```

(b) The names of the months will be printed with no space between each name. There should be a space after **JANUARY** and another after **MAY** in line 40.

```
40 DATA JANUARY ,MAY ,SEPTEMBER
```

(c) The three words will be printed with no space between each word. There are a number of solutions, two of which are shown below.

```
10 LET B$='BLACK '          10 LET B$='BLACK '
40 PRINT B$;'AND ';W$        20 LET W$=' WHITE'
```

5. Programs are written for a computer that leaves one space before a positive number and one space after any number.

2. (a) **Using the INPUT Statement**

```
01 REM D$--DAY OF THE WEEK
02 REM M$--MONTH
03 REM D--DAY OF THE MONTH

10 PRINT
20 PRINT "DATE";        ←—— Optional
30 INPUT D$,M$,D
40 PRINT D$;M$;D
99 END

RUN

DATE? MONDAY ,JANUARY,1
```

(b) **Using the READ/DATA Statements**

```
10 READ D$,M$,D
20 DATA MONDAY ,JANUARY,1
30 PRINT
40 PRINT D$;M$;D
99 END
```

(c) **Using LET Statements**

```
10 LET D$="MONDAY "
20 LET M$="JANUARY"
30 LET D=1
40 PRINT
50 PRINT D$;M$;D
99 END
```

3. (a) **Using the INPUT Statement**

```
01 REM I$--I SCORED
02 REM N--NUMBER OF POINTS
03 REM P$--POINTS

10 PRINT
20 PRINT "SCORE";      ←—— Optional
30 INPUT I$,N,P$
40 PRINT I$;N;P$
99 END
```

```
RUN

SCORE? I SCORED,24,POINTS
```

(b) Using the READ/DATA Statements

```
10 READ I$,N,P$
20 DATA I SCORED,24,POINTS
30 PRINT
40 PRINT I$;N;P$
99 END
```

(c) Using LET Statements

```
10 LET I$='I SCORED'
20 LET N=24
30 LET P$='POINTS'
40 PRINT
50 PRINT I$;N;P$
99 END
```

4.

```
01 REM N$--NAME

10 DIM N$(6)
20 PRINT
30 FOR I=1 TO 6
40    READ N$(I)
50    DATA ANNE ,CRAIG ,BARRY ,ROGER ,LAU
RIE ,TRACY
60 NEXT I
70 PRINT N$(1),N$(3),N$(5)
99 END
```

5.

```
01 REM N$--NAME

10 DIM N$(2,3)
20 PRINT
30 FOR I=1 TO 2
40    FOR J=1 TO 3
```

```
50      READ N$(I,J)
60      DATA ANNE ,CRAIG ,BARRY ,ROGER ,L
AURIE ,TRACY
70    NEXT J
80 NEXT I
90 PRINT N$(1,1);N$(1,3);N$(2,2)
99 END
```

12.3 PROCESSING STRINGS

Before the processing of strings is discussed, you should be aware of how information is stored in a computer. Each character (digit, letter, or other symbol) is stored as a series of ones and zeros. These ones and zeros are representative of the two states of the computer's electronic circuitry, which can be either on or off. Conventionally, a 1 signifies that the circuit is on, while a 0 signifies that the circuit is off. The 1 and the 0 are referred to as bits (**b**inary dig**its**). The order of their sequence is the numeric equivalent of a particular character. For example, the number 1 is represented by the seven bits 0110001, the letter A is represented by 1000001, and the bit pattern for the letter Z is 1011010. To standardize these numeric codes, several encoding systems have come into existence. One of these is the seven-bit ASCII code. ASCII is the acronym for **A**merican **S**tandard **C**ode for **I**nformation **I**nterchange. In ASCII, the digits 0 through 9 precede the letters of the alphabet as shown on page 586.

Since the base two numbering system is an awkward system with which to work, the binary codes are usually converted to their base ten equivalent (decimal notation) or base eight equivalent (octal notation) or base sixteen equivalent (hexadecimal notation). The notation used depends on the computer system.[6] Base ten uses the ten digits 0 through 9; base eight uses the eight digits 0 through 7. To represent values in hexadecimal notation, 16 one-digit symbols are required. Since only ten are available in the decimal system, the letters A, B, C, D, E, and F are used to represent the values 10, 11, 12, 13, 14, and 15.[7]

The process of converting letters, digits, and other characters to their ASCII codes is referred to as **encoding**. Translating the ASCII codes into their corresponding characters is called **decoding**. There are many ASCII codes. These include codes that represent system commands, such as the code for a carriage return which is shown on the following page in two notations.[8]

6. This book uses decimal notation to represent the ASCII codes for letters, digits, special characters, and system commands.

7. The intent of this unit is merely to introduce you to hexadecimal notation. If you wish a more detailed discussion on hexadecimal representation, refer to a Mathematics book or to a Data Processing text.

8. A code that represents a system command does not have a corresponding character.

```
10 PRINT CHR$(13)    Decimal notation
10 PRINT HEX(0D)     Hexadecimal notation
```

These two statements cause a carriage return. **CHR$** and **HEX** are special functions that enable a programmer to use an ASCII code in a program. The following table lists the ASCII codes in octal, decimal, and hexadecimal translations for the characters most often used.

Character	Octal	Decimal	Hexadecimal
space	040	32	20
"	042	34	22
#	043	35	23
$	044	36	24
'	047	39	27
(	050	40	28
)	051	41	29
*	052	42	2A
+	053	43	2B
,	054	44	2C
-	055	45	2D
.	056	46	2E
/	057	47	2F
0	060	48	30
1	061	49	31
2	062	50	32
3	063	51	33
4	064	52	34
5	065	53	35
6	066	54	36
7	067	55	37
8	070	56	38
9	071	57	39
:	072	58	3A
;	073	59	3B
<	074	60	3C
=	075	61	3D
>	076	62	3E
A	101	65	41
B	102	66	42
C	103	67	43
D	104	68	44
E	105	69	45
F	106	70	46
G	107	71	47
H	110	72	48
I	111	73	49
J	112	74	4A
K	113	75	4B
L	114	76	4C

Character	Octal	Decimal	Hexadecimal
M	115	77	4D
N	116	78	4E
O	117	79	4F
P	120	80	50
Q	121	81	51
R	122	82	52
S	123	83	53
T	124	84	54
U	125	85	55
V	126	86	56
W	127	87	57
X	130	88	58
Y	131	89	59
Z	132	90	5A

Notice the hierarchical ordering of the ASCII codes. The space and a number of special characters precede the digits. The digits are followed by other symbols, which, in turn, are followed by the capital letters. This hierarchy makes it possible to compare strings by using the same relational operators that are used to compare numbers. The computer compares two strings by comparing one character at a time, moving in a left-to-right direction until a difference is found. Here are some examples. For each relational expression, the answer is either true or false. Consult the ASCII list of codes for the numerical equivalent of a character. The codes shown below are in decimal notation.

1. Is **JANSEN** equal to **JANZEN**?

J A N S E N = J A N Z E N
74 65 78 (83)   74 65 78 (90)

   False.   83 (the code for **S** in **JANSEN**) is not equal to 90 (the code for **Z** in **JANZEN**).

2. Is **STEPHENS** less than **STEVENS**?

S T E P H E N S < S T E V E N S
83 84 69 (80)   83 84 69 (86)

   True.   80 (the code for **P** in **STEPHENS**) is less than 86 (the code for **V** in **STEVENS**).

3. Is **BROWNE** greater than **BROWN**?

B R O W N E > B R O W N
66 82 79 87 78 (69)   66 82 79 87 78 (32)

True.   69 (the code for **E** in **BROWNE**) is greater than 32 (the code for the space following **BROWN**).

The remaining relational operators work in a similar manner. By using these operators, it is possible to sort strings alphabetically in much the same way as numbers were sorted in the Sorting Program in Chapter Seven.

12.3 PROCESSING STRINGS—Sample Programs

1. This program compares the two names **AIKEN** and **AITKEN** and prints them in alphabetical order.

```
10 PRINT
20 LET A$="AIKEN "
30 LET B$="AITKEN "
40 IF A$<=B$ THEN 70

50 PRINT B$;A$
60 GO TO 99
70 PRINT A$;B$
99 END

RUN

AIKEN AITKEN
```

— Leaves a blank line.
— Assigns **AIKENb** to the string variable **A$**.
— Assigns **AITKENb** to the string variable **B$**.
— Compares the two strings:
   (i) If the value of **A$** is less than or equal to that of **B$**, control is transferred to the PRINT statement, which prints the value of **A$** before the value of **B$**.
   (ii) If the value of **A$** is greater than that of **B$**, the computer proceeds to the next statement, which prints the value of **B$** before the value of **A$**.
— Prints the value of **B$**, then the value of **A$**.
— Transfers control to the END statement.
— Prints the value of **A$**, then the value of **B$**.
— Terminates program execution.

Notice the trailing space after each name. This space is necessary, otherwise the semicolon in the executed PRINT statement causes the two names to be printed with no space between them.

2. This program illustrates how a string variable can be compared with a string.

```
01 REM D$--DAY

10 PRINT
20 FOR I=1 TO 4
30   READ D$
```

— Leaves a blank line.
— Sets up a loop.
— Reads 4 strings one at a time and assigns each string to the variable **D$**.

```
40      DATA SUNDAY,TUESDAY,THURSDAY,SATURD
AY
50      IF D$="SATURDAY" THEN 90




60 NEXT I
70 PRINT "SATURDAY NOT FOUND"

80 GO TO 999

90 PRINT "IT'S SATURDAY"
999 END

RUN

IT'S SATURDAY
```

— Supplies the READ statement with 4 strings.
— Tests the value of **D$**:
  (i) If its value is **SATURDAY**, control is transferred to line 90 which prints a message.
  (ii) If its value is not **SATURDAY**, the computer proceeds to the next statement.
— Transfers control back to line 20.
— Prints the string **SATURDAY NOT FOUND**.
— Transfers control to the END statement.
— Prints the string **IT'S SATURDAY**.
— Terminates program execution.

In line 50, the string **SATURDAY** is enclosed in quotes. Most computer systems require these quotes whenever a string is compared with another value in an IF/THEN statement. Also, no trailing space is left after the name of each day in the DATA statement, since these strings are not printed.

3. In this program, a counter (K) keeps track of how many times the word YEAR is entered into the computer.

```
01 REM S$--STRING

10 LET K=0
20 FOR I=1 TO 5
30    READ S$



40    DATA THIS,YEAR,AND,LAST,YEAR

50    IF S$<>"YEAR" THEN 70





60    LET K=K+1
70 NEXT I
80 PRINT
90 PRINT "'YEAR' IS ENTERED";K;"TIMES"
```

— Initializes a counter to zero.
— Sets up a loop.
— Reads 5 strings one at a time and assigns each string to the variable **S$**.
— Supplies the READ statement with 5 strings.
— Tests the value of **S$**:
  (i) If its value is not **YEAR**, control is transferred to line 70 to resume reading.
  (ii) If its value is **YEAR**, the computer proceeds to the next statement.
— Increments the counter by one.
— Transfers control back to line 20.
— Leaves a blank line.
— Prints the number of times **YEAR** is entered into the computer.

```
99 END                              —Terminates program execution.

RUN

'YEAR' IS ENTERED 2 TIMES
```

As in the previous program, there is no need to code a space after each string in the DATA statement since these words are not printed.

4. Strings can be transferred or **copied** from one storage location to another without altering the contents of the first location.

```
10 LET A$="TORTOISE"    —Assigns TORTOISE to A$.
20 LET B$="HARE"        —Assigns HARE to B$.
30 LET B$=A$            —Copies the string that is stored in A$ and places it in B$.
40 PRINT                —Leaves a blank line.
50 PRINT A$,B$          —Prints the values of A$ and B$ widely spaced.
99 END                  —Terminates program execution.

RUN

TORTOISE   TORTOISE
```

The string **HARE** in variable **B$** has been replaced by the string **TORTOISE**. **TORTOISE** is now stored in two locations, **A$** and **B$**. Since a comma is used in the PRINT statement, there is no need for a trailing space after each string in the LET statements. The second item is automatically printed in the next available print zone.

5. Two strings can be added, although the computational procedure is not the same as that performed on numeric data. The process is referred to as **concatenation**. Here is a comparison of the two types of addition.

(a) Addition on Strings   (b) Addition on Numeric Values

```
10 LET A$="111"          10 LET A=111
20 LET B$="222"          20 LET B=222
30 LET C$=A$+B$          30 LET C=A+B
40 PRINT                 40 PRINT
50 PRINT C$              50 PRINT C
99 END                   99 END

RUN                      RUN

111222                   333
```

The addition in Program (a) attaches 222 to the tail end of 111, which produces 111222. The addition in Program (b) is a numeric addition which produces the sum 333.

Some systems require the use of the **STR** function to concatenate strings. Here is an example.

```
10 LET A$="111"        — Assigns the string 111 to A$.
20 LET B$="222"        — Assigns the string 222 to B$.
30 STR(C$,1,3)=A$      — Sets the first, second, and third characters of C$ to 111.
40 STR(C$,4,3)=B$      — Sets the fourth, fifth, and sixth characters of C$ to 222.
50 PRINT               — Leaves a blank line.
60 PRINT C$            — Prints the concatenated string.
99 END                 — Terminates program execution.

RUN

111222
```

6. Care must be taken when words are concatenated, for no space is left between the words after they are ''attached.'' Examine the results of the following programs.

Using the "+" Operator

```
10 LET B$="BASIC"      — Assigns the string BASIC to B$.
20 LET C$="COBOL"      — Assigns the string COBOL to C$.
30 LET S$=B$+C$        — Concatenates the two strings.
40 PRINT               — Leaves a blank line.
50 PRINT S$            — Prints the concatenated string.
99 END                 — Terminates program execution.

RUN

BASICCOBOL
```

Using the STR Function

```
10 LET B$="BASIC"      — Assigns the string BASIC to B$.
20 LET C$="COBOL"      — Assigns the string COBOL to C$.
30 STR(S$,1,5)=B$      — Sets the first character through and including the fifth character of
                         S$ to BASIC.
40 STR(S$,6,5)=C$      — Sets the sixth character through and including the tenth character
                         of S$ to COBOL.
50 PRINT               — Leaves a blank line.
60 PRINT S$            — Prints the concatenated string.
99 END                 — Terminates program execution.
```

```
RUN

BASICCOBOL
```

How can the programs be modified so that there is a space between the two words?

```
********************
10 LET B$="BASIC"
20 LET C$=" COBOL"
```
↑
Space before **COBOL**

A leading space is coded in the string **COBOL** (" COBOL"). In the function method, line 40 would be changed to **40 STR(S$,6,6)=C$**. An alternative method is to code a trailing space in the string **BASIC** ("BASIC ") with no space in the string **COBOL** ("COBOL").

7. It is possible to **accumulate** strings. The programs shown below accumulate the five letters B, A, S, I, and C in the string variable **W$**. When using the "+" operator, the accumulation is similar to the way numbers are added on the computer. The variable in which the letters are accumulated is first initialized to the **null** string (**LET W$=""**), much like setting a numeric variable to zero before numbers are summed (**LET S=∅**). When using the STR function to accumulate strings, initialization is to the "blank" character rather than to the null string.

Using the "+" Operator

```
01 REM W$--WORD
02 REM L$--LETTER

10 LET W$=""            —Initializes the string variable W$ to the null string.
20 FOR I=1 TO 5         —Sets up a loop for the five letters.
30    READ L$           —Reads the letters one at a time.
40    DATA B,A,S,I,C    —Supplies the READ statement with the letters.
50    LET W$=W$+L$      —Concatenates the letters one at a time and stores the accumulated
                         result in W$.
60 NEXT I               —Transfers control back to line 20.
70 PRINT                —Leaves a blank line.
80 PRINT W$             —Prints the concatenated word.
99 END                  —Terminates program execution.

RUN

BASIC
```

Using the STR Function

```
01 REM W$--WORD
02 REM L$--LETTER

10 LET W$=" "          — Initializes the string variable W$ to blank.
20 FOR I=1 TO 5        — Sets up a loop for the five letters.
30    READ L$          — Reads the letters one at a time.
40    DATA B,A,S,I,C   — Supplies the READ statement with the letters.
50    STR(W$,I,1)=L$   — Concatenates the letters one at a time in the variable W$ by
                         setting the first character of W$ (I=1) to the first letter read, the
                         second character of W$ (I=2) to the second letter read, etc.,
                         until the loop is complete (I=5).
60 NEXT I              — Transfers control back to line 20.
70 PRINT               — Leaves a blank line.
80 PRINT W$            — Prints the concatenated word.
99 END                 — Terminates program execution.

RUN

BASIC
```

8. String variables may not be compared with numeric variables. The following program produces an error message which will be either the one shown below or something similar.

```
10 PRINT                          — Leaves a blank line.
20 LET A=123                      — Assigns a numeric value to a numeric variable.
30 LET B$="123"                   — Assigns a string to a string variable.
40 IF A=B$ THEN 70                — Attempts to compare a numeric value with a
                                    string; produces an error message.
50 PRINT A;"IS NOT EQUAL TO ";B$
60 GO TO 99
70 PRINT A;"IS EQUAL TO ";B$
99 END

RUN

?TYPE MISMATCH ERROR IN  40
```

12.3 PROCESSING STRINGS – Your Turn

1. State whether the following relational expressions are true or false. Write the ASCII code beneath each character until you find a difference in the two strings.

(a) SPARKES<SPARKS   (d) KRUEGER<>KRUGER

(b) LINDSAY=LINDSEY   (e) LYNN<=LYNNE

(c) FREDERICK>=FREDRICK   (f)   PHILIPS>PHILLIPS

2. Fill in the missing lines.

```
(a) 10 PRINT
    20 LET A$="ANDERSEN "
    30 LET B$="ANDERSON "
    40 IF A$>=B$ THEN 70
    50
    60 GO TO 99
    70
    99 END

    RUN

    ANDERSEN ANDERSON
```

```
(b) 10 PRINT
    20 FOR I=1 TO 4
    30    READ P$
    40    DATA MERCURY,VENUS,EARTH,MARS
    50
    60    PRINT "I LIVE ON THE PLANET EARTH"
    70 NEXT I
    99 END

    RUN

    I LIVE ON THE PLANET EARTH
```

3. Indicate the errors, if any, in the programs shown below. If there is an error, make the necessary correction; if there is no error, show the RUN.

```
(a) 10 PRINT
    20 LET G$="GREAT DANE"
    30 IF G$>CHIHUAHUA THEN 60
```

```
40 PRINT "CHIHUAHUA"
50 GO TO 99
60 PRINT G$
99 END
```

```
(b) 10 LET K=0
    20 FOR I=1 TO 8
    30    READ A$
    40    DATA A,B,D,B,F,C,A,B
    50    IF A$="B" THEN 70
    60    GO TO 80
    70    LET K=K+1
    80 NEXT I
    90 PRINT
    100 PRINT "B APPEARS";K;"TIMES"
    999 END
```

4. Write a program that concatenates the three strings **PRO-GRAMS, IN, BASIC**. Assign each string to a string variable by means of a LET statement.

```
RUN

PROGRAMS IN BASIC
```

12.3 PROCESSING STRINGS – Solutions for "Your Turn"[9]

1. (a) S P A R K E S < S P A R K S
       83 80 65 82 75 ⑥⑨   83 80 65 82 75 ⑧③
       True

   (b) L I N D S A Y = L I N D S E Y
       76 73 78 68 83 ⑥⑤   76 73 78 68 83 ⑥⑨
       False

   (c) F R E D E R I C K > = F R E D R I C K
       70 82 69 68 ⑥⑨   70 82 69 68 ⑧②
       False

9. The codes shown for Problem 1 are in decimal notation.

(d) K R U E G E R < > K R U G E R
   75 82 85 ⑥⑨   75 82 85 ⑦①
   True

(e) L Y N N   < = L Y N N E
   76 89 78 78 ③②   76 89 78 78 ⑥⑨
   True

(f) P H I L I P S > P H I L L I P S
   80 72 73 76 ⑦③   80 72 73 76 ⑦⑥
   False

2.

(a)
```
50 PRINT A$;B$
70 PRINT B$;A$
```

(b)
```
50 IF P$<>"EARTH" THEN 70
```

3. (a) The string **CHIHUAHUA** in line 30 should be enclosed in quotation marks.

```
30 IF G$>"CHIHUAHUA" THEN 60
```

(b) Nothing is wrong.

```
RUN

B APPEARS 3 TIMES
```

4. Using the "+" Operator

```
01 REM C$--CONCATENATED STRING

10 LET P$="PROGRAMS"
20 LET I$=" IN"
30 LET B$=" BASIC"
40 LET C$=P$+I$+B$
50 PRINT
60 PRINT C$
99 END
```

Using the STR Function

```
01 REM C$--CONCATENATED STRING
```

```
10 LET P$="PROGRAMS"
20 LET I$=" IN"
30 LET B$=" BASIC"
40 STR(C$,1,8)=P$
50 STR(C$,9,3)=I$
60 STR(C$,12,6)=B$
70 PRINT
80 PRINT C$
99 END
```

12.4 EXTRACTING SUBSTRINGS[10]

Until now, you have been working with a string in its entirety. There may be occasions when you want to access just part of a string. Suppose each string consists of a person's first name, last name, address, and telephone number. You may want to extract just the last name from each string so that the names can be sorted alphabetically, or perhaps you may want to extract the last name and the telephone number from each string. The piece of string that is extracted is called a **substring**. There are several different ways by which the various versions of BASIC extract substrings. Some of the variations are given in this chapter. If you find that none of them work on your computer system, check your manual. A feature that does affect the way a substring is extracted is the method by which characters in a string are numbered. Some systems consider the left-most character as character number zero; others consider it as character number one.

A substring may be comprised of one of the following:

1. Any number of left-most characters of a string.
2. Any number of right-most characters of a string.
3. Any series of characters from within a string.

You will be shown two basic methods of extracting substrings. One is called the function method, which uses a built-in function followed by arguments in parentheses, and the other is called the subscript method, which uses a string variable followed by subscripts in parentheses. Two examples are shown below.

Function Method   **Subscript Method**

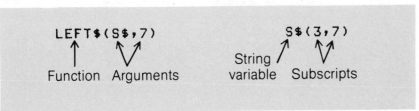

Although two basic methods of extracting substrings exist, the interpretation of the arguments, the interpretation of the subscripts,

10. Some versions of BASIC do not extract substrings from strings. Check your computer manual, and if your system does not support this operation, you may omit this section.

and the name of the function vary widely among computers. Shown below are different versions of the two methods along with their interpretations. The string **PLAYING WITH WORDS** has been assigned to **S$** in the examples. Either the string variable or the string itself (enclosed in quotation marks) may be used as the argument of a function. To simplify the examples, the string variable has been used.

I. To extract the left-most characters

xx LET S$ = "PLAYING WITH WORDS"

Example	Interpretation	Result
Function Method		
`LEFT$(S$,7)`	Extract the 7 left-most characters.	`PLAYING`
`SUBSTR(S$,1,7)` `STR(S$,1,7)`	Extract 7 characters starting at the first.	`PLAYING`
Subscript Method		
`S$(1,7)`	Extract 7 characters starting at the first	`PLAYING`
	or	
	Extract the first character through and including the seventh.	`PLAYING`

II. To extract the right-most characters

xx LET S$ = "PLAYING WITH WORDS"

Example	Interpretation	Result
Function Method		
`RIGHT$(S$,10)`	Extract the 10 right-most characters.	`WITH WORDS`
`SUBSTR(S$,9,10)` `STR(S$,9,10)`	Extract 10 characters starting at the ninth.	`WITH WORDS`
`SUBSTR(S$,9)` `STR(S$,9)`	Extract the ninth character through and including the last.	`WITH WORDS`
Subscript Method		
`S$(9,10)`	Extract 10 characters starting at the ninth.	`WITH WORDS`
`S$(9,18)`	Extract the ninth character through and including the eighteenth.	`WITH WORDS`

S$(9)	Extract the ninth character through and including the last.	WITH WORDS

III. To extract any series of characters

xx LET S$= "PLAYING WITH WORDS"

Example	Interpretation	Result

Function Method

MID$(S$,5,10)	Extract 10 characters starting at the fifth	ING WITH W
	or	
	Extract the fifth character through and including the tenth.	ING WI
MID$(S$,5)	Extract the fifth character through and including the last.	ING WITH WORDS
SUBSTR(S$,5,10) STR(S$,5,10)	Extract 10 characters starting at the fifth.	ING WITH W

Subscript Method

S$(5,10)	Extract 10 characters starting at the fifth	ING WITH W
	or	
	Extract the fifth character through and including the tenth.	ING WI

Notice that the first numeric argument in **MID$(S$,5,10)** and the first subscript in **S$(5,10)** indicates the starting point of the extraction. The argument or subscript that follows is the one that is interpreted differently by the various computer systems. Below is a review of the interpretation of these two examples.

1. **S$** indicates the string upon which the extraction will be performed.
2. The 5 indicates where the extraction begins. This argument or subscript is usually interpreted in the same way by all computers. In this case, the extraction begins at the fifth character of the string stored in **S$**.
3. The last argument or subscript is the one that is interpreted differently by the various systems. It may mean:
   (a) *Extract 10 characters* starting at the fifth, or
   (b) Extract the fifth character *through and including the tenth*.

One more comment before going on to some sample programs. If the arguments or subscripts are negative or greater than the length of the string (or greater than what is left in the string), an error message will likely result. Remember, some computer systems consider the left-most character of a string as character number zero. This means that the argument or subscript indicating the start of an extraction of the left-most characters would be zero.

12.4 EXTRACTING SUBSTRINGS – Sample Programs

The programs that follow use the features listed below.

1. The left-most character of a string is considered character number one.
2. The functions **RIGHT$**, **LEFT$**, and **MID$** are used to extract substrings with variations shown either alongside the statements or below the program. Refer to your manual if the ones given cannot be used on your computer system.
3. The third argument of the MID$ function indicates the number of characters to extract — that is, the count. For example, **MID$(S$,7,3)** means "extract *three* characters starting at the seventh."
4. In the variations:
   (a) The third argument in the function method indicates the number of characters to extract (the count). For example, **SUBSTR(S$,9,4)** means "extract *four* characters starting at the ninth."
   (b) The second subscript in the subscript method indicates where the extraction ends. For example, **S$(4,8)** means "extract the fourth character through and *including the eighth*."

I. This program extracts the seven left-most characters from a string. The function is coded in a LET statement. A string variable is used as an argument.

```
                                           Variations

10 LET S$='PLAYING WITH WORDS'         20 LET L$=STR(S$,1,7)
20 LET L$=LEFT$(S$,7)                   20 LET L$=SUBSTR(S$,1,7)
30 PRINT                                20 LET L$=S$(1,7)
40 PRINT L$
99 END

RUN

PLAYING
```

II. In this program, the ten right-most characters are extracted. Instead of the string variable, the actual string (in quotes) is coded as an argument of the function. The function is coded in a PRINT statement.

```
10 PRINT
20 PRINT RIGHT$("PLAYING WITH WORDS",10)
99 END

RUN

WITH WORDS
```

Variations

```
  20 PRINT SUBSTR("PLAYING WITH WORDS",9,10)
or 20 PRINT SUBSTR("PLAYING WITH WORDS",9)

  15 LET S$="PLAYING WITH WORDS"
  20 PRINT S$(9,18)  or  20 PRINT S$(9)

  20 PRINT STR("PLAYING WITH WORDS",9,10)
or 20 PRINT STR("PLAYING WITH WORDS",9)
```

III. This program extracts a substring of four characters, starting at the ninth character of the initial string. The function is coded in both an IF statement and a PRINT statement. Notice the quotation marks around the string **WITH** in line 20.

```
10 LET S$="PLAYING WITH WORDS"
20 IF MID$(S$,9,4)="WITH" THEN 40
30 GO TO 99
40 PRINT
50 PRINT MID$(S$,9,4)
99 END

RUN

WITH
```

Variations

```
20 IF STR(S$,9,4)="WITH" THEN 40
50 PRINT STR(S$,9,4)

20 IF SUBSTR(S$,9,4)="WITH" THEN 40
50 PRINT SUBSTR(S$,9,4)

20 IF S$(9,12)="WITH" THEN 40
50 PRINT S$(9,12)
```

IV. This program finds how many **A**'s there are in the name **BAR-BARA**. Here are the instructions.

(a) Use a counter to keep track of the number of **A**'s found.

(b) Use a FOR/NEXT loop to control the testing of each letter in the name.

(c) Use the MID$ function to test each letter. The function's arguments should be the following:

  (i) A string variable in which the name is stored.

 (ii) The index of the FOR statement, say I. This is the starting point of the substring in each test.
When I is 1, the substring starts at **B**;
When I is 2, the substring starts at **A**;
When I is 3, the substring starts at **R**, etc.

(iii) The number 1, which indicates the length of the substring. In this case, only one letter is extracted at a time.

(d) If the extracted letter is **A**, increment the counter; if it is not, test the next letter.

(e) After all the letters in the name have been tested, print the message as shown in the RUN.

```
01 REM K--COUNTER
02 REM N$--NAME

10 LET K=0
20 LET N$="BARBARA"
30 FOR I=1 TO 7
40    IF MID$(N$,I,1)="A" THEN 60
50    GO TO 70
60    LET K=K+1
70 NEXT I
80 PRINT
90 PRINT "NO. OF A'S IN BARBARA IS:";K
99 END

RUN

NO. OF A'S IN BARBARA IS: 3
```

Variations

```
40 IF STR(N$,I,1)="A" THEN 60
40 IF SUBSTR(N$,I,1)="A" THEN 60
40 IF N$(I,I)="A" THEN 60
```

12.4 EXTRACTING SUBSTRINGS—Your Turn

1. The following is a list of members who belong to the social committee of a local community club. Write a program that

determines the number of members whose first names are Allan and prints the names of these members with a running counter alongside each name.

Allan Smith, Laureen Peters, Allan Mills, Sandra Campbell, Allan Webster, Mary Williams

(a) Initialize a counter to 1.
(b) Use a FOR/NEXT loop to control input.
(c) Use the READ/DATA statements to enter the names in first name first order.
(d) Use the LEFT$ function in an IF/THEN statement to extract the first five characters of each name. In the same statement, determine whether or not the substring is **ALLAN**. If it is, transfer control to a statement that prints the name and the running counter as shown in the RUN. Immediately after this statement, increment your counter.

```
RUN

1        ALLAN SMITH
2        ALLAN MILLS
3        ALLAN WEBSTER
```

2. One of the "Your Turn" programs on page 594 compared the two names Andersen and Anderson to determine which one was greater, then printed the names alphabetically. Rewrite the program, this time comparing the last three characters of each name. In one IF/THEN statement, perform the following:

(a) Extract the three right-most characters of each name by means of the RIGHT$ function.
(b) Compare the substrings using a relational operator.
(c) Branch to the appropriate PRINT statement.

```
RUN

ANDERSEN ANDERSON
```

3. Write a program that performs the following operations:

(a) Divides the string 5671234 into the two substrings 567 and 1234, by using the LEFT$ function and the RIGHT$ function.
(b) Determines which substring is the greater.
   (Hint: This does not mean greater numerically.)
(c) Branches to the appropriate PRINT statement to print the greater of the two substrings.

```
RUN

567
```

4. In Chapter Nine on pages 409 and 412, you were shown how to reverse the order of the digits of a number. The same thing can be done with the characters of a string. Write a program that prints each of the names Michael, Suzanne, and William with their letters in reverse order. Notice that each name has seven letters. To reverse the order of the letters in names that have various lengths, the number of characters in each name must first be determined. This is explained in the next section.

  (a) Use nested FOR/NEXT loops:
    (i) One loop controls the entering of data.
    (ii) The other controls the isolating and printing of each letter.
  (b) Use the READ/DATA statements to enter the data.
  (c) To print the letters of a name in reverse order:
    (i) Set the initial value of the FOR statement in the inner loop to 7 (the length of each name), then work backwards to 1 (the STEP value should be − 1). This means that you will be working from the last letter in a name to the first letter.
    (ii) Use the MID$ function to isolate each letter. Assign the isolated letter to a string variable. The arguments of the MID$ function should be the string variable in which the name is stored, the index of the inner loop, and the number 1, which extracts one letter at a time.
    (iii) Print the value of the string variable that stores the isolated letter. End the PRINT statement with a semicolon so that each letter is printed on the same line with no intervening spaces.

```
RUN

LEAHCIM
ENNAZUS
MAILLIW
```

Problem 4

N$ — NAME   L$ — LETTER

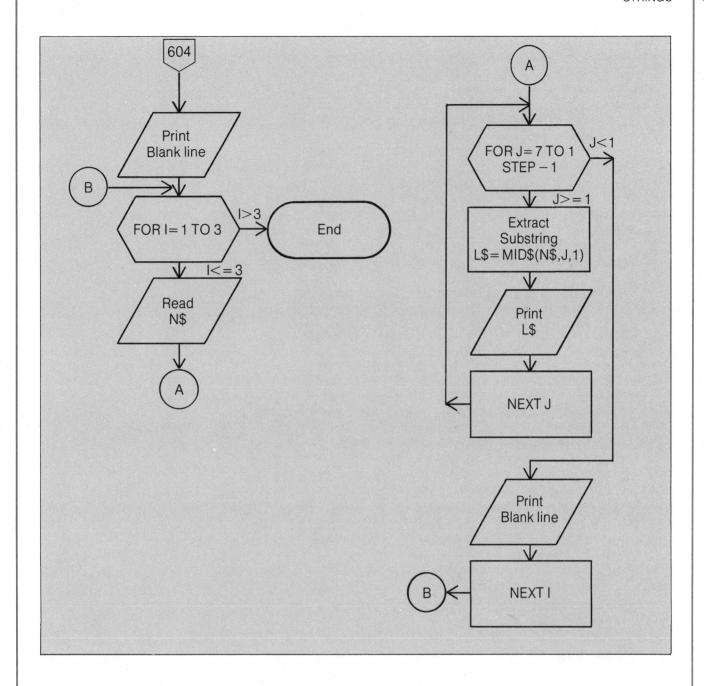

12.4 EXTRACTING SUBSTRINGS—Solutions for "Your Turn"

1.

```
01 REM N$--NAME

10 PRINT
```

```
   20 LET K=1
   30 FOR I=1 TO 6
   40    READ N$
   50    DATA ALLAN SMITH,LAUREEN PETERS,ALL
AN MILLS,SANDRA CAMPBELL,ALLAN WEBSTER
   60    DATA MARY WILLIAMS
   70    IF LEFT$(N$,5)="ALLAN" THEN 90
   80    GO TO 110
   90    PRINT K,N$
  100    LET K=K+1
  110 NEXT I
  999 END
```

Variations

```
   70 IF STR(N$,1,5)="ALLAN" THEN 90
   70 IF SUBSTR(N$,1,5)="ALLAN" THEN 90
   70 IF N$(1,5)="ALLAN" THEN 90
```

2.

```
   10 PRINT
   20 LET M$="ANDERSEN "
   30 LET N$="ANDERSON "
   40 IF RIGHT$(M$,3)<=RIGHT$(N$,3) THEN 70
   50 PRINT N$;M$
   60 GO TO 99
   70 PRINT M$;N$
   99 END
```

Variations

```
      40 IF STR(M$,6,3)<=STR(N$,6,3) THEN 70
   or 40 IF STR(M$,6)<=STR(N$,6) THEN 70

      40 IF SUBSTR(M$,6,3)<=SUBSTR(N$,6,3) THEN 70
   or 40 IF SUBSTR(M$,6)<=SUBSTR(N$,6) THEN 70

      40 IF M$(6,8)<=N$(6,8) THEN 70
   or 40 IF M$(6)<=N$(6) THEN 70
```

3.

```
   01 REM S$--STRING
   02 REM L$--LEFT SUBSTRING
   03 REM R$--RIGHT SUBSTRING
```

```
   10 PRINT
   20 LET S$='5671234'
   30 LET L$=LEFT$(S$,3)
   40 LET R$=RIGHT$(S$,4)
   50 IF L$>=R$ THEN 80
   60 PRINT R$
   70 GO TO 99
   80 PRINT L$
   99 END
```

Variations

```
   30 LET L$=STR(S$,1,3)
   40 LET R$=STR(S$,4,4)
or 40 LET R$=STR(S$,4)

   30 LET L$=SUBSTR(S$,1,3)
   40 LET R$=SUBSTR(S$,4,4)
or 40 LET R$=SUBSTR(S$,4)

   30 LET L$=S$(1,3)
   40 LET R$=S$(4,7)
or 40 LET R$=S$(4)
```

4.

```
   01 REM N$--NAME
   02 REM L$---LETTER

   10 PRINT
   20 FOR I=1 TO 3
   30    READ N$
   40    DATA MICHAEL,SUZANNE,WILLIAM
   50    FOR J=7 TO 1 STEP -1
   60       LET L$=MID$(N$,J,1)
   70       PRINT L$;
   80    NEXT J
   90    PRINT
   100 NEXT I
   999 END
```

Variations

```
   60 LET L$=STR(N$,J,1)
   60 LET L$=SUBSTR(N$,J,1)
   60 LET L$=N$(J,J)
```

12.5 OTHER FUNCTIONS

Several other string-handling functions are available in most versions of BASIC. Although the disparities are not as great as in the extraction of substrings, some of the ones shown below may need an alternative. Refer to your manual if the following functions cannot be used on your computer system.

I. LEN

LEN(N$)   LEN("MAUREEN")

↑   ↑

String variable   String

This function counts the number of characters in a string. RUN the following program using your first name as data, to produce the number of characters in your name.

```
10 READ N$          — Reads your name.
20 DATA MAUREEN     — Supplies the READ statement with your first name.
30 LET L=LEN(N$)    — Counts the number of characters in your name and stores the
                      result in a numeric variable.
40 PRINT            — Leaves a blank line.
50 PRINT L          — Prints the number of characters.
99 END              — Terminates program execution.

RUN

   7
```

II. VAL

VAL(S$)   VAL("2468")

↑   ↑

String variable   String of digits

The **VAL** function converts a string that consists of digits to its numeric value. For example, the string "2468" is converted to 2468. If the string contains a non-numeric character, the computer converts only those digits to the left of the character or gives an error message. Some computers use **NUM** instead of VAL.

```
10 LET S$="2468"   — Assigns a string of digits to S$.
```

```
20 LET N=VAL(S$)        — Converts the string to its numeric value.
30 PRINT                — Leaves a blank line.
40 PRINT N              — Prints the numeric value.
99 END                  — Terminates program execution.

RUN

 2468
```

Depending on your computer system, a space may or may not be left before the printed number.

III. STR$

STR$ is the opposite to VAL. It converts a number to its string equivalent.

```
10 LET N=2468           — Assigns a number to N.
20 LET S$=STR$(N)       — Converts the number to a string.
30 PRINT                — Leaves a blank line.
40 PRINT S$             — Prints the string.
99 END                  — Terminates program execution.

RUN

 2468
```

Computers that leave a space before a positive number will leave a space before its string equivalent. This is because the computer considers the space for the assumed plus sign as part of the number and when the number is converted to a string, the space becomes part of the string. When the **LEN** function is applied to the string stored in **S$(ƀ2468)**, the computer will return a length of 5.

The last two functions may be confusing. The following will help you remember what each one does.

(a) VAL resembles value — it changes its argument to a numeric value.

(b) STR$ resembles string — it changes its argument to a string.

IV. CHR$

```
CHR$(C)                        CHR$(65)

  ↑                               ↑
Numeric variable              Numeric value
```

This function converts a number to its ASCII character equivalent. The number must be an ASCII code, otherwise the result will likely be an error message. If the code represents a system command, no character is displayed. For example, the number 13 is the decimal notation for a carriage return. Nothing is displayed when 13 is converted to its ASCII character.

```
10 LET C=65            — Assigns an ASCII code (in decimal notation) to C.
20 LET C$=CHR$(C)      — Converts the number to its ASCII character equivalent.
30 PRINT               — Leaves a blank line.
40 PRINT C,C$          — Prints the code and its ASCII character.
99 END                 — Terminates program execution.

RUN

  65        A
```

V. ASC

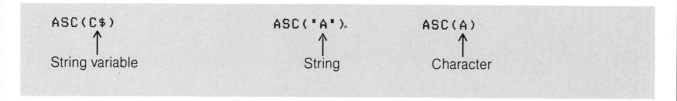

```
ASC(C$)                    ASC("A")        ASC(A)

  ↑                           ↑              ↑
String variable            String         Character
```

ASC is the opposite to CHR$. It converts a single character to its ASCII code. If the argument consists of a series of characters, only the first character of the string is converted. Some systems do not accept a string variable as the argument of the ASC function. Instead, a single character (without quotes around it) is required.

```
10 LET C$="A"          — Assigns the character A to C$.
20 LET C=ASC(C$)       — Converts A to its ASCII code equivalent.
30 PRINT               — Leaves a blank line.
40 PRINT C$,C          — Prints the character A and its ASCII code.
99 END                 — Terminates program execution.
```

```
RUN

A            65
```

The following will help you differentiate between CHR$ and ASC.

(a) CHR$ resembles character — it changes its argument to an ASCII character.
(b) ASC resembles ASCII — it changes its argument to an ASCII code.

The five functions just shown may also be used with subscripted variables. The following program determines the length of each of the five words that are stored in the one-dimensional array W$.

```
10 DIM W$(5)                          — Reserves storage locations
                                        for five words.
20 PRINT                              — Leaves a blank line.
30 FOR I=1 TO 5                       — Sets up a loop.
40    READ W$(I)                      — Reads the words from the
                                        DATA statement one at a time
                                        and stores each word as an
                                        element of array W$.
50    DATA VARIABLE,FUNCTION,SUBSCRIPTED,   — Supplies the READ statement
ARRAY,SUBROUTINE                              with the words.
60    LET L=LEN(W$(I))               — Determines the length of each
                                        word and stores the length
                                        in a numeric variable.
70    PRINT W$(I);TAB(20);L          — Prints the word and its length.
80 NEXT I                            — Transfers control back to
                                        line 30.
99 END                               — Terminates program execution.

RUN

VARIABLE          8
FUNCTION          8
SUBSCRIPTED       11
ARRAY             5
SUBROUTINE        10
```

12.5 OTHER FUNCTIONS — Your Turn

1. What is the output of each of the following programs?

```
(a) 10 LET A$="NUMBERS AND STRINGS"        (d) 10 READ A
    20 LET L=LEN(A$)                           20 DATA 67
    30 PRINT                                    30 PRINT
    40 PRINT L                                  40 PRINT A,CHR$(A)
    99 END                                      99 END

(b) 10 LET A$="5789"                       (e) 10 READ A$
    20 PRINT                                    20 DATA T
    30 PRINT VAL(A$)                            30 PRINT
    40 PRINT A$                                 40 PRINT A$,ASC(A$)
    99 END                                      99 END

(c) 10 LET A=3456
    20 PRINT
    30 PRINT STR$(A)
    40 PRINT A
    99 END
```

2. Write a program that converts each of the strings "24" and "25" to its numeric value, then adds the two numbers.

   (a) Use the READ/DATA statements to read in the two strings.
   (b) Use three PRINT statements in addition to the one that leaves a blank line:
      (i) The first one prints the strings.
      (ii) The second one prints the numbers.
      (iii) The third one prints the sum.

```
RUN

24          25
 24          25
 49
```

3. Write a program that converts the decimal numbers 65 through 90 to their ASCII character equivalents.

   (a) Use a FOR/NEXT loop. Set the initial value in the FOR statement to 65 and the test value to 90.
   (b) Use the index as the argument of the function that converts each number to its ASCII character. Assign the character to a string variable.
   (c) Print the value of the index and its ASCII character on one line widely spaced.

```
RUN
```

```
65          A
66          B
67          C
--          --

--          --
90          Z
```

4. Write a program that converts each character of the string **SEA FLOOR SPREADING** to its ASCII code equivalent as follows.[11]

   (a) Assign the string to a string variable.
   (b) Set up a FOR/NEXT loop whose FOR statement has an initial value of one and a test value that is equal to the number of characters in the string (use the LEN function).
   (c) Extract each character of the string one at a time by means of the MID$ function. Assign the character to a string variable. See Problem 4 on page 604 if you need help with the arguments of the MID$ function.
   (d) Convert each character to its ASCII code by means of the ASC function and assign the code to a numeric variable.
   (e) Print the character and its ASCII code on one line widely spaced.

```
RUN

S          83
E          69
A          65
           32
F          70
--         --
--         --
G          71
```

Problem 4

S$ — STRING
A$ — SUBSTRING   A — ASCII CODE

11. If your computer system does not accept a string variable as the argument of the ASC function, you may omit this question.

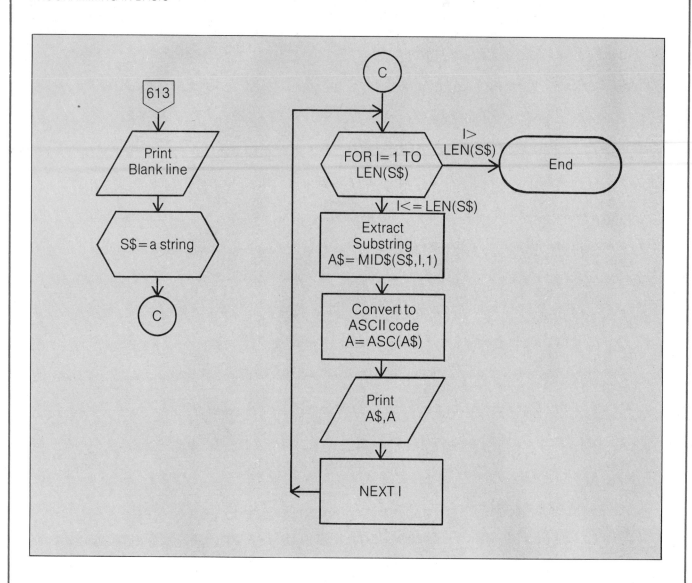

12.5 OTHER FUNCTIONS — Solutions for "Your Turn"[12]

1.

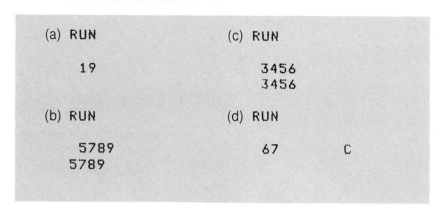

(a) RUN

   19

(b) RUN

   5789
 5789

(c) RUN

   3456
   3456

(d) RUN

  67   C

12. The spacing in your output may differ from the ones shown.

(e) RUN

```
   T              84
```

2.

```
10  READ A$,B$
20  DATA "24","25"13
30  LET A=VAL(A$)
40  LET B=VAL(B$)
50  LET C=A+B
60  PRINT
70  PRINT A$,B$
80  PRINT A,B
90  PRINT C
99  END
```

3.

```
10  PRINT
20  FOR I=65 TO 90
30     LET C$=CHR$(I)
40     PRINT I,C$
50  NEXT I
99  END
```

4.

```
01  REM S$--STRING
02  REM A$--SUBSTRING
03  REM A--ASCII CODE

10  PRINT
20  LET S$="SEA FLOOR SPREADING"
30  FOR I=1 TO LEN(S$)
40     LET A$=MID$(S$,I,1)
50     LET A=ASC(A$)
60     PRINT A$,A
70  NEXT I
99  END
```

Variations

```
40  LET A$=STR(S$,I,1)
40  LET A$=SUBSTR(S$,I,1)
40  LET A$=S$(I,I)
```

13. The programs in this book need quotes around strings that consist of numbers.

A SHORT SUMMARY

Strings give the means by which alphabetic and alphanumeric data can be manipulated. Many of the operations performed on numeric data can also be performed on strings. Strings may be assigned to string variables by using the same statements that assign numeric data to numeric variables. The relational operators that are used to compare two numbers may also be used to compare two strings. However, substrings are extracted from strings differently than the way digits are separated from numbers. Two basic methods exist — the function method and the subscript method. The function method uses built-in functions, while the subscript method uses subscripted string variables. Substrings may be formed by extracting any number of left-most characters from a string, any number of right-most characters from a string, or any series of characters from within a string. The arguments or subscripts indicate where the extraction begins and where it ends. It is also possible to isolate a single character. However, many disparities exist among the different versions of BASIC in the interpretation of the arguments and subscripts. The function name also differs among computers.

Several functions are available on most computers to enable the user to perform special operations on strings, such as finding the length of a string, converting a string that consists of digits to its numeric value, and converting an ASCII code to its character equivalent. The reverse of the last two operations is also available.

Strings are used in many applications. Some of the more common ones are the sorting of names, the printing of address labels, the search for a particular name or word, and, along with numeric data, the maintenance of payroll records and the control of inventory.

Questions and Exercises

1. Explain how a string variable is coded.
2. Write three programs that print your name and the current date. Each program prints the items on one line closely spaced and each program enters the data in a different way. The first program uses the INPUT statement (without a prompt), the second program uses the READ/DATA statements, and the third program uses LET statements. The date consists of two strings: (a) the month and the day of the month, and (b) the day of the week. An example is shown below.

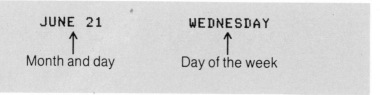

```
        JUNE  21              WEDNESDAY
           ↑                      ↑
     Month and day         Day of the week
```

Assign your name to one string variable, the month and day of the month to another string variable, and the day of the week to a third string variable. Show your response to the INPUT statement. Below is a sample line of output.

```
JOHN SMITH JUNE 21 WEDNESDAY
```

3. (a) Explain how a character (digit, letter of the alphabet, or other symbol) is stored in a computer.
   (b) State the reason for this method of storage.
4. (a) What do the letters ASCII represent?
   (b) What is an ASCII code? Define base two (binary), base ten (decimal), base eight (octal), and base sixteen (hexadecimal) representations of numbers.
   (c) What is the hierarchical order of the ASCII codes listed on page 586?
5. State whether the following relational expressions are true or false. Write the ASCII code beneath each character until you find a difference in the two strings. Refer to page 586 for the ASCII codes.

   (a) GRAHAM<GRAHAME   (c) THOMPSON>=THOMSON

   (b) FRANCIS<>FRANCES   (d) HUTCHESON<=HUTCHISON

6. What is wrong with each of the following programs? Make the necessary corrections. Several items printed on one output line must be separated by one or more spaces.[14]

```
(a) 10 PRINT
    20 PRINT "NUMBER,STREET";
    30 INPUT N,S
    40 PRINT N;S
    99 END

    RUN

    NUMBER,STREET? 123,MAIN STREET

(b) 10 LET N=123
    20 LET S$=MAIN STREET
    30 PRINT
    40 PRINT N,S$
    99 END

(c) 10 PRINT
    20 FOR I=1 TO 5
```

14. If you are not using an interactive system, you may omit question 6 (a).

```
30    READ W$
40    DATA NUMBER,SEVEN,IS,THE,WINNER
50    PRINT W$;
60 NEXT I
99 END
```

(d)
```
10 PRINT
20 LET A$="789 "
30 LET B=789
40 IF A$=B THEN 70
50 PRINT A$;"IS NOT EQUAL TO";B
60 GO TO 99
70 PRINT A$;"IS EQUAL TO";B
99 END
```

(e)
```
10 PRINT
20 FOR I=1 TO 2
30    READ A$,B
40    DATA STEVEN,4598,MICHAEL,2485
50    PRINT A$,B$
60 NEXT I
99 END
```

(f)
```
10 PRINT
20 LET B$="BASIC"
30 LET P$="PROGRAMMING"
40 PRINT
50 PRINT B$;P$
99 END
```

(g)
```
10 LET S$="SOMETHING WRONG"
20 LET L=LEN$(S$)
30 PRINT
40 PRINT L
99 END
```

(h)
```
10 LET N=1234
20 PRINT
30 PRINT VAL(N)
99 END
```

(i)
```
10 LET N$="90"
20 PRINT
30 PRINT CHR$(N$)
99 END
```

(j)
```
10 READ N
20 DATA 5678
30 PRINT
40 PRINT STR(N)
99 END
```

7. What is the output of each of the following programs?

(a)
```
10 PRINT
20 LET A$="MICRO"
30 LET B$="MINI"
40 IF A$>=B$ THEN 70
50 PRINT A$,B$
60 GO TO 99
70 PRINT B$,A$
99 END
```

(b)
```
10 PRINT
20 LET C$="COMPUTER"
30 FOR I=1 TO LEN(C$)
40   LET L$=MID$(C$,I,1)
50    PRINT L$;" ";
60 NEXT I
99 END
```

(c)
```
10 READ A
20 DATA 9753
30 PRINT
40 PRINT A
50 PRINT STR$(A)
99 END
```

(d)
```
10 READ N
20 DATA 54
30 PRINT
40 PRINT N
50 PRINT CHR$(N)
99 END
```

(e)
```
10 LET S$="STRING HANDLING"
20 LET L=LEN(S$)
30 PRINT
40 PRINT L
99 END
```

(f)
```
10 LET S$="5432"
20 PRINT
30 PRINT S$
40 PRINT VAL(S$)
99 END
```

(g)
```
10 LET Z$="Z"
20 LET C=ASC(Z$)
30 PRINT
40 PRINT Z$,C
99 END
```

Programming Problems

1. In Section 12.4 page 604 you wrote a program that printed three names with their letters in reverse order. Each name had seven letters. Rewrite the program, this time using the words **PRO-GRAMMER**, **BASIC**, and **COMPUTER** as your data. Notice that the words have different lengths, which means that you will need the LEN function to determine the number of characters in each word.

   (a) Use nested FOR/NEXT loops:
      (i) One loop controls the entering of data.
      (ii) The other controls the isolating and printing of each letter.

(b) Use the READ/DATA statements to enter the data.
(c) To print a name in reverse order:
   (i) Use the LEN function as the initial value of the inner loop to set the index first to the number of characters in a word, then work backwards to 1 (the STEP value should be − 1). This means that you will be working from the last letter in a word to the first letter.
   (ii) Use the MID$ function to isolate each letter. Assign the isolated letter to a string variable.
   (iii) Print the value of the string variable.

```
RUN

REMMARGORP
CISAB
RETUPMOC
```

2. The program in Problem 1 prints one letter at a time in reverse order. It is possible to accumulate the letters by concatenation much like you accumulate a sum of numbers. Replace the statement that isolates each letter by a statement that performs the following:

(a) Isolates each letter of the word by means of the MID$ function.
(b) Concatenates this isolated letter to the string variable that accumulates the letters.
(c) Stores the result in the same string variable (similar to **xx LET S=S+N** when adding numbers).

Don't forget to set the string variable that accumulates the letters to the null string. Do this between the two FOR statements so that the string variable is nullified before each word is reversed. Should you need some help, refer to page 592, where a similar program illustrates how to set a string variable to the null string and how to accumulate the letters.

If you are using a computer that requires the STR function to concatenate strings, set the string variable that accumulates the letters to blank. Use the following statement to concatenate the letters instead of a statement that uses the MID$ function.

```
xx STR(R$,LEN(W$)+1-J,1)=STR(W$,J,1)
```

where **W$** is the word read into the computer, **R$** is the word with its letters in reverse order, and **J** is the index of the inner loop. As the value of **J** changes, the expression **LEN(W$)+1−J** sets the first character of **R$** to the last letter of **W$**, the second character of **R$** to the second last letter of **W$**, etc.

Print the results as shown below. Remember, there is no space printed before and after a string. To make sure that your words in the output line do not run together, code a space after the word **OF**, a space before **IS**, and a space after **IS** in your PRINT statement.

```
RUN

THE REVERSE OF PROGRAMMER IS REMMARGORP
THE REVERSE OF BASIC IS CISAB
THE REVERSE OF COMPUTER IS RETUPMOC
```

Problem 2

R$ — REVERSE
W$ — WORD

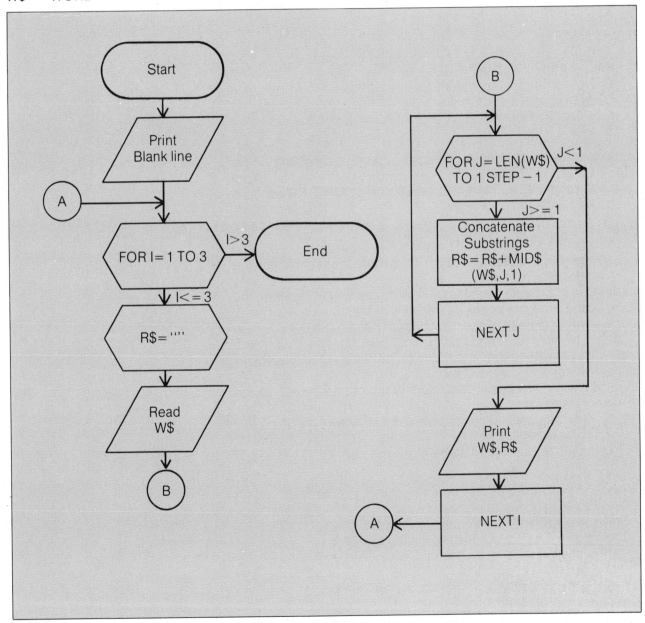

3. Write a program that reads the names of the twelve months of the year into a 3× 4 two-dimensional array. Print the names in matrix form. Perform the read and write operations by rows in one set of nested FOR/NEXT loops.

   Note: If your computer does not require quotes around strings in the DATA statement and if it allows only two lines of data in the statement, perform the following when more data items are to be coded:

   (a) In the second line of the first DATA statement, place quotes around the last string and its trailing space.
   (b) The line should not end with a comma.
   (c) Code the next string in a new DATA statement.

   This gives a space in the output between the last string of the first DATA statement and the first string of the second DATA statement.

   ```
   RUN

   JANUARY FEBRUARY MARCH APRIL
   MAY JUNE JULY AUGUST
   SEPTEMBER OCTOBER NOVEMBER DECEMBER
   ```

4. The program for Problem 6 in Chapter Four (Page 146) determined the largest sale made by a salesperson. Something similar can be done with strings. Write a program that finds which of the three words PROGRAMMER, BASIC, or COMPUTER contains the greatest number of letters.

   (a) Use a FOR/NEXT loop to control input.
   (b) Use the READ/DATA statements to enter the data.
   (c) Assign a low value (say L = − 1) to a numeric variable outside your loop.
   (d) Use the LEN function in an IF/THEN statement to compare the number of characters in a word with the current value of L.
      (i) If the number of characters is greater than the current value of L, replace L by the LENgth of the word just read. Save this word (which is currently the longest) in another string variable, say L$.
      (ii) If the number of characters is not greater, go on to the next word.
   (e) Print the data and the longest word as shown below. (Hint: Notice the space after IS: in the output. This space should be coded in your PRINT statement.)

   ```
   RUN

   PROGRAMMER
   BASIC
   COMPUTER

   THE LONGEST WORD IS: PROGRAMMER
   ```

Problem 4

L — LENGTH
W$— WORD
L$ — LONGEST WORD

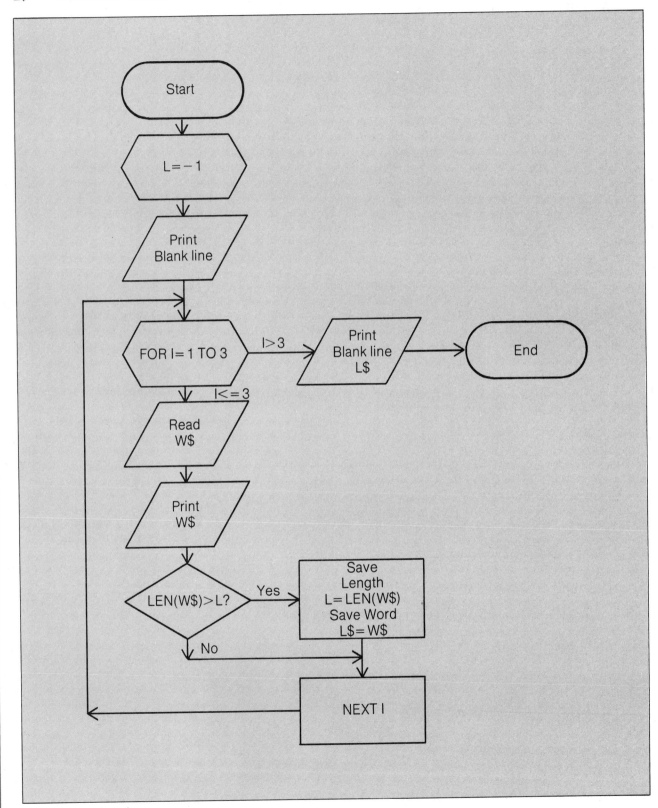

5. In Chapter Seven, a program was listed that sorted numbers in ascending order. Write a similar program, this time sorting the names Nancy, James, Tracy, Alexander, Gayle, and Edward alphabetically.

(a) Use a separate FOR/NEXT loop to read the names into a one-dimensional array, say N$. Sort the names in a subroutine that is called immediately after all the names have been read. Perform the printing of the names in its own loop in the main program after control RETURNS from the subroutine.

(b) To sort the names, use nested FOR/NEXT loops:
   (i) The outer loop controls the sorting of the six names.
   (ii) The inner loop sorts two adjacent names. Set its test value one number less than the number of names, since you will be comparing the name stored in **N$(J)** with the one stored in **N$(J+1)**. If the two names are in order, no exchange is made; if they are not in order, the names must be interchanged. To perform this, you must place the first name of a pair in temporary storage, the second name of the pair in the current variable (**N$(J)**), and the name that is in temporary storage in the next variable (**N$(J+1)**).

```
xx LET T$=N$(J)         — Places the first name of a pair in temporary storage.
xx LET N$(J)=N$(J+1)    — Places the second name of the pair in the current variable.
xx LET N$(J+1)=T$       — Places the name that is in temporary storage in the next variable.
```

Suppose **J** = 1. This is what happens with the first pair of names.

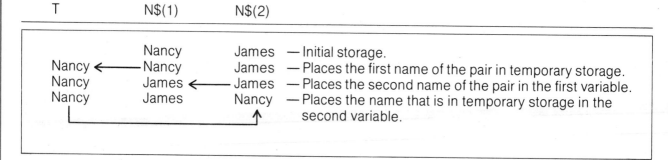

T	N$(1)	N$(2)	
	Nancy	James	— Initial storage.
Nancy	Nancy	James	— Places the first name of the pair in temporary storage.
Nancy	James	James	— Places the second name of the pair in the first variable.
Nancy	James	Nancy	— Places the name that is in temporary storage in the second variable.

The first pair of names is now in alphabetical order.

(c) Refer to the sorting program in Chapter Seven, page 290, if you need some help.

```
RUN

ALEXANDER
EDWARD
GAYLE
```

```
JAMES
NANCY
TRACY
```

Problem 5
N$ — NAME
T$ — TEMPORARY STORAGE

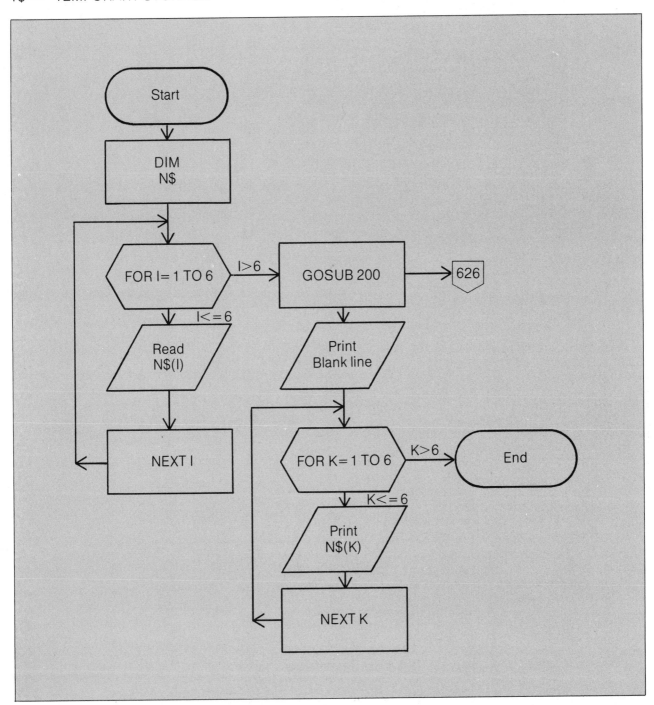

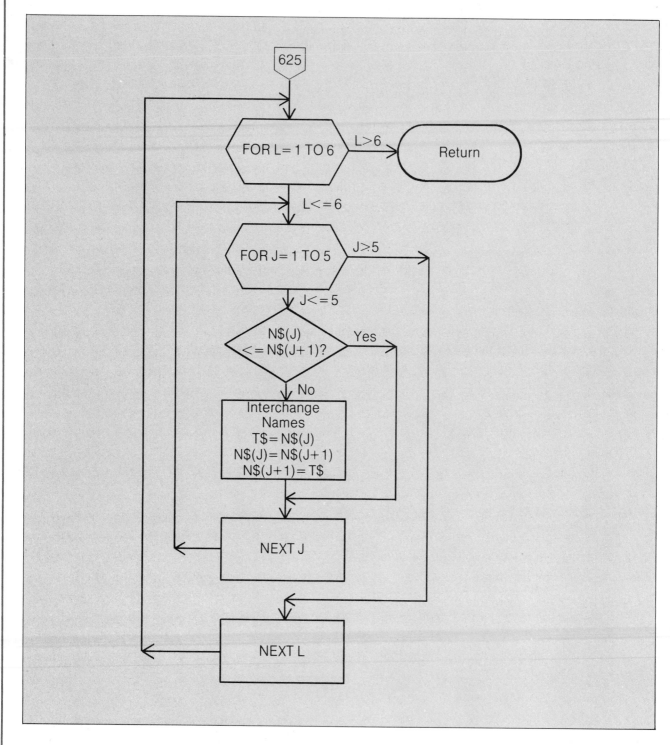

6. Write a program that reads the names of the following five people in first name first order, with one space between the first name and the last name.

Arthur Brown, James Anderson, Ellen Miller, Steven Taylor, Allan Fraser

Print their names in this manner: last name, comma, first name.

(a) Use nested FOR/NEXT loops:

(i) The outer loop controls the reading of the names. (Hint: Do not leave a space after each last name in the DATA statement.)

(ii) The inner loop locates the space between a first name and a last name. To find the space:

— Use J as the index of the FOR statement.

— Use the LEN function as the test value in the FOR statement. (The argument of the LEN function is the string variable that stores a name.)

— Use the MID$ function to check each character of a name for the space ('' ''). The arguments of the MID$ function should be the string variable that stores a name, the index of the inner loop, and the number 1. When the space is found, the value of the index is the number of characters in the first name plus the space. Transfer control to a statement that extracts the first name. This should be followed by a statement that extracts the last name.

(b) To extract the first name:

(i) Use the LEFT$ function and assign the substring to a string variable, say **L$**.

(ii) The arguments of the LEFT$ function should be the string variable that stores a name and the index of the inner loop. The value of the index is the number of characters in the first name plus the space.

Example: |ARTHUR |BROWN
The value of the second argument (**J**) is 7.

(c) To extract the last name:

(i) Use the RIGHT$ function and assign the substring to another string variable, say **R$**.

(ii) The arguments of the RIGHT$ function should be the string variable that stores a name and the LEN function minus the index of the inner loop. The latter argument is the length of the name minus the number of characters in the first name and the space.

Example: ARTHUR |BROWN|
Length of name = 12.
Length of first name and space = 7.
Length of last name is 12−7=5.

The value of the second argument (**LEN(N$)−J**) is 5.

(d) Print the substring extracted by the RIGHT$ function, a comma, then the substring extracted by the LEFT$ function.

(e) Continue with the next name.

```
RUN

BROWN,ARTHUR
ANDERSON,JAMES
MILLER,ELLEN
TAYLOR,STEVEN
FRASER,ALLAN
```

Problem 6

N$ — NAME
L$ — LEFT SUBSTRING (FIRST NAME)   R$ — RIGHT SUBSTRING (LAST NAME)

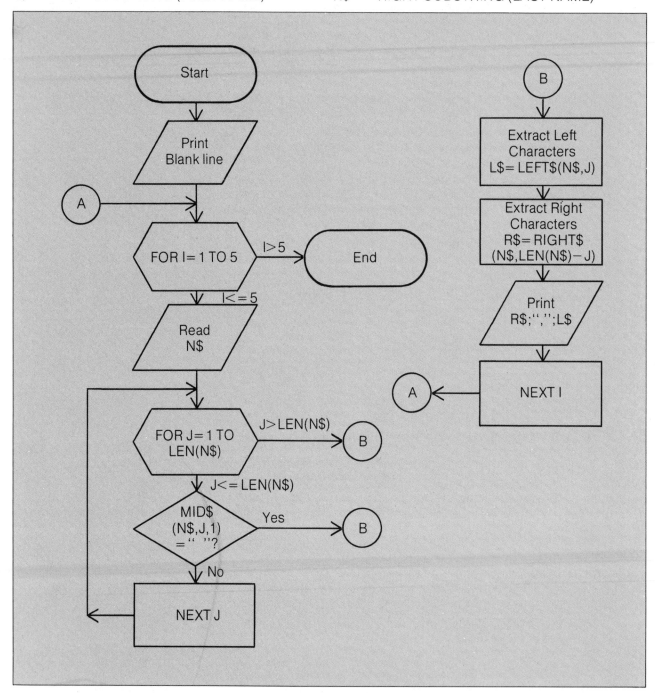

7. It is possible to align the decimal points of numbers by using the TAB function along with several of the functions learned in this chapter. Align the numbers 9.67, 3125.49, .26, 85.17, 123.45, 14.21. The procedure is as follows:

(a) Set up an outer loop to control the reading of the numbers. Convert each number to a string immediately after the number is read in.

(b) Set up an inner loop with a FOR statement that has an initial value of 1 and a test value equal to the length of the string. Use J as the index.

(c) Find the position of the decimal point by using the MID$ function to check each character of the string. This statement is similar to the one used in Problem 6, where each character in a name was checked for a space. When the decimal point is found, transfer control to the PRINT statement that produces the RUN shown below. The value of J at this point is the number of characters up to and including the decimal point.

(d) Print the number stored as a string in the string variable and the number stored in the numeric variable on one line widely spaced. Use the TAB function to align the number stored in the string variable. If your computer leaves a space before a positive number, this space is included as the first character of the string. Since the longest number entered has six characters up to and including the decimal point (b3125.), the argument of the TAB function should be 6−J. Thus, the first character of the string b3125.49 will be positioned in column zero.

```
RUN

      9.67    9.67
   3125.49    3125.49
       .26    .26
     85.17    85.17
    123.45    123.45
     14.21    14.21
```

8. Write a program that decodes the following ASCII codes (in decimal notation) into their ASCII character equivalents. Use the READ/DATA statements to enter the numbers.

   67, 79, 77, 80, 85, 84, 69, 82, 32, 76, 73, 84, 69, 82, 65, 67, 89

9. Write a program that reads the five numbers 20, 15, 25, 40, and 60 into a one-dimensional array, then converts each number to its string equivalent. Remember, some computer systems include a leading space in the string equivalent, while others do not. Thus, your output may differ from the one shown below.

```
RUN

   20
   15
   25
   40
   60
```

10. Write a program that uses a FOR/NEXT loop to control the following operations:[15]
    (a) Generates fifteen random whole numbers ranging from 49 to 57 inclusive.
    (b) Changes each of these numbers to its ASCII character equivalent.
    (c) Converts the ASCII character to its ASCII code equivalent.
    (d) Prints the ASCII character and its code widely spaced. Refer to Chapter Nine, page 415, if you need help in generating random numbers.

```
RUN          (Sample RUN)[16]

6            54
8            56
1            49
--           --
--           --
9            57
```

11. Modify your program for the above problem so that it generates twenty-six random whole numbers ranging from 65 to 90 inclusive.

```
RUN          (Sample RUN)

E            69
G            71
L            76
--           --
--           --
A            65
```

15. If your computer system does not accept a string variable as the argument of the ASC function, you may omit this problem.
16. Remember, decimal notation is used for the ASCII codes.

Index